Ioannis Miltoni Effigies Ætat: 62.
1670.

JOHN MILTON

FROM AN ORIGINAL ENGRAVING BY WILLIAM FAITHORNE

THE LIFE RECORDS OF

John Milton

VOLUME V

1670-1674

AND ADDITIONS

EDITED BY J. MILTON FRENCH

RUTGERS UNIVERSITY PRESS

NEW BRUNSWICK, NEW JERSEY

1958

PREFACE

THIS volume, which concludes *The Life Records of John Milton*, covers (1) Milton's life from the beginning of 1670 to his death in 1674, (2) some facts in his life to which no definite date can be assigned, (3) the history of his family before his birth, (4) the history of his family after his death, and (5) additions and corrections to Volumes I-IV.

I wish to thank a number of people for unusual helpfulness. I fear I have never adequately thanked two great Milton scholars from whom I have received incalculable aid and encouragement, both from their books and personally. David H. Stevens's *Reference Guide to Milton* gave me clues to many items in my book. James Holly Hanford's *Milton Handbook* was perhaps one of the earliest influences on my search for Miltoniana and has remained one of the most constant aids, as he himself has become one of my most highly valued friends. Mr. William Sloane, Director of the Rutgers University Press, and Miss Helen A. Stewart, Executive Editor of the Press, have both given me most generously both time and advice. Dean Thomas C. Pollock and Professor Oscar Cargill of New York University, by inviting me to act as Berg Visiting Professor of English there during the year 1956-1957, not only paid me a high honor but also for that year took me away from administrative responsibilities so that I was able to complete this volume in a fraction of the time which it would otherwise have required. The Rutgers University Research Council has generously supported the preparation and the publication of this as well as preceding volumes. My debt to William R. Parker, Maurice Kelley, and Edward L. Ruhe is so pervasive that I have used a shorthand method of acknowledging it by adding the appropriate last initial in parentheses after many items, especially in the fifth part. (See also p. 357 below.) Professor Parker, especially, has devoted himself in extraordinary measure to friendly cooperation with me in improvement of this work, not only by sending me many indispensable notes on the earlier volumes but also, despite other heavy commitments, by generously reading the proof of this volume and thus giving me the benefit of the editorial skill which he achieved so remarkably as editor of *PMLA*. My debts to other sources will be plain on almost every page.

J. MILTON FRENCH

Rutgers University
January 1, 1958

A NOTE ON THE FRONTISPIECE

The frontispiece of the present volume is a reproduction of what is undoubtedly the best known portrait of Milton, engraved by William Faithorne and first published in *The History of Britain* in 1670. It is taken from a copy of that book in the Rutgers University Library.

THE LIFE RECORDS OF
John Milton

The Life Records of John Milton

LIVES FOR A TIME WITH BOOKSELLER MILLINGTON.

One that had Often seen him, told me he us'd to come to a House where He Liv'd, and he has also Met him in the Street, Led by *Millington*, the same who was so Famous an Auctioneer of Books about the time of the Revolution, and Since. This Man was then a Seller of Old Books in *Little Britain*, and *Milton* lodg'd at his house. This was 3 or 4 Years before he Dy'd. he then wore no Sword that My Informer remembers, though Probably he did, at least 'twas his Custom not long before to wear one with a Small Silver-Hilt, and in Cold Weather a Grey Camblet Coat. his Band was Usually not of the Sort as That in the Print I have given, That is, as my Original is, but like What are in the Common Prints of him, the Band usually wore at That time; to have a more Exact Idea of his Figure, let it be remembered that the Fashion of the Coat Then was not Much Unlike what the Quakers Wear Now. . . . about 1670 I have been told by One who Then knew him, that he Lodg'd Some time at the House of *Millington* the Famous Auctioneer Some Years ago, who Then Sold Old Books in *Little Britain*, and who us'd to Lead him by the Hand when he went Abroad.

Richardson, pp. iii-iv, xciii; Masson, VI, 650-651; Darbishire, pp. 203, 275. Edward Millington was a bookseller and the chief auctioneer of his time from 1670 to his death in 1703 (Henry R. Plomer, *Dictionary of the Printers and Booksellers . . . 1668-1725*, Oxford, 1922, p. 207).

TUTORS SIR WILLIAM DAVENANT'S SON WILLIAM, WHO READS TO HIM.

. . . [in] the life of Thomas Elwood writ by himself . . . he

[1]

says p. 154. he had always a man to read to him wch was usually ye Son of some gentleman of his acquaintance whom in kindnes he took to improve in his learning. in confirmation of this last J can give you this true account.

J was very intimately acquainted when young with one m^r William Davenant 2^d Son to Sr William ye Poet, this Gentleman was after of magdalen Hal in Oxford & published a Book printed there being a translation relating to old Authors in 80. He was after unfortunately dround in france as he was Swiming. This mr Davenant told me that mr milton helped him in his study of ye lattin & Greke Authors, to whom he used to goe in order to his Learning—That when his father was in the tower he was very much assisted by mr milton in his gaining his Liberty, & if J am not very much mistaken he at the same time told me his father in return upon ye restoration was very helpfull to milton, & milton was very acknowledging for it & uppon that score offered his assistance [willingnes *added above the line*] in doing any thing that shoud be gratefull to S^r. William—Jt was a litle after miltons death he told me this, J had a mind to have seen miltons Books & mr Davenant went with me in order to it; J was then in my prentiship . . . mr milton was some time before then removed from Jewin street to moorfields near ye Artillery ground. . . .

From Jacob Tonson's letter to his nephew, date about 1731-1732, now in the Pierpont Morgan Library; Helen Darbishire, *The Manuscript of Milton's Paradise Lost Book I*, 1931, p. xiv. I have already quoted a small part of this section at III, 257. The date is impossible to determine with any accuracy. But we can set outside limits. It could hardly have been earlier than about 1663, since Davenant, who matriculated at Magdalen Hall, Oxford, on August 1, 1673, at the age of 16, could not have begun his schooling much before that year; and of course it could not have been later than 1673, when he entered college. Alfred Harbage, who scouts the whole story of the Milton-Davenant mutual aid, does not mention this phase of it. Arthur H. Nethercot, on the contrary, who accepts it, is more specific than he gives any authority for being. After telling how William's older brother Charles was sent out of the city during the plague of 1665 to study at Cheam, Surrey, he continues: "But while Charles was laying the foundations of his academic career in the country under the tutelage of Master George Aldrich, of Cambridge, his next brother, William, continued his studies under . . . John Milton . . . [who] helped him in his study of the Latin and Greek authors." However, this account cannot be exactly right, for Milton himself left London during the plague. For lack of specific data the entry is here placed in 1670. See Joseph Foster, *Alumni Oxonienses*, I (1891), 376, under William Davenant; Alfred Harbage, *Sir William Davenant*, Philadelphia, 1935, pp. 115-116; Arthur H. Nethercot, *Sir William D'Avenant*, Chicago, 1938, p. 406. William Davenant is here called the elder Davenant's second son, probably not because he was actually the second son born to the dramatist, but because he was the second son of that name. Sir William had had an earlier son William by his first wife, but this William had died. The visit of Tonson and Davenant to Milton's house may well have occurred in 1676. Tonson was an apprentice from 1670 to 1677, taking up his freedom on December 20 of the latter year (Henry R. Plomer, *A Dictionary of Booksellers and Printers . . . 1668-1725*, London, 1922, *s.v.* Tonson). According to Foster, Davenant was "of Gray's Inn" in 1676. Three years after publishing a translation of *Notitia Historicorum Selectorum* (1678), the book probably referred to by Tonson, Davenant was drowned in the Seine in 1681 (*DNB*).

RIDICULED FOR BLINDNESS IN *POOR ROBIN*.

Blind Milton

Poor Robin, 1670, under date of November 2; see above under date of 1664 for the first of this series of snubs. The entry is printed in red.

DAUGHTERS LEAVE HIM (?).

[Christopher Milton, the poet's brother, testified that] he knoweth not how the ptyes ministring these interryes [Milton's daughters] frequent the Church or in what manner of behaviour of life and conversaēon they are of they liveing a pte from their father fowr or five yeares last past and as touching his the deceasedꝑ displeasure with them he only herd him say at the tyme of declareing of his will that they were vndutifull and vnkind to him not expressing any pticulars—but in former tymes he hath herd him complaine that they were careles of him being blind and made nothing of diserteing him.

From Christopher Milton's answers to interrogatories about Milton's will on December 5, 1674, in the Deposition Book, 1674, f. 239, in the Prerogative Court of Canterbury, London; Warton, 1791, p. xxxiii; Todd, 1 (1826), 274; Masson, VI, 737-738; CM, XVIII, 371. The last two quote only part. More material from the investigation into Milton's will will be given later. The extent of the daughters' leaving of Milton is not made clear. But the following items are somewhat more specific. See also above under 1663 for other similar records.

[Milton's daughters' duty of reading to him without understanding what they read] must needs be a Tryal of Patience, almost beyond endurance; yet it was endured by both for a long time, yet the irksomeness of this imployment could not be always concealed, but broke out more and more into expressions of uneasiness; so that at length they were all (even the Eldest also) sent out to learn some Curious and Ingenious sorts of Manufacture, that are proper for Women to learn, particularly Imbroideries in Gold or Silver.

Phillips, p. xlii; Darbishire, pp. 77-78.

We are Now therefore in the Year 62. Then, and Soon after we are Assur'd he had Plenty of Other Assistance, and in a few Years after, by that time they were about 20 Years of Age, their Father, Partly from Their Complaints, Partly from his Own Reflections, Acquitted them of This Duty.

Richardson, p. xxxiv; Darbishire, pp. 227-228.

[Thomas Birch says of Milton's granddaughter Elizabeth Foster:] In my first visit to her on the 11th of February, 1737-8, she gave the following particulars, which she had often heard from her mother, Mrs. Clarke, who meeting with very ill treatment from Milton's last wife, left her father, and went to live with a lady, whom she called Merian. This lady going over to Ireland, and resolving to take Milton's daughter with her, if he would give his consent, wrote a letter to him of her design, and assured him, that 'as chance had thrown his daughter under her care, she would treat her no otherwise than as his daughter and her own companion.' She lived with that lady, till her marriage, and came over again to England during the troubles in Ireland, under king James II.

[4]

Milton, *A Complete Collection of the . . . Works*, ed. Thomas Birch,
I (1753), lxxvi; Masson, VI, 741 (brief summary); CM, XVIII, 263.

[On a visit from Thomas Birch to Milton's granddaughter
Elizabeth Foster on November 13, 1750:] She gave me a particular Account of the Severities of her Grandfather's last Wife
towards his three Daughters by his first, the two eldest of whom
she bound prentices to Workers in Gold-Lace, without his
knowledge; & forc'd the younger to leave his Family. M^rs.
Foster confess'd to me, that he was no fond Father, but assur'd
me that his Wife's ill Treatment of his Children gave him
great uneasiness; tho' in his State of Health & Blindness he
could not prevent it.

I am indebted to my colleague, Mr. Edward Ruhe, for the transcript
of this note from Birch's account in the British Museum, Add. MS.
35,397, f. 321v, from a letter of Birch to Yorke dated from London,
November 17, 1750. The visit had taken place on the thirteenth. This
matter of unkindness to the daughters, being a continuous affair (if
true), cannot be more definitely dated than as following the marriage.

His 3^d wife. Had no children by her. Very cruel to her children in law. Either now living or but lately dead at Chester.
born about the year 1642. His papers came all into her hands.

From John Ward's notes in the British Museum, Add. MS. 4320,
f. 232, as transcribed by Mr. Edward Ruhe. Ward makes numerous
errors in his account, such as saying that Milton died at the age of 63
(actually 65, almost 66), and that he lost his sight at the age of 40
(actually 43). But since his statement about Elizabeth Minshull's unkindness agrees substantially with Birch's, it deserves consideration. For
further information about Milton's daughters and his relations with them,
see the section on undated material below.

DIVORCE VIEWS ATTACKED BY JOHN EACHARD.

*I am not I'le assure you, any of those occasional Writers,
that missing preferment in the Vniversity can, presently write
you their new ways of Education; or being a little tormented
with an ill chosen Wife, set forth the Doctrine of Divorce to
be truly Evangelical.*

John Eachard, *The Grounds & Occasions of the Contempt of the
Clergy and Religion*, 1670, sigs. A4v-[A5]; Todd, I (1826), 64-65;

[5]

Raymond, p. 269; Parker, *Milton's Contemporary Reputation*, p. 110. This book was so popular that it reached its eighth edition in 1672, but Wing's *STC* notes only one edition (1671) between. The ninth edition did not appear until 1685.

SELDOM SEES MARVELL NOW.

[Speaking of Part I of *The Rehearsal Transpros'd*, published 1672:] For by chance I had not seen him of two years before; but after I undertook writing, I did more carefully avoid either visiting or sending to him, least I should any way involve him in my consequences.

Andrew Marvell, *The Rehearsal Transpros'd*, Part II, 1673, p. 377; Masson, VI, 707.

EARLY UNKNOWN ISSUE OF *ART OF LOGIC* (?).

Lowndes, *Bibliographer's Manual*, ed. Bohn, 1900, III, 1567, says that there was an edition of this date. Masson, VI, 686, declares this statement a mistake, and says there is none known before 1672. I have never seen any other evidence of an issue of 1670.

REVISED EDITION OF L'ESTRANGE'S *TOLERATION DIS-CUSS'D* ATTACKING *THE TENURE OF KINGS*.

[1] Every Worthy Man, *in* Parliament, *may, for the* Publique Good, *be thought a fit* Peer, *and* Judge *of the* King. P. 24.

[Marginal note:] Tenure of Kings. 1649.

[2] *It is lawful for* any, *who have the* Power, *to call to* Accompt, *a* Tyrant, *or* Wicked King; *And after due* Conviction, *to* Depose, *and put him to* Death, *if the* Ordinary Magistrate *have* Neglected, *or* Deny'd *to do it.*

[Marginal note:] Tenure of Kings. 1649.

Sir Roger L'Estrange, *Toleration Discuss'd*, 1670, pp. 64, 65. Though bearing the same title as L'Estrange's book of 1663 (*q.v.*), this volume is radically revised and almost rewritten. Professor Sensabaugh, who discusses the 1663 edition on pp. 32-35 of *That Grand Whig Milton*, does not mention that of 1670.

RECEIVES GIFT OF WATCH FROM FRENCH NOBLEMAN
(?).

MILTON'S WATCH FOUND.

IN POSSESSION OF A CHICAGO ANTIQUARIAN.

HE DISCOVERED THE POET'S TREASURE IN A ST. LOUIS PAWNSHOP.

RAISED FIGURES ON ITS DIAL MARK THE HOURS OF THE DAY.

Chicago, Sept. 25.—The ponderous silver watch, upon whose raised dial Poet John Milton felt the time during several of the years of his blindness that afflicted him toward the end of his life, is now in possession of a Chicago antiquarian, who found it recently in the shop of a St. Louis pawnbroker.

About 10 months ago a foreigner entered the store of B. Zuckerman in St. Louis, and laid upon the counter a leather case containing a big silver watch and a collection of ancient coins.

The stranger proved to be the Marquis Costello de Shamer of Verona, Italy. He said he had lost all his money, and offered to part with his treasures for $500, but declared the watch was priceless, as it had been the property of John Milton. The coins, also, were of great value.

After the usual amount of haggling, Mr. Zuckerman secured the watch and coins at much less than $500, and having sold the coins at a handsome advance, readily parted with the watch to a Chicago collector who had discovered its value.

Aside from its historic associations the timepiece is very interesting. The watch is about three times the thickness of an ordinary timepiece, and extremely heavy.

A tiny bell strikes the hours in silvery tones that must have delighted the blind poet's ear. The most interesting feature, however, is the face.

Around the centre-pin is a small brass dial upon which the hours are marked in Arabic numerals. Surrounding this is a porcelain dial bearing the Roman symbols from I. to XII. in black ink. These numerals are slightly raised, and upon them Milton's fingers traced the hours when his eyes could not distinguish day from night.

The watch was made for the poet by order of a French nobleman and presented to him in 1670, when he had been blind for 16 years. When he died four years later it was found under his pillow. In time it was sold, and at last it has come to Chicago.

This story, however credible it may be, comes from a source which I am unable to identify. It is an anonymous newspaper clipping, not bearing the name or date of the newspaper, from a Milton collection of Mr. Abram G. Cutter, lent to me in 1940 by the kindness of a mutual friend, Mr. Clement K. Stodder of Boston. From the advertisements on the back of the clipping, which relate to real estate for sale in Boston and surrounding towns, and which mention both horse cars and electric cars as then in operation, I judge that it comes from a Boston paper of about 1900. This watch apparently has no connection with that mentioned above under 1631 (I, 225). Its present location is unknown.

PORTRAIT DONE BY WILLIAM FAITHORNE.

Ioannis Miltoni Effigies Ætat: 62. 1670. Gul. Faithorne ad Vivum Delin. et sculpsit.

Inscription on the portrait of Milton used as a frontispiece for the first edition of his *History of Britain*, 1670; see John F. Marsh, "On the Engraved Portraits and Pretended Portraits of Milton," *Transactions of the Historic Society of Lancashire and Cheshire*, XII (1860), nos. 24 ff.; Williamson, *Milton Tercentenary*, pp. 6-7, 48-58; Masson, VI, 755-756. There are good reproductions in Williamson, facing p. 5; CM, X, frontispiece; and Fletcher facsimile, III, 62. One has also appeared as the frontispiece of the present volume. In addition, there are of course endless other discussions and reproductions of it. The legend quoted above (in which italic letters simulate the effect of handwriting in the original) appears in two sections. The first part ("*Ioannis . . . 1670*") is inscribed on the front of the base supporting the oval con-

[8]

taining the portrait; the second is written in smaller letters above the top of the base, part on the left and part on the right of the oval. There is said to be also an early state of the engraving misdated 1607.

The original portrait by Faithorne has disappeared from sight, though it must have been in existence at least as late as 1760. In that year the engraver Cipriani made an etching of it for Thomas Hollis, bearing the inscription: "Iohn Milton Drawn and etched MDCCLX by I. B. Cipriani a Tvscan at the desire of Thomas Hollis F. R. and A. SS. from a portrait in crayons now in the possession of Mess. Tonson Booksellers in the Strand London." Cipriani's etching, which is very like the above engraving, is noticeably different from the two portraits immediately to be described below as numbers 1 and 2. Cipriani's words show also that the original was in crayons and not in oils. Closely related to this drawing are the following:

1. The Baker or Bayfordbury crayon drawing, said to be by Faithorne and to have been drawn from life. After belonging to the Tonsons, it descended on the death of Richard Tonson (1772) to his nephew William Baker of Bayfordbury Park, Hertfordshire, in whose family it remained until Air Marshal Sir Brian Baker had it sold at Christie's in 1953. The present owners, Messrs. William H. Robinson (1953), have most courteously provided me with an excellent photograph of it, which appeared as the frontispiece of Volume IV of the present work. They have also given me a good deal of information about it with which to supplement that given by Marsh (p. 165), Masson (VI, 755-756), Williamson (pp. 9, 34), and others. Reproductions of it may also be found in Sotheby's *Ramblings* (frontispiece), in Williamson (facing p. 9), in Richard Garnett and Edmund Gosse's *English Literature An Illustrated Record* (III [New York and London, 1906], frontispiece, reproduced in color), and elsewhere. Louis Fagan, in his *Descriptive Catalogue of the Engraved Works of William Faithorne* (1888) and in his article on him in the *DNB* (1889), makes no question that this and the next following number are by Faithorne. Marsh thinks it not by Faithorne but an eighteenth-century copy (p. 165). Masson wavers, Fagan gives it unquestioningly to Faithorne, Williamson thinks it "probably" by Faithorne, and Messrs. Robinson are sure that it is by him, and that it is the picture about which Milton's favorite daughter Deborah exclaimed with so much emotion (see below). It now carries on the back a printed card of about 1800-1810, quoting Newton that two Milton portraits are of greater value than all the others and are undoubted originals: the Onslow portrait (see above, I, 206-207; II, frontispiece) and the Richardson-Tonson crayon (so called because it was owned by Jonathan Richardson before it came to the Tonsons). The card continues: "THIS is the Crayons Picture above mentioned." The drawing measures 10 5/8" by 8 1/8". Messrs.

Robinson consider Williamson's facsimile "a very poor reproduction indeed" photographically. I am grateful to them for aid, and also to Lady Rosa A. Clinton-Baker of London, Miss Winifred M. Baker of Hertford, and Messrs. T. Agnew and Sons of London.

2. The Hobart painting. Sotheby's catalogue of its sale (March 5-6, 1934, item 355) calls it a "Bust portrait in oils, full face, with long flowing hair, dark dress and white collar, framed and glazed, oval canvas, 23 in. by 18 in." A reproduction faces that page. This portrait, which Williamson ranks "next in position to the Bayfordbury drawing," is said to be traced back through Sir Robert H. Hobart, Bart., to his maternal uncle, Mr. Edmund F. Moore, great-great-grandson of Sir Thomas Moore of Sayes Court, Chertsey, son of David Moore and Anne Agar, who was the daughter of Anne Milton Agar, the poet's sister. It came later to Lt. Col. Sir Vere Hobart, called the senior surviving representative of the Milton family, from whose collection it was sold at Sotheby's in 1934 and came to Mr. Arthur Pforzheimer of Woodmere, New York. At his death it was sold, but I have not been able to discover who now owns it. It is described by Williamson (pp. 7, 37), and reproduced by him facing p. 7. The reproduction in the Sotheby catalogue, though obviously the same picture, is much softer, clearer, and more attractive. This picture was exhibited at the South Kensington Museum in 1866. I am greatly indebted for attempts to locate it to Mr. E. Byrne Hackett of New York, Messrs. Sotheby and Company of London, Miss Emily Driscoll of New York, and Mrs. Pforzheimer, who tried in vain to ascertain who bought it from her late husband's estate.

3. The engraving for the *History of Britain* quoted above as the main text for the present entry. According to the legend Faithorne himself engraved it, and presumably from his own original portrait.

4. The print made in 1671 by Dolle as a frontispiece for Milton's *Art of Logic*, 1672, and for *Paradise Lost*, 1674. These will be described in their appropriate places below.

5. The frontispiece to *Paradise Lost*, 1688, fourth edition, by White. Reproduced in Williamson, *Milton Tercentenary*, facing p. 117.

In summary, the Baker and Hobart portraits are much alike, and the three frontispieces are also much alike. In position, clothing, and expression the frontispieces are more like one another than like the portraits; and the portraits similarly are more like each other than like the frontispieces.

[Likeness of John Milton at the age of 62, in 1670. William Faithorne drew it from the life and engraved it.]

the Picture in Crayons I have of him was shown her [Milton's daughter Deborah] After several Others, or which were

Pretended to be His; when Those were shown, and She was Ask'd if She could recollect if She had ever seen Such a Face. No, No. but when This was Produc'd, in a Transport,—— 'tis My Father, 'tis my Dear Father! I see him! 'tis Him! and then She put her Hands to several Parts of Her Face, 'tis the very Man! Here, Here——

Richardson, p. xxxvi; Darbishire, p. 229. The reference could be to either the lost Faithorne or the Baker-Bayfordbury drawing described above as number 1. According to the card on the latter, it must have been that one. Somewhat similar anecdotes may be found in Marsh, pp. 137-139, and elsewhere.

JANUARY. "MILTON'S CASE" MENTIONED IN LEGAL PROCEEDINGS.

. . . This is the Very same with Miltons Case Lately in Starr [?]: where it was Adjudged that an Jndeb Assumpsitt will not Lye, in this Case. (And J thinke hee Added that the Verdict would nott helpe.). . .

Public Record Office, SP 29/272, ff. 231-231v; *CSP Dom, 1670,* p. 46. This obscure reference to one Milton, probably not the poet, is part of a long collection of material described by *CSP* as "portion of the pleadings . . . on a legal case referring to the King's right of presentation." The reference may possibly be to a William Milton, who was defendant in a case in the Star Chamber in 1634; see *CSP Dom, 1634-1635,* pp. 256, 290. William Milton's name also occurs frequently in the lists of plaintiffs and defendants in Chancery pleadings.

MARCH (?). IS CONSULTED ABOUT DIVORCE PROCEEDINGS FOR LORD ROOS.

And when the Subject of Divorce was under consideration with the Lords, upon the account of the Lord Ross, hee was consulted by an Eminent Member of that house.

The "earliest" biography, f. 144; Darbishire, p. 33; Masson, VI, 572-574, 639-640. The Roos story is sordid and complicated, but must be told in some detail to clarify this reference.

John Manners, Lord Roos (or Ross), son of the Earl of Rutland, had married Anne, daughter of Henry Pierrepont, Marquis of Dorchester. This lady and her father and her husband were all unusual people. She was self-willed and unfaithful; her husband was apparently impotent and weak; and her father was violent. As early as 1660 the Marquis had challenged his son-in-law to a duel for ill treatment of the lady, and had published the abusive letters written by each man to the other, in which the father called the son-in-law a whelp and a coward, and the son-in-law branded the father a fool and an ass. This quarrel, though patched up by wiser friends, smoldered for some time until the lady, after having casually left her husband and spent some months in London, returned home pregnant. When he complained, she, far from denying the fact, boasted of it and taunted him with the fact that the child, if a boy, would succeed to the title of Earl of Rutland. Lord Roos's mother, the Countess of Rutland, took over at this point and held the wife virtually prisoner until the baby was born. She then turned her out, but not before the expectant mother had so worked on the feelings of her susceptible father that he considered her the innocent victim of outrageous abuse.

The new baby, a boy, was named Ignoto—the unknown. After the lady's return home, her father made a great stir in her behalf. He had already consulted lawyers about the possibility of removing her by force from Roos's home, but no one could find a legal pretext. A similar appeal to the king had met failure. But after her return home, he obtained a hearing before the king and numerous bishops and lords. To his surprise and humiliation the inquiry revealed the facts of his daughter's waywardness, which she continued shortly afterwards by running away from his home. In atonement for his former mistakes he apologized to the Earl of Rutland, both privately and in the House of Lords.

But the story has only begun. Without opposition now from her father, Lord Roos brought in a bill into the Court of Arches, an ecclesiastical court, for separation on the grounds of her adultery. He won his plea, probably some time in 1661.

To prevent the new baby from inheriting the Rutland title, Lord Roos or his friends next introduced into the House of Lords on April 19, 1662, a bill to declare Ignoto illegitimate and a bastard incapable of inheritance, with a like bar against any future children which the Lady Roos might bear. Both fathers supported the bill in the House. But some members were distrustful of such an innovation. After a month or so of inactivity the bill drops out of sight from the records.

Some four years later, however, on October 22, 1666, the same or a similar bill was introduced as if nothing had happened. This time the mother was invited to the hearing, but it was soon reported that she had fled to Ireland—with the father of Ignoto. So the bill moved along quickly towards passage until one day it met an unexpected obstruction. On November 29, 1666, the Duke of Buckingham suddenly opposed the bill for the trivial reason that it named the husband Lord

Roos, a title which he claimed in his own family though everyone had been giving it to its present carrier. Though few members sympathized with the Duke, he stoutly insisted on his point until everyone was tired of it. On December 19, 1666, indeed, he and the Marquis of Dorchester climaxed the squabble by calling each other liars and other insulting names so heatedly that both men were committed to the Tower. On January 11, 1667, Lord Roos swore under examination that he could not be the child's father because since March 4, 1659, and indeed since several months earlier, he had had "no carnal Knowledge of his Wife, the Lady *Anne Ross*." Shortly afterwards, on February 8, 1667, after consent from both Houses, the king gave the bill for denying legitimacy to Ignoto his consent.

But on March 5, 1670, the struggle broke out again, this time in the form of a bill in the House of Lords to enable Lord Roos to marry again. It took over a month of debating, some of it causing a considerable stir, before this bill could pass. Indeed, John Evelyn attended the session of March 22, 1670, when the king himself was present, and later wrote in his diary: "Such an occasion and sight had not been seene in England since the time of Hen. VIII." The concurrent debates in the House of Commons, which have been preserved in detail, were heated, including the remark of Sir Charles Harbord that "the worst of whores is a wife-whore." The bill eventually passed both houses and was signed into law by the king on April 11, 1670.

This account is based on the *Journals* of the Houses of Commons and Lords for the periods indicated (Lords: XI, 433-450; XII, 15-110, 191, 300-350; Commons: VIII, 675-685); Clarendon's *Life* by himself, 1817, II, 331-337; Wood's *Fasti*, ed. Bliss, II (1820), 37, under "Pierpont, Robert"; the *DNB* under "Pierrepont, Henry"; John Harold Wilson, *A Rake and his Times: George Villiers, 2nd Duke of Buckingham*, 1954, pp. 64-65; and the letters of Roos and Dorchester published in 1659.

Interesting as these proceedings were in themselves, they were far more so as a trial balloon to discover the feasibility of a divorce for Charles II from his barren queen. As Burnet reveals in his *History of his Own Time* (I [1815], 337-338), many courtiers had long been urging Charles to put away his wife and take another, one strong contender for this choice being the mother of the Duke of Monmouth. There were schemes for getting rid of the queen in various ways. When the Roos separation was granted, it seemed providential to the supporters of the bill; and when the bill to allow Roos to marry again was under debate, Burnet says the king was "earnest in the setting it on." After its passage everything seemed ready for putting through the royal bill. But for some unknown reason, three days before the date set, the king withdrew it, and nothing more came of it.

Milton's connection with this notorious event poses several questions. First, when did it happen? Second, who suggested asking his help? Third, what help did he give? None of these questions is answered in any accounts of the proceedings which I have seen; indeed, none mentions Milton's name at all. But we can make some guesses.

First, as to the date, he might have come in (1) between April 19 and May 7, 1662, when the bill for branding the child Ignoto illegitimate was being considered in the House of Lords; (2) between October 22, 1666, and February 8, 1667, when the second similar bill was in debate; or (3) between March 5 and April 11, 1670, during the debate on the bill to allow Lord Roos to remarry. His advice as a famous student of divorce might have been useful at any of these points. But the first two, being concentrated chiefly on the legitimacy of the baby, are less likely than the third, which concerned Lord Roos's permission to marry again. The last named was also certainly the occasion of the widest public interest of the three. It is the part selected for full report in the debates of the House of Commons (March 30-31, 1670), and it was the one about which Evelyn exclaimed (March 22). This note is therefore filed under March, 1670, as the likeliest date. Masson similarly dates it.

Second, who proposed consulting Milton? Again, we can only guess. Both the anonymous biographer and Wood (quoted below) merely mention "an Eminent Member" of the House of Lords, though Wood adds "a chief Officer of State" as a second participant. The Earl of Bridgewater certainly knew Milton as the author of *Comus*, in which he had acted as a youth, and may conceivably have advised seeing him. The Earl of Anglesey, to whom Edward Phillips says Milton gave the unlicensed papers of his *History of Britain*, is another candidate—and Masson's. Masson questions whether Lord Keeper Bridgman may have been the "chief Officer." Conceivably the Duke of York, who visited Milton as described above, might have carried this message along with others. Finally, if the idea could have come through the House of Commons to the Lords, since the Commons debated the bill vigorously, the likeliest person to have started the notion would of course have been Andrew Marvell, who actually spoke several times as mentioned in the records. He referred to the affair half a dozen times in his letters; see Margoliouth's edition, 1927, pp. 102, 103, 105, 301, 303.

Third, what help did Milton give? Again, we have to guess. If his advice had been contrary to the king's wish, we might find here some slight reason for the Duke's sour account of his encounter, if he was the agent. But on the basis of Milton's previous ideas and writings, it seems almost inevitable that he should have favored the divorce, especially in view of the flighty character of the Lady Roos. Much of the debate in the House of Commons, incidentally, turned on interpretations of Biblical passages about marriage and divorce, of which Milton was a master if anyone was. It is therefore not an unreasonable guess that his information and opinion may have had some weight in gaining the passage of the bill of 1670.

It would be most interesting if further information about Milton's part in this action could be discovered.

. . . after his Majesties Restauration, when the subject of Divorce was under consideration with the Lords upon the account of *John* lord *Ros* or *Roos* his separation from his Wife *Anne Pierpont* eldest daughter to *Henry* Marquess of *Dorchester*, he was consulted by an eminent Member of that House, as he was about that time by a chief Officer of State, as being the prime person that was knowing in that affair.

Wood, 1, 882; Darbishire, p. 41.

ABOUT APRIL 28. JOHN AUBREY QUOTES FROM AND REFERS TO MILTON'S *HISTORY OF BRITAIN*.

CHIPPENHAM . . . .

(K. Edgar) 'The Twelve-tyde following, all oathes forgotten, the Danes came to Chippenham in Wiltshire, dispeopling the country round, dispossessing some, driving others beyond the sea. A.D. 878.'—*J. Milton's History*. . . .

HUBBA'S-LOWE. (In Chippenham.)

'In the reign of King Ethelred, Hinguor and Hubba, two brothers, Danes, Leaders, who had gott footing among the E. Angles. These Pagans, Asserius saith, came from Danubius. Bruern, a nobleman, whose wife King Osbert had ravished, called in Hinguor and Hubba to revenge him.'—*J. Milton's History, page* 233. 8vo. . . .

[In connection with King Athelstan and his laws and William of Malmesbury:] V. Jo. Milton's Hist.

John Aubrey, *Wiltshire. The Topographical Collections*, ed. Jackson, Devises, 1862, pp. 66, 74, 258. Though this work was first published in 1862, Aubrey's preface is dated April 28, 1670. This entry is therefore so dated. The first entry is a fairly correct quotation from Milton's *History of Britain*, CM, X, 213, and the second similarly from p. 207. Both are slightly altered to fit the sentences. The third may be a reference to p. 238. Aubrey is not quoting from the 1670-71 edition, but from 1677, 1678, or 1695.

There was heretofore (vide J. Milton) a great fight with the Danes, which made the inhabitants give it that name [Slaughtersford.]

Aubrey, *Natural History of Wiltshire,* ed. John Britton, 1847, p. 50; quoted also in Aubrey's *Remaines of Gentilisme and Judaisme,* ed. James Britten, Publications of the Folk-Lore Society, IV (1881), 239. The date of composition is unknown; it is put here for convenience with Aubrey's other references. The editor says Aubrey began it in 1656 and finished it in 1686, with some additions up to 1691. It was first published in 1847. Though Milton does not use the name Slaughtersford, the reference seems to be to CM, X, 258-259.

MAY(?). NEPHEW EDWARD PHILLIPS EXALTS *PARADISE LOST* IN BUCHLER'S *THESAURUS.*

Joannes Miltonius, præter alia quæ scripsit elegantissima, tum Anglicè, tum Latinè, nuper publici juris fecit Paradisum Amissum, *Poema, quod, sive sublimitatem argumenti, sive leporem simul, et majestatem styli, sive sublimitatem inventionis, sive similitudines et descriptiones quam maximè naturales, respiciamus, verè Heroicum, ni fallor, audiet: plurium enim suffragiis qui non nesciunt judicare, censetur perfectionem hujus generis poematis assecutum esse.*

Edward Phillips, "Compendiosa Enumeratio Poetarum," in John Buchler's *Phrasium Poeticarum Thesaurus,* 17th edition, 1669, p. 270; William Godwin, *Lives of Edward and John Phillips,* 1815, p. 145; Masson, VI, 635-636; Parker, *Milton's Contemporary Reputation,* pp. 109-110. This is the first edition of Buchler's book to carry Phillips's supplement. The mention of Milton remains practically unchanged in the 1679 edition, p. 399. Though the title page is dated 1669, the Term Catalogues (I, 40) carry the book under date of the Easter term, 1670. It is therefore here dated accordingly.

[John Milton, in addition to other most elegant books which he has written, both in English and in Latin, has lately presented to public opinion *Paradise Lost,* a poem which, whether we regard the sublimity of the subject, or the combined pleasantness and majesty of the style, or the sublimity of the inven-

[16]

tion, or the supremely natural images and descriptions, will, if I am not mistaken, be received as truly heroic; for by the votes of the many who are not ignorant how to judge, it is deemed to have achieved perfection in this kind of poetry.]

MAY 29. *PARADISE REGAINED* ALREADY IN PRINT(?).

In an advertisement of this and two other books by Milton appended to Benjamin Priolo's *History of France under the Ministry of Cardinal Mazarine,* 1671, quoted below under that date, is the statement about two books on the list: "In the Press 29th. *May,* 1670." This note seems to indicate that the whole list was made up at that time. If it was, then Milton's poem must then already have been in print or at least well enough along toward publication so that its publisher could plan to advertise it. No copy of the poem dated 1670 has however been found. It is of course possible that 1670 is a misprint for 1671, or there may be some other mistake in the catalogue of Starkey's books. But the simplest interpretation of the fact would seem to be that the poem was in print at that date. What delayed its appearance until the following year I have no idea.

JULY 2. *PARADISE REGAINED* LICENSED BY TOMKYNS.

Licensed, *July* 2. 1670.

Endorsement on flyleaf opposite title page of first edition of *Paradise Regained,* 1671; Masson, VI, 651; CM, II, 541; Fletcher facsimile, IV, 50. Though Tomkyns's name does not appear here, it does on the entry in the Stationers' Registers; see below, September 10, 1670.

SEPTEMBER 10. *PARADISE REGAINED* AND *SAMSON AGONISTES* REGISTERED.

Septemb. 10 1670

Master John Starkey. Entred ... under the hands of Master THO: TOMKYNS and Master Warden ROPER a copie or booke intituled *Paradise regayn'd*; A Poem in 4 Bookes. The Author, **John Milton.** To wch is added *Samson Agonistes*, A drammadic Poem, by the same Author. ... vj^d

Stationers' Registers, II, 415; Masson, VI, 651; Fletcher facsimile, IV, 15. Masson somehow alters the date to September 20. The word "drammadic" is preceded in the register by "dramma," canceled.

BEFORE NOVEMBER (?). AGREES TO SUPPRESS PASSAGES IN MANUSCRIPT OF *HISTORY OF BRITAIN*; THE "DIGRESSION."

The Reader may take notice, That this Character of Mr. Miltons was a part of his History of Britain, *and by him designed to be Printed: But out of tenderness to a Party,* [*whom neither this nor much more Lenity has had the luck to oblige*] *it was struck out for some harshness, being only such a Digression, as the History it self would not be discomposed by its omission.*

Milton, *Character of the Long Parliament*, 1681, "To the Reader," sig. A2; CM, XVIII, 247. Though no date for this action is given, it must have been previous to, and presumably not long before, publication of the *History*, which is assigned here to November, 1670. It is not even sure that the *Character* constitutes all of the portion struck out; see CM, XVIII, 519. Masson deals with this problem at some length at VI, 806-812, where he assumes that the *Character* was not the passage primarily objected to, but that the passages which are said to have come to the Earl of Anglesey are other sections or even perhaps doctored passages which Milton refused to accept in their changed form. Masson also interprets the "Party" mentioned here as "the Presbyterians and other old Parliamentarians." Benjamin Boyce (*The Polemic Character*, 1955, p. 43) asserts that the deleted section, despite its published title, is not a true character, doubts that Milton ever gave it such a label, and suggests that Milton wrote it as a corrective to the digression in praise of Parliament which he had included in his *Apology*. But in view of Milton's constant deference to Parliament as the lawgiving body of English, the third point seems hard to accept.

The Digression.
in Miltons History of England.
To come in Lib. 3. page 110. after these words.

Heading to Harvard College Library manuscript, shelf mark 14496.34, corresponding for the most part with the published *Character of the Long Parliament*; CM, X, 317-325, with some corrections at XVIII, 645-646, and changes in the manuscript recorded at XVIII, 515-516 and 654. The first 400 words, or thereabouts, have no corresponding passage in the *Character*. The manuscript consists of 12 pages, about six by seven and a half inches. The property of Thomas Mostyn in 1744, advertised by the London bookseller Ellis in the early twentieth century, it was bought for Harvard in 1926. See Stevens,

Reference Guide, No. 84; French, "The Autographs of Milton," No. 50; CM, as indicated. Emma Unger and William A. Jackson, in *The Carl H. Pforzheimer Library*, No. 710, state that there are several early manuscripts of this digression, but give no locations for them.

In the year 70 also came abroad his *History* of *Britain*, whereof we had occasion to speak before. He deduc'd it only to the *Norman* Conquest, and yet we have it not as it came out of his hands; for the Licensers, those sworn Officers to destroy Learning, Liberty, and good Sense, expung'd several passages of it wherin he expos'd the Superstition, Pride, and Cunning of the Popish Monks in the *Saxon* Times, but apply'd by the sagacious Licensers to *Charles* the Second's Bishops.

Milton, *Works*, ed. Toland, 1698, I, 43; Darbishire, p. 185.

NOVEMBER(?). PIERRE DU MOULIN ATTACKS MILTON AND GIVES SOME HISTORY OF THE *CLAMOR* CONTROVERSY.

Duabus istis rationibus adductus Religionem & Ecclesiam mihi vindicandas esse duxi, quod solutâ potissimùm oratione pleniùs exequi conatus sum Gallicâ Diatribâ justi voluminis & libello cui titulus est Clamor Regii sanguinis ad Cœlum, *in cujus calce* Oden *ad* Salmasium, & Iambum *ad* Miltonum *apposueram, quæ cum aliis ejusdem argumenti versibus hîc etiam exhibeo. Quòd stimulis non pepercerim, & omnem vehementiam nimis lenem existimaverim quâ tam criminosa & portentosa vesania sugillaretur, nemo opinor qui Dei gloriæ zelo accenditur, Religionémque sartam tectam & Ecclesiam cupit incolumen, me inclementis & immoderati animi reum faciet. Quid nobis reliquum erat, rebus perduellium prosperè fluentibus, & parricidio triumphante, latámque portam ad Regum Majestatem violandam omnibus populis apierente; quàm ut grandem invidiam Religioni creatam, & paucorum hypocritarum crimine bonorum omnium capitibus impendens periculum quàm maximâ aversatione & detestatione amoliremur. . . .*

[19]

In impurissimum Nebulonem Joannem Miltonum,
Parricidarum & Parricidii Advocatum.
Quò quò citato ruitis injussi pede
Acres Iambi? . . .
                    Crux mala,
Hos candidatos, & tuos mando tibi. . . .

Epistolam quam Iambo in MILTONUM *Author subjunxe-
rat, per operarum nostrarum festinantiam prætermissam, hîc
exhibemus; ad paginam 36 Libelli secundi referendam.*

In quod periculum me conjecerit prima hujus carminis cum
Clamore Regii sanguinis editio, publicâ notitiâ dignum haud
existimarem, nisi divini præsidii miraculum quo servatus sum
incolumis, communi bonorum admiratione & summi Liberatoris
laude dignissimum esset . . . At *Morus*, tantæ invidiæ impar,
in Regia causa frigere cœpit, & *Clamoris* Authorem *Miltono*
indicavit. Enimvero in sua ad *Miltoni* maledicta responsione,
duos adhibuit testes, præcipuæ apud perduelles fidei, qui Authorem probè nôssent, & rogati possent revelare. Unde sanè
mihi & capiti meo certissimum impendebat exitium. At magnus
ille justitiæ vindex, cui & hanc operam & hoc caput libens de-
voveram, per *Miltoni* superbiam salutem meam asseruit; ut ejus
sapientiæ solemne est ex malis bona, ex tenebris lucem elicere.
Miltonus enim qui plenis caninæ eloquentiæ velis in *Morum*
invectus fuerat, quique id ferme unicum *Defensionis secundæ*
suæ fecerat argumentum, ut *Mori* vitam atque famam laceraret;
adduci nunquam potuit ut se tam crassè hallucinatum esse fa-
teretur. Scilicet metuens nè cæcitati ejus populus illuderet, eúm-
que compararent Grammaticorum pueri Catulo illi cæco apud
Juvenalem qui piscem *Domitiano* donatum laudaturus
                    plurima dixit
    In lævum conversus, at illi dextra jacebat
    Bellua.
Perseverante igitur *Miltono* totum illud periculosi in Regem
amoris crimen *Moro* impingere, non poterant cæteri perduelles

sine magna boni patroni sui injuria alium à *Moro* tanti criminis reum peragere. Cúmque *Miltonus* me salvum esse mallet quàm se ridiculum, hoc operæ meæ præmium tuli, ut *Miltonum* quem inclementiùs acceperam haberem patronum, & capitis mei sedulum ὑπασπιστήν. Parce risu, Lector; & Deo Liberatori, Optimo, Maximo, & Sapientissimo, summas mecum gratias age.

Pierre du Moulin, ΠΑΡΕΡΓΑ. *Poematvm Libelli Tres*, 1670, Book II, sigs. F8-F8v and pages 36-42; Book III, pages 141-142; Masson, v, 219-221 (most of the selection); Parker, *Milton's Contemporary Reputation*, pp. 110-111 (almost all this quotation). The poem "In impurissimum Nebulonem Joannem Miltonum," of which only the first and last sentences are given here, is quoted extensively above under date of August, 1652, in the entry for the publication of *Regii Sanguinis Clamor*. In the same entry is the section omitted a few lines later between "dignissimum esset" and "At *Morus*." It tells how du Moulin sent the copy for his book to More, who arranged for its printing; how Milton decided that More was the author; and how amused du Moulin felt about the affair. Latin copies of du Moulin's poems appear in British Museum Burney MS. 406, ff. 64v-71v (numbered from the back). An English translation appears in British Museum Add. MS. 24,501, ff. 70 ff. The French book referred to is his *Apologie de la Religion Reformée*. This entry is dated from its appearance in the *Term Catalogues* (I, 59) under date of November 22, 1670.

[Induced by these two reasons, I considered that religion and the church ought to be vindicated by me, a task which with the freest possible style I tried to follow more fully with a French treatise and with a book which has the title *The Cry of the Royal Blood to Heaven*, in the heel of which I had put an ode to Salmasius and iambics to Milton, which I present here also with other verses on the same subject. Because I had not spared the goads, and had not considered any vehemence too strong by which so criminal and horrible madness might be reviled, no one, I believe, who is kindled with zeal for the glory of God, and who desires religion put in order and defended and the church preserved, will accuse me of an unkind and immoderate spirit. What was left to us, while the enemy's affairs were flowing prosperously, and parricide triumphant and opening to all nations a broad doorway to the

violation of the majesty of kings, except with the greatest aver-
sion and detestation to repel the great enmity created against
religion and the danger hanging over the heads of all good men
through the crime of a few hypocrites? . . .

> To the beastly blackguard John Milton,
> Advocate of parricides and parricide.
> Where, where, my sharp iambics, do you rush
> Unordered, on quick foot? . . .
> Evil gallows,
> I deliver to you these your candidates. . . .

I give here the letter which the author had submitted to
Milton in iambic meter, omitted by the haste of my works;
to be referred to page 36 of the second book.

The peril into which the first publication of this poem with
The Cry of the Royal Blood threw me I should have considered
hardly worth public notice, if the miracle of divine guidance by
which I was kept safe had not been most worthy of the general admiration of good men and of their praise of the most
high Saviour. . . . But More, unequal to such hatred, began to
grow cold in the royal cause, and indicated to Milton the author of the *Cry*. For truly in his reply to Milton's foul language he brought two witnesses highly regarded among the
enemy, who might well have known the author, and who might,
if asked, have been able to reveal him. Thus there truly hung
over me and my head most certain ruin. But that great Vindi-
cator of justice, to whom I had freely devoted both this work
and this head, saved my life through Milton's pride; as it is
the custom of His wisdom to draw good out of evil, light out
of darkness. For Milton, who had been carried against More
by the full sails of his snappish eloquence, and who had made
it almost the only point of his *Second Defense* to pull to pieces
the life and fame of More, could never be brought to confess
himself to be so grossly deceived. Evidently fearing that the
people would jeer at his blindness, and that the children of the

grammarians might compare him to that Catullus in Juvenal, who, about to praise the fish given to Domitian, "made most of his speech while turning to the left, but the monster lay at his right hand." As Milton thus persisted in laying that whole crime of the dangerous love of the king on More, the rest of the enemy could not without great injury to their good patron continue the prosecution of any other defendant than More for so great a crime. And since Milton preferred to have me safe rather than himself ridiculous, I got this reward for my work, that I had Milton, whom I had treated pretty roughly, as my patron and as the solicitous shield-bearer for my head. Spare the laugh, reader; and give the highest thanks with me to God the best, greatest, and most wise Deliverer.]

NOVEMBER (?). PUBLISHES *HISTORY OF BRITAIN*.

The History of Britain, That part especially now call'd England. From the first Traditional Beginning, continu'd to the Norman Conqvest. Collected out of the antientest and best Authours thereof by John Milton. London, Printed by J.M. for James Allestry, at the Rose and Crown in St. Paul's Church-Yard, MDCLXX.

Title page of first edition; CM, X, facing p. 1. The date comes from that of the Term Catalogues in which it is announced; see below. See also above, II, 218 and 233, for entries about Milton's first beginning of the writing of this book. The text of the *History* is given in CM, X, 1-328, with brief notes at pp. [385]-[386]. CM, XVIII also contains a number of passages relating to it at pp. 256-257 (Toland's additions to the first edition), 467-483 (the index, presumed to be at least in part Milton's own work), 514-519 (notes on *The Character of the Long Parliament*), 633-634 (notes on the index), and 645-647 (notes on the *History*). Important articles on the *History* are by Charles H. Firth in *Proceedings of the British Academy*, III (1908), 225-257; by Harry Glicksman in *PMLA*, XXXV (1920), 116-122; and by Harris Fletcher in *Journal of English and Germanic Philology*, XXXV (1936), 405-414. See also J. M. French, "Milton as a Historian," *PMLA*, L (1935), 469-479; Masson, VI, 642-649. Prefixed to the *History* is the 1670 engraving of Milton by Faithorne described above under date of 1670; CM, X, frontispiece. The date of publication may conceivably have been earlier.

. . . hee finish'd [various works] after the Restoration: As also the *Brittish history* down to the Conquest. . . .

The "earliest" biography, f. 143; Darbishire, p. 29.

9 The History of Britain, from yᵉ first Tradiconall beginning, cōtinued to the Norman Conquest. 4ᵗᵒ Lōdon MDCLXX. for James Alestry Rose & Crowne Ps ch-yard. Scripsit ꝑut ꝑ Effigiem [sed falsam] 1670. ætate 62.

Aubrey, f. 68v; Darbishire, p. 9. The brackets are Aubrey's. The Latin at the end may be translated: "He wrote it, according to his portrait [i.e., the frontispiece], which is false, in 1670 at the age of 62." Though the "sed" in the brackets is so blotted as to be illegible, a bit of the lower end of the long s and of the upper end of the d are still visible, so that this reading, which is that of Miss Darbishire and of Clarke in his edition, is reasonably certain.

Here [in Bunhill] it was also that he finisht and publisht his History of our Nation till the Conquest, all compleat so far as he went, some Passages only excepted, which being thought too sharp against the Clergy, could not pass the Hand of the Licencer, were in the Hands of the late Earl of *Anglesey* while he liv'd; where at present is uncertain.

Phillips, p. xxxix; Darbishire, p. 75.

The History of *Brittain*, that part especially now called *England*: From the first Traditional Beginning, continued to the *Norman* Conquest. Collected out of the Ancientest and best Authors thereof, in 4ᵗᵒ.

Phillips, p. [lii]; not in Darbishire.

(25) *History of Britany from the first traditional beginning, continued to the Norman Conquest.* Lond. 1670, qu. This History when it first came abroad, had only the reputation of the putting of our old Authors neatly together in a connex'd story, not abstaining from some lashes at the ignorance, or I know not what, of those times.

Wood, I, 883; Darbishire, p. 46.

Hist of Engl.

British Museum Additional MS. 28,954, f. 9.

J think Mr Martyn printed his History of England & y^t it came out before ye P. Regained, & Starkey printed that, & they were most likely to employ another printer they were used to & Symonds might be dead

From Jacob Tonson's letter to his nephew, date about 1731-1732, now in the Pierpont Morgan Library; Helen Darbishire, *The Manuscript of Milton's Paradise Lost Book I*, 1931, p. xii. Professor Parker scouts the idea that John Martin printed the first edition, though he did acquire the rights on December 29, 1672 (*q.v.*); he thinks the printer was John Macock. Masson (VI, 646-647) toys oddly with the notion that the initials J. M. on the title page may refer to Milton himself, but does not really accept it. Yet he casually mentions Martin in the same paragraph, though without saying that he printed this book.

NOVEMBER. CONTEMPORARY ANNOTATED COPIES OF AND MANUSCRIPT COMMENTS ON *HISTORY OF BRITAIN*.

Professor Parker writes (*Milton's Contemporary Reputation*, pp. 52-53): "I have a copy of the *History of Britain*, 1670, on the title-page of which a contemporary owner expressed the situation [of Milton's reputation] nicely: 'A good Author though an ill subject to his Prince.' . . . My own copy is heavily annotated on both front and back fly-leaves in what appears to be a contemporary hand. B. M. Sloane MS 1030 f. 90^v is an early extract in French; Sloane MS 1506 contains notes taken from it." Though none of these items is dated, and though all may be later, it is quite possible that one or more of them is within a year or so at least.

AFTER NOVEMBER 22. *HISTORY OF BRITAIN* AND *PARADISE REGAINED* AND *SAMSON AGONISTES* ADVERTISED IN TERM CATALOGUES.

The History of *Britain*, that part especially now called *England*, from the first traditional beginning, continued to the Norman Conquest. Collected out of the Antientest and best Authors thereof, by **John Milton**. In Quarto. Price, bound, 6s. Printed for **Spencer Hickman** at the Rose in St. *Paul's* Churchyard.

From *Numb. 3 A Catalogue of Books Printed and Published at London in Michaelmas Term, 1670. Licensed Novemb. 22. 1670.*

Roger L'Estrange, as reprinted in the *Term Catalogues*, I, 54-63. The entry of Milton's *History* comes on p. 56. The book appears under the division entitled "History." See Parker, *Milton's Contemporary Reputation*, pp. 111-112. The title page represented in this advertisement is new and different from the first in that the publisher has changed from James Allestry to Spencer Hickman. James Allestry had died on November 3, 1670, according to Richard Smith's Obituary, quoted in Henry A. Plomer's *Dictionary of the Booksellers and Printers . . . 1641 to 1667*, pp. 2-3. According to Plomer's similar *Dictionary* for 1668-1725, p. 153, Spencer Hickman was at the Rose 1670-1672. See also Masson, VI, 647. The only title pages which have been recorded with Hickman's name on them are dated 1671.

PARADISE Regain'd. A Poem, in Four Books; to which is added, *Samson Agonistes*, a Dramatick Poem. The Author, Jo. Milton. In Octavo. Price, bound, 4s. Printed for *John Starkey* at the Mitre in *Fleet street*.

From the same catalogue as the preceding entry, same page, under the category of "Poetry and Plays." Masson (VI, 651), on the basis of the license date of July 2, 1670, for these two poems, suggests that they may actually have been published in 1670 though all known title pages bear the date 1671. This entry lends force to the assumption. Harris Fletcher (Facsimile, IV, 16) suggests that perhaps there was unexpected delay in the publication of the volume, but that it may actually have come out late in 1670, but not earlier than "a little before or during the Christmas season of 1670." But see the entry above under date of May 29, 1670.

NOVEMBER 27. BROTHER CHRISTOPHER'S SON THOMAS ADMITTED TO INNER TEMPLE.

Special admission of Thomas Milton, eldest son of Milton of the bench, at the request of his father.

F. A. Inderwick, *A Calendar of the Inner Temple Records*, III, 74. Thomas was called to the bar on November 29, 1677 (*ibid.*, p. 119).

AFTER NOVEMBER (?). PREPARES REVISIONS FOR NEW EDITION OF *HISTORY OF BRITAIN*.

CM, XVIII, 516-517, summarizes the evidence that Milton may have done some work toward preparing for a new and revised edition of the *History of Britain*. First, Toland's version of the *History*, published in his edition of Milton's *Works* in 1698, makes a considerable number of additions to the original edition; these additions are gathered on pp. 256-257. Toland described his text as from a copy "corrected by the Author himself." Second, it is quite possible that if Milton had put out a second edition, he might have at least tried to put back in some of the passages which had been stricken out of the first. Third, he would of course have seen to it that the errata (pp. 517-519) would be incorporated in the new text. Milton's own actual marked copy of the first edition is not known to survive. Though the date when he did this work is not known, it must have been between November, 1670, when the first edition appeared, and 1674, the date of his death. Harry Glicksman, in a work already mentioned (*PMLA*, xxxv [1920], 116-122) is confident that Toland had Milton's copy; Stevens (*Reference Guide*, No. 65) labels his theory "conjectural." It may be added that a copy which might answer such a theory was listed in Sotheran's Catalogue 819 (1930), item 756, where it was described as being interleaved and as having numerous additions in seventeenth-century handwriting. See French, "The Autographs of John Milton," No. 49. But its present location is not known.

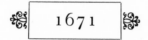

WILLIAM DOLLE MAKES COPY OF FAITHORNE PORTRAIT.

Ioannis Miltoni Effigies Ætat. 63. 1671. W. Dolle sculpsit.

Inscription on the portrait of Milton used as the frontispiece for Milton's *Artis Logicæ*, 1672, and apparently with no important change again for *Paradise Lost*, 1674. It is discussed in Marsh (no. 28), Williamson (pp. 49, 116), and Fletcher (Facsimile, iii, 60-61). It is reproduced by Fletcher at iii, 63. It is an unusually close copy of the Faithorne portrait used as the frontispiece for the *History of Britain* described above, but reduced in size and with the inscription altered to fit the new date. Even the lettering keeps as close to Faithorne as possible. Marsh says that the original measures 5.1 by 3.1. Fletcher points out that because the print was slightly too large for the *Artis Logicæ*, it had to be trimmed to fit. He also points out some almost invisible changes between the two appearances of the Dolle illustration, but thinks that they were probably made on the same plate. When in 1671 Dolle did this work, and whether he means 1671/2 by his date, we cannot tell.

[Likeness of John Milton at the age of 63, 1671. W(illiam) Dolle engraved it.]

BROTHER CHRISTOPHER NAMED AMONG GENTRY OF SUFFOLK.

Gentry of Suffolk, 1671. . . . Christopher Milton, of Ipswich, Esqʳ.

British Museum Add. MS. 19,142, f. 79v.

ATTACKED BY PETER BARWICK.

[Hugh Peters was infamous,] id quod Miltonus ipse negare non ausus erat; cùm Apologiam dedita operâ in hoc ipsum scriberet; ut conjuratorum immanissimos & hunc inter primarios, nominatim ab Adversariis . . . defenderet. . . .

Peter Barwick, *Vita Johannis Barwick*, 1721, p. 202; White Kennet, *Register*, 1728, p. 777. The date comes from the statement of G. F. Barwick, who edited the book in 1903 (p. xviii), that the writer began it in 1671. It is of course not necessarily certain that he wrote this particular part in 1671, but this year is as suitable a place for it as any.

[. . . a fact which *Milton* himself (a very good Advocate for a very bad Cause) did not dare to deny, when he purposely wrote his Apology for this very end, to defend even by Name (as far as was possible) the very blackest of the Conspirators, and *Hugh Peters* among the chief of them. . . .]

The Life Of the Reverend Dr. John Barwick . . . Translated into English, 1724, p. 296.

HISTORY OF BRITAIN REISSUED.

The History of Britain, That part especially now called England. From the first Traditional Beginning, Continued to the Norman Conqvest. Collected out of the Antientest and best Authors thereof: By John Milton. London, Printed by J. M. for Spencer Hickman, at the Rose in St. Paul's Church-Yard, MDCLXXI.

Title page of the 1671 edition; CM, x, 385; Masson, vi, 647. For a discussion of the relation between this and the first appearance of this book, see above under date of November, 1670.

PUBLISHES *PARADISE REGAINED* AND *SAMSON AGONISTES.*

Paradise Regain'd. A Poem. In IV Books. To which is added Samson Agonistes. The Author John Milton. London, Printed by J. M. for John Starkey at the Mitre in Fleetstreet, near Temple-Bar. MDCLXXI. . . .

Samson Agonistes, A Dramatic Poem. The Author John Milton. Aristot. Poet. Cap. 6. Τραγωδία μίμησις πράξεως σπυδαίας, &c. Tragœdia est imitatio actionis seriæ, &c. Per misericordiam & metum perficiens talium affectuum lustrationem. London, Printed by J. M. for John Starkey at the Mitre in Fleetstreet, near Temple-Bar. MDCLXXI.

Title pages of the whole volume and of the section containing *Samson Agonistes*, which has a separate title. The capital I following the last date and on the line below it is not part of the title but merely a signature mark. These title pages are reproduced in CM, II, 404, and I, 330; also in Fletcher facsimile, IV, 51 and 177. The text of *Paradise Regained* is in CM, II, 405-482; of *Samson Agonistes* in CM, I, 331-399. The date of publication of this volume is not certain. The license on the flyleaf facing the title page is dated July 2, 1670, as already noticed above. The book may have appeared any time between that date and November 22, 1670, the license date of the catalogue advertising it (*q.v.*). The time of composition is still less certain. Allan H. Gilbert (*Philological Quarterly*, XXVIII [1949], 98 ff.) thinks that Milton wrote *Samson* early and brought it out of his notes to help fill up the present volume. On the other hand, Hughes (ed. *Paradise Regained* and other poems, 1937, p. 422) believes that Milton "wrote the tragedy, probably in close succession to *Paradise Regained*." And to assume that the latter poem dates from much earlier compels us to reject Thomas Ellwood's circumstantial account of it completely (see above, 1666). See also Masson, VI, 651-678.

After he was blind he wrote, these following Bookes viz. . . .

Paradise regained. . . .

Paradise . . . regaind 4ᵗᵒ. Edw. Philips his cheif Amanuensis.

Aubrey, ff. 63, 68v; Darbishire, pp. 3, 9. Aubrey does not mention *Samson*.

. . . hee finish'd [various works] after the Restoration: As also . . . *Paradise regaind, Samson Agonistes*, a Tragedy. . . .

The "earliest" biography, f. 143; Darbishire, p. 29.

It cannot certainly be concluded when he wrote his excellent Tragedy entitled *Samson Agonistes*, but sure enough it is that it came forth afert his publication of *Paradice lost*, together with his other Poem call'd *Paradice regain'd*, which doubtless was begun and finisht and Printed after the other was publisht, and that in a wonderful short space considering the sublimeness of it; however it is generally censur'd to be much inferiour to the other, though he could not hear with patience any such thing when related to him; possibly the Subject may not afford such variety of Invention, but it is thought by the most judicious to be little or nothing inferiour to the other for stile and decorum.

Phillips, p. xxxix; Darbishire, pp. 75-76.

Paradice regain'd, a Poem in four Books; to which is added *Samson* Agonistes. *Octav.*

Phillips, p. [lii]; not in Darbishire.

(24) *Paradise regain'd*: a Poem in four books. *Lond.* 1670. qu.

Wood, I, 883; Darbishire, p. 46. Wood does not mention *Samson*.

I think Mr Martyn printed his [Milton's] History of England & y^t it came out before ye P. Regained, & Starkey printed that, & they were most likely to employ another printer they were used to & Symonds might be dead.

From Jacob Tonson's letter to his nephew, date about 1731-1732, in the Pierpont Morgan Library; Helen Darbishire, *The Manuscript of Milton's Paradise Lost Book I*, 1931, p. xii.

PRESENTS COPIES OF *PARADISE REGAINED* AND *SAMSON AGONISTES* TO COOK AND OTHERS.

Sum Shadracis Cooke, Christ's Coll: Cantab. ex dono authoris.

Inscription reported to be written on an old flyleaf inserted in a copy of *Paradise Regained* and *Samson Agonistes* sold at Sotheby's in 1923 for £12. Its present location is unknown. See *Book Auction Records*, xx (1923), 648; French, "The Autographs of John Milton," no. 51; CM, XVIII, 550. Cooke (1655-1724) was admitted to Christ's College in 1670 and matriculated in 1671. He was ordained in 1676 (Venn, *Alumni Cantabrigienses*, I, 387).

[I belong to Shadrach Cook of Christ's College, Cambridge, by gift of the author.]

m/Jo.

In 1820 Charles Lamb gave William Wordsworth a copy of the 1671 edition of *Paradise Regained* which bore these initials, supposed to represent Milton's signature on a copy given to an unknown friend. See *Notes and Queries*, VI, vii (1883), 466-467; *Works of Charles and Mary Lamb*, ed. E. V. Lucas, VII (1905), 912; Lamb's *Letters*, ed. Lucas, III (1935), 372. This entry is rather dubious.

E[?] dono Joanis Miltoni.

Mr. Donald S. Robertson of Trinity College, Cambridge, owns a copy of *Samson Agonistes*, 1671, which contains this entry on the first page. The letter after the initial E, though no doubt an x, is undecipherable. I am grateful to Mr. Robertson for informing me of this copy and for allowing me to publish this note. He tells me that there is no note at the beginning of *Paradise Regained*, but suspects that a flyleaf bearing an inscription may have been torn away. It might conceivably be the sheet noted above, bearing the name of Shadrach Cook.

MAKES MANUSCRIPT CORRECTIONS IN *PARADISE RE-GAINED* (?).

For God of old hath for His people wrought
Things as incredible; what hinders now?

This changed reading of lines 1532-33 of *Samson Agonistes* is one of a number of manuscript corrections and changes said to have been found in copies of *Paradise Regained* and *Samson* (1671); it is the only one definitely quoted. Other copies have been reported sold at Sotheby's in 1916 and in 1925 (not necessarily but possibly the same copy), listed in the catalogue of George Daniel's Library, and advertised for sale by both Maggs and Quaritch. For a list of references for these various items see French, "The Autographs of John Milton," Nos. 52 and 52a; CM, XVIII, 550, 644.

IS SAID TO HAVE PREFERRED *PARADISE REGAINED* TO *PARADISE LOST*.

In the year 1670 he publish'd his *Paradise Regain'd*, consisting of four Books; but generally esteem'd much inferior to *Paradise Lost*, which he could not endure to hear, being quite of another mind: yet this occasion'd som body to say wittily enough that *Milton* might be seen in *Paradise Lost*, but not in *Paradise Regain'd*.

Toland, I, 43; Darbishire, p. 185; CM, XVIII, 380. See also the quotation from Phillips to the same effect above in the note on the publication of the poem. Toland evidently echoed Phillips's phrase that Milton "could not hear with patience any such thing [as people's preference for *Paradise Lost*] when related to him."

. . . *Paradise Regained* was, in the poet's own opinion, the better poem, though it could never obtain to be named with *Paradise Lost*; and that Milton gave this reason for the general dislike, namely, *That the people had a general sense of the loss of Paradise, but not an equal gust for the regaining of it.*

Todd, 1 (1826), 210, from a manuscript note which Todd says a friend of his found written in a copy of Toland's life of Milton; CM, XVIII, 393.

JOHN STARKEY ADVERTISES *TETRACHORDON*, *PARADISE REGAINED*, AND *ACCEDENCE COMMENCED GRAMMAR* FOR SALE.

Quarto's.

Tetrachordon: Expositions upon the four cheif places in Scripture, which treat of marriage, or nullities in Marriage On *Gen* I 27.28. compar'd & explain'd by *Gen.* 2, 18 23.24. On *Deut.* 24.1.2. On *Matth.* 5 31.32. with *Mat.* 19. from the 3d. v. to the 11th. On 1 *Cor.* 7. from the 10th. to the 16th. Wherein the Doctrine and Discipline of Divorce, as was lately publish'd, is confirm'd by explanation of Scripture, by testimony of ancient Fathers, of civil Laws in the Primitive Church, of famousest Reformed Divines. And lastly, by an intended Act of the Parliament and Church of *England* in the last year of *Edward* the sixth. By the Author *J. Milton*, price 1*s.* 6*d.* . . .

Paradice regain'd, a Poem in four books, to which is added *Samson Agonistes.* The Author, *John Milton*, price bound 2*s.* 6*d.* . . .

Twelves. . . .

Accidence commenc'd Grammer, and supply'd with sufficient Rules; or a new and easie Method for the learning the *Latine Tongue*. The Author *John Milton*, price bound 8*d*.

From "*A Catalogue of Books Printed for* John Starkey *Bookseller, at the* Mitre *in* Fleetstreet *near* Temple Bar," appended to Benjamin Priolo's *History of France under the Ministry of Cardinal Mazarine*, 1671, sigs. A2v, A3v, A4; Fletcher facsimile, IV, 13. This advertisement was probably made up early in 1670; on the last page it bears, before the last two titles, the notation: "In the Press 29th. *May*, 1670." This notice probably appeared in a good many books. Professor Fletcher states that he has found it in (1) a copy of *Paradise Regained*, 1671, and (2) Paul Rycaut's *History of the Turkish Empire*, 1680. I may add that in the Rycaut volume it is entirely reprinted, not the same printing. The signature marks in the Priolo volume quoted above are erroneous, as Fletcher points out, in that the first leaf is numbered R and the second A. Since the third and fourth pages are not marked, I cannot tell (working from a microfilm) which is correct. Incidentally, in the Rycaut volume no prices are given.

JUNE 10. BROTHER-IN-LAW THOMAS AGAR MAKES WILL.

Thomas Agar of London Gentleman . . . And first I give and bequeath vnto Edward Phillipps my sonn in Law Two Hundred Pownd℘ To be laid out in the purchase of an Annuity for his life or some place of imployment for his better subsistence which shall seem most for his benefitt wherein I desire my dearly and intirely beloued and most deserving nephew Mr Thomas Agar whome J declare nominate and appoint my Executor of this my last will and Testamt to be assistent to him my said sonn in Law, requiring and enioyning him my said sonn in Law to be ordered and gouerned herein by him my said Nephew who J am assured hath much loue and kindnes for him Provided that if before my decease J procure the Kings Mts Graunt of my Office of ingrossing of Appealls to be made and passed vnder the great Seale of England to him Then this my bequest to him before mentioned to cease and be vtterly void. Jtem, J gyve and bequeath vnto my Grandsonn Thomas

Moore To be paid him by my Executor at his full age of One and Twenty yeares ffyue Hundred Pownds of lawfull English money And my intent Will and meaning is that one full Moyety of such my Estate as shall remain besides Debtꝑ buriall expences and what I haue and shall bequeath by this my last will otherwaies vpon a cleere and iust Accompt thereof to be made by my Executor within One yeare next after my decease shall be paid and disposed to such Trustee or Trustees as my deare Daughter Mrs Ann Moore shall direct and appoint to remaine in his or their handꝑ for the intentꝑ and purposes following That is to say ffor her sole and seperate vse notwithstanding her present Coverture with her present or any other husband wherein her said husband shall not any way intermeddle nor haue to doe nor any other with whome she shall happen to intermarry. . . .

Prerogative Court of Canterbury, 142 Pye; Masson, VI, 771-775 (quoting somewhat more than is given above, though the present text follows the original manuscript). Masson notes that Milton's sister Ann, Agar's wife, may have died any time between 1637 and 1671. The Ann Moore mentioned is their daughter Ann Agar, now married to David Moore. A codicil of October 27, 1673, will be mentioned later, as will the proving of the will on November 5, 1673.

BEFORE AUGUST 24. HICKMAN ASSIGNS HIS RIGHTS IN MILTON'S *HISTORY OF BRITAIN* TO JOHN DUNMORE (?).

. . . an assignment under the hand and seale of JOHN DUN-MORE, citizen and stacōner of London, bering date the fowre and twentith day of August 1671; and unto wch assignemt the hand of Master Warden MEARNE is subscribed . . . **Milton's** *History of England.* . . .

From the entry in the *Stationers' Registers* on December 29, 1672, *q.v.* The wording is not quite clear. But since on the latter date Sir Thomas Davies entered the *History* by virtue of Dunmore's assignment, the meaning seems to be that by August, 1671, Dunmore had gained control of the rights from the previous holder, who was Spencer Hickman.

COMUS ADVERTISED FOR SALE.

Milton's Masque.

As in 1661, this entry occurs on page 10 of Francis Kirkman's *Catalogue* of dramatic works for sale. In 1661 Kirkman's "A True, perfect, and exact Catalogue" etc. was printed with *Tom Tyler and His Wife*. (P)

BOINEBURG REPROACHES MILTON'S CRITICISM OF SALMASIUS.

Miltonus exprobravit nimis acerbe Salmasii errores quos ipse ubique non vitavit.

From *Johann Christian Baronis de Boyneburg, Epistolae ad J. C. Dietericum*, 1705, p. 270, as quoted in Stern, II, iii, 263. I have not seen the original book. The date, not given, was at least before Boineburg died in 1672. Probably the date is given more exactly in the original.

[Milton reproached too sharply the errors of Salmasius which he himself did not everywhere escape.]

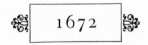

JOHN EACHARD'S ATTACK ON MILTON'S POSITION ON DIVORCE AND ON EDUCATION REPRINTED.

I am not, I'll assure you, any of those occasional Writers, that missing preferment in the Vniversity can presently write you their new ways of Education; or being a little tormented with an ill chosen Wife, set forth the Doctrine of Divorce to be truly Evangelical.

John Eachard, *The Grounds & Occasions of the Contempt of the Clergy and Religion*, 8th edition, 1672, sigs. A3-A3v. See the entry of the original edition under date of 1670 above.

RIDICULED FOR CONDEMNING IN SALMASIUS THE
GRAMMATICAL MISTAKES WHICH HE HIMSELF MAKES.

[After talking about solecisms in Beza, Scaliger, Casaubon,
and others:] Præfervido autem & præcipiti Salmasio solœcis-
morum affatim provenisse minus miror. quam illi copiam & se-
getem vitiorum, probri loco Joannes Miltonus objicit, in libro,
contra Carolum eo nomine regem Britanniæ primum, scripto.
Sed illud mirum pariter & festivum quod is quo loco & quibus
plane verbis attribuit Salmasio, solœcismos, iisdem ipse solœcis-
mum, aut solœcismo flagitium non minus admittat: cum quidem
dicat, vapulandum se præbuit.

Francis Vavassor, *De Epigrammate Liber*, 1672, pp. 301-302; Milton's *Works* (Pickering edition), 1851, p. clxxii. There was a later
edition in 1678.

[I am less surprised that plenty of solecisms proceed from
the hot and headstrong Salmasius than that John Milton, in his
book written against Charles, the first king of Britain of that
name, casts at him as a form of insult this copious crop of faults.
But it is equally amazing and funny that in the very place and
in the very words in which he attributes solecisms to Salmasius,
he himself in the same places permits no less solecism or disgrace by solecism; when he speaks, indeed, he offers himself
to be flogged.]

ALLEGED SLAP AT MILTON IN NEPHEW JOHN PHIL-
LIPS'S *MARONIDES*.

In his *Lives of Edward and John Philips*, 1815, p. 148, William
Godwin asserts that John Phillips's *Maronides or Virgil Travestie: Being
a new Paraphrase Upon the Fifth Book of Virgils Æneids*, 1672, is
written "in an express spirit of spite and malignity against Milton." Actually, though it is riotously anti-Puritan and mentions many conserva-
tives by name, I can find no references in it which could be called specifically attacks on Milton. The tenor of the book undoubtedly was
unwelcome to Milton, but that is a different thing from calling it an attack on him.

Sᴙ HENRY WOTTON'S LETTER TO MILTON REPRINTED.

To Mr. *MILTON*.

Heading of the letter in Wotton's *Reliquiæ Wottonianæ*, third edition, 1672, p. 342; Parker, *Milton's Contemporary Reputation*, p. 85. The letter is undated in this edition, but is found among other letters of 1637. For the text see above, I, 361-363.

Aʟᴇxᴀɴᴅᴇʀ ᴙᴏss's *PANSEBEIA*, REBUKING MILTON, REPRINTED.

Q. 10. *What other Sects and opinions are there now stirring amongst us?* . . . there are amongst us *Divorcers*, who hold that men may put away their Wives upon small occasions. We have also *Soul-Sleepers*, who with the *Arabick* Hereticks, hold that the soul dieth or sleepeth with the body. . . .

Q. 17. *What are the opinions of the* Independents? . . . 8. They permit divorces in slight cases.

Ross, *Pansebeia*, 1672, pp. 376 and 389. For the first edition of this work see above under date of June 7, 1653.

J. H. BOECLER'S CRITICISMS OF MILTON REPRINTED.

Boecler's *Museum ad Amicum*, first issued in 1663, was reprinted in 1672. The references to Milton, practically unchanged from the earlier edition, appear on pp. 31-46. Christian Gryphius quotes Boecler in his *Apparatus*, 1710, pp. 333-335.

Aʟʟᴇɢᴇᴅ ɪɴꜰʟᴜᴇɴᴄᴇ ᴏɴ ᴍᴀʀᴠᴇʟʟ's *REHEARSAL TRANSPROSED.*

. . . there are many *Miltons* in this one Man.

Richard Leigh, *The Transproser Rehears'd*, 1673, p. 147; for further quotations from this book see below under date of May 6, 1673. The writer finds echoes from several of Milton's books in Marvell's. *The Rehearsal Transprosed* appeared in 1672. Marvell's discussion of the pros and cons of licensing books undoubtedly owes something to *Areopagitica*.

. . . our author Parker being esteemed by the nonconformists a forward, proud, ambitious and scornful person, was taken to task, purposely to clip his wings or take him shorter, by their buffooning champion Andrew Marvell sometime one of John Milton's companions, in a book which he published entit. *The Rehearsal transpos'd: or animadversions upon a late Book entit. A Preface shewing*, &c. Lond. 1672. oct.

Wood, *Athenae Oxonienses*, III (1820), 230, *s.v.* Parker. Though Wood does not specifically say that Marvell copied from or was influenced by Milton, he calls him a disciple, and his statement therefore seems to belong with the preceding one from Leigh. C. H. Firth (on Marvell in *DNB*) says: "Rumour credited Milton with a share in the composition of the 'Rehearsal Transprosed,' and he was consequently attacked with great virulence by Parker and Parker's allies."

FEBRUARY 15. BROTHER CHRISTOPHER ONE OF LEADERS OF INNER TEMPLE PARLIAMENT.

Parliamentum ibm̄ tentum [decimo] quinto die Februarij Anno dnī [1671] Annoqz dnī Regis Caroli secundi Vicesimo quarto Coram Edr̄o: Thurland Mił Xp̄ofero Milton Ar̄ Edr̄o Pecke Ar̄ et alijs. [Marginal note:] Jnterius Templū Heneag[s]. Finch Mił & Barront[s]. Attorñ Generał. Thesaurar̄. ibm̄./ 1671./

Records of the Inner Temple; printed in F. A. Inderwick, *A Catalogue of the Inner Temple Records*, III, 84. Christopher was to serve in this capacity a number of times. Words in brackets are no longer visible but can be deduced from the context.

[Parliament held in the same place on February 15, 1671/2, and in the twenty-second year of our lord King Charles II, before Edward Thurland, Knight; Christopher Milton, Esquire; Edward Pecke, Esquire; and others. (Note:) Inner Temple: Heneage Finch, Knight and Baronet, Attorney General, Treasurer of the same, 1671.]

ABOUT FEBRUARY 22. DUKE OF RICHMOND GIVES MILTON WRITING CASE.

I Richard Lovekin of Namptwich in the County of Chester, do affirm, and will make Oath if need be, that a Tortoise Shell Case containing, a Pen, Pensil, 3 Leaves of Ivory, and a Pair of Dividers; and a Fish Skin Case in which is contained 3 Ivory Leaves, late in my Possession, and now the Property of Jos[h]:

Massie, were given me by my Aunt M^rs. Milton Widdow of Poet Milton, sometime before her Death, who informed me that both of the Cases abovementioned belonged to her deceased Husband M^r. Milton, and that he used the raised oval at the Bottom of the Tortoise Shell Case as a Seal, also that he did intend to have had his own Coat of Arms engraved on it: in witness whereof I have hereunto sett my hand this Twenty first Day of October A. D. 1742.

Richd Lovekin. . . .

This Box was given to Mr Milton when ye Duke of Richmond was sent ambassador to France, he gave it him and Mrs Streeter gave it me April 22 1807

(The above memo. was written by the late William Milton Bridger Esqr. of Halvaker, Sussex, d. 1862.

L[owther] B[ridger]
1863.

These affidavits accompany a mottled red case about 4 inches by 1½ by 1½ and a fishskin case containing a pair of dividers, a protractor, and one or two other drawing instruments, now in the Bodleian Library; *Academy*, LIII (1898), 663; *Daily News* (London), June 10, 1898, p. 6d; Williamson, *Milton Tercentenary*, 1908, p. 160; Raymond, p. 327; CM, XVIII, 393, 584, 610. Though I have been able to find no Duke of Richmond who was ambassador to France, Charles Stuart, third Duke of Richmond, was commissioned ambassador to Denmark on business pertaining to France on February 22, 1672; see *CSP Dom, 1671-1672*, p. 153. This item is therefore dated accordingly. The Duke died on December 12, 1672.

MAY (?). *ART OF LOGIC* PUBLISHED.

Joannis Miltoni Angli, Artis Logicæ Plenior Institutio, ad Petri Rami Methodum concinnata, Adjecta est Praxis Annalytica & Petri Rami vita. Libris duobus. Londini, Impensis Spencer Hickman, So-cietatis Regalis Typographi, ad insigne Rosæ in Cæmeterio, D. Pauli. 1672.

Title of the book; facsimile in CM, XI, p. [vi]. The work is reprinted, with English translation, in CM, XI, 1-515. Milton had probably written this work many years earlier; see, for example, above under date of 1630 in I, 214. The date of appearance must have been some time in May or near to it, because the book catalog which first advertised its appearance (an excerpt from which is given below) was licensed on May 13, 1672. Facing the title page of the first edition is Dolle's portrait of Milton based on the Faithorne portrait first used in *The History of Britain*, 1670. There has been some little talk about the theory that the original manuscript of the book is still in existence, but no trace of it has been found in recent times; see French, "The Autographs of Milton," No. 53, and CM, XVIII, 557. See also French, "Milton, Ramus, and Edward Phillips," *Modern Philology*, XLVII (1949), 82-87, for some discussion of the relations between Milton's work, a briefer one by his nephew Edward Phillips, and Ramus. See also Wilbur S. Howell, *Logic and Rhetoric in England, 1500-1700*, Princeton, 1956.

[John Milton Englishman's fairly full presentation of the art of logic prepared according to the method of Peter Ramus. Added to it are an analytical exercise and the life of Peter Ramus. In two books. London, printed by Spencer Hickman, printer to the Royal Society, at the sign of the Rose in St. Paul's Churchyard, 1672.]

Joannis Miltoni Angli, *Artis Logicae Plenior Institutio, ad* Petri Rami *Methodum, concinnata.* Adjecta est *Praxis Analytica* et Petri Rami *Vita. Libris Duobus.* In Twelves. Price, bound, 2s.

Term Catalogues, I, 105, from *A Catalogue of Books*, No. 9, London, 1672, licensed May 13, 1672; Parker, *Milton's Contemporary Reputation*, p. 112.

. . . hee finish'd after the Restoration . . . *Logica.* . . .

The "earliest" biography, f. 143; Darbishire, p. 29.

His Logick.

Aubrey, ff. 64, 68v; Darbishire, pp. 9, 11. The same entry occurs on two different pages.

Johannis Miltoni Angli Artis Logicæ Plenior Institutio ad Petri Rami Methodum Concinnata: Adjecta est Praxis Annalytica & Petri Rami vita libris Duobus. *Twelves.*

Phillips, p. liv; not in Darbishire.

(26) *Artis logicæ plenior institutio ad Petri Rami methodum concinnata.* Lond. 1672. in tw.

Wood, I, 883; Darbishire, p. 46.

Logick.
British Museum, Add. MS. 28,954, f. 9.

MAY 1. BROTHER CHRISTOPHER AGAIN ONE OF LEADERS OF INNER TEMPLE PARLIAMENT.

Parliamentum ibm̄ Tentum Primo [die] Maij Anno Dnī 1672. Annoqz Regni [Regis?] dnī Caroli scdī Vicesimo quarto Coram [Edr̄o?] Thurland mił xp̄ofero Milton Edr̄o Pecke et Alijs. [Marginal note:] Jnterius Templū. Heneag⁸. Finch Mił. & Barronett⁸ Attorn̄ Geñał Thesaurar⁸.

Records of the Inner Temple; printed in F. A. Inderwick, *A Calendar of the Inner Temple Records*, III, 84. The words in brackets are illegible because of the worn-off edge of the page, but they are reasonably certain from the context.

[Parliament held in the same place May 1, 1672, and in the twenty-fourth year of the reign of our lord and king Charles II, before Edward Thurland, Knight; Christopher Milton; Edward Pecke; and others. (Note:) Inner Temple. Heneage Finch, Knight and Baronet, Attorney General, Treasurer.]

MAY 13. BROTHER CHRISTOPHER DEPOSES IN COURT ABOUT HIS WORK AS A LAWYER IN ADVISING SIR ROBERT CLENCH ABOUT HIS WILL.

13° Maij 1672 Annoqz   Ex Parte Elizabethe Cobb Spinster
R° R Car' secd xxiiij°   p Guardian̄ Deft ads Nicholai
                                 Wilton Jur' Testes Examinati p
                                 Robtm Peyton mr̄ in Cancell'
                                 Examinatorem

Christopher Milton of Jpswich in the County of Suffolke Esqʳ. aged 55 yeares or thereaboutp beeing p̠duced &c'

1 That hee hath seene yᵉ Complt Nicholas Wilton but yᵉ other Complt Thomazine his wife this deponᵗ hath knowne for about 15 or 16 yeares but yᵉ Defᵗ Elizabeth Cobb this deponᵗ knoweth not.

2 3 That hee well knew sʳ Robᵗ Clench late of Holbrooke in

[41]

yᵉ County of Suffolke deced & in yᵉ Arcle' inquired of when hee
was liueing and soe knew him for about 10 yeares before hee
dyed and saith yᵗ it is as this depᵗ beleiues about 7 yeares since
yᵉ decease of him yᵉ said sʳ Robᵗ clench And saith yᵗ hee yᵉ said
sʳ Robt clench had att his death 3 children to witt 3 daughters
one whereof was called Meriell clench one called ffrances clench
and yᵉ other called Thomazine clench All wᶜʰ said 3 daughters
this deponᵗ well knew . . .

9 That yᵉ paper writeing now ꝑduced & shewed vnto him
this deponᵗ Conteineing twoe sheetꝑ & a halfe of written Paper
and affixed & sealed together att yᵉ Top thereof is yᵉ Last will
& Testamᵗ of yᵉ said sʳ Robᵗ Clench And this deponᵗ saith yᵉ hee
this Deponᵗ was pʳsent when hee yᵉ said sʳ Robᵗ Clench did signe
seale publish & declare yᵉ said ꝑduced will to bee his last will
and Testamᵗ And in Testimony thereof hee this deponᵗ did sub-
scribe his name among others on yᵉ last sheet of yᵉ said ꝑduced
will in such manner as is now there to bee seene And this deponᵗ further saith yᵗ hee yᵉ sᵈ sʳ Robᵗ Clench was att yᵉ tyme of
his said signeing sealeing & publishing of his sᵈ will of a good
sound & ꝑfect memory & vnderstanding in his this deponᵗꝑ
Judgemᵗ & apprehension And more saith not

10 11 That hee was sent for by the sᵈ sʳ Robᵗ Clench to aduise
about a draught of his will wᶜʰ some other pson had drawne . . .
for this deponᵗ saith yᵗ vpon this deponᵗꝑ pusall of yᵉ sᵈ Draught
hee this deponᵗ obserueing the wordꝑ of yᵉ said draught as to
yᵗ pticuler did aske yᵉ said sʳ Robᵗ whether hee did intend yᵗ if
his elder daughters should marry & dye Leaueing issue before
yᵉ younger should attaine to yᵗ age such issue should bee barred
of any share of his estate hee yᵉ sᵈ sʳ Robt thereto answered this
Depᵗ thus vizᵗ God forbid J intend noe such thing [And yᵉ
sᵈ sʳ Robᵗ] Reply'd in such manner as yᵉ draught is now penned
there might bee some doubt whether such issue of his daughter
soe dyeing might not bee Excluded or to yᵗ effect then sayd yᵉ
sᵈ sʳ Robᵗ Lett my will bee soe worded yᵗ such mischeife of bar-
ring my daughters issue may bee pʳvented yett doe it as Couertly

as you can for J thinke it tyme enough for my eldest daughters
to marry when my youngest will bee of 21 yeares of age & J
would not haue her encouraged to marry before or vsed words
to y^t or ye like effect whereupon hee this Depon^t as to y^t Clause
wch concerns ye settlem^t of his estate after the Paym^t of his debtȝ
& Legacies worded it in such manner as it is Expressed in ye said
will now ꝑduced & afterwardȝ read ye same over to ye said s^r
Robert whoe well approued of the same . . .

Chr̄ Milton

Public Record Office, Chancery Town Depositions, C24/974/13;
not previously published. This document was discovered by Mr. Charles
V. Bernau, to whom I am grateful for permission to use it. I have given
somewhat longer excerpts from it than might seem warranted because
it gives a detailed picture of the sort of work which Christopher Milton
did as a lawyer. A few words about three quarters of the way through
are given in brackets because they are worn off the original and have
been supplied partly by guess and partly from the clues furnished by a
few still readable curls at the tops of some letters. In the original the
numbers preceding paragraphs are in the margin. The omitted portions
give details about Clench's heirs.

[The notes at the beginning may be translated as follows:
May 13, 1672, in the 24th year of the reign of King Charles II.
On the part of Elizabeth Cobb, spinster, through her guardian,
defendant against Nicholas Wilton, witnesses sworn and examined by Robert Peyton, Master in Chancery, Examiner.]

NOVEMBER 9. JOHN BRAMHALL'S *SERPENT SALVE*,
WITH SLUR ON MILTON, REGISTERED FOR REPUBLICA-
TION.

𝕹obember 9tȟ 1672 . . . .

Master   Entred . . . under the hands of Master THOMAS
Ben. Tooke TOMKINS and Master Warden ROPER one copie
           or booke intituled *The Serpent Salve, or the
           Remedy for the biting of an Aspe*; by **John
           Bramhall**, D. D. Lord Primate of Ireland . . .
           . . . . . vj^d

Stationers' Registers, II, 447. This book first appeared in 1643; see above, II, 83. I have found no record of republication in the seventeenth century such as the present would indicate.

NOVEMBER 12 (?). ELIE BOUHEREAU PRAISES MILTON HIGHLY.

L'ouvrage de Milton contre Morus m'estant tombé en main durant les vendanges, je l'ay leu avec un très grand plaisir, mais par malheur pour toy, il m'a fourni matiere de continuer a te fatiguer de mes questions. . . . Il est par tout si brillant et il dit des injures de si bonne grace que quelque peu malin que tu sois, tu ne laisseras pas de t'y divertir. Celuy dont je me suis servi est l'impression de Londres de l'année 1654. . . . Je suis ravi de voir avec quelle liberté d'esprit et quelle constance il respond au reproche que l'on luy fait de la perte de sa veue: *Non est miserum esse caecum, miserum est, caecitatem non posse ferre.* . . . Consulte, je te prie, Mr Richard ce que devint Milton. Le sejour que il a fait en Angleterre luy aura peutestre fait connoistre et sa personne et ses ouuvrages. Demande luy s'il estoit en vie dans le temps que le Roi fut restabli. Il paroit par son ouvrage que s'il estoit bel esprit, il n'estoit pas prophete, et il n'avoit pas le moindre soupçon de ce qui est arrivé depuis. . . . On ne peut pas nier que cet Anglois n'eût infiniment de l'esprit, beaucoup de belles lettres, et de la vertu extraordinairement si il l'en faut croire.

From a letter of Elie Bouhereau to Marquis Turon de Beyrie, the original manuscript of which is in Marsh's Library in Dublin; printed in the *Proceedings of the Huguenot Society of London*, IX (1909-1911), 241-242. Milton's work referred to must be the *Defensio Secunda*. The Latin sentence quoted is from CM, VIII, 62. The letter was dated from Pau, November 22, 1672, which is probably November 12 in English dating.

[Milton's work against More having fallen into my hands during the harvest season, I have read it with a very great pleasure, but unfortunately for you, it has provided me with material to continue to weary you with my questions. . . . He is everywhere so brilliant and he says insults with so beautiful grace that, however little malicious you may be, you won't stop being diverted with it. The edition which I have used is the London one of the year 1654. . . . I am ravished to see with what freedom of wit and what firmness he answers the reproach which they have made against him for the loss of his eyesight: "It is not wretched to be blind; it is wretched not to be able to bear blindness." . . . Ask Mr. Richard, I beg you, what has become of Milton. The visit which he made in England will perhaps have allowed him to become acquainted with both his person and his works. Ask him whether he was alive at the time when the king was restored. It appeared by his work that even if he was a wit, he was no prophet, and he had not the least suspicion of what has happened since. . . . No one can deny that this Englishman had infinite wit, a fine knowledge of literature, and extraordinary virtue if it is necessary to believe him about it.]

DECEMBER 29. *HISTORY OF BRITAIN* ENTERED SUCCESSIVELY TO SIR THOMAS DAVIES AND TO JOHN MARTIN.

December 29ᵗʰ 1672

Sir Tho. Davies   Entred for his copies by vertue of an assignement under the hand and seale of JOHN DUNMORE, citizen and stacõner of London, bering date the fowre and twentith day of August 1671; and unto wch assignemt the hand of Master Warden MEARNE is subscribed, all his estate, right and title of, in & to the severall bookes or copies & parts of bookes or copies, hereafter menconed, That is to say . . . . vˢ vjᵈ [plus "vjˢ" later in the margin]. . . .
  [Then follow 23 titles, one of which is:]
Milton's *History of England*.

Stationers' Registers, II, 451; Masson, VI, 647. Almost immediately after this entry (p. 452) is the record of a second assignment of the same titles, this time from Sir Thomas Davies to John Martin. Thus, to add slightly to Masson's note, the copyright or ownership of Milton's *History of Britain* had belonged within two years to five stationers: James Allestree (see above under date of November, 1670), Spencer

Hickman (see above under date of 1671, the reissue), John Dunmore, Sir Thomas Davies, and John Martin.

Master John Martin	Entered for his copies by vertue of an assignemt under the hand and seal of Sʳ THOMAS DAVIES knight and Alderman of the City of London, bering date the fowr and Twentith day of August, 1671, and unto wch assignemt the hand of Master Warden MEARNE is subscribed, all his estate, right and title of, in and to the severall books or copies and parts of bookes or copies hereafter menconed, That is to say . . . xjˢ vjᵈ.

. . .

Milton's *History of England.*
Ibid., II, 452.

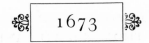

1673

DRYDEN VISITS HIM AND ARRANGES TO TRANSFORM *PARADISE LOST* INTO A DRAMA; WALLER ACCOMPANIES HIM; THEY DISCUSS ENGLISH POETRY.

Jo: Dreyden Esq Poet Laureate, who very much admires him: & went to him to have leave to putt his Paradise-lost into a Drama in Rhyme: Mʳ Milton recieved him civilly, & told him he would give him leave to tagge his Verses.

Aubrey, f. 63v; Darbishire, p. 7; CM, XVIII, 373. The point of the word "tagge," which is not clear to the modern reader, becomes obvious in Richardson's version quoted below. Though the date of Dryden's visit is not given, it is most likely to have been about this time, if not earlier. Hugh Macdonald (*John Dryden A Bibliography*, Oxford, 1939, p. 115) thinks that Dryden may have written his version (*The State of Innocence*) for the wedding festivities of the Duke of York and Mary of Modena, who were married November 21, 1673. But it was not performed. A. W. Verrall (*Lectures on Dryden*, 1914, p. 220), who dates the composition of *The State of Innocence* 1674-1677, rejects Aubrey's story of the "tagging" as apocryphal. Morris Freedman's Columbia dissertation on Milton and Dryden (1953) gathers most of the available information and offers some interesting interpretations.

Milton was the Poetical Son of *Spencer*, and Mr. *Waller* of *Fairfax*; for we have our Lineal Descents and Clans, as well as other Families. . . . *Milton* has acknowledg'd to me, that *Spencer* was his Original.

Dryden, *Fables Ancient and Modern*, 1700, Preface, sig. *A; *Essays of John Dryden*, ed. W. P. Ker, II (1926), 247; Masson, VI, 682; CM, XVIII, 381. Though this remark may not have come up at the same meeting with the preceding one, it is given here for lack of specific indication to the contrary.

We shall here beg the Reader's Pardon for mentioning a Passage told a Gentleman of our Society almost Forty Years since by Mr. *Dryden*, who went with Mr. *Waller* in Company, to make a visit to Mr. *Milton*, and desire his Leave for putting his *Paradise lost* into Rhime for the Stage. Well, Mr. *Dryden*, says *Milton*, it seems you have a mind to *Tagg* my Points, and you have my Leave to *Tagg* 'em, but some of 'em are so Awkward and Old Fashion'd that I think you had as good leave 'em as you found 'em.

The Monitor, Vol. I, No. 17, April 6-10, 1713; *Review of English Studies*, I (1925), 80-81; Darbishire, p. 335; CM, XVIII, 382.

Morris Freedman has made a good study of this episode in "Dryden's 'Memorable Visit' to Milton," *Huntington Library Quarterly*, XVIII (1955), 99-108.

. . . *Dryden* had . . . *Rim'd Milton* in his *State of Innocence*, *Tagg'd his Lines*, as *Milton* said. the Fashion was in those days to wear much Ribbon, which Some Adorn'd with Taggs of Metal at the Ends.

Richardson, p. cxx; Darbishire, p. 296.

I think my self oblig'd to render them [the readers] *a Reason, why I publish an* OPERA *which was never acted. . . . I was also induc'd to it in my own defence: many hundred Copies of it being dispers'd, abroad without my knowledge or consent: so that every one gathering new faults, it became at length a Libel against me; and I saw, with some disdain, more nonsence than either I, or as bad a Poet, could have cram'd into it, at a*

Months warning, in which time 'twas wholly Written, and not since Revis'd. After this, I cannot without injury to the deceas'd Author of Paradice Lost, *but acknowledge that this POEM has receiv'd its entire Foundation, part of the Design, and many of the Ornaments, from him.* . . . *The Original being undoubtedly, one of the greatest, most noble, and most sublime POEMS, which either this Age or Nation has produc'd.*

Dryden, *The State of Innocence*, 1677, "The Authors Apology for Heroique Poetry," sig. b; Masson, VI, 776-777 (in part). In Dryden's *Dramatic Works*, III (1932), 490 ff., Montague Summers, the editor, mentions at least five extant or known manuscript copies of Dryden's dramatization of Milton's poem. They are (1) in the Harvard College Library (with some writing in Dryden's own hand), (2) Bodleian MS. Rawl. C. 146, (3) British Museum Add. MS. 37,158, (4) one mentioned in Thomas Rodd's *Catalogue of a Collection of Manuscripts*, 1838, No. 325, and (5) Thomas Corser's copy.

Mr. *Dryden* in his Preface before *the State of Innocence* . . . at that time knew not half the Extent of his [Milton's] Excellence, as more than twenty Years afterwards he confess'd to me, and as is pretty plain from his writing *The State of Innocence.*

John Dennis, *Original Letters*, I (1721), 75, a letter dated May 25, 1719, and addressed to Judas Iscariot, Esq.; quoted in Milton's *Works*, ed. Mitford, I (1851), cvii.

BROTHER CHRISTOPHER AND BROTHER-IN-LAW RICHARD POWELL APPEAR IN BLOME'S *BRITANNIA*.

Christopher Milton of *Ipswich* Esq. . . . .
Richard Powell of *Forest-hill* Esq.

Richard Blome, *Britannia*, 1673, pp. 430, 417; Mark Noble, "Pedigree of Milton," *Monthly Mirror*, New Series, VII (1810), 17-20, 92.

ATTRIBUTED EPITAPH ON MADAME ELIZABETH SWETTENHAM.

An Epitaph on Madam Elizabeth Swettenham. . . .
If chearfull, chast as [are] the snows . . .
No soul can be more bless'd than this,

Whose sacred reliques in this urn
Are kept until the soul's return
To reunite itself to its known mate,
And raise these reliques to an happyer state.

These are the first line and the last five lines of a fourteen-line poem quoted as perhaps by Milton in the *Sixth Report of the Commission on Historical Manuscripts*, Appendix, p. 343; CM, XVIII, 599. This entry is dated 1673 because one Elizabeth Swettenham, who of course may or may not be the one in question here, died in 1673. There is hardly any evidence to connect Milton with these verses except the remote fact that the Swettenham family of Cheshire was related to the Minshull family of Milton's third wife.

TWITTED IN *S'TOO HIM BAYES*.

[Writer derides Marvell:] Come, you had all this [*The Rehearsal Transprosed*] out of the Answerer of *Salmasius*.

John Dryden (?), *S'Too him Bayes*, 1673, p. 130; Parker, *Milton's Contemporary Reputation*, p. 112; Sensabaugh, *That Grand Whig Milton*, p. 37. In *John Dryden: A Bibliography*, 1939, p. 196, Hugh Macdonald notes that this book "has been attributed to Dryden himself"; and Parker states that the author may "possibly" be Dryden. Macdonald describes at some length the antagonism between Dryden and Marvell in his edition of *The Poems of Andrew Marvell*, 1952, p. 176, and thinks that Dryden's attempt to "tag" Milton's *Paradise Lost* for a drama may have been partly accountable for Marvell's hostility. As Macdonald points out in the *Bibliography*, p. 209, Dryden wrote in the Preface to *Religio Laici* of Marvell as "Martin Mar-Prelate (the Marvel of those times) . . . the first Presbyterian Scribbler who sanctified Libels and Scurrility to the use of the Good Old Cause."

BEFORE FEBRUARY 7. JEERED AT IN *A COMMON-PLACE-BOOK OUT OF THE REHEARSAL TRANSPROS'D*.

[Marvell] . . . seems to have learned his *Accidence*, but *Grammar* . . . for your farther satisfaction in the Grammatical part I refer, when you next see him, to blind *M*. who teaches School about *More-fields*.

Sir Roger L'Estrange (?), *A Common-place-Book out of the Rehearsal Transpros'd*, 1673, pp. 35-36; Masson, VI, 704 (merely mentioned); Parker, *Milton's Contemporary Reputation*, p. 112; Sensabaugh, *That Grand Whig Milton*, p. 37. Sensabaugh mentions an early note in the Huntington copy of this book which calls L'Estrange the author; Parker thinks also that L'Estrange "may have been" the writer. The date of appearance of the book must have been before February 7, which is the date of licensing of the Catalogue in which it was advertised; see *Term Catalogues*, I, 128.

BEFORE FEBRUARY 7. *ART OF LOGIC* REISSUED.

Joannis Miltoni Angli, Artis Logicæ Plenior Institutio, ad Petri Rami Methodum concinnata. Adjecta est Praxis Annalytica & Petri Rami vita; Libris duobus. Londini, Impensis S. H. Prostant pro R. Boulter ad Insigne Capitis Turcæ exadversum Mercatorio Regali in Vico vulgò Cornhill dicto, 1673.

Title page of second issue; mentioned but not given in detail in Masson, VI, 687, and CM, XI, 519. J. W. McCain describes both issues in *Notes and Queries*, CLXV (1933), 56-59. The text seems to be identical with that of 1672. Presumably "S. H." is Spencer Hickman, publisher of the first issue.

[John Milton Englishman's fairly full presentation of the art of logic prepared according to the method of Peter Ramus. Added to it are an analytical exercise and the life of Peter Ramus. In two books. London, printed for S(pencer) H(ickman) and are to be sold for R. Boulter at the sign of the Turk's Head over against the Royal Exchange in the street vulgarly called Cornhill, 1673.]

Johannis Miltoni, Angli, *Artis Logicæ plenior Institutio ad* Petri Rami *methodum concinnata*. Adjecta est *Praxis Analytica et* Petri Rami *vita, Libris duobus*. In Twelves. Price, bound, 2s. Printed for *Robert Boulter* at the Turk's Head in *Cornhill*.

A Catalogue of Books, no. 12, 1673, licensed February 7, 1673; *Term Catalogues*, I, 128; Parker, *Milton's Contemporary Reputation*, p. 112. Milton's book, to be included in this catalogue, must have appeared before the date of licensing. Since the title as given here practically repeats that of the title page, translated above, it seems unnecessary to translate it again.

BEFORE MAY 6. SAMUEL PARKER SCORCHES MILTON IN ANSWER TO MARVELL.

[In connection with a text discussing rebellion of subjects

against their prince:] . . . you know a friend of ours that has vindicated its true meaning against a learned Man abroad that indiscreetly and injudiciously enough objected it against the late Rebellion. . . . [p. 125]

With what zeal and courage have you asserted its Liberty [of the press] from the bondage of *Imprimaturs* and the Inquisition of Prelates? What stiff and stubborn Homilies have you made to make it good that the suppression of a good Libel is *no less than Martyrdom,* [marginal note: Areo pag Pag. 4.] *and if it extend to the whole Impression a kind of Massacre, whereof the Execution ends not in the slaying of an Elemental Life, but strikes at that ethereal and fifth essence, the breath of Reason it self, slays an Immortality rather than a Life?* Such fustian bumbast as this past for stately wit and sence in that Age of politeness and reformation. . . . [p. 191]

And if we take away some simpering phrases, and timorous introductions, your Collection will afford as good Precedents for Rebellion and King-killing, as any we meet with in the writings of *J.M.* in defence of the Rebellion and the Murther of the King. . . . [p. 212]

[Speaking of ministers and tithes,] And yet a goodly Casuist of the Modern Reformation, *viz.* from the bondage of Prelatical and Regal Tyranny, has set it down for a certain rule of Conscience, that in Ministers of the Gospel, contention (that is demanding their Tythes) though for their own Right is scarce allowable. These things certainly are too fond and unreasonable of themselves to be seriously believed by those that pretend them. But they are resolved to be dishonest. . . . [p. 340]

Samuel Parker, *A Reproof to the Rehearsal Transprosed,* 1673, pages as indicated; Masson, VI, 703-705 (one brief quotation); Parker, *Milton's Contemporary Reputation,* pp. 116-117; Sensabaugh, *That Grand Whig Milton,* pp. 37-38. Mr. Parker gives almost all of these quotations and somewhat more; Mr. Sensabaugh gives only a few phrases. The date comes from the date of licensing of the Catalogue in which this title is advertised; see the *Term Catalogues,* I, 134. The book was entered in the Stationers' Registers on March 15 under the hands of Parker himself and of "Master Warden ROPER." See also

Marvell's references to Parker's work in the quotation below from his *Rehearsal Transpros'd: The Second Part.*

BEFORE MAY 6. JEERED AT IN *THE TRANSPROSER REHEARS'D.*

[Marvell] might as well have cal'd him *Bayes Anonymus* in imitation of *Miltons* learned Bull (for that Bulls in *Latin* are *learned* ones, none will deny), who in his Answer to *Salmasius,* calls him *Claudius Anonymus.* . . . [p. 9]

I dare assure you Sir, the work would have been more gratefully accepted than *Donns Poems* turn'd into *Dutch,* but what talk I of that, then *Prynnes Mount Orguil,* or *Milton's Paradise lost* in blank Verse. . . . [p. 30]

'Tis his scolding Common-place-book, which acquaints him with all the Moods and Figures of Railing; here he has all the terms of that Art which *Smectimnuus, Marchmont Needham, J. Milton,* or any other of the Professors ever thought of. . . . [p. 32]

. . . the *blind* Author of *Paradise lost* (the odds betwixt a *Transproser* and a *Blank Verse Poet,* is not great) begins his third Book thus, groping for a beam of *Light.*

> *Hail, holy Light, Off-Spring of Heav'n first born,*
> *Or of th' Eternal Coeternal beam.*

And a little after,

> ———*thee I revisit safe,*
> *And feel thy Sov'raign vital Lamp; but thou*
> *Revisitst not these eyes, that rowl in vain*
> *To find thy piercing Ray, and find no dawn;*
> *So thick a drop Serene hath quencht their Orbs,*
> *Or dim suffusion veil'd.*———

No doubt but the thoughts of this *Vital Lamp* lighted a *Christmas* Candle in his brain. What dark meaning he may have in calling this *thick drop Serene,* I am not able to say; but for his *Eternal Coeternal,* besides the absurdity of his inventive Divinity, in making *Light* contemporary with it's Creator, that jingling in the middle of his Verse, is more notoriously ridiculous, because the *blind Bard* (as he tells us himself in his Apology for writing in blank Verse) studiously declin'd Rhyme as a *jingling sound of like endings*. Nay, what is more observable, it is the very same fault, which he was so quick-sighted, as to discover in this Verse of *Halls Toothless Satyrs*.

  To teach each hollow Grove, and shrubby-Hill.

This, *teach each*, he has upbraided the Bishop with in his *Apology* for his *Animadversions on the Remonstrants Defence against Smectymnuus.* . . . [pp. 41-43]

Once, perhaps in a Century of years, there may arise a *Martin-Mar-Prelate*, a *Milton*, or such a Brave as our present Author. . . . [p. 55]

This Doctrine of *killing Kings in their own Defence*, you may safely vindicate as your own, it was never broacht before. . . . Which, if I understand not amiss, is nothing but *Iconoclastes* drawn in Little, and *Defensio Populi Anglicani* in Miniature. . . . [p. 72]

Nay, *Milton* holds, that the Legislative Power is in the Parliament exclusively, and the Executive only in the King. . . . [p. 98]

. . . concurring rather with your *Dear Friend* Mr. *Milton*: who says, that the only true Religion if commanded by the Civil Magistrate, becomes Unchristian, Inhumain and Barbarous. . . . [p. 110]

. . . an ingenious Writer against Mr. *Milton*, concerning the Rise and Fall of Republicks, He tells us, That it was not the Tyranny of *Spain*. . . . [p. 113]

. . . his *Accidence* (whether it be the same with *Miltons Accidence commenc'd Grammer*, I know not. . . . [p. 126]

Which is almost as apposite a Description of an *Independent*, as his Friend Mr. *Milton* has given us of a *Bishop*, who in his *Apology for his Animadversions upon the Remonstrants Defence against Smectymnuus*, says, that *a Bishops foot that hath all his Toes maugre the Gout, and a linnen Sock over it, is the aptest*

Emblem of the Bishop himself; who being a Pluralist, under one Surplice which is also linnen (and therefore so far like the Toe-Surplice, the *Sock*) *hides four Benefices besides the Metropolitan Toe*. So that when Arch-Bishop *Abbot* was suspended, we might say in Mr. *Miltons* style, his *Metropolitan Toe* was cut off. But since *Milton* is so great an Enemy to *great Toes* (however dignified or distinguisht, be they *Papal* or *Metropolitan*) we would fain know, whether his are all of a length, since the Leveller (it seems) affects a Parity even in Toes. Whether now his *Bishop* with a *Metropolitan Toe*, or our Authors *Congregational Man* with ten *Fingers* and long *Nails* upon all, be the fitter Monster to be shown, is hard to say. . . . [pp. 126-127]

But if *Milton's Sock* will not well endure a comparison with the *Surplice*, what think you of our Animadverter's joyning the *White-Surplices* and the *White-Aprons* in one period, *pag.* 195. (observe *John Milton*, they are both *Linnen* and both *White*). . . . For unluckily, among other Calamities of late, there has happen'd a prodigious Conjunction of a *Latin Secretary* and an *English School-master*, the appearance of which, none of our Astrologers foretold, nor no Comet portended. . . . [p. 128]

. . . his Discourse of the Liberty of Unlicens'd Printing *p.* 6. (which is little else but Milton's *Areopagitica* in short hand). . . . [p. 131]

If you will have it in his Elegancy, I never saw a man in *so high a Salivation*. If in *Miltons* (I know he will be proud to *lick* up his *Spittle*) *He has invested himself with all the Rheume of the Town, that he might have sufficient to bespaul* the Clergy. But enough of these two loathsome Beasts, and their spitting and spauling. . . . [p. 132]

As for his wonderful Gift in Rhyming, I could furnish him with many more of the *Isms* and *Nesses*, but that I should distast a *Blank Verse* Friend of his, who can by no means endure a Rhyme any where but in the middle of a Verse, therein following the laudable custom of the *Welsh Poets*. . . . [p. 133]

> *O marvellous Fate. O Fate full of marvel;*
> *That* Nol's Latin *Pay two* Clerks *should deserve ill!*
> *Hiring a* Gelding *and* Milton *the* Stallion;
> *His* Latin *was gelt, and turn'd pure* Italian.

Certainly to see a *Stallion* leap a *Gelding*, (and this *leap't* fair, for he *leapt* over the *Geldings* head) was a more preposterous sight, or at least more *Italian*, then what you fancy of *Father Patrick's bestriding Doctor Patrick*. Neither is it unlikely but some may say in defence of these Verses, that *Nol's Latin Clerks* were somewhat *Italianiz'd* in point of Art as well as Language, and for the proof of this refer those that are curious to a late Book call'd the *Rehearsal Transpros'd*, where p. 77. the Author or some body for him asks his Antagonist if the *Non-conformists must down with their Breeches as oft as he wants the prospect of a more pleasing* Nudity. And for his fellow Journeyman, they may direct the *Leaf-turners* to one of his books of *Divorce*, (for he has learnedly *parted Man and Wife* in no leas then four Books) namely, his *Doctrine* and *Discipline*, where toward the bottom of the second *Page*, they may find somewhat which will hardly merit so cleanly an Expression as that of the *Moral Satyrist*, *words left betwixt the Sheets*. Not but that he has both *excus'd* and *hallow'd* his Obscenity elsewhere by pleading Scripture for it, as *pag*. 24, 25. *Of his Apology for his Animadversions upon the Remonstrants Defence against Smectymnuus*. And again in his *Areopagitica*, p. 13. for Religion and Morality forbid a Repetition. Such was the Liberty of his Unlicenc'd Printing, that the more modest *Aretine* were he alive in this Age, might be set to School again, to learn in his own Art of the *Blind School-master*. . . . [pp. 135-137]

His Malicious and Disloyal Reflections on the late Kings Reign, traducing the Government of the best of Princes, and defaming his faithful Councellors in so foul a manner, as if he had at once made use of *Miltons* Pen, and *Gerbier's* Pencil. So black a Poyson has he suckt from the most virulent Pamphlets, as were impossible for any Mountebank but the Author of *Icono-clastes* to swallow, without the Cure of Antidotes. And certainly if that Libeller has not clubb'd with our Writer (as is with some reason suspected) we may safely say, there are many *Miltons* in this one Man. [pp. 146-147]

Richard Leigh (?), *The Transproser Rehears'd*, 1673, on the pages indicated; Masson, VI, 703-706 (somewhat less extensive selections); Parker, *Milton's Contemporary Reputation*, pp. 112-116; Sensabaugh, *That Grand Whig Milton*, 1952, pp. 38-39 (a few quotations). This attack on Marvell's *Rehearsal Transprosed* is generally thought to have been written by Richard Leigh. Parker (pp. 50-51) questions whether Leigh may perhaps be the "scribing quack" mentioned by Edward Phillips (p. xl); see above under date of 1660. The date of the present entry comes from the fact that *The Transproser Rehears'd* is announced for sale in a catalogue licensed on May 6, 1673; see *Term Catalogues*, I, 135. The curious reader who may wish to look up some of the Milton allusions in this passage will find Milton's strictures on Hall's "teach each" in CM, III, 343; those on the "Metropolitan Toe" at III, 308; those on the "Rheume of the Town" at III, 134; and that from *Areopagitica* at IV, 312. The chief object of attack in the book is Andrew Marvell. Paul B. Anderson (*Studies in Philology*, XLIV [1947], 504-518) attributes *The Transproser Rehears'd* to Samuel Butler.

MAY 1 (?). MARVELL DEFENDS MILTON'S CHARACTER AGAINST PARKER'S ATTACKS.

You do three times at least in your *Reproof*, and in your *Transproser Rehears'd* well nigh half the book thorow, run upon an Author *J.M.* which does not a little offend me. For why should any other mans reputation suffer in a contest betwixt you and me? But it is because you resolved to suspect that he had an hand in my former book, wherein, whether you deceive your self or no, you deceive others extreamly. For by chance I had not seen him of two years before; but after I undertook writing, I did more carefully avoid either visiting or sending to him, least I should any way involve him in my consequences. And you might have understood, or I am sure your Friend the Author of the *Common Places* could have told you, (he too had a slash at *J.M.* upon my account) that had he took you in hand, you would have had cause to repent the occasion, and not escap'd so easily as you did under my *Transprosal.* . . . But because in your 115 *p.* you are so particular *you know a friend of ours,* &c. intending that *J.M.* and his answer to *Salmasius,* I think it here seasonable to acquit my promise to you in giving the Reader a short trouble concerning my first acquaintance with you. *J.M.* was, and is, a man of great Learning and Sharpness of wit as any man. It was his misfortune, living in a tumultuous time, to be toss'd on the wrong side, and he writ *Flagrante bello* certain dangerous Treatises. His Books *of Divorce* I know not whether you may have use of; but those upon which you take him at advantage were of no other nature then that which I mentioned to you, writ by your own father; only with this difference, that your Fathers, which I have by me, was written with the same design, but with much less Wit or Judgment, for which there was no remedy: unless you will supply his Judgment with his High Court of Justice. At His Majesties happy Return, *J.M.* did partake, even as you your self did for all your huffing, of his Regal Clemency and has ever since expiated himself in a retired silence. It was after that, I well remember it, that being one day at his house, I there first met you and accidentally. Since that I have been scarce four or five times in your Company, but, whether it were my foresight or my good fortune, I never contracted any friendship or confidence with you. But then it was, when you, as I told you, wander'd up and down *Moor-fields* Astrologizing upon the duration of His Majesties Government, that you frequented *J.M.* incessantly and haunted his house day by day. What discourses you there used he is too generous to remember. But he never having in the least provoked you, for you to insult thus over his old age, to traduce him by your *Scaramuccios,* and in your own person, as a School-Master, who was born and hath lived much more ingenuously and Liberally then your self; to have done all this, and lay at last my simple book to his charge, without ever taking care to inform your self better, which you had so easie opportunity to do; nay, when you your self too have said, to my knowledge, that you saw no such great matter in it but that I might be the Author: it is inhumanely and inhospitably done, and will I hope be a warning to all others, as it is to me, to avoid (I will not say such a *Judas*,) but a man that creeps into all companies, to jeer, trepan, and betray them.

Andrew Marvell, *The Rehearsall Transpros'd, The Second Part,* 1673, pp. 377-380; Masson, VI, 707-708; Parker, *Milton's Contemporary Reputation,* pp. 117-119; Sensabaugh, *That Grand Whig Milton,* p. 39 (a few phrases). I have already quoted some parts of this passage above. The date comes from what looks like a mock license printed in the front of the book. The book appears in the *Term Catalogues* (1, 134) under license of May 6, 1673.

Before May 6. Publishes *of true religion.*

Of True Religion, Hæresie, Schism, Toleration, And what best means may be us'd against the growth of Popery The Author J. M. London Printed in the Year, 1673.

Title page of the first edition; Masson, VI, 687; CM, VI, 165-180, with facsimile of title page facing p. 165. The date comes from the next following entry.

Of true Religion, Heresie, Schism, Toleration; and what best means may be used against the growth and increase of Popery. The Author, **J. Milton.** In Quarto. Sold by **T. Sawbridge** in *Little Britain.*

Term Catalogues, I, 135, from a catalogue of books licensed on May 6, 1673, so that Milton's book must have been published on or before that date; Parker, *Milton's Contemporary Reputation,* pp. 50, 117. The catalogue is Number 13.

Of Toleration Heresie & Schisme.

Aubrey, f. 64, apparently in Edward Phillips's hand; Darbishire, p. 11.

His Treatise of true Religion, Heresy, Schism and Toleration, &c. was doubtless the last thing of his writing that was publisht before his Death.

Phillips, p. xl; Darbishire, p. 76.

Of True Religion, Heresie, Schism, Toleration, and what best means may be used against the growth of Popery. 4*to.*

Phillips, p. [li]; not in Darbishire.

(27) *Of true Religion, Heresie, Schism, Toleration, and what best means may be used against the growth and increase of Popery.* Lond. 1673. qu.

Wood, 1, 883; Darbishire, p. 46.

24 of tru Relig. Heresy, schisme & toleracōn wth ye means to p^rvent Popery.

British Museum Add. MS. 28,954, f. 9v.

AUGUST 22 (OR 12?). ELIE BOUHEREAU PRAISES MILTON HIGHLY.

Je suis bien ayse de ne m'estre trompé dans le jugement que j'avois fait des ouvrages de l'autheur anglois, et que tu l'ayes authorisé par le tien. je le trouve si brillant et si agreable partout, que j'aymerois mieux lire des volumes entiers de luy qu'une seule page de son adversaire qui me paroit par tout fort pedant et peu spirituel.

From a letter of August 22, 1673, written by Elie Bouhereau to Marquis Turon de Beyrie as printed in the Proceedings of the Huguenot Society of London, IX (1909-1911), 241-242. The original, which I have not seen, is said to be in Marsh's Library in Dublin. We may probably assume that the Count had answered Bouhereau's former letter of November 22, 1672, endorsing his views of Milton. If the date is New Style, the English date is August 12. The "adversaire" is of course Salmasius or Du Moulin.

[I am very glad not to have been deceived in the judgment which I had made of the works of the English author, and that you have supported it by your own. I find him so brilliant and so agreeable everywhere that I should prefer to read entire volumes of his rather than a single page by his adversary, who seemed to me everywhere very pedantic and not at all witty.]

OCTOBER 27. BROTHER-IN-LAW THOMAS AGAR ADDS CODICIL TO WILL.

The will is given above under date of June 10, 1671. The codicil of October 27, 1673, makes various changes, but none of them affects Milton or people close to him. The bequest of £200 to Edward Phillips remains unchanged. See Masson, VI, 773-774.

NOVEMBER. ENGAGES ELIZABETH FISHER AS MAID.

... this Deponent [Elizabeth Fisher] was servant unto Mr John Milton the Testator in this Cause deced for about a yeare before his death who dyed vpon a Sunday the fifteenth of November last at night.

From Elizabeth Fisher's deposition of December 15, 1674, *q.v.* See below under November 9, 1674.

NOVEMBER. MAKES ACQUAINTANCE OF MARY FISHER, ELIZABETH'S SISTER.

Maria Fisher soluta famul' domestica Johīs Batten ... antea cum Johanne Bayley infra Oppidum Milton in Com. Stafford per spacium duorum annorum, ante cum Johanna Baddily infra parochiam de Milton præd. per spacium trium annorum, et antea cum quodam Rogers Hargrave infra parochiam de Milton præd. per spacium duorum annorum ... ætatis 23 aut eo circiter ... this Deponent knew and was well acquainted with the arlāte John Milton the Testator in this Cause deced for about a twelve moneth before his death who dyed about a moneth since to the best of this Deponent's remembrance. ...

From Mary Fisher's deposition of December 15, 1674, *q.v.* Presumably she and her sister Elizabeth came to know Milton at about the same time, namely when Elizabeth became his maid. It is an interesting coincidence that Mary had formerly been a servant for several years in a town named Milton. The word "arlāte," which Todd expands to "articulate," probably means articled or mentioned.

[Mary Fisher, free domestic servant of John Batten ... formerly with Joan Bayley in the town of Milton in co. Stafford for the space of two years, previously with Joan Baddily in the parish of Milton aforesaid for the space of three years, and before that with a certain Rogers Hargrave in the parish of Milton aforesaid for the space of two years ... of the age of 23 or thereabout. ...]

NOVEMBER. BROTHER CHRISTOPHER'S SON THOMAS SUCCEEDS POET'S BROTHER-IN-LAW THOMAS AGAR IN CROWN OFFICE.

...*Thomas Agar* ... held [the position of Secondary of the Crown Office in Chancery] for many Years, and left it to Mr. *Thomas Milton* (the Son of the aforementioned Sir *Christopher*) who at this day executes it with great Reputation and Ability.

Phillips, p. vii; Darbishire, p. 53; Masson, VI, 774. This arrangement must have been informal, for it seems not to be mentioned in Agar's will of June 10, 1671. But if Phillips is correct, presumably Thomas Milton must have come into this office upon Agar's death, which occurred November 1. Masson, however, seems to say that Milton had already been in the office with Agar before his death, though he gives no basis for such a view. His words are as follows: "Thomas Milton was already [in 1674] a person of some consequence. Having been taken into the Crown Office in Chancery under his uncle Mr. Thomas Agar, Deputy Clerk of the Crown, he had, on Mr. Agar's death in 1673, succeeded him in the Deputy Clerkship" (VI, 763). As for the later fortunes of the family of Anne Milton Phillips Agar, Elizabeth Foster, the poet's granddaughter, told Thomas Newton about 1749 that "She knows nothing of her aunt Philips or Agar's descendants, but believes that they are all extinct" (*Paradise Lost*, ed. Newton, 1749, I, lix). Birch reports this statement, with the addition of some weird spellings, in his 1753 edition of Milton's prose *Works* (I, lxxvii).

NOVEMBER 5. BROTHER-IN-LAW THOMAS AGAR'S WILL PROVED.

The will of June 10, 1671, was proved on November 5, 1673, by Agar's son Thomas. See Masson, VI, 774. This action cleared the way for Milton's nephew Edward Phillips to receive his legacy of £200, and for Christopher Milton's son Thomas to succeed to Agar's office as Deputy Clerk of the Crown Office.

BEFORE NOVEMBER 24. SECOND EDITION OF *POEMS* PUBLISHED.

Poems, &c. upon Several Occasions. By Mr. John Milton: Both English and Latin, &c. Composed at several times. With a small Tractate of Education To Mr. Hartlib. London, Printed for Tho. Dring at the Blew Anchor next Mitre Court over against Fetter Lane in Fleet-street. 1673.

[Alternate imprint on some copies:] Printed for Tho. Dring at the White Lion next Chancery Lane End, in Fleet-street. 1673.

[Title page preceding Latin poems:] Joannis Miltoni Londinensis Poemata. Quorum pleraque intra Annum ætatis Vigesimum Conscripsit. Nunc primum Edita. [ornament] Londini, Excudebat W. R. Anno 1673.

Title page of 1673 edition; that of the Latin part is on sig. [L4]; Masson, VI, 687; reproduced in facsimile in CM, I, facing p. 46 (the "Blew Anchor" issue); also in Fletcher facsimile, I, 11 (both issues); the titles of the Latin section are reproduced in CM, I, 154 verso, and in Fletcher facsimile, I, 99. This edition of 1673 is the basis of the CM text; it is reproduced entire in Fletcher facsimile, I, 11-145. Fletcher thinks it almost certain that the W. R. of the Latin title page, who also probably printed the whole volume, is William Rawlins (I, 7-8). The date is determined by that of its entry in the *Term Catalogues* (see next item). Though Fletcher (I, 10) thinks it impossible to determine which of the two imprints on the title page came first, Emma Unger and William A. Jackson (*Catalogue of the Carl H. Pforzheimer Library*, II, 733), state that the "White Lion" is the earlier. This volume carries, in addition to the poems in the 1645 volume, the following: "On the Death of a fair Infant," sonnets XI-XIX, "The fifth Ode of Horace," "At a Vacation Exercise," "On the new forcers of Conscience," Psalms 1-8 and 80-88, "Apologus de Rustico & Hero," "Ad Joannem Rousium," and "Of Education" (not in Fletcher facsimile).

[Translation of Latin title page: Poems of John Milton of London. Most of which he wrote before the age of twenty. Now first published. London. W. R. printed them in the year 1673.]

Poems, etc. upon several occasions. By Mr. **John Milton.** Both English and Latine, etc., composed at several times. With a small Tract of Education, to Mr. *Hartlib.* In Octavo. Price, bound, 2s. 6d. Printed for **Th. Dring,** at the Blew Anchor, over against *Fetter lane*, in *Fleet street.*

Term Catalogues, I, 151, from *A Catalogue of Books*, No. 15, licensed November 24, 1673; Parker, *Milton's Contemporary Reputation*, p. 117.

1 Poems 8° printed at . . . . twice printed ⎰Some writt but
⎱at 18. . . .
10 A Letter, of Education to Mr S. Hartlib. [wth his Poëms]

Aubrey, f. 68v; Darbishire, p. 9. The dots following "printed at" are Aubrey's own; apparently he intended to fill in the name later but never did so. The brackets at the end are also his.

. . . Mr. *Cyriak Skinner* whom he honoured with two Sonnets, one long since publick among his Poems; the other but newly Printed. . . .

Poems upon several Occasions, both *English* and *Latin*, &c. Composed at several times.

Phillips, pp. xxxvii and [lii]; Darbishire, p. 74 (first quotation only). In the second quotation, if Phillips is copying from the title instead of writing from memory, he is referring to 1673 and not to 1645, which lacks the words "upon several Occasions." The first quotation must refer to 1673, however, because the Skinner sonnets were written long after the publication of the 1645 volume.

[He made friends in Italy.] The reputation hee had with them they express'd in several Commendatory Verses, wch are extant in his book of Poems. . . .

. . . an elegant Copy of Verses entitl'd Mansus wch is extant amongst his other latin Poems.

The "earliest" biography, ff. 140v and 141; Darbishire, pp. 20, 21. Though these references might be to either edition of Milton's poems, they are likelier to refer to the later one, especially since the writer speaks of the poems as being "extant."

(28) *Poems, &c. on several occasions, both English and Latin, &c. composed at several times*. Lond. 1673-4. oct. Among these are mixed some of his Poems before mention'd, made in his youthful years.

Wood, I, 883; Darbishire, pp. 46-47.

AFTER NOVEMBER 24. ASSOCIATION COPIES OF MIL-
TON'S *POEMS*.

Two copies of the 1673 *Poems* which belonged to contemporaries of Milton and which they very likely bought or acquired shortly after publication have come down to fairly recent times. Another copy with manuscript corrections which may date from Milton's lifetime has also survived.

(1) Edmund Waller's copy with his autograph belonged to Richard Heber and appeared in his sale catalogue, *Bibliotheca Heberiana, Catalogue of the Library of the late Richard Heber . . . which will be sold by auction . . .* 1835-6, part 8, item 1650. It came up for sale again at Sotheby's on March 29, 1928, and was sold to Pearson for £60. Its present location is unknown. See *Book Auction Records,* xxv (1928), 282.

(2) John Evelyn's copy, with his monogram in gold on the sides and the back, formerly in the Currer collection, was sold at Sotheby's on July 2-4, 1894, to Quaritch for £63. It had previously belonged also to Sir Joseph Hawley, Bart. See *Book Prices Current,* viii (1895), 424. Its present location is unknown.

(3) The Yale University Library possesses a copy which contains many notes in what looks like seventeenth-century handwriting. Some are in red ink, others in black. They supply the dates of some poems, supply some missing lines, and correct some errors of spelling and punctuation and the like. There is no clue to the identity of the scribes.

DECEMBER 23. FRIEND SIR PETER WENTWORTH LEAVES MILTON £100 IN WILL.

. . . And alsoe I giue to my worthy and verie learned Friend Mr John Milton (who writt against Salmatius) one hundred pounds of like money.

Prerogative Court of Canterbury, 26 Bence; *Notes and Queries,* v, vii (1877), 166; Masson, vi, 719; CM, xviii, 626. Wentworth had been for several years a member of the Council of State (see Masson's index), and had been present at some of the meetings which Milton also had attended. He had upon occasion opposed Cromwell, who had ruthlessly squelched him. Wentworth's will includes many other legacies large and small, one being for £50 to a Mr. or Dr. Needham, who may be Milton's old associate Marchamont Needham. Since Wentworth survived Milton, and since his will was not proved until February 24, 1676, Milton never received any financial advantage from this bequest. But he must have appreciated the kindness which prompted it.

ADVERSE CRITICISMS OF *PARADISE LOST* FOR SUPERNATURAL SUBJECT (?).

 ... neither had he [Horace] *now liv'd, would he have tax'd* Milton, *as our false Critiques have presum'd to do, for his choice of a supernatural Argument.*
 Dryden, "The Authors Apology for Heroique Poetry; and Poetic Licence," prefixed to *The State of Innocence,* 1677, sig. c2v; Dryden's *Dramatic Works,* ed. Montagu Summers, III (1932), 424; Dryden's *Essays,* ed. W. P. Ker, I (1926), 190. Through a good deal of this prefatory essay Dryden seems to assume a considerable body of hostile criticism of Milton's epic.

HENRY HAMMOND'S ATTACK ON MILTON'S DIVORCE VIEWS REPRINTED.

 The first open attempt that I remember that way [*i.e.,* in loose, licentious, wishful thinking], was made in a Discourse purposely on that *subject,* and presented to the *Parliament,* at the beginning of these *licentious* times; and the *special* artifice made use of, was that, of bringing back *Christ* unto *Moses,* or interpreting the restraint laid on this matter in the *New Testament,* by *analogie* with the *Judaical permission* in the *Old.* . . .
 [Marginal note:] A Plea for Divorces.
 Henry Hammond, *A Letter of Resolution to six Quaeres,* 1652, reprinted in his *Workes,* I (1674), 457; Parker, *Milton's Contemporary Reputation,* p. 93. See above under date of November 1, 1652.

BELITTLED IN SECOND EDITION OF FOULIS'S HISTORY.
 [Among a list of inhuman defenders of rebellion:] And the unparallel'd murther of his Sacred Majesty, could not want vindications, whilst *Milton, Goodwin,* and their associates, could command the Press. . . .
 How *Cromwel's* Faction spread abroad Pamphlets against King, City, and Parliament, [1647.] that the people might

take the Army for honest-men, is somewhat pointed at by Mr.
Walker. And since that, What scurrilous Book have been con-
trived by *Needham, Goodwin, Milton, Rogers* and such like
Billingsgate Authors, is not unknown to any. . . .

Henry Foulis, *The History of the Wicked Plots and Conspiracies Of
Our Pretended Saints . . . The Second Edition,* 1674, pp. 4, 24. For
the first edition see above under date of 1662. The date 1647 in brackets
stands thus in the original.

SATIRIZED IN *POOR ROBIN* FOR BLINDNESS.

Blinde Milton

Poor Robin, 1674, under date of November 2; see above under date
of 1664 for the beginning of this series of gibes. This entry is printed
in red ink. Despite Milton's death in 1674 similar entries continued in
1675, 1676, and 1677.

MARVELL REFERS SATIRICALLY TO DRYDEN'S DRAMATI-ZATION OF *PARADISE LOST* (?).

Or if a Work so infinite he [Milton] spann'd,
Jealous I was that some less skilful hand
(Such as disquiet always what is well,
And by ill imitating would excell)
Might hence presume the whole Creations day
To change in Scenes, and show it in a Play.
Pardon me, Mighty Poet, nor despise
My causeless, yet not impious, surmise. . . .
Well mightst thou scorn thy Readers to allure
With tinkling Rhime, of thy own sense secure;
While the *Town-Bayes* writes all the while and spells,
And like a Pack-horse tires without his Bells:
Their Fancies like our Bushy-points appear,
The Poets tag them, we for fashion wear.
I too transported by the Mode offend,
And while I meant to Praise thee must Commend.
Thy Verse created like thy Theme sublime,
In Number, Weight, and Measure, needs not Rhime.

A. M.

John Milton · 1674

From Andrew Marvell's commendatory verses prefixed to Milton's *Paradise Lost*, 1674, sig. [A3]; Masson, VI, 715-716; CM, II, 3-5; Fletcher facsimile, III, 69-70. Masson pronounces these verses "a studied combination of eulogium on Milton for his *Paradise Lost* with rebuke to Dryden for his impudence in attempting a dramatic and rhymed transversion of such an epic." A. W. Verity (ed. *Paradise Lost*, Cambridge, 1910, p. 366) considers the reference to Dryden here "not to be mistaken." The expressions "ill imitating," "show it in a Play," "*Town-Bayes*," and "Poets tag them" seem to fit Dryden's work too closely to be merely a general apprehension of some future attempt not actually done at the time of Marvell's writing.

SOME OF MILTON'S BOOKS READ AND STUDIED IN NEW-INGTON GREEN AND OTHER ACADEMIES (?).

Milton's Apology was in *Deliciis* with most of us, I am apt to believe poor *W. J.* formed his Latin Stile very much by reading him, for he had a very good one. We had also *Eiconoclastes*, some of the lads had *Meursii Elegantiae* . . . and the most lewd abominable Books that ever blasted Christian Eye: These you'll believe our Tutors knew not of, nor did they direct us to the former. All the Reports since spread about the King's Book were then common among us, and Bishop *Gauden's* Son was quoted as their Author; we all esteemed very meanly of the Father. . . .

From Samuel Wesley's *A Letter from a Country Divine to his Friend in London. Concerning the Education of the Dissenters, in Their Private Academies*, 1703, pp. 14-15, as quoted by Lew Girdler in "Defoe's Education at Newington Green Academy," *Studies in Philology*, L (1953), 575. The editor comments that "Since curricula change slowly, it can be assumed that most books used in Wesley's time (1680-1683) were also used in Defoe's (1675-1680)," *ibid.*, p. 574. If this assumption is correct, there is no reason to assume that the same might not also be true a year earlier in 1674, and perhaps in other schools. The entry is therefore given here tentatively as a guess based on rather strong foundations. See below, p. 420.

FIRST EDITION OF *PARADISE LOST* ADVERTISED.

Poetry in Quarto. *Price of each 3s.* . . .

Milton's *Paradise lost*: A Poem in ten Books. Printed for *S. Simmons.*

[67]

Robert Clavel, *The Catalogue of all the Books printed in England, Since the Dreadful Fire in 1666,* 1675, p. 82; Todd, 1 (1826), 194. Though the date of the catalogue is given as 1675, the fact that Milton's epic is described as being in ten books rather than in twelve makes it necessarily a reference to the first edition and therefore probably at least prepared if not printed before the second edition of the poem in the middle of the year.

DUTCH PRINTER ELZEVIR ADVERTISES MILTON'S POEMS AND SOME PROSE WORKS FOR SALE.

Miltoni (Joan.) Poëmata, 8. Lond. 1645.

.... Defensio Populi Anglicani, 12. Amst. 1651.

.... eadem, 4. Lond. 1651.

.... Defensio pro se contra Alex. Morum, 8. ibid. 1655.

........................eadem, 12. Hagae Comitis, 1655.

.... Defensio secunda pro Populo Anglicano contra Alex. Morum, 8. Lond. 1654.

.... eadem, 12. Hagae-Comitis, 1654.

Catalogus Librorum Qui In Bibliopolio Danielis Elsevirii venales extant [Catalogue of books which are offered for sale in Daniel Elzevir's bookshop], Amsterdam, 1674, p. 121; Parker, *Milton's Contemporary Reputation,* p. 119.

[John Milton, *Poems,* octavo, London, 1645.

> *Defense of the English People,* duodecimo, Amsterdam, 1651.

> The same, quarto, London, 1651.

> *Defense of himself against Alexander More,* octavo, the same place, 1655.

> The same, duodecimo, the Hague, 1655.

> *Second Defense of the English People against Alexander More,* octavo, London, 1654.

> The same, duodecimo, the Hague, 1654.]

ACQUAINTED WITH "OBITUARY" SMYTH.

A Catalogue of All Such Persons Deceased whome I knew in their life time . . . John Milton.

The Obituary of Richard Smyth, ed. Sir Henry Ellis, Publications of the Camden Society, No. 44, 1849, pp. 1, 104. This volume is a transcript of British Museum Sloane MS. 886. Though the heading and the entry give no indication how long Smyth had known Milton, at least the acquaintance must have existed in the last year of Milton's life. Among other friends of eminence or of some interest in connection with Milton whose deaths Smyth records are Sir James Leigh, Earl of Marlborough (March 14, 1629), Sir Henry Wotton (February 21, 1638), Sir (and Dr.) Arthur Duck (December 16, 1648), Alexander Rosse (February 24, 1654), John Selden (November 30, 1654), Archbishop James Ussher (March 22, 1656), Oliver Cromwell (September 3, 1658), John Bradshaw (October 31, 1659), Humphrey Moseley (January 31, 1661), Thomas Fuller (August 16, 1661), Isaac Pennington (December 17, 1661), Sir Robert Pye (May 20, 1662), Bishop John Gauden (September 19, 1662), the Countess of Bridgewater (June 13, 1663), George Thomason (buried April 10, 1666), George Wither (May, 1667), Jeremy Taylor (August 13, 1667), William Prynne (October 23, 1669), George Monck, Duke of Albemarle (January 3, 1670), the Lady Brackley (March 4, 1670), Edward Hyde, Earl of Clarendon (November 9, 1674). Smyth is sometimes wrong in his dates.

BECOMES ACQUAINTED WITH DANIEL SKINNER.

And though I happen'd to be acquainted with Milton in his lifetime, (which out of mere love to learning I procur'd, and noe other concerns ever pass'd betwixt us but a great desire and ambition of some of his learning,) I am, and ever was, soe farr from being in the least tainted with any of his principles, that I may boldly say, none has a greater honour and loyalty for his Majesty, more veneration for the Church of England, and love for his countrey then I have.

From a letter of Skinner to Samuel Pepys, November 9/19, 1676, now in the Bodleian, MS. Rawl. A 185, ff. 271 ff.; Hamilton, p. 38; Samuel Pepys, *Letters and the Second Diary*, ed. R. G. Howarth, London, 1933, 57-62. The text above is that of Howarth. The date is merely a guess and may be some time earlier. Milton may possibly have given to Skinner at this time the manuscripts of his *Letters of State* and *Christian Doctrine* which he tried to publish in 1676 (*q.v.*), or they may have come to him indirectly.

HAS *LETTERS OF STATE* PREPARED FOR PUBLICATION AT URGING OF DANISH RESIDENT.

The *Danish* Resident prevail'd with *Milton* to get the Letters of State (formerly mention'd) transcrib'd, and which were publisht after his death; as were also his *Familiar Letters* in 74. . . .

Toland, p. 44; Darbishire, p. 188; Masson, VI, 720-722. The amanuensis who transcribed them was probably Daniel Skinner. See French, "That Late Villain Milton," *PMLA*, LV (1940), 102-115. For further details about this work see below under date of 1676. The Danish resident at this time was Marcus Gioé (*CSPD, 1673-1675*, p. 26. But Ethel Seaton identifies the man who talked to Milton as Simon de Petkum; see her *Literary Relations of England and Scandinavia in the Seventeenth Century*, Oxford, 1935, pp. 142-143, and the additional entry for IV, 394 (before August 1, 1663). The quotation from Toland of course gives no date for the conversation, which is here filed under 1674 for lack of more specific information.

EDWARD PHILLIPS CONTINUES TO VISIT MILTON.

Thus have I reduced into form and order what ever I have been able to rally up, either from the recollection of my own memory, of things transacted while I was with him, or the Information of others equally conversant afterwards, or from his own mouth by frequent visits to the last.

Phillips, p. xliii; Darbishire, p. 78; CM, XVIII, 378.

HELPS NEPHEW EDWARD PHILLIPS COMPILE *THEATRUM POETARUM* (?).

AS oft as I seriously consider with My self most worthy Associates in Learning and Vertue, and My most honour'd Friends, what a vast difference there is, or at least seems to be, between one part of Mankind and the other; how near the Intelligence of Angels the one, how beneath the Ingenuity and Industry of many Brute Animals the other; how aspiring to the Perfection of knowledge the one, how immers't in swinish sloth and ignorance the other; I am apt to wonder how it could possibly be imagin'd that the same rationality of Soul should inform alike,

as we are oblig'd to beleive by the authority of Sacred Scrip-
tures, and the Doctrine of the Souls Immortality, the whole
masse & frame of Human Nature, and not rather that there
should be a gradation of Notion from the lowest brute up to
the Angelic Region. . . .

Edward Phillips, *Theatrum Poetarum, or a Compleat Collection of*
the Poets, 1675, sigs. *2-*2v. Many critics have believed that Milton contributed something to this book, of which I give above the first sentence
of the prefatory essay addressed to Thomas Stanley and Edward Sherburn. Todd says (1 [1826], 228) that ". . . traces of Milton's hand
may certainly be discovered in this interesting volume," especially in the
section on Shakespeare. Masson (vi, 765) unhesitatingly pronounces
that the book conveys "opinions about poets which Phillips must have
imbibed from Milton, with sometimes, perhaps, as in the sketches of
Euripides, Marlowe, Shakespeare, Ben Jonson, Drummond, Waller,
Cowley, and Dryden, a phrase lent by Milton or recollected from his
talk. The Prefatory Discourse opens with a strain of expression so Miltonic, so much above Phillips's usual range, that one is obliged to fancy
either that Milton actually dictated some of the sentences, or that Phillips had Milton's ideas and voice in his mind and was trying to echo
them." I may add one other opinion, that of William Lowndes, written
in a copy of the book which I now own: "The hand of Milton may be
often discovered in this publication of his elder nephew. Among many
criticisms in this volume which must be attributed to Milton those on
Shakespeare & Marlowe are eminently conspicuous. In the Preface are
more manifest marks of Miltons hand than in the book itself. . . . Lowndes." On the basis of these and other such statements the sections on
Marlowe, Shakespeare, Jonson, and Dryden were included in the Columbia edition of Milton; see CM, XVIII, 460-461, 628-629. This book
was licensed for publication on September 14, 1674 (verso of title page),
and advertised in the bookseller's catalogue on June 19, 1675 (*Term*
Catalogues, I, 212). In the original text, instead of the comma after
"vast difference there is," the printer mistakenly put a single quotation
mark or an inverted comma, which I have corrected in this transcript.
It should be added that the book is a compilation of brief remarks, seldom
over a page in length and usually only a few lines, about the great poets,
and many lesser ones, of European countries since the beginnings. The
one dissenting voice about Miltonic participation or influence is that of
William R. Parker, who records his skepticism in the London *Times*
Literary Supplement for February 28, 1942, p. 108. Professor Parker
points out that many men whom Milton would very likely have wanted
to include (as for example Wotton, Marvell, Diodati, and Gill) do
not appear in the collection, whereas on the other hand Phillips does

bring in some of Milton's worst enemies, like Pierre du Moulin. At the other end of the scale is Professor Harris Fletcher, who claims (*Journal of English and Germanic Philology*, LV, 1956, 35-40) that "perhaps as much as nine-tenths of the work was almost beyond doubt done by Milton. As I now see the *Theatrum*, it stands out as a work almost completely produced by Milton, though not of course in the form in which it was printed." See also the entry below for the publication of the *Theatrum* in May (?), 1675.

GIVES BRABAZON AYLMER MANUSCRIPT OF *HISTORY OF MOSCOVIA* FOR PUBLICATION (?).

ADVERTISEMENT.

This Book was writ by the Authour's own hand, before he lost his sight. And sometime before his death dispos'd of it to be printed. But it being small, the Bookseller hop'd to have procured some other suitable Piece of the same Authour's to have joyn'd with it, or else it had been publish'd 'ere now.

Milton, *A Brief History of Moscovia*, 1682, sig. A4v; CM, X, 329. Though Aylmer, who printed this volume, does not say that Milton gave the manuscript to him, it seems most likely that he did, since we know from the printer's note to the reader in Milton's *Epistolarum Familiarium* in 1674 that Milton gave him his private letters and his college prolusions and probably would have given him the letters of state had not the authorities objected. Probably Milton sent the manuscript to Aylmer by the same common friend who conducted those other negotiations. The date is vague, but I should guess that Aylmer had already received the *Letters and Prolusions* and was engaged in printing them before he received this new manuscript.

MAKES PLANS WITH BRABAZON AYLMER TO PUBLISH PRIVATE LETTERS.

Typographus LECTORI.

FActa spes erat aliquandiu, Lector Benevole, *fore ut hujus Authoris Epistolæ cum Publicæ tum Familiares, uno volumine excudendæ mihi permitterentur. Verum de Publicis, postquam eos, per quos solos licebat, certas ob causas id nolle cognovi, concessa parte contentus, Familiares tantum in lucem emittere satis habui. Eas cum aliquanto pauciores esse, quam pro Volumine satis concinno, reperirem; agendum cum Authore per Amicum*

*utriq; summum statui, ut, siquid haberet apud se Opusculi forte
repositi, ad pensandam vel saltem explendam Epistolarum pau-
citatem, quasi cumulum adjicere ne gravaretur. Ille hortatoris
Authoritate adductus, excussis Chartulis, in hæc forte juvenilia
hic illic disjecta tandem incidit, & flagitanti Amico morem gessit.
Hæc itaque, cum & commune Amico, cujus in judicio acquievi,
satis probata, Authori non pœnitenda videri animadverterem,
non dubitavi, quantumvis juvenilia, in lucem edere; sperans,
quod mea maxime refert, non minus fore mihi vendibilia, quam
Auditoribus olim fuerint, cum recitarentur, non injucunda.* Vale.

Milton, *Epistolarum Familiarium,* 1674, sigs. A3-A3v; CM, XII, 2.
In the original there is a second superfluous comma after "Benevole,"
which I have omitted. Though Aylmer does not say just when he carried on these negotiations with Milton, it is likely that they took place
not too long before the actual printing of the book, some time before
May 26 (see below). One would like to know who the unnamed friend
was who acted as intermediary between Milton and Aylmer. The letters of state, which Aylmer had hoped to include in this volume, were
not published until 1676, and then surreptitiously. The volume was
filled out to publishable size by inclusion of Milton's college exercises or
prolusions. Aylmer may also have procured at the same time with these
pieces the manuscript of the *History of Moscovia,* for, though he did
not publish it until 1682, he says in his advertisement to it (CM, X, 329)
that Milton "before his death dispos'd of it to be printed."

[It was my hope for a while, gentle reader, that I should be
allowed to print this author's letters, both public and private,
in one volume. But after I found out about the public ones that
those men by whom alone permission could be given did not
want to give it, I considered it enough, content with the permission given, to bring only the private ones to the light. When I
found them to be somewhat fewer than I consider enough to
make a volume, I decided that the most important thing to do
was to negotiate with the author through a common friend, so
that if he had about him any little work perhaps laid aside, he
might not be unwilling to add some weight, as it were, to com-
pensate for or at least to fill out the slimness of the letters. He,
persuaded by the authority of the encourager, at length fell
upon these perhaps youthful compositions, scattered here and

there among the writings which he had composed, and complied with the wishes of our importunate friend. And so when I found that these were sufficiently approved by our common friend, in whose judgment I acquiesced, and that they seemed not objectionable to the author, I did not hesitate, however youthful they are, to bring them to light; hoping (what concerns me most) that they will be no less salable for me than they were not unpleasing formerly to their hearers when they were recited.

Farewell.]

JANUARY 30. SLIGHTINGLY ALLUDED TO BY ROYALIST PREACHER(?).

[Deposition of rulers is not lawful because it is not really the will of the people.] No, so far was it from any of this, that the ablest Writer that was to be had for money, to defend the Villany to the World, being pinched, with the fewness and despicableness of those who were engaged in it, hath nothing to return to it, but that sneaking Blasphemy, That it was the Mysterious Will of the Lord, and so *not many Wise, not many Mighty, not many Noble* were *called* to it.

Richard Meggott, *A Sermon Preached before the Right Honourable The Lord Major and Aldermen, &c. At Gvild-Hall Chappel, January the 30th 1673/4*, London, n.d. [1674], pp. 45-46; Sensabaugh, *That Grand Whig Milton*, pp. 50-51. Though Milton is nowhere mentioned by name, Sensabaugh feels sure that the reference is to him. A possible reference, though less clear, occurs on p. 33.

FEBRUARY 1. BROTHER CHRISTOPHER AGAIN ONE OF LEADERS OF INNER TEMPLE PARLIAMENT.

Parliamentum ibm̄ Tentum Primo Die ffebruarij Anno Dnī 1673. Annoqz Regni Regis Dnī Caroli scdī nunc Anglie &cs Vicesimo sexto Coram Francō Philipps xpōfero Milton Edr̄o Pecke Arīs et Alijs. [Marginal note:] Jnterius Templum Johēs Heath Miles. Attornat' Ducat' Lancastr' et Thesaur' ibm̄.

Records of the Inner Temple; printed in F. A. Inderwick, *A Calendar of the Inner Temple*, III, 94.

[Parliament held in the same place on February 1, 1673/4, and in the twenty-sixth year of the reign of our lord and king Charles II now of England etc., before Francis Phillips, Christopher Milton, Edward Peck, Esquires, and others. (Note:) Inner Temple. John Heath, Knight, Attorney of the Duchy of Lancaster and Treasurer of the same.]

FEBRUARY 11. BROTHER CHRISTOPHER AGAIN ONE OF LEADERS OF INNER TEMPLE PARLIAMENT.

Parliamentum ibm̃ Tentum vndecimo die ffebruarij Anno Domini 1673. Annoqz RRρ Dnī Caroli scdī nunc Angl' &cs xxvj°. Coram xp̄ofer Milton Edr̃o Pecke Thoma Farrar Aris et Alijs. [Marginal note:] Jnterius Templum Johēs Heath Miles Attornat' Ducat' Lanc: Thesaurar'.

Records of the Inner Temple; printed in F. A. Inderwick, *A Calendar of the Inner Temple Records*, III, 95.

[Parliament held in the same place on February 11, 1673/4, and in the twenty-sixth year of the reign of our lord and king Charles II now of England etc., before Christopher Milton, Edward Pecke, Thomas Farrar, Esquires, and others. (Note:) Inner Temple. John Heath, Knight, Attorney of the Duchy of Lancaster and Treasurer.]

MARCH 25. RATED FOR FOUR HEARTHS FOR TAX.

St Giles Criplegate . . . Artillery Wall . . . John Melton—4.

Public Record Office, E179/143/370, m. 57: "A true View of All the ffire Hearthes and Stoves within the County of Middlesex . . . for one Yeare Ended at our Lady Day one thousand Six hundred Seaventy and fower, And p^{r}sented . . . the twelueth day of Aprill . . . 1675"; Hunter, *Milton*, p. 43; Masson, VI, 717-719. The number 4 after Milton's names indicates the number of hearths and stoves recorded as in his possession as of the date given. The title quoted, which appears at the foot of the last membrane, gives the date presented as well as that on which the survey was based. The amount of the tax is not stated, but it would have been proportionate to the number. As Masson notes, Milton had as low a rating as any of his neighbors, some of whom had five or six hearths. Why the eight hearths of 1665 (IV, 418) should have shrunk to four is not clear.

MARCH 25. BROTHER CHRISTOPHER AND SON RICHARD RATED FOR TAX.

Richard Milton 2 [hearths]. . . .

Chris. Milton Esq. 9.

Public Record Office, Hearth Tax returns for the year ending Lady Day (March 25), 1674, as quoted in *Suffolk in 1674, being the Hearth Tax Returns*, in *Suffolk Green Books*, Number 11, Volume 13, 1905, pp. 77, 165. Richard appears under the location of Cockfeild in Babergh, and Christopher under St. Margarett, Ipswich. The return is signed by three justices of the peace: Thomas Edgar, Edward Mann, and "Chr. Milton" (p. 1). Richard is among those "certified," which the editor interprets (p. xxxii) as meaning that he had a "certificate of poverty." This compilation is evidently part of the same action as that in which John Milton is included in the preceding entry, but I did not find the present entry in the Public Record Office when I was searching for the poet's.

APRIL 17. DRYDEN'S DRAMATIZATION OF *PARADISE LOST* REGISTERED.

17ᵗʰ Aprill 1674

Master Hen. Entred . . . under the hands of ROGER L'ES-
Herringman TRANG Esqʳ and Master Warden MEARNE,
a booke or coppy entituled *The Fall of Angels and man in innocence, An heroick opera* Written to [*sic*] **John Dreyden,** servant to his Matie . . . . . . vjᵈ.

Stationers' Registers, II, 479; Masson, VI, 710.

MAY 10. BROTHER CHRISTOPHER AND HIS SON RICHARD SIGN INDENTURE WITH FRANCIS AND ELIZABETH HALY AND OTHERS.

This Jndenture tripartite made the tenth day of May in the six and twentieth year of the raigne of our Soūaigne Lord Charles the second by the grace of God of England Scotland ffrance and Ireland King defender of the faith etc Annoqz Dni 1674 Between Nicholas Haly late of [Nacton] in the County of Suff Gent and ffrances Dixon the widd and relict of ffennor

Dixon late of Stoak next Jpswich in the said County Gent dcd
of the first part ffrancis Haly eldest Sonne and heir apparent of
the said Nicholas Haly and Elizabeth his Wife onely Daughter
and Heir of the said ffennor Dixon and ffrances his Wife of the
second part And Christopher Milton of Jpswich aforesaid Esq'
and Richard Milton his Sonne of the third part Witnesseth That
Whereas a marriage hath lately been had and solempnized between the said ffrancis Haly and the said Elizabeth his Wife
Now it [is] hereby mutually covenanted . . . That one or more
fine or fines . . . shall be had acknowledged and levied by the
said Nicholas Haly ffrances Dixon ffrancis Haly and Elizabeth
his Wife to the said Christopher Milton and Richard Milton
and the heires of the said Christopher before his Maties Justices
of the Co^{rt} of comon pleas at Westm̄ in due forme of Law before the end of Trinity Terme now next ensuing the date of
these p^rñtₚ Of all and singular the Messuages ffarmes Lands
and Tenem^{ts} hereafter mencōned That is to say Of All That
capitall Messuage or Tenem^t and ffarme called or known by the
name of Goodlesford Andrews āls Godlesford Andrews āls
Gusford Hall . . . in Stoak and Belsted or in Washbrooke or
Sproughton w^{th}in the said County . . . late in the tenure or occupacōn of the said ffennor Dixon but now in the occupacōn
of the said ffrances Dixon and ffrancis Haly or their Assignes
And Of All that Messuage . . . scituate lying or being in Crans-
ford w^{th}in the said County and now or late in the occupacōn of
John Dowsing or his Assignes And of those two Messuages . . .
in the seūall occupacōns of John Chandler and Robert Kemp
or their Assignes and scituate lying or being in Parham w^{th}in
the said County of Suff And lastly Of all that messuage . . .
scituate lying or being in Nacton aforesaid and in the tenure or
occupacōn of the said Nicholas Haly or his Assignes . . . Jn
Witnesse whereof the said parties to these p^rnts Have hereunto
enterchangably sett their hands and seales the day and year first
abovewritten.

[Signed]   Chr̄ Milton   Richd̄ Milton

[77]

[Endorsed on the back:] Sealed and deliūed by the wthin-named Nicholas Haly ffrances Dixon ffrancis Haly and Eliza-beth his Wife in the p^{r}sence of us   [not signed]

                    Sealed and deliūed by the
wthinnamed Christopher Milton and Richard Milton in the p^{r}sence of us./

         [Signed] Laurence Mollyner   John Whiting
              10 May 1674

      Nich: Halie & alī ⎫
              to   ⎬   Jnd^r. to lead the vses of a ffine:
      Chris: Milton & alī ⎭

Original document in the Morgan Library, New York; described in *Notes and Queries*, xi, vi (1912), 100. I have left out many of the repetitive phrases which always pad out any such document, and a con-siderable part which states that the estates in question are for the use and benefit of the newly married couple, their heirs, and so forth. The purpose of the transaction as it concerns Christopher and Richard Mil-ton seems to be their transfer of the properties to the Halys. In the Maggs Brothers catalogue for 1919 (item 562) in which this document was advertised Christopher and Richard Milton are said to have signed as "trustees." There are clippings from this catalogue in the Milton col-lection of manuscript material in the New York Public Library. The anonymous author of the article in *Notes and Queries* already men-tioned thinks that Richard Milton wrote Anne Milton's signature on the document drawn up by her concerning the poet's will on February 22, 1675, by which she surrendered to Milton's widow her rights under his will. The two handwritings certainly do look very much alike. In-cidentally, there may well have been some relationship between the Ha-lys concerned in the present transaction and the Richard Hayley of Idlestreet, co. Hertford, who gave bond to John Milton the poet on July 24, 1674 (*q.v.*).

MAY 10. BROTHER CHRISTOPHER REAPPOINTED A LEADER OF INNER TEMPLE PARLIAMENT.

Parliamentum ibm̄ Tentum Decimo die Maij Anno Dnī 1674. Annoqz Regni Regis Dnī Caroli scdī nunc Angl' &cs vicesimo sexto Coram xp̄o Milton Ed̄ro Pecke et Thoma ffarrar Armiger' et alijs. [Marginal note:] Jnterius Templum Johēs Heath Miles (Attorn' Ducat' Lanc') et Thesaurar' ibm̄

Records of the Inner Temple, printed in F. A. Inderwick, *A Calendar of the Inner Temple Records*, III, 95.

[Parliament held in the same place May 10, 1674, and in the twenty-sixth year of the reign of our lord and king Charles II now of England etc., before Christopher Milton, Edward Pecke, and Thomas Farrar, Esquires, and others. (Note:) Inner Temple. John Heath, Knight, Attorney of the Duchy of Lancaster, and Treasurer of the same.]

MAY 13. BROTHER CHRISTOPHER AND HIS SON RICHARD WITNESS AN INDENTURE.

Sealed and deliūed in the pʳsence of us./:

Chr̄. Milton

Richard Milton

Endorsement on an indenture in the British Museum, Add. Chart. 10,260. I believe this document has not previously been mentioned in print. It is an indenture between Robert York of Kirton, co. Suffolk, tailor, and Edmond Waller of Kaesgrave, also co. Suffolk, gentleman, by which for £100 York assigns to Waller properties in Kirton. The amount of the sale plus £2-14-6 interest was paid in full, according to an endorsement, on October 25, 1675. The writing of the document seems to be in the hand of Richard Milton.

ABOUT MAY 26. FAMILIAR LETTERS AND PROLUSIONS PUBLISHED.

Joannis Miltonii Angli, Epistolarum Familiarium Liber Unus: Qvibvs Accesserunt, Ejusdem, jam olim in Collegio Adolescentis, Prolusiones Quædam Oratoriæ. Londini, Impensis Brabazoni Aylmeri sub Signo Trium Columbarum Via vulgo Cornhill dicta, An. Dom. 1674.

Title page of the first edition; Masson, VI, 722-724; CM, XII, frontispiece (facsimile of title page), 1-285 (Latin text and translation). For the date, see the next following entry. Though this book is called "Liber Unus," no additional book appeared.

[One book of the familiar letters of John Milton, Englishman, to which have been added certain oratorical exercises of the same writer, done formerly when he was still a youth in college. London, printed for Brabazon Aylmer at the sign of the Three Pigeons in the street commonly called Cornhill, in the year 1674.]

Joannis Miltoni Angli *Epistolarum Familiarum liber unus.* Quibus accesserunt *Ejusdem jam olim in Collegio Adolescentis prolusiones quædam oratoriæ.* In Octavo. Printed for **B. Aylmer** at the Three Pidgeons in *Cornhill.*

From *A Catalogue of Books,* No. 17, London, 1674, licensed May 26, 1674, and published in Easter term, 1674, as quoted in *Term Catalogues,* I, 172; Parker, *Milton's Contemporary Reputation,* p. 119. For the translation, see the preceding entry.

7 Latin Epts̄. 8°. $\begin{cases} \text{Familiar.} \\ \text{Politique.} \end{cases}$

Aubrey, f. 68v; Darbishire, p. 9.

Johannis Miltoni Angli Epistolarum Familiarium Liber unus: Quibus Accesserunt, jam olim in Collegio Adolescentis, Prolusiones Quædam Oratoriæ. *Octavo.*

Phillips, p. [liv]; not in Darbishire.

(29) *Epistolarum familiarium lib.* I. Lond. 1674. oct. (30) *Prolusiones quædam Oratoriæ in Coll. Christi habitæ.* printed with the *familiar Epistles.*

Wood, I, 883; Darbishire, p. 47. Wood adds the phrase *"in Coll. Christi habitæ"* (held in Christ's College), which occurs nowhere in the original title.

AFTER MAY 26 (?). CORRECTS MISTAKES IN *EPISTOLARUM FAMILIARIUM* (?).

[There is said to have been a copy of this book] corrected in some places with his own hand.

From a letter said to have been written by Roger Comberbatch to William Cowper, quoted in Francis Peck, *New Memoirs of . . . Milton,* 1740, p. 97; French, "The Autographs of John Milton," No. 53a; CM, XVIII, 553. If there ever was such a volume, it has long since been lost. Comberbatch is said to have received the volume from Milton's widow and to have lent it to a Dr. Lancaster. Milton could hardly have corrected it "with his own hand," of course, being blind; but it is possible, even if not convincing, that he may have authorized some corrections in a copy now lost. Roger Comberbatch, or Comberbach, could easily have had such a volume from Milton's widow if there was one, since as Masson shows (1 [1881], 9) both father and son of that name were antiquarians in Nantwich and were therefore unlikely not to have known the widow. In this connection may be mentioned one of the British Museum copies of this work (shelf mark G3546), which is neatly and briefly annotated in what looks like a seventeenth-century hand, with regular references to "Milton's Life."

AFTER MAY 26. ASSOCIATION COPIES OF *EPISTOLARUM FAMILIARIUM*.

At least two copies of this work are known to have been in the possession of interesting contemporaries of Milton. (1) One belonging to Nicholas Heinsius is entered in the catalogue of his library: *Bibliotheca Heinsiana, sive Catalogvs Librorvm Quos magno studio & sumptu, dum viveret, collegit vir illustris Nicolaus Heinsius, Dan. Fil.*, Leyden, 1682, Part II, p. 47, item 460 (misprinted 360). The title is given as "Epistolae . . . J. Miltonii & Prolusiones Oratorię. Lond. 1674." (2) Another belonging to Milton's friend and correspondent Emeric Bigot is listed in the catalogue of his library: *Bibliotheca Bigotiana . . . Joannes, Nicolaus, & Lud. Emericus Bigotii . . . Horum fiet Avctio die I. mensis Julii 1706*, Part III, p. 192, item 4799. The title here is given as "Miltoni Epistolarum liber, *in 12. Londini. 1674.*" The titles may be translated as (1) "The Heinsian library, or a catalogue of the books which that illustrious man Nicholas Heinsius, son of Daniel, collected with great zeal and expense while he lived"; (2) "The Bigot library . . . John, Nicholas, and Lewis Emeric Bigot . . . a sale of these will be held on July 1, 1706."

MAY 31. BROTHER CHRISTOPHER AND BROTHER-IN-LAW RICHARD POWELL LEADERS IN INNER TEMPLE PARLIAMENT.

Parliamentum ibm̄ Tentum Tricesimo Primo die Maij Anno Dnī 1674. Annoqz RRę Caroli &c scdī vicesimo sexto Coram xp̄o Milton Ricō Croke et Ricō Powell Arīs et Alijs. [Marginal note:] Jnterius Templum Johēs Heath Miles (Attorn̄ Ducat' Lancastr'.) et Thesaurar' ibm̄.

Records of the Inner Temple; printed in F. A. Inderwick, *A Calendar of the Inner Temple Records*, III, 96. This is the last time during the poet's lifetime that Christopher held this office, though he continued in it fairly regularly until 1685. On May 31 Christopher also participated in two room-admittances.

[Parliament held at the same place on May 31, 1674, and in the twenty-sixth year of the reign of King Charles II etc., before Christopher Milton, Richard Croke, and Richard Powell, Esquires, and others. (Note:) Inner Temple. John Heath, Knight, Attorney for the Duchy of Lancaster, and Treasurer of the same.]

JULY. PROMISES HIS WIFE HIS ESTATE AFTER HIS DEATH; SUFFERS FROM GOUT BUT REMAINS PLEASANT.

[His maid Elizabeth Fisher deposed that] on a day hapning in the moneth of July last the time more certainly shee remembreth not this Deponent being then in the decēdǫ lodging Chamber (hee the said decēd and the pty Producent in the Cause his wife being then alsoe in the said Chamber at Dinner together and the said Elizabeth Milton the pty Producent having pvided something for the decēdǫ Dinner which hee very well liked) hee the said deceased then spoke to his said wife these or the like words, as neare as this Deponent can remember vizt God have mercy Betty J see thou wilt pforme according to thy promise in providing mee such Dyshes as J think fitt whilst J live, and when J dye thou knowest that J have left thee all, there being noe body p^{r}sent in the said Chamber with the said decēd and his wife but this Deponent And the said Testator at that time was of pfect mind and memory and talked and discoursed sensibly and well but was then indisposed in his body by reason of the distemper of the Gout which hee had then vpon him ffurther this Deponent saith that shee hath seūall timeǫ heard the said decēd since the said time above deposed of declare and say that hee had made provision for his Children in his life time and had spent the greatest part of his estate in pvideing for them and that hee was resolved hee would doe noe more for them liveing or dyeing, for that little pte which hee had left hee had given it to his wife ye arlāte Elizabeth the producent or hee vsed wordǫ to that effect And likewise told this Deponent that there was a thousand poundǫ left in M^r

Powell's hands to be disposed amongst his Children hereafter
. . . hee was at that time very merry and not in any passion or
angry humor neither at that time spoke any thing ag^t. any of
his Children that this Respondent heard of.

From Elizabeth Fisher's deposition of December 15, 1674, *q.v.* The
Mr. Powell mentioned here must be the poet's brother-in-law Richard;
and the thousand pounds is presumably Mary Powell's dowry, the "lost
dowry" interestingly described by David H. Stevens in *Milton Papers*,
1927 (Modern Philology Monographs of the University of Chicago),
pp. 7-13. See also Masson, VI, 730-731; CM, XVIII, 372.

He was very healthy, & free from all diseases, seldome tooke
any Physique, only sometimes he tooke Manna. only towards
his later end he was visited wth the Gowte spring & Fall: he
would be chearfull even in his Gowte-fitts: & sing.

Aubrey, f. 68; Darbishire, p. 5. The best study of Milton's gout is an
article by Edward Block in the *Bulletin of the History of Medicine*,
XXVIII (1954), 201-211. Mr. Block thinks that Milton probably first
developed gout about 1664-1666, that during his last four years he
probably suffered from it almost constantly, that during the latter part
of this period he probably lost almost all ability to walk, and that he
probably died of heart failure resulting from hardening of the arteries
rather than from the gout itself. He emphasizes that Milton was extraordinary in being able to remain serene and cheerful despite cruel suffering.

J U L Y (?). PUBLISHES *DECLARATION* . . . *OF* . . . *PO-
LAND.*

A Declaration, or Letters Patents of the Election of this
present King of Poland John the Third, Elected on the 22^d
of May last past, Anno Dom. 1674. Containing the Reasons of
this Election, the great Vertues and Merits of the said Serene
Elect, His eminent Services in War, especially in his last great
Victory against the Turks and Tartars, whereof many Particulars are here related, not published before. Now faithfully
translated from the Latin Copy. London, Printed for Brabazon
Aylmer, at the Three Pigeons in Cornhil, 1674.

Title page of the original edition; Masson, VI, 725-727; Parker,
Milton's Contemporary Reputation, p. 50; CM, VI, 273-284. A copy

in the British Museum (shelf mark C.55.d.18) has a manuscript note on the title page in a more or less contemporary hand: "By John Milton." Bernard Halliday's Catalogue 111 (1929), item 100, advertised a copy said to be inscribed on the title page: "John Phillips, J.M., 1674." The writer of the catalogue suggested that it might have been a presentation copy and that the writing might perhaps have been in the hand of either John Phillips or Mrs. Milton. The price asked was £12-10-0. See CM, XVIII, 553. This book is Milton's translation from the Latin original. No satisfactory explanation for his having performed this unusual task at this period in his age has been offered. The date is Masson's.

A Declaration, or Letters Patents of the Election of *John* King of *Poland*. A Translation.

Phillips, p. [liii]; not in Darbishire.

. . . he translated out of *Latin* into *English* the Declaration of the *Poles* concerning the Election of their King *John* the Third, containing an Account of the Virtues and Merits of the said Prince. . . .

From Toland's edition of Milton's prose works, 1698, I, 44; Darbishire, p. 188. Toland prints the *Declaration* on pp. 839 ff.

JULY 1. *FAMILAR LETTERS* REGISTERED.

1ˢᵗ July 1674

Master	Entred . . . under the hands of Master ROGER
Brabazon	L'ESTRANG and Master Warden MEARNE
Aylmer	a book or copy intituled **Joannis Miltonii** *Angli*
	Epistolarum familiarum Liber unus quibus acces-
	serunt eiusdem jam olim in Collegio adolescentis
	prolusiones quaedam oratoriae . . . vjᵈ.

Stationers' Registers, II, 481; Masson, VI, 722. Either the registration occurred after the date of publication of the letters, or else the catalogue from which I have quoted the entry regarding publication appeared considerably later than the date of its being licensed; see above under date of May 26, 1674. The Latin is translated in that entry.

BEFORE JULY 6. MARVELL WRITES POEM IN PRAISE OF *PARADISE LOST*.

ON Paradise Lost.

WHen I beheld the Poet blind, yet bold,

In slender Book his vast Design unfold,
Messiah Crown'd, Gods Reconcil'd Decree,
Rebelling Angels, the Forbidden Tree,
Heav'n, Hell, Earth, Chaos, All; the Argument
Held me a while misdoubting his Intent,
That he would ruine (for I saw him strong)
The sacred Truths to Fable and old Song
(So *Sampson* groap'd the Temples Posts in spight)
The World o'rewhelming to revenge his sight.

   Yet as I read, soon growing less severe,
I lik'd his Project, the success did fear;
Through that wide Field how he his way should find
O're which lame Faith leads Understanding blind;
Lest he perplex'd the things he would explain,
And what was easie he should render vain.

   Or if a Work so infinite he spann'd,
Jealous I was that some less skilful hand
(Such as disquiet always what is well,
And by ill imitating would excell)
Might hence presume the whole Creations day
To change in Scenes, and show it in a Play.

   Pardon me, Mighty Poet, nor despise
My causeless, yet not impious, surmise.
But I am now convinc'd, and none will dare
Within thy Labours to pretend a share.
Thou hast not miss'd one thought that could be fit,
And all that was improper dost omit:
So that no room is here for Writers left,
But to detect their Ignorance or Theft.

   That Majesty which through thy Work doth Reign
Draws the Devout, deterring the Profane.
And things divine thou treatst of in such state
As them preserves, and thee, inviolate.
At once delight and horrour on us seise,
Thou singst with so much gravity and ease;

And above humane flight dost soar aloft
With Plume so strong, so equal, and so soft,
The Bird nam'd from that Paradise you sing
So never flaggs, but always keeps on Wing.

Where couldst thou words of such a compass find?
Whence furnish such a vast expence of mind?
Just Heav'n thee like *Tiresias* to requite
Rewards with Prophesie thy loss of sight.

Well mightst thou scorn thy Readers to allure
With tinkling Rhime, of thy own sense secure;
While the *Town-Bayes* writes all the while and spells,
And like a Pack-horse tires without his Bells:
Their Fancies like our Bushy-points appear,
The Poets tag them, we for fashion wear.
I too transported by the Mode offend,
And while I meant to Praise thee must Commend.
Thy Verse created like thy Theme sublime,
In Number, Weight, and Measure, needs not Rhime.

A. M.

Milton, *Paradise Lost*, 1674, sigs. A3-A3v; Fletcher Facsimile, III, 69-70; Marvell's *Miscellaneous Poems*, 1681, pp. 61-62; Marvell's *Poems*, ed. Margoliouth, 1927, pp. 131-132; CM, II, 3-5. Marvell is generally agreed to be the author. Margoliouth thinks that lines 25-26 suggest that Dryden had decided against publishing or performing his opera based on the poem. The date of composition is uncertain. Masson discusses this poem at VI, 710, 715-716.

BEFORE JULY 6. SAMUEL BARROW WRITES POEM IN PRAISE OF *PARADISE LOST*.

IN Paradisum Amissam Summi Poetæ JOHANNIS MILTONI.
QVi legis Amissam Paradisum, grandia magni
Carmina Miltoni, *quid nisi cuncta legis?*
Res cunctas, & cunctarum primordia rerum,
Et fata, & fines continet iste liber.
Intima panduntur magni penetralia mundi,
Scribitur & toto quicquid in Orbe latet.

Terræque, tractusque maris, cœlumque profundum
  Sulphureumque Erebi, flammivomumque specus.
Quæque colunt terras, Portumque & Tartara cæca,
  Quæque colunt summi lucida regna Poli.
Et quodcunque ullis conclusum est finibus usquam,
  Et sine fine Chaos, & sine fine Deus:
Et sine fine magis, si quid magis est sine fine,
  In Christo erga homines conciliatus amor.
Hæc qui speraret quis crederet esse futurum?
  Et tamen hæc hodie terra Britanna *legit.*
O quantos in bella Duces! quæ protulit arma!
  Quæ canit, & quanta prælia dira tuba.
Cœlestes acies! atque in certamine Cœlum!
  Et quæ Cœlestes pugna deceret agros!
Quantus in ætheriis tollit se Lucifer *armis!*
  Atque ipso graditur vix Michæle *minor!*
Quantis, & quam funestis concurritur iris
  Dum ferus hic stellas protegit, ille rapit!
Dum vulsos Montes ceu Tela reciproca torquent,
  Et non mortali desuper igne pluunt:
Stat dubius cui se parti concedat Olympus,
  Et metuit pugnæ non superesse suæ.
At simul in cœlis Messiæ insignia fulgent,
  Et currus animes, armaque digna Deo,
Horrendumque rotæ strident, & sæva rotarum
  Erumpunt torvis fulgura luminibus,
Et flammæ vibrant, & vera tonitrua rauco
  Admistis flammis insonuere Polo:
Excidit attonitis mens omnis, & impetus omnis
  Et cassis dextris irrita Tela cadunt.
Ad pœnas fugiunt, & ceu foret Orcus asylum
  Infernis certant condere se tenebris.
Cedite Romani *Scriptores, cedite* Graii
  Et quos fama recens vel celebravit anus.

[87]

Hæc quicunque leget tantum cecinesse putabit
Mæonidem *ranas*, Virgilium *culices*.

S. B. M. D.

Milton, *Paradise Lost*, 1674, sigs. A2-A2v; Fletcher Facsimile, III, 67-68; CM, II, 1-2. Masson gives a brief account of this poem (VI, 714-715). He also refers several times in Volume V (pp. 476, 499, 500, 528, 534) to Barrow as physician to General Monck's army in Scotland. The identification of "S. B." with Barrow goes back at least to Toland (Darbishire, p. 184).

[On the *Paradise Lost* of the greatest poet, John Milton.

You who read *Paradise Lost*, the grand poem of the great Milton, why do you read it except complete? This book contains complete things, and origins of complete things, and fates, and ends. The intimate secrets of the great world are thrown open, and whatever is concealed in the whole world is written: the lands and the stretches of the sea, the profound Heaven and the sulphurous Hell, and the fire-vomiting cave; whatever things inhabit the earth, the harbor, and the blind infernal regions; whatever things inhabit the bright kingdoms of the highest Heaven; and whatever is included anywhere within any bounds, and Chaos without end, and God without end; and, what is more without end, if anything is more without end, love obtained in Christ towards men. Who would believe that there would be anyone who would hope for these things? And yet the land of Britain is reading these things today. O what leaders in war he has brought forth! what arms! what songs he sings, and what dire battles on the trumpet! Celestial armies! and Heaven in conflict! And what a battle would fit the celestial fields! What a Lucifer raised himself in ethereal arms! And he walks hardly less great than Michael himself! With how great and how fatal wraths the battle is joined while the latter fiercely defends the stars and the former snatches at them! While they hurl the beardless mountains or the alternating weapons, and rains fall from above with immortal fire, Olympus stands doubtful to which side it will yield itself, and it feared it might not win its battle. But at the same time the symbols

of the Messiah gleam in the heavens; and the living chariots, the arms worthy of God, and the wheels grate terribly, and the raging lightnings of the wheels burst out in fierce flashes, and the flames quiver, and real thunders mixed with flames resounded in the hollow sky. All mind falls away from the thunderstruck ones, and all weapons of attack drop powerless from their broken hands. They flee to their punishments; and as if Hell were a refuge, they strive to hide themselves in infernal shades. Yield, you Roman writers; yield, you Greeks, and those whom recent or ancient fame has celebrated. Whoever reads these lines will think that Homer sang only of frogs, Virgil only of fleas.
     S(amuel) B(arrow), Doctor of Medicine.]

ABOUT JULY 6. *PARADISE LOST* APPEARS IN SECOND EDITION.

Paradise Lost. A Poem in Twelve Books. The Author John Milton. The Second Edition Revised and Augmented by the same Author. London, Printed by S. Simmons next door to the Golden Lion in Aldersgate-street, 1674.

Title page of original edition; CM, II, 1-401, with facsimile reproduction of title page on p. 484; Masson, VI, 712-717; Fletcher facsimile, III, the entire volume. Aside from a few lines called for by the redivision of the poem into twelve books instead of the original ten, the only substantial justifications of the "Revised and Augmented" of the title are the Dolle portrait of Milton, based on Faithorne's of 1670 for the *History of Britain*, and the commendatory verses by S[amuel] B[arrow] and A[ndrew] M[arvell]. The date comes from the entry in the *Term Catalogues* given below. The Columbia text, like that of most editions, is this of 1674, though collated in the notes with the first and others. The commendatory verses, which as Fletcher points out are among the earliest printed appreciations of the poem, are highly laudatory. Unfortunately, almost no editor translates Barrow's, which are in Latin.

Paradise Lost. A Poem, in Twelve Books; Revised and Augmented by the Author, **John Milton**. Price 3s.

A Catalogue of Books, licensed July 6 and published in Trinity term, 1674, as quoted in *Term Catalogues*, I, 181; Parker, *Milton's Contemporary Reputation*, p. 119.

the first Edition was Printed in Quarto by one *Simons* a Printer in *Aldersgate-Street*, the other in a large Octavo, by *Starky* near *Temple-Bar*, amended, enlarg'd, and differently dispos'd as to the Number of Books, by his own Hand, that is by his own appointment. . . .

Phillips, pp. xxxviii-xxxix; Darbishire, p. 75. Phillips is of course mistaken is naming Starkey as the printer; he probably confused this edition of *Paradise Lost* in his own mind with *Paradise Regained*, which Starkey published. Otherwise his description is reasonably accurate. This is the only definite mention of the 1674 edition in the early biographies. British Museum Egerton MS. 203 is a neat copy of the whole poem in twelve books and with the prefixed poems of Barrow and Marvell, with no title page but with faintly visible impressions of one still remaining on the opposite page.

JULY 14. BROTHER CHRISTOPHER'S SON RICHARD (?) MAKES WILL.

In the Prerogative Court of Canterbury the will registered as 109 Bunce is that of a Richard Milton of Colfield, Essex, dated July 14, 1674. I am not sure whether this Richard is the son of Christopher or not, though we have seen that he did have a son of that name. I am rather doubtful of their identity. This Richard makes various small bequests to two sisters whose last names are Sanders and Poulter, to his brothers William and Samuel, to William's son Richard, to William's daughter Prudence, and to one or two others. The will was witnessed by Stephen Waterworth and Robert Elkin, and proved by Prudence Milton on September 24, 1674. Though Christopher had a son Richard, Perceval Lucas's account of the rest of the family (*Notes and Queries*, XI, vii, 1913, 21-22) shows no William or Samuel.

JULY 20 (?). MAKES ORAL WILL WITH HELP OF BROTHER CHRISTOPHER; IS SERIOUSLY UNWELL.

[Christopher Milton deposed on December 5, 1674] that on or about the twentith day of July 1674 the day certaine he now remembreth not this dep^t. being a pratizer in the Law. and a bencher in the Inner Temple but living in vacations at Jpsw^{ch} did vsually at the end of the terme visite John Milton, his this dep^{te} brother the testator arlāte deceased before his goeing home, and soe at the end of Midsomer terme last past he this dep^t. went to visit his said brother and then found him in his chamber within his owne house scituate on Bunhill within the pish of St Giles Creplegate London And at that tyme he the s^d testator being not well and this dep^t being then goeing into the Country in a serious manner with an intent as he beleeveth that what he then spoke should be his will if he dyed before his this dep^{te} comeing the next Terme to London declared his will in these very wordϱ as neare as this dep^t cann now call to mynd vizt brother the por$\bar{c}$on due to me from m^r Powell, my former wives father, J leave to the vnkind children J had by her but J have receaved noe part of it and my will and meaning is they shall have noe other benefit of my estate then the said por$\bar{c}$on and what J have besidϱ don for them. they haveing ben very vndutiful to me. And all the residue of my estate J leave to the disposall of Elizabeth my loveing wife. she the sd Elizabeth his the deceasedϱ wife, and Elizabeth ffisher his the deceasedϱ then maideservant was at the same tyme goeing upp & downe the roome but whether she then heard the sd dec^d. soe declare his will as above or noe he knoweth not And the sd testator at the p^{r}misses was of pfect mind and memory and talked and discoursed sensibly and well. . . .

Ch$\bar{r}$. Milton

From Christopher Milton's deposition about Milton's will on December 5, 1674, in the Prerogative Court of Canterbury, Deposition Book, 1674, f. 238v; Warton, pp. xxvii-xxxii; Todd, i (1826), 271-274; Masson, vi, 735-739; cm, xviii, 371. For Milton's possessions at the time of his death and preceding, see the inventory of his widow's holdings in Masson, vi, 747-748. Christopher's two datings of the will do not quite agree, since Midsummer (Trinity) Term ends 25 days after Trinity Sunday; in 1674 this would be July 9. Which date is more accurate is impossible to say.

MEMORANDUM, that JOHN MILTON, late of the parish of St. Giles Cripplegate in the Countie of Middlesex Gentleman, deceased, at several times before his death, and in particular, on or about the twentieth day of July, in the year of our Lord God 1674, being of perfect mind and memorie, declared his Will and intent as to the disposall of his estate after his death, in these words following, or of like effect: *The portion due to me from Mr. Powell, my former wife's father, I leave to the unkind children I had by her, having received no parte of it: but my meaning is, they shall have no other benefit of my estate than the said portion, and what I have besides done for them; they having been very undutifull to me. All the residue of my estate I leave to disposall of Elizabeth my loving wife.* Which words, or to the same effect, were spoken in the presence of

CHRISTOPHER MILTON.

Nov. 23, 1674.   X [Mark of] ELIZABETH FISHER.

From the original record of the will in the Prerogative Court of Canterbury as published for the first time in Warton, pp. xxvii–xxviii; Masson, VI, 735; CM, XVIII, 424, 621. When I visited the Court, I was unable to find this part of the record, though it undoubtedly was (or has been) there. The original manuscript would undoubtedly have differed widely from Warton's version in details of spelling, punctuation, and the like. Most succeeding versions have been based on Warton's or on Masson's, which in turn comes from Warton. Further details about this will (which was not admitted to probate, though the poet's widow was able to obtain letters of administration) appear in the lengthy testimonies of the widow and of Elizabeth and Mary Fisher on December 5 and 15, 1674, and in the grant of letters of administration on February 25, 1675; see Warton, pp. xxviii–xlii.

JULY 27. RECEIVES BOND OF £40 FROM RICHARD HAYLEY.

Noverint universi per p'sentes me Richardū Hayley de Idlestreete alias Ilstreye in Comīt Hertfořd Yeoman teneri et firmiter obligari Iohanni Milton de London Armigeř in Quadringentis libris legalis monetæ Angliæ solveñd eidem Iohanni Milton aut suo certo Attornāt Executōr vel Administř suis Ad quamquidem Soluc̄onem bene et fideliter faciend Obligo me herēd Executoř et Administř meos firmiter per presentes Sigillo meo Sigillāt. Dāt Vicesimo Septimo die Julij Anno Domī 1674 Annoqz Regni Domī nrī Caroli secundi Dei gratia Angliæ Scotiæ ffranciæ et Hiberniæ Regis fidei Defensoř &c Vicesimo Sexto./

John Milton · JULY 1674

The Condicõn of th'above written Obligacõn is such That if th'above bounden Richard Hayley his heires Executorp Admini͏ʳˢ. and Assignes and every of them doe and shall well and truly pay observe performe fulfill and keepe all and every the payments Covenants Graunts Articles Clauses Provisoes Condicõns and Agreements which on his and their parts and behalfes are and ought to be paid observed performed fulfilled done and kept mencõned specifyed and comprized in one paire of Indenturep bearing the date above written Expressed to be made betweene the said Richard Hayley of th'one part And th'above named Iohn Milton of th'other part And that in and by all things according to the purport true intent and meaning of the same Indentures Then th'above written Obligacõn to be voyd or else it shall stand in full force and vertue./

Sealed and deliūed in yᵉ
presence of

Hen: Bosworth   Richard Haley   [two seals]

Joseph Beane ⎫
Ioceb Bosworth ⎬ Servᵗˢ. to Geo:
Daniel Alford ⎭   Peryer Scrʳ.

Original bond in the manuscript department of the New York Public Library; mentioned by J. F. M[arsh?] in *Notes and Queries*, I, i (1850), 366, and in *Chetham Miscellanies*, 1 (1851), 2; mentioned in Sotheby's *Ramblings*, p. 122; French, "Autographs of John Milton," item 129; printed in full in CM, XVIII, 623. Masson overlooked this item. The indentures themselves have disappeared. The owners of these and other Milton family papers, with the dates of sale as given by Sotheby, are as follows: James Boswell, Jr., Thorpe (1825), Evans, Pickering (1833), Mr. Anderdon, John Fitchett Marsh (1860).

[Know all men by these presents that I, Richard Hayley of Idlestreet, alias Ilstreye, in the county of Hertford, yeoman, am bound and firmly obligated to John Milton of London, gentleman, in the sum of forty pounds of legal money of England, to be paid to the said John Milton or to his certain attorney, his executors, or his administrators; for the making of which payment well and faithfully I obligate myself, my heirs, my executors, and my administrators firmly by these presents. Sealed

[93]

with my seal. Given on the twenty-seventh day of July in the year of our Lord 1674 and in the twenty-sixth year of the reign of our lord Charles the Second, by the grace of God King of England, Scotland, France, and Ireland, Defender of the Faith, etc.]

AUGUST (?). PLANS BEQUEST TO BROTHER CHRISTOPHER'S CHILDREN (?).

[Christopher Milton testified on December 5, 1674, that] since this rond^te. comeing to London this Michas Terme last paste this Rond^te sister the pty now producent in this cause told this Rep^t that the deceased his brother did after his this rond^te. goeing into the Country in Trinity vacacon last say [?] that if she should have any overplus above a 1000 ł come to her hand℘ of this the deceased℘ estate she should give the same to this rond^te children but the deceased himselfe did not declare any such thing to this Rond^t at the tyme of his declaring his will the tyme above deposed of.

From Christopher Milton's deposition on December 5, 1674, *q.v.* The "sister" mentioned is Christopher's sister-in-law, the poet's wife. The "rond^t" or "Rep^t" is the respondent in the questioning, Christopher himself. The date is somewhat vague, but it must be later than the time when the poet declared his will to Christopher, and therefore probably the latter part of July or some time in August. The conversation part of this section is quoted in CM, XVIII, 371.

SEPTEMBER 14. NEPHEW EDWARD PHILLIPS'S *THEATRUM POETARUM* LICENSED.

Licensed *September the* 14th 1674. *RO. L'ESTRANGE.*

From Edward Phillips, *Theatrum Poetarum*, 1675, sig. *v. For a discussion of Milton's possible contributions to this book see above under date of 1674.

OCTOBER 15 (?). MERRILY PROMISES HIS WIFE HIS ESTATE AFTER HIS DEATH.

[Mary Fisher deposed on December 15, 1674, that] on a day hapning about two moneths since as neare as this Deponent can remember this Deponent being then in the kitchen of the house of the foresaid John Milton scituate ag^t. the Attillery Ground neare Bunhill feild꞉ and about noone of the same day the said Decēd and the Producent Elizabeth his wife being then at Dinner in the said kitchen Hee the said decēd amongst other discourse then had betweene him and his said wife did then speake to his said wife and vtter these words vizt Make much of mee as long as J live for thou knowest J have given thee all when J dye at thy disposall there being then p^rsent in the said kitchen this Deponent꞉ sister and contest namely Elizabeth ffisher And the said decēd was at that time of pfect mind and memory and talked and discoursed sensibly and well and was very merry, and seemed to be in good health of body. . . .

[She also testified that] the decēd when hee declared the words p^rdeposed was then at Dinner with his wife the pty Producent and was then very merry and seemed to be in good health of body but vpon what occasion hee spoke the said word꞉ shee knoweth not. . . .

From the deposition on December 15, 1674, of Mary Fisher, sister of the Miltons' maid Elizabeth Fisher, *q.v.*; quoted in part in CM, XVIII, 373. The word "contest" means fellow-witness.

NOVEMBER 2. NUMEROUS OF HIS BOOKS AND A PROCLAMATION AGAINST HIM ADVERTISED.

History in Quarto. . . . Price *6s.* **Milton**'s *History of Britain,* especially that part now called *England,* from the first traditional beginning; continued to the *Norman* Conquest. Collected out of the ancientest and best Authors thereof. . . .

Miscellanies in Quarto. . . . *Price of each 3d* . . . **Milton** *of true Religion,* Heresie, Schism, Toleration, and what best means may be used against the growth and increase of Popery. Printed for *T. Sawbridge.* . . .

Proclamations since his Majesties Restauration. . . . For calling in and suppressing two Books written by *John Milton,* and a third by *John Goodwin.* . . .

Poetry in Quarto. *Price of each* 3*s.* . . . **Milton**'s *Paradise lost*; A Poem in ten Books. Printed for *S. Simmons.* . . .

Poetry in large Octavo. . . . *Price of each* 2*s.* 6*d.* **Milton**'s *Paradise regain'd*; a Poem: in four Books: to which is added, *Sampson Agonistes*; a Dramatic Poem. Printed for *J. Starkey.* . . .

Milton's *Poems*, &c. upon several occasions, both English and Latin; with a small Tract of Education to Mr. *Hartlib.* Printed for *T. Dring.* . . .

A Catalogue of School Books, with their Prices. . . .

Milton's Grammar	0	0	8
-- -- -- *Logick*	0	2	0

Libri Lat. in small Octavo. . . . *Price of each* 1*s.* . . . **Joannis Miltoni** Angli Epistolarum familiarum liber unus. Quibus accesserunt, ejusdem, jam olim in Collegio adolescentis, prolusiones quædam oratoriæ. Printed for *Brab. Aylmer.* . . .

Libri Lat. in large Twelves. . . . *Price of each* 2*s.* . . . **Joannis Miltoni** Angli, Artis Logicæ plenior institutio, ad Petri Rami Methodum concinnata. Adjecta est praxis Analytica & Petri Rami vita libris duobus. Printed for *R. Boulter.*

From *The General Catalogue Of Books Printed In England Since the Dreadful Fire of London, 1666. To the End of Trinity Term, 1674.* . . . *Collected by Robert Clavel*, London, 1675, pp. 34, 47, 76, 82, 83, 102, 104, 112, 113. The unsigned leaf (A2?) following the title page, addressed "To the Reader," is dated "Novemb. 2. 1674." Dr. Parker does not give this allusion in his *Milton's Contemporary Reputation*, probably because it was not published until 1675. Only two of the nine titles quoted here (*The History of Britain* and *Of True Religion*) are in the index to the *General Catalogue*. The figures following the titles of the *Grammar* and the *Logic* give the prices in pounds, shillings, and pence.

ABOUT NOVEMBER 9. DIES IN BUNHILL.

He died in Bunhill opposite to the Artillery-garden-wall. . . .

He died of ye gowt—struck in the 9th or 10th of Novemb 1674, as appeares by his Apothecaryes Booke.

Aubrey, f. 68; Darbishire, pp. 4-5. In the second entry, which is about half a page below the first, Aubrey first wrote "He died of a feaver: at his house in Juinn street about the 64th yeare of his age." He then crossed out all but "He died of," and finished it as above. It is difficult to set the exact date of Milton's death. Masson (VI, 731) gives it with complete assurance as "on Sunday, the 8th of November, late at night." But none of the early lives gives this date, which must have been an inference from the date of his burial on the 12th. Richard ("Secondary" or "Obituary") Smith gives the date as November 15, which must be impossible. But anywhere from the 8th to the 10th would be appropriate. Masson chooses November 8 because it was Sunday, the day of the week when Elizabeth Fisher said Milton died.

1674 . . . November.—Nov. 19, Th[ursday]., in a letter from Mr. ⟨Thomas Blount⟩, 'tis said that . . . Milton was dead neare London. See Sir Walter Raleigh ⟨in the Ath.⟩.

Anthony Wood's record in his diary as printed in *Life and Times* of Wood, II, 297. All the brackets are as in the original.

In these Works, and the instruction of some Youth or other at the intreaty of his friends, hee in great Serenity spent his time & expir'd no less calmly in the Yeare 1674. . . .

Hee dy'd in a fitt of the Gout, but with so little pain or Emotion, that the time of his expiring was not perceiv'd by those in the room. And though hee had bin long troubl'd with that disease, insomuch that his Knuckles were all callous, yet was hee not ever observ'd to be very impatient.

The "earliest" biography, ff. 143, 144; Darbishire, pp. 29, 33.

He died in the year 1673. towards the latter end of the Summer. . . .

Phillips, p. xl; Darbishire, p. 76. As often elsewhere, Phillips is mistaken about the date.

At length this great Scholar and frequent Writer dying in his house at *Bunhill* near *London* in a fit of the Gout, but with so little pain, that the time of his expiring was not perceived by those in the room, on the ninth or tenth day of *Novemb.* 1674. . . .

Wood, I, 883; Darbishire, p. 47.

1674 . . . Novem 15 Iohn Milton. Died at Bunhill near morefields in Criplegate Parish. blind some time before he Died.

British Museum Sloane MS. 886, f. 73v ("A Catalogue of all such Persons deceased whome I knew in their Life time . . . from the year of our Lord M.DC.XXVIII"); *The Obituary of Richard Smyth*, 1849 (Publications of the Camden Society, No. 44), p. 104. As mentioned above, this date is obviously wrong. It is, however, interesting to note that both Elizabeth and Mary Fisher testified that Milton died on Sunday, November 15. There may be some connection between their mistake and Smith's.

NOVEMBER 12. BURIED IN ST. GILES CRIPPLEGATE.

L John: Milton Gentleman Buried. Nov. 12. 1674. Consumpcōn Chancell 12 Milton.

From the original entry in the parish register of St. Giles Cripplegate, London, procured on microfilm through the good services of University Microfilms. The underlining is as in the original. The initial L probably refers to "liberty" (of the parish); it occurs before the majority of the names on this page. "Chancell" indicates the part of the church used for burial; Milton is the only one on this page (containing about 40 names) so labeled. The "12" is the day of the month; Milton is one of seven entered for this day. The "Buried. Nov. 12. 1674" in the middle and the "Milton" at the end are unique, at least on this page. They may also be in a different hand, though the rest of the entry seems to be in the same hand as all the others on the page. Evidently Milton stood out as a person of unusual importance, whose burial deserved special attention. Some years ago the Rev. Everett G. Turner, then Vicar of the parish, kindly sent me a reproduction of this and several other burial entries made up for book publication, but I am glad to have been able to verify the details by a new photographic reproduction. Todd (1, 1826, 217) remarks that the name "Milton" (in its first occurrence in the entry) was originally written "Melton" and then altered "in fresher ink, to Milton." The photograph supports his reading, though it is difficult to be sure. The cause of death given, consumption, occurs several other times on the same page (November 2-16), along with such other causes as flux, teeth, griping, aged, fever, chrisom, convulsion, and others. Through the entry for Milton there seems to be a somewhat lighter band as if it had at some time been cleaned, whereas the entry following it is so darkened as to be almost unreadable. See also *Gentleman's Magazine*, LVII (1787), 779; J. P. Malcolm, *Londinium Redivivum*, III (1803), 300; W. Denton, *Records of St. Giles' Cripplegate*, 1883, p. 27; Masson, VI, 731-732. Masson, in *Good Words*, XXXIV (1893), 238, 240, 241, describes the church and and gives some pictures of it.

M^r J: Milton is buryed at St Giles Criplegate, wch J will also see.

From a letter of January 12, 1674/5, from Aubrey to Wood, Bodleian MS. Wood F. 39, f. 288; Darbishire, p. 334.

Hee had this Elogy in common with the Patriarchs and Kings of Israel that he was gather'd to his people; for hee happen'd to bee bury'd in Cripplegate where about thirty yeer before hee had by chance also interrd his Father.

The "earliest" biography, f. 144; Darbishire, p. 34. The author originally wrote instead of "was gather'd to his people": "slept with his Fathers." For the poet's father's burial in the same church see above, II, 182. Both were buried in the chancel of the church. A small stone now marks the site of the poet's grave. Before the last war busts or statues of him stood both outside and inside the church, but both were broken during the war by bombings.

He lies buried in St Giles Cripplegate upper end of chancell at the right hand mdm̄ his stone is now removed; about 2 yeares since [now 1681] the steppes to the com̄union table were raysed. J ghesse Jo: Speed & He lie together.

Aubrey, f. 68; Darbishire, p. 5; CM, XVIII, 539. The words "upper end of" were added over a caret. After "the right hand" are "v. his stone" and above that "gravestone" canceled. Before "about" is the word "for" canceled. The bracketed "now 1681" is in the original.

He . . . had a very decent interment according to his Quality, in the Church of St. *Giles Cripplegate*, being attended from his House to the Church by several Gentlemen then in Town, his principal wellwi-shers and admirers.

Phillips, p. xl; Darbishire, p. 76. The peculiar spelling of "wellwi-shers" stands thus in the original.

[He] was buried in the grave of his Father (who died very aged about 1647) in the Chancel of the Church of S. *Giles* near *Cripplegate, London.*

Wood, I, 883; Darbishire, p. 47.

All his learned and great Friends in *London*, not without a friendly concourse of the Vulgar, accompany'd his Body to the Church of S. *Giles* near *Cripplegate*, where he lies buried in the Chancel, and where the Piety of his Admirers will shortly erect a Monument becoming his worth, and the incouragement of Letters in King *William*'s Reign.

Milton's prose works, ed. Toland, 1698, 1, 46; Darbishire, p. 193.

An antient bookseller afterwards a pension[er] in y[e] Charterhouse brought M[rs]. Clarke a printed life of M[r] Milton, which she thought better than what had been drawn up by others. He held up y[e] paul at M[r] Miltons funeral, and as he said wrote y[e] life himself.

From John Ward's notes in British Museum Add. MS. 4,320, f. 232v. I owe this note to the courtesy of my colleague Mr. Edward L. Ruhe, who believes that the bookseller in question who was one of Milton's pallbearers was Brabazon Aylmer, who published several of Milton's later books. What "printed life" of Milton Aylmer could have written is not clear. Ward's notes are so full of errors of various kinds that this whole business may be wrong.

ITEMS WITHOUT DATE

Though many of the items given in Volumes I-IV have been hard to date, and though a considerable number have been placed hesitantly, there remain a number for which it seems impossible to assign even an approximate date. These are therefore gathered together here at the end. For the sake of a certain attempt at logic I have arranged them in categories as follows:

Appearance
Disposition and behavior
Intellectual powers
Temperance
Sense of dedication
Amanuenses and servants
Relations with daughters
Schedule of work and other activities
Writings, genuine or attributed
Friends and visitors
Alleged unorthodox religious ideas, especially Catholicism
Allusions
Reading and library
Relics
Portraits
Autobiography

APPEARANCE.

He was scarce so tall as J am. [added above after a pointing hand:] q quot feet J am high? Resp. of middle stature he had light browne [added above:] abroun hayre, his complex very [added above:] exceeding faire#. ovall face. [added above:] his eie a darke gray His widowe has his picture drawne very well & like when a Cambridge schollar [#he was so faire, y^t they called him the lady of X^ts coll:] She has his picture when a cambridge schollar, wch ought to be engraven: for the Picturs before his bookes are not *at all* like him. . . .

he was a Spare man. . . .

His harmonicall, and ingeniose soule dwelt [added above:] did lodge in a beautifull & well proportioned body—In toto nusquā corpore menda fuit. Ovid.

Aubrey, ff. 63, 68; Darbishire, pp. 3, 4. Aubrey rewrote his notes so much that it is impossible to be sure just how much of his jottings above he wished to delete and how much to keep, or in what order exactly he intended the words to come. But we can get the general drift without much trouble. The Latin may be translated: "There was no blemish anywhere in his whole body." The symbol resembling our # is evidently intended to bring together two statements about Milton's fair complexion.

Hee was of a moderate Stature, and well proportion'd, of a ruddy Complexion, light brown Hair, & handsom Features; save that his Eyes were none of the quickest. But his blindness, which proceeded from a Gutta serena, added no further blemish to them. His deportment was sweet and affable; and his Gate erect & Manly, bespeaking Courage and undauntedness (or a Nil conscire) On which account hee wore a Sword while hee had his Sight, and was skill'd in using it.

The "earliest" biography, f. 143v; Darbishire, p. 32. The Latin phrase means "to be conscious of nothing."

He was of a moderate Stature, and well proportion'd, of a ruddy Complexion, light brown hair, and had handsome features, yet his eyes were none of the quickest. When he was a Student in *Cambridge* he was so fair and clear, that many called him the *Lady of Christs Coll.* His deportment was affable, and his gate erect and manly, bespeaking courage and undauntedness. On which account he wore a sword while he had his sight, and was skill'd in using it.

Wood, I, 883-884; Darbishire, pp. 47-48.

I have heard many Years Since that he Us'd to Sit in a Grey Coarse Cloath Coat at the Door of his House, near *Bun-hill* Fields Without *Moor-gate*, in Warm Sunny Weather to Enjoy the Fresh Air, and So, as well as in his Room, receiv'd the Visits of People of Distinguish'd Parts, as well as Quality. and very Lately I had the Good Fortune to have Another Picture of him from an Ancient Clergy-man in *Dorsetshire*, Dr.

Wright; He found him in a Small House, he thinks but One Room on a Floor; in That, up One pair of Stairs, which was hung with a Rusty Green, he found *John Milton*, Sitting in an Elbow Chair, Black Cloaths, and Neat enough, Pale, but not Cadaverous, his Hands and Fingers Gouty, and with Chalk Stones. among Other Discourse He exprest Himself to This Purpose; that was he Free from the Pain This gave him, his Blindness would be Tolerable.

Richardson, pp. iv-v; Darbishire, pp. 203-204; Masson, VI, 679; CM, XVIII, 386.

DISPOSITION AND BEHAVIOR.

Extreme pleasant in his conversation, & at dinner supp &c: but *Satyricall*. He pronounced yᵉ letter R very hard# [added in margin: "Litera Canina"] [added on f. 68: "a certaine signe of a Satyricall Witt. frᵒ Jo: Dreyden".] . . .

As he was severe on one hand, so he was most familiar and free in his conversation to those to whome most severe in his way of education. . . .

Of a very cheerfull humour. . . . he would be chearfull even in his Gowte-fitts: & sing.

Aubrey, ff. 63v, 64v, 68; Darbishire, pp. 6, 12, 5; CM, XVIII, 373 (the first section only).

He was affable in Conversation, of an equal and chearful Temper, and highly delighted with all sorts of Music, in which he was himself not meanly skil'd. He was extraordinary temperat in his Diet, which was any thing most in season or the easiest procur'd, and was no Friend to sharp or strong Liquors.

Toland, p. 46; Darbishire, p. 194.

He was a Chearfull Companion; but no Joker: his Conversation was Lively, but with Dignity. and as he was whilst Young, he Continu'd to be in his more Advanc'd Age. . . .

He had a Gravity in his Temper, Not Melancholly, or not 'till the Latter Part of his Life, not Sour, Morose, or Ill-Natur'd; but a Certain Severity of Mind, a Mind not Condescending to Little things.

Richardson, pp. vii, xv; Darbishire, pp. 206, 212; CM, XVIII, 387 (the first section only).

That Daughter [Deborah] . . . when she gave Accounts of *Milton's* Affairs to the Many Enquirers Lately . . . spoke of him with Great Tenderness; particularly I have been told She said He was Delightful Company, the Life of the Conversation, and That on Account of a Flow of Subject, and an Unaffected Chearfulness and Civility.

Richardson, p. xxxvi; Darbishire, p. 229; CM, XVIII, 387.

INTELLECTUAL POWERS.

Hee had naturally a Sharp Witt, and steddy Iudgment; which helps toward attaining Learning hee improv'd by an indefatigable attention to his Study. . . .

The "earliest" biography, f. 143; Darbishire, p. 29.

To conclude, he was a person of wonderful parts, of a very sharp, biting and satyrical wit. He was a good Philosopher and Historian, an excellent Poet, Latinist, Grecian and Hebritian, a good Mathematician and Musitian, and so rarely endowed by nature, that had he been but honestly principled, he might have been highly useful to that party, against which he all along appeared with much malice and bitterness.

Wood, I, 881; Darbishire, p. 39.

JOH. MILTONI *Epistolæ Familiares* extant libello exiguo. (*hhh*) Non ignobilis fuit Autor Miltonus, qvod è scripto Anti-Salmasiano constat, qvem ille exagitarat, argutiis & salibus causam commendans, à Salmasio non iis, qvibus poterat, argumentis defensam. *Id singulare in illo notari potest, freqventum illum esse in Solœcismis & Barbarismis Salmasio objiciendis, cum tamen & ipse sit σόλοικος sæpe & barbarus, ut qvadret hîc illud Juvenalis, Sat. II.

Loripidem rectus derident, Æthiopem albus.
Ejus commatis sunt illa in præfatione: *Tuis Grammatistis te vapulandum propino,* & pag. II. *populus assentitus est,* & pag. 142. *res nostras hallucinante.* Sed talia Viris doctis interdum

præter intentionem excidunt, qvalia in Scaligero & Casaubono
non pauca notavit Scioppius, delicatus illarum sordium collector,
qvi ingens domi sterqvilinium talium Observationvm habuit,
quod publicari voluit cum titulo Herculis κοπροφόρου. *QVicqvid tamen ejus sit, ostendunt Miltoni scripta Virum vel in ipsâ
juventute: qvæ enim ille adolescens scripsit carmina Latina,
unà cum Anglicis edita, ætatem illam longè superant, quâ ille
Vir scripsit poëmata Anglica sed sine rhythmis, qvos ut pestes
carminum vernaculorum abesse volebat, qvale illud 13. libris
constans, *the paradise lost*. Plena ingenii & acuminis sunt, sed
insuavia tamen videntur ob rhythmi defectum, qvem ego abesse
à tali carminum genere non posse existimo, qvicqvid etiam illi,
& Italis nonnullis, & nuper Isaaco Vossio in libro *de poëmatum
cantu*, videatur. Epistolæ ejus paucæ sunt, in qvibus tamen non
pauca de Autoribus veteribus, recentioribus, domesticis, exteris
judicia, qvæ legere & nosse operæ pretium est. Editæ sunt Londini an. 1647. in 8. . . .

. . . in Epico Carminum genere, *Joh. Miltoni* insigne poëma
The Paradise Lost Gallos omnes in epicis infeliciores longo post
se intervallo reliquit. . . .

Ab Anglis commendari *Joh. Miltonus*, ut in Anglicis, ita in
Latinis poematibus, solet.

Daniel George Morhof, *Polyhistor Literarius*, 1714, Tome I, Book
I, chapter 24, paragraphs 80-82; *ibid.*, I, iv, iv, 19; *ibid.*, I, i, vii, 17.
This reference comes from Toland, who says: ". . . the judicious *Morhof*, in his *Polyhistor Literarius*, says, that *Milton's* Writings shew him
to have bin a Man in his very Childhood; and that these Poems are exceedingly above the ordinary Capacity of that Age"; from Toland, pp.
6-7; Darbishire, p. 87. The text of the quotation given here is from
the edition of 1714, but it checks with that of 1695 except that the
latter does not contain the two small passages at the end. I have not
been able to check the first edition of 1688-1692. The date 1647 for
Milton's letters is obviously a misprint for 1674. Isaac Vossius's book,
De Poematum Cantu, was published in London in 1673. The "(*hhh*)"
near the beginning of the first selection refers to a footnote stating that
Milton's letters of state have been published by Pritius in 1690: "qvæ
lectionem, ob stylum pariter atqve Argumenta, merentur" (which deserve reading on account equally of their style and the subject matter).
Vossius's book seems to have no reference to Milton by name.

[John Milton's *Familiar Letters* are published in a small book. The author Milton was not undistinguished, as appears from his writing against Salmasius, whom he harassed, commending the cause with shrewdness and wit, a cause not defended by Salmasius with those arguments that he could have used. *This fact can be especially noticed in the former, that he abounds in the solecisms and barbarisms to be exposed in Salmasius, though nevertheless he is often ungrammatical and barbarous, so that that line of Juvenal's second satire is appropriate here: "the perfect man scorns the crooked-footed, the white man the Ethiopian." Samples of that imperfection are those in the preface: "I deliver you to your grammarians to be flogged"; and on page 2: "The people have consented"; and on page 142: "talking our affairs wildly." But such things happen occasionally to learned men contrary to their intention, not a few of which Scioppius noticed in Scaliger and Casaubon—a voluptuous collector of that filth, who had at home a huge dunghill of such observations, which he wanted to publish with the title of "The dung-basket of Hercules." *But whatever may be said of *him*, Milton's writings show him as a man even in his very youth; for the Latin songs which he wrote as a youth, together with the English poems which he published, rise far above that age in which that man wrote the English poems, but without the rhythms which he wanted absent as the plague of vernacular poetry, like that harmonious work in thirteen books, *the Paradise Lost*. They are full of genius and wit, but nevertheless they seem unrefined because of the lack of rhythm, which I think cannot be missing from such a kind of songs, however it may seem to him and to some Italians, and recently to Isaac Vossius in his book, *Of the Singing of Poems*. His letters are few, but in them are not a few judgments about authors old, recent, domestic, and foreign: works which it is worth while to read and know. They were published in London in the year '47 in octavo. . . .

. . . in the epic form of poetry John Milton's famous poem,

The Paradise Lost, has left all French writers, more unskillful in epics, at a long distance behind him. . . .

By the English, John Milton is accustomed to be praised, as in English poems, so also in Latin.]

He had a very good memory: but J beleeve yᵗ his excellent method of thinking, & disposing did much to helpe his memorie.

Aubrey, f. 68; Darbishire, p. 4. Aubrey first wrote "extraodinary" before "memory" but then crossed it out and substituted "very good."

TEMPERANCE.

[He was witty] and was supported in that by a Temperance, allways observ'd by him, but in his Youth even with great Nicety. . . .

This his Sincerity, and disentanglement of any private ends with his Sentiments relating to the Public, proceeded no doubt from a higher Principle, but was in great part supported, and temptations to the contrary avoided by his constant Frugality; which enabl'd him at first to live within compass of the moderate patrimony his Father left him, and afterwards to bear with patience, and no discomposure of his way of living, the great losses which befell him in his Fortunes. . . .

His moderate Estate left him by his Father was through his good Oeconomy sufficient to maintain him.

The "earliest" biography, ff. 143, 143v; Darbishire, pp. 29, 31, 32.

[Elizabeth Foster told Thomas Newton that Milton] was very temperate in his eating and drinking, but what he had he always loved to have of the best. . . .

Milton, *Paradise Lost,* ed. Newton, 1749, I, lviii.

SENSE OF DEDICATION.

Yet did hee not reckon of this Talent but as intrusted with him; and therefore dedicated all his labours to the glory of God, & some public Good; Neither binding himselfe to any of the gainfull Professions, nor having any worldly Interest for aim in what hee taught.

The "earliest" biography, f. 143; Darbishire, p. 29.

AMANUENSES AND SERVANTS.

The Youths that hee instructed from time to time servd him often as Amanuenses, & some elderly persons were glad for the benefit of his learned Conversation, to perform that Office.

The "earliest" biography, f. 144; Darbishire, p. 33.

Milton had a Servant, who was a very Honest, Silly Fellow, and a Zealous and Constant Follower of these [fanatic] Teachers; when he came from the Meeting, his Master would frequently Ask him What he had heard, and Divert Himself with Ridiculing Their Fooleries, or (it may be) the Poor Fellow's Understanding; both One and t'other Probably; However This was so Grievous to the Good Creature, that he left his Service upon it.

Richardson, p. xlvii; Darbishire, p. 238; CM, XVIII, 387. Though one may be tempted to wonder whether the silly fanatic was Thomas Ellwood the Quaker, Richardson admired Ellwood as an honest, sincere man.

RELATIONS WITH DAUGHTERS.

He had three Daughters who surviv'd him many years (and a Son) all by his first Wife (of whom sufficient mention hath been made.) *Anne* his Eldest as abovesaid, and *Mary* his Second, who were both born at his House in *Barbican*; and *Debora* the youngest, who is yet living, born at his House in *Petty-France*; between whom and his Second Daughter, the Son, named *John*, was born as above-mention'd, at his Apartment in *Scotland Yard.* . . . those he had by the First he made serviceable to him in that very particular in which he most wanted their Service, and supplied his want of Eye-sight by their Eyes and Tongue; for though he had daily about him one or other to Read to him, some persons of Man's Estate, who of their own accord greedily catch'd at the opportunity of being his Readers, that they might as well reap the benefit of what they Read to him, as oblige him by the benefit of their reading; others of younger years sent by their Parents to the same end, yet excusing only the Eldest Daughter by reason of her bodily Infirmity, and difficult utterance of Speech, (which to say truth I doubt was the Principal cause of excusing her) the other two were Condemn'd to the performance of Reading, and exactly pronouncing of all the Languages of what ever Book he should at one time or other think fit to peruse. *Viz.* The *Hebrew* (and I think the *Syriac*) the *Greek*, the *Latin*, the *Italian, Spanish* and *French*. All which sorts of Books to be confined to Read, without understanding one word, must needs be a Tryal of Patience, almost beyond endurance; yet it was endured by both for a long time, yet the irksomeness of this imployment could not always be concealed, but broke out more and more into expressions of uneasiness; so that at length they were all (even the Eldest also) sent out to learn some Curious and Ingenious sorts of Manufacture, that are proper for Women to learn, particularly Imbroideries in Gold or Silver. It had been happy indeed if the Daughters of such a Person had been made in some measure Inheritrixes of their Father's Learning; but since Fate otherwise decreed, the greatest Honour that can be ascribed to this now living (and so would have been to the others had they lived) is to be Daughter to a man of his extraordinary Character.

Phillips, pp. xl-xlii; Darbishire, pp. 76-78.

M^rs. Clarke read to h^r husband in 8 languages, but w^thout understanding any but English. Hebrew. Greek, Latin. Italian. Spanish. French. Dutch. English. which she could read with equal facility. The daughters were never sent to school, but taught by a governess at home.

From John Ward's notes in British Museum Add. MS. 4,320, f. 232. I wish to thank Edward L. Ruhe for his kindness in letting me use his transcript of this passage. The word "husband" in the first line must undoubtedly be a slip for "father," since it was Deborah's reading to her father which was being discussed here.

[John Ward writes to Thomas Birch about Deborah:] She informed me, that she and her sisters used to read to their father in eight languages; which by practice they were capable of doing with great readiness and accuracy, though they understood what they read in no other language but English; and their father used often to say in their hearing, "one tongue was enough for a woman." None of them were ever sent to school, but all taught at home by a mistress kept for that purpose. Isaiah, Homer, and Ovid's metamorphoses were books, which they were often called to read to their father; and at my desire she repeated a considerable number of verses from the beginning of both these poets with great readiness. I knew who she was, upon the first sight of her, by the similitude of her countenance with her father's picture. And upon my telling her so, she informed me, that Mr. Addison told her the same thing, upon her going to wait on him. For he, upon hearing she was living, sent for her, and desired, if she had any papers of her father's she would bring them with her, as an evidence of her being Mr. Milton's daughter. But immediately upon her being introduced to him, he said, "Madam, you need no other voucher; your face is a sufficient testimonial whose daughter you are."

From John Ward's letter of February 10, 1738, to Thomas Birch, printed in Birch's Life of Milton prefixed to his edition of Milton's prose, 1753, I, lxxvi; Masson, VI, 753-754. The interview described here took place "not long before her death," which occurred on August 24, 1727. A part of this passage is quoted in CM, XVIII, 392. Other interviews with Elizabeth Foster brought out similar details; they are reported in Birch and in Newton's edition of *Paradise Lost*. I give one below.

[Milton] would not allow them to learn to write, which he thought unnecessary for a woman: that her mother [Deborah] was his greatest favorite, and could read in seven or eight languages, tho' she understood none but English.

From Birch's interview with Elizabeth Foster, daughter of Deborah Milton Clarke, on February 11, 1738, recorded in Birch, I (1753), lxxvii, and in Newton's edition of *Paradise Lost*, I (1749), lviii-lix. In spite of the supposed prohibition on writing, it is worth noting that by 1675 two of the daughters, Mary and Deborah, were at least able to sign their names to their releases to the poet's widow; see Masson, VI, 740-741.

Deborah Milton. Her I knew and often releivd. She is very like her Fathers picture; from her I had many particulars of her father's life. Though she could read Greek and Latin she understood not one word.

From what is said to be a pencil note by Robert Harley, Earl of Oxford, in his copy of Wood, which belonged in 1915 to Douglas Macleane, as reprinted in the *Saturday Review*, cxix (1915), 114-115.

Anne Milton is Lame but hath a trade and can live by the same, which is the making of gold and silver lace and wch the deced bred her vp to.

From Elizabeth Fisher's deposition about Milton's will on December 15, 1674; Todd, 1 (1826), 286; Masson, vi, 738.

[Christopher Milton testified on December 5, 1674, that at the time of making his will the poet had] complained, but without passion, that his children had been unkind to him, but that his wife had been very kind and careful of him; and he . . . only heard him say at the tyme of declareing of his Will, that they were undutifull and unkind to him, not expressing any particulars; but in former tymes he hath herd him complaine, that they were careless of him being blind, and made nothing of deserteing him. . . .

[Elizabeth Fisher testified on December 15, 1674, that Milton had told her] that, a little before hee was marryed to Elizabeth Milton his now relict, a former maid servant of his told Mary one of the deceased's daughters . . . that shee heard the deceased was to be marryed, to which the said Mary replyed to the said maid servant, that that was noe news to heare of his wedding, but if shee could heare of his death that was something: and further told this respondent, that all his said children did combine together and counsel his maid servant to cheat him the deceased in her markettings, and that his said children had made away some of his bookes and would have sold the rest of his bookes to the dunghill women. . . .

From the original documents as reprinted by John F. Marsh in "Papers Connected with the Affairs of Milton and his Family," in *Remains Historical & Literary Connected with the Palatine Counties of Lancaster and Chester Published by the Chetham Society*, xxiv (1851), 39, 43. See also above under date of 1670.

[Deborah Milton] could repeat the first lines of Homer, the "Metamorphoses," and some of Euripides, by having often read them. Yet here incredulity is ready to make a stand. Many repetitions are necessary to fix in the memory lines not understood; and why should Milton wish or want to hear them so often? These lines were at the beginning of the poems.

Samuel Johnson, life of Milton in *Lives of the Poets*, "World's Classics" edition, I, 113.

SCHEDULE OF WORK AND OTHER ACTIVITIES.

He was an early riser, sc: at 4 a clock manè. yea, after he lost his sight: He had a man read to him: the first thing he read was the Hebrew bible, & yt was at 4ʰ. mane ½ʰ†. then he contemplated. At 7 his man came to him again & then read to him and wrote till dinner: the writing was as much as the reading. His da: Deborah, (2) maried in Dublin to one Mʳ Clarke [a Mercer sells silke &c] very like her father could read to him Latin: Jtal. & French, & Greeke. The other sister is Mary (1), more like her mother. After dinner he usd to walke 3 or 4 houres at a time; he alwayes had a Garden where he lived: went to bed about 9. *Temperate*, rarely dranke between meales. . . . He had a *delicate tuneable* Voice & had good skills his Father instructed him: he had an Organ in his house: he played on it most. His exercise was chiefly *walking*.

Aubrey, f. 63v; Darbishire, p. 6. I have arranged in readable order a text which in the manuscript is full of backing and filling, writing above the line, etc. The brackets are in Aubrey's original manuscript.

Hee rendred his Studies and various Works more easy & pleasant, by allotting them thir several portions of the day. Of these the time friendly to the Muses fell to his Poetry; And hee waking early (as is the use of temperate men) had commonly a good Stock of Verses ready against his Amanuensis came; which if it happend to bee later then ordinary, hee would complain, Saying *hee wanted to bee milkd*. The Evenings hee likewise spent in reading some choice Poets, by way of refreshment after the days toyl, and to store his Fancy against Morn-

ing. Beside his ordinary lectures out of the Bible and the best
Commentators on the week day, That was his sole subject on
Sundays. And Davids Psalms were in esteem with him above
all poetry.

The "earliest" biography, f. 144; Darbishire, p. 33.

His Recreations, before his Sight was gon, consisted much in
feats of Activity, particularly in the exercise of his Arms, which
he could handle with dexterity.

Toland, p. 46; Darbishire, p. 194.

Hee had an excellent Ear, and could bear a part both in Vocal
& Instrumental Music.

The "earliest" biography, f. 143v; Darbishire, p. 32.

He had a delicate tuneable voice, an excellent ear, could
play on the Organ, and bear a part in vocal and instrumental
Musick.

Wood, I, 884; Darbishire, p. 48.

[Milton] after dinner played on the organ, and either sung
himself or made his wife sing, who (he said) had a good voice
but no ear; and then he went up to study again till six, when
his friends came to visit him and sat with him perhaps till eight;
then he went down to supper, which was usually olives or some
light thing; and after supper he smoked his pipe, and drank
a glass of water, and went to bed. . . . After his severer studies,
and after dinner as we observed before, he used to divert and
unbend his mind with playing upon the organ or bass-viol,
which was a great relief to him after he had lost his sight; for he
was a master of music as was his father, and he could perform
both vocally and instrumentally, and it is said that he composed
very well, tho' nothing of this kind is handed down to us. It is
also said that he had some skill in painting as well as in music,
and that somewhere or other there is a head of Milton drawn
by himself. . . .

Milton, *Paradise Lost*, ed. Newton, 1749, I, xlviii, li; CM, XVIII,
389, 390 (with some omissions). On the possibility of Milton's having
done a portrait of himself, see above, II, 134-135.

I remember a Story I had from a Friend I was Happy in for many Years, and who lov'd to talk of *Milton*, as he Often Did. *Milton* hearing a Lady Sing Finely, *now will I Swear* (says he) *This Lady is Handsom*. his Ears Now were Eyes to Him.

Richardson, p. vi; Darbishire, p. 204; CM, XVIII, 386.

Whatever he Undertook was Dispatch'd as soon as possible. He was Always in Hast. *Cosa Fatta Capo hà* is an old *Florentine* Proverb. a thing Done has a Head; the Finishing Stroke is the principal One, the Work is Nothing without it.

Richardson, p. viii; Darbishire, pp. 206-207. Richardson supports his statement by a reference to Milton's letter of September 2, 1637, to Diodati; see above, I, 343.

WRITINGS, GENUINE AND ATTRIBUTED.

APOLOGUS DE RUSTICO ET HERO

Rusticus ex malo sapidissima poma quotannis. . . .

Poems, 1673, part 2, p. 44; CM, I, 230-231. There seems to be no means of dating this poem aside from the facts that it appears in the 1673 edition and is not in that of 1645. But since Milton gives no further clue himself than simply the title and the poem, and since it has little perceptible connection with any events of his life or with his other writing, it seems to fit best here as an undated work. It is a brief twelve-line poem on a theme similar to the familiar story of the man who killed the goose that laid the golden eggs. Professor MacKellar (*The Latin Poems of John Milton*, p. 39) finds the same story in both verse and prose renderings in William Bullokar's *Aesop's Fables in True Orthography*, London, 1585, and says that they are "both so close to Milton's Latin version that this last might well be a translation." There is no question that it is a genuine poem by Milton. Harris Fletcher (*The Intellectual Development of John Milton*, I [Urbana, 1956], 237, 240, 263) is convinced that Milton wrote it in grammar school, and finds a more likely source in Mantuan's *Sylvarum*, Book 4.

ON DAY BREAK

Welcome, bright chorister, to our hemisphere. . . .

This poem was published as perhaps Milton's in the *Gentleman's Magazine*, LVI (1786), 698-699, with a further note on p. 755. It is a poem of 42 lines in rhyming couplets, describing the dawning of the day and assuring God that though the writer is "dark," he sees with "intellectual eyes"; and that night is "a noon-tide blaze, illumin'd by/

The glorious splendour of thy Majesty." It is reprinted in CM, XVIII, 594, with the opinion that it is probably not by Milton. It was ascribed to Milton by a self-styled "Oxonian," who sent the verses to the magazine with the note that he found them in his copy of *Paradise Lost* (in *ten* books), written as he thought "by a female," and followed by the note: "*Dictated* by J. M." Inasmuch as the original has never appeared and Milton never to our knowledge spoke of them as his own, these lines are probably a hoax, or at least written by one of the many other people of that time or later with the initials J. M.

An EXTEMPORE upon a Faggot, by MILTON.
Have you not in a Chimney seen. . . .

A poem of eight lines of octosyllabic couplets with this title and first line was published in *Oxford and Cambridge Miscellany Poems*, undated but assigned by the Bodleian catalogue (for its copy bearing the shelf-mark 2805. e. 110) to about the year 1710. The volume was edited by, or at least contained a dedicatory epistle by, Elijah Fenton. It appears on pp. 286-287. See *Notes and Queries*, IV, iv (1869), 195, 370, 421; CM, XVIII, 603. The poem is coarse and erotic, far more likely to have been the composition of a man like the Earl of Rochester than of Milton. Todd (I, 1801, cxxxi) has ascribed it to Rochester; and it appears in *The Works of the Right Honourable the Earls of Rochester, and Roscommon*, London, 1709 (third edition), p. 76, under the title "A Description of a Maidenhead." It also appears in later collections of Rochester's writings. It is highly unlikely that Milton wrote it.

UPON A FLY THAT FLEW INTO A LADY'S EYE, AND THERE LAY BURIED IN A TEAR.

Poor envious soul! what couldst thou see. . . .

A poem of 44 lines in octosyllabic couplets first attributed to Milton in *Notes and Queries*, v, iii (1875), 368; CM, XVIII, 602. On p. 398 of the same volume of *Notes and Queries* a contributor states (correctly) that it appeared in *The Works of Mr. John Cleveland*, 1687, pp. 231-232. The note in CM points out that though it does not occur in Berdan's edition of Cleveland and may therefore not certainly be Cleveland's composition, there is no reason to think it the work of Milton.

De Tribus Impostoribus.

Henry Charles Lea says that a work by this title has been attributed to many writers, including Milton. But since it is highly doubtful that any such book was ever written, except after the tradition had existed long enough to prompt willing hands to manufacture it, we need think no further about Milton's authorship. It was rumored to be a book about Moses, Christ, and Mahomet as three impostors. See Lea's *History of the Inquisition of the Middle Ages*, III (1888), 560. I thank Professor Francis L. Utley for this note. (P)

FRIENDS AND VISITORS.

His *familiar learned Acquaintance* were

Mr Andrew Marvell. Mr Skinner, Dr Pagett M. D.

Mr. . . . Skinner, who was his disciple.

Jo: Dreyden Esq Poet Laureate, who very much admires him: & went to him to have leave to putt his Paradise-lost into a Drama in Rhyme: Mr Milton recieved him civilly, & told him he would give him leave to tagge his Verses.

His widowe assures me that Mr Hobbs was not one of his acquaintance: y^t her husband did not like him at all: but he would acknowledge (grant) him to be a man of great parts, & a learned man. Their Jnterests & tenets were diametrically / . did run Counter to each other v. Mr Hobbes Behemoth.

Aubrey, f. 63v; Darbishire, p. 7. The word "grant" appears in the manuscript written above "acknowledge" as an afterthought or revision, but without the cancelation of the original. The sign which here appears as a slant bar looks in the original like that sign with a tiny circle on each end. It seems to mean "opposite."

[Milton's widow] has a great many letters by her from learned men his acquaintance, both of England & beyond sea.

Aubrey, f. 68; Darbishire, p. 4. Unfortunately, all but a few of Milton's letters have disappeared.

The said Earl of *Anglesy* whom he presented with a Copy of the unlicens'd Papers of his History, came often here (Jewin Street, Bunhill) to visit him, as very much coveting his society and converse; as likewise others of the Nobility, and many persons of eminent quality; nor were the visits of Foreigners ever more frequent than in this place, almost to his dying day.

Phillips, pp. xxxix-xl; Darbishire, p. 76.

[Milton] lived many years much visited by all strangers, and much admired by all at home for the poems he writ, tho' he was then blind; chiefly that of *Paradise Lost*, in which there is a nobleness both of contrivance and execution, that, tho' he affected to write in blank verse without rhyme, and made many new and rough words, yet it was esteemed the beautifullest and perfectest poem that ever was writ, at least in our language.

Thomas Burnet, *Bishop Burnet's History of His Own Time*, I (1724), 163; Raymond, p. 267.

Sir *Robert Howard* . . . was a great admirer of *Milton* to his dying day; and, being his particular Acquaintance, would tell many pleasant Stories of him, as that he himself having demanded of him once what made him side with the *Republicans?* *Milton* answer'd, among other Reasons, because theirs was the most frugal Government; for that the Trappings of a Monarchy might set up an ordinary Commonwealth.

Toland, p. 43; Darbishire, pp. 185-186; CM, XVIII, 380.

. . . our Author bestow'd a Copy of the unlicens'd Papers of his History on the Earl of *Anglesey*, who, as well as several of the Nobility and Gentry, was his constant Visitor.

Toland, p. 43; Darbishire, p. 186; CM, XVIII, 378.

But he was led out sometimes for the benefit of the fresh air, and in warm sunny weather he used to sit at the door of his house near Bunhill Fields, and there as well as in the house received the visits of persons of quality and distinction; for he was no less visited to the last both by his own countrymen and foreigners, than he had been in his florishing condition before the Restoration.

Paradise Lost, ed. Newton, 1749, I, xlix; CM, XVIII, 389. A similar statement appears on p. lviii (CM, XVIII, 392). Newton says this remark was made by Elizabeth Foster to Thomas Birch on February 11, 1738, and that she got it from her mother. But of course it does hardly more than repeat what previous writers, quoted above, have said.

Dryden used sometimes to visit him, but he thought him no poet, but a good rimist: but this was before Dryden had composed his best poems.

Paradise Lost, ed. Newton, 1749, I, lvi-lvii. Newton says this information came from Milton's widow, though not necessarily directly to him.

. . . M^r. Joyner who was intimately acquainted with M^r. *Milton.* . . .

From *Remarks and Collections of Thomas Hearne*, I, 288. A more extensive quotation from this passage, with a brief note on it, appears below under the section on Milton's supposed Catholicism, *q.v.* The reference is to William Joyner (or Lyde *alias* Joyner).

[He] was generous in relieving the wants of his Friends.

The "earliest" biography, f. 143v; Darbishire, p. 31.

[Richard Dugard was an] Intimate friend of Milton.

John and J. A. Venn, *Alumni Cantabrigienses*, II, 72. No source of the information is given, and it is possible that the compilers confused Richard Dugard with his nephew William (see above, II, 226-228, 301, etc.). Richard (B.A., 1609-1610; M.A., 1613; B.D., 1620, Sidney Sussex College, Cambridge; later fellow) is said by the Venns to have been a famous College tutor. From 1636 to his death in 1654 he was rector of Fulletby, Lincolnshire. (P)

This may be as appropriate a place as any to record the fact that Sir Charles Sedley, though we have no proof that he knew Milton, at least collected some of his books. *A Catalogue of the Books of Sir Charles Sidley, B^{nt} Dec. with the Addition of part of a Library of a Late Eminent Divine, to be sold by auction Mar. 23, 1702/3*, as reprinted (in selections) in V. de Sola Pinto's *Sir Charles Sedley*, 1927, pp. 324-336, contains the following titles: "Miltonij pro Populo Angl. Def. 7d." (p. 328), "Literae Cromwellij &c. Scripta a Jo. Miltono 4d." (*ibid.*), and "Milton's Eiconoclastes *Lond.* 1649" (p. 330).

ALLEGED UNORTHODOX RELIGIOUS IDEAS, ESPECIALLY CATHOLICISM.

From so Christian a Life, so great Learning, and so unbyass'd a search after Truth it is not probable any errors in Doctrine should spring. And therefore his Iudgment in his Body of Divinity concerning some speculative points, differing perhaps from that commonly receivd, (and which is thought to bee the reason that never was printed) neither ought rashly to bee condemnd, and however himselfe not to bee uncharitably censur'd; who by beeing a constant Champion for the liberty of Opining, expressd much Candor towards others.

The "earliest biography," f. 143v; Darbishire, p. 31.

Milton was a known frequenter of a Popish Club.

Titus Oates, *True Narrative of the Horrid Plot and Conspiracy of the Popish Party*, 1679, dedication to Charles II, sig. (a)2; Todd, I (1826), 216; Sensabaugh, *That Grand Whig Milton*, p. 115. This is the first of a number of quotations to be given on this subject. Though no serious student of Milton has ever found any good foundation for the rumors, they were widespread and therefore cannot be omitted from a book like the present. Sensabaugh explains the movement as part of a Tory "concerted campaign of vilification and falsehood" (p. 114). One has only to remember Milton's many denunciations of Catholicism during his life to realize the unlikelihood of his turning to that faith. The fact that most of the later mentions of Milton's supposed Catholicism rest on this allegation of Titus Oates takes away most of whatever credibility it might otherwise obtain.

[After a tirade against Catholics:] Now all this is agreeable to the Principles of the *Jesuits* and the *Kirk-men*, and the rest of that Clan, *viz.* that *the King is onely a Son of the Church, notwithstanding his Kingship*; that *their power is of Divine Institution, whereas the Kings authority is onely by compact with the people*; and *so, much inferiour to theirs, being onely Fiduciary*; and *upon that score he may be brought to account, and tryed*; and *every worthy man in Parliament may, for the publick good, be thought a fit Peer, and Judge of the King*, saith *Milton*. This puts me in mind what Mr. *Oates* hath discovered of that great *Oracle*, Mr. *Milton*; namely, that he was a member of a *Popish* Clubb. The thing is credible enough, that he was a *Jesuit in disguise*.

Edward Pelling, *The Good Old Way*, 1680, p. 115; George W. Whiting, in *Notes and Queries*, CLXVIII (1935), 150-151; Sensabaugh, *That Grand Whig Milton*, pp. 110, 118. A marginal note opposite the first occurrence of Milton's name in the quotation above reads: "*Tenure of Kings*, p. 24."

I have told you what *White* the *Jesuit* did, and that wretched *Milton*, *Cromwel's* Secretary, who had been at *Rome*, and in his writings speaks of great *kindness* received *there*; and holding correspondence with some *Italians*, could have no other design in printing those books of *Divorce*, against *Tythes* and *Clergymen*, and to justifie the *Regicides*, but to bring us to *Atheism*

[119]

first, and then to Confusion. He was by very many suspected to be a *Papist*; and if Dr. *Oates* may be believed, was a known frequenter of the *Popish Club*, though he were *Cromwell's* Latine Secretary.

Thomas Long, *A Compendious History of all the Popish & Fanatical Plots*, 1684, p. 93. Sensabaugh, *That Grand Whig Milton*, p. 124. Long charges that Cromwell's favor to the Independents proves his *"connivance"* with the Catholics.

Lambert, a Papist this thirtie yeer, and John Milton a frequenter of a clubb of Papists.

From the *Diary of the Rev. John Ward*, ed. Charles Severn, 1839, p. 141; mentioned in J. S. Smart, *Shakspere Truth and Tradition*, 1928, pp. 83-84.

No[vember]. 17, 1698. . . . Milton a good Grammarian, a schoolm^r, He practis'd y^e Doct$^r̄$ Divorce upon own wife, at last taken to be und^r Secretary to Oliver, vindicated y^e Cutting of Ch Head ag^t Salmasius, for wch never call'd to Account, but He had a brother y^t was a Papist, and he ('twas thot) dyed one.

From an anonymous manuscript diary in the Bodleian, MS. Rawl. D. 1120, f. 67v; identified in *Catalogi Codicum Manuscriptorum Bibliothecæ Bodleianæ Partis Quintæ Fasciculus Quartus*, Oxford, 1898, col. 303, as the notebook of Zachary Merrill. This is the earliest of these quotations to associate in any way the known Catholicism of Christopher Milton with the alleged Catholicism of the poet.

He ever exprest the profoundest Reverence to the Deity as well in Deeds as Words; and would say to his Friends, that the Divine Properties of Goodness, Justice, and Mercy, were the adequat Rule of human Actions, nor less the Object of Imitation for privat Advantages, than of Admiration or Respect for their own Excellence and Perfection. In his early days he was a Favorer of those Protestants then opprobriously cal'd by the name of *Puritans*: In his middle years he was best pleas'd with the *Independents* and *Anabaptists*, as allowing of more Liberty than others, and coming nearest in his opinion to the primitive practice: but in the latter part of his Life, he was not a profest Member of any particular Sect among Christians, he frequented none of their Assemblies, nor made use of their peculiar Rites in his Family. Whether this proceded from a dislike of their uncharitable and endless Disputes, and that Love of Dominion, or Inclination to Persecution, which, he said, was a piece of Popery inseparable from all Churches; or whether he thought one might be a good Man, without subscribing to any Party; and that they had all in som things corrupted the Institutions of Jesus Christ, I will by no means adventure to determin: for Conjectures on such occasions are very uncertain, and I never met with any of his Acquaintance who could be positive in assigning the true Reasons of his Conduct.

Toland, p. 46; Darbishire, pp. 194-195; CM, XVIII, 381 (in part). It is interesting to note that Toland, like the "earliest" biographer, pays no attention to the rumor of Milton's Catholicism. Samuel Johnson (*Lives of the Poets*, World's Classics edition, 1906, I, 111) disapprovingly interpreted the "nor . . . Rites" part as meaning that "there was no hour of prayer, either solitary, or with his household; omitting public prayers, he omitted all." But this interpretation seems far-fetched.

. . . a Popish Judge in a late Reign declar'd publickly, as of his own Knowledge, that the great Champion of the Cause, and who is suppos'd to have writ himself blind, in the defence of it, was a Roman Catholick.

[Footnote to the above:] Judge *Milton*, a profess'd Papist, in his Circuit, at *Warwick*, affirm'd to several Gentlemen and Justices that his Brother *Milton* the famous Author, was of his Religion.

Dean William Binckes of Lichfield, *A Sermon Preach'd before the Honourable House of Commons . . . Novemb. 5. 1704*, London, 1705, p. 16; *Notes and Queries*, VII, xi (1891), 306 (in part); CM, XVIII, 612 (in part); Sensabaugh, *That Grand Whig Milton*, p. 125 (mention only, but no quotation). The footnote is tied to the passage in the text by a symbol composed of three dots and resembling the geometrical symbol for "therefore."

Mr. Wm. Joyner told me that Mr. Selden writ ye Life of Fryer Bacon. But he cannot tell where 'tis now. At ye same time he gave large Encomiums of Mr. Milton: but denyes that he died a Papist. . . .

Dr. Hudson has often inquir'd of Mr. Joyner who was intimately acquainted with M^r. Milton whether ye said M^r. Milton dyed a Papist or No? To wch M^r. Joyner constantly reply'd y^t he was sure he did not. Yet for all this 'tis credibly reported y^t Sir Xtopher Milton his Brother made a Judge in K. James's Reign declar'd publickly in Company that his Brother died a Papist & had liv'd in y^t Communion for above ten years. For further satisfaction ab^t this consult a sermon printed by D^r. Binks now Dean of Lichfield, wch was preach'd at ye Assize at Warwick.

Entries under dates of July 4, 1705, and September 16, 1706, in *Remarks and Collections of Thomas Hearne*, ed. C. E. Doble, Oxford Historical Society Publications, I (1885) I, 288-289; quoted earlier in *Gentleman's Magazine*, Third Series, II (1857), 261; mentioned in Sensabaugh, *That Grand Whig Milton*, p. 125. Wood (*Athenae*, 1721, II, 1013-1014) has a one-column article on William Joyner (or Lyde *alias* Joyner) (1622-1706), who resigned his fellowship in Magdalen College, Oxford, became a Catholic, was abroad for a number of years, and spent many of his later years at Horsepath (co. Oxon.) and nearby Ickford (co. Bucks). He comes into the story of the law-suit of Milton and the Copes in a minor way; see my *Milton in Chancery*, pp. 139, 178, 200, 204, 383. It is perfectly possible that he may have known Milton for most of their lives, since he came from country near Wheatley and Forest Hill. But no details of their friendship have been found.

ALLUSIONS.

Jhon Milton Jhon Turner George Harrison.

A marginal note by Charles, second Lord Stanhope, in his copy of Cresacre More's *Life and Death of Sir Thomas More*, 1642 (now in the Folger Shakespeare Library), f. Bb2r. Dr. James M. Osborn mentioned this fact in a letter in the London *Times Literary Supplement*, January 4, 1957, p. 16, taking it from G.P.V. Akrigg's "The Curious Marginalia of Charles, Second Lord Stanhope," in *Joseph Quincy Adams Memorial Studies*, ed. McManaway, Dawson, and Willoughby, Washington, 1948, p. 789. This Lord Stanhope was born in 1608 and died in 1675. I am grateful to both Dr. Osborn and Dr. McManaway for help on this item, though there is of course no certainty that it refers to the poet, and though it is in any case merely a mention of his name. R. A. Sayce notes a similar allusion in another of Stanhope's books (*Times Literary Supplement*, October 11, 1957, p. 509), this one in a book in the library of Worcester College, Oxford. It reads: "Jhon Mil-

ton gentleman by my fathers procurement fellow first of kinges colledge in Cambridge & afterwards of Eaton colledge." Mr. Sayce identifies this reference as to a John Milton who came up from Eton to
King's College in 1594. Probably, therefore, the first allusion is to the
same John Milton.

A ghost of an allusion appears in *Notes and Queries*, II, v (1858),
363, where a writer says that among various other writers who attacked Milton was one named Tyffe. No date is given, and no title;
and I have been unable to find any writing by any person named Tyffe
attacking Milton. There is no Tyffe in Wing's *STC*.

DANISH STUDENT OLAUS BORRICHIUS DISAPPROVES MILTON.

[Borrichius coupled Milton and Hobbes as, despite their
learning,] zealous in malignity, or scandalous in boasting.

From Borrichius's *Dissertationes*, Copenhagen, 1715, I, 119-120,
as given by Ethel Seaton in her *Literary Relations of England and
Scandinavia in the Seventeenth Century*, Oxford, 1935, p. 168. The
date may be after the writer's visit to England in 1663, but since he
is evidently thinking of Milton's political writings chiefly, it may of
course be earlier, or even later. (P)

READING AND LIBRARY.

. . . and being asked whether he did not often read Homer
and Virgil, she [his widow] understood it as an imputation
upon him for stealing from those authors, and answered with
eagerness that he stole from no body but the Muse who inspired
him; and being asked by a lady present who the Muse was, replied that it was God's Grace, and the Holy Spirit that visited
him nightly. She was likewise asked whom he approved most
of our English poets, and answered Spenser, Shakespear, and
Cowley: and being asked what he thought of Dryden, she said
Dryden used sometimes to visit him, but he thought him no
poet, but a good rimist: but this was before Dryden had composed his best poems, which made his name so famous afterwards.

Milton, *Paradise Lost*, ed. Newton, 1749, I, lvi-lvii; CM, XVIII,
390. This list, which is hardly more than a sample, could be increased
almost indefinitely. Milton must, of course, have been familiar with

and to some extent admired the authors whom he had his nephews read, as described in Phillips, pp. xvii-xix (Darbishire, pp. 60-61). The same holds true of the list of authors which he gives in his *Of Education*. Many of the so-called sources of *Paradise Lost* and of his other poems which scholars and others have pointed out during the years must have been familiar to him, and he must have owned copies of a good many. Eleven folios of common law books which were in the inventory of Milton's widow must have belonged to him. He bought a whole box of music books in Italy. He refers, of course, to hundreds of books in his prose writings. He is said to have been able to recite most of Homer by heart and a good deal from Ovid and Euripides. Todd reports that he "was a great admirer of Taylor, and studied his works," as he no doubt did those of dozens of other theologians of the time. His *Commonplace Book* is another index to his wide reading. But there is no room, and no justification, to do more here than to give the above quotation as a token text with the understanding that though it is a ridiculous understatement, we have neither the materials nor the space for anything accurate and adequate.

Yett he was not sparing to buy good Books, of which hee left a fair Collection. . . .

The "earliest" biography, f. 143v; Darbishire, p. 31.

Towards the latter part of his time he contracted his Library, both because the Heirs he left could not make a right use of it, and that he thought he might sell it more to their advantage than they could be able to do themselves. His Enemies reported that Poverty constrain'd him thus to part with his Books: and were this true, it would be indeed a great disgrace, not to him . . . but to any Country that should have no more regard to Probity or Learning.

Toland, pp. 45-46; Darbishire, pp. 192-193; CM, XVIII, 381. The following list of books which belonged, or may have belonged, to Milton is supplementary to those which have occurred from time to time during these four volumes, and for which, unlike these, some grounds for dating could be found. Like the others, these vary from those which we can be reasonably sure Milton owned and wrote in to those whose chance of genuineness is remote. They are arranged alphabetically, with a key word (from either author or title) to identify each. An excellent account of Milton's activities as a collector of books is James Holly Hanford's "Milton among the Book Collectors," *Newberry Library Bulletin*, IV (1956), 97-109. Fletcher (*The Intellectual Development of John Milton*, I, 1956) has a short chapter on Milton's book-buying before 1625 (chapter 25).

[1. Beza.] Joannes Miltonus. . . . Sit hoc tuum in primis verum et immortale decus, Anglica, quod Ioanem Wiclefum edideris, primum ausum romanæ meretrici bellum palam indicere.

Signature and note alleged to have been in a "book of portraits of reformers" by Theodore Beza, published in Geneva in 1580. It is described in CM, XVIII, 581, from *Inventaire des Autographes . . . Reunis par M. Benjamin Fillon*, Paris, 1879, part II, item 1436. Its later history has not been traced. The Latin inscription on the title page, quoted above, may be translated: "Let this be your true and immortal honor among the first, England, that you brought forth John Wycliffe, who first dared to proclaim war openly on the Roman prostitute."

[2. Bibles.]

a. Wynne Baxter, in *Notes and Queries*, XI, iii (1911), 109-110, described all the Bibles known to him to have any connection with Milton. The first was a Geneva Bible of 1560 said to have been the property of the poet. It was sold several times between 1901 and 1907, the signature was declared a forgery, and later W.A. Wright identified it as that of Major John Milton of the Training Bands. It has dropped out of sight since 1911. Baxter quotes Wright from the *Daily News* of November 12, 1907.

b. William Jaggard reported in the *Athenaeum*, 1916, I, 251, that he had found a Bible printed by Henry Middleton and Thomas Vautrollier in 1581, which bore the signature "Jhon Milton" on the title page in a hand resembling Milton's. See French, "The Autographs of John Milton," no. 68; CM, XVIII, 564. The book was said to contain a large number of marginal annotations and a longish prayer written on a blank leaf, the latter of which is quoted in CM. In a letter to one of the editors of CM, XVIII, Mr. Jaggard added that the manuscript comments which he considered Milton's were on 123 pages, in Latin and Greek and English and Hebrew, and in an almost microscopic hand. He also corrected the first reading of Milton's name to "Melton."

c. Within four years George Offor described two Bibles in his possession with autographs of Milton. In *Notes and Queries*, II, iv (1857), 334-335, he told of one published in 1614; in the same journal, II, xii (1861), 233, he said he had one of 1613. One may suspect that by a slight error he was describing the same volume in both places, but there may have been two. At any rate, of the 1614 edition he said that his copy had the signature "John Milton" on the back of the title page of the New Testament and also on the reverse of the concordance of 1615 bound with it. See French, "The Autographs of John Milton," no. 70; CM, XVIII, 562. Sotheby reproduced the signature in his *Ramblings*, facing p. 124, but doubted whether it was the poet's. Since the volume is thought (perhaps both volumes, if there are two) to have been destroyed in the fire in Sotheby's in 1865, there is neither opportunity nor incentive for further investigation of it.

d. A contributor to *Notes and Queries*, CXLIII (1922), 31, who signed himself R. S. M. described a Bible dated 1629 which he owned. He said it contained signatures or names of James, Robert, Elizabeth, and Ann Milton, with at least one date of 1682. See CM, XVIII, 564. The connection with the poet, if any, is apparently very remote.

[3. William Browne, *Britannia's Pastorals*, 1613-1616.]

A copy of this book, with an entry to the effect that Milton wrote the numerous notes in it and that it was originally sold in London by a distant relative of Milton, was again sold at Sotheby's in 1911. It later came to Lucius A. Wilmerding of New York, who made it available to the editors of CM, XVIII. It is discussed in Sotheby's *Ramblings*, pp. 97-104, with a facsimile facing p. 98; in Stern, I, i, 175; in French, "The Autographs of John Milton," no. 66; and in CM, XVIII, 336-340, 570-571. Though the volume contains no signature by Milton, its genuineness as a book from his library seems acceptable. It was sold again at the Parke-Bernet Galleries with other books from Mr. Wilmerding's library on November 27-29, 1950 (*United States Cumulative Book Auction Records*, 1950-1951, p. 278), for $1,000. The present owner is Dr. Otto O. Fisher of Detroit.

[4. Thomas Cooper, *Thesaurus Linguæ Romanæ et Britannicæ*, 1573.]

A copy of this book which has been alleged to have belonged to Milton and to contain notes by him is now in the New York Public Library. It is described in Milton's *Commonplace Book*, ed. A. J. Horwood for the Camden Society, 1877, p. viii; in French, "The Autographs of John Milton," no. 57; and in CM, XVIII, 581. Though J. Payne Collier, who owned it in 1875, claimed that it contained more than 1500 notes written by Milton, Horwood rejected it, as most scholars since have done.

[5. *Les Delices de la Suisse*.]

All that is known of this book comes from a letter of Thomas De Quincey, of May 25, 1809, probably to Dorothy Wordsworth, quoted in Horace A. Eaton's *Thomas De Quincey*, 1936, p. 181, and in CM, XVIII, 575. The passage concerning this volume reads: ". . . if Mr. Heber by the strength of his purse had not prevented me, I should have bought a book (Les Delices de la Suisse) with Milton's M.S. notes on the margin." The catalogue of Heber's library (*Bibliotheca Heberiana*, 1834, II, 81, item 1571) shows this title, but with no mention of any writing of Milton's in it.

[6. Sir Anthony Fitzherbert, *La Vievx Natura breuium*, 1584.] Johēs Milton me possidet. . . . Det Christus studijs vela secunda meis.

Inscriptions on the front leaves of a copy of Fitzherbert now in the New York Public Library; described in Hunter, *Milton*, 1850, p. 22; Sotheby, *Ramblings*, pp. 125-126 (with some reproductions facing p. 124); Stern, I, i, 159, 320; French, "The Autographs of John Milton," no. 59; CM, XVIII, 516. There are also several additional notes. The book contains also signatures of John Marston. It is said to have come from Milton's widow through Joshua Eddowes, a bookseller in Shrewsbury, Rev. Thomas Stedman of Shrewsbury, and Sir William Tite to its present location. There is no way of being sure that it was the poet who owned this book, but the evidence seems favorable. There is also a note about this volume in British Museum Add. MS. 24,501, f. 76; though it does not seem to be in Hunter's handwriting, it is part of his collection of records, and he uses most of the details in his book. Sotheby and others have thought that the owner may have been the poet's father. Either of them had enough experience with the law to justify his having such a work for reference.

[John Milton owns me. . . . May Christ give favorable progress to my studies.]

[7. Nicodemus Frischlin, *Operum Poeticorum*, Strassburg, 1595.] I: M.

A copy of this book with these initials on the title page is now in the Harvard College Library; see French, "The Autographs of John Milton," no. 65; CM, XVIII, 578. Aside from the initials and some underlinings, there are no notes of any importance in the book. It is enclosed in an oak case said to have been made of wood from Milton's house in the Barbican, demolished in 1865. A certificate to this effect, signed by the bookseller John Wallen, 1866, is pasted inside.

According to a clipping in the New York Public Library Manuscript Room this volume, as part of the Charles F. Gunther collection, was offered for sale at the American Art Association on November 12, 1925.

[8. James I, *A Remonstrance . . . for the Right of Kings . . . against an Oration of the Cardinal of Perron*, Cambridge, 1619.]

A copy of this book said to contain the initials J. M. and two pages of manuscript notes by the poet was sold at Sotheby's in 1908, but has not since been traced. See CM, XVIII, 575.

[9. James V of Scotland, *La Navigation du roy d'Ecosse Jacques, cinquiesme du nom, autour de son royaume*, Paris.]

This title is mentioned in the same catalogue as the Beza volume above (no. 1). It is said to have contained the signature of Milton and two lines in his handwriting. Like the Beza, it has vanished. Another unnamed book accompanied these two.

[10. Olaus Magnus, *Historia de Gentibus Septentrionalibus*, Antwerp, 1558.] JM.

The Milton Cottage at Chalfont St. Giles has this volume with this monogram. It is mentioned in French, "The Autographs of John Milton," no. 60, and in CM, XVIII, 579. There is no further proof either for or against its connection with the poet.

[11. J. B. Marliani, *Urbis Romæ Topographia*, Venice, 1588.] Jo. Milton.

A copy of this title, bearing on the title page Milton's signature in the form given, is listed in the *Catalogue of the Library of . . . Wynne E. Baxter*, 1921, item 172. It is also mentioned in French, "The Autographs of John Milton," no. 62, and in CM, XVIII, 576. It is probably the same work as Joannes Bartholomaeus Marlianus' *Antiquae Romae Topographia*, Rome, 1534 (*CBEL*, I, 778), but a later edition. This copy has not been traced since 1921.

[12. Montaigne, *Essays*, translated by John Florio, 1613.]

This volume is said to have contained the signatures of Milton and of an Anthony Pembruge on the title page. Nothing has been heard of it since 1858, when it was mentioned in *Notes and Queries* (II, v, 115). See French, "The Autographs of John Milton," no. 64, and CM, XVIII, 580.

[13. Marc Antoine Muret, *Variarvm Lectionvm Libri XV*, Paris, 1586.]

[a] Joannes Milton   pre: 2^s 6^d

[b] N.B. y^e. above is y^e. Autograph of y^e famous Milton. I. Bromehead.

[c] Sum Rich: King Exoniēsis.

I wish to thank Mr. Arthur Swann of the Parke-Bernet Galleries for allowing me to see this volume while it was in his possession in 1950. Except for the entry of its sale at those Galleries on May 7-8, 1945, for $350 (*United States Cumulative Book Auction Records*, v, part iii, 59), I believe this possible volume from Milton's library has not been mentioned in print. The first two items given above are on

[128]

the front flyleaf and the third on the title page. Though the signature looks genuine, there has been some question about it. The volume also contains a Greek phrase written on the title page and another signature of Joseph Bromehead. The first item gives the price of the book as 2s. 6d. The third means: "I am the book of Richard King of Exeter," who is probably Richard John King the antiquary (1818-1879), who took his B.A. from Exeter College, Oxford, in 1841 (*DNB*). The volume bears the bookplate of John Gribbel.

[14. *Negotiation de la Paix*, 1576.] J:M.

These initials, on the title page of this volume, were identified as Milton's in G. H. Last's Catalogue 221, 1936, item 234; it is mentioned in French, "The Autographs of John Milton," item 58, and in CM, XVIII, 578. Professor Thomas O. Mabbott, who owned the volume for a time, thought that though there were hundreds of other J.M.'s in England, these initials might be the poet's. The volume is now in the Library of Congress.

[15. Blaise Pascal, *Les Provinciales, or, The Mystery of Jesvitisme*, London, 1658.] J.M.

What was said to be Milton's copy of this volume, with the above initials on the title page, was offered in George Bates' Catalogue 16, 1937, item 216, for £40; the catalogue contains a facsimile of the title page. The volume is said to contain also the signature of John Newton, the divine and friend of Cowper. It is mentioned in CM, XVIII, 581, as "indubitably Miltonic."

[16. John Pits, *Relationum Historicarum de Rebus Anglicis*, Tome I, Paris, 1619.] JM

This volume, containing the above monogram which may be Milton's, belonged to the bookseller Blackwell in 1940. It is described in the Second Supplement to CM in *Notes and Queries*, CLXXIX (1940), July 13. The book contains also the signature of Peter Wentworth, probably Milton's friend. This connection increases the likelihood that the book belonged to the poet.

[17. John Sleidan, *De Statv Religionis et Reipvblicae*, Strassburg, 1555.]

The New York Public Library copy of this work (shelf mark *KB+1555) has been thought to come from Milton's library. Miss Ruth Mohl, editor of Milton's *Commonplace Book* for the *Complete Prose Works of John Milton*, I (1953) says (p. 373): "Marginal notes . . . are, I am convinced, in Milton's own handwriting." The volume contains no signature of Milton but has that of Jacobus Krüegerus on the title page. There are many annotations in the book, which seem to be in more than one hand. Some seem to belong to Krüegerus, and others are different. A number may well be Milton's, though most of them can be identified as German script by the little lines above the u's. Almost as good a case for Miltonic ownership could be made for the 1559 edition of Sleidan, also in the New York Public Library (KB 1559). But the Miltonic-looking annotations were probably made by the "Jo Fri Gregorii" whose signature is on the title page.

[18. Thucydides, *De Bello Peloponnesiaco Libri Octo*, Basel, 1564.]

A copy of this book, bound with Francis Irenicus' *Germaniæ Exegeseos Volumina Duodecim*, Basel, 1567, with the signature of John Milton on the title page and a few notes in what may be his hand, was recently in the possession of Dr. Rosenbach in New York. It bore the bookplate of Thomas Wentworth, Earl of Strafford. It is described in French, "The Autographs of John Milton," no. 78, and in CM, XVIII, 344-345, 572. In Rosenbach's catalogue, *English Poetry to 1700*, 1941, item 507, it was offered for sale for $2,750.

In addition to the above autographed books from Milton's library, the Morgan Library in New York used to have a detached signature reading "Liber Jo Milton." It was on a slip of paper about 2" by ½", mounted on a sheet 5" by 3½", and that in turn on another 15" by 8". Though the handwriting looked a good deal like Milton's, the librarian was not very confident of the genuineness of the writing. See CM, XVIII, 582, and French, "The Autographs of John Milton," no. 93.

One further word may be said about books which Milton is known to have used and the editions of them which have been identified from his references to them. Important works like those of Homer, Virgil, Dante, and the like we may take for granted that he owned, even though the copies may not survive or may not have come to light. Miss Mohl, for example (see the note to number 17 above), has patiently identified editions of many works which Milton abstracted in his *Commonplace Book*. In *Milton's Rabbinical Readings* (1930) Harris Fletcher proves pretty conclusively that Milton knew and used Buxtorf's *Lexicon* of 1639-1640, his rabbinical Bible of 1618-1619, and certain other associated works. Nathan Dane (*Modern Language Notes*, LVI, 1941, 278-279) identifies Milton's edition of Callimachus from the marginal notes in his copy of Pindar. Harris Fletcher similarly identifies his Homer (*Journal of English and Germanic Philology*, XXXVIII, 1939, 229-232). Toland's statement (*Vindicius Liberius, or Defence of himself*, 1702, p. 8, as quoted in Todd, 1, 1826, 366) that Milton "often read Plautus, in order the better to rail at Salmasius" makes it certain that Milton must have owned a copy of Plautus. The Callimachus edition is that of Antwerp, 1514; Homer, that of Basel, 1560-1569.

RELICS.

A number of objects which had some personal association with Milton either still survive or survived for a considerable time after his death, or have been said to do so. Portraits, which might well be included, are in a separate section following this one.

An interesting basis of comparison with the present list is the inventory of the possessions of the poet's widow, made on August 26, 1727, from which a selection appears below under that date. References to this inventory appear in some of the sections immediately following.

I have divided this subject of relics into three parts: (1) *household objects*, (2) *personal articles*, and (3) *bodily remains*.

[I. HOUSEHOLD OBJECTS.]

[1. China dishes.]

Two china dishes said to have belonged to the poet were exhibited at Christ's College in 1908; see *Milton Tercentenary*, p. 160. They are said to have come down through Milton's niece to Mr. A. E. Shipley, who lent them for this exhibit. They were on stands made of oak from Milton's house in the Barbican. The only dishes mentioned in Mrs. Milton's inventory were of pewter: "8 Pueter Plates," "2 Pueter Dishes," etc.

[2. Knife and fork.]

Mrs. Milton's inventory mentions "A Totershell Knife & ffork wth other odd Ones," which may have been her husband's. In 1857 Joseph Hunter described this set as owned then by Thomas Wyndham Jones of Nantwich. The handles are described here as "clouded agate," which may be the same as the tortoise shell of the inventory. They were traced back from Mr. Jones to the Hassalls of Nantwich, who got them from a Miss Elizabeth Webb, whose grandfather had received them from Milton's widow, his friend. Hunter describes them in his manuscript, British Museum Add. MS. 24,501, ff. 82-83, and gives a sketch of them, showing some odd devices on the sides of the knife. Their story is fairly completely told in the *Archaeological Journal*, XIV (1857), 89-91, and J. Hall's *Nantwich*, 1883, p. 474. They are mentioned in CM, XVIII, 583.

[3. Coffee pot.]

J. S. Howson mentions this article and a walking stick of Milton's in "On the Associations of Milton with the River Dee and Cheshire," *Journal of the Architectural, Archaeological, and Historic Society, for* the County, City, and Neighborhood of Chester, III (1885), 409-418. Among rambling notes on other matters he says (p. 416) that Milton was "connected with this county by a very close personal link. . . . My illustrations now are a walking-stick . . . and a coffee-pot, the presence of which I owe to the kindness of Mr. WILBRAHAM TOLLEMACHE, of NANTWICH." Mrs. Milton's inventory lists "1 Tin Coffee Pott," which could be this item.

[4. Bed.]

Francis Blackburne, in *Memoir of Thomas Hollis*, 1780, I, 111, says that on June 12, 1761, Thomas Hollis bought the bed on which Milton died and presented it to the poet Mark Akenside. The story is repeated in Milton's *Poetical Works*, ed. Mitford, 1852, I, xci, and in CM, XVIII, 584. This could possibly be the first article quoted from the inventory below.

[II. PERSONAL ARTICLES.]

[1. Snuff box or tobacco box.]

What is called sometimes Milton's snuff box and sometimes his tobacco box was mentioned in Mrs. Milton's inventory and has been known for a long time. It was exhibited as early as 1908 in the Milton Tercentenary (Williamson, p. 160) as the property then of Lowther Bridger, a descendant of Milton's brother Christopher. It had been described in the *Daily News* of June 10, 1898. It had been deposited in 1905 by Bridger in the Bodleian, where it remained on loan for many years and finally was presented to the library in about 1951 or 1952. It is made of tortoise shell, is circular, about 3½" in diameter and about 1" deep, and is said to have been used by Milton up to the time of his death. It is mentioned in Raymond, p. 327; in CM, XVIII, 584; and in the *Seventeenth-Century News-Letter*, X (1952), 3.

[2. Writing case.]

The Bodleian now possesses a tortoise-shell case said to have belonged to Milton and to have contained originally six ivory tablets, a pair of dividers, a pen, a pencil, and some other objects. It is described in *Academy*, LIII (1898), 663, in *Notes and Queries*, X, x (1908), 388; and in CM, XVIII, 393, 584, 610. Accompanying it is a document signed by Richard Lovekin of Nantwich, dated October 1, 1742, nephew of Milton's widow, certifying its genuineness. When I saw it in 1935, it contained only three ivory tablets and a smaller case containing the dividers and a protractor. Apparently the latter case had at one time become separated from the former, because the outer case was said to have been deposited in 1905 by Lowther Bridger, and the smaller one to have been given to the library in 1923 by Mrs. Mary G. T. Stonehouse. Both are now owned by the Bodleian. The outer case, measuring about 4″ x 1½″ x ½″, has a raised oval on the bottom on which Milton is said to have intended to have his coat of arms fastened for use as a seal but never did so. Milton received this case as a gift from the Duke of Richmond; see above under February 22, 1672.

[3. Clothing.]

According to the inventory of Milton's widow's possessions, she had a "Blew shagg Coat," valued at one shilling; "yᵉ Best Shute head Cloathes" (a puzzling term usually interpreted as "the best suit of broadcloth" or of "twad" cloth), valued at three shillings; and "yᵉ Worser Ditto," valued at 1/6. Though "head cloths" could be cloths to be hung at the head of the bed, I cannot offer a convincing interpretation of the term, but in any case I have seen no reference to any such clothes of the poet as being extant since 1727.

[4. Spectacles.]

The inventory mentions "2 Pair Spectables," which may have been Milton's. But they too have not appeared since.

[5. Walking stick.]

J. S. Howson mentions Milton's walking stick as the second of two articles connected with Milton. See the note above about his coffee pot (1, 3). The stick does not appear in the inventory.

[6. Seal] The arms that *Joh. Milton* did use and seal his Letters with, were *Argent a spread Eagle with two heads gules, legg'd and beak'd sable.*

Wood, 1, 880; Darbishire, p. 35. Compare Aubrey's note (Darbishire, p. 1) that Milton's crest was "an Arme dexter holding an Eagles head & Neck erased G." Two principal types of seals of Milton need to be considered. One is that bearing his portrait, which is dealt with below under the section on portraits. The other is that bearing his family arms, which was briefly mentioned above (11, 337-338), but which needs further attention here.

Known samples of the two-headed eagle seal as used by Milton occur on the Foxcroft bond (111, 29), on some of his letters to Mylius (111, 100, 117, 165, 173, 175, 193), and on the agreement for *Paradise Lost* (1v, 431). An enlargement of the latter decorates the covers of the volumes of the present work. But since the impression shown on these instances seems not to be exactly like that of the actual known instrument itself as it survived at least well into the middle of the nineteenth century, it is quite likely that Milton had more than one seal bearing this device. In fact, Masson, in his edition of Milton's *Poems* (1874, 1, 5-6), describes a second in addition to the foregoing: "out of a wreath, a lion's gamb couped and erect azure, grasping an eagle's head erased gules": see also *Notes and Queries*, 111, vii (1865), 504.

It may be that Masson was thinking of the actual silver seal itself, which in a sense combines the two descriptions. Indeed in his *Life* (1881 edition, I, 5-7) he shows side by side the example from the agreement for *Paradise Lost* and that which I am about to describe. Francis Blackburne mentions (*Memoir of Thomas Hollis*, II, 526) that Hollis purchased Milton's "bed and his silver seal." One of the earliest descriptions of it which I have found is that in the *Archaeological Journal*, VI (1849), which comes from the speech of John Disney to the Archaeological Institute on May 4, 1849. He exhibited at that meeting a "silver seal, well authenticated as having been used by Milton. The impress is a coat of arms, a double-headed eagle displayed; the shield is surmounted by a helm, lambrequins, and crest, which appears to be a lion's gamb grasping the head of an eagle, by the neck, erased." Disney explained that this relic had come, on the death of Thomas Foster, husband of the poet's granddaughter Elizabeth Foster, to John Payne, who sold it to Thomas Hollis in 1761. On Hollis's death it went to his protégé Thomas Brand Hollis, from whom Disney's father inherited it. Marsh reproduced this material with several additions. In his "Papers Connected with the Affairs of Milton and his Family," Publications of the Chetham Society, XXIV (1851), 21, he speculated that Thomas Foster had probably received the seal from his mother-in-law Deborah Clarke, Milton's daughter, who in turn probably received it from her mother, whose favorite daughter she was. Both of these publications reproduced the seal itself, both side view and bottom view. It is of course not a photograph; Marsh described his method of reproduction as having been made from a stereotype from the woodcut in the *Journal*. If I read correctly the microscopic legend under Marsh's reproduction, it says that A. Way drew it and O. Jewitt engraved it. Masson (*Life*, 1881, I, 5-7) added that at the time of his writing the seal belonged to Disney's son Edgar of the Hyde, Ingatestone, co. Essex. He also said that Hollis had paid Payne three guineas for it in 1761. Williamson (*Milton Tercentenary*, p. 79) barely mentions this seal, as does Miss Darbishire (p. 339), but neither gives any further information as to its present location. Incidentally, Blackburne, who devotes a long section (II, 533*-584*, inserted between pp. 532 and 533) to a spirited attack on Samuel Johnson's derogatory remarks about Milton, reproduces this seal but in a form very different from that given by Marsh and Masson. It is similar to but not identical with that given by Toland in his edition of Milton's prose works, 1698, beneath the portrait on the frontispiece of Volume I. Where the original seal is at present I cannot say.

But E. K. Adams, Esq., Assistant Keeper of the National Portrait Gallery, suggests to me that some of the references to Milton's seal may possibly, by a slight extension of the term, be to the Commonwealth Great Seal of England of 1651, which may have been used to stamp some of the letters of state which he put into Latin for sending to foreign countries. Mr. Adams kindly sent me a reproduction of the silver electrotypes of this seal in the Gallery, which he informs me were made from the original wax impression in the British Museum. The legend below these reproductions states that this seal was done by Thomas Simon, that it shows on one side a map of England and Ireland and on the other a scene of Cromwell addressing the House, and that these electrotypes were presented in May, 1885, by George Scharf, Esq., C.B., F.S.A. The obverse side, showing Cromwell in the House, has been reproduced, though apparently from a drawing and not directly, in *English Literature and its Backgrounds*, ed. Grebanier, Middlebrook, Thompson, and Watt (Dryden Press, New York, revised edition, 1949, I, 527). There is, however, of course nothing personal to Milton about this seal, and it has no relation to the ones just described.

[III. BODILY REMAINS.]

[I. Hair.]

A lock of Milton's hair which probably came to Addison from the poet's daughter Deborah has multiplied numerically by being divided by various owners, so that it has become at least three. It belonged successively to Addison, Johnson, John Hoole, and Dr. Robert (?) Batty. Batty divided the original lock in two and gave half to Leigh Hunt, who divided his again to give part to Browning. Hunt's letter to Browning was printed in the *Athenaeum*, 1883, II, 15-18. Both Hunt and Keats wrote poems about this lock. Hunt's, all addressed to Dr. Batty though without naming him, and all published in *Foliage* (1818, pp. cxxxi-iii), begin: "I felt my spirit leap, and look at thee"; "It lies before me there, and my own breath"; and "A liberal taste, and a wise gentleness." Keats's, beginning "Chief of organic numbers!" and mentioned in his letter of January 23, 1818, is published in his *Complete Poetical Works and Letters* (ed. Horace E. Scudder, Cambridge Poets edition, 1899, pp. 39, 284). A letter from Benjamin Bailey to R. M. Milnes about Keats's poem, which Keats sent to him, is quoted in *The Keats Circle*, ed. Hyder E. Rollins, 1948, II, 283. One of these three locks is now in the Miriam Lutcher Stark Collection at the University of Texas; a second belongs to Dr. Dallas Pratt; and a third is in the Keats Memorial House in Hampstead. One of them belonged in 1918 to Sir Charles Wakefield, who bought it for £15 (London *Times*, March 15, 1918, p. 5f, and March 29, p. 2d). Still another piece of Milton's hair, which has no known relation with the foregoing three, is in the Chalfont St. Giles Cottage, the gift of Mrs. Barchard of the Lee, co. Bucks, who had it from her great-grandfather, Dr. George Gregory, lecturer at St. Giles Cripplegate. It is said to have been taken from Milton's head at the time of his disinterment. See CM, XVIII, 583;

Trevor R. Leigh-Hunt in the *John Keats Memorial Volume*, London, 1921, pp. 107-109. I am grateful for assistance to Professor Thomas O. Mabbott and to Miss Fannie Ratchford of the University of Texas Library.

[2. Bones.]

The most gruesome relic of Milton, according to Philip Neve's *Narrative of the Disinterment of Milton's Coffin* (1790), was his body itself, or at least parts of it. In Neve's account and other later amplifications Milton's body was dug up, dealt out in pieces to gay young blades at a party, and later hawked about and exploited by peddlers and janitors for the benefit of the curious. Hair, teeth, fingers, ribs, leg-bones, and other sections turned up endlessly. Some critics assailed Neve's account; others defended him. The best recent discussion is A. W. Read's "Disinterment of Milton's Remains," *PMLA*, XLV (1930), 1050-1068. Read thinks that the story is credible. None of these particular relics seem to have been traced to recent times.

PORTRAITS.

Some genuine and numerous doubtfully attributed portraits of Milton have appeared in the present and previous volumes. They can easily be traced in the indexes under "Milton: Portraits." It now remains to enter the large number of undated and mostly uncertain pictures. Most of them have already been included in the two books which are the standard treatments of this subject, and which I shall refer to by the names of the authors below. These are (1) John Fitchett Marsh, "On the Engraved Portraits and Pretended Portraits of Milton," a paper read to the Historic Society of Lancashire and Cheshire on May 3, 1860, and printed in its *Transactions*, XII (1860), 135-188; and (2) George C. Williamson, *Milton Tercentenary The Portraits, Prints and Writings of John Milton . . . Exhibited at Christ's College, Cambridge*, 1908. Since Williamson includes most of Marsh's and considerable additional material, I have previously given references usually only to the later book, but not without realizing the great contribution which Marsh made. I hope that the present section may be useful to students of Milton because it brings many of the notes down to the present date from the almost fifty years ago where Williamson left them.

The important basic documents about Milton portraits, aside from the pictures themselves, are the references by the early biographers, which can be found in Darbishire, pp. 3, 202, 229, 333-334; Vertue's letter of August 12, 1721, printed in Masson, I, 309n, and in Marsh, pp. 137-138; and Blackburne's note about Vertue's visit to Deborah Clarke in 1725, printed in Marsh, pp. 138-139. Masson also has comprehensive discussions at I, 66-68, 308-310, and at VI, 754-758.

The following list includes only portraits which we may assume to have been made before Milton's death or to reflect others which were, and about which we cannot be sure. Some may in fact be later, but in case of doubt my principle is to include the items. A few additional portraits will be mentioned later among posthumous events, as for example the Rysbrack monument in Westminster Abbey. The present group may very likely include some repetitions due to scanty information. But whenever possible I have traced the pictures down to their present owners and locations. I wish to offer here my most grateful thanks and appreciation to the many kind people in many parts of England and this country who have helped me in this search. One of the deep satisfactions of scholarship is that of experiencing this sort of courtesy and cooperation. I have attempted to record my obligations under the individual entries below, but what little I can say is inadequate.

What may well be the best single collection of prints of portraits of Milton ever formed is that made by the late Beverly Chew and bequeathed by him to the New York Public Library. It contains between 350 and 400 prints. When exhibited at the Grolier Club in 1908-1909, it was catalogued under the title: "Catalogue of an Exhibition Commemorative of the Tercentenary of the Birth of John Milton," of which the Library has an annotated copy.

1. A portrait by Mary Beale, 19 or 20 inches by 15 inches, on canvas, with brown dress, open collar, and long reddish hair; Williamson, pp. 22, 35. This picture was exhibited at the South Kensington Museum in 1866. In 1908 it was at Knole, Sevenoaks, in the collection of Lord Sackville. Williamson does not consider it to be of Milton. Neither does Gery Milner-Gibson-Cullum in his article on Mary Beale in the *Proceedings* of the Suffolk Institute of Archaeology and Natural History, XVI (1918), 234.

2. A picture of a man with a beard, at Lord Braybrooke's residence at Audley End, Essex, in 1850; Milton's *Poetical Works*, ed. John Mitford, I (1852), xc; Marsh, p. 186. The present Lord Braybrooke kindly informs me that it is still in the possession of the family at Audley End, and that it is described in item 21 of a catalogue compiled by the Ministry of Works staff, who look after ancient monuments and historic buildings. At his request Mr. Richard J. B. Walker, Curator of Pictures for the Ministry of Works, has sent me the following description of it: "canvas, 30 inches by 25, half-length to left, black coat, white linen collar (similar to Faithorne but no bands) and tassels, brown grizzled beard and drooping moustache, long curly chestnut hair, large grey (?) eyes, long and rather lean face, surly expression, age about fifty, faint resemblance to Charles I but not actually of him, painted about 1650 or later; 18th or 19th century inscription JOHN MILTON at top left; no clue on back." He says that it belonged at one time to George

Berkeley (1763-1793), and that at his death it may have been bought by Lord Howard de Walden, who then owned Audley End and who bought a number of pictures. He says, however, that neither he nor the Director of the National Portrait Gallery believes it to be a picture of Milton. The photograph which Mr. Walker has kindly sent me amply supports his decision that the picture is not of Milton, whom it does not in the least resemble.

3. A bust, said to be of marble, in the Print Room of the British Museum about 1860; Marsh, p. 187. Mr. P. Lasko, Assistant Keeper of the Department of British and Medieval Antiquities at the Museum, kindly informs me that what Marsh probably saw was a plaster bust, still in the Museum, which is a copy of the Roubilliac terracotta now in the Scottish National Gallery (see below, number 31). The photographs which I have received of the two busts make them appear identical.

4. A miniature long said to be of Milton and owned and shown by George Chapman at a meeting of the Society of Antiquaries in 1861; *Gentleman's Magazine*, Second Series, x (1861), 286.

5. An engraving (?) published in 1777 and labeled "From an Original in Ld Chesterfield's Collection"; size 4 3/4 inches by 2 7/8 inches. A young man with long hair, gown, white collar, and white cuff, with his right arm resting on a book, and his hand raised to support his head. Marsh, nos. 152-154; Williamson, pp. 18, 84. What may be a reproduction, said to be from Faithorne, is said to be in the *Imperial Dictionary of Universal Biography*, III (1865), 374-378. The engraver was Cook, perhaps Henry (1642-1700).

6. An oil portrait attributed to Samuel Cooper (1609-1672) and lent by J. G. Fanshawe to the South Kensington Museum in 1865; Williamson, p. 23.

7. A miniature, painted in oil on copper, attributed to Samuel Cooper, and said to have been painted about 1654 or 1655. It was lent to the South Kensington Museum in 1865 by the then owner, W. Phillips; Williamson, p. 23. It measures 3 1/3 inches high by 2 1/3 inches across. The present owner, Oliver Watney, Esq., writes to me that it came to his father, Vernon Watney, from the collection of Dr. Propert. To the best of my knowledge it has not been reproduced; and Mr. Watney tells me that it is not feasible for him to have a photograph made for me. I am grateful to him for giving me information about it.

8. Another miniature said to be by Samuel Cooper, showing Milton as a young man; Marsh, p. 187; Williamson, p. 22, with reproduction facing p. 21. This picture, which belonged to the Duke of Buccleuch and Queensberry at Montagu House in 1908, is still in the possession of the present Duke, to whom I am grateful for further information about it. It is a water-color, signed "S. C.," oval, and 3 inches high by 2.4 inches wide. It represents the poet as a young man, painted full

face, with long fair hair falling over his shoulders. The present Duke's great-grandfather bought it at the sale of the effects of a Mr. Villiers of Tours. The present Duke is very certain that it is of Milton. An entry in Michael Bryan's *Biographical and Critical Dictionary of Painters and Engravers*, revised by George Stanley, London, 1853, pp. 181-182, says that Cooper's portrait of Milton "was recently discovered, and is now in the possession of the Duke of Buccleuch. His Grace owes it to the country to have it engraved."

9. A portrait now in the possession of Sir John Dashwood of West Wycombe Park, Buckinghamshire; reproduced with a brief note in *Time*, March 2, 1953, p. 53. The owner has kindly told me that, though he does not yet have all the details of its previous history, Milton was his uncle in the eleventh line of descent [through Sir John Dashwood King, who in 1790 married Sarah Moore, the granddaughter of Milton's sister]. Dr. French Fogle of the Huntington Library kindly tells me that this portrait came to light some twenty years ago when Sir John's father was having some portraits cleaned. In the process this picture, then apparently merely a piece of whitewashed canvas, proved after the application of cleaner to have the word "Milton" on it. Thomas Langley's *History and Antiquities of the Hundred of Desborough, and Deanery of Wycombe, in Buckinghamshire* (London, 1797, p. 417) mentions a "Milton, fine, supposed to be original," closely resembling the Faithorne. Though the reproduction in *Time* does not closely resemble other known portraits of Milton, Sir John is carrying on investigations about it.

10. A portrait said formerly to be of Milton by William Dobson (1610-1646), and now in Dr. Williams's Library in London; Marsh, no. 158; Williamson, pp. 19, 86. It shows a man in a gown with plain wide square collar and voluminous folds, and wearing very long hair. Roger Thomas, Esq., the Librarian, kindly writes to me that his staff has long been satisfied that it is not a picture of Milton, and that there is no record of how it came to the Library. For that matter, neither Marsh nor Williamson believed it to be of Milton. Though it has been reproduced as such in a drawing by J. Thurston engraved by J. T. Wedgwood and published in 1820 by Walker and printed by B. McQueen, it can be definitely eliminated from the list of genuine Miltons.

11. Another portrait by Dobson, measuring 7 7/8 inches by 5 3/8 inches and matching the description of the preceding, and recently in the collection of the late Booth Tarkington. It was reproduced in color in his *Some Old Portraits*, 1939, facing p. 40; and in black and white as the frontispiece of Dora Neill Raymond's *Oliver's Secretary*, 1932. Though both Mr. Tarkington and his secretary, Miss Elizabeth Trotter, gave me generous information about his picture and firmly believed

[139]

that it was of Milton, I cannot agree with them. It bears almost no resemblance to the other known representations of him.

12. A picture in the possession of the Reverend J. Elderton of Bath and described by him in the *Gentleman's Magazine*, LXI (1791), 39, and reproduced at LXII (1792), plate 3, facing p. 17. He said that it had belonged to his child's ancestor Sir Edward Seymour [1633-1708?]. A discussion of it in later issues of the same journal (LXI, 399, 603-605, 885-887) suggested variously that the picture was a fraud, that it was of Selden, and that it was of Milton. It is mentioned in Marsh, no. 150, and in Williamson, pp. 18, 83. It has not been heard of in recent years.

13. A full-length standing figure, showing a man with curly hair, in a long cloak, knee breeches, stockings, and shoes, with white bands about his neck; inscribed: "Milton. J. Fougeron sculp.," and measuring 4¼ inches by 2½ inches; Williamson, p. 89.

14. A portrait lent in 1908 by Major Galton of Hadzor; Williamson, p. 36. Through the kindness of the Postmaster of Droitwich, Worcestershire (Mr. J. F. Ballard) I learn that Major Galton's paintings were sold at the time of his death some thirty years ago. Though Lady Sandys, a descendant of the Galton family, has generously tried to trace it, she kindly informs me that she has been able to find no trace of it.

15. A portrait lent in 1908 by E. Garnett, Esq., of Horsforth; Williamson, p. 36. His son David Garnett, Esq., kindly writes me that he knows of no such picture and thinks the attribution must be an error.

16. A painting said to have belonged to a bookseller named Graves; Marsh, p. 187. This may possibly be the same as the Walker described below (no. 44).

17. A portrait said to have been done between 1650 and 1670 painted "within the separable sides of a Spanish dollar," exhibited by a Mr. Gray at a meeting of the Archaeological Section of the Historic Society of Lancashire and Cheshire on December 6, 1855, and mentioned in the Society's *Transactions*, VIII (1856), 228.

18. A seal ring said to be Milton's. R. Grindall wrote to John Wilkes on April 15, 1780, sealing his letter with "a head of Milton": "This seal Ring of Milton is yours if I die first"; *Fourth Report of the Royal Commission on Historical Manuscripts* (papers of Colonel Macaulay), 1874, p. 399. This may have some relation to the steel puncheon described above at II, 337-338.

19. An alleged portrait by James Houseman (Jacob Huysmans, d. 1696), listed in a catalogue of Chinnock and Galsworthy in 1860; Marsh, p. 187n.

20. A portrait by an unknown artist, of unknown date, of dubious authority, now in the Huntington Library. Dr. French Fogle kindly informs me that it is based on Faithorne, but that the artist has added

hands, the right one resting on a large red volume, perhaps the Bible, and bearing a small gold band on the little finger. Its history before Mr. Huntington acquired it from Stevens and Brown in London in 1922 is vague.

21. A marble bust said to have been made from life by an Italian sculptor during Milton's visit to Italy; Marsh, p. 187. Thomas Hollis searched in vain for it in 1762, but a Mr. Labouchere purchased it in 1850 for 200 guineas. What is presumably the same bust is mentioned in the Pickering edition of Milton's *Works*, 1851, I, clxxx, as belonging to the Reverend Charles Woodward of Manchester Square.

22. The portrait by an unknown artist once owned by Charles Lamb and reproduced above as the frontispiece to Volume III; see also III, vi. A further word about this interesting portrait is needed. Its history before Lamb acquired it is unknown, but it is enough like other pictures of Milton to deserve careful consideration. Neither Marsh nor Williamson mentions it. Lamb apparently picked it up in 1815 for a few shillings, or rather his brother did so and turned it over to him. He mentioned it in several letters to Wordsworth as undoubtedly genuine, one of his greatest treasures, and the first thing which he put carefully in place when he moved from one residence to another. He gave it to Emma Isola as a marriage portion, with the idea apparently that it would eventually go to Wordsworth. After a period of obscurity it appeared in 1881 and was bought for the New York Public Library, which now owns it. Among possible painters mentioned for it are Van Dyck and Sir Peter Lely. See E. V. Lucas's edition of Lamb's *Letters*, 1935, II, 154, 159, 320, 407, and III, 127, 372. Lucas reproduced it in the 1905 edition of the *Letters*, VI, facing p. 460.

23. A portrait lent in 1908 by Lord Leconfield; Williamson, pp. 25, 35. The present Lord Leconfield kindly informs me that this portrait now belongs to his nephew, Mr. John Wyndham. It is an oil painting measuring 18 inches by 14½ inches, nearly full face, with dark coat and deep white collar and tassel. Lord Leconfield regards it as by a seventeenth-century, though unknown, painter. His family has regularly believed that it formed part of the collection of pictures bought by Algernon Percy, tenth Earl of Northumberland [1602-1668], a nobleman of Parliamentary sympathies. He also pronounces it an entirely different picture from (and inferior to) that reproduced as from the collection of a former Lord Leconfield in Richard Garnett and Edmund Gosse's *English Literature An Illustrated Record*, III (1906), 17, which closely resembles the Faithorne engraving.

From the photograph which Lord Leconfield has kindly sent me, however, I believe that his portrait is genuinely of Milton and that it is closely related to the Bayfordbury and the Faithorne pictures (see above under 1670) and to the Lamb portrait (see the preceding item).

24. A full-face portrait of a blind man with black vest, gown, white collar with tassels, and long hair; inscribed: "Marckl d. Mad Ethiou," measuring 3½ by 3½ inches; Williamson, pp. 20, 89.

25. A print engraved by R. Page "from an original painting." Marsh, no. 160; Williamson, pp. 20, 87. Williamson calls it absurd.

26. A miniature said to have belonged to the Duchess of Portland, showing Milton's face "severe in youthful beauty"; Todd, 1 (1826), 236; Marsh, p. 186. My letter to the present Duke of Portland brought me an answer from Francis Needham, Esq., former librarian at Welbeck. Mr. Needham informed me that a sale catalogue of the Portland family in 1786 carried an entry of this miniature and a corresponding one of Milton's mother in a tortoise-shell case. But he called my attention to the fact that in 1916 the late R. W. Goulding said in *The Welbeck Abbey Miniatures* (Walpole Society, IV, 14) that the miniature was then at Belvoir Castle. He thinks that it may still be there, though his requests for information have brought no reply.

27. A portrait formerly in the Examination Hall of Queen's College, Belfast, Northern Ireland; Williamson, p. 25. The present Librarian of the University, Mr. J. J. Graneek, kindly informs me that this portrait is now in the University Library, and that it has been in the possession of Queen's College since its foundation in 1849. He says that it professes to be a portrait of Milton at the age of 62, in 1670, and that it measures 26 inches high by 23 3/8 inches wide. I am indebted to P. A. Larkin, Esq., Sub-Librarian of the University, for an excellent photographic reproduction. Though at first it appears to be very different from other portraits of Milton, it looks more like the Faithorne engraving the more one looks at it. I suspect it is a poor copy, but I have no idea when it was made.

28. An engraving by W. Ridley, printed for C. Cooke, 17 Paternoster Row, in 1800, said to be taken from a bust in the possession of the proprietor, and published in *Cooke's Pocket Edition of Select English Poets*; Marsh, no. 128; Williamson, p. 77. The bust has not been located.

29. An excellent original painting, conjectured by some to be by Riley or Dobson, belonging early in the nineteenth century to John Charnock, Jr., Esq., of Greenwich; Todd, 1 (1826), 240; Marsh, pp. 185-186.

30. An oil painting on canvas measuring 54 by 60 inches, showing the subject seated at a table with his hand resting on a book; mentioned in a catalogue of H. Rodd in 1824 and priced at 15 guineas; Williamson, p. 26.

31. A terra-cotta bust by Roubilliac, now in the Scottish National Portrait Gallery; London *Times*, August 17, 1925, p. 13e. Mr. R. E. Hutchison, Keeper, kindly writes me that the Gallery acquired this bust

in 1925 from a London dealer who had bought it in the Caledonian Market. It is likely that it may have been originally in the collection of William Benson (1682-1754). This is the original of no. 3 above. It bears a considerable resemblance to the Faithorne engraving.

32. A portrait which in 1908 was in the collection of Lord Sackville at Knole, Sevenoaks; Williamson, pp. 22, 35. It is said to be in grisaille, 7 feet 1 inch by 4 feet 10 inches. Williamson says it may be by De Wit.

33. A bust said to have been made while Milton was visiting Manso in Naples in 1638. Denis Saurat, who reproduced it as the frontispiece of the 1944 edition of his *Milton Man and Thinker*, says (p. v) that it was bought in Italy about 1880-1890 by a clergyman, from whom it passed to Émile Mond and later to himself. It somewhat resembles the Christ's College bust (above, II, 337). M. Saurat has kindly written to me that he has since presented the bust to the National Portrait Gallery. He considers it of remarkable beauty, giving a unique impression of Milton as a young man. D. T. Piper, Esq., Assistant Keeper of the National Portrait Gallery, kindly informs me that the bust is of marble, 18½ inches high, showing Milton clean-shaven and with long hair. He believes that it may have been done in the early eighteenth century but that it descends from the Faithorne engraving.

34. A portrait in oil on mahogany panel, measuring 2 feet 11 inches by 2 feet 5 inches, belonging in 1908 to the late Arthur E. Shipley, Esq., Master of Christ's College, Cambridge; Williamson, p. 34. It is said to have come down from Sir John Ryther, a gentleman of Cromwell's court and a personal friend of Milton. The grounds of the latter assertion are not given. The present Master of Christ's College, Brian W. Downes, Esq., kindly informs me that despite his attempts and those of relatives of Dr. Shipley to locate this picture among members of the Shipley family, he cannot discover what became of it after 1908. Nor does he remember ever having seen it in Dr. Shipley's rooms, though he frequently visited there from 1911 onwards.

35. A seal, perhaps by Thomas Simon, which may or may not be identical with one of those mentioned above at II, 337-338. It is very small, measuring only about 7/16 inch wide by ½ inch high. It shows a youthful face, turned slightly to its right; the gown is tightly buttoned, with a very narrow collar. Though the seal itself seems to be lost, a wax impression survives in the Hunter Coin Cabinet of the Hunterian Museum in Glasgow. Miss Anne S. Robertson, Curator of the Cabinet, who very kindly sent me a plaster cast of the impression, thinks that it must have belonged to William Hunter before his death in 1783. I am grateful to Dr. Thomas O. Mabbott for first calling my attention to this seal.

36. A life-sized portrait in oils partly inlaid in the paneled wainscot at Stansted Park, Sussex, belonging in 1860 to a Mr. Way; Marsh,

p. 187. Frank O'B. Adams, Esq., kindly writes to me from the Post Office at Rowlands Castle, Hampshire, that Stansted House burned down in 1900, and that probably the portrait, like practically all the other contents of the house, was destroyed at that time.

37. A portrait in oil on canvas, said to have been painted by Robert Streater (1624-1680), now in the Metropolitan Museum of Art in New York but for the last several years on loan to Fairleigh Dickinson College. It is in oil on canvas, measuring 27¼ inches by 21½ inches; it is listed on p. 93 of the Museum's catalogue of European paintings. Presented to the Museum in 1908 by Mrs. Wheeler Smith, it is thought to have been previously in the collection of Robert Gilmor of Baltimore. Mr. Theodore Rousseau, Jr., Curator of Paintings at the Museum, kindly tells me that it originally came to the Museum as a Van Dyck, that it was later attributed to the Flemish school, and that it was finally considered to be by Streater. It was reproduced in the *Burlington Magazine for Connoisseurs*, LXXXIV (1944), facing p. 151, as a picture of John Lilburne or possibly of John Milton. It seems to me sufficiently different from the other known pictures of the poet to be difficult to accept as genuinely of Milton.

38. A picture belonging to Lord Townshend at Raynham, Norfolk, about 1850; Milton's *Poetical Works*, ed. Mitford, 1 (1852), xc; Marsh, p. 186. The present Lord Townshend has kindly answered my inquiry by reporting that he has no record of any picture of Milton as ever having been in his family's possession. He has a portrait of a man in seventeenth-century Puritan dress, which could conceivably have been said to be of Milton, but there is no evidence that it is such.

39. A half-length portrait, formerly thought to be of Milton, by Pieter van der Plas, now in the National Portrait Gallery in London; Marsh, nos. 156-157; Williamson, pp. 19, 85, with reproduction facing p. 19. It shows a man in a plain buttoned coat and a simple white collar, with a pilgrim's staff and bottle in the background on one side and a representation of the risen Christ on the other. D. T. Piper, Esq., Assistant Keeper of the Gallery, kindly informs me that it was left to the National Gallery by Capel Lofft in 1839 and was deposited on loan in the National Portrait Gallery in 1883. It was attributed to Milton in an engraving published by W. Stevenson of Norwich in 1794. But according to Mr. Piper, the identification of the portrait as Milton has long been discredited; indeed it is uncertain whether Pieter van der Plas (whichever of that name the painter may be) or any of his family ever visited England; and the subject may very likely be a Dutch pilgrim. Further references to this picture may be found in the *Gentleman's Magazine*, LXVII (1798), 940; *Academy*, LI (1897), 356; *Notes and Queries*, x, x (1908), 481-482; *Time*, March 17, 1941, p. 97, and April 7, 1941, p. 4.

40. A miniature portrait on vellum on card, measuring 3 inches by 2¼ inches, of a man in a black doublet and plain collar, signed "S. C." This portrait, now in the Victoria and Albert Museum, is a part of the Jones Bequest and is catalogued as No. 607-1882. Leigh Ashton, Esq., the Director and Secretary, considers it an eighteenth-century imitation of a seventeenth-century work, possibly copied after Samuel Cooper or possibly merely worked up from the imagination. From the photograph which Mr. Ashton kindly sent me, it bears no resemblance to any other known picture of Milton.

41. A portrait said to be of Milton in middle age and belonging in the early nineteenth century to a Mr. Waldron; Todd, 1 (1826), 143, 146.

42. A portrait said to be by Robert Walker (d. 1658?) and to have belonged early in the nineteenth century to Sir Joseph Banks and later to Archdeacon Bonney of Lincoln; Marsh, p. 187. This may be identical with that shown in the exhibition of 1908 by the Reverend C. P. Jones; Williamson, p. 36. A correspondent in *Notes and Queries*, II, xii (1861), 2, states that Milton's daughter Deborah, when she met Vertue on August 12, 1721, rejected Walker's portrait as not of her father; but Vertue's account as given by Masson (1, 1881, 309) does not mention Walker's name. Mrs. J. Varley, Archivist of the Lincolnshire Archives Committee, kindly writes that the picture is now untraceable. Canon A. E. Kaye of Lincoln, to whose brother, the late Archdeacon Kaye, the portrait came upon the death of Archdeacon Bonney, has generously sent me further information. He says that an amateur who treated the portrait found a painting of a cavalier underneath, but spoiled the Milton in the process. Even the discovery of the picture would therefore now be of no use.

43. A full-faced portrait (also by Walker?) on a panel measuring 17½ inches by 14½ inches, formerly in the collection of Sir Thomas William Holburne, 5th and last Baronet of Menstrie, and now in the Holburne of Menstrie Museum of Art in Bath; Williamson, p. 25. The present curator of the Museum, Hugo Burrow, Esq., informs me that, though this portrait was formerly thought to be contemporary, that view is now open to question. The photograph which he has kindly supplied to me differs considerably from other recognized portraits of Milton, though it bears a very distant resemblance to the Lamb portrait (above, no. 22).

44. A portrait said to be by Walker and now in the W. A. Clark Library in Los Angeles. Dr. French Fogle of the Huntington Library kindly informs me that it came in 1922 from the Burdett-Coutts family, who had owned it since 1851. It measures 22½ inches by 17½ inches. It is said to have been found by a Mr. John Burrows in a tavern called the St. John of Jerusalem in St. John's Street, Clerkenwell, in

1800. The landlord at that time said that it had been in the tavern for many years and was an authentic portrait of Milton. Through various other hands it came about 1850 to Messrs. Graves of Pall Mall, who restored it and pronounced it an authentic portrait of Milton by Walker. Though it bears some resemblance to the Faithorne engraving, it differs enough so that it may possibly be of some other person than Milton. It may possibly be the same picture as that mentioned above in number 16.

45. A portrait lent in 1908 by Mr. W. Webber, slightly resembling the Onslow portrait; Williamson, p. 37.

46. A so-called fine original portrait of Milton at West Wycombe Manor House, Buckinghamshire; Todd, 1 (1826), 240; Marsh, p. 186. This may be the same as number 9 above.

47. An engraving showing the half-length figure of a man seated in a chair, wearing buttoned vest, gown, white collar with tassels, and long hair; Williamson, p. 89. It measures 2½ inches by 2 inches. Williamson gives no location.

AUTOBIOGRAPHY (?).

q̄ Mʳ Allam of Edm: hall Oxon. of Mʳ. J. Milton's life writt by himselfe. v. pagg.

Aubrey, f. 66v; Darbishire, p. 15. Though these words could mean that Aubrey was searching for a manuscript autobiography, he more probably had in mind asking Andrew Allam some question about Milton's *Defensio Secunda*, which in the Hague editions contains exactly five leaves (not pages) of autobiography. John Diekhoff's *Milton on Himself* (1939) gathers in one volume Milton's many references to his own life scattered through his writings.

MILTON'S FAMILY BEFORE HIS BIRTH

1485. MILTON FAMILY ENGAGED IN WARS OF ROSES;
ORIGINS IN OXFORDSHIRE.

... he [the poet Milton] is said to have been Descended of
an Ancient Family of the *Miltons*, of *Milton*, near *Abington*
in *Oxfordshire*; where they had been a long time seated, as appears by the Monuments still to be seen in *Milton*-Church, till
one of the Family having taken the wrong side, in the Contests
between the Houses of *York* and *Lancaster*, was sequestred of
all his Estate, but what he held by his Wife.

Phillips, p. iv; Darbishire, p. 51; Masson, 1 (1881), 10. This account, vague though it is, is not too convincing. Masson reported as
long ago as 1859 (I, 10) that no trace of the monuments in the Milton
church was then in existence; and he noted that Newton had had the
same experience 100 years earlier. How much truth there may be in the
details of the rest of the account we cannot be sure. Our earliest tan-
gible hold on Milton's family comes with the poet's father's grandfather
Henry Milton (see below under date of November 21, 1558) and with
his mother's grandfather John Jeffrey (below, February 22, 1550/1).
But the above entry, together with the corresponding one immediately
below from the "earliest biography," helps to preserve a biographical
tradition.

The learned Mr John Milton, born about the yeer sixteen
hundred and eight, is said to bee descended from an antient
Knightly Family in Buckingamshire, that gave name to the
chief place of thir abode.

The "earliest" biography, f. 140; Darbishire, p. 18.

   Mr *John Milton*
was of an Oxfordshire familie.

Aubrey, f. 63; Darbishire, p. 1; Masson, 1 (1881), 8.

[He was] descended from those of his name who have lived
beyond all record at *Milton* near *Halton* and *Thame* in *Oxfordshire*.

Wood, I, 880; Darbishire, p. 35.

1551. FEBRUARY 22. MOTHER'S FATHER'S FATHER
JOHN JEFFREY MAKES WILL.

Jn the name of god Amen The xxijth daye of ffebruary Anno

dnī Millimo quingentesimo quīquagesimo . . . J John Jefferye
of Est Hanyngfeld in the Countie of Essex yoman . . . do make
this my present testament and last will . . . [bequeaths income
from certain property] vnto my sonne Paule and his assignes
. . . Also J do gyve vnto my sonnes John Paule and Thomas the
younger. that ys to saye to eūyone of them a fetherbedd a Mat-
teris two payre of sheetɋ one payre of blankettɋ. a boulster a
Coūlet and Sixe pecɋ of pewter egallye to be destributed/ And
to eūy of my said sonnes J give a sylū sponē/ all Whiche premisses . . . J will yt shalbe egally distributed vnto my said Chil-
dreñ by my said wyf . . . Jn witnes whereof to this my present
testmᵗ J haue setto my signe & Seale the daye and yere abovesaid in the presens of thes psones vnderwrytten/ Robert [blank].
John Steward Thomas Jeffery Richard Jefferie John Jefferie.
Johañ Jefferie Thomas Blakmore William Bright tenñtɋ/
Thomas Wardall and me Dauid Sympson and other

This Codcill indented made the daie and yere above wryten
. . . Jtem J giue vnto my sonne Paule ffyftie poundɋ of good
and lawfull money of England/ and one specialtie of the some
of xiijˡⁱ vjˢ viijᵈ wherin oñ Richard Bourne standeth bounden.
vnto my sonne in lawe David Sympson whiche specialtie ys Annexed vnto the said Paules. Jndenture/ Also J giue more vnto
the said Paule in redy money fyve m̄rkɋ/ to be delyūed vnto
my said sonne Paule by my said wyff or her assigñ when he shall
come to thage of xxjᵗⁱ yeres/. . .

Probatum fuit testamentū vnacū Codicillo annex̄ coram dnō
Cant' Archiepō apud London xxj° die Menss Marcij Anno dñi
Millimo quingentesimo quīquagesimo Juramento Executorū in
hmoī testamento noīatorɋ/ Ac approbatū et insinuatū Comissois
fuit admīstracō omī bonorū &c' dcī defuncti p̄fat'/ ex̄/ De bene
et fidelir' Admīstrand eadem/ Ac de pleno Jnuʳⁱᵒ &c' exhibend/
Ad sancta dei Euñgelia Jurat'

Prerogative Court of Canterbury, 9 Bucke; Joseph Lemuel Chester
in the *Athenaeum*, 1880, I, 696; Masson, I (1881), 34, 38. In this
long and detailed will, containing many bequests, the testator names a
large number of members of his family and various estates in East Han-

ningfield and in Chelmsford, co. Essex. Those mentioned include his wife Johan; his sons John, Thomas the elder, Thomas the younger, Richard, and Paul; his son-in-law David Sympson; his sisters Bridget, Mary, Johan Tyrrell (with her children John the elder, John the younger, Richard, and Alice), and Alice Webb (with an unnamed daughter); and various friends and employees. This Paul is almost surely the father of the poet's mother. A brief genealogical chart based on this will and on Chester and Masson may clarify the relationships.

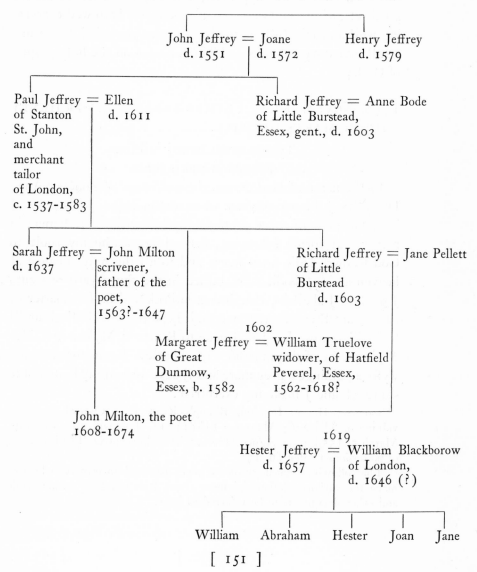

Some of the above material comes also from the 1634 Visitation of Essex, Publications of the Harleian Society, XIII (1878), i, 427.

[This will, together with the annexed codicil, was proved before the lord Archbishop of Canterbury in London on the 21st day of the month of March in the year of our Lord 1550 (i.e., 1550/1) on the oath of the executors named in a will of this sort. And it was approved, and administration of all the goods etc. of the said deceased aforesaid was bestowed concerning well and faithfully administering the same and concerning a full inventory etc. to be exhibited. Sworn on the holy gospels of God.]

1558. NOVEMBER 21. FATHER'S GRANDFATHER HENRY MILTON MAKES HIS WILL.

Testamentum henrij millton

de Stanton Sancti Johīs

In the name of God Amen, the xxi[th] daye of nouēber Anno D[ni] 1558 J Henry Mylton of Staunton Saynt Jonis sicke of body but pfect of mynd do make my last will and testament in maner and forme foloweing, fyrst J bequeathe my soule to God to owre ladie saynt marie and to all the holy cōpanye of heaven and my bodie to be buried in the churchyard of stantō J geue to Jsabell my daughter a bullock and half a quarter of barley and Richard my sonne shall kepe the sayd bullock untill he be iij yeares olde Jtm̄ J geue to Rowland Mylton and Alys Mylton eche of theym halffe a q[r] of barleye J geue to Agnes my wyffe a geldinge a grey mare and ij keye and all my householde stuffe whome J make my executrixe.

Somerset House, London, Bishop's Registry of Oxford, Series 1, volume 6, folio 236; Masson, 1 (1881), 14. This will was proved on March 5, 1558/9, by Agnes Milton, wife and executrix. The inventory of possessions totaled £6. 19s.

The following genealogy of the poet's paternal ancestry will help to make the various relationships more clear. It is based on various wills and other documents to be referred to later.

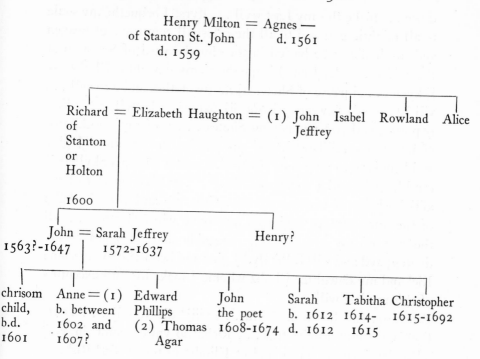

Henry Milton = Agnes —
of Stanton St. John   d. 1561
d. 1559

Richard = Elizabeth Haughton = (1) John   Isabel   Rowland   Alice
of   Jeffrey
Stanton
or
Holton

1600

John = Sarah Jeffrey   Henry?
1563?-1647   1572-1637

chrisom   Anne = (1) Edward   John   Sarah   Tabitha   Christopher
child,   b. between   Phillips   the poet   b. 1612   1614-   1615-1692
b.d.   1602 and   (2) Thomas   1608-1674   d. 1612   1615
1601   1607?   Agar

1559. FEBRUARY 17. MOTHER'S FATHER PAUL JEF-
FREY TAKES FREEDOM AS MERCHANT TAILOR.

Jeoffrey, Paulus. Ricum Bourne. 17 febru 1558 5 & 6 P & M.

I am grateful to Mr. Fairfax Lucy, Clerk of the Company of Merchant Taylors in 1939, for sending me this transcript of the entry in
the records of the Company. Hyde Clarke had mentioned it in the
Athenaeum for 1879, II, 464-465. The telegraphic entry may be explained as meaning that Paul Jeffrey, who had been apprenticed to
Richard Bourne, was admitted to the freedom of the Company on
February 17, in the 5th and 6th years, respectively, of Philip and Mary,
which was 1559. The entry comes from the Book of Admissions.

1561. MARCH 9. FATHER'S GRANDMOTHER AGNES MIL-
TON MAKES WILL.

Testamentum Agnete mylton de Staunton Sñcti Johanñis
Jn the name of god amen the ix^th daye of m̄che anno dnī 1560.
J agnes mylton of Staunton Saynt Jonys in the cow̄t oxon wy-

dowe . . . make this my Last wyll . . . ffyrst J bequethe my soule
to all mightie god and to all the celestiall companye of heaven
and my bodie to be buried in the churche yard of Staunton at
the belferye ende, Jtem J bequethe to my dawghter Elsabz my
ij kyen . . . xi payre of Shetes iiij meate clothes and a towell . . .
viij platters ij Sawcers a bason iiij pannes, a kettell, a Skyllett
ij pottes, and two wynnoying Shetes . . . v of my smockẹ two
of my best candillstickẹ, and the whele; ffurthermore J giue
and bequethe to my sonne Richard. a pott a pānne a Skyllett ij
candill stickẹ and a wynnynge Shete . . . halffe a quarter of the
xiiij bushellẹ of barleye wch he owithe me and twoo bushellẹ
of the same barleye J giue to my sonne willm howse . . . All
the rest of my goodes both moueable and vnmoueable my
deptes payd and will fullfyllyd J giue and bequethe to my sonne
Ric' and my dawghter Elsabz whome J make my full executors
of this my last will . . .
Probatum fuit hoc testamentū . . . xiiij° die Junnij . . . 1561.
Cõmissaqz erat administra° . . . Richardo vni executor' in Tes-
ta^to noiat' in psona propri[a] et Elisabz in psona dict' Ric^t . . .
[Jn]uentariū ————————————————— vij^li iiij^s iii[j^d]

Bodleian Library, MS. Wills Oxon 184, ff. 2-2v; Masson, 1 (1881),
15. Agnes Milton was the widow of Henry, whose will is given above
under date of November 21, 1558. In Masson's time this will, like
others of the Bishop's Registry of Oxford, was kept in Somerset House
in London.

[This will was proved on June 14, 1561. Administration
was given to Richard (Milton), one of the executors named in
the will, in his own person, and to Elizabeth in the person of
the said Richard. Inventory: £7 4s. 4d.]

1563. POET'S FATHER BORN.

(2) That his Father *Joh. Milton* . . . was a Native of *Halton*
in *Oxford*shire. . . .

Wood, 1, 880; Darbishire, p. 35; Masson, 1 (1881), 8. There seems
to be no dependable basis for deciding when the poet's father John Milton the scrivener was born. Many statements about his age appear in
records printed in these volumes, but they are not consistent. The best

we can do is to collect all these references, chiefly from depositions in Chancery actions, but occasionally from other sources, and estimate the probabilities. References to his age appear in Volume I on pp. 5, 24, 25, 34, 44, 56, 63, 66, 218, 276, 284, 285, and 292. They also occur below under dates of July 3, 1604, October 23, 1604, January 4, 1605, January 21, 1605, April 24, 1605, and May 15, 1612. Of these 19 mentions, 5 put his birth in 1563, 3 in 1564, 6 in 1565, 1 in 1566, 1 in 1567, 2 in 1568, and 1 in 1569. In addition, the statements of Christopher Milton (I, 320) and of Aubrey (III, 199) also point towards 1563.

The place of his birth has been troublesome. For some odd reason Milton's granddaughter Elizabeth Foster informed Thomas Birch (*A Complete Collection of the . . . Works of John Milton*, 1738, I, lxii) that *"Milton's* Father was born in *France."* But she later told Newton (*Paradise Lost*, ed. Newton, 1749, I, lix) that "she was mistaken in informing Mr. Birch, what he had printed upon her authority, that Milton's father was born in France; and a brother of hers who was then living was very angry with her for it, and like a true-born English-man resented it highly, that the family should be thought to bear any relation to France." Professor Parker suggests to me that perhaps the elder Milton did not actually know the date of his own birth until some-how along about the 1620's he found it out and that thereafter he gave his age accurately. This theory fits with the facts as we now have them, but I fear that it does not work very consistently with the general prac-tice in depositions. Christopher Milton, for example, who could surely have ascertained the date of his own birth easily from the family Bible in his own brother's possession, more often than not was off a year or more in his statements. Of four depositions made in 1658, 1663, 1672, and 1674 (all given in volumes IV and V of this present work), he erred by a year or more in three. More glaring is the inaccuracy of the poet himself in giving his age for the allegation on his third marriage. Though he called himself "aged about 50 yeares" (above, IV, 381), he was at that time actually 54 years and 2 months old. In short, any age which depends upon the statement of the person himself, during the period here concerned, is likely to be only approximately correct.

Mr Milton lived next Towne to Fosthill. within ½ a mile [Holton]. . . .

Aubrey, f. 68v; Darbishire, p. 8. The square brackets are in Aubrey. He first wrote "like Holton," then crossed out "like," and added the brackets. This note comes beside the line for the poet's grandfather in Aubrey's little genealogical chart.

John and *Christopher* [Milton] were Sons of *John Milton* of *Halton*, of *Christ-church* in *Oxon*, (as 'tis said) Son of *John Milton* of *Halton* near to *Forshill*, Ranger or Sub-Ranger of *Shotover*. . . .

John Guillim, *A Display of Heraldry*, 1724, p. 210; quoted in British Museum Add. MS. 19,142, f. 79. The reference to Christ Church is puzzling for two reasons: first, because there is no such town or city known in Oxfordshire, and second, because it suggests a possible confusion with the assertion (given below) that the poet's father was educated at Christ Church in Oxford. But it is remotely possible that both statements are confused ways of stating that he was born and grew up within the diocese of the Cathedral of Oxford, which is part of Christ Church, Oxford.

1572. MOTHER BORN.

Though no record of Sarah Milton's birth has been found, it seems likely that it took place in 1572. For evidence, see the entries below under dates of April 11, 1572, and February 11, 1573.

1572. MARCH 9. MOTHER'S FATHER'S MOTHER JOAN JEFFREY MAKES WILL.

Jn yᵉ name of god amē: J Jone Jeffery wyddow of yᵉ towne of Est hanningfeld in yᵉ coūty: of Essex . . . do ordeyne & make this my wil and testymēt yᵉ ixᵒ die of march Aᵒ Doṁ 1572 . . . al yᵉ Rest of my goodꝑ boeth moveables and vnmoveables J wil & bequeth to Jhon Jeffery my sonne whō J mak my ful executor. . . .

Essex Record Office, D/ABW 21/88, 1573; first described by J. L. Chester in the *Athenaeum* for 1880, I, 696. The older reference for this document was the Commissary Court of London, Essex, and Herts. Joan seems to have been the widow of John Jeffrey, whose will appears above under date of February 22, 1551. According to Colonel Chester their son John's will, given above under date of February 11, 1573, mentions the present will, so that Joan must have been dead before that date. The date 1572 here must therefore mean 1571/2, as Chester says, rather than 1572/3, under which the Essex Record Office files the will. Joan Jeffrey leaves bequests to John and Richard, sons of her son Richard Jeffrey; to Richard, Thomas, Edward, William, Joan, and Prowe (Prue?), children of her son Thomas; and to her son John as above. But common given names like John, Thomas, Richard, and the like occur so often in families that it is difficult to be sure of identifications.

[156]

1572. APRIL 11. MOTHER'S RELATIVE JOHN JEFFREY
MAKES WILL.

Jn the name of god amen The xi^th daie of Aprill 1572 . . .
J John Jeffrey of the pishe of Childerdiche in the countie of Essex . . . declare this my present testament . . . [with bequests
to:] Jvlyan my Wief . . . Thomas Jeffrey my sonne . . . my
sone John Jeffrey . . . my daughter Marye . . . Henry Jeffrey of
little bursted in the Countie of Essex [later called "my cozen"]
. . . eache of my wyeves children . . . my three poore systers
Agnes Jone and Katherin . . . euerie one of my seruñtp as well
men as maydes . . . my brother Stewarde . . . my brother Hale
. . . Richard Jeffries wief . . . to Pawle Jeffries wife twentie
shillingep . . . my brother Johnson . . . my Cosyn John Rogers
. . . my brother Lawrence . . . And . . . J do make & ordeine my
saied wief and my brother in lawe John Lawrence my execu-
tours but my Wieff onelie J will to haue all the profittp duringe
hir liffe. . . .

Probatū fuit Hmoī Testamentū Coram Dnō Cantuarieñ
Archiepō apud Londoñ xiij° Junij anno dnī 1572 . . . Juliane
relcē et exᶜᵖ . . . Johī Lawrence eх̄. . . .

[A will of this sort was proved before the Lord Archbishop
of Canterbury at London on June 13, 1572 . . . by Juliana, relict
and executrix, . . . (and by) John Lawrence, executor. . . .]

Principal Probate Registry, London, 19 Daper; Masson, 1 (1881),
36. The will is fairly long, with many bequests in addition to the few
listed above, which are chosen because the recipients are all designated
as relatives. The word "brother" as used for several men here includes
the wider meanings of brother-in-law etc. Paul Jeffrey, whose wife here
received twenty shillings, was named with several others as an overseer
of the will. Masson believes that the Henry Jeffrey named was probably a nephew; see his will under date of February 23, 1579. The exact
relationship of this John Jeffrey to the poet is not clear.

1573. FEBRUARY 11. MOTHER'S UNCLE JOHN JEFFREY
MAKES WILL.

Jn the name of God Amen the xj^th Day of ffebruary in the
yere of oʳ lorde God 1572 J John Jefferey of Esthanñyngfeld

[157]

in the Countie of Essex . . . geue & bequeth vnto my brother pawle Jefferey the Some of lxvj li xiijs iiijd lawfull englishe money to be p^d vnto hym hys executors or assignes W^{t}in one yere after my buryall/ Jtm J geue vnto Sara Jefferey the doughter of my brother paule Jefferey. the Some of C s^s to be p^d vnto hyr at hyr fulle age of xxj yeres . . . Jtm J geue & bequeth . . . to my brother paule Jefferey hys wyffe xxs. which J will shalbe payd vnto them w^{t}in one monthe after my buryall.

. . .

Essex Record Office, D/ABW 21/87; described by J. L. Chester in the *Athenaeum* for 1880, 1, 696; Masson, 1 (1881), 35, 38. The older reference for this document was the Commissary Court of the Bishop of London. The importance of this document is that it shows that the poet's mother Sarah was living by this date, and that presumably she was then an only child, since the testator provided that if she died before reaching the age of 21, the bequest should go to "the nexte chylde that shalbe lawfully begotton by my seyd brother paule Jefferey." Moreover, since the will of John Jeffrey of Childerditch, made on April 11, 1572, named Paul but none of his children, it is at least a fair guess that Sarah had been born since that date. John Jeffrey names also in his will his mother Joan, now deceased; his brothers Thomas the elder, Thomas the younger, and Richard; Thomas the elder's children Richard, Thomas, Edmund, William, Grace, and Joan; Thomas the younger's children Lettice, Joan, and Bridget; Richard's sons John and Richard; his brother-in-law Davy Sympson; and several cousins. Paul Jeffrey was one of several witnesses.

1577. GRANDFATHER RICHARD MILTON AN UNDER-RANGER OF SHOTOVER (?).

(3) That his Grandfather *Milton* whose Christian name was *John*, as he thinks, was an Under-Ranger or Keeper of the Forest of *Shotover* near to the said Town of *Halton*, but descended from those of his name who have lived beyond all record at *Milton* near *Halton* and *Thame* in *Oxfordshire*.

Wood, 1, 880; Darbishire, p. 35. The "he" in the second line probably refers to John Aubrey, from whom Wood got much of his material about Milton. Masson (1, 1881, 19) reminds us that no one has found any documentary proof of such an appointment. Wood's "John" is presumably an error for "Richard."

John Milton, of *Halton* near to *Forshill*, Ranger or sub-Ranger of *Shotover*, his Ancestors lived at *Milton* near to *Halton*, Rom. Cath.

John Guillim, *A Display of Heraldry*, 1724, p. 210. This entry is quoted substantially verbatim in Add. MS. 19,142, f. 79.

1577. OCTOBER 3. GRANDFATHER RICHARD MILTON ASSESSED IN STANTON ST. JOHN.

Oxoñ

This Jndenture made the thirde Day of October in the xix^th yere of the Reygñe of ou^r Souereygñe Ladye Elizabethe. . . .
The hundred of Bolington. . . .

Staunton   Rychard Mylton in goodẹ — iij^li — iij^s
St Johns

Public Record Office, Subsidy Rolls, E 179/162/341; mentioned in Hunter's MS. Add. 24,501, f. 13; Hunter, *Milton*, p. 4; Masson, 1 (1881), 16; Brennecke, p. 33. It is now generally accepted that this Richard Milton was the father of John the scrivener and the grandfather of the poet. The meaning of the entry is that Richard was assessed 3 shillings on a valuation of 3 pounds on his property in Stanton St. John. Brennecke says that the assessment was 5 pounds, though he does not refer to a source.

1579. FEBRUARY 23. MOTHER'S FATHER'S FATHER'S BROTHER HENRY JEFFREY MAKES WILL.

Jn the name of God Amen The Three and Twentieth daye of ffebruarye/ in the year of oure Lorde god after the Computacõn of Englande, One Thowsande ffyue hundred Seaventie Eight/ J Henry Jeffrie of litle birsted in the Countie of Essex yõman . . . doe ordaine and make this my last will and Testament . . . Jtem J geue vnto my Cosin Paule Jeffrie of London Three poundes, and to his wief Twentie shillinges, and to Sara his daughte^r ffourtie shillinges/ and to his yongest daughter Twentie shillinges, meaning them twoo that be nowe lyvinge at this pñte requiringe my Executor to paye it so shortlie as he maye conveniently . . . Theis beinge witnesses to this will Robert Carensdale, Robert Barrett, John Wells, Richard Bragge, Josias Hollengton. . . .

Probatum fuit hmoi Testamentum Apud London Coram ma-
gr̄o Willm̄o Drurye legum Doctore Curie Prerogatiue Cantua-
reū Commissario Decimo tertio Die mensis Maij Anno Dnī mil-
lim̄o Quingentesimo Septuagesimo nono/ Juramento magr̄i Ed-
wardi Orvell Notarij publici procuratoris Johannis Rogers Ex-
ecutoris in hmoī testamento noīat' Cui comissa fuit Adcō &cọ
De bene &cọ/ Ad Sancta Dei Euñgelia Jurat'/. . . .

Prerogative Court of Canterbury, 17 Bakon; Joseph Lemuel Chester
in the *Athenaeum*, 1880, 1, 696; Masson, 1 (1881), 36-38. Henry
Jeffrey seems to be a brother of the John Jeffrey whose will is given
above under date of February 22, 1551, and is therefore an uncle of
the poet's mother's father Paul Jeffrey. Henry Jeffrey's will is far too
long even to summarize. He names endless uncles, aunts, and especially
cousins; and he disposes of many properties in Essex and Suffolk. But
we may list a few names here: his beloved mother Julian Jeffrey (who
married his uncle Jeffrey!); his uncle John Jeffrey, late of Stratford,
with his sons John and Thomas, the first of whom may be Paul's father;
his brother-in-law John Rogers, whom he named as executor of his
will; numerous brothers-in-law named Morse; various cousins named
Jeffrey, including two Richards, one John of Harifeld, and one Thomas
of Chensford; and his wife, who remains unnamed. The cousin Paul
mentioned in the passage quoted is presumably the poet's mother's father.

[A will of this sort was proved at London before Master
William Drury, Doctor of Laws and Commissary of the Prerogative Court of Canterbury, on the 13th day of the month of
May in the year of our Lord 1579, on the oath of Master Edward Orvell, Notary Public and agent of John Rogers, the
executor named in a will of this sort; to whom was committed
administration etc. sworn on the holy gospels of God concerning
well etc. . . .]

1580. FATHER ALLEGEDLY ATTENDS CHRIST CHURCH, OXFORD.

His father was brought-up in yᵉ Univʳsity of Oxōn: at Christ-
church.

Aubrey, f. 63; Darbishire, p. 1; Masson, 1 (1881), 23. As Masson
points out, there is no evidence either for or against Aubrey's statement,
except that the absence of the father's name from the registers of the

University weighs somewhat heavily against it. But Ernest Brennecke (pp. 5-6) accepts Aubrey's statement almost conclusively, adds the hypothesis that Milton was a boy chorister at Oxford, and devotes nearly twenty pages (3-24) to a description of his activities on that assumption. He even goes further in saying, "It was nothing less than a master stroke to get the boy admitted as a chorister of Christ Church," because his "training both as a boy chorister and as a student would account most satisfactorily for the known details of his later career." In addition, he repeats, though skeptically, the rumor that Milton "may also have been resident at Magdalen College for some time" (p. 25). Mark Noble (*Monthly Mirror*, N. S. VI [1809], 202) asserts that it is "evident" that Milton so attended, though Noble gives no proof. Henry Foley (editor, *Records of the English Province of the Society of Jesus*, London, I [1877], 466-468; from Fletcher's *Contributions*, p. 56) suggests that Anthony Greenway, alias Tilney, who was at Magdalen College at about this period, may have been a schoolfellow of Milton. This suggestion may have been the basis of the guess that Milton was of Magdalen.

Even if we accept the guess that Milton went to Christ Church, we cannot assign a correct date. Masson quite plausibly gives the ages of fifteen to twenty as the likely times, and no one can do better. This wobbly hypothesis is therefore entered under the compromise date of 1580.

I should add that some earlier students have thought, like Professor Brennecke, in terms of the elder Milton's period at Oxford as having been that of a choir-boy in the church, but they usually think of it as replacing the idea of him as a student at the college. Both Mark Pattison, for example (*Milton*, 1901 [first edition, 1879], p. 3), and Hyde Clarke (in the *Athenaeum*, March 13, 1880, p. 344) put forward this theory.

Wood, the authority on Oxford, omits this note from Aubrey.

1582. MAY 11. GRANDFATHER RICHARD MILTON PROCLAIMED AS RECUSANT, AND EXCOMMUNICATED.

Vndecimo die Mensis Maij Ao *1582* in visitacōe nr̄a Archinali apud Oxoñ./

Jn dei noīe Amen. Nos Thomas Glasier l̄l doctor Archidiaconatus Oxoñ Officialis ltīme constitutus rite et ltime procedentes prunciamus omnes et singulos quorū noīa et cognoiā inferius describuntur vīz. Citatos pᵣconizatos non comparentes propter eorum manifestam contumaciam in non comparend in visitacoē nr̄a Archinali ad hos diem et locum sibi assignatos contumaces (iusticia id poscente et in paenā contumaciarū suarū hmoī excōmunicandos provt excōmunicavimus in his scriptis./

Mr Robertū Brian Rect S^{cti} Clemētᴇ

Dm̄y Willm̄ Lane Curatū oīm S^{ctorū}

Dm̄y [blank] Little Curatū de Haliewell

Dm̄y [blank] Heale Curat Staunton S^{cti} Jhōis

M^{rm̄} Thomam Elye Curat. de Horsepath

Josephū Barnes Gard. oīm S^{ctoru}. dimiss:/

Edwardū Turley ⎱ gard. de Haliwell,/
Ricm̄ Hoare —— ⎰

ffranciscū Gennis gardianū S^{cti} martini

Ricm̄ milton ⎱ gardianos Stantoñ S^{cti} Jhōis
Jhōem White ⎰

Henricū Hampton ⎱ ga^rdianos de Cuddesdon
Wilmū Pokius —— ⎰ comparuit Pokius et suscepit pro Hampton et habet ad inducend presentacionem die sabboti p^re [?] ad septimanam

Willm̄ Curtes ⎱ ga^rdianos de Culuehm[?]
Jhōem Powell, ⎰

Jta est.   [signed] Tho. Glasier./

Bodleian, MS. O.A.P. Oxon. e. 11, f. 182v; Hyde Clarke in the *Athenaeum* for 1880, I, 760-761; Masson, I (1881), 16; I believe this document was first found and published by W. H. Allnut in *Notes and Queries*, VI, i (1880), 115, with the query whether this Richard Milton could be the poet's grandfather. Both Clarke and Masson felt sure that he was. Clarke said that Mr. Sides of the Bodleian found opposite Richard Milton's name the notation "cōt" for "contumax" (refractory, obstinate). But no such notation appears on the photostat which (through the kindness of Professor William R. Parker) I have. However, Richard is stated in the document to be contumacious, so that no further note is needed. Masson thinks that Richard's election as churchwarden ("gardianos" in the manuscript) may have brought him into general notice and been partly the cause for his troubles. Brennecke (pp. 41, 43, 52) adopts this idea, thinks that Richard's conversion to Roman Catholicism must have come after his election as churchwarden, and asserts (without reference) that Richard "remained a bitter adherent to the Popish tenets to the end."

[May 11, 1582, in our archdiaconal visitation of Oxford.

In the name of God, Amen. We, Thomas Glasier, LL. D., Archdeacon of Oxford, legally chosen for this office and proceeding legally, pronounce that all and singular of those whose names and cognomens are listed below—that is to say, those summoned and proclaimed who have not appeared—shall for their manifest contumacy in not appearing during our archdiaconal visitation on the day and place assigned them, be considered contumacious (justice demanding it), and shall be excommunicated as punishment for their contumacy, as we have hereby excommunicated them in these writings:

Mr. Robert Brian, rector of St. Clements.

Mr. William Lane, curate of All Saints.

Mr. —— Little, curate of Holywell.

Mr. —— Heale, curate of Stanton St. John.

Mr. Thomas Elye, curate of Horsepath.

Joseph Barnes, churchwarden of All Saints, dismissed.

Edward Turley and Richard Hoare, wardens of Holywell.

Francis Gennis, warden of St. Martin's.

Richard Milton and John White, wardens of Stanton St. John.

Henry Hampton and William Pokius, wardens of Cuddesdon.

(Pokius appeared and undertook for Hampton, and has until a week from Sunday to appear and to induce him to appear.)

William Curtes and John Powell, wardens of Cowley (?).

This is correct.

Thomas Glasier.]

[The poet's] Grandfather . . . [a Rom: Cath:] of *Holton* in Oxfordshire neer Shotover.

<small>Aubrey, f. 63; Darbishire, p. 1. The first brackets are mine, the second Aubrey's. For the last phrase Aubrey first wrote "neer Whateley."</small>

1583. FATHER DISINHERITED AND MOVES TO LONDON TO BECOME A SCRIVENER.

. . . his Father was entitled to a true Nobility in the Apostle Pauls Heraldry; having bin disinherited about ye beginning of

Queen Elizabeths reign by his Father a Romanist, who had an estate of five hundred pound a yeer at Stainton St John in Oxfordshire, for reading the Bible. Upon this occasion hee came yong to London, and beeing taken care of by a relation of his a Scrivenor. . . .

The "earliest" biography, f. 140; Darbishire, p. 18. Mark Noble (*Monthly Mirror*, N. S. VI [1809], 202) scouts the idea of disinheritance and asserts that under-rangers do not leave considerable estates. But most students accept it. Masson (I, 1881, 24) dates the move about 1585, as does Brennecke (pp. 42-45). It has usually been assumed that Milton became apprenticed to scrivener James Colbron about 1595, that being the date of Colbron's admission to the Company of Scriveners, and that Milton himself was admitted in 1600. But Professor William R. Parker has made a convincing case for the earlier date in his "John Milton, Scrivener, 1590-1632," *Modern Language Notes*, LIX (1944), 532 ff. From the records of Chancery suits in which Milton participated, and particularly from quotations given in my *Milton in Chancery*, pp. 271-272, in which Milton and his servant-partner Thomas Bower both agree that Milton had been investing money for John Cotton for nearly thirty-five years before these two men became partners in 1625 (see above, I, 86, 88), we come to the conclusion that Milton must have begun an independent career at least by 1590. If so, he would probably have been apprenticed about seven years earlier, 1583. Parker says there are many instances of scriveners who began to practise long before they troubled to become freemen of the Company. Parker also raises the interesting question (p. 536) whether there could be any relation between the alleged but unidentified Castons of the poet's mother's family and the Baldwin Castleton who was the master of James Colbron as an apprentice, who in turn was master of the poet's father on his admission into the Company. The above statements are not intended to contradict the indisputable fact of Milton's admission to the freedom of the Company in 1600 (see below). Hyde Clarke put forth even a different theory in the *Athenaeum* for March 13, 1880, p. 344. It was that Milton began his apprenticeship under another master, switched in 1595 to Colbron, and finished on time in 1600. A further avenue for speculation opens when we learn of a connection, however distant, between Colbron and the Powell family of Forest Hill. A Thomas Archdale (Anne Powell's mother was an Archdale), citizen and draper of London, whose will (102 Wood) was dated March 5, 1609, and proved December 3, 1611, left bequests of £6-13-4 each to James Colbron and his son Thomas; see Henry F. Waters, *Genealogical Gleanings in England*, I (1901), 317.

. . . his gr:father disinherited him because he kept not the
Catholique Religion q. he found a Bible in English in his chamber. so therupon he came to London, and became a Scrivener
[brought up by a friend of his, was not an Appentice]. . . .

Aubrey, f. 63; Darbishire, p. 1. The square brackets appear thus in
Aubrey's manuscript. The "him" in the first line refers to the poet's
father.

Which Grandfather being a zealous Papist, did put away, or,
as some say, disinherit, his Son, because he was a Protestant,
which made him retire to *London*, to seek, in a manner, his fortune.

Wood, 1, 880; Darbishire, p. 35.

His Father . . . [was] cast out by his Father, a bigotted *Roman
Catholick*, for embracing, when Young, the Protestant Faith,
and abjuring the Popish Tenets. . . .

Phillips, pp. iii-iv; Darbishire, pp. 50-51.

1583. MARCH 14. COMMISSION ISSUED TO ADMINIS-
TER MOTHER'S FATHER'S ESTATE.

Joseph Lemuel Chester states in the *Athenaeum* for 1880, 1, 696,
that a commission to administer the estate of Paul Jeffrey, late of the
parish of St. Swithin, who died intestate, was issued from the Commissary Court of London on March 14, 1582/3, to Paul's relict Ellen;
Masson, 1 (1881), 36-37. I regret that I have been unable to find the
original document, though I searched for some time; but there is no
reason to doubt the accuracy of Colonel Chester's report.

1590. FATHER BEGINS TO HANDLE INVESTMENTS OF
JOHN COTTON.

. . . this def^t . . . doth beleeve and hath beene enformed by
the said Mr Milton that the said John Cotton for thirty yeares
or thereabout$_e$ did ymploye the said John Milton to lett out att
interest diuerse great somēs of money after the rate of Tenne
and eight in the hundred & accordingly the said John Milton
by the direccōn and assent of the said John Cotton did lett out
the said somēs to sundry persons But this defendant denyes
that the said John Milton and this def^t or this defendant onely

hadd w^{th}in five or six yeares last past putt into the handꝑ of them or this defendant by the said John Cotton or his assignes any somē or somēs of money whatsoeū to be lett out att interest. . . .

From Thomas Bower's answer to Sir Thomas Cotton's bill, April 8, 1637, *q.v.* According to Bower's chronology, the period covered by Milton's (and his own) relations with Cotton as investment advisers must be from about 1600 to about 1630. But see the following entry.

. . . this defend^t. sayth that before this defend^t. became partner wth the other defend^t. Thomas Bower and after their Copartnership vizt, in all, for the space of neere fforty yeares the said John Cotton did dispose of and lend at the shop of this defend^t scituate in Bredstreete in London divers somes of money vnto a good value about Three thousand poundꝑ . . . wch manner of Dealinge betwixt this defend^t and the said John Cotton did Continue before the Copartnershipp Betwixt this Deffendaunt and the said Thomas Bower about the space of thirty and ffive yeares, as this Defendaunt taketh it, and after this Copartnershipp for the space of Two yeares or thereaboutꝑ. . . .

From Milton's answer to Cotton's bill, April 13, 1637, *q. v.* If we take Milton's dates literally, and subtract 35 from 1625 (the year of his partnership with Bower; see 1, 88, above), we come to 1590 as the beginning of his association with Cotton. See also the first note to the entry above under 1583.

1595. DECEMBER 11. MOTHER'S RELATIVE (?) JOHN JEFFREY OF HOLTON MAKES WILL.

Jn the name of god Amen. The xj^{th} day of December in the xxxviij^{th} yeare of the Raigne of our soueraigne Lady Elizabeth queene of England . . . J John Jeffery of Halton in the county of Oxoñ husbandman . . . make this my laste will . . . Jtm̄ J make and appoynte Elizabeth Jeffery my wiffe my full & whole executrix . . . Jtm̄ J geue and bequeath vnto xp̄ofer Jeffery my cosene thone halfe or moytye of all my goodꝑ w^{th}out doores after the decease of Elizabeth my wiffe . . . Jtm̄ J geue vnto Henry Jeffery fourty shillingꝑ of lawfull English money . . .

Jtm̄ J geue vnto margaret Jeffery my kinswomā vj^l xiij^s iiij^d
... Jtm̄ J appoynte xp̄ofer Jeffery & Raphe Barnarde [?] to
be my overseers of this my last will & testamente ...

Probatm̄ erat hoc Testm̄ ... xvj° die menss' martij Anō dnī
1595. Ac ... administra° ... Executrici in eodem nōiatæ ...
Jnventariū ———————————————— lxxv^l viij^s vij^d

Bodleian Library, MS. Wills Oxon 37 (no page number on my
photostat); Masson, I (1875), 14-15. There is a copy of this will in
MS. Wills Oxon 190, ff. 147-147v. The relationship of this John Jeffrey to the poet's mother is not clear, but the kinswoman Margaret
whom he mentions may be her sister. Masson gave this item as a possible lead in the 1875 edition of his volume, but dropped it in the 1881
edition on finding better ones.

[This will was proved on March 16, 1595 (i.e., 1595/6),
and administration granted to the executrix named in the same.
Inventory: £75 8s. 7d.]

1600. FATHER MARRIES SARAH JEFFREY.

No record of this marriage has been found, but since the first child
of the union of which we know was an infant buried on May 12, 1601,
the year 1600 is as good a guess as any. For a brief characterization of
the poet's mother, see below under 1608. For a careful discussion of
Sarah Jeffrey's pedigree, see the various entries about her family above,
and Masson, I (1881), 30-39.

1600 (?). FEBRUARY 27. FATHER ADMITTED TO COMPANY OF SCRIVENERS.

[1] 27 Feby 1599 Admission of Iohn Milton Son of Richard
Milton of Stanston. C°. Oxon Yeoman Apprentice to Iames Col-
bron, Cit^n and Court Letter Writer This Iohn Milton, was the
Father of Milton

[2] 162 Et ego Johēs Miltoñ filius Riċhd Miltoñ de Staunston
in Com̄ Oxoñ Yeomañ App^{r}nticius Jacobi Colbroñ Civis et Scr'
Lrē Curiāl Londoñ, satis faciens Juramēt quod modo p'stito
fore p̄quam necessariū. Et ea esse intencōne p̄viss' et edit' idem p̄
virib^9 (Deo volente) inviolabiliter obsvare intendo. Jgitur ad

singulas ordinacōnes artem pᵣd' nrām Concernantes manu mea propria hic subscripsi Die et Anno infer script'

p̄ me Johem̄ Miltoñ

[In margin:] Jo Milton

From the records of the Company of Scriveners, London, who kindly provided me, through University Microfilms, Ltd., with photographic reproductions. The second has not, to the best of my knowledge, previously been published. The first looks like writing of the eighteenth or even nineteenth century; the second, except for the marginal signature, is all in the same hand, presumably that of the elder Milton. The marginal signature looks like his usual signature to documents. Whether the figure 162 is a page number or some other identification is not clear, since my photograph shows only this entry alone with the rest of the page cut off. I have found no official record of action on Milton's application, if this can be called such, other than that given below; nor does either that or Milton's application give any date beyond the year. In response to my request for reproductions of the entries in the Company's records concerning Milton's admission, these two were all that were sent to me, and therefore presumably all that are now in the holdings of the Company. But there is no reason to doubt that the first of the records printed above is correct.

[And I, John Milton, son of Richard Milton of Stanton in County Oxford, yeoman, apprentice of James Colbron, citizen and writer of the court letter of London, satisfying the oath which according to established custom is extremely necessary, intend to observe inviolably according to my powers (God willing) those provisions carefully laid down in the same. Therefore I have subscribed to each of the regulations concerning our aforesaid art here with my own hand on the day and year written below.

By me, John Milton.]

The copy of the record is, that on the 27th of February 1599, John Milton, son of *Richard* Milton, of Stanston [*sic*], Co. Oxon, and late apprentice to James Colbron, citizen and writer of the Court Letter of London [scrivener], was admitted to the freedom of the Company.

Hyde Clarke published this entry in the *Athenaeum*, March 19, 1859, p. 390, saying that it came from the records of the Company of Scriv-

[168]

eners, but giving no identification; Hamilton, p. 43; Masson, 1 (1881), 25; Brennecke, p. 50. Clarke interprets this record as nullifying Aubrey's "inference" that Milton "became a scrivener by purchase, without serving an apprenticeship." The brackets are Clarke's.

1599 ... John Milton ——— of James Colebron ——— 1595.

Bodleian MS. Rawl. Misc. 51, f. 27v, "An Annual Catalogue ... of the Company of Scriveners"; Henry J. Sides in the *Athenaeum*, May 1, 1880, pp. 565-566. The second date, 1595, is that of the admission of Colbron himself, which is given on f. 27. Colbron had been an apprentice of Baldwin Castleton, who was made free of the Company in 1577.

[The poet's father] became a *Scrivener* [brought up by a friend of his, was not an Appentice] and gott a plentifull estate by it. ...

Aubrey, f. 63; Darbishire, p. 1. The second brackets are Aubrey's.

... beeing taken care of by a relation of his a Scrivenor, hee became free of that profession. ...

The "earliest" biography, f. 140; Darbishire, p. 18.

His Father *John Milton*, an Honest, Worthy, and Substantial Citizen of *London*, by Profession a Scrivener, to which Profession he voluntarily betook himself, by the advice and assistance of an intimate Friend of his, Eminent in that Calling. ...

Phillips, pp. iii-iv; Darbishire, p. 50. Brennecke (p. 48), without even mentioning Phillips, assumes that the intimate friend was Colbron, and tells how the two men "discussed the situation and finally evolved a solution for Milton's predicament" of being rather old to begin an apprenticeship, and how they "managed to persuade the officers of the Company to accept from him a reduced period of five years as apprentice, with a money payment as partial compensation." He gives no basis for this theory, though it is very probable that the friend was Colbron.

J, John Milton, do sweare vpon the Holy Evangelist, *to be true and faithfull vnto our Soveraigne Lord the King his heires and successors kings and Queenes of England and* to be true and iust in myne office and scyence and to doe my dilligence that all the deeds wch J shall make to be sealed shall be well and truely done after my learning skill and scyence and shalbe duely & advisedly read over and examined before thensealing of the

same And especially J shall not write nor suffer to be written
by any of mine to my power or knowledge any deed or wryting
to be sealed wherein any deceite or falsehood shalbe conceived
or in my conscience suspected to lye nor any deed bearing date
of long tyme past before th'ensealing thereof nor bearing any
date of any tyme to come neither shall J testifie nor suffer any
of mine to testify to my power or knowledge any blanck Charter
or deed sealed before the full wryting thereof, and neither for
hast nor for coveteousness J shall take vpon me to make any deed
touching inheritance of landę or estate for life or yeares nor any
deed of great charge whereof J have not cunning w^{th}out good
advice and informacoñ of Councell And all the good rules and
ordinances of the Society of Scrivenors of the citty of London
J shall well and truely keepe and observe to my power so farr
as god shall give me grace So help me god and the holy contents of this booke.

"The forme of every freemans Oath," from the constitution of the
guild as promulgated in 1619, in British Museum Harl. MS. 2,295,
f. 23; Masson, 1 (1881), 29. I have substituted Milton's name for the
impersonal "N.D." of the original.

1601. FATHER'S MUSIC PUBLISHED IN MORLEY'S *MADRIGALS*.

Iohn Milton.

Fayre *Orian* in the morne,
before the day was borne,
With veluet steps on groūd,
which made nor print nor soūd,
Would see hir Nymphs a bed,
what liues those Ladies led,
The Roses blushing sayd,
O stay thou shepherds mayd,
And on a sodain all,
They rose & heard hir call.
Then sang those shepherds and Nymphs of *Diana*,
Long liue faire *Oriana*.

[170]

Thomas Morley, *Madrigales The Triumphes of Oriana, to 5. and 6. voices,* 1601, number 18; Masson, I, 30-33; Brennecke, pp. 53 ff. This title is a book in six parts, one for each of the six singing voices. Milton presumably wrote the words as well as the music. A similar manuscript version appears in British Museum Add. MSS. 37,402-37,-407, inclusive, #19, except that this collection gives the music alone without the words. The text given above is from the cantus volume.

Grove's Dictionary of Music and Musicians, ed. H. C. Colles, v (1928), 385, *s.v.* "Triumphes of Oriana," says that Morley's book, though dated on the title page 1601, was probably not published until 1603, after the death of Queen Elizabeth, whom this series of songs was intended to honor. Brennecke (p. 58) repeats this assertion, which seems to be based on the fact that the volume was not entered in the Stationers' Registers until October 15, 1603. But entry in the Registers is not a reliable test of the date of publication; so the item is here assigned to the year 1601. Grove mentions two "issues" in 1603, which Brennecke changes to "editions." I have found only the one edition, which is all the *STC* mentions. Brennecke gives facsimiles of the title page (facing p. 54) and of the tenor part (facing p. 58). He adds that the "Triumphs" "has enjoyed a greater vogue in modern times than any other contemporary collection of English vocal music" (p. 58). He describes the music in some detail, adding a highly imaginative account of Morley's visits to Milton during its composition (pp. 53-60), and speculates as to whether through Morley's association with Shakespeare the elder Milton may have met the dramatist. Other musicians whose music appeared in the same collection with Milton's were Thomas Tomkyns, John Wilbye, Thomas Weelkes, and Morley himself.

He has a madrigal for five voices, among the numerous contributions of the most capital performers, in the TRIUMPHS OF ORIANA, published by Morley in 1601. . . . This collection is said to have been planned by the earl of Nottingham, lord High Admiral; who, with a view to sooth queen Elizabeth's despair for the recent execution of lord Essex by flattering her preposterous vanity, gave for a prize-subject to the best poets and musicians, whom he liberally rewarded, the beauty and accomplishments of his royal mistress, now a decrepit virgin on the brink of seventy.

Warton, p. 523; quoted in Todd, vi (1826), 336. Warton gives no source for his story.

His father . . . was an ingeniose man, delighted in Musiq.

composed many Songs (now in print especially that of Oriana.
. . .

ꝗ Mʳ J. Playford—ꝑ Wilby's sett of *Oriana's*.

Aubrey, ff. 63, 65; Darbishire, pp. 1, 13. No music of Milton's in
Wilbye's books is known. Brennecke's explanation is therefore probable
(p. 55): "Wilbye's contribution became so famous [in Morley's book]
that the whole collection was sometimes ascribed to him rather than to
Morley. This would account for Phillips's curious statement [see be-
low] that three or four of Milton's 'songs' were 'still to be seen in the
old Wilby's set of Airs.' Aubrey mentions 'Wilby's Set of Orianas.' "

Masson (1, 1881, 51) makes a statement which is almost certainly
true, but without definite evidence: "An organ and other instruments
were part of the furniture in the house in Bread Street. . . ." Perhaps
this is a slight wrenching of Aubrey's statement (see above, 1, 22) that
the poet "had an Organ in his house." But Aubrey's pronouns are none
too clear.

Milton John, a musitian living in the reigne of qu. Elizab.
& K. Jam. 1 wee have some of his compositions in yᵉ publick
musick school at Oxon, but whether he hath any extant J cannot
tell.

Bodleian MS. D. 19 (4), f. 91v; Warton, p. 523; Todd, VI
(1826), 336; Stern, 1, i, 301. The reference may or may not be to
the manuscripts in Christ Church, Oxford, described above at 1, 260.
Warton speaks of the manuscript in the Bodleian as Mus. MS. Ashm.
D. 19. 4to.

. . . yet did he not so far quit his own Generous and Ingenious
Inclinations, as to make himself wholly a Slave to the World;
for he sometimes found vacant hours to the Study (which he
made his recreation) of the Noble Science of Musick, in which
he advanc'd to that perfection, that as I have been told, and as
I take it, by our Author himself, he Composed an *In Nomine*
of Forty Parts: for which he was rewarded with a Gold Medal
and Chain by a *Polish* Prince, to whom he presented it. However, this is a truth not to be denied, that for several Songs of
his Composition, after the way of these times, three or four of
which are still to be seen in Old *Wilby's* set of Ayres, besides
some Compositions of his in *Ravenscrofs* Psalms, he gained the

Reputation of a considerable Master in this most charming of all the Liberal Sciences. . . .

Phillips, pp. iv-v; Darbishire, p. 51; Brennecke, pp. 34-41. Brennecke suggests that the Polish prince may have been Albertus Alasco, free baron of Lasco and vaiode or count palatine of Siradia, a duchy in Lower Poland, who visited London and Oxford in 1583. He describes the visit in considerable detail. He also speculates that, in view of the baron's shortness of money, Milton had been obliged to return the reward for the baron to use to satisfy a disgruntled creditor. He also raises the question whether Aubrey and Phillips may have given two confused descriptions of the same episode when Aubrey described (see above, I, 4) Milton's musical composition for a Landgrave of Hesse. In any case, no "In Nomine" of any such complication as that mentioned by Phillips has been found, though Brennecke gives the shorter form of such a composition at pp. 139-142, with reproductions of the music facing p. 142 and on pp. 208-211.

1601. MAY 12. OLDER BROTHER OR SISTER BURIED.

The xij^th of maye A° 1601 was buried A Crysome Childe of m^r John myltons of this pishe scriveno^r.

Parish registers of All Hallows, Bread Street, London; Masson, I, 23; Publications of the Harleian Society, XLIII (1913), 169. Though the date of birth is not given, it must have been very shortly before the date of burial. A chrisom child is one in its chrisom, hence a babe or infant; the chrisom is a white cloth thrown as a sign of innocence over a child when baptized.

1601. JULY 13. GRANDFATHER RICHARD MILTON CONVICTED OF RECUSANCY.

Dct'us Spencer nup de waterpary in com p̄dcō yoman' cxx. 1s'. viz' lx. ls'. inde virtute actus p̄dict' Eo qd' ip̄e non accessit ad' eccliam pochialem de Waterpary p̄d' nec alicui alr ecclīo capella aut vsuali loco coīs p̄cacoīus ad' aliquod tempus infra tres mens' p'xim' sequen' sextam diem Decembr Anno xliij^cio Regine huius Et lx. ls'. Rcs' de die lune xiij^mo die Julij Anno xliij^cio p̄dcō quo die convict' fuit vsqz quartam diem Octobr̄ ex tnno px'im' sequen' sclt p tribz mens' Eo qd' ipe' non fecit submission' et devenit confirmabilr scdm' veram Intenc' actus p̄liament' Anno xxiij^cio eda' et puis

Alicia Bullyn' nup de Woln'cote in com' p̄dco' Vid' cxx. ls' p consili

Ricus milton' nup de Staunton' Sci' Jōhnis in com' p̄dc̄o yōm cxx. ls' p consili.

Public Record Office, Exchequer Recusant Rolls, E377/29d/10; Hunter, pp. 1-4; Hamilton, pp. 42-43; Masson, 1 (1881), 17; Brennecke, p. 42. It is also mentioned in Hunter's manuscript, British Museum Add. MS. 24,501, f. 13. Presumably the details about Milton follow those given for Spencer.

[The said Spencer late of Waterperry in the said county, 120 pounds, viz.: 60 pounds by virtue of the aforesaid act in that he did not come to the parish church of Waterperry aforesaid nor to any other church, chapel, or usual place of meeting proclaimed at any time within the three months next following the 6th day of December in the 43rd year of this queen (1600). And 60 pounds more from Monday, July 13, in the aforesaid 43rd year (1601), the day on which he was convicted, to the 4th day of October of the term next following; that is, for three months, in that he did not make submission and become conformable according to the true intention of the Act of Parliament published and provided in the 23rd year (1580).

Alicia Bulleyn late of Woolvercot in the aforesaid county, widow, 120 pounds through counsel.

Richard Milton late of Stanton St. John in the aforesaid county, yeoman, 120 pounds through counsel.]

1602 (?). SISTER ANNE BORN.

[The poet's father and mother had] an onely Daughter *Ann*.

Phillips, p. v; Darbishire, p. 52; Masson, 1 (1881), 39. Though no entry for Anne Milton's birth has appeared, it seems to be generally agreed that she was older than the poet, and therefore born some time between 1602 (a year after the "chrisom child" mentioned above) and 1607 (a year before the birth of the poet). But almost any date within these limits, and perhaps even outside them, is possible.

1602. AUGUST 28. FATHER WITNESSES TRUELOVE-JEF-
FREY MARRIAGE ALLEGATION.

28° mensis Augusti 1602/

This daie appeared psonally before m^r doctor Stanhope
Willm̄ Trulove gent' of the pishe of Hatfeild Peverell in the
Countie of Essexe Widowe^r and so hathe byn about a yeare
past aged 40 yeres or theraboutp and alleageth that he intendeth to marrye one Margarett Jeffraye maiden of Newton
hall in the pishe of great Dunmowe in the Countie of Essexe
aforesaid aged 20 yeres the naturall and lawfull daughter of
Paule Jeffraie while he liued of the pishe of St Swythins London m^rchant Taylor deceased And at the same tyme appeared
John milton of the pishe of Alhollowes in Bredstreete Londoñ who married the sister of the same Margarett Jeffery and
both the mother of the same Margaret & her mistris one mrs
Kindlemarshe of milton hall aforesayd are now in London
wth her & giue their Consentp to this marriage offering to depose for the Consent of Ellen Jeffraye widowe mother of the
saide maiden to this intended mariage And the saide pties desire licence to be maried in the pishe Churche of Christchurche
London

p Wm Treuloue

Jo: milton.

Jurat' [sworn] 28 Aug^i. 1602

From the original document in the Bishop of London's Registry;
Publications of the Harleian Society, xxv (1887), 271; *Miscellanea
Genealogica et Heraldica*, ed. J. J. Howard, II (1876), 131; *Athenaeum*, 1868, II, 603; Masson, I (1881), 37; Brennecke, p. 61. The
word "milton" after the name of Mrs. Kindlemarshe is probably a slip
of the pen for "Newton." The whole section from "who married the
sister" through "to this marriage" is a marginal addition with a caret
to mark its position. Howard breaks it into two parts, placing "and both
the mother . . . to this marriage" after "to this intended marriage," a
placing which makes smoother reading, since "offering to depose" belongs with "John Milton"; but the manuscript gives no authorization
for this division. It does, however, show two canceled readings, one
of which is interesting, the other a mere rearrangement. The descriptive

phrase applied to William Truelove, "Widowe[r] and so hathe byn about a yeare past" is written in above the canceled description of him as "Baccheler and at his owne goverment." Preceding the last five words of the text are the canceled "Christchurch pishe London." The Harleian Society transcript wrongly reads the duration of Truelove's widowerhood as seven years.

1603. FATHER ACQUAINTED WITH SCRIVENER GEORGE BROOME.

George Broome of the p[r]cinct of Blackfriers London scriuen' ... hath knowne ... the def[t] Milton some 27 or 28 yeares or thereaboutᵽ. ...

From Broome's deposition of September 19, 1631; see above, I, 247. The date is of course only approximate, but subtracting 28 from 1631 gives us 1603.

1603. FEBRUARY 17. MOTHER'S COUSIN RICHARD JEFFREY MAKES WILL.

Jn the name of god Amen J Richard Jeffrey of Little Bursted in the county of Essex gent' ... will & bequeathe vnto my welbeloued wyf Jane Jeffrey all that my capitall messuage wherin J now dwell ... dureing the mynority of John Jeffrey my sonne ... Jtem J will & bequeathe vnto my sayd wyf all my customary landes & tenēntᵽ in Easthanningfeild with their apptenaunces for the terme of tenne yeares paying my debtes and bringing vp of my children Richard & Hester Jeffrey ... and of this my p[r]sent last will & testament J make my wyfe & my sonne John my Joynt executors Jn witnesse wherof J the sayd Richard Jeffrey have herevnto sett my hand & seale the 17 day of ffebruary in the five & fourtethe yeare of her ma[ties]: reigne and in the yeare of our Lord 1602/

[Signed:] Richard Jeffery

Essex Record Office, D/ABW 21/211, 1603; first described by J. L. Chester in the *Athenaeum* for 1880, I, 563. The older reference for this document was Commissary Court of London, Essex, and Herts. This Richard Jeffrey is evidently the son of Richard, brother of the poet's mother's father Paul; see the genealogy above under date of

February 22, 1551. This document is unusual in that it is the original will rather than a copy, bearing the shaky signature of Richard Jeffrey at the end and the signatures of three witnesses.

1603. MARCH 4. FATHER WITNESSES HEIGHAM-SPARROW-SANDERSON BOND.

Nou^rint vniūsi per presentes nos Thomam Heigheham de Bednollgreene in cõm Midds' Armigeȓ et Richaȓd Sparrowe Ciuem et Aurifabrū london Teneri et firmiter obligari Johñ Sanderson de London generū: in [blank] libris . . . dat' quarto die Martij *1602*. Annōqz RReg^{ne} Elizabethe ect' Quadragesimo Quinto./

Sealed and deliu^red in the   Thomas Heigham.
p^rsence of Jo Milton Scr'.   Richard Sparrow.

The condition of this obligation is sutch that yf the wthin bound Thomas Heigham & Richard Sparrowe there executors or assignes doe well & treuelie pay or cause to be paid vnto the wthin named John Sanderson his executors or assignes at the nowe shop of John Milton scrivener in Bread Street london. the some of [blank] poundȝ & shillinges of good & lawfull mony of England one the 5th day of May next insuinge the date wthin written. that then this obligation to be voyd or else it to stand in full force./.

British Museum, Lansdowne MS. 241, f. 58 (John Sanderson's record book from 1560 to 1610); George F. Warner in the *Athenaeum* for 1880, I, 375-376; Masson, I (1881), 4-5; Brennecke, p. 53. Presumably the date of 1602 means 1602/3; see also below under date of April 2, 1603. Masson, who in his earlier editions read the "nowe" shop of Milton as the "newe" shop (1859, p. 1; 1875, pp. 1-2) and speculated about the change of residence involved, corrected himself on the basis of Warner's article. This document appears to be only a copy and not the original bond; the signatures are therefore not in the hands of either the contracting parties or Milton.

[Know all men by these presents that we Thomas Heigham of Bethnal Green in co. Middlesex, Esquire, and Richard Sparrow, citizen and goldsmith of London, are held and firmly obligated to John Sanderson of London, gentleman, in (blank)

[177]

pounds. . . . Givén on the fourth day of March, 1602, and in the forty-fifth year of the reign of Queen Elizabeth, etc.]

1603. APRIL 2. FATHER'S SERVANT PETER JONES WITNESSES SPARROW-SANDERSON BILL OF SALE.

Be it knowne vnto all men by thes psentp that J richard sparowe citizen & gouldsmith of L°. for the some of 50ˡ: of lawfull mony of Jngland to me by John sanderson of london drap in hand paid have bargained sould & dl vnto the said John sanderson in plaine and open markett wᵗʰin the citie of London. a Collett of gould sett wᵗʰ a great Rubie . . . in wittness wherof J the said richard sparowe have hearvnto sett my hand & seale the second day of aprill in the yeare of our lord one thousand six hundreth & three.

Sealed & dl in the psence of   Richard Sparrowe

peter Jones seruant to   [sketch of seal]

John milton scrivener.

Nouʳint vniuʳsi p pñtes me Richm̄ Sparrowe Ciuem et Aurifabrū london: Teneri et firmiter obligari Johñ Sanderson de london pannaꝛ in Quinquagint' libris lēglis monete Anglī . . . dat' Secundo die Aprilli Anno Dñi Millesimo sexcentesimo Tertio

The condition of this obligation is sutch . . . .

Sealed & deliuered in the psence   Richard Sparrow

of Peter Jones seruant to   [sketch of seal]

John milton scrivner

British Museum Lansdowne MS. 241, f. 363; Masson, 1 (1881), 4. This manuscript is not the original bill of sale but a copy. The Latin is so close to the English of the preceding section that a translation of it would be superfluous. The omitted section explains, according to the usual custom, that if Sparrow pays Sanderson £52 10s. on the ensuing October 3, at Sparrow's shop in Cheapside, the bill of sale is to be void. See also the entry of March 4, 1603, above, concerning Sparrow and Sanderson.

1604. TWO OF FATHER'S MADRIGALS (?) PUBLISHED BY THOMAS BATESON.

[1] This song should haue bene printed in the set of *Orianas*.

When *Oriana* walkt to take the aier . . .
Long liue faire *Oriana*, faire *Oriana*.
[2] *Orianas* farewell.
Hark, heare you not, heare you not a heauenly har-
      mony . . .
In heauen liues Oriana.

From Thomas Bateson's *The First Set of English Madrigales*, 1604,
sigs. A4v and D3v; Brennecke, p. 58. This volume was entered in the
Stationers' Registers on October 15, 1603. Though Brennecke names
these songs in his discussion of Milton's contributions, he does not say
that they were by Milton, and there is no evidence that they were.

1604. JANUARY 14. FATHER WITNESSES INVENTORY.

Leases left in the hands of Richard Prowde goldsmith dwelling in Cheapeside at the Corner of Breadstreete london: the
xiiijth of January 1603 for the vse of Mary Edmondꝑ./ [Then
comes a list of the contents of five boxes containing about thirty
transactions] . . . Teste me Jo: Milton: scr.

Westminster Abbey Muniment #9588. I do not believe that this document has been previously mentioned in print. If Richard Prowde was
related to the Prowdes of Shrewsbury, he and the Milton family were
soon to be more closely connected, for Edward Phillips, who was to
marry Anne Milton, daughter of the scrivener and sister of the poet, in
1623, was the son of a father of the same name and Catherine Prowde,
daughter of George Prowde, mercer, of that city. There may conceivably already have been a distant connection on the side of the poet's
mother, for Catherine Prowde's brother Thomas had a cousin Robert
Jeffreyes. See Walter Goodwin Davis's "Ancestry of Thomas Lewis
. . . ," in the *New England Historical and Genealogical Register*, CI
(1947), 10. Richard Prowde had four children who were baptized between 1599 and 1606 in Milton's church of All Hallows, Bread Street,
where Prowde was buried in 1609 (*Registers*, Harleian Society Publications, XLIII, 14, 15, 173).

1604. APRIL 20. FATHER SUMMONED FOR JURY SERV-
ICE BUT DOES NOT RESPOND.

Et postea . . . die Jovis xix° die Aprilis Anno secundo . . .
p̄ceptū fuit . . . p̄fat' Nichō Holmes ad tunc vni sʳvień ad Cla-
vam p̄dcī Willī Romeny . . . quod ipē . . . sumoñ et venire fa-

ceret coram p̄fact' Willō Romeny . . . in Guihāld prēd vizᵗ die
veñis xx° die Aprilis . . . vigint' quatuor p̨bos et leglēs hoīnes
wārd de Bredstrete Ciuit̨ London ac de vicenet' eiusdem Wārd
quor' quīlt &c herēt terr' et tēnta bona seu Cattāll ad valenc'
quadraginta m̄car' . . . ad faciēnd Jūr inter ptes prēd. . . . Nichās
Holmes . . . retorñ et Certificavit . . . quod ipē prēd vigint'
quatuor p̨bos et leglēs hoīnes . . . quor' noīa patebant in quodam
pannell' Cuῗ prēd p ip̄m tunc et ib̄m exhibit' venire fecit et
sumoñ . . . quor' noīa sequntʳ. vizᵗ Rōbtus Keasar, Johñes Melton, Ricūs Hatche, Willm̄s Lawrence, Willm̄s Ellis. Johñes
Langley, Johñes Dunster, Georgius Wallmisley. Ricūs Prowde,
Oswald' Blunte. Johñes fflood, Thom̄s Thompson. Johñes Snelling. Polecarpus Dawkins. Willš Woodcocke, Jeroīmus Lawes,
Abraham ffoythe, Johñes Mason Johñes Preston, Ricūs Grenegras, Robtūs Longrove Humfrūs Ambler, Willm̄s Awdley,
Esdras ffairmands. . . . Et . . . die m̄tis dcō viij° die Maij . . .
p̄ceptū fuit . . . Nichō Holmes . . . quod ipē . . . sumoñ et venire
faceret . . . m̄curij nono die Maij . . . eosdem viginti quatuor
p̨bos et leglēs hoīnes. . . . Et . . . Nichās Holmes . . . retorñ
et Certificavit . . . quod ipē prēd vigint' quatuor p̨bos et leglēs
hoīnes . . . venire fecit et sumoñ. . . . Et . . . p̄dcī vigint' quatuor
. . . hoīnes . . . solempnitʳ exact' fuer' et non compuerunt sed defalt' fecerunt Jdeo quīlt eor' p defalt' faciēnd in Mrī &c. . . . Et
. . . die Jovis xvij° die Maij . . . preceptū fuit p̄fat' Nichō Holmes
. . . quod ipē . . . summoñ et venire faceret . . . die veñis xviij°
die Maij . . . prēd vigint' quatuor . . . hoīnes . . . ac etiam quod
sumoñ et venire faceret . . . sex tlēs p̨bos et leglēs hoīnes wārd
prēd. . . . Et p̄dcūs Nichās Holmes . . . Certificavit . . . quod ipē
prēd vigint' quatuor . . . hoīnes . . . sumoñ et venire fecit. Ac
etiam [sex tlēs] p̨bos et leglēs hoīnes . . . quor' noīa sic sequntʳ
[vizᵗ] Mathews Smyth, Georgius Chapman. Edward Smyth
Jeremias [Lewes, Walters̄] Lewes, ffranciscus Sherwood . . .
et duodecim illor' vizᵗ Robtūs Keasar [Willm̄s] Ellis. Polecarpus Dawkins Willms Woodcock Johñes[Mason?] Esdras
ffairmands, Mathews Smyth, Georgius Chapman [Johñes?]

Smyth Jeremias Loggyn, Walter' Lewes et ffranciscus Sherwood compuerunt qui in Jūr prēd ad veritat' dicēnd . . . tunc et ibm̄ . . . Jurat' fuerunt. . . .

Corporation of London Records Office, Sheriffs' Court Roll, 1604, Symes vs. Barley. I am indebted to Professor Mark Eccles for giving me this reference and for helping me to work it out; as also to the officials of the Records Office for providing me with a photostatic copy of it.

In brief, this long and wordy though incomplete document recounts the law-suit brought by Valentyne Symes against William Barley, the latter of whom part way through the proceedings requested trial by jury. Sir William Romney, a sheriff of London, thereupon gave orders through Nicholas Holmes, sergeant at mace, for the parties to appear at the Guildhall and for a jury to be summoned. Though Holmes tried faithfully, most of the 24 men on his original list, including the elder Milton, failed to appear. But by adding six more men to his list he was able to form a jury of twelve, who decided against Barley and charged him damages and costs and in addition 48 shillings for the plaintiff's expenses. The translation below is slightly condensed from the Latin and is printed continuously instead of being continually punctuated with ellipses like the original.

[And later on Thursday, April 19, in the said second year (of James I: 1604), Nicholas Holmes, then a sergeant at mace of Sir William Romney, was ordered to summon and to cause to come before the said Sir William Romney in the Guildhall on Friday, April 20, twenty-four good men and true of the ward of Bread Street of the city of London and of the vicinity of the same ward, each of whom held lands and tenements, goods or chattels, to the value of forty marks, in order to give judgment among the parties. Nicholas Holmes certified that he had summoned the said twenty-four men, whose names appeared in a certain panel of the court by him then and there exhibited, and whose names follow: Robert Keasar, John Melton, Richard Hatche, William Lawrence, William Ellis, John Langley, John Dunster, George Wallmisley, Richard Prowde, Oswald Blunte, John Flood, Thomas Thompson, John Snelling, Polecarp Dawkins, William Woodcock, Jerome Lawes, Abraham Foyth, John Mason, John Preston, Richard Grenegras, Robert Longrove, Humphrey Ambler, William Awdley, and

Ezra Fairmands. And on Tuesday, May 8, Nicholas Holmes
was ordered to summon on Wednesday, May 9, the same twenty-four men. And Nicholas Holmes certified that he had summoned the twenty-four men; and the twenty-four men were
solemnly demanded and did not appear but made default, thus
each of them for his default throwing himself on the mercy
(of the court). And on Thursday, May 17, Nicholas Holmes
was ordered to summon on Friday, May 18, the said twenty-
four men and also six more such men of the same ward. And
Nicholas Holmes certified that he had summoned the said twenty-four men and also six more such good men and true, whose
names follow: Mathew Smith, George Chapman, Edward
Smith, Jeremiah Lewes, Walter Lewes, and Francis Sherwood.
And twelve of them (Robert Keasar, William Ellis, Polecarp
Dawkins, William Woodcock, John Mason (?), Ezra Fairmands, Mathew Smith, George Chapman, John Smith, Jeremiah
Loggyn, Walter Lewes, and Francis Sherwood) appeared and
were sworn in the court to speak the truth.]

1604. JULY 3. FATHER TESTIFIES IN COURT ABOUT IN-VESTMENTS FOR SKYNNER, EVANS, AND GARSTACKE IN 1601.

Capta coram me Otho: Nicholson
    in absenc' Mri Robertson
John Mylton of the pishe of Allhollowes in Bredstreete London Scrivener aged 40 yeares or thereaboutp sworne & exaīed
the 3ᵈ. day of July Aᵒ pʳdcī. Deposeth & saith

. 8 . That about some 3 yeares nowe laste paste Robert Skynner nowe
deceased in ye Jnter' named came vnto this deponᵗ. and towlde
this deponᵗ that he had some money in his handp of a kinsemans
of his (meaninge the nowe complt as it did afterwardp appeare)
and that he was to put it out for his saide kinseman. and that he
woulde be as carefull in doinge of it, for him as he woulde be
for him self. and then willed this Depont to make a bonde for
fforty or ffiftie powndp from one Mʳ Mowntney wᶜʰ was then

to have the saide money for a Certeyne tyme. wch bonde was maide by this Depon^t accordinge to the direccions of the saide Robert Skynner in the name of the Compl^t. as by this Depon^{te} Note booke wherein all such matters are entered more playnely maye appeare, And whereunto this Depon^t for the Certeyne some, the tyme, and the manner of makinge the saide bonde, doth referre himself. And further this Depon^t saith, that after the makinge of the bonde from Mr Mowntney as aforesaide, the saide Robert Skynn' came to this Depon^t, and gave this Depon^t instructions for the makinge of an assignment, of a Certeyne Tenem^t in Crutched ffryers London from one Richard Evans wch this Depon^t taketh to be one of the nowe Defen^{te}. wch assignment was made in Consideracōn and for the saide Robert Skynners assurance of the sōme of xx^{li}. wch the saide Evans was to have of him the saide Robert Skynner. And as this Depon^t remembrethe the same was made absolute without any Condicion, but wheather the same xx^{li} was pte of such money as the saide Robert Skynner had in his handꝑ of the nowe Compl^{te}. or wheather it was his owne money or noe this depon^t can not Certenly sett downe for that he did not heare the saide Robert Skynner to vse any speeches that mighte manifeste the same. And further this Depon^t saith that about ffebruary nowe laste paste (as this Depon^t nowe remembrethe.) but sure he is it was since the deathe of the saide Robert Skynner, Ames Garstacke one other of the now def^{te}. came vnto this Depon^{te} shopp. (havinge noe busines so farr as this depon^t coulde ꝑceave, but onely to talke with this Depon^t about matters betweene the nowe compl^t. and the saide Robert Skynner. And after diūse speeches passed, about that busines this Depon^t (havinge formerly made a lrē of Attorney from the said Richard Evans vnto the saide Robert Skynner to recive of one (whose name this depon^t dothe not nowe remember,) the some of xxx^{li}. wch was due vnto the saide Evans, and wch xx^{li} thereof to dischardge the saide assignment, and the other x^{li} to be paied backe to the saide Evans. and beinge desierous to knowe what had beene done therein:

he this depon^t asked the said Garstacke yf the saide Robert
Skynner had received the saide money by vertue of the saide
lrē of Attorney. whereunto the saide Garstacke awnsweared
that he had received it, then (qth this Depon^t) What is become
of the x^{li} overplus that (qth the saide Garstacke) was paied over
to the saide Evans. Then this Depon^t (pceivinge by the saide
Garstackẹ speeches, that the writingẹ were in his handẹ. notwith-
standinge the paym^t of the saide xx^{li}.) asked the said Garstacke
Whie the writingẹ weare not deliūed backe againe, to the said
Evans. whereunto the saide Garstacke made a very vnpfecte
awnsweare in so much as this depon^t did suspecte some ill dealinge in that matter. And afterwardẹ this depon^t vrginge him
againe whie he kepte the saide Writingẹ in his handẹ. the saide
Garstacke (as this deponent conceived) havinge forgott his
former speeches towlde this Depon^t, that the saide Robert Skynner did before his deathe deliū them vnto him. and willed him
to helpe himself by those writingẹ. for the debt wch he did owe
him but what the same debt was this depon^t knoweth not: but
hathe heard it was about 3^{li}. And more to this Jnter' he can not
depose/

p me [signed] Jo: milton:

Public Record Office, Chancery Town Depositions, C24/309/70;
not previously published. Though the year does not appear on this record,
it is likely that it was 1604, since Milton was probably about 40 years
old in that year. The introductory lines may be translated: "Taken before me, Otho Nicholson, in the absence of Master Robertson." I have
given this document entire because it presents so vividly the actions, including even the conversations, of the elder Milton as he engaged in
his business as a scrivener. The figure 8 at the beginning refers to the
question, or interrogatory, which he is here answering. For this document, as for several other similar ones, I am indebted to the researches
of Mr. Charles A. Bernau. Lacking the Chancery action of which this
deposition is part, I cannot be sure of the year. But 1604 is probably
close. It would be worth while some time for some scholar to search out
the Chancery actions pertaining to this and other depositions of Milton's
father to be named later in this section in order to discover such additional facts about his career as may be given in them. As usual, Milton
signed his name at the foot of each page.

1604. OCTOBER 23. FATHER TESTIFIES IN COURT ABOUT
INVESTMENT FOR ANNE EDWARDS.

Jhon Milton of the pishe of all Hallowes in Breadstreete London Schrivenoᵉ of the age of 40 yeares or thereaboutꝑ sworne &
ēxd the 23ᵗʰ of Octobeʳ Año 2° Jacobi Regꝑ deposeth & sayeth.
That he knoweth the Compᵗ & Defᵗ & did knowe Anne late wief 1
to the Defᵗ.

That he this depᵗ can not now certainely remember what seũall 2
somes of money the Compᵗ did from tyme to tyme bringe to
this depᵗꝑ shoppe, nor to what ꝑson or ꝑsonꝑ the same were lent
and deliũed, nor vppon what specialtyes pawnes plate or Jewellꝑ
they were lent, but he sayeth that he hath kepte a note in his
booke of all such somes of money as came to this depᵗꝑ handꝑ
at any tyme from the sᵈ Compᵗ. albeit yt is not precisely expressed in the same note what severall somes the Compᵗ himselff did bring to the shoppe of this Depᵗ, but he remembreth
that the Compᵗ did bringe divers somes of money to his shoppe
and he sayeth that all the specialtyes & securityes made for the
same wᶜʰ the compˡᵗ himselff brought were made in the Compᵗꝑ
owne name, but howe longe or to whose vse this depᵗ knoweth
not. And as he thinketh the specialtyes & pawnes for the same
viz for thos that the compˡᵗ. himself brought were deliũed to
the Compᵗꝑ owne handꝑ. And he further sayeth that nether the
defᵗ nor any other in his name to this depᵗꝑ now remembrance
did at any tyme chalenge any proꝑtye trust or confidence in the
s̄d money or at any tyme intermedled wᵗʰ the loane & employment of any money brought by the compˡᵗ or lent in his name.
And he further sayeth that the paiment of the sᵈ money at yᵉ
day limitted in yᵉ sᵈ specialtyes was appointed in yᵉ beginninge
to be made & doñe in this depᵗꝑ shoppe, but for whose vse he
knoweth not nether doth he remember vnto what grosse some
in ende the same did amounte vnto in the wholle And for further answer to the true drifte and meaninge of this interr' (as
this depᵗ taketh yt) he sayeth That divers somes of money then
(besides such as were deliũed to this depᵗ by the sᵈ Compᵗꝑ owne

handₚ) were deliūed vnto him or his servant by Anne Edwardₚ
late Wief of the now Def'; and all the specialtyes & pawnes for
the same were for some certeyne tyme wch he nowe remembreth
not tyme taken in the Compᵗᵖ name but deliūed to the s^d Anne
Edwardₚ so longe as she lived, And shortely after the decease
of the s^d Anne Edwardₚ as this dep^t taketh yt the def^t did come
to this depᵗᵖ shoppe and challenged & claimed as his owne all
such somͤs of money for the wch security or pawnes were then
taken in the Compᵗᵖ name, and as they or any of them grew
due, made them in his owne name. (as more plainly & pticularly
doth appere by this depᵗᵖ note booke) then now he can sett
downe. And this is all that he doth remember for the satisfyinge
of this interr'

3 That he did not from tyme to tyme as the paymentₚ or renuyngₚ
of the p^rmiss happend goe or send to the Comp^t only, either to
receive the money due or to take order for the renuyngₚ thereof,
but also went and sent to the s^d Anne Edwardₚ duringe her lyfe
& afterwardₚ to her husband the def^t. And he sayeth that in the
beginninge he this dep^t in the absence of ye Comp^t did renue
various specialtyes in the Compᵗᵖ name but by ye consent of y^e
s^d Anne Edwardₚ as he remembreth, and he sayeth that vppon
his now remembrance he cannot certainely sett downe vnto
whome he delivered them or sent the same, or vnto whose vse
they were.

4 That he knoweth not what plate & Jewels are mentioned in the
deftₚ answere, because he never read the same And therefore
he cannot satisfye any of the severall demaundₚ of this interr'.

5 That the Comp^t did of late tell him this dep^t that the def^t vppon
an agrement betwixt them had, made him a Bill for the payment of two hundred poundₚ & gave his worde for the vse
money. And more or otherwise this dep^t cannot depose to any
of y^e questions in this interr' for oughte he now remembreth.

6 That he remembreth not that any such promisse was made as is
mentioned in this article, but he sayth that so much money as

[186]

this Jnter' speeketh of this dep^t. received so longe as the s^d
Anne Edward$\wp$ lived from tyme to tyme

That to his remembrance he nether had to doe wth the def^t 7
duringe his s^d wifes lyfe for any somes of money made in the
Comp^{te} name but afterwardes, he dealte only wth y^e def^t touch-
inge those somes formerly made in y^e Comp^{te} name, & wth none
other, & for ought this dep^t knoweth all the s^d somes are now
still remayninge in the deft$\wp$ hand$\wp$ or at his disposinge.

That he verily thinketh y^t he did put forth money for the def^t 8
him selfe & in his name wthout any mention made of y^e Comp^t
& at no pte of y^e foresayd money before the death of the s^d Anne
the deft^e wyef. but for more certainty thereof he referreth him
self to his note booke wch hee wilbee ready to shew forth yf occasion requyre.

That he cannot directly answer to this interr' because he know- 9
eth not what plate or Jewell$\wp$ are expressed in the s^d bill & Answer.

That he cannot depose. vide postea+   10

That true yt is that y^e def^t shortely after the decease of the s^d 11+
Anne Edward$\wp$ his late wife did come vnto this dep^t to vnder-
stande what money & specialtyes this dep^t did knowe of w^{ch}
then went in the Comp^{te} name. And this dep^t sayeth that as
he now remembreth he did then certifye the Def^t of the whole
Value of the same & also did then tell the Def^t that the Comp^t
vsed to take but after nyne in the hundreth interest for one
hundred pound$\wp$ of the s^d money: Wherevppon the Def^t replyed & sayed that then all was his & he would have after tenne
pound$\wp$ in the hundred, or to the like effect. And lastely he sayeth
that xx^s was formerly allowed vnto him this dep^t for his care &
paynes in kepinge & continuinge in loane & vse the plate & Jewels wch wente in the Comp^{te} name.

That Peter Jones this dept$\wp$ servaunt about the tyme mentioned 12
in this interr' as he remembreth did write a note in this dept$\wp$
booke to make a bill obligatorye from the def^t to the Comp^t
to the effect mentioned in this interr'. but he knoweth not what

moved the def^t not to seale the same bill in this dep^{te} shoppe, yet he hearde yt reported that y^e def^t did seale y^e like Bill to y^e Comp^t aboute the same tyme at one Dims shoppe a Sriveno^r neere Cheape syde.

21 That he can say nothinge savinge that the s^d Anne the Deft^e
22 late Wyfe was put in trust wth divers somes of money, wch were putt forth in the name of the Comp^t, but whether the s^d trust were comitted vnto her by the Comp^t or the Def^t this dep^t knoweth not.

23 That the def^t had certaine somes of money in other mens hand^e at the tyme mentioned in this interr', & yt he deliūed the money him selfe & tooke the specialtyes there vppon made in his owne name & that this dep^t deliūed the s^d specialties vnto the Deft^e owne handes as he verily thinketh. & that ye Def^t disposed there-of alwayes at his owne pleasure wthout mention made of the Comp^t, in that behaulfe. And he sayeth that he doth not cer-tainely remember what some or somes of money the Def^t did so dispose of, but referreth him selfe to his note booke where the same is certainely sett downe.

24 That he never heard to his remembrance y^t ye Def^t trusted the Comp^t wth ye layinge out or keepinge of any of ye s^d Deft^e prop good^e or that he trusted the Comp^t to take securitye for the s^d good^e in his owne name.

28 That vppon his now remembrance he cannot more say then he
30 hath alreddy deposed in his answers to the other interr' savinge that he sayeth that he never hearde to his remembrance that the Def^t made any clame to the s^d money plate or Jewels put forth & taken in the Comp^{te} name duringe the lyfe of the sayd Anne his wief.

To the rest not exd by dirrection

[signed] Jo: milton

Public Record Office, Chancery Town Depositions, C24/312/55; not previously published. The manuscript has been much written over and revised, so that it is hard to read; and the answers to questions 9, 10, and 11 come at the end with lines to indicate where they belong. As usual, the deponent signs his name at the bottom of each page.

1605. JANUARY 4. FATHER TESTIFIES IN COURT ABOUT
FINANCIAL TRANSACTIONS FOR JOHN CHESEWRIGHT,
AGNES BIRD, AND ROBERT PYNFOLD IN 1600.

4° Januarij anno. 2. Jacobi Regis   ꝑ Pynfold
John Mylton̄ Citizen and wryter of the Courte lr̄e of the Citty
of London of the age of 40. yeres or therabtꝑ sworne &c vppon
the 1 & 25 Jnterr̄s

Jnter'. That he knoweth the partyes to this sute bothe p̄ltꝑ and 1
deftꝑ.

That abowte fyve yeres past as he best remembreth John Chese- 25
wright one of the now dēftꝑ gaue this dēpt dyreccons for the
drawing and makeing of a lease in wryting betwene him the s̄d
Chesewright and a wydowe woman then dwelling in a Corner
howse as he taketh it wch is scituat ptely in ffanchurche street &
partelye in Gracions strete London whervppon he this dēpt dyd
accordingly drawe & make the s̄d lease bering date the xvth day
of July 1600 wherby the s̄d wydow woman whose name was
Agnes Bird together wth Rychard Pynfold one of the now
Com̄pltꝑ dyd demise the shoppe of the s̄d howse together w^{th}
two back romes or warehowses & one voyde rome or entery in
the same howse vnto the s̄d John Chesewright his executo^{rs} ad-
minstrators & assignes . . . for the yerly rent of one peper Corne
. . . But he well rembreth that at suche tyme as the s̄d Jndenture
of lease was made There was likewise an Jndenture of Covenantꝑ
made . . . wherin the s̄d John Chesewright dothe Covenant to
paye vnto the s̄d Agnes Bird her Executors or Assignes the
sum̄e of Cxl^{li} of lawfull money of England for the s̄d demised
p^{r}misses in nature of a ffyne at the shopp before menconed . . .
And morover this dep^{t} sayth that as he best rembreth yt was
furth^{r} agreed betwene the s̄d Agnes Byrd & the s̄d John Chesewright by word of mouthe abowte the tyme of the makeing of
the s̄d lease that he the sayd Chesewright should paye vnto the
s̄d Agnes Bird in Consideracōn of the s̄d demise forty shillingꝑ
yerly or the valew therof and more &c.

                     [signed] Jo: milton:

Public Record Office, Chancery Town Depositions, C24/311/76; not previously published. The corner of Grace Church Street and Fenchurch Street, here mentioned, is about half a mile east from Milton's office in Bread Street. The phrase "writer of the court letter" used in the opening lines is simply another term for "scrivener." See Masson, I (1881), 25.

1605. JANUARY 21. FATHER AGAIN TESTIFIES ABOUT INVESTMENTS FOR ANNE EDWARDS AND ALSO ABOUT HIS "FALSE AND LOOSE" APPRENTICE PETER JONES.

21. Januarij anno .2. Jacobi Regis. p̃ Edwardp̃

John. Myltoñ of Londoñ Scryvenoʳ dwelling in Bredstreete of the age of 40 yeres or thereabtp̃ sworne &c vppon the .1.2.3.6. 7.8.10. & 13 Jnterrs. 1 Jnter'.

1 That he knoweth the partyes to this sute bothe plt & dẽft and hath knowne them thes fower or five yeres past and dyd know Anne Edwardp̃ named in the Jnter' when she lyved for the space of two yeres or therabtp̃ as he taketh it before her decease

2 That he knoweth that in the lief tyme of the s̃d Anne Edwardp̃ late wief of the now dẽft there were dyvers & sundry sumes of money delyvred owte and lent somtymes by the s̃d Comp̃lt John Johanes & somtymes by the sayde Anne Edwardp̃ some vppon bondp̃. and some vppon pawnes of plate & Jewells for wᶜʰ there were made bills of sale all wᶜʰ bondp̃ and bills were made in the name of the s̃d John Joanes from the tenth of June 1600. vntill the viijᵗʰ day of September *1601.* . . . .

3 That he this dep̃t being the man that dyd make the bondp̃ and bills of sale for dyvers sũmes of money lent as afores̃d somtymes by the p̃ltp̃ delyvery and somtymes by the delivery of the s̃d Anne Edwardp̃ dyd as occason served somtymes goe him self to the s̃d Anne & somtymes sent his srvant to her & to the Com̃plt for moneyes to be lent vnto dyvers p̃sons somtymes vppon bond & somtymes vppon pawnes by bills of sale. . . .

7 That the dẽft hath hertofore shewed vnto this dep̃t an obligacoñ wherin as yt semed the p̃lts stode bound to the dẽft for paymẽt

[190]

of a Certen sume of money wch as he rembreth was two hundred poundꝑ or therabtꝑ. . . .

That Peter Joanes named in this Jnter' ys at this p^rsent s^rvant to this dept whose Credyt this dept cannot comend for that he hath knowne him bothe a faulse & lose fellowe hertofore and hathe bene in some trouble for yt but being a young fellowe this dept hath bene & ys contented to kepe him still vppon hope of amendemēt and his promise to become a reformed mañ but hertofore he hath throughe yll Companye & Counsell as this Dēpt supposeth behaved him self very lewdly in fylching bothe from this dēpt & others and hath bene a very disobedyent srvant and somtymes over taken wth drinke. and more to thes Jnterr̄s he cannot depose nor more &c

{ 10
13 }

[signed] Jo: milton.

Public Record Office, Chancery Town Depositions, C24/315/20; not previously published. What relation there may have been between the "lewd" servant Peter Jones and the plaintiff in the suit John Johanes or Jones remains a mystery.

1605. APRIL 24. FATHER TESTIFIES IN COURT ABOUT INVESTMENTS FOR JOHN WILLIAMS, EDWARD RYDER, AND OTHERS.

24 Aprilis Anno .3. Jacobi Regis   ꝑ Rider.
John Miltoñ Citizen & Wryter of the Court lrē of Londoñ of the age of 40 yeres or therabtꝑ sworne &c. 1 Inter'. That he knoweth all the ptyes to this sute both p̄lt & dēftꝑ And hath knowne them all for dyvers yeres past.

That abowte two yeres now past the now deft John Williams 2 dyd lend vppon the ioynt & seūall bond of Edward Ryder Roger Walmesly & George Walmeslye named in this Jnter'. the sume of one hundred poundꝑ. . . .

That he herd the s̄d George Walmesly saye that he dyd receive 3 some pte of the s̄d hundred poundꝑ when yt was lent but he sayd he knewe not well whether yt were fyftie poundꝑ, more or lesse.

. . .

4 That after the s̄d hundred poundȝ wᵗʰ interest for the same
was due to the s̄d John Willm̄s by the Condicoñ of the s̄d obligacoñ the s̄d Edward Ryder came to this dept & towld him that
he could provide but threescore poundȝ towardȝ the paymēt
of the s̄d hundred poundȝ & therfore desyred this dept to helpe
him to forty poundȝ towardȝ the paymēt therof vppon the bond
of him the s̄d Ryder & George Walmesly. Whervppon this dept
procured from Rōbt Est in the Jnter' named the sum̄e of forty
poundȝ vppon the bond of the s̄d Ryder & George Walmesly
and thervppon the same forty poundȝ and the sum̄e of three
score poundȝ more & some odd money to the valew of fyve or
sixe poundȝ or therabtȝ was payd by the s̄d Ryder to the s̄d John
Williams wᶜʰ the sayd Williams dyd receyve but dyd not accept therof as in full satisfaccoñ of the s̄d bond for that the s̄d
John Willm̄s required a further Consyderacoñ for his often
com̄ing to towne in the heate of the last sycknes of the plague
and his attendance there & Charge of him self wᵗʰ a man and two
geldingȝ at a Com̄on Jnne wᵗʰowte Bishopsgate still expecting
paymēt of the s̄d hundred poundȝ & interest according to manye
promisses of the s̄d Ryder as the s̄d John Willm̄s affirmed in
pʳsence & hering of this dept. . . .

6 That to the knoledg of this dept the s̄d John Willm̄s hathe not
assigned the s̄d obligacon of CCˡⁱ wherin the s̄d Ryder wᵗʰ the
s̄d Roger & George Walmesly stand bound for paymēt of the
s̄d Cˡⁱ & interest for the same As by the artycle ys intended for
this dept thinketh that he hathe that bond in his Custodye. . . .

[signed] Jo: milton:

Public Record Office, Chancery Town Depositions, C24/317/63;
not previously published.

1607. JANUARY 21. FATHER WITNESSES SCUDAMORE-
CALTON INDENTURE.

This Jndenture made the one and twentith day of January
one thowsand six hundreth and six . . . Between Richard Scudamor of London Gentleman on the one part And Thomas Calton

of Dulwich in the parishe of Camberwell in the Countie of Surrey Gentleman on the other part. [Scudamore transfers to Calton his lease, from Sir Frances Calton and Thomas Hopkins, of several parcels of land in Dulwich in return for £40 to be paid by Calton in four installments, of which the last is due on April 8, 1609.] ... Jn witnes whereof the parties aforesaid to these Jndentures Enterchangeably haue sett their handꝑ and seales yeouen the day and yeare first aboue written

Sealed and deliūed in the p̄sence of

[signed:] Jo: milton: scr

Richard Scudamor

John Roch [?]

[Signed also below:] Richard Scudamor

[Memorandum on the back:] The xxth day of december *1608*

M^r that J the wthinnamed Richard Scudamo^r doe hereby acknoleg to haue received of the wthin named Thomas Calton the three first somes of mony on the dayes wthin specified and doe herby acknowledge to haue receivd of the s̄d Thomas Calton on the day afores̄d. the some of tenn poundꝑ residue of the said some of ffourty poundꝑ wthin mencōed wch shoold be paid on the viiith day of Aprill next as is wthin mencōed J say Re^{cd} x^{li}.

[Signed:] Richard Scudamor

Witnes Edward Ouerey

[Beside this memorandum:] Sealed and deliūed in the p̄nce of [signed] Jo: milton: scr.

[Also beside the memorandum:] x^{li}

Dulwich College Muniment 503; mentioned by George F. Warner in the *Athenaeum* for 1880, 1, 376; Masson, 1 (1881), 4; partial facsimile in Brennecke, facing p. 50. I am grateful to Dulwich College and to its librarian, W. S. Wright, for information about this record and for a photostatic copy of it. Though Mr. Wright reads the third signature as "John Roch," as I have given it above, it is difficult to see this name in the reproduction, which looks more like Jolyon Ross. It should be noticed that the poet's father signed this document in two places and at two different dates: the first on January 21, 1607, and the second on December 20, 1608, the day of the young poet's baptism.

1607. MAY 12. FATHER WITNESSES WILLIAMS-SHEL-
LEY DEED.

[On May 12, 1607, John Williams of London gave a deed of assignment of property in St. John's Street, Clerkenwell, to Richard Shelley of Itchingfield. One of the witnesses who signed the document was] Jo: Milton: scr.

Perceval Lucas described this deed, then in his own possession, in *Notes and Queries*, XI, ii (1910), 427; French, *Milton in Chancery*, p. 13. Nothing further seems to have been heard of this record.

1607. JULY 20. FATHER'S SERVANTS WITNESS THROCK-
MORTON-HUNTLEY BOND.

Noverint Vniūsi per pñtes me Nicholañ Throckmorton de Mitcham in Com̃ Surr' Generosum teneri et firmiter obligari Johñi Huntley de Wallington in dict' Com̃ Surr' generoso in Centum Libris . . . Dat' Vicesimo die Julij 1607 Annoqz Regni dnī nrī Jacobi dei grā Anglie & ffranc' et Hibñie Regis fidei defensor' &c' Quinto Ac Scotie Quadragesimo:/:/

[signed] N Throckmorton

Sigīll et delīv in pnc̃:
Law: Edwards svien̄ Johīs Milton scr
Jo: ffippes srvieñ dict' scr

[In lower right hand corner:] M̃ʳ Thorckmortō 55ˡⁱ the xxjᵗʰ of July *1608* 5: 9°. 1°.

[On the back:] The condicoñ of this obligacoñ is such That yf the wᵗʰin bound Nicholas Throckmorton his heires executors admīstrators or assignes doe well and truly pay or cause to be paid vnto the wᵗʰin named John Huntley his executors admīstrators or assignes Att or in the now dwelling house of the said John Huntley in Wallington wᵗʰin written the sōme of ffiftie and ffyve poundes of good and lawfull money of England On the One and twentith daye of Julie wᶜʰ shalbe in the yere of oʳ Lord God One thowsand six hundred and eight That then this obligacoñ to be void and of none effect Or ells it to stand in full force and vertue:/:/

British Museum Additional Charter 23,573; mentioned by George F. Warner in the *Athenaeum* for 1880, I, 376. I am not certain whether the note at the bottom is a record of payment or a reminder of the date due. Additional Charter 23,574 is so similar to the above document that it is easy to confuse the two. They are both between the same parties, of the same date, and signed by the same witnesses in virtually identical signatures. But curious changes occur. In 23,574 Throckmorton appears as "Militem" (soldier, knight) rather than as "Generosum" (gentleman); Huntley is of Binderton rather than of Wallington; and the amount of money is £120 rather than £100. In addition, though the signatures are closely alike, the texts are obviously written by two different scribes. Minor variations also appear, but the foregoing are the only ones of significance. I have no explanation of the divergences, and presumably they have no bearing on Milton.

[Know all men by these presents that I, Nicholas Throckmorton of Mitcham in co. Surrey, gentleman, am held and firmly obligated to John Huntley of Wallington in the said co. Surrey, gentleman, in one hundred pounds. . . . Given on the twentieth day of July, 1607, and in the fifth year of the reign of our lord James by the grace of God defender of the faith of England and France and Ireland, and in the fortieth year of Scotland.

N. Throckmorton.

Sealed and delivered in the presence of Lawrence Edwards, servant of John Milton, scrivener, and of John Fippes, servant of the said scrivener.]

1608. FATHER'S CONDITION AND POSITION AT TIME OF POET'S BIRTH.

Londini sum natus, genere honesto, patre viro integerrimo. . . .

Milton, *Defensio Secunda*, London, 1654, pp. 81-82; CM, VIII, 119.

[I was born in London, of an honorable family, my father being a man of the highest integrity. . . .]

[His father was a scrivener] and gott a plentiful estate by it & left it off many yeares before he dyed. . . .

[His father lived] at yᵉ Spread Eagle, wᶜʰ was his house,

he had also in y^t street another house the Rose and other houses in other places.

Aubrey, f. 63; Darbishire, p. 1. This entry has been so marked over that it is almost incoherent. But it is reasonably understandable.

[As a scrivener his father] was so prosperous in it, and the Consortship of a prudent virtuous Wife, as to bee able to breed up in a liberal manner, and provide a competency for two Sons, and a Daughter. . . .

The "earliest" biography, f. 140; Darbishire, p. 18.

[His father was a scrivener;] this Vocation he followed for many Years, at his said House in *Breadstreet*, with success suitable to his Industry, and prudent conduct of his Affairs. . . .

Yet all this while, he managed his Grand Affair of this World with such Prudence and Diligence, that by the assistance of Divine Providence favouring his honest endeavours, he gained a Competent Estate, whereby he was enabled to make a handsom Provision both for the Education and Maintenance of his Children. . . .

Phillips, pp. iv-v; Darbishire, pp. 51-52.

(2) That his Father *Joh. Milton* who was a Scrivner living at the *Spread Eagle* in the said street. . . .

Wood, I, 880; Darbishire, p. 35. An asterisk in the original after *"Spread Eagle"* refers to a note on the family coat of arms, which will be described below. Brennecke (pp. 50-51) quotes from Stow's *Survey of London* that at about this time Bread Street was "now wholly inhabited by rich merchants."

1608. CHARACTER AND POSITION OF MOTHER AT TIME OF POET'S BIRTH.

Londini sum natus . . . matre probatissima, & eleemosynis per viciniam potissimùm notà.

Milton, *Defensio Secunda*, London, 1654, pp. 81-82; CM, VIII, 119. Wood (as quoted above, I, 367) repeats the statement about the poet's mother's charities.

[I was born in London . . . of a most virtuous mother, especially known for her charities throughout the vicinity.]

his mother was a *Bradshaw*. Crest an Arme dexter holding
an Eagles head & Neck erased G. . . . q̄.Xpr: Milton [his brother the Jnner Temple] Bencher. . . .

Sarah Bradshaw

Aubrey, ff. 63, 68v; Darbishire, pp. 1, 8. The first paragraph consists of two notes written in as afterthoughts at the two upper corners
of the page; the second is simply the name of the elder Milton's wife
as given in Aubrey's genealogy. On the left corner of the first page is
a rough copy of a shield showing a spread eagle as described; in the
top middle is one consisting of two diagonal bars s[able] on a field
a[rgent]. Aubrey's editor Clark (1, 61) renders it "argent, 2 bendlets
sable." The former is presumably the Milton arms, the latter the Bradshaw. Aubrey's entries are much written over.

As the earlier entries in this section show, the poet's mother was almost certainly a Jeffrey rather than either a Bradshaw or a Caston
(as Phillips says). However, it is highly likely that there were Bradshaws and Castons in her family, as well as probably Haughtons. By
a slight slip either Phillips or some member of the family to whom he
talked could easily have given one of the closely related names as the
actual maiden name of Sarah Jeffrey. Masson (1, 1881, 30-39) gives
a thorough discussion of this whole problem.

his mother had very weake eies, & used spectacles pʳsently
after she was thirty yeares old.

Aubrey, f. 68; Darbishire, p. 5. If, as I have speculated above, she
was born in 1572, she must have begun wearing glasses about in 1602,
and thus would have been doing so from the time of her son's earliest
recollection. In this sentence Aubrey probably means "consequently"
by "presently." The relation between the weak eyes of mother and son
is easy to see.

[The poet's father was so prosperous in his work as a scriv-
ener] and the Consortship of a prudent virtuous Wife, as to
bee able to breed up in a liberal manner, and provide a competency for two Sons, and a Daughter.

The "earliest" biography, f. 140; Darbishire, p. 18.

. . . his Mother named *Sarah* was of the antient Family of
the *Bradshaws*.

Wood, 1, 880; Darbishire, p. 35.

[The poet's father had three children,] all by one Wife,
Sarah, of the Family of the *Castons*, derived originally from

Wales. A Woman of Incomparable Vertue and Goodness; *John* the Eldest, the Subject of our present Work. *Christopher*, and an onely Daughter *Ann.*

Phillips, p. v; Darbishire, p. 52.

JOHN MILTON, the Son likewise of *John Milton*, and *Sarah Caston*, a Woman exemplary for her Liberality to the Poor. . . .

Toland, p. 6; Darbishire, p. 85.

1608. FATHER'S COAT OF ARMS.

["In MS. Aubr. 8, fol. 63, Aubrey gives in trick the coat for Milton:"] argent, a double-headed eagle displayed gules legged and beaked sable.

Crest an Arme dexter holding an Eagles head & Neck erased G.

Aubrey, f. 63; Darbishire, p. 1. The first paragraph quoted above is not what Aubrey wrote, but the interpretation of the drawing in his manuscript by A. Clark in his edition of Aubrey's *Brief Lives*, II (1898), 61; the second paragraph is actually Aubrey's wording. Masson discusses the Milton arms at I (1881), 5-9. He also describes (*ibid.*, pp. 5-7) two of Milton's seals, one known from the Simmons agreement of 1667, and the other thought to be then in the possession of Edgar Disney, Esq. He reproduces both on p. 6.

Argent, an Eagle display'd with two heads *Gules*, member'd *Sable.* This Coat was born by *John Milton*, Author of *Paradice lost and re-gain'd.* . . .

This was us'd also by *Christopher Milton* (Brother of the said Poet). . . .

John Guillim, *A Display of Heraldry*, 1724, p. 210. Guillim gives as his source for the first part "M.S. *of* Ant. à Wood, *F.* 3. p. 168." This note is repeated in British Museum Add. MS. 19,142, f. 79.

Mylton.

324. E[nglish]. A. a double headed Eagle displaid G bequed & membred B

L[atin]. Aquilam bicipitem coccinei coloris expansam rostro & crucibus tamen coeruleis in campo candido

F[rench]. D'argent à l'aigle eploie aux deux tétes de gueules. bequé & membré d'azure.

To . . . Mylton aḽs Mytton of Coṁ. Oxoñ. . . . of ye abovesd Arms & Crest vizt Out of a wreath a Lyons gamb coup'd & erect A. grasping an Eagles head erased G.

British Museum Add. MS. 12,225 ("Aspidora Segariana"), number 324; Hunter, p. 8; Masson, 1 (1881), 6. Masson points out that Segar was Garter King-at-Arms from 1603 to 1633; that this is one of a list of grants and confirmations of arms made by Segar; that the entry shows that someone from Oxfordshire applied to the College of Arms for either a grant or a confirmation; and that the applicant could have been Milton's father. Since Segar died in 1633, this transaction must at least have preceded that date though in the manuscript it is undated.

The Arms that *Joh. Milton* did use and seal his Letters with, were *Argent a spread Eagle with two heads gules, legg'd and beak'd sable.*

Wood, 1, 880; Darbishire, p. 35. This statement is a footnote, connected with asterisks, to Wood's mention of the Spread Eagle as the poet's father's residence.

Mr. *Milton's* Mother (I am informed[4]) was a *Haughton* of *Haughton-Tower* in *Lancashire*; as appears by the arms of his father & mother in pale, upon a board, a quarter of a yard square, some time since in possession of his widow. Where, under his father's arms, is wrote *Milton* [of *Milton* near *Abingdon*] in *Com. Oxon.* &, under his mother's, *Haughton* of *Haughton-Tower* in *Com. Lanc.*

[Footnote:] 4. From a Letter of *Roger Comberbach* of *Chester* Esq; to *William Cowper* Esq; Clerk of the Parliament, dated 15. *Dec.* 1736.

Francis Peck, *New Memoirs of . . . Milton,* 1740, p. 1; Milton, *A Complete Collection of the . . . Works,* ed. Thomas Birch, 1753, 1, ii; Masson, 1, 9. The brackets are in Peck. On Comberbach, see above, 1, 206.

Milton, the proud republican, had a coat of arms; he bore on a field, sa. an eagle, arg^t. doubled headed, gu, beak and legs. sa.—

Ibid. [Chateaubriand's *Sketches of English Literature*, Vol. II], p. 146.

Chateaubriand's heraldry is incorrect, as may be seen from the above quotation from Gwillim.

British Museum Add. MS. 19,142, f. 79v. In this note Joseph Hunter is referring back to his previous copy of Guillim's note, given above.

JOHN MILTON
Born 1608, died 1674

Argent a double headed eagle displayed gules beaked and legged azure

A Patent of confirmation of these Arms with the grant of a Crest, by Sir William Segar, Garter, to "Mylton *alias* Mytton of . . . Co. Oxford," is recorded. This is undoubtedly John Milton's father, who named his inn in Bread Street the Spread Eagle. A "Painter's Work Book" in the College of Arms (I. B. 7, fo. 46b) records the use of these Arms at "the funerall of Secretary Milton his wife her name Woodcock" in 1658. The coat is based, without historical justification, on that of Mytton of Shropshire.

Anthony R. Wagner, *Historic Heraldry of Britain*, Oxford, 1939, p. 80, number 93. I am grateful to Professor Henry L. Savage of Princeton University for calling this item to my attention, and to Mr. Wagner himself for his kindness in answering some questions of mine and for procuring for me a copy of the entry in the "Painter's Work Book" which he here describes. The written part of that entry is given above under date of February 10, 1658, the day of Milton's second wife's funeral. Like the other entries in the Work Book, this one is accompanied at the side by what Mr. Wagner identifies as a "rough trick" of the combined spread-eagle arms of Milton and those of the Woodcock family. Facing page 80 in Mr. Wagner's book is a beautiful reproduction in black and white of Milton's spread-eagle arms.

1608. FEBRUARY 27. FATHER ARRANGES SHERES-WALTHEW BOND.

. . . the Defft Robert Walthewe by an obligacōn dated the xxvij[th] day of ffebruary Aō Dnī 1607. did become bound to the

plt in the penall somme of fower hundred poundℓ condicōned
for the paymt of CCxx^{li} to the complt at the shoppe of the depont in Breadstreete london vpon the first day of March Ao
Dnī 1608 . . .

From the elder Milton's deposition in a later Chancery suit over
this loan on October 8, 1623, *q.v.* It is interesting to note that as late
as 1623, as usual, Milton refreshed his memory by referring to "a note
in a booke wch he keepeth for such purposes," and that "for more cer-
tenty he doeth referre himself" to this book. Neither the book nor the
bond, so far as is known, is now extant. According to Milton's testimony
the debt was reasonably well paid "at or about the tyme lymitted for
the payment thereof" and presumably at the shop in Bread Street.

MILTON'S FAMILY AND AFFAIRS
AFTER HIS DEATH

Only in the narrowest sense do the life records of Milton end with his death and burial in early November, 1674. Some of his writings remained unpublished until years later, and members of his family lived on. As Masson and others have realized, it would be shortsighted to stop at this point.

Yet it would be difficult for any six people to agree what to include and what to exclude in Milton's posthumous record. Many items could be justified on one basis or another. Important and often interesting allusions to his life and his poetry invite acceptance. The story of the growth of appeal of his writings, as evidenced in growingly frequent editions of them, is hard to reject. But for the present work I have decided to limit the coverage to (1) biographical data about Milton's immediate family (with a few concessions to the Powell family), (2) the first publications of posthumous works, (3) the first publications of English translations of books not appearing in English in the poet's lifetime, and (4) the first appearance of a few important early biographies.

Many facts which are of great interest even though we cannot find room for them here have been gathered in the following publications, which deal with the first fifty or a hundred years after Milton's death. All of them have discovered new references to Milton during this period, which all succeeding biographies have freely incorporated to whatever extent they have found appropriate. They are here listed chronologically in order of appearance.

1. William Godwin, *Lives of Edward and John Philips*, London, 1815.

2. J. G. Robertson, "Milton's Fame on the Continent," *Proceedings of the British Academy*, III (1908), 319-340.

3. G. Waterhouse, *The Literary Relations of England and Germany in the Seventeenth Century*, Cambridge, 1914.

4. John W. Good, *Studies in the Milton Tradition*, Urbana (University of Illinois Studies in Language and Literature, Volume I, numbers 3 and 4), 1915.

5. George Sherburn, "The Early Popularity of Milton's Minor Poems," *Modern Philology*, XVII (1919-20), 259-278 and 515-540.

6. Raymond D. Havens, *The Influence of Milton on English Poetry*, Cambridge, Massachusetts, 1922.

7. C. A. Moore, "Miltoniana (1679-1741)," *Modern Philology*, XXIV (1926-27), 321-339.

8. Alfred Gertsch, "Der steigende Ruhm Miltons," Leipzig (Kölner Anglistische Arbeiten, Number 2), 1927.

9. H. Scherpbier, *Milton in Holland*, Paris, 1933.

10. William R. Parker, *Milton's Contemporary Reputation*, Columbus, Ohio, 1940.

11. George F. Sensabaugh, *That Grand Whig Milton*, Stanford, California (Stanford University Publications, University Series, Language and Literature, Volume XI), 1952.

I wish to record my appreciation of all these books, together with many others which I may have occasion to notice more specifically.

1674. NOVEMBER 23. BROTHER CHRISTOPHER WRITES AND FILES POET'S NUNCUPATIVE WILL.

. . . he this rond[t]. did draw vpp the very will extēd in this cause & write it with his owne hand when he came to this Court about the 23th of November last past and at that tyme this rond[t] did read the same all over to Elizabeth ffisher the sd deceasedρ late maid servant and she said she remembred the same and in confirmation thereof set her marke thereto in manner as on the same will exted in this cause is now to be seen. and this rond[t] waited on the sd deceasedρ Widdow once at Docr Extons chambr about this suite at w[ch] tyme she wanted some halfe Crowneρ and this rond[t] lent her then two halfe Crownes but more he hath at noe tyme paid either to Docr or Proctor in this cause.

From Christopher Milton's answers to interrogatories on December 5, 1674, *q.v.* Elizabeth Fisher's "memorandum" about the poet's oral directions for the disposition of his estate has already been quoted above under date of July 20, 1674. Probably "extēd" in the first line stands for exhibited and not, as Warton transcribes it, executed. A proctor, mentioned near the end, is a lawyer who represents a client in a canon court as an attorney or solicitor does in other courts. Dr. Exton named here is probably Sir Thomas Exton (1631-1688), admiralty lawyer, who received the degree of LL.D. from the University of Cambridge in 1662, and who was knighted and made an admiralty judge some time before 1678 (*DNB*). But Venn says he was knighted in 1675 and appointed judge of the Admiralty in 1686. The third word in the text means "respondent."

1674. DECEMBER 1 (?). ALLEGATION PROPOUNDING MILTON'S WILL.

Negotium Testamentarium, sive probacionis Testamenti nuncupativi, sive ultimæ Voluntatis, JOHANNIS MILTON, nuper dum vixit parochiæ S. Ægidii *Cripplegate* London generosi, defuncti, habent, &c. promotum per Elizabetham MILTON Relictam, et Legatariam principalem nominatam in Testamento nuncupativo, sive ultima Voluntate, dicti defuncti, contra Mariam, Annam, et Deboram MILTON, filias dicti defuncti.

THOMPSON.   CLEMENTS.

Secundo Andreæ, A. D. 1674. Quo die . . . Thompson, nomine, procuratione, ac ultimus procurator legitimus, dictæ Elizabethæ MILTON, omnibus melioribus et effectualioribus [efficacioribus] via, modo, et meliori forma, necnon ad omnem juris effectum, exhibuit Testamentum nuncupativum dicti JOHANNIS MILTON defuncti, sic incipiens, 'MEMORANDUM, that JOHN MILTON, late of the parish of S. Giles, Cripplegate, &c.' Which words, or words to the same effect, were spoken in the presence of Christopher MILTON, and Elizabeth Fisher; et allegavit consimiliter, et dicens prout sequitur. I. Quod præfatus JOHANNES MILTON, dum vixit, mentis compos, ac in sua sana memoria existens, . . . Testamentum suum nuncupativum modo in hoc negotio exhibitum . . . tenoris schedulæ . . . testamentariæ condidit, nuncupavit, et declaravit; cæteraque omnia et singula dedit, donavit, reliquit, et disposuit, in omnibus, et per omnia, vel similiter in effectum, prout in dicto Testamento nuncupativo continetur, ac postea mortem obiit: ac Principalis Pars ista proponit conjunctim, divisim, et de quolibet. II. Item, quod tempore conditionis, declarationis, nuncupationis Testamenti, in hoc negotio exhibiti, præfatus JOHANNES MILTON perfecta fruebatur memoria; ac proponit ut supra.

Warton, 1791, pp. xxviii-xxix, from "Registr. Cur. Prærog. Cant." (Registry of the Prerogative Court of Canterbury); it has been repeated by Todd (I, 1826, 263-287), Marsh (*Papers*, 1851, pp. 36-44), and elsewhere, with the other papers in this business. Unfortunately, though I found most of these papers on a visit to London some years ago, and hence am able to give more exact copies than Warton's (since he modernizes and spells out rather than presenting the record as it stands), I missed this one and several others. When I have tried recently to get photostats of the entire series, the searcher selected by University Microfilms was able to find only one brief record, that of the letters of administration of February 25, 1674/5. I shall therefore be obliged at times to fall back, as here, on Warton's transcript. Warton adds one interesting note which deserves republication, that "this cause, the subject of which needed no additional lustre from great names, was tried by that upright and able statesman, Sir Leoline Jenkins, Judge of the Prerogative Court, and Secretary of State; and that the depositions were taken in part before Dr. Trumbull, afterwards Sir William Trumbull, Secretary of State, and the celebrated friend of Pope" (p. xxviii).

Warton's explanation of the proceedings may also be helpful: "This Will was contested by Mary, Deborah, and Anne Milton, daughters of the poet's first wife Mary, daughter of Mr. Richard Powell, of Forresthill in Oxfordshire. The cause came to a regular sentence, which was given against the Will; and the widow, Elizabeth, was ordered to take Administration instead of a Probate." Masson (VI, 735-744) gives the history in detail.

The "efficacioribus" in brackets is Warton's emendation.

[They (the undersigned Thompson and Clements?) have the business concerning the will, whether of the probating of the nuncupative testament or of the last will of John Milton, recently while he lived gentleman of the parish of St. Giles Cripplegate, London, deceased, etc.; the business being directed by Elizabeth Milton, relict and principal legatee named in the nuncupative testament or last will of the said deceased against Mary, Anne, and Deborah Milton, daughters of the said deceased.

Thompson.   Clements.

The day after St. Andrew's Day (November 30), 1674. On which day . . . Thompson, in the name and at the expense of and as last legal administrator for the said Elizabeth Milton, in all the better and more effective ways, means, and better form, also to the entire satisfying of the law, exhibited the nuncupative will of the said John Milton, deceased, beginning thus: "Memorandum, that John Milton, late of the parish of St. Giles Cripplegate, etc." Which words, or words to the same effect, were spoken in the presence of Christopher Milton and Elizabeth Fisher, and he alleged to the same effect, speaking as follows: 1. That the aforesaid John Milton, while he lived, being of sound mind and being in his right mind . . . gave, testified, and declared as his nuncupative testament that now exhibited in this business . . . of the tenor of a . . . testamentary schedule; and gave, donated, left, and disposed of all and singular other things in all and through all things, or to the same effect, as is contained in the same nuncupative testament, and therupon died; and the principal party proposes those things, together, separately, and however. 2. Also that at the time of the giving, declaring, and speaking of the testament exhibited in this business, the aforesaid John Milton enjoyed perfect memory; and he proposes as above.]

1674. DECEMBER 2. BROTHER CHRISTOPHER AND HIS SON RICHARD PURCHASE PROPERTY IN OXFORDSHIRE.

This Jndendenture made the second day of December in the six & twentieth yeare of our Soūaigne Lord Charles the second . . . Annoqz Dnī 1674, Betweene Joseph horneby Cittizen & Goldsmith of London Nathaniel horneby Cittizen and haberdasher of London & John Orton Cittizen & haberdasher also of London of th'one parte and Christopher Milton of the Jnner Temple London Esqz & Richard milton soñe of the said Christopher of th'other parte witnesseth that whereas by one Jndenture bearing date the six & twentieth day of September in the ffoure & twentieth yeare of the Reigne of our said Soūaigne

Lord Charles the second over England &c Annoqz Dnī 1672
& inrolled in Chancery the one & twentieth day of November
then next following the right honoᵇˡᵉ ffrancis Lord Sr' Charles
harbord knᵗ his maᵗⁱᵉ Surveyor Geñall Sr' Willm̄ haward Of
Tandridge in the County of Surry knᵗ Sr' John Talbott of
Lacock in the County of Wiltꝑ knᵗ & Willm̄ harbord of Graf-
ton Parke in the County of Northtōn Esqz surviveing Trustees for the sale of ffee ffarm rentꝑ & other rentꝑ . . . did . . .
grant . . . vnto Sr' John Banckꝑ of Aylesford in the County of
Kent Baronett & henry ffisher of Aylesford . . . Aɫɫ that Annuaɫɫ or ffee ffarme rent of three poundꝑ eight Shillingꝑ reserved & Issueing out of or for a Watermill lying & being in
Watlington Within the County of Oxoñ and aɫɫ that Annuaɫɫ
or ffee ffarme rent of ffive poundꝑ reserved or issueing out of
or for hedgrowes called Jeneper hiɫɫ Cocklehiɫɫ & Dottereale
in the said County of Oxoñ And alsoe aɫɫ that yearly rent or
tenth of three poundꝑ seaven shillingꝑ and one penny reserved
& Jssueing out of & for the demesne landꝑ of the late monargey
[?] of Dorchester in the said County of Oxoñ . . . for and in
consideracōn of the sume of One hundred Ninety & nine poundꝑ
& ten Shillingꝑ of lawfull English monie by the said Christopher
milton & Richard milton to the said Joseph horneby Well &
truly paid and of six shillingꝑ of like lawfuɫɫ monie to the said
Nathaniell hornby & John Orten or one of them in hand paid
. . . they hereby . . . discharge them the sd Xpōfer milton &
Richard milton . . . To have and to hold aɫɫ & singuler the said
ffee ffarm rentꝑ . . . Jn Wittnes Whereof the said ꝑties to these
ꝑsentꝑ have herevnto interchangeably sett their handꝑ & seales
. . . Jur' tertio die Decembr' Anno p̄dcō . . . Exˡᵉ

Public Record Office, Close Rolls, C54/4405/13. I think that this
document is now first published. I have left out as much as possible
without losing the main points.

1674. DECEMBER 5. DEPOSITIONS ON MILTON'S WILL
BEGIN; BROTHER CHRISTOPHER TESTIFIES.

Decemb. 5, 1674. Interrogatoria ministrata et ministranda ex
parte Annæ Mariæ et Deboræ Milton, testibus ex parte Elizabethæ MILTON productis sive producendis sequuntur. [Questions
asked and to be asked on the part of Anne, Mary, and Deborah
Milton, of witnesses brought in or to be brought in on the part of
Elizabeth Milton follow.]

Imprimis, Aske each witnesse, what relation to, or dependance
on, the producent, they, or either of them, have; and to which
of the parties they would give the victory were it in their power?
Et interrogatur quilibit testis conjunctim, et divisim, et de quolibet. [And let any of the witnesses be questioned together and
separately and any way.]

2. *Item,* Aske each witnesse, what day, and what time of the
day, the Will nuncupative was declared; what positive words
did the deceased use in the declaring thereof? Can you positively
sweare, that the deceased did declare that hee did leave the residue of his estate to the disposall of his wife, or did hee not
say, "I will leave the residue of my estate to my wife?" *Et
fiat ut supra.* [And let it be done as above.]

3. *Item,* Upon what occasion did the Deceased declare the
said Will? Was not the Deceased in perfect health at the same
time? Doe you not think, that the Deceased, if he declared
any such Will, declared it in a present passion, or some angry
humour against some or one of his children by his former
[first] wife? *Et fiat ut supra.*

4. *Item,* Aske each witnesse, whether the parties ministrant
were not and are not greate frequenters of the Church, and
good livers; and what cause of displeasure had the Deceased
against them? *Et fiat ut supra.*

5. *Item,* Aske Mr. [Christopher] MILTON, and each other
witnesse, whether the Deceased's Will, if any such was made,
was not, that the Deceased's wife should have £.1000, and the

children of the said Christopher MILTON the residue; and whether she hath not promised him that they should have it, if shee prevailed in this Cause? Whether the said Mr. MILTON hath not since the Deceased's death confessed soe much, or some part thereof? *Et fiat ut supra.*

6. *Item*, Aske each witnesse, whether what is left to the Ministrants by the said Will, is not reputed a very bad or altogether desperate debt? *Et fiat ut supra.*

7. Aske the said Mr. MILTON, whether he did not gett the said Will drawn upp, and inform the writer to what effect he should draw it? And did he not enquire of the other witnesses, what they would or could depose? And whether he hath not solicited this Cause, and payd fees to the Proctour about it? *Et fiat ut supra.*

8. *Item*, Aske each witnesse, what fortune the Deceased did in his life-time bestowe on the Ministrants? And whether the said *Anne* MILTON is not lame, and almost helplesse? *Et fiat ut supra.*

9. *Item*, Aske each witnesse, what value is the Deceased's estate of, as neare as they can guess? *Et fiat ut supra.*

Warton, 1791, pp. xxix-xxxi, from the Prerogative Court of Canterbury. I have not been able to check this document and to give it in the original form, though there is no reason to doubt the substantial accuracy of Warton's transcript. The bracketed "first" in the third interrogatory and "Christopher" in the fifth are Warton's.

Elizabetha Milton relcā et legataria prinlīs Johis Milton dēft con Mariam Annam et Deboram Milton filias eiusd^m. dēft. Thompson Clem^tp. | Sup allnē arlata et testō nuncupativi Johīs Milton dēft ex pte Elizabethæ Milton prēd in hoc negotio 2do. Andreæ 1674 dat et ext/

5to. Decembris 1674.

Chrūs Melton villæ Gipwici in cõm suff' Ar. ortus infra poañm omī storum Bredstreet London. etaz 58 annorz aut eo circa testus &c/ Ad omnes artōs dce allnis et ad testum nuncupativum Johis Melton geñ dēft in hoc negotio dat et ext deponit et dicit that on or about the twentith day of July 1674 the day certaine he now remembreth not this dep^t. being a pratizer in the Law. and a bencher in the Inner Temple but living in vacations at Jpsw^{ch} did vsually at the end of the terme visite John Milton, his this dept♀ brother the testator arlāte deceased before his goeing home, and soe at the end of Midsomer terme last past he this dep^t. went to visit his said brother and then found him in his chamber within his owne house scituate on Bunhill within the pish of S^t. Giles Creplegate London And at that tyme he the s^d testator being not well and this dep^t being then goeing into the Country in a serious manner with an intent as he beleeveth that what he then spoke should be his will if he dyed before his this dept♀ comeing the next Terme to London declared his will in these very word♀ as neare as this dep^t cann now call to mynd vizt brother the porc̄on due to me from m^r Powell, my former wives father, J leave to the vnkind children J had by her but J have receaved noe part of it and my will and meaning is they shall have noe other benefit of my estate then the said porc̄on and what J have besid♀ don for them, they haveing been very vndutiful to me. And all the residue of my estate J leave to the disposall of Elizabeth my loveing wife. she the sd Elizabeth his the deceased♀ wife, and Elizabeth ffisher his the deceased♀ then maideservant was at the same tyme goeing upp & downe the roome but whether she then heard the sd dec^d. soe declare his will as above or noe he knoweth not And the sd testator at the p^{r}misses was of ꝓfect mind and memory and talked and discoursed sensibly and well, et aliter nescit deponere.

Chr̄. Milton

AD INTERROGATORIA.

Ad I^m. Interr. *respondet*, that the party producent in this cause was and is the relict of the said deceased, who was his this respondent's brother; and the parties ministring these interrogatories were and are in repute, and soe he beleeveth his the said deceased's children by a former wife: and for his part, he wisheth right to take place, and soe would give it if in his power; and likewise wisheth that his brother's will might take effect.

Ad 2ᵐ. Interr. *respondet*, that on what day of the moneth or weeke the said deceased declared his will, as is above deposed, he now remembreth not precisely; but well remembreth, that it was in a forenoone, and on the very day he this deponent was goeing in the country in [the] Ipswich coach, which goeth not out of towne till noone or thereabout: and he veryly beleeveth in his conscience, that the residue of his estate he did then dispose of in these very words, viz. "And all the residue of my estate I leave to the disposall of Elizabeth my loving wife;" or he used words to the selfe same effect, *et aliter referendo se ad pe. depos. nescit respondere.*

Ad 3ᵐ. Interr. *respondet*, that the said deceased was then ill of the goute, and what he then spake touching his will was in a very calme manner; only [he] complained, but without passion, that his children had been unkind to him, but that his wife had been very kind and careful of him; and he believeth the only reason induced the said deceased at that time to declare his will was, that he this deponent might know it before his goeing into the country, *et aliter referendo se ad pe. deposita, nescit respondere.*

Ad 4ᵐ. Interr. *respondet*, that he knoweth not how the parties ministring these interrogatories frequent the church, or in what manner of behaviour of life and conversacion they are of, they living apart from their father four or five yeares last past; and as touching his the deceased's displeasure with them, he only heard him say at the tyme of declareing of his will, that they were undutifull and unkind to him, not expressing any particulars, but in former tymes he hath herd him complaine, that they were careless of him being blind, and made nothing of deserteing him, *et aliter nescit respondere.*

Ad 5ᵐ. Interr. *respondet*, that since this respondent's comeing to London this Michaelmas Terme last paste, this respondent's sister, the party now producent in this cause, told this respondent, that the deceased his brother did after his this respondent's goeing into the country in Trinity vacacion last summer [say,] that if she should have any overplus above a 1000*l.* come to her hands of his the deceased's estate, she should give the same to this respondent's children: but the deceased himselfe did not declare any such thing to this respondent at the tyme of his declaring his will, the tyme above deposed of.

Ad 6ᵐ. Interr. *respondet,* that he beleeveth that what is left to the parties ministring these interrogatories by the said deceased's will, is in the hands of persons of ability abell to pay the same, being their grandmother and uncle; and he hath seen the grandfather's will, wherein 'tis particularly directed to be paid unto them by his executers, *et aliter nescit respondere.*

Ad 7ᵐ. Interr. *respondet.* that he this respondent did draw upp the very will executed in this cause and write it with his owne hand, when he came to this court, about the 23d. of November last past, and at that tyme this respondent did read the same all over to Elizabeth Fisher the said deceased's late maid servant, and she said she remembered the same, and in confirmation thereof set her marke thereto in manner as on the same Will executed in this cause is now to be seen. And this respondent waited on the said deceased's widdow once at Doctor Exton's chambers about this suite, at which tyme she wanted some halfe crownes, and this respondent lent her then two halfe crownes, but more he hath at noe tyme paid either to Doctor or Proctor in this cause.

Ad 8ᵐ. Interr. *respondet.* that he knoweth of noe fortune given by the said deceased to the parties ministring these interrogatories, besides the portion which he was promised with his former wife in marriage, being a 1000*l.* which is still unpaid besids the interest thereof for about twenty yeares, saveing his charges in their maintenance and breeding, *et aliter nescit respondere,* saveing that Anne Milton interr. is lame and helples.

Ad ult. reddit causas scientiæ suæ ut supra.

Die prid.

Repetit. cor. Doctore.   CHR. MILTON.

    Lloyd Surroḡ.

Prerogative Court of Canterbury, Deposition Book, 1674, ff. 238v ff.; Warton, 1791, pp. xxviii-xxxiv; Masson, VI, 736-738. I have been able to take Christopher Milton's deposition directly from the original documents. But for the interrogatories and his answers to them I have had to depend on Warton. The differences in rendering are obvious.

[Elizabeth Milton, relict and principal legatee of John Milton, deceased, against Mary, Anne, and Deborah Milton, daughters of the same deceased.

On the articled allegation and the nuncupative will of John Milton, deceased, on behalf of the aforesaid Elizabeth Milton, given and exhibited in this business the day after St. Andrew's (November 30), 1674.

December 5, 1674. Christopher Milton of the town of Ipswich in county Suffolk, esquire, born within the parish of All Hallows, Bread Street, London, aged 58 years or thereabouts, witness, etc. To all the articles of the said allegation, and to the nuncupative will of John Milton, gentleman, deceased, given and exhibited in this business, deposes and says.

(The separate answers end with some version of) And, referring himself to the depositions, he cannot respond further.

To the last he gives the causes of his knowledge as above.

Christopher Milton. On the preceding day he was brought before Dr. Lloyd, Surrogate.]

1674. December 15. Mary Fisher examined about Milton's will.

Milton coñ Milton et Milton Thompson — Clementᵖ

sup Allⁿᵉ arlāta et Testamᵗᵒ nuncupativo Johīs Milton defuncti ex ᵽte Elizabethe Milton in huiōi causa dāt et admiss's examināt

15° Dec 1674

Maria Fisher soluta famūl domestica Johīs Batten habitañ in vico vocat Bricklane in Oldstreete vbi moram fecit ᵽ spacium sex hebdomadarum aut eo circ̄ antea cum Benjamino Whitcomb Mercatore habitañ in vico vocat Colemanstreete Londoñ

p̄ spacium 3ᵐ mensium, antea cum Guiddoñ Culcarꝑ infra locum vocat Smock Alley ꝑpe Spittlefeildꝑ p̄ spacium vnius anni
aut eo circr, antea cum Johanne Bayley infra Oppidum Milton
in Com̄ Staffoȓd p̄ spacium duorum Annorum, antea cum Johanne Baddily infra poām de Milton pʳd p̄ spacium trium
Annorum, et antea cum quōd Rogero Hargrave infra poām de
Milton pʳd p̄ spacium duorum annōr aut eo circȓ orta infra
poām de Norton in Com̄ Staffoȓd Dict̄ ætatis 23 aut eo circȓ
testis &c.

Ad omnes articulos dictæ Allⁿⁱˢ. et ad testamentum nuncupativum Johan. Milton testatoris in hac causa defuncti in hujusmodi negᵒ. dat. et exhibit. *deponit* et *dicit*, that this deponent
knew and was well acquainted with the articulate John Milton
the testator in this cause deceased, for about a twelve moneth
before his death, who dyed about a moneth since to the best of
this deponent's remembrance; And saith, that on a day hapning
about two moneths since as neare as this Deponent can remember this Deponent being then in the kitchen of the house of the
foresaid John Milton scituate agᵗ. the Attillery Ground neare
Bunhill feildꝑ and about noone of the same day the said Decēd
and the Producent Elizabeth his wife being then at Dinner in
the said kitchen Hee the said decēd amongst other discourse
then had betweene him and his said wife did then speake to his
said wife and vtter these words vizᵗ Make much of mee as long
as J live for thou knowest J have given thee all when J dye at
thy disposall there being then prsent in the said kitchen this
Deponentꝑ sister and contest namely Elizabeth ffisher And the
said decēd was at that time of p̄fect mind and memory and
talked and discoursed sensibly and well and was very merry,
and seemed to be in good health of body, *et aliter nescit.*

Signum

MARIÆ FISHER.

AD INTERROGATORIA.

Ad primum Interr. *respondet*, that this respondent hath noe
relation or dependance on the producent Elizabeth Milton, that

it is indifferent to this respondent which of the parties in this suite obtaine, and would give the victory in this cause if in her power to that party that hath most right; but which party hath most right thereto this respondent knoweth not, *et aliter nescit.*

Ad secundum Interr. *respondet,* that this respondent doth not remember the day when the deceased declared the words by her pre-deposed, but remembreth that it was about noone of such day that the words which hee then declared were these, viz. "Make much of mee as long as I live, for thou knowest I have given thee all when I dye at thy disposall;" then speaking to his wife Elizabeth Milton the party producent in this cause, *et aliter nescit.*

Ad tertium Interr. *respondet,* that the decēd when hee declared the words pʳdeposed was then at Dinner with his wife the pty Producent and was then very merry and seemed to be in good health of body but vpon what occasion hee spoke the said wordꝑ shee knoweth not, *et aliter nescit.*

Ad quartum Interr. *respondet,* that this respondent knoweth neither of the parties ministrant in this cause saving this respondent once saw Anne Milton one of the ministrants, *et nescit respondere per parte sua.*

Ad quintum Interr. nescit respondere.

Ad sextum Interr. nescit respondere.

Ad septimum Interr. non concernit eam, et nescit respondere.

Ad octavum Interr. *respondet,* that this roñdent once saw the interr' Anne Milton but doth not remember whether shee was Lame or helplesse, *et aliter nescit.*

Ad 9ᵐ. Interr. *respondet,* that this respondent knoweth nothing of the deceased's estate or the value thereof, *et aliter nescit.*

Eodem die   Signum

Repetit coram Doctore.   Mariæ Fisher,

Digby Surro. &c. pnte.

Tho. Welham, N. P.

Prerogative Court of Canterbury, Deposition Book, 1674, ff. 311v-312; Warton, 1791, pp. xxxv-xxxvi; Masson, VI, 737. I have been able to give a transcript of the original document for the most part through the main statement by Mary Fisher, whereas for the text of her answers to the questions I have had to draw mostly on Warton.

[Milton vs. Milton and Milton. Thompson and Clements. On the articled allegation and the nuncupative will of John Milton, deceased, on behalf of Elizabeth Milton, given, admitted, and examined in a case of this sort.

December 15, 1674.

Mary Fisher, free domestic servant of John Batten, living in the street called Brick Lane in Old Street, where she has stayed for the space of six weeks or thereabouts; previously with Benjamin Whitcomb, merchant, living in the street called Coleman Street, London, for the space of three months; previously with Guiddon Culcares (or Culcap) in the place called Smock Alley near Spittlefields for the space of one year or thereabouts; previously with John Bayley in the town of Milton in county Stafford for the space of two years; previously with John Baddily in the parish of Milton aforesaid for the space of three years; and previously with a certain Roger Hargrave in the parish of Milton aforesaid for the space of two years or thereabouts; born in the parish of Norton in county Stafford aforesaid; of the age of 23 or thereabouts; witness, etc.

To all the articles of the said allegation and to the nuncupative will of John Milton, testator in this case, deceased, in the business of this sort given and exhibited, deposes and says. . . .

The mark of Mary Fisher. She was brought the same day before Dr. Digby, Surrogate, etc., in the presence of Thomas Welham, Notary Public.]

1674. DECEMBER 15. ELIZABETH FISHER, MILTON'S SERVANT, EXAMINED ABOUT HIS WILL.

Eodem die [as Mary Fisher]

Elizabetha Fisher famula Domestica Elizabethæ Milton ptiꝑ Producentis in hac causa cum qua et Johanne Milton ejus marito defuncto vixit ꝑ spacium 13 mensium, antea cum quodam Thoma

[219]

Adams apud Bagnall^m Com̄ Staffoꝶd p spacium trium annorum
et sex mensium, antea cum W^mo Bourne gen' infra poam̄ de
Woolstilstan in Com̄ Staffoꝶd p̄^rd p spacium duorum Annorum
ortus infra poam̄ de Norton in Com̄ p̄^rd ætatis 28 Annorum aut
eo circr testis &c

Ad omnes artōs dictæ All^nis. et ad testamentum nuncupativum
Johan. Milton testatoris in hac causa defuncti in hujusmodi negotio dat exhibit et admiss. *deponit* et *dicit,* that this deponent was
servant unto Mr. JOHN MILTON the testator in this cause deceased for about a yeare before his death, who dyed upon a
Sunday the fifteenth of November last at night, And saith that
on a day hapning in the moneth of July last the time more certainly shee remembreth not this Deponent being then in the
decēdꝑ lodging Chamber (hee the said decēd and the ꝑty
Producent in the Cause his wife being then alsoe in the said
Chamber at Dinner together and the said Elizabeth Milton the
ꝑty Producent having ꝑvided something for the decēdꝑ Dinner
which hee very well liked) hee the said deceased then spoke to
his said wife these or the like words, as neare as this Deponent
can remember vizt God have mercy Betty J see thou wilt ꝑforme
according to thy promise in providing mee such Dishes as J
think fitt whilst J live, and when J dye thou knowest that J
have left thee all, there being noe body p^rsent in the said
Chamber with the said decēd and his wife but this Deponent
And the said Testator at that time was of ꝑfect mind and memory and talked and discoursed sensibly and well but was then
indisposed in his body by reason of the distemper of the Gout
which hee had then vpon him ffurther this Deponent saith
that shee hath seūall timeꝑ heard the said decēd since the said
time above deposed of declare and say that hee had made provision for his Children in his life time and had spent the greatest
part of his estate in ꝑvideing for them and that hee was resolved
hee would doe noe more for them liveing or dyeing, for that
little pte which hee had left hee had given it to his wife ye arlāte
Elizabeth the producent or hee vsed wordꝑ to that effect And

[220]

likewise told this Deponent that there was a thousand poundꝑ left in Mr Powellꝑ hands to be disposed amongst his Children hereafter By all which words this respondent verily beleeveth that the said testator had given all his estate to the articulate Elizabeth his wife, and that shee should have the same after his decease, *et aliter nescit respondere*, saving that the said deceased was at the sevral times of declaring the words last predeposed alsoe of perfect mind and memory.

Signum

ELIZAB. FISHER.

AD INTERROGATORIA.

Ad primum Interr. *respondet*, that this respondent was servant to the deceased in his life time and is now servant to the producent and therefore hath a dependency upon her as her servant, that if the victory were in this respondent's power shee would give the deceased's estate equally to be shared betweene the ministrants and the producent, *et aliter nescit*.

Ad secundum Interr. *respondet*, that this respondent doth not remember on what day the deceased declared the words first by her afore deposed, but it was about noone of such day when hee was at dinner that the precise words as neare as this respondent can remember which the deceased used at that time were these, viz. "God have mercy Betty (speaking to his wife Elizabeth Milton for soe hee usually called her) I see thou wilt performe according to thy promise in providing mee such dishes as I think fitt whilst I live and when I dye thou knowest that I have left thee all," *et aliter nescit*, saving that this respondent well remembreth that the deceased declared the words last by her deposed to the articles of the allegation to this respondent once on a Sunday in the afternoone, but on what day of the month or in what month the said Sunday then happened this respondent doth not remember.

Ad tertium Interr. *respondet*, that the occasion of the deceased's speaking of the words deposed by this respondent in her answer to the next preceedent interrogatory was upon the producent's provideing the deceased such victuals for his dinner as hee liked and that he was then indifferent well in health saving that some time he was troubled with the paine of the gout and that hee was at that time very merry and not in any passion or angry humour neither at that time spoke any thing against any of his children that this respondent heard of, *et aliter nescit.*

Ad quartum Interr. *respondet,* that this Respondent hath heard the decēd declare his displeasure agᵗ the pties Ministrant his Children and pticulerly the decēd declared to this Respondent that a little before hee was marryed to Elizabeth Milton his now Relict, a former Maidservant of his told Mary one of the decēds Daughters and one of the Ministrantꝑ that shee heard the decēd was to be marryed, to wᶜʰ the said Mary replyed to the said Maidservant that that was noe News to heare of his wedding but if shee could heare of his death that was something,—and further told this Respondent that all his said Children did combine together and counsell his Maidservant to cheat him the decēd in her Markettings, and that his said children had made away some of his bookes and would have sold the rest of his bookes to the Dunghill women or hee the said decēd spoke wordꝑ to this Respondent to the selfe same effect and purpose: that this respondent knoweth not what frequenters of the church, or what good livers, the parties ministrant or either of them are, *et aliter nescit.*

Ad quintum Interr. *respondet,* that this respondent doth not know that the deceased's wife was to have 1000*l.* and the interrogative children of Christopher Milton the residue nor doth this respondent know that the said Elizabeth, the deceased's wife, hath promised the interrogative Christopher Milton or his children any such thing in case shee should prevaile in this cause, that the said Mrs. Milton never confessed soe much in this respondent's hearing, or to any body else that this respondent knoweth of, *et aliter nescit.*

Ad sextum Interr. *respondet,* that this respondent believeth that what is left the deceased's children in the will nuncupative in this cause executed and mencioned therein to be due from Mr. Powell, is a good debt; for that the said Mr. Powell is reputed a rich man, *et aliter nescit.*

Ad septimum Interr. *respondet,* that this respondent did voluntarily tell the interrogative Mrs. Milton, what shee heard the deceased say which was to the effect by her predeposed *et aliter nescit.*

Ad octavum Interr. *respondet,* that this respondent knoweth not what the deceased did in his life time bestow on the ministrants his children, and that the interrogative Anne Milton is Lame but hath a trade and can live by the same, which is the making of gold and silver lace and wch the deceͩ bred her vp to, *et aliter nescit.*

Ad nonum Interr. *respondet,* that this respondent knoweth not the deceased's estate, or the value thereof, *et aliter nescit.*

<table>
<tr><td>Eodem die</td><td>Signum</td></tr>
<tr><td>Repetit coram Doctore</td><td>ELIZABETHÆ FISHER.</td></tr>
<tr><td>*Trumbull* Surrō. &c.</td><td></td></tr>
</table>

Tho. Welham, N. P.

GEORGE GOSLING,
JAMES TOWNLEY, } DEPUTY REGISTERS.
ROBERT DODWELL.

Prerogative Court of Canterbury, Deposition Book, 1674, ff. 312-313v; Warton, 1791, pp. xxxvii-xl; Masson, VI, 738-739. My text, as with the preceding one for Mary Fisher, is partly from the original and partly from Warton.

[The same day (as Mary Fisher).

Elizabeth Fisher, domestic servant of Elizabeth Milton, the party producent in this case, with whom and with John Milton her husband, deceased, she has lived for the space of 13 months; previously with a certain Thomas Adams in Bagnall in county Stafford for the space of three years and six months; previously with William Bourne, gentleman, in the parish of Woolstilstan (Woolaston?) in county Stafford aforesaid for the space of two years; born in the parish of Norton in the county aforesaid; aged 28 years or thereabouts; witness, etc.

To all the articles of the said allegation and to the nuncupative will of John Milton, testator in this case, deceased, given, exhibited, and admitted in business of this sort, deposes and says. . . .

The mark of Elizabeth Fisher. She repeated it on the same day before Dr. Trumbull, Surrogate, etc.; Thomas Welham, Notary Public.]

1675. DAUGHTER DEBORAH MARRIES ABRAHAM CLARKE.

. . . Abraham Clarke of the Citty of Dublin in ye Kingdome of Jreland Weavor and Deborah his wife one of the daughters of John Milton. . . .

From the release of Deborah and her husband dated March 27, 1675, *q.v.* We know next to nothing about this event: when it took place, where it occurred, how Deborah met Clarke, and so on. It is mentioned here for lack of a better place, but it may perfectly well have taken place before Milton's death. But it must at least have come before March 27, 1675. At some unknown date after 1688 Abraham Clarke died. He must have been living until about that date, for their daughter Elizabeth (later Mrs. Foster) was born in November, 1688, in Ireland, *q.v.* We hear no more about him after 1688.

1675. MR. ELLIS'S MANUSCRIPT BIBLIOGRAPHY OF MILTON'S WRITINGS.

I. Milton's

Hist of Engl. 2. Logick. 3. Accid^{ce}. comenc'd Gramar. 4. Pro pop. angl. ɔtra Salmas. 5. Defensio 2da. 6. defensio pro se. 7. I. Philipps' angl. Responsio. 8. Of civil Power in Eccles. causes. 9. ag^t. Hirelings. 10. Of a comonwth. wth. y^e. dang^r. of readmitting k.ship. 11. Εἰκονοκλάστης. 12. Tenure of Kings & Magistrates. 13. P^rlat^{ll}. Episcopacy. 14. Areopagitica for unlicenc'd Printing. —15. Doct^{ne}. & Discip^{ne}. of Divorce. 16. Iudgem^t. of M. Beucer. 17. χολαστεριον. 18. Tetrachordon. 19. Notes on a sermon entit. The fear of God and ye K. 20. Reformacon touching church discipl. 21. Reasons of Ch. Goverm^t. ag^t. P^rlacy. 22. animadv. upon the Remonstrants def^{ce}. ag^t Smectimnuus. 23 apolog. for y[e] animadv. 24 of tru Relig. Heresy, schisme & toleraĉon w[th] y[e] means to p[r]vent Popery.

British Museum, Add. MS. 28,954, ff. 9-9v (the commonplace book of one Ellis, secretary). I believe this list of Milton's writing has not been published except as I have drawn on it in previous volumes of the present work. The date may perhaps be 1676. The list is remarkable for its omission of Milton's poetry completely, and of all titles later than 1673. With this catalogue should be compared the two in Aubrey (ff. 64 and 68v; Darbishire, pp. 11 and 9) and that in Phillips (pp. [xlix]- [liv], not in Darbishire).

1675. REISSUE OF *PARADISE LOST* (?).

Paradise Lost . . . Printed by S. Simmons, and to be sold by T. Helder, at the sign of the Angel in Little Britain, 1675.

From the title page of a copy in the library of the University of Illinois, as described by Harris Fletcher in *Papers of the Bibliographical Society of America*, XLIII (1949), 173-178. Professor Fletcher hesitates to assert whether this unique copy of a title page dated 1675 means an actual reissue or merely a bibliographical sport. But as he describes it, and as one can see from the photographic reproduction of the title page, it seems to bear the same relation to the first issue of 1674 that the later issues of the first edition bear to that of 1667. Though the title page itself is partly or entirely reset, Mr. Fletcher says that the text follows that of 1674, with the second states of pages in which he noted variants in his facsimile edition. This particular volume formerly belonged to John Disney, whose monogram is on the front cover and whose bookplate is inside.

1675. FEBRUARY 22. BROTHER CHRISTOPHER GIVES BOND TO RICHARD POWELL.

. . . One Bond or Obligaĉon Dated y[e] two & twentieth day of ffebruary now last past of y[e] penall Sume of Two Hundred Pounds entred into by Christopher Milton of y[e] Jnner Temple London Esq[r] Vnto Richard Powell of the same Jnner Temple London Esqr.

From Deborah Clarke's discharge of March 27, 1675, *q.v.* The purpose of the bond is not stated, but we may guess that it is in some way related to the payments to the daughters.

1675. FEBRUARY 22. DAUGHTER ANNE, IN RETURN
FOR £100, SIGNS RELEASE TO STEPMOTHER.

To all Christian people to whom this pʳsent Writeing shall
come Anne Milton of London Spinster one of the Daughterᵱ
of John Milton late of Bunhill ᵱish of Sᵗ Gyleᵱ Cripplegate
Gent' Deceased sendeth Greeting Whereas Elizabeth Milton
Relict of the said John Milton hath before th'Ensealing and
delivery hereof Secured to be payd unto the said Anne Milton
the suɱe of one hundred poundᵱ of Lawfull money of England
As her the Said Anne Miltonᵱ part & Share of the Estate of
the said John Milton her Late ffather To the end the said One
hundred poundᵱ may by and with the Consent and approbaācon
of Christopher Milton and Richard Powell both of the Jnner
Temple London Esqzᵱ be layd out & disposed off for and in the
purchaseing of A Rent Charge or Aɲuity for her the sayd Anne
Milton dureing her naturall Life or otherwise as they Shall
judge to be for the best benefitt and Advantage of the said Anne
Now the said Anne Milton doth hereby Acknoweledge herselfe
fully Sattisfyed of her Share and Distribuācon of her said late
ffatherᵱ Estate (Except such Share or part thereof as Shee the
said Anne doth or may Clayme or demand by force or Colour
of one bond or Obligaācon bearing even date with these pʳsentᵱ
of the penall suɱe of two hundred poundᵱ Entred into by the
above named Christopher Milton Esqz unto the said Richard
Powell or of the Condiācon thereunder Written) And doth
hereby acquitt and discharge her the said Relict her Executorᵱ
& Admrᵱ & eūy of them of and from her sayd Share & Distribuācon (Except as is before Excepted) And of and from all Bondᵱ
& Obligaāconᵱ Entred or to be Entred into by the sayd Relict
for or concerning the same, And of & from all Acāonᵱ Suiteᵱ
& Demandᵱ in Relaācon thereunto And the said Anne doth
hereby promise and Agree to and with the said Relict That Shee
the said Anne her Executorᵱ & Admrᵱ shall and will upon the
reasonable Request And at the Costs and Chargeᵱ in the Law

of her the said Relict, doe any other Reasonable Act or thinge for the Releasing & Discharging her said Share and Distribuçon (Except as before is Excepted) which is hereby Expressed or intended to be Released and Discharged Jn witness whereof the ptye hereunto have Sett her hand and Seale this Twenty Second Day of ffebruary *1674*

Sealed & Delivered in	Signum
the pˢence of us	[mark]
Hen Bosworth	Anne Milton
Richard Milton	[seal]
Thomas Robinson	
Jacob Bosworth	

[At the bottom:] Anne Miltons Release to Elizabeth Milton for 100ˡⁱ/

New York Public Library Manuscript Room; Marsh, *Papers*, pp. 16-18; Masson, VI, 740-743. Marsh speculates whether the daughters may have received more than the £100 represented by this receipt and those of Mary and Deborah to be given later (Mary's under the same date and Deborah's under that of March 27, 1675), on the theory that some at least of the unpaid Powell dowry may have come through, but he admits that it is purely speculation. He also speculates, but as we know now with considerable accuracy, that the Richard Milton who signed as a witness was perhaps a son of Christopher's still unknown of in Marsh's time; he is also undoubtedly correct in saying that Anne's signature was written by him. The mark which she made is a mere scrawl. The figure on the seal is almost undistinguishable, but Sotheby (*Ramblings*, p. 176) gives a sketch which is fairly plain. He also reproduces Mary's signature and seal on p. 177, and those of Deborah and her husband on p. 179. The bond from Christopher Milton to Richard Powell has not been found.

I wish here to express my deep gratitude to the staff of the Manuscript Room of the New York Public Library for courteous help and interest in connection with this manuscript and other papers in the same package. As Marsh pointed out in his *Papers* (pp. 1-2), these papers were at one time in the possession of James Boswell, second son of the biographer of Samuel Johnson, at the dispersion of whose library in 1825 they were sold. A clipping from a Quaritch catalogue of 1882 shows that they were then advertised for sale for 42 pounds. The contents of the collection, now in the New York Public Library, are as follows:

1. Milton's letter to Carlo Dati, April 21, 1647 (see above, II, 185 ff.).

2. Dati's letter to Milton, November 1, 1647 (above, II, 201 ff.).

3. The Milton-Hayley bond of July 27, 1674.

4. Anne Milton's release, February 22, 1675.

5. Mary Milton's release, February 22, 1675.

6. Deborah Clarke's release, March 27, 1675.

7. Richard Minshull's bond to Mrs. Milton, June 4, 1680.

8. Minshull's bond to Robert Cudworth, July 6, 1674.

9. Minshull's agreement with Cudworth, December 5, 1674.

10. Mrs. Milton's bond to Randle Timmis, April 11, 1713.

11. Mrs. Milton's agreement with John Darlington, October 22, 1720.

12. Mrs. Milton's new agreement with Darlington, June 16, 1725.

13. A true copy of Mrs. Milton's will, August 22, 1727.

14. A true copy of the inventory of Mrs. Milton's estate, August 26, 1727.

15. A certificate of probate of Mrs. Milton's will, October 10, 1727.

Of numbers 3-15 above, which have not been included in previous volumes of the present work, all but numbers 8 and 9 are reprinted, in whole or in part, in the present volume. Numbers 8 and 9, which are mentioned under number 10, have no immediate connection with the Milton family and are therefore omitted.

1675. FEBRUARY 22. DAUGHTER MARY SIGNS RELEASE TO ELIZABETH MILTON.

To all Christian people to whom this p'sent Writeing Shall come Mary Milton of London Spinster one of the Daughters of John Milton late of Bunhill in the pish of S‍t. Gyles Cripplegate Gent' Deceased Sendeth Greeting. . . .

Mary millton
[seal]

New York Public Library Manuscript Room; Marsh, *Papers*, pp. 18-19; Masson, VI, 740-743. As Marsh says, the text of this document, except for trivial variations in spelling, punctuation, and the like, is identical with that for Anne Milton just preceding. He fails to point out, however, one interesting difference. The words "for and in the purchaseing of A Rent Charge or Añuity for her the sayd Anne Milton dureing her naturall Life or otherwise" does not appear in this paper concerning Mary. I judge that Christopher Milton, Richard Powell, and the others who were assisting Milton's widow in this business made some special arrangement for Anne which they thought unnecessary or unsuitable for Mary. Another difference, which Marsh does notice, is that Mary signed her own name whereas Anne merely made her mark. Since the text of this paper is so similar to that of Anne's, it seems unnecessary to take up space by inserting it here.

1675. FEBRUARY 25. WIDOW GETS LETTERS OF ADMINISTRATION FOR SETTLING ESTATE.

Mense Februarij 1674/5 . . .

Johannes Milton./. Vicesimo quinto die emanavit Como Elizabethæ Milton Relictæ Johannis Milton nuper Parochiæ Sancti Egidii Cripplegate in Com' mīd defunct' hēntis &c ad Administrañd bona jura et credita dicti defunct' de bene &c: jurat'. Testamento Nuncupativo dict' defuncti alr̄ per antedictam Elizabetham Milton allegato nondum probato

vlt Julij

vlt Decʳ

[Marginal note:] p̄ decret verbo (ab intestato) deceden' in Adcone omisso.

Prerogative Court of Canterbury, Administration Act Book, 1675, f. 14; Francis Blackburne, *Memoir of Thomas Hollis*, 1780, ii, 628; Warton, 1791, p. xli; Masson, vi, 739-740. Warton thinks (p. xlii) that Milton's nuncupative will was held invalid by the court because (1) Milton never told his listeners that he was going to deliver his will; (2) the witnesses spoke of two declarations of Milton, made at two separate times, whereas the law requires that three witnesses must testify to the same words spoken at the same time; and (3) Milton was not in his last sickness, as the law requires of a nuncupative will. Hence, Warton concludes, Sir Leoline Jenkins as judge rejected the will and decreed administration instead. Masson finds no such definite rejection of probate, but thinks that the various parties concerned (the widow, the daughters, Christopher Milton, Richard Powell, and Anne Powell) all reached an understanding, as the result of which the widow withdrew her claim for probate and agreed to be content with administration of the poet's effects. The latter course gave her, says Masson, two thirds of the estate (with one third to the daughters) as against the whole estate through probate. Warton omits the note in the left margin, but adds at the end the names of three people whom he identifies as "deputy registrars": George Gostling, James Townley, and Robert Dodwell. These names do not occur in Todd, in Masson, or on my photostatic copy of the original document.

[The month of February, 1674/5. John Milton. On the 25th day there issued a commission to Elizabeth Milton, relict of John Milton, late of the parish of St. Giles Cripplegate, county Middlesex, deceased, to have etc. for administering the goods, rights, and credits of the said deceased, of well, etc., sworn; the nuncupative will of the said deceased, alleged otherwise by the aforesaid Elizabeth Milton, having not yet been proved.

(In the right margin:) the last day of July; the last day of December.

(In the left margin:) by decree; the word of the intestate deceased having been omitted in administration.]

1675. MARCH 27. DAUGHTER DEBORAH AND HER HUSBAND SIGN RELEASE TO WIDOW.

To all to whom these shall come Abraham Clarke of the Citty of Dublin in ye Kingdome of Jreland Weavor and Deborah his wife one of the daughters of John Milton late of Bunn Hill in ye pish of S^t: Giles Criplegate London Gent' Deced sendeth greeting Know yee that for & in Consideraͨon of the full and Just Suͫe of One Hundred Pounds Sterling paid by Elizabeth Milton relict and also Administratrix of the goods and Chattles of the said John Milton Vnto John Burrough of Corne Hill London Cabbinet Maker for the Vse and by the Appointment of the said Abraham Clarke and Deborah his said wife And of the delivery Vnto ye said John Burrough for the Vse and by the like Appointment of seuerall Goods late of ye said John Milton Deceased by ye said Elizabeth Milton, They the said Abraham Clarke & Deborah Doe hereby Acknowledge that ye said monies soe paid and ye said Goods soe delivered were soe paid and delivered by ye direction and Appointment of them the said Abraham Clarke and Deborah, And that by ye said payment of the said Suͫe of One Hundred Pounds and delivery of ye said Goods as aforesaid, they ye said Abraham Clarke and Deborah his said wife & each of them are & is fully

Satisfyed of & for all Such share proporcõn part & Distribucõn
of all Such Estate of w^ch: ye said John Milton decēd dyed possessed or any way interested in as in any wayes due or to bee
due or claymable or demandable by ye said Deborah as Daughter of ye said John Milton or by the said Abraham Clarke in
right of ye said Deborah his said wife (Except Such share thereof
as ye said Deborah or as ye said Abraham Clarke in right of y^e
said Deborah doth or may clayme or Demaund by force or
Colour of One Bond or Obligacõn Dated ye two & twentieth
day of ffebruary now last past of ye penall Sumē of Two Hundred Pounds entred into by Christopher Milton of ye Jnner
Temple London Esqr Vnto Richard Powell of the same Jnner
Temple London Esqr. or of ye Condicõn thereunder written)
And ye said Abraham Clarke & Deborah his said wife doe and
each of them doth hereby Acquitt release & Discharge her y^e
said Elizabeth Milton her Executo^r?. & Adm^r?. & every of them
of & from his ye said Abraham Clarkes and her ye said Deborahs
said share part proporcõn & distribucõn (Except as before is Excepted) And of & from all Bonds & Obligacõns entred or to bee
entred into by the said Elizabeth for or concerning the same or
in relacõn thereunto And also of and from all Accoñs and
Suites cause and causes of Accoñs & Suites claimes & Demaunds
whatsoever as well in Law as in Equity in relacõn thereunto
And the said Abraham Clarke doth hereby promise & agree to
& with ye s^d Elizabeth her Executo^rs and Adm^rs. that hee y^e
said Abraham Clarke and ye said Deborah his said wife & either
of them & ye Executo^rs. & Adm^rs. of them & either of them shall
& will from time to time and at all tymes hereafter at ye request & at ye proper Costs & Charges in ye Law of ye said Elizabeth her Executo^rs. or Adm^rs. or any of them doe and execute
any further or other reasonable Act or thing Acts or things for
ye furthe & better releaseing and Dischargeing his and her said
share part proporcõn & Distribucõn (Except as is before Excepted) w^ch: is hereby Expressed or mencõned to bee released

& Discharged, Jn Witnesse whereof yᵉ said Abraham Clarke &
Deborah have hereunto putt their Hands and Seales yᵉ Twentie
Seaventh day of March 1675 Annoqᶻ Rñi Rḡs Caroli Sc̄di Vice-
simo Septimo./

Sealed and delivered   Abraham Clarke [seal]
   in the presence of.

Thomas Hackett

Edmond Loftus   Deborah Clarke [seal]

John. Price/.

Tho: Sisson: Notʳᵘˢ:Publ̄:

   [Note at bottom:] Deborah Daughter of Inᵒ Milton. receipt or release

   New York Public Library Manuscript Room; Marsh, *Papers*, pp. 19-
23; Masson, VI, 740-742. The handwriting of this document is entirely
different from that of the releases of Anne and Mary Milton given
above under date of February 22, 1675, as is the list of witnesses. Marsh
and Masson both think it was probably prepared and signed in Dublin.
Though neither of them says so, the reason why this release is a month
later than theirs is probably in considerable part due to the distance between London and Dublin; the additional arrangements about property
to be given to them, and the fact that they were a married couple rather
than single individuals like the other sisters, would also tend to slow
the process. Masson reads Deborah's signature as "Deboroh," but the
last vowel is near enough to an a so that I think we can safely assume
that she spelled her own name correctly. But she did have trouble with
the last name, apparently writing it first as "Clarkk" and then rewriting
the last letter. I should guess that the handwriting of the body of the
document is that of Thomas Sisson, the notary who signed it. He blun-
dered in writing the year 1675 near the end of the document and rewrote it, for the sake of clearness, in the margin.

1675. MAY 16. BROTHER CHRISTOPHER PRESIDES OVER PARLIAMENT AT INNER TEMPLE.

   From the records of the Inner Temple as printed by F. A. Inderwick
in *A Calendar of the Inner Temple Records*, III, 100. This entry is
similar to several preceding ones already given, for example under date
of May 31, 1674. I shall not take up unnecessary space in giving further
items of this sort except when they are of special interest. But I will give
here a very brief summary of those which Mr. Inderwick has collected,

which can easily be found in his book. I will give first the page in Inderwick, Volume III, next the date, and finally the action.

100	1675	May 16.	On Parliament.
		June 13.	Ditto.
101		June 20.	Ditto.
103		July 25.	On committee about drains and about a petition about repairs to church.
102		October 30.	Ditto.
105		November 28.	On Parliament.
	1676	January 30.	Ditto.
106		May 7.	Ditto.
		June 11.	Ditto.
109		November 26.	Son Richard Milton called to bar.
110	1677	May 27.	On Parliament.
111		June 24.	Ditto.
119		November 29.	Son Thomas Milton on standing committee on expenses of buttery; called to bar.
121	1678	February 10.	On committee about site of office for King's Bench.
122		June 9.	On Parliament.
123		June 19.	Ditto.
124		November 3.	On committee about burned buildings.
124-125		November 9.	On committee about King's Bench.
131	1679	January 26.	On Parliament.
132		May 18.	Ditto.
137		November 6.	Ditto.
151		November 12.	In arrears for dues. See below under date.
		November 13.	Ditto. See below under date.
		November 14.	Ditto. See below under date.
146		November 28.	Ditto.
152	1680	February 2.	Ditto. See below under date.
		February 6.	Ditto.
159	1681	February 17.	On Parliament.
		June 5.	Ditto.
161		November 13.	Ditto.
162		November 20.	Ditto.
163		November 27.	Ditto.
173	1682	May 21.	Ditto.
174		June 25.	Ditto; also on committees about insolvent accounts and saving expenses.
175		July 4.	On Parliament.
		July 6.	Ditto.

186   1682   November 23.   Ditto.
                November 27.   Ditto.
187   1683   February 4.   Reports as member of committee on im-
                proved training of law students.
196   May 8.   On committee about setting up an organ.
201   November 25.   On Parliament.
203   1684   February 10.   Ditto.
                February 14.   Ditto.
206   June 15.   Ditto.
218   1685   February 10.   Ditto.
238   1686   November 4.   Treasurer's account for preceding 12
                months includes paying ironmonger for
                work in "Baron" Milton's room.
249   1687   November 19.   Inquiry to be made of him when he in-
                tends to move out of his chambers. See
                below under date.

Except for the short term during which he was irritating the treasurer by failing, for some unknown reason, to pay his dues (a failing far from uncommon in the records) this record seems to show that Christopher Milton was an active, highly regarded member of the Inner Temple. The entry for November 19, 1687, is the last one in the books. Though he lived over five years longer, he probably retired from active participation in affairs of the Inner Temple at about this time.

1675. MAY 18. ANDREW MARVELL PROMISES TO WRITE MILTON'S LIFE.

London May 18. 1675./

Mr Wood:./

. . . Mr Marvell has pmised me to write *minutes* for you of M^r Jo: Milton who lyes buryed in St Giles Cripplegate ch:— J shall tell you where. . . .

Jo: Aubrey

From the original letter of Aubrey to Wood, Bodleian MS. Wood. F. 39, ff. 296-297; Masson, 1 (1881), vii, and vi, 778. Marvell, who died about three years later, apparently never lived to complete his task, unless he is the author of the anonymous life.

This is perhaps an appropriate place to mention two other lives of Milton either written or planned or at least rumored. Among Aubrey's notes on Milton (f. 66v; Darbishire, p. 15) is the following cryptic entry: "q̄ Mr Allam of Edm: hall Oxon. of Mr J. Milton's life writt by himselfe. v. pagg." This sounds like Aubrey's reminder to himself to ask Andrew Allam about Allam's life of Milton, with a cross reference to a page in Aubrey's notes which he never filled in. In his edition of the *Brief Lives* (II, 72) Clarke explains this as meaning a life written by Allam (1655-1685), who was well known to Wood, who mentions him a number of times in his *Life and Times of Anthony Wood* (ed. Clarke, 5 vols., Oxford, 1891-1900). But no life by Allam is known unless, as some have thought, he may be the author of the anonymous "earliest" biography. However, the wording of Aubrey's note could also mean that he intended to ask Allam something about Milton's autobiography: *i.e.*, the *Defensio Secunda*. But the ambiguity is intriguing.

The other reference I owe to my friend Mr. Edward L. Ruhe, who pointed it out to me in John Ward's notes about Milton's family (British Museum Add. MS. 4,320, f. 232v). Ward says: "An antient bookseller afterwards a pension[er] in y[e] Charter-house brought Mrs. Clarke [Milton's daughter Deborah] a printed life of M[r] Milton, which she thought better than what had been drawn up by others. He held up y[e] paul at M[r] Miltons funeral, and as he said wrote y[e] life himself." Mr. Ruhe identifies the bookseller-pallbearer as Brabazon Aylmer, the publisher of Milton's *Epistolarum Familiarium*. Aylmer is thus still another candidate to join Mr. Parsons' long list of possibilities for the anonymous life (*English Historical Review*, XVII, 1902, 95-110) or to provide some future scholar with an additional source of information about the poet. See also the entry below about the Anonymous Life under the date 1687.

1675. MAY (?). PUBLICATION OF EDWARD PHILLIPS'S *THEATRUM POETARUM*, WITH PERHAPS SOME WRITING OF MILTON.

Theatrum Poetarum, Or A Compleat Collection of the Poets, Especially The most Eminent, of all Ages. The Antients distinguish't from the Moderns in their several Alphabets. With some Observations and Reflections upon many of them, particularly those of our own Nation. Together With a Prefatory Discourse of the Poets and Poetry in Generall. By Edward Phillips. [Greek motto from Hesiod] . . . London, Printed for Charles Smith, at the Angel near the Inner Temple-Gate in Fleet-Street. Anno Dom. M. DC. LXXV.

Title page of my own copy; Masson, VI, 776-777; CM, XVIII, 460-461, 628-629. The date on the title page of my own copy, used above, is perfectly clear, though in many it is not. For Milton's possible contributions to this volume, see entry above under date of 1674.

Iohn Milton, the Author (not to mention his other Works, both in Latin and English, both in strict and solute Oration, by which his Fame is sufficiently known to all the Learned of Europe) of two Heroic Poems, and a Tragedy; namely *Paradice lost*, *Paradice Regain'd*, and *Sampson Agonista*; in which how far he hath reviv'd the Majesty and true *Decornm* of Heroic Poesy and Tragedy: it will better become a person less related then my self, to deliver his judgement.

Phillips, *Theatrum Poetarum*, 1675, II, 113-114; Masson, VI, 777. Phillips's high praise of the epic poem here makes it important for us to notice that he spends almost all of his preface on that type. His complimentary reference to an unnamed *"English Heroic Poem, which came forth not many years ago."* (sig. **4v) may be to *Paradise Lost*.

John Philips, the Maternal Nephew and Disciple of an Author of most deserved Fame late deceas't, being the exactest of Heroic Poets, (if the truth were well examin'd, and it is the opinion of many both Learned and Judicious persons) either of the Ancients or Moderns, either of our own or what ever Nation else; from whose Education as he hath receiv'd a judicious command of style both in Prose and Verse. . . .

Phillips, *Theatrum Poetarum*, 1675, II, 114-115. Phillips continues with about the same amount more of discussion of his brother's own accomplishments. Sidney Lee (*DNB*) interprets the section from "exactest" to "else" as applying to John Phillips rather than to Milton.

. . . [Milton] had 2 nephews both indifferent Authors, Phillip's; one wrot the English Dictionary folio. and published a thick twelves, an Account of ye Poets antient & modern, if in that milton shoud be mentioned it may be relyd upon.

From Jacob Tonson's letter to his nephew, date about 1731-1732, in the Pierpont Morgan Library; Helen Darbishire, *The Manuscript of Milton's Paradise Lost Book I*, 1931, p. xiv.

1675. JULY 6. BROTHER CHRISTOPHER'S DAUGHTER THOMASINE BURIED.

[1675] Julye the 6. thomising Duater of n^r [?M^r] Melton burried.

Parish Register of St. Nicholas, Ipswich, as printed by E. Cookson for the Parish Register Society, 1897, p. 157; Perceval Lucas in *Notes and Queries*, XI, vii (1913), 21-22. The "?Mʳ" in brackets is Cookson's.

1676. BEFORE OCTOBER 18. *LETTERS OF STATE* PUBLISHED.

Literæ Pseudo-Senatûs Anglicani, Cromwellii, Reliquorumque Perduellium nomine ac jussu conscriptæ A Joanne Miltono. [Ornament] Impressæ Anno 1676.

Title page of my own copy; reproduced in CM, XIII, facing p. xiv; Masson, VI, 793. The long and complicated story of the publication of these letters is told in great detail in Masson, VI, 790-806; CM, XIII, 593-600; French, "That Late Villain Milton," *PMLA*, LV (1940), 102-115; and other places. A quick review of this event is therefore all that is needed here. These are the Latin letters which Milton wrote while Secretary for the Foreign Tongues from 1649 to 1659, which he planned to publish with his *Familiar Letters* in 1674 as the result of the urging of the Danish Resident, but which in the end he left to Daniel Skinner instead, along with the manuscript of his treatise on Christian doctrine. Skinner attempted to have them published by the Dutch printer Daniel Elzevir, but the pressure of political conditions in England made Elzevir change his mind about printing the material. Meanwhile Moses Pitt, a London printer, had apparently acquired somehow another copy of the manuscript and wanted to make an agreement with Elzevir to print it. Just who actually was responsible for the publication is not quite clear, but the letters actually appeared in two editions with the same date. The printer seems to have been E. Fricx of Brussels (CM, XIII, 645-646). One (the above) bears a cut of a face on the title page; the other has a representation of fruit. They are virtually identical. The Columbia edition reprints all the letters, together with several others which may be Milton's and which have been gathered from various sources; and it provides careful collation from all known sources, including the original letters when they could be found. The date of appearance is fairly well settled by Skinner's statement printed below, and by a sentence from his letter of November 9/19, 1676, to Samuel Pepys: "About a moneth agoe there creeps out into the world a little imperfect book of Miltons state letters, procur'd to be printed by one Pitts a bookseller in London." Neither edition bears any place of publication on the title page; the title pages are otherwise identical in every way that the bibliographer can easily describe, though a careful comparison of the two side by side shows that they were separately printed. Bruce Harkness ("The Precedence of the 1676 Editions of Milton's *Literae Pseudo-Senatus Anglicani,*" *Studies in Bibliography*, VII, 1955, 181-185) argues that the edition with the face on the title is a reprint of that with the fruit, which must therefore be the first edition. His argument is based on facts concerning watermarks, line-justification, errors in printing, etc.

Meanwhile Skinner, after considerable negotiating, had returned the manuscript of the letters of state, along with that of the essay on Christian doctrine, to England, where apparently Sir Joseph Williamson or someone else in the government had stowed them away in the archives. After a century and a half of total neglect, they came to light in 1823. The Christian doctrine was published in 1825, but it was another quarter of a century before anyone paid further attention to the letters. In 1859 W. D. Hamilton, of the State Paper Office, described the collection, published some which had not previously been printed, offered variant readings from some others, and added a number of letters of the period concerning them (*Original Papers Illustrative of the Life and Writings of Milton, Publications of the Camden Society*, LXXV, 1859, 1-42). The Columbia edition (CM, XIII) offers variant readings from all the letters in the manuscript, as well as from those in the Columbia Manuscript and all other sources then known. In the present work references to this manuscript by number are given, as for the Columbia, for all letters contained in it.

Mr Skinner's informaċon
Octr. 18th. 1676

That Mr Pitts Bookseller in Pauls Churchyard to the best of my remembrance about 4 or 5 moneths agoe told me he had mett withall and bought some of Mr Miltons papers, and that if I would procure an agreement betwixt him And Elseviere at Amsterdam (to whose care I had long before committed the true perfect copy of the state letters to be printed) he would communicate them to my perusall; If I would not, he would proceed his own way and make the best advantage of 'em; So that in all probability I not procuring Elsevieres concurrance with him, and 'tis impossible it should be otherwise, Mr Pitts has been the man by whose meanes this late imperfect surreptitious copy, has been publish't.

I attest This to be truth

Octr. 18th. 1676   Dan: Skinner

Public Record Office, SP Dom 29/386/65; Hamilton, pp. 30-31; *CSP Dom* 1676/7, p. 372; Masson, VI, 794-795; French, "That Late Villain Milton," p. 104 (incomplete). The two lines given here at the top appear in the original as an endorsement on the outside. The whole document is in the same handwriting, including the signature, but excluding the date. This statement by Skinner makes it clear that the book had already been published before October 18, 1676, but probably not long before.

1677. DAUGHTER ANNE HAS BY NOW MARRIED, HAD A CHILD, AND DIED IN CHILDBED, TOGETHER WITH THE CHILD.

Anne married a master builder she died in childbed of her first child: A beautiful woman. Her child died wth her

British Museum Add. MS. 4,320, f. 232 (John Ward's notes for Thomas Birch); reprinted without much change by Birch in Milton's *A Complete Collection of the . . . Works*, I (1738), lxi; Masson, VI, 750. See below under date of February 10, 1738. Though Ward gives no dates, Anne must have been dead before October 24, 1678, because Anne Powell's will of that date speaks of her sisters Mary and Deborah as the only surviving children. The entry is here filed under 1677 as an approximation.

1677. FEBRUARY(?). DRYDEN'S *STATE OF INNO-CENCE*, BASED ON *PARADISE LOST*, PUBLISHED.

The State of Innocence and Fall of Man. An Opera written in Heroic Verse; and dedicated to her Royal Highness the Dutchess. By **John Dryden,** Servant to his Majesty. In Quarto. Price, sticht, 1s. Sold by **H. Herringman** at the Anchor in the New Exchange.

Term Catalogues, I, 266; Fletcher Facsimile, III, 12. This entry occurs among the list of books issued in Hilary Term, 1676/7, which was in February. The book was licensed on February 12. In a doctoral dissertation on *Milton and Dryden* (1954), Mr. Morris Freedman makes an interesting case for the possible relation of both *Paradise Lost* and *The State of Innocence* to the current debate over the relative merits of rhyme and blank verse. He also finds more political significance in Milton's writing than most previous commentators have.

1677. DECEMBER 10. BROTHER CHRISTOPHER'S SONS
THOMAS AND RICHARD SIGN INDENTURE WITH JOHN
PEED ABOUT PROPERTY IN SUFFOLK.

This Jndenture triptite made the tenth day of December . . .
One thousand six hundred seaventy & seaven Between Thomas
Milton of the Jnner Temple London Esq' of the first pte John
Peed of Hopton in the County of Suff yeoman of the second
pte, And Richard Milton of Jpswich in the said County of Suff
Esq' brother of the said Thomas Milton of the third pte Witnesseth that for . . . seaven poundę two shillingę & six pence
. . . by the said John Peed to the said Thomas Milton in hand
paid . . . and of the sume of thirteen poundę of like money by
him the said John Peed to the said Richard Milton . . . being
the residue & whole remainder of the money mencōned and
reserved to be paid . . . [by] an Jndenture of Lease . . . dated
the thirtieth day of May . . . One thousand six hundred seaventy
& six . . . of the mesuages . . . granted . . . He the said Thomas
Milton hath granted . . . (by & with the consent & direction
of the said Richard Milton . . .) . . . to the said John Peed . . .
All that mesuage late conveyed or granted by the said John
Peed to the said Thomas Milton . . . scituate . . . in Corton in
the County of Suff . . . lately conveyed to him the said Thomas
Milton by the said John Peed . . . Except only all those two
tenemtę . . . in Lowestoft . . . Which said two excepted tene-
mentę the said Thomas Milton & John Peed . . . have lately
bargayned & sold . . . Of wch said mesuages . . . the said John
Peed is now in full and peaceable possession & seisin by virtue
of a bargayn & sale for a yeare thereof to him made by the said
Thomas Milton by Jndenture dated the eighth day of this instant December . . . To have & to hold . . . for ever . . . And
that he the said Thomas Milton and Martha his wife . . . shall
& will . . . within seaven yeares next ensewing . . . make . . .
such further & other lawfull & reasonable act & acts . . . [pro-
vided they] be not for the doing thereof compelled . . . to tra-
vaile above one mile . . . Jn witnesse whereof vnto the ptę of this

Jndenture the parties above named have interchangeably put their hand℘ & seales Dated the day & yeare first abovewritten./

[Signed and sealed by] Tho: Milton   Riċhd Milton

[On the back are signatures of witnesses and a receipt for £7-2-6 signed:] Tho: Milton

From the original document now in the Library of the University of Illinois. I am grateful to the Librarian for making me a photostatic copy of this document and granting me permission to publish it. I am also grateful to Maggs Brothers in London for helping me to find the document. I first noticed it in their *Mercurius Britannicus*, Number 77 (1943), item 422. Though Christopher is nowhere named in the indenture, we need not fear to identify Richard and Thomas as his sons, because we meet them in the records of the Inner Temple, and because they are from his city of Ipswich.

1678. THIRD EDITION OF *PARADISE LOST*.

Paradise Lost. A Poem In Twelve Books. The Author John Milton. The Third Edition. Revised and Augmented by the same Author. London, Printed by S. Simmons next door to the Golden Lion in Aldersgate-street, 1678.

From the title page of my own copy; Masson, VI, 779.

1678. OCTOBER 24. MOTHER-IN-LAW ANNE POWELL MAKES WILL, LEAVING BEQUESTS TO POET'S DAUGHTERS MARY AND DEBORAH.

Jn the Name of God Amen J Anne Powell of London Widdow and Relict of Richard Powell late of fforresthill in the County of Oxford Esqʳ deceased . . . Doe make and ordeine this my last will and testament . . . Jtem J give vnto my sonne Richard Powell of the Inner temple . . . Esqʳ one bond or obligacoñ of the penalty of one hundred and twenty pounds . . . wherein hee standeth bound vnto mee . . . which bond beareth date on or about the eighth day of July which was in the yeare of our Lord one thousand Six hundred Sixty and five . . . Also I give vnto my said sonne Richard Powell one little Gold Ring, which was his Grandmother Archdalls and also all such goods householdstuffe vtensills and implements of House or hus-

bandry which at any time heretofore were myne . . . Jtem J
give vnto Anne the wife of my said sonne Richard the Picture
of my said sonne which J have and is sett in a case or frame of
Gold or Enamell also J give vnto my Grandchild Richard
Powell eldest sonne of my said sonne Richard Powell twenty
shillings to buy him a Ring . . . Jtem J give vnto my daughter
Anne Kinaston wife of Thomas Kinaston of London Merchant
ffifty pounds . . . Also . . . the further summe of ffifty pounds,
vpon trust . . . for . . . my daughter Sarah Peirson wife of
Richard Peirson Gent' and her sonne Richard Peirson . . . and
to my two daughters Elizabeth Howell wife of Thomas Howell
Gent' and Elizabeth Holloway wife of Christmas Holloway
Gent' vnto each of them fifty pounds . . . Jtem J give vnto my
two Grandchildren Mary Milton Spinster and Deborah Clarke
the wife of [blank] Clarke of [blank] in the Kingdome of Jreland being the two Surviveing daughters of my late daughter
Mary Milton deceased vnto each of them tenne pounds a peece
. . . Also J give vnto my loveing cousen M^{rs}. Elizabeth Lewis
Widdow Tenne shillings . . . and to her Sister M^{rs}. Martha
[blank] wife of [blank] of the Borough of Southwarke tenne
shillings . . . And to my loveing freinds Richard Cox of Stanton
S^t. Johns in the county of Oxoñ Gent' and Mary his wife tenne
shillings a peece and to their two Sonnes Richard and Nicholas
Tenne shillings a peece . . . Jtem my will is that in case any
money shall bee recovered vpon a bond formerly entred into
by Martin Dawson Gent' deceased vnto one William Dew
Gent' in trust for mee . . . then the money soe recovered . . .
shall bee equally divided . . . betweene my said sonne Richard
Powell and my said foure daughters . . . Lastly I give and devise all and sin̄gler my goods and chattells . . . vnto my said
Daughter Anne Kinaston whom J make and ordeine sole Executrix of this my last will and testament . . . Jn witnesse whereof
J have herevnto sett my hand and seale the twentie fourth day
of October . . . one thousand Six hundred Seaventie and eight

Anne Powell, Signed . . . in the presence of Henr' Waldron John Meres Tho: Sorell

Probatum fuit humoi testum Londini Coram venli viro Henrico ffauconberge legum Doctore Surrogato venlis et egregij viri Domini Leolini Jenkins Militis legum etiam Dcoris Curiæ Prrogativæ Cantuarien Magistri Custodis sive Commissarij ltime constituti Sexto die mensis Novembris Anno Dni Millesimo Sextenmo Octogemo Secundo Juramento Annæ Kinaston Executricis in dicto testamento nominat' Cui Commissa fuit Administratio omniū et singulorum bonorum Juriū et Creditorum dicti defuncti De bene et fidelr Administrando eadem ad Scta Dei Evangelia Jurat'. Ex^r

Prerogative Court of Canterbury, 138 Cottle; Masson, VI, 750-751 (summary). I have omitted as much as possible of the cumbrous phraseology of the original without sacrificing the names of any legatees. The omission of any mention of the poet's daughter Anne indicates that she was dead by this date. The Anne Kinaston who proved the will on November 6, 1682, apparently was also known as Anne Kingston; see the will of Richard Powell entered below under date of December 29, 1693.

[A will of this sort was proved in London before the worshipful man Henry Falconberg, Doctor of Laws, Surrogate to the worshipful and excellent Master Leoline Jenkins, Knight, also Doctor of Laws, Master Keeper or Commissary, legally constituted, of the Prerogative Court of Canterbury, on the sixth day of the month of November in the year of our Lord 1682, by the oath of Anne Kinaston, executrix named in the said will, to whom administration of all and singular the goods, chattels, and credits of the said deceased was granted, she being first sworn on the Holy Gospels of God to administer the same well and faithfully. Let it (the record) be exhibited.]

1679. JANUARY 7. DR. NATHAN PAGET BEQUEATHES £20 TO POET'S WIDOW.

In the Name of God Amen The Seaventh day of January . . . Annoqz Dni One Thowsand Six Hundred Seaventy Eight

J Nathan Pagett of London in the Parish of S^t. Stephens Cole-manstreete Doctor of Phisick . . . doe make this my last Will and Testament . . . Jmprimis J giue and bequeath all that ffarme and Messuage . . . Oakes Hall being in the Parish of ffonsbury in Shropshire . . . vnto my loving brother Thomas Pagett Clerk . . . Jtem J giue and bequeath those my Two ffarmes in Weston with the appurtennces in the Parish of Hodmitt in the County of Salop . . . vnto my loving sister Elizabeth Johnson . . . And J doe likewise giue and bequeath vnto my loving brother Thomas Pagett All that Messuage or Tenement . . . now in the occupacōn of Richard Mart situat in St Stephens Coleman-streete . . . Jtem J doe giue and bequeath vnto my said brother Thomas Pagett and his heires foreuer All that Messuage with the appurtennces which J now dwell in being situat in S^t. Stephens Colemanstreete as aforesaid Also J doe giue to my said brother Thomas Pagett fforty volumes out of my study of Bookes such as he shall be pleased to choose . . . Jtem whereas J am possessd of a terme of yeares by the Assignement of Richard Corseige in seuerall Messuages in Petty ffrance in little Moore feilds London J will and devise to the Trustees of the Poore of the Parish of St Stephens Colemanstreete London All those said Messuages for so long terme as J haue by my Assigne-ment . . . Jtem J doe bequeath to my Cosen Elizabeth Milton the sumē of Twenty Pownds . . . And J doe Constitute and ap-point my said brother Thomas Pagett Clerke and my Cosen John Goldsmith of the Middle Temple Gent' the Executors of this my last Will and Testament . . . Nathan Pagett./ . . . Signed sealed . . . in the presence of Heze: Burton Wal: Need-ham Edward ffowler./

Probatum Londini fuit huiusmodi Testamentum . . . Decimo Quinto die Mensis Januarij Anno Dnī (stilo Angliæ) Mille-simo Sexcentesimo Septuagesimo Octavo Juramentis Thomæ Pagett Oliviri et Johannis Gouldsmith Executorum in huius-modi Testam^{to}: nominatorum Quibus Comīssa fuit Administra-tio. . . .

Prerogative Court of Canterbury, 9 King; Masson, VI, 744 (brief summary). Among the omitted portions of the will are bequests to Pagett's sister Elizabeth Johnson and her children Thomas and Elizabeth, his cousin John Goldsmith (one of the executors), and the president and fellows of the College of Physicians (for twenty pounds a year). I have left out also some of the verbiage of the probate. The name of Oliver Goldsmith as one of the executors is interesting. Though we do not know what books Thomas Pagett selected from his brother's collection, Dr. James Holly Hanford has described the sale catalogue of the library in 1681 in the *Bulletin of the Medical Library Association*, XXXIII (1945), 91-99. It included numerous copies of Milton's books.

[A will of this sort was proved in London . . . on the fifteenth day of the month of January in the year of our Lord (in English style) 1678, on the oaths of Thomas Pagett and of Oliver and John Goldsmith, executors named in the will of this sort, to whom was committed administration. . . .]

1679. NOVEMBER 12. BROTHER CHRISTOPHER REMISS IN TEMPLE DUES.

Att the Bench Table Novem̃ the 12ᵗʰ 1679. . . .

Ord^{red}. that the Head Buttler attend Mʳ Milton of the Bench for payement of his duties and Pencoñˢ forthwith otherwise the Lawes of the House must been proceeded against him.
. . .

Ordred that the Cheife Buttler likewise demand the summe of fower pound of Mʳ. Milton his sonne for his Caution money wch should haue been paid att his Call to the Barr.

From the records of the Inner Temple, f. 16v; *A Calendar of the Inner Temple Records*, ed. F. A. Inderwick, III (1901), 151. The son mentioned might be either Thomas, who had been called to the bar on November 29, 1677, or Richard, who had been called to the bar about a year earlier, November 26, 1676. For a summary of the Inner Temple records of Christopher and his sons, see above under date of May 16, 1675. Caution money is money deposited as a guarantee of good behavior, especially by students. There are numerous records of about this date concerning the unpaid dues of members of the society; apparently there was a financial crisis which called for quick money, which was hard to raise. In these entries, as usual in these records, the substance of the entry is repeated in the margin as a quick guide to the contents; I shall not give these marginal summaries.

1679. NOVEMBER 13. INNER TEMPLE AUTHORITIES BE-
COME INCREASINGLY SEVERE WITH BROTHER CHRIS-
TOPHER.

Att y^e. Bench table Novemb^r. 13th. 1679

Ordered att y^e. Bench table that M^r. Milton bee once more
attended by the Cheife Butler to pay his duties And yf hee
refuse to pay the same by Satturday next the table will then
proceede according to y^e. Orders of y^e. house to padlock vpp
his Chambers And the table doe not thinck fitt to allow any
of M^r. Milton his share in repayring of his Chambers vnlesse
Mr. Milton then better reasons.

From the records of the Inner Temple, f. 16v; Inderwick, III, 151.
See the preceding item.

1679. NOVEMBER 14. BROTHER CHRISTOPHER STILL
REMISS IN PAYMENTS; BROTHER-IN-LAW RICHARD
POWELL IN SIMILAR TROUBLE.

Att the Bench Table ye 14th. of Nov. 1679.

Ordered by the Table this day y^t M^r. Milton Mr Powell
two of the Masters of the Bench have notice by the Cheife
Butler to bee at the Table to morrow att Dinner to giue theire
finall Answeare not payeing of their Dutyes.

From the Records of the Inner Temple, f. 16v; Inderwick, III, 151.
See the preceding items.

This is perhaps an appropriate place for a brief summary of the career
of Milton's brother-in-law Richard Powell as revealed in these records.
It is rather similar to that of Christopher Milton as given above under
date of May 16, 1675. I will give it here in the same form as that,
showing first the page in Inderwick, Volume III, then the date, and then
the action. First, however, may be mentioned two actions in Inderwick's earlier Volume II. One (p. 307) is the treasurer's report for the
year from November 3, 1652, to November 7, 1653, listing among others the receipt of £4 from Powell. The other (p. 308) is the notice
of Powell's being called to the bar, given above under date of November 24, 1653 (III, 347-348).

20	1663	January 10.	On a committee.
13		February 4.	Called to the bench.
35	1665	February 12.	Recommends repair to room.

36		May 28. On committee.
40	1666	October 28. On committee.
42		November 30. On committee.
45	1667	April 28. "Special admission of . . . Richard Powell, at the request of his father, Powell of the bench."
47		May 13. On committee.
47		November 3. Chosen auditor.
51	1668	June 7. To hear, with others, a petition.
52		November 3 and 6. On committee.
52		November 8. Chosen auditor.
60	1669	February 7. On committee.
61		February 15. On committee.
64		May 10. On committee.
61		May 23. On committee.
69	1670	February 11. On committee.
70		April 24. Attendant to reader.
71		November 6. Auditor.
71		November 20. Chosen to inspect bonds.
80		November 25. On committee.
80	1671	February 10. On committee.
74		February 12. On committee.
75		May 24. Chosen reader.
77		June 4. On committee.
79		October 29. Chosen auditor.
81		October 29. Mentioned in treasurer's report for preceding year for £60 for attendance of stewards at his reading.
83		November 12. On committee.
83		November 26. Attendant to reader.
84	1672	February 15. On committee.
85		June 10. On Parliament.
86		June 10. Requests special admission of Richard Cooke.
87		November 3. Chosen auditor.
88	1673	February 5. Argument over prices of rooms referred to other members.
87		February 15. On committee.
89		Expense of glazing chamber reported.
91		June 15. On committee.
93		November 23. On committee.
96	1674	May 31. On Parliament.
97		July 5. On committee.
100	1675	May 16. On committee.
103		June 16. To seize and view a chamber.
101		June 20. To hear a petition.

103		July 25. On committee.
104		June 26. On committee. (An error for July?)
105	1676	January 30. On Parliament.
105		February 6. On Parliament.
106		April 16. On Parliament.
112		October 28. Chosen treasurer.
110		November 26. Son Richard called to the bar.
113	1677	May 7. On committee.
118		November 4. Treasurer.
118		November 18. Treasurer.
118		November 25. Treasurer.
119		November 29. Treasurer and on committee.
115		December 11. On committee.
120	1678	January 27. Treasurer.
120		February 10. Treasurer.
126		February 15. Treasurer.
121		April 28. Treasurer.
121		May 14. Treasurer.
122		June 9. Treasurer.
122		June 16. Treasurer.
123		June 19. Treasurer.
124		November 3. Treasurer.
127		November. Account as treasurer.
131	1679	January 26. On Parliament.
138		February 3. His chamber mentioned.
141		May 21. On committee.
142		June 30. Ordered to pay indebtedness shown in treasurer's account before next parliament.
144		November. "Powell's Building" mentioned.
145		November. Account for him mentions coach hire to the Duke of Monmouth's.
151		November 10. Consulted about conveyance.
151		November 14-15. In trouble over unpaid dues.
207	1684	November 6. His eldest son Poole admitted as of Easter term, 1682.
241	1687	October 30. On Parliament.
259	1689	Record that he attended two parliaments during year.
272	1690	Record that he attended three parliaments during year.
288	1691	Record that he attended three parliaments during year.
306	1694	February 7-8. Baron Powell asked to give further time to Grant's business. This is the final entry.

1679. DECEMBER 15. TREASURY ORDER FOR PAYING BROTHER CHRISTOPHER'S SON £144-13-6.

[Marginal note:] Thomas Milton gent 144:13:6

After &c[a]. By vertue of his Ma[ts]. gen[ll]. Lrēs Patents dormant beareing date y[e] 24th. day of July last past These are to pray and require yo[u]. to draw one or more Orders for payment of y[e] summe of One Hundred forty foure pounds thirteene shillings six pence to Thomas Milton Gent Deputy Clerke of y[e] Crowne or to his assignes without Account for ffees and charges due to himselfe & others in passing two Comissions for executing the Office of Treār of the Excheq[r]. And let y[e] same bee paid out of any his Ma[ts]. Treār now or hereafter being and Remaineing in y[e] Receipt of the Excheq[r]. not appropriated to pticuler uses by Act of Parliam[t]. And for soe doeing &c[a]. 15° Dec[r]. 79.

LH ED SG SF

[In margin:] To S[r] Robert Howard &c

Public Record Office, Treasury 53, Vol. I, p. 286; *Calendar of Treasury Books 1679-1680*, p. 305. The initials at the end are not signatures, being all in the same handwriting. This document, like most of the similar ones to be given here, seems to be a copy and not the original.

1679. DECEMBER 16. ORDER FOR PAYMENT TO THOMAS MILTON REPEATED.

[Note in margin:] M[r]. Tho: Milton for y[e] charge of passing two Comissions for y[e] Office of Treār of y[e] Excheq[r]. 144:13:6.

Order dated xvj° day of December 1679 By Dormant Lrēs Patents dated xxiiij° Julij last To Thomas Milton gent Deputy Clerke of y[e] Crowne or to his assignes y[e] Summe of One hundred fforty four Pounds thirteene shillings six pence w[th]out accompt for Fees & Charges due to himselfe & others in passing two Comissions for executeing y[e] Office of Treār of y[e] Excheq[r]. &c[a]. 144:13:6.

LH JE ED SG SF

Public Record Office, Treasury 60, Vol. 38, p. 58; *Calendar of Treasury Books 1679-1680*, p. 305.

[In margin:] S^r. Robt. Howard.

S^r. Out of the summe of 682:3:4 that remaines undisposed of ye 8000^{li} lately sent by M^r. Kent & M^r. Duncombe The Lords Com^{rs}. of ye Treāry desire yo^u. make these following paym^{ts}. . . .

<table>
<tr><td></td><td>li</td><td>s</td><td>d</td></tr>
<tr><td>To M^r. Milton of ye Crowne Office - - - </td><td>144</td><td>:13</td><td>: 6</td></tr>
</table>

. . . J am S^r. &c. HG 16°. Decem^{br}. 1679.

Public Record Office, Treasury 27, Vol. 5, p. 307; *Calendar of Treasury Books 1679-1680*, p. 310.

1680. FEBRUARY 2. BROTHER CHRISTOPHER AGAIN IN ARREARS IN INNER TEMPLE.

Att the Bench Table the 2^d. ffeb^{ry}. 79[80].

Ordered that S^r. Thomas ffoster and M^r. Milton doe pay their duties before the next Parliament otherwise their Chambers to bee Seized

From the records of the Inner Temple, f. 17; Inderwick, III, 152. After another similar action on February 6, this sort of record disappears and is no more heard of.

1680. APRIL 15. BROTHER CHRISTOPHER CONDUCTS HEARING ON A RIOT NEAR FELIXSTOWE IN SUFFOLK.

[In margin] suff: ss

The Jnformacōn & Examinacōn of Willm Parsons of ffelixtwo Husbandman taken vpon Oath before Chr̄. Milton Esqz one of his Ma^{ts} Justices of ye Peace of this County the 15th. Apr. 1680/.

This Jnformant vpon his exam̄ sayth That in Augt. last he heard that 20 hh^s of wine were landed at Bardsey fferry And ye next day being satturday this Jnformant was told that ye sayd Wines were seized by Mr Cooke one of ye officers of ye Custome-house after they were brought in Robert Baggotts Cart into Jo^n. Waggers Barne and there left in ye Custody of

Nicholas Swann by the Ord^r. of ye sayd Mr Cooke This Examinant hearing that the sayd wynes thus remained in the sayd Barne went thither vpon the then next Sunday about two of ye Clock afternoone. and found there in the sayd Barne wth the sayd wines the sayd Nicholas Swann Robert Blomfeild & Jo^n Scott the Constable of the Towne of ffelixtwo who was there to see ye peace kept and then the sayd Nicholas Swan desired the sayd Exam^{nt}. to stay there to helpe loade the sayd Wines when the Carts should Come to fetch them away for his Ma^{ts} vse This Exam^{at}. further sayth That about ten of ye Clock the same Sunday at night came seuerall psons to a great number wth Carts some of wch persons were souldiers then belonging to Landgard-ffort there close by the names of wch sõld are as follows . . . This Exam^{at}. saith that Tho. Mayhews sayd to his Masters shearers vpon friday in ye afternoone That if they cutt downe all the Corne then standing they could not carry it because they had other loading to load theire Carts w.thall anon. But what this mans name is they cannot tell ffurther this Exam^{at}. sayth That vpon ye appch of this great Company he runn away for feare, and hath heard since that if he had not soe done he had been shott because he was there to guard the wine but from whom he heard this or how they should know that he was there to guard ye wine he cannot tell, onely there was one John Gardner of Trymly who was vp & Downe about ye Barne in ye afternoone but for what purpose he this Exam^{at}. cannot tell nor whither he was one of ye Company at night This Exam^{at}. last sayth That he lay in a Bush afterwards about eight rods frõ ye Barne and heard blowes & saw a gunñ and afterwards found ye Constable & swann lye bound neck & heades in ye feild neare the Barnes and likewise heard the sayd wines driuen away in ye Carts.

[Signed:] Chr̄ Milton

Signum

W^m.   X   Parsons

Public Record Office, Treasury 27, Vol. 5, pp. 489-491; *Calendar of Treasury Books 1679-1680*, pp. 530-531. The signature of Christopher Milton seems to be in the same hand as the rest of the entry, which in turn seems identical with such preceding and following pieces as are included in my photostatic copy. It is quite likely that a good deal of the writing in these books may be in Christopher's hand. The portion which I have omitted is merely a catalogue of names. Probably I should have omitted more than I have, but the account is sufficiently interesting to invite lengthy quotation. The paragraph preceding this account in the manuscript is a copy of a letter of transmittal of this report from H. G. (Henry Guy?) to Sir Charles Littleton dated May 11, 1680.

1680. APRIL 28. BROTHER CHRISTOPHER'S SON THOMAS SIGNS RECEIPT FOR FEES FROM JUDGE GEORGE JEFFREYS.

Chester & Sir George Jefferyes ffees

fflint		li	s	d
Hanap Office		05:	13:	04
Crowne Office & Greate Seale		07:	00:	00:
Pryvate Seale		02:	00:	00:
Attendance		01:	00:	00:
		15:	13:	04:

Denbigh &
Mountgom^{r}y: the like ffees 15   13. 04

To the Clarke of the C$\bar{r}$ for swearing 02: 00. 00:

Tot. .33. .06. 08

xxviijth: Aprill: 80:
Rec^d: then the abovesaid ffees
p̱ me Tho: Milton

From the original document in the Library of the University of Illinois. I thank the Librarian for providing me with a photostatic copy of it; and Maggs Brothers in London (in whose *Mercurius Britannicus*, Number 77, 1943, item 421, I first learned of it) for kindly informing me of its location. This judge is he of the notorious "Bloody Assizes" reputation.

1680. JUNE 4. WIDOW RECEIVES BOND FROM HER BROTHER RICHARD MINSHULL.

Noverint Vniu'si p p'ñtes me Ricūm Minshull de Wisterson in Com Cestr̄ fframe work knitter Teneri et firmiter obligari Elizabethe Milton de Ci^te. London vid' in Trecent' libr' bone et leḡlis Monet' Angl solvend' eid' Elizabethe Executor' Administr' vel Assignat' suis Ad quam quidem solucōnem bene et fideliter faciend' Obligo me hered' Executor' et Administr' meos firmiter p p'ntes S'gillo meo sigillat' Dat' quarto die Junii Anno Regni Regis Carōl scdī nunc Anḡl &c' Tricesimo scdō Annoqz Dnī 1680.

The Condition of the aboue written obligation is such That Whereas the aboue bounden Richard Minshull for & in Consideration of the sume of one hundred & ffifty pounds in hand payd or secured to be payd by the aboue named Elizabeth Milton vnto him the sayd Richard Minshull (att the Request & ffor the vse of the sayd Elizabeth Milton) hath lately heretofore granted & surrendered vnto Sr Thomas Wilbraham Barronett All that Messuage and Tenement with thappurtenances and diverse lands therevnto belonging or therewith vsed, late in the possession holding or occupation of George Henshaw late of Namptwich in the sayd County of Chester yeoman deceased & now or late in the possession of the sayd Richard Minshull or his vndertenants scituate lying & beinge in Brindley in the sayd County of Chester ffor the Terme of the life of Mary Minshull wife of the sayd Richard Minshull To the intent and purpose to enable the sayd Sr Thomas Wilbraham to make a pfect lease of the p'misses vnto the sayd Elizabeth Milton ffor the Terme of Nynty & Nyne yeares if the sayd Elizabeth Milton, Mary Minshull & Richard Minshull sonne of the sayd Richard and Mary or any of them did or should soe long live. Now Therefore if the sayd Elizabeth Milton her Executo^rs Administrato^rs & Assignees & eūy of them shall . . . quietly and peaceably have hold occupy possesse and enjoy the sayd

Messuage . . . Then this p^rsent obligation to bee voyd or els the same to Remaine & be in ffull power & virtue.

Sealed & delev^red in the
 p^rsence of

Edw: Miñshull   [signed:] Richard Mynshull [seal]
Tho: Wright
Willī Meakin

[Endorsed:] Richard Minshull his bond to save Mrs Melton harmeles. &c̄

From the original document now in the New York Public Library Manuscript Room; first described by John F. Marsh in the *Athenaeum*, September 22, 1849, p. 954; Marsh, *Papers*, pp. 23-24 (in full); referred to in British Museum Add. MS. 24,501 (Hunter's collection), f. 44; summarized in Masson, VI, 745. I have left out a few lines which, though probably important to a lawyer, add no important information for the ordinary reader. Masson interprets this action as Mrs. Milton's provision for a home for herself after her retirement to Nantwich; but he adds that she did not actually occupy it. Masson gives the amount of money in the Latin paragraph as thirty rather than, correctly, three hundred pounds.

This might be an appropriate place to mention two documents in the same collection which do not warrant inclusion as texts because they have no real connection with the Milton family, though they do concern Mrs. Milton's brother. They are both papers signed by Richard Minshull, and both dated 1674. In one, dated July 6, he binds himself in the sum of £860 to Robert Cudworth of Newhall, co. Chester, conditioned on the observance of an indenture of the same date between (1) himself, his wife Mary, and his mother Anne, and (2) Cudworth. In the second, dated December 5, he and his wife Mary state that whereas at the last Assizes or General Sessions (September 21) they levied a fine to Robert Cudworth on property in Stapeley, they now release him from it. Neither Marsh nor Masson mentions either of these documents.

[Know all men by these presents that I, Richard Minshull of Wistaston in the county of Chester, frame work knitter, am bound and firmly obligated to Elizabeth Milton of the city of London, widow, in three hundred pounds of good and legal money of England, to be paid to the said Elizabeth, her executors, administrators, or assigns, to the making of which payment well and faithfully I obligate myself, my heirs, executors, and administrators firmly by these presents. Sealed with

my seal. Given the fourth day of June in the thirty-second
year of the reign of King Charles the Second, now of England,
etc., and in the year of our Lord 1680.]

1680. JULY 12. BROTHER CHRISTOPHER TO MAKE FURTHER EXAMINATION ABOUT RIOT IN FELIXSTOWE.

[Marginal address and summary:] Govern' Landgard ffort
ābt a Royot by yᵉ soldierꝑ ābt wines &c at felixton

Sʳ The ComʳꝒ. of his maᵗꝒ Customes haue yᵉ 10ᵗʰ of May
last layd before the Lords ComʳꝒ. of his MaᵗꝒ Treāry the Copy
of an Affidauit of Wᵐ: Parsons concerning a Ryott comitted at
ffelixton in yᵉ County of Suffolke & seuerall Wines seized ꝑ
Isaac Cooke Survey' of the Port of Jpswich & Nich: Swan
Boatman in yᵉ said Port rescued in yᵉ Moneth of August last
by Jnº: Adams Gunner Tho: Hall Peter Cramocke & Tho:
ffosdicke Souldiers then belonging to Landguard ffort That
they desire you forthwᵗʰ to send yᵉ said George Adams to Mʳ
George Gosnell Collector of his Maᵗˢ Customes at Jpswich
to be in his presence examined by mʳ Milton one of his Maᵗˢ.
Iustices of yᵉ Peace in Jpswich in order to the ꝑsecution of yᵉ.
Rioters at yᵉ next assizes at Bury Sᵗ. Edmunds

I am

Treāry Chamber   yoʳ most humble servᵗ
12 Iuly 1680   H: Guy

Public Record Office, Treasury 27, Volume 6, p. 36; *Calendar of
Treasury Books 1679–1680*, p. 620. For the earlier part of this action
see above under date of April 15, 1680. The present document is a
copy, not an original letter.

1680. DECEMBER 21. WIDOW RECEIVES £8 FROM SAMUEL SYMMONS AND RELEASES ALL HER RIGHTS IN *PARADISE LOST* TO HIM.

I do hereby acknowledge to have received of Samuel Sy-
m̄onds Cittizen and Staċoner of London, the sum̄ of Eight
pounds: which is in full payment for all my right, Title, or
Jnterest, which J have, or ever had in the Coppy of a Poem

Jntitled Paradise Lost in Twelve Bookes in 8ᵘᵒ. By John Milton Gent: my late husband. Wittness my hand this 21ˢᵗ. day of December 1680.

Wittness William Yapp   [Signed:] Elizabeth Milton
       Ann Yapp

The original of this receipt is in the Library of Christ's College, Cambridge; Sotheby, facing p. 136 (facsimile); Masson, VI, 779; CM, XVIII, 620; Fletcher Facsimile, III, 15. There were two copies of this document, one belonging to Sir Thomas Gery Cullum and the other to Dawson Turner. There was some question for a time as to which was the original, but it seems reasonably clear now that Cullum's was the original and Turner's a copy. See the discussion in the *Athenaeum* for September 17, October 1, and October 15, 1859, pp. 375, 432, and 499. Masson gives a facsimile of the signature.

1681. HAAK TRANSLATES *PARADISE LOST* INTO DUTCH OR GERMAN.

Mdm̄ Mʳ Theodore Haak R.S.S. hath translated halfe his Paradise lost into High Dutch in such blank verse, wᶜʰ is very well liked of by Germanus Fabricius Professor at Heidelberg, who sent to Mʳ Haak a letter upon this Translation—Jncredibile est quantum nos omnes effecerit gravitas style, & copia lectissimorum verborum et. . . . v. the letter.

Aubrey, f. 68; Darbishire, p. 5. One could make an endless list of editions and translations, but this book is not the place for them. The present note is included because it seems fair to include everything that the early biographers put in, since readers might miss it otherwise. Haak's translation was apparently not published. But it must have been done by 1681, the date which may safely be assigned to Aubrey's work. Whether the language was actually Dutch or German is open to question. Wood, who repeats this story almost verbatim in his life of Haak (*Athenae Oxonienses*, 1692, II, 643) lists many translations by Haak from and into both German and Dutch.

The Latin may be translated: "It is incredible how much the solemnity of his style and his command of the most choice words has affected us all."

1681. WIDOW REMOVES TO NANTWICH.

Masson, VI, 745: "It seems to have been in or about 1681 that the widow, then in her forty-third year, made up her mind to leave London

and retire to her native Cheshire." Darbishire, p. 334. There seems to
be no documentary evidence of this date. But presumably the agreement of June 4, 1680, with Richard Minshull of Wistaston (above)
and the release of April 29, 1681, to Samuel Symmons (below) were intended to pave the way for her to leave London and go back to her childhood section of the country. Later records of April 11, 1713, and subsequent dates (given below) speak of her as of Nantwich. Whatever the
exact date, therefore, there is no doubt of the action itself. Masson repeats a saying which became current about her in that town, indicating
her frugality, saying of people in straitened circumstances, "They have
had Mrs. Milton's feast, enough and no more." But with any rumors
of this sort it is always well to remember G. Gray's letter of July 30,
1731, to his brother Zachary Grey (quoted in Marsh's *Papers*, p. 34):
"There were three Widow Miltons there, [at Nantwich] vizt. the
Poet's widow, my Aunt, and another. . . ." The pinching Mrs. Milton
could have been any one of these or of many others, since Nantwich
and the surrounding country were full of Miltons.

1681. JOHN AUBREY VISITS WIDOW AND WRITES BIO-GRAPHICAL NOTES ON MILTON.

His widowe has his picture drawne very well & like when a
Cambridge-scholler. . . . She has his picture when a cambridge
schollar, wch ought to be engraven: for the Pictures before his
bookes are not *at all* like him./ He mar^d his 2^d *wife* M^ris Eliz:
Minshull A°. the yeare before the sicknesse. a gent. person a
peacefull & agreeable humour. . . .

His widowe assures me that Mr Hobbs was not one of his
acquaintance: y^t her husband did not like him at all: but he
would acknowledge grant him to be a man of great parts, a
learned man. . . .

vidua Affirmat she gave all his papers [among wch this Dict:
imperfect] to his Nephew, that he brought up, a sister's son:—
Philips, who lives neer the Maypole in the *Strand* q She has a
great many letters by her from learned men his acquaintance,
both of England & beyond sea.

Aubrey, ff. 63, 63v, 68; Darbishire, pp. 3, 7, 4. Masson (VI, 744)
points out that Aubrey must have visited the widow to have written as
he did; and the deduction seems sound. Miss Darbishire also thinks (p.
12n.) that the line recording the day and hour of Milton's birth is in

Mrs. Milton's hand; it is certainly different from the rest of the passage and like her signatures to the receipts to Samuel Simmons. The present entry is dated by Aubrey's notes on his manuscript. Andrew Clarke (*Brief Lives*, I, 13-15) quotes one as "Pars . . . iii^{tia} 1681." Another is Aubrey's entry on f. 4: "Auctarium vitarum a JA collectarum, anno Domini 1681" (the overplus of the lives collected by John Aubrey, A.D. 1681). Clarke also quotes (I, 14) a letter from Wood to Aubrey acknowledging the receipt of the manuscript in September, 1681. See also Darbishire, p. xi. The brackets above are in Aubrey. The "q" after "*Strand*" appears directly above that word in the manuscript. Aubrey's visits to the widow may of course have been made earlier, but probably not much. The section of Aubrey's manuscript notes dealing with Milton covers ff. 63-68v of MS. Aubrey 8 in the Bodleian. It is transcribed in Clarke, II, 60-72, and in Darbishire, pp. 1-15. Aubrey heads it: "Mr *John Milton*." He evidently added a few notes (like that on the *History of Moscovia* below) later.

1681. APRIL 29. WIDOW GIVES MORE FORMAL RELEASE TO SYMMONS.

Know all men by these p^rsents that J Elizabeth Milton of London widdow, late wife of John Milton of London Gent: deceased have remised released and for ever quitt claimed And by these p^rsents doe rm̄ise release and for ever quitt clayme vnto Samuell Symonds of London Printer his Heires Executo^rs and Administrato^rs All and all manner of Accōn and Accōns Cause and Causes of Accōn Suites Bills Bonds writings obligatorie Debts Dues Duties Accompts Sum̄e and Sum̄es of money Judgments Execucōns Extents Quarrells either in Law or Equity Controversies and demands And all and every other matter cause and thing whatsoever which against the said Samuell Symonds J ever had And which J my heires Executors or Administrato^rs shall or may have clayme psecute challenge or demand for or by reason or meanes of any matter cause or thing whatsoever from the beginning of the World vnto the day of the date of these p^rsents Jn wittnes whereof I have herevnto sett my hand and Seale the twenty ninth day of April in the thirty third Yeare of the Reigne of our Soveraigne Lord Charles a by the grace of God of England Scotland ffrance

and Ireland King Defender of the ffaith &c Annoqz Dni 1681
Sealed and delivered
in the p'sents of

Jo: Leigh   [Signed:] Elizabeth Milton [seal]
Wm Wilkins

The original document is in the Library of Christ's College; facsimile in Fletcher Facsimile, III, 17, with transcript on p. 16; Masson,
VI, 780 (brief mention); CM, XVIII, 620 (text). The letter "a" after
"Charles," which makes no sense, may be a mere scribal flourish but is
a perfect letter "a." This document is a prepared form, though hand
written, in which only the immediate names and dates are filled in for
the present transaction.

1681. APRIL (?). *CHARACTER OF THE LONG PARLIA-
MENT* PUBLISHED.

Mr John Miltons Character of the Long Parliament and
Assembly of Divines. In MDCXLI. Omitted in his other
Works, and never before Printed, And very seasonable for
these times. [device] London: Printed for Henry Brome, at
the Gun at the West-end of St. Pauls. 1681.

Title page of the first edition; Masson, VI, 806; CM, XVIII, 247 ff.,
with facsimile of title page on p. 247. The substance of this pamphlet,
though from a manuscript version, is introduced into the Columbia edition of Milton's *History of Britain* as a supplement (CM, X, 317-325),
with directions to insert it about twelve pages after the beginning of
Book III, on p. 114 of the Columbia text; the printed text, however,
when included in editions of Milton's *History*, has usually come on what
corresponds to p. 103. Masson, who discusses this piece at considerable
length (pp. 806-812), is not sure that it is Milton's or that it fits ap-
propriately in the *History*. For further discussion see above under the
entry for the *History* in November, 1670. Though Professor William
A. Jackson says that several early manuscripts of this piece are known
(*The Carl H. Pforzheimer Library*, II, 721, #710), I know of only
that at Harvard which is printed and collated in CM. Wing (*STC*,
T.3590) catalogues this title under Sir James Tyrrell as well as under
Milton (M2098).

The Reader may take notice, That this Character of Mr.
Milton's *was a part of his History of* Britain, *and by him designed to be Printed: But . . . it was struck out for some harshness. . . .*

Character of the Long Parliament, 1681, sig. A2; CM, XVIII, 247.

Mr. **John Milton's** Character of the Long Parliament and Assembly of Divines, 1641; omitted in his other Works, and never before printed. Quarto. Price 2d.

Term Catalogues, I, 443, under Easter Term, 1681, which gives us April or May as the date of publication.

(32) *Character of the Long Parliament and of the Assembly of Divines.* Lond. 1681, in 2 sheets in qu. In which book is a notable account of their Ignorance, Treachery, and Hypocrisie.

Wood, I, 883; Darbishire, p. 47. None of the other early biographers mentions this work.

1682. LETTERS OF STATE TRANSLATED INTO ENGLISH.

Milton's Republican-Letters or A Collection of such as were written by Comand of the Late Commonwealth of England, from the year 1648. to the Year 1659. Originally writ by the learned John Milton, Secretary to those times, and now translated into English, by a Wel-wisher of English honour. Printed in the Year 1682.

Title page of the copy in the British Museum; Parker, *Milton's Contemporary Reputation*, p. 53; apparently not mentioned in Masson or in Wing's *STC*. An anonymous manuscript note inserted in the British Museum copy suggests that the book was printed abroad. Except for a multitude of mistakes it follows the edition of 1676.

1682. FEBRUARY(?). *HISTORY OF MOSCOVIA* PUBLISHED.

A Brief History of Moscovia: and Of other less-known Countries lying eastward of Russia as far as Cathay. Gather'd from the Writings of several Eye-witnesses. By John Milton. London, Printed by M. Flesher, for Brabazon Aylmer at the Three Pigeons against the Royal Exchange. 1682.

Title page of the 1682 edition; text in CM, X, 327-382; Masson, VI, 812-813. The date comes from the entry in the Term Catalogues, which follows. See also the entry about this book under 1674.

A brief History of *Muscovia*; and of other less known Countries lying Eastward of *Russia*, as far as *Cathay*. Gathered from the Writings of several Eye-Witnesses. In Octavo. By **John Milton,** before he lost his Sight. Printed for **B. Aylmer** at the Three Pidgeons in *Cornhill.*

Term Catalogues, I, 472, under date of Hilary Term, 1682.

11 A Brief History of Muscovia: and other less known Countries lyeing Eastward. Advertisement. writt by the Author's owne hand before he lost his Sight: and intended to have printed it before his death.

Aubrey, f. 68v; Darbishire, p. 9.

(33) *Brief History of Muscovia and of other less known Countries, lying eastward of Russia as far as Cathay,* &c. Lond. 1682. oct.

Wood, I, 883; Darbishire, p. 47.

A brief History of *Muscovia,* and of other less known Countries, lying *Eastward* of *Prussia,* as far as *Cathay;* gathered from the writings of several Eye-witnesses. *Oct.*

Phillips, p. [liii]; not in Darbishire.

1682. MARCH 7. BROTHER CHRISTOPHER ORDERED TO PREPARE REPORT.

At an Assembly held 7 March 1682, Mr. Recorder, Mr. Milton, Mr. Ventris, & Mr. Golty [?] the Town Counsel & Lecturer was required to prepare a Letter to the Master & Fellows of Pembroke Hall, to be signed by the Bailiffs of Ipswich concerning the 4 Scholarships belonging to the Town.

British Museum Add. MS. 19,142, f. 78, said to be based on Batley's Ipswich Charters, p. 303. I have not looked up this reference. The year may be either 1682 or 1683, depending on whether the writer is using Old or New Style.

1683. FEBRUARY 19. BROTHER CHRISTOPHER'S DAUGHTER ANNE GETS LICENSE TO MARRY JOHN PENDLEBURY (?).

1682-3 . . . Feb. 19 John Pendleberry, of Enfield, Middx., Bach[r], 24, & Anne Milton, of S[t] Dunstan in the West, London, Sp[r], 22, her parents dead; at S[t] Sepulchre's, London.

Allegations for Marriage Licences issued from the Faculty Office of the Archbishop of Canterbury, London, *1543-1869* (Publications of the Harleian Society, Vol. XXIV, 1886), p. 165; Perceval E. Lucas in *Notes and Queries*, XI, vii (1913), 21-22. I have not seen the original documents. Anne's father Christopher was of course actually to live for another ten years. But since her fiancé was a Protestant minister, she may have wanted to conceal her father's Catholicism.

1683. JUNE 15. BROTHER CHRISTOPHER'S SON THOMAS ORDERED TO PREPARE REPORT AS DEPUTY CLERK OF THE CROWN.

[Marginal note:] M^r. Milton Dep^{ty} Clerke of y^e. Crowne

S^r/ The Lords Com^{rs}. of his Ma^{ts}. Treāry desire you forthwith to send to M^r. Langford at the Treary Chambers a List of the severall Lord Leiu^{ts}. of England and the countyes under their respective care, J am S^r &c H: G. Treary Chambers 15th. Iune 1683./

Public Record Office, Treasury 27, Vol. 7, p. 170; *Calendar of Treasury Books, 1681-1685*, part 2, p. 841.

1683. JULY 21. SOME OF HIS POLITICAL BOOKS BURNED AT OXFORD.

The Judgment and Decree of the University of Oxford Past in their Convocation July 21. 1683, Against certain Pernicious Books and Damnable Doctrines Destructive to the Sacred Persons of Princes, their State and Government, and of all Humane Society. Rendred into English, and Published by Command. . . . Printed at the Theater, 1683. . . .

[Among the heresies listed are two naming Milton:] 3. That if lawfull Governors become Tyrants, or govern otherwise then by the laws of God and man they ought to do, they forfeit the right they had unto their Government.

> *Lex Rex. Buchanan de Jure Regni. Vindiciæ contra tyrannos. Bellarmine de Conciliis, de Pontifice. Milton. Goodwin. Baxter H. C. . . .*

26. King Charles the first was lawfully put to death, and his

murtherers were the blessed instruments of Gods glory in their Generation.

Milton. Goodwin. Owen....

[Selections from the judgment on these books follow:]

We decree, judge and declare all and every of these Propositions to be false, seditious and impious; and most of them to be also Heretical and Blasphemous, infamous to Christian Religion, and destructive of all Government in Church and State.

We farther ... interdict all members of the University from the reading the said Books, under the penalties in the Statutes exprest.

We also order the before recited Books to be publicly burnt, by the hand of our Marshal in the court of our Scholes.

Likewise we order ... these our decrees ... publicly affixt in the Libraries, Refectories, or other fit places, where they may be seen and read of all.

Title page and selections from pp. 3, 7, 8 of the original pamphlet, a photostatic copy of which I have through the courtesy of the Keeper of Printed Books of the Bodleian; reprinted in *Somers Tracts*, VIII (1812), 421-424; Sensabaugh, *That Grand Whig Milton*, pp. 90, 111. Though no titles of Milton's works are named here, presumably the objects of the University's wrath were his political pieces, especially the *Eikonoklastes* and the first *Defensio*. In *A Bodleian Guide for Visitors* (Oxford, 1906, p. 110), however, Andrew Clark names the *Tenure of Kings* and the first two *Defenses*, though without naming the source of his information.

Saturday, 21 July, 1683 ... after which the Convocation was dissolved, and the vice-chancellor, bishop, Drs. and Mrs. in their formalities, went into the School quadrangle, where a bonfier being prepared in the middle thereof, were severall books, out of which those damnable tenets and propositions were extracted, committed to the flames by Gigur, the Universitie bedell of beggars. The scholars of all degrees and qualities in the meane time surrounding the fier, gave severall hums whilst they were burning. [Among the 23 books by Buchanan, Hobbes, Baxter, Owen, Knox, Bellarmine, and others, number 14 is:] John Milton's pieces in defence of the king's murder.

The Life and Times of Anthony Wood, ed. Andrew Clark, Oxford Historical Society, 1891-1900, III, 63-64. In the same work Wood notes under date of September 6, 1683, that James Parkinson, fellow of Lincoln College, was ejected because "he commended to some of his pupils Milton as an excellent book and an antidote against Sir Robert Filmer, whom he calls 'too high a Tory.'"

1683. JULY 24. PRINTER BRABAZON AYLMER REGISTERS *PARADISE LOST*.

24th July 1683

Master   Entred . . . booke or coppy entituled *Parri-*
Brabezon Aylmer   *dise lost, in* 12 *bookes,* by **John Milton,**
                        wch booke is by vertue of one assignmt
bearing date the 27th of October, Ano 1680, under the hand
of Master Sam[1] Simmons, assigned over to the said Brabezon
Aylmer .... vj[d]
Witnes. Martin Newton
Stationers' Registers, III, 176.

1683. AUGUST 17. AYLMER SELLS HALF RIGHT IN *PARADISE LOST* TO TONSON.

. . . and Aylmer afterwards sold it [the rights to *Paradise Lost*] to old Jacob Tonson at two different times, one half on the 17th of August 1683, and the other half on the 24th of March 1690, with a considerable advance of the price. . . .

Milton, *Paradise Lost*, ed. Thomas Newton, 1749, I, xxxviii; Masson, VI, 782. There seems to be no record of this transaction in the Stationers' Registers. Fletcher (*Facsimile*, III, 19) calls Newton's statement "the earliest authority extant today." Yet the extract from the Tonson letter given just below, though undated itself and giving no dates for the transaction, is undoubtedly earlier and at least states that the transaction was made.

. . . y[e] 1st edition [of *Paradise Lost*] . . . was assigned over with the bond when Symonds sold ye Coppy &c to Aylmere of whome I bought it. . . . If M[r]. Aylmer is yet Living he may give you some account of this matter & particularly of Symons y[e] printer &c.

[264]

From Jacob Tonson's manuscript letter to his nephew, written probably about 1732; reprinted in Helen Darbishire's *The Manuscript of Milton's Paradise Lost Book I*, p. xii.

1683. AUGUST 21. ROBERT SCOTT REGISTERS *HISTORY OF BRITAIN*.

21ᵗʰ Augᵗ Anno 1683

Master Robt Scott. Entred then for his Bookes or Coppyes by vertue of an assignmt under the hand and seale of Mʳˢ SARAH MARTIN, relict and executrix of the last will and testamᵗ of John Martin late Cittizen and Stationer of London, deceased, her late husband, bearing date the fourteenth day of June Anno Doṁ 1681, and by order of Court of the seaventh of Novemʳ, 1681, these severall bookes or coppyes or parts of bookes or coppyes hereafter mencōned wch did formerly belong to the said John Martin decd. Salvo jure cujuscunque, viz: . . .

> **Milton's** *History of Brittaine.* . . .
> **Salmasij** *responsio ad Miltonum.*

Stationers' Registers, III, 181-185; Fletcher Facsimile, III, 19. These two titles are part of a very long list, covering nine pages in the printed registers. No price for this entry is given.

1684. EDWARD PHILLIPS PUBLISHES TWO DICTIONARIES USING MILTON'S COLLECTIONS.

Mr. *Phillips* hath also written . . . *Enchiridion Linguæ Latinæ* . . . Lond. 1684. oct.

Speculum Linguæ Latinæ . . . *Lond.* 1684. oct. These two last were all or mostly taken from the *Latin Thesaurus,* writ by *Joh. Milton* Uncle to *Edw. Phillips.*

Wood, *Athenae Oxonienses,* 1721, II, 1118; Masson, VI, 813; CM, XVIII, 631. A fuller entry appears above under the date 1655. I have never seen copies of either of these dictionaries, which are not in Wing's *STC.*

1684. FEBRUARY 26. BROTHER CHRISTOPHER PRO-
VIDES GROUNDS FOR ROYAL WARRANT AGAINST IPSWICH.

Articles ag^t ye Town of Jpswich whereon to ground a Quo Warranto

1 The major pte of ye Portmen & four & twentie being of phana-
tique principles in matters relateing to ye Kings service, still
bandy ag̅^{t} & overvote ye Loyall ptie.

2 . . . few or none of ye s̅d Offenders [non-attenders of church,
etc.], have been punish't or proceeded ag^t according to law, but
secretly dismiss't wthout much punishm̅^{t}. . . .

3 Seūall Quakers now com̄itted to ye Town gaol, are pmitted to
goe at large all ye week. . . .

J humblie conceive these or some of these Articles are sufficient grounds for a Quo warranto. Et quæ non psunt singula,
cuncta juvant [and what they don't accomplish singly they do
together]

ffeb 26th 1683./   [Signed:] Chr̄. Milton.

Public Record Office, SP 29/436/144, p. 97; *CSP Dom, 1683-
1684*, pp. 291-292; Arthur D. Matthews, "Christopher Milton v.
Ipswich," *Notes and Queries*, CXCVI (1951), 205. The document contains nine articles. The remaining six assert that an advocate of the murder of the Duke of York escaped with only a slight fine, that an innocent man accused foolishly of theft was kept in prison for over a year
without bail or trial, that the bailiffs have illegally coined farthings, that
the town has regularly held three fairs a year whereas only one is allowed in the charter, that unjust fines have been imposed, and that
justice has been delayed and denied. Whether true or false, these accusations against officials of his own town give a new insight into Christopher's character. Mr. Matthews, who summarizes the whole affair
capably, misdates the action 1685 rather than 1684. He calls Milton
a hireling tool of James II in preparing this document. The editor of
CSP (p. xiii) points out that Ipswich was only one of numerous towns
whose municipal franchises were being systematically attacked by similar
means, which assured the crown of a veto on the choice of local officers
and hence of control of local politics. Part of Christopher's reward for
this service may have been his appointment as Deputy Recorder of Ipswich on July 8, 1685 (*q.v.*). A "quo warranto" was a King's Bench
writ by which people were called to show by what right they held offices
or franchises. The manuscript is all in the same hand, and since the

signature is like many others of Christopher Milton's, it is presumably all his writing.

1684. NOVEMBER 14. BROTHER CHRISTOPHER WRITES TESTIMONIAL FOR GEORGE RAYMOND.

The *United States Cumulative Book Auction Records 1940-45* (New York, 1946, p. 1293) records the sale on December 4-5, 1944, at the Parke-Bernet Galleries, of a "D. s. testimonial for Geo. Raymond, 4to. N. p. Nov. 14, 1684," for $7.00. I have not discovered its purchaser or present location. Raymond is very likely related to the distinguished legal family of Sir Thomas Raymond (1627-1683), lawyer and judge.

1685. BROTHER CHRISTOPHER'S WIFE THOMASINE DIES.

Thomasine da. of Willm. Webber of London; dyed before her husband was made a Baron, bur^d. in S^t. Nich^s. Parish Ipswich.

British Museum Add. MS. 19,142, f. 78 (Joseph Hunter's notes); Hamilton, p. 64; Masson, vi, 762. Hunter gives several references for the little genealogy from which this item is taken, so that it is uncertain which was the chief source. But presumably it is Harl. MS. 5802. I have not found the record of the burial of Mrs. Milton. The present date is only a guess, but it must be before the spring of 1686, when Christopher was created baron.

1685. JULY 8. BROTHER CHRISTOPHER NAMED DEPUTY RECORDER OF IPSWICH.

Et ulterius volumus ac p p'sentes p nobis hered' & Successor' nris ordinamus & declaramus quod post mortem vel' amoco'em Christopheri Milton ab Officio Deputat' Recordator' Vill eide' Burgi p'ditt' luctum sit & erit tam p'fat' Robto B'roko quam eīdz. . . . et Christopherus Milton in hijs p'sentibz constitut' & nominat' fore Deputat' Recordator' Ville eide Burg' p'ditt'. . . .

Public Record Office, C66/3241, number 6, 36 Car. ii; Hamilton, p. 64 (passing mention); Todd, i (1826), 259-260. July 8, 1685, was the date of the charter of Ipswich from Charles II, from which this extract is taken. Masson (vi, 727) uses the title for Christopher Milton in connection with the discussion of Milton's will in 1674, but he may not necessarily have meant that he thought Christopher held the appointment at that time. Arthur D. Matthews ("Christopher Milton

v. Ipswich," *Notes and Queries*, CXCVI, 1951, 205) gives some interesting notes about Christopher, but chides Todd for calling him Deputy Recorder rather than more accurately Recorder; but the present quotation makes it quite clear that at this time his appointment was as deputy recorder. I shall not translate the above selection because the following excerpt does so and adds a few lines which I should have taken from the original charter but neglected to do. The Venns (*Alumni Cantabrigienses*, III, 193) date this appointment 1674. Though Charles II had died on February 6, 1685, this charter is described as issuing from him.

[Sir Robert Brooke is named Recorder.] And also we . . . do . . . nominate . . . Our beloved Subject *Christopher Milton*, Esq. to be the first and new *Deputy-Recorder* of the Town or Borough aforesaid. . . . And further, We will, and by these Presents for Us, *etc*. do declare and ordain, that after the Death or Removal of *Christopher Milton* from the Office of Deputy-Recorder of the Town or Borough aforesaid, it may and shall be lawful as well for the aforesaid *Robert Brooke* . . . to have, nominate, and make any other sufficient and discreet Man . . . to be his Deputy. . . . And further, *etc*. We do grant . . . the aforesaid *Robert Brooke* . . . and *Christopher Milton* . . . may and shall be our Justices . . . to preserve and keep Our Peace. . . . And by these Presents We make, ordain, create, and constitute them . . . Our Justices. . . . And further, for Us, *etc*. We ordain, and command that the Bailives aforesaid . . . shall take their corporal Oaths before the said *Robert Brooke* or *Christopher Milton*, or one of them. . . .

Richard Canning, *The Principal Charters . . . of Ipswich in Suffolk*, London, 1754, pp. 48-68 (the charter of 36 Car. II, July 8, 1685); my selections are from pp. 52, 59, 60, 63. John Wodderspoon, in his *Memorials of . . . Ipswich*, 1850, pp. 91-92, summarizes this charter inaccurately, stating the Milton appointment as: "Christopher Milton, esq. to be appointed Recorder." He describes the process by telling how Charles II had granted a charter to the town of Ipswich on February 11, 1665, but that near the end of his reign "the corporation were intimidated to surrender their charters, franchises, and privileges to the king, by formal deed under their common seal. They were then newly incorporated by the charter of Charles II, 1685." Later, he says, this charter in turn was revoked (1688), and "the rights and liberties of the Corporation were restored" (p. 93). The chief defect of the 1685 charter was that it gave the king full power to remove summarily almost any officer of the town. John Oldmixon, in his *History of England* (1730, p. 708) goes even further. He states that Charles II, resolved to have judges who would "sell him their Consciences," turned out of office "the Tools which he had hitherto work'd with . . . and put other Tools still more wicked and more worthless in their Places; which was done against *Easter-Term, April* 21. [1686]." Among the new appointees whom he names is "*Christopher Milton* Esq;." Of him Oldmixon continues: "The latter, *Christopher Milton*, was an unworthy Brother of the great Poet *John Milton*. He starv'd by his Practice, and to mend his Market, turn'd Papist. He was one of the dullest Fellows that ever appear'd with a Bar-Gown upon his Back in *Westminster-Hall*." Much of this attack must of course be taken with a grain of salt as part of a political campaign against the Stuarts; see the article on Oldmixon in the *DNB*.

1686. APRIL (?). BROTHER CHRISTOPHER SUPPORTS KING'S DISPENSING POWER.

Whith^r his M$\bar{a}^{tie}$ may dispense wth y^e penalties in y^e late Acts of y^e 25th & 30th yeares of our late Soveraign King Charles y^e 2^d for p^{r}venting dangers from popish Recusants./

J humbly conceive he may

ffor that all those penalties are grounded only vpon Malum 1 politicū, & not vpon any thing ratione intrinsica Malum.

for that ye transgression of these lawes, can not be to ye damage 2 of any ptcular Subject, if to any at all, so as to entitle any of them, to any ptcular remedie, and if any wrong be done, by transgressing ye s̄d lawes, it must be to ye king, who may dispense wth his own rights

Because ye forfeiture of 500^l. in these acts, are recoūable by ac- 3 c̄on popular, eūie man is entitled to bring ye acc̄on, wch ye king vndoubtedly may p^{r}vent by his dispensation, ceding themselves

Seūall dispensations are comp^{r}hended in ye s̄d acts, wch shewes 4 that they contain matters dispensable

Jt is ye just p^{r}rogative of ye King to dispense wth penall lawes 5 where it is no p^{r}judice to private interests. This is granted by ye comōns in parlam^t H 5 cited by Rolls, in ye case of pmitting Aliens to continue in England, so y^t to deny this were to restrain ye kings just power

6 The transgression of these acts is so far from entrenching vpon bonū publicum, that an inconvenience rather accrues to a considerable number of his Mā^ties loyall Subjects, if the ẽd acts be strictly observ'd, by depriveing y^e ẽd subjects, of their best Birthright, wch is a capacitie to serve their Soveraign wth those endowm^ts & talents, wch god hath bestow'd vpon them, and consequently of that p^rferm̄^t from their Prince, wch may be ye reward of their service

7 Jt appears from ye Records in 4 of Ed 1 reported by Rolls, that it was thus ruled Ad Regiæ celsitudinis potestatem ptinet, leges justas et vtiles ratas habere, illas autem quæ Regni robur, diminuere potius, quam augere videntur, aboleri convenit, aut in melius com̄utare

8 The stat of Don̄ con̄d made by a wise king, & for a pious end vt voluntas donatoris observetur, is yet in a manner eūie day dispens't w^th, by ye provident invention of ye Judges, only to avoyd inconveniences not foreseen by ye makers of that law./

These reasons J humbly offer as consonant to ye distinction & resolutions of Sorrells & reported by my Lord Vaughan
Lastly ye king as head of ye Church may dispense wth ye subject matters of those Acts

[Signed:] Chr̄. Milton

From a photostatic copy of the original document, now in the Library of the University of Illinois, furnished to me by the kindness of the Librarian. I first learned of its existence through an advertisement in Maggs Brothers' *Mercurius Britannicus*, Number 77, 1943, item 420; and Messrs. Maggs kindly informed me who had bought it. The word "themselves" in section three, which makes no particular sense where it is, may belong after "acts" in section 4; the manuscript is not clear. But the end of number 3 is obscure in either case. The last sentence looks like an afterthought, crowded into a space too small for it. Though undated, this piece of writing must be part of the struggle about the dispensing power which was seething at about this time, and which Macaulay describes vividly in his *History of England*, chapter VI. Macaulay tells how James II dismissed a number of high judges—Chief Justice Jones, Chief Baron Montague, Neville, Charlton, and Heneage Finch, Solicitor General; and would have dismissed Sawyer, the Attorney General, if he could have found a worthy successor, since it was necessary, in the selfish interests of the Crown, "that one at least of the Crown lawyers should be a man of learning, ability, and experience; and no such man was willing to defend the dispensing power" (*History of England*, World's Classics edition, ed. T. F. Henderson, II, 71). Pointing out that Christopher Milton "had scruples about communicating with the Church of England, and had therefore a strong interest in supporting the dispensing power," he implies that Christopher's action was partly spineless and partly self-seeking. In a time of so intense a struggle it seems likely that the characteristic which counted most in the mind of the king, and which probably won for Christopher the promotions which he was about to receive, was rather his willingness to support the King in his radical moves than any legal skill. Further interesting information about the dispensing power and especially about the test case of Arthur Godden, coachman to Sir Edward Hales, his employer, whom Godden brought into court because James II had given him dispensation from the statute of 25 Charles II requiring all subjects to receive the sacrament every three months, may be found in [Cobbett's] *A Complete Collection of State Trials*, compiled by T. B. Howell, XI (1811), 1166-1315, and in the notes on Hales and on Sir John Street in the *DNB*.

[1. . . . political evil . . . evil on intrinsic grounds. . . .

7. It pertains to the power of the royal majesty to keep just laws and useful rates, but it is fitting to abolish or change for the better those which are seen to weaken rather than to build up the strength of the kingdom.

8. . . . as the will of the donor is observed. . . .]

1686. APRIL 21. BROTHER CHRISTOPHER MADE SERJEANT-AT-LAW.

Westminster, April 23. Sir *John Holt* Recorder of *London*, Sir *Ambrose Philips, Christopher Milton* Esq; *John Powell* Esq; *John Tate* Esq; *William Rawlinson* Esq; *William Killingworth* Esq; *Hugh Hodges* Esq; *Thomas Geeres* Esq; and *George Hutchins* Esq; being called by the Kings Writ to take upon them the State and Degree of Serjeants at Law, they accordingly appeared the first day of the Term at the *Chancery* Bar, where having taken the Oaths according to Custom, the Lord Chancellor made a short Speech to them; After which the new Serjeants delivered a Ring to his Lordship, praying him to present it to the King, with their Duty and most humble

Thanks for the Honor his Majesty had been pleased to confer upon them. And this day the new Serjeants having met and performed in the *Inner Temple* Hall (the Lord Chief Justice of *England* being of that Society) the Ceremony of Counting, and had their Quoifs put on by the Judges, walked from thence, being cloathed in Party-coloured Robes, Violet and Purple, accompanied by a great many Gentlemen of the Long Robe out of the several societies in the usual manner to *Westminster*; Being come into the Hall, they were brought, each between two Senior Serjeants, to the Bar of the *Common-Pleas*, where they again Counted in their order before all the Judges; and then gave Rings with this Motto, *Deus, Rex, Lex.* After which the Court rose; and the new Serjeants entertained the Lord Chancellor, with many of the Nobility, the Judges, and other Persons of Quality, at a Splendid Dinner in *Serjeants Inn* in *Fleetstreet*.

London Gazette, April 22-26, 1686; Add. MS. 19,142, f. 78; Masson, VI, 762. The date is arrived at in the following way. In 1686, Easter Day fell on April 4; therefore the Easter Term began on April 21; and since the new serjeants were appointed, according to the above account, "the first day of the Term," April 21 must have been the day. For helpful tables in finding these days see John J. Bond, *Handy-Book of Rules and Tables*, London, 1869, especially pp. 178, 286. White Kennett (*A Complete History of England*, III, 1706, 451-452) gives the date as April 23, as it would be very easy to do. The *Shorter Oxford English Dictionary* defines the position of serjeant as a "member of a superior order of barristers (abolished in 1880), from which, until 1873, the Common Law judges were always chosen." The appointment of Christopher was presumably made in preparation for that of judge a few days later.

1686. APRIL 24. BROTHER CHRISTOPHER APPOINTED BARON OF THE EXCHEQUER.

Jacobus Secundus dei grā Anglie . . . Sciatis quod nos . . . Constituimus dīlcum et fidelem nrum Edrūm Atkins mīl nū Baron' Sccij nrī Capītlm Baronem de Sccio nrō . . . Teste me ipō apūd Westm̄ vicesimo primo die Aprilis Anno Regni nrī sc̄do. p̣ ipm̄ Regem. . . .

S^r. Thomas Ienner the like patent to be Baron of the Excheq^r. dated 10th. ffēbrij 1685

Rich^d. heath Serj^t. at Law the like patent dated the 24th. Aprill 1686

Christopher Milton Serj^t. at Law the like dated [blank]

Public Record Office, T 52/10, p. 424. The warrant for Atkins is given in full, though I have quoted only enough to show the basic meaning, which is his promotion from Baron to Chief Baron. The present selections about Jenner, Heath, and Milton, which are given just as they stand, assume similar warrants for them. This manuscript is merely a record of the warrants issued, not the original warrants. Heath may be related to Milton's former pupil; see above, III, 282-286.

[James II, by the grace of God of England . . . know ye that we . . . have appointed our beloved and faithful Edward Atkins, knight, now Baron of our Exchequer, to be Chief Baron of our Exchequer. . . . Witness myself at Westminster, April 21, in the second year of our reign. By the king himself.]

Royal Letters Patent, April 24, 1686, constituting Richard Heath and Christopher Milton, Sergeants at Law, barons of exchequer.

Calendar of Treasury Books, 1685-1689, part 2, p. 711; Masson, VI, 762. Masson says he was sworn as baron on April 24 and knighted on the following day.

Whitehall, April 26. His Majesty has been pleased to constitute Sir *Christopher Milton* one of the Barons of the Exchequer; And Sir *John Powell* one of the Justices of the Common-Pleas; And to make Sir *Thomas Powis* His Sollicitor General, in the place of *Heneage Finch* Esq; . . .

London Gazette, April 26-29, 1686. The same information is available in several other places, including Harl. MS. 5802, f. 16v (giving date as April 25); John Nichols, *The History and Antiquities of Leicestershire*, III (1800), 413; Thomas B. Macaulay, *History of England*, London, 1849, II, 83; Add. MS. 19,142, f. 78 (quoting most of the foregoing). The Harleian manuscript gives a brief genealogy of Christopher Milton.

1686 . . . June 2nd . . . New Judges also here, amongst wch was Milton, a Papist (brother to that Milton who wrote for y^e

Regicides), who presum'd to take his place without passing ye Test.

John Evelyn, *Diary*, ed. Bray, III (1879), 162; ed. E. S. De Beer, Oxford, 1955, IV, 514.

At the time mentioned . . . four new Iudges were appointed, who had taken the royal test by declaring their belief in the unlimited, illimitable, & eternal nature of the dispensing power. One of these was the brother of the Author of 'Paradise Lost,' & of the 'Defence of the People of England for putting Chas. 1. to death.' Sir Christopher Milton, recommended by Herbert, was in all respects a striking contrast to Iohn, as he was not only a favourer of Popery, & a friend to arbitrary power, but the dullest of mankind.

John Lord Campbell, *The Lives of the Chief Justices of England*, II (1849), 86-87, as quoted in Add. MS. 19,142, f. 79v.

[As a lawyer Christopher] came to no Advancement in the World in a long time, except some small Employ in the town of *Ipswich*, where (and near it) he lived all the latter time of his Life. For he was a person of a modest quiet temper, preferring Justice and Vertue before all Worldly Pleasure or Grandeur: but in the beginning of the Reign of K. *James* the II. for his known Integrity and Ability in the Law, he was by some Persons of Quality recommended to the King, and at a Call of Serjeants received the Coif, and the same day was Sworn one of the Barons of the Exchequer, and soon after made one of the Judges of the Common Pleas. . . .

Phillips, pp. vi-vii; Darbishire, pp. 52-53.

1686. MAY 15. WARRANT FOR SALARY TO BROTHER CHRISTOPHER.

[In margin:] S^r. Thomas Jenner Dorm^t Warr^t.

After &^a. By vertue of his Ma^ts. Letters Patents authorizing ye paym^t. of the yearly Sallarys to the Judges, These are to pray and req^r. you to make & pass debentures for paym^t. of such Sumes of money as are and shall from time to time be due to

S^r. Thomas Jenner kn^t. one of the Barons of his Ma^{ts}. Court of Excheq^r. upon his Sallary of 1000^{li} p anñ according to the direccōn of the said Letters Patents, and lett the same be satisfied out of any his Ma^{ts}. Treasure now or hereafter being and remaining in the Rec^t of the Excheq^r. not appropriate to particular uses by act of Parliam^t. ffor wch. this shalbe your Warr^t. Whitehall Treāry Chambers the 15th. day of May *1686*. Rochester, To S^r. Robt. Howard &^{a}.

[In margin:] Christopher Milton Serj^t. at Law & one of the Barons of ye Excheq^r. Richard Heath serj^t. at Law & one other of the Barons of ye Excheq^r.

[After a bracket from the preceding:] The like Warr^{ts}. of the same date mutatis mutandis

Public Record Office, Treasury 53, Vol. 6, p. 315; *Calendar of Treasury Books, 1685-1689*, part 2, p. 741.

1686. JUNE 21-24. BROTHER CHRISTOPHER ASSIGNED TO MIDLAND CIRCUIT.

Midland Circuit.

Lord Chief Baron *Atkins*.

Mr. Baron *Milton*.

Northampton, Wednesday, *July* 14. at *Northampton*.

Warwick, Monday, *July* 19, at *Warwick*.

City of *Coventry*, Wednesday, *July* 21, at the City of *Coventry*.

Leicester, Thursday, *July* 22. at the Castle of *Leicester*.

Borough of *Leicester*, the same day at the Borough of *Leicester*.

Derby, Monday, *July* 26. at *Derby*.

Nottingham, Thursday, *July* 29, at *Nottingham*.

Town of *Nottingham*, The same day at the Town of *Nottingham*.

Lincolne, Monday, *August* 2. at the Castle of *Lincolne*.

City of *Lincolne*, The same day at the City of *Lincolne*.

Rutland, Friday, *August* 6. at *Oakham*.

London Gazette, June 21-24, 1686. This section is headed: "The Circuits appointed for this Summer-Assizes, are as followeth. . . ." In quoting other similar entries below, I will omit a good deal and summarize, since the form used here is repetitious. But the first one given should show how the entry appears in the original.

1686. OCTOBER 2. BROTHER CHRISTOPHER'S SON RICHARD LEASES NORWOODS MANOR, SPROUGHTON, SUFFOLK.

. . . it was alleged that a certain indenture had been made on October 2, 1686, between the said William Burrough of Ipswich aforesaid, grocer, and Charles Burrough on the one part and Richard Milton of Ipswich aforesaid, gentleman, on the other part. . . .

From the translation of the grant of administration of Richard Milton's estate given below under date of August 12, 1713.

1687. ANONYMOUS ("EARLIEST") LIFE OF MILTON WRITTEN.

The Life of Mr John Milton

Bodleian MS. Wood. D. 4, ff. 140-144; first printed by Edward S. Parsons in the *English Historical Review*, XVII (1902), 95-110; reprinted in Darbishire, pp. 17-34.

The authorship of this biography is a much-debated but still unresolved question. Malone, who is the first recorded writer to have noticed it, and who had plans for publishing it which he never carried out, did not try to assign an author (Bodleian MS. Eng. Misc. d. 26, as quoted in Darbishire, p. 337). Mr. Parsons, in his introduction, proposed numerous candidates, but eliminated most of them. Charles G. Osgood (*Journal of English and Germanic Philology*, VI, 1906-1907, 133-139) suggested the possibility that Andrew Allam wrote it, chiefly on the basis of Allam's discussion with Aubrey. Aubrey himself hints at a different author in a letter of May 18, 1675, to Anthony Wood (Bodl. MS. Wood. F. 39, ff. 296-297; Masson, I, 1881, vii): "Mr. Marvell has promised me to write minutes for you of Mr. Jo. Milton, who lies buried in St. Giles Cripplegate Church." Pierre Legouis (*André Marvell*, Paris and Oxford, 1928, p. 232, with references to Aitken's edition of Marvell, 1892, I, lxvii, and to Augustine Birrell's *Andrew Marvell*, New York and London, 1905, p. 199) also mentioned this possibility. Miss Darbishire, in the introduction to her edition of the lives (pp. xiv-xxvii) asserted that John Phillips was the author. Parsons soon argued against this theory (*PMLA*, L, 1935, 1057-1064). Allen R. Benham (*ELH*, VI, 1939, 245-255) wrote about the manuscript, but chiefly to argue

[276]

against its being earlier than Wood's life. William R. Parker (*Milton's Contemporary Reputation*, p. 6n) again proposed serious consideration of Allam as author. Harris Fletcher (editor of Milton's *Complete Poetical Works*, Houghton Mifflin, 1941, p. 3) strongly supported this view. Parsons (*ELH*, IX, 1942, 106-115) returned to the question of date, maintaining that the manuscript was earlier than Wood's, a theory which Benham (*ibid.*, pp. 116-117) rejected. Here the argument rests at present, except for a casual question tossed out by James Holly Hanford at an MLA meeting in 1954, whether the author was perhaps Daniel Skinner.

Though I cannot settle the debate, I am inclined to discard Allam as a candidate, chiefly because I fear some previous adherents of his have misunderstood Aubrey's statement (Aubrey, f. 66v; Darbishire, p. 15): "q̄ Mr Allam of Edm-hall Oxon. of Mr J. Milton's life writt by himselfe. v. pagg." The "himselfe" could of course be either Allam or Milton, but in view of the fact that Milton actually wrote a short autobiography in his *Defensio Secunda*, probably Aubrey merely intended to ask Allam some question about it. He may even not have known where to find it, and may have wanted to ask Allam what book it might be in. Andrew Clark (ed. Aubrey's *Brief Lives*, II, 72 n.) identifies "himselfe" as Allam.

The case against Allam is perhaps slightly strengthened by a document (Bodleian MS. Ballard 14, f. 134; old numbering 83) which I believe has not been printed before. In a letter of December 20, 1681, one Jo. Gregorius writes to Anthony Wood: ". . . pray remember me very kindly to Mr Allam: J am exceedingly taken with his ingenuity, and obligeingnesse. pray aske him where Mr J. Milton speakes of his owne life & ye pagg. . . ." Here the phraseology, somewhat similar to Aubrey's, unmistakably refers to Milton's own life of himself, presumably in his *Defensio Secunda*. It seems also to prove that a literate man of this time like Aubrey could know that Milton had written something autobiographical but might not know just where to find it. This John Gregory is probably the man of that name mentioned by Wood (*Fasti Oxonienses*, 1721, II, 147), whose father of the same name wrote *A Discourse of the Morality of the Sabbath*, which the son published posthumously in 1681 with a dedication to John, Lord Scudamore.

The evidence which Miss Darbishire adduces in support of John Phillips seems inadequate. It is based chiefly on similarity of handwriting, which is always a weak argument because there are so many thousand other hands no longer surviving which might claim attention. The other basis of attribution is the supposedly peculiar spelling of *their-thir*, which similarly depends on the need of consulting thousands of handwritings no longer extant and on assumptions as to the strictness of seventeenth-century spelling which are hard to accept. And the pronounced antipathy between the characters and writings of Phillips and Milton render it unlikely that Phillips would have written a biography so sympathetic as this one. Maurice Kelley (*Modern Philology*, LIV, 1956, 20-25) has made strong cases against both Phillips and Allam: against Phillips because the handwriting is not like his, and against Allam because he was born in 1655, too late to have been the amanuensis of sonnets 21 and 22, on which Miss Darbishire bases so heavy a burden of her case about the authorship, and which must have been written about 1655 and not about 1672-1673. He proposes as a possibility Cyriack Skinner, whom Professor Hanford also tells me that John Smart once suggested to him in a letter.

If one must choose, the evidence for Marvell seems somewhat stronger than at least that for Allam or Phillips. Milton and Marvell were close friends, fellow-poets, and fellow-members of the Administration. The handwriting of the manuscript is reasonably close to Marvell's, at least as shown by the facsimile in Margoliouth's edition. And of course Marvell's promise would fit perfectly with this fulfillment. Though I cannot regard this theory as very convincingly proved, it at least seems to me to explain the facts better than any other yet proposed.

See also the entry about Marvell in connection with a proposed life of Milton under date of May 18, 1675, above.

Since this note was printed, Professor William R. Parker has made out a very strong case (London *Times Literary Supplement*, September 13, 1957, p. 547) for the authorship of Cyriack Skinner. He believes that a comparison of the handwritings of sonnets 21 and 22 in the Cambridge Manuscript, of Skinner's letter of March 23, 1668/9, in the archives of Kingston upon Hull, and of the present biography "leaves not the slightest doubt that all three were written by the same hand." Though Mr. R. W. Hunt, Keeper of Western Manuscripts in the Bodleian, questions Parker's ascription (ibid., October 11, 1957, p. 609), the likelihood of Skinner's writing such a piece combines with the evidence of the handwriting to give him the leading place as candidate for authorship.

1687. PUBLICATION OF *THE STATE OF CHURCH AFFAIRS* ATTRIBUTED TO BROTHER CHRISTOPHER.

The State Of Church Affairs In this Island of Great Britain Under the Government of the Romans, And British Kings. London, Printed by Nat. Thompson for the Author, and are to be Sold by the Booksellers of London, Anno MDCLXXXVII.

A book with this title page is attributed to Christopher Milton by Wing (*STC*, M2085) and various others. It is a quarto book (or folio in 4's) of 178 pages. Professor Hanford tells me that he has found at least two copies with the attribution to Milton written in very old hands. It contains no preface or introduction with any references to the author by which he can be identified. From the many enthusiastic references to various "Holy Popes" it is obvious that the writer was a Roman Catholic. The many detailed accounts of miracles throughout, as well as this pro-Catholic tone, eliminates any idea that it could perhaps have been a book put together from notes of John Milton that Christopher might have found and thought worth publishing. I know of no supporting evidence in any records about Christopher Milton to guarantee his authorship. Robert Watt, *Bibliotheca Britannica*, II, 672p) attributes the book to John Milton.

1687. JANUARY 31-FEBRUARY 3. BROTHER CHRISTOPHER ASSIGNED TO NORFOLK CIRCUIT.

Norfolk Circuit.

Lord Chief Justice *Bedingfield*.

Mr. Baron *Milton*.

London Gazette, January 31-February 3, 1686/7. The assignments were for Aylesbury, Bucks, on March 1; Bedford on March 3; Huntingdon on March 5; Cambridge on March 7; Norfolk on March 10; Norwich on March 10; and Ipswich on March 16.

1687. FEBRUARY 10-14. BROTHER CHRISTOPHER'S SCHEDULE ALTERED.

In the *London Gazette* of this date the timetable given above is partially altered. Christopher is now to be at Aylesbury on February 28, at Bedford on March 2, at Huntingdon on March 4, and at Cambridge on March 5. The other assignments are unchanged except that the meeting-place for Suffolk is changed from Ipswich to Bury St. Edmunds.

1687. FEBRUARY 15. TREASURY ORDER TO BROTHER CHRISTOPHER AND OTHER JUDGES.

Whereas Wee are credibly Jnform'd that divers Mischiefes and abuses are practised & Comitted by the Clerkes of Assize in the severall Counties . . . to the great losse of his Ma^{ts} Revenue . . . therefore we doe most Earnestly recõmend to yor Lordp̄s that you doe in yor Circuit in every place where you shall sitt, require a true Copie or Duplicate frõ the respective Clerkes of ye Assizes of all ffines, Jssues, fforfeitures, Amerciam^{ts}. and other Duties. . . . We remaine, Our very good Lords yor Lordp̄s humble Serv^{ts}. Godolphin, Dover, J Ernle: S ffox:

[In margin:] Whitehall Treāry Cham^{rs}. 15th: ffeb^{r}y 1686./.

[Among those addressed are:] Mr Baron Milton Norfolk Circuit. . . . M^r. Justice Powell./. North^n. Circuit.

Public Record Office, Treasury 27, Vol. II, p. 33; *Calendar of Treasury Books, 1685-1689*, part 3, p. 1199.

1687. APRIL 14. BROTHER CHRISTOPHER APPOINTED JUSTICE OF COMMON PLEAS.

Royal Letters Patent constituting Sir Christopher Milton, Baron of the Exchequer, to be one of the Justices of Common Pleas during pleasure.

Calendar of Treasury Books, 1685-1689, part 3, p. 1304; Masson, VI, 762. Masson, on what grounds I do not know, gives the date as April 18 and the rank as Chief Justice. Others give other dates.

1687. MAY 10. WARRANT FOR BROTHER CHRISTOPHER'S SALARY.

. . . These are to pray and req^r. you to make and pass Debentures for paym^t. of such Sum̄es of money as are and shall from time to time be due to S^r. Robt. Wright Kn^t. Lord Cheife Iustice of his Ma^{ts}. Court of Kings Bench or his assignes upon his Sallary of 1000^{li} p ann̄. . . . Whitehall Treāry Chambers the 9th: day of May 1687 Belasye, Godolphin, JE, S Fox To Sr Robt. Howard. . . .

S^r. Edwd. Herbert Kn^t Lord Cheife Iustice of ye Common Pleas, the like warrant, mutatis mutandis, dated the 10th. of May 1687.

Sr Christopher Milton one of ye Iustices of y^e. Common Pleas, like warr^t. of ye same date wth Lord Cheife Iustice Herberts.

Public Record Office, Treasury 53, Vol. 8, p. 141; *Calendar of Treasury Books, 1685-1689*, part 3, p. 1353.

1687. MAY 11. BROTHER CHRISTOPHER RECOMMENDS DISPENSATION FOR IPSWICH TEACHER.

My Lord

Mr Samuel Reynolds Vsher of ye free School at Jpswich & Batchello^r of art of two yeares standing a very sober man & a good scholler, is in prospect of a good p^{r}ferment but is incapable of it for want of Orders, wch my Lord Bishop of Norwich will not confer vpon him wthout your Graces dispensation, in regard he lacks a year of three & twentie years of age. My Suit to your Grace is for your Dispensation in this behalfe wch if your Grace shall be pleas'd to grant you will very much oblige

My Lord

May ye 11th Your Graces most humble Servt

1687   Chr̄ Milton

Bodleian, Tanner MS. 41, f. 118; *Suffolk Records*, III, 332. The letter, though it bears no name of addressee, is said to have been written to Archbishop Sancroft. In the book the letter is mistakenly dated 1678. Venn says that Reynolds was admitted to Pembroke College, Cambridge, on March 29, 1682, from Ipswich School at the age of 16, and that he proceeded B.A. in 1685-6.

1687. JUNE 6-9. BROTHER CHRISTOPHER ASSIGNED TO NORFOLK CIRCUIT.

Norfolk Circuit.

Lord Chief Baron *Atkyns*.

Mr. Justice *Milton*.

London Gazette, June 6-9, 1687. The specific places and dates are: Chipping Wycombe, Bucks, July 4; Ampthill, Bedfordshire, July 7; Huntingdon, July 9; Cambridge, July 11; Ipswich (changed in issue of June 16-20 to Bury St. Edmunds), July 14; Norfolk, July 19; Norwich, the same day.

1687. NOVEMBER 12. BROTHER CHRISTOPHER TRANSFERS PROPERTY IN RUSHMERE.

Hec est finalis concordia fat.' in cur Dn̄i Regis apud Westm̄ in Crastino st̄i Martin̄i Anno regnor Jacob̄i . . . t'cio Coram Edwardo Herbert Thoma Street Edro' Lutwich & Cristofero

Miltoñ Justic̄ & Alijs . . . Jnt Jōhem Wallace in medicinis
D'torem querz et Cristoferum Miltoñ Militem Vnu' Justic̄ Dnī
Regis de Banco & Johem Alleñ & Elizabeth Vxem̄ eius deforc'
de tribz mesuagijs . . . cum ptiñ in Rushmerz Clopton' & De-
bach Vnde Plitm' Conuenco' is sum' fuit int' eos in eadem Curz'
Scīlt qd' p̄dcī Cristoferus & Jōhes Alleñ & Elizabēth recogñ
p̄dca teñ cum ptiñ esse ius ipiūs Johīs Wallace Vt iłł que idem
Johēs hēt de dono p̄d'corz Cristoferī & Johīs Alleñ & Eliza-
bēth Et iłł remiserz & quiet' clam̄ de ipīs Cristofero & Johē
Allēn & Elizabēth . . . Et p̨ hac recogñ remissione quiet' clam̄
Warant' fine & Concordia idem Johēs Wallace dedit p̄dcis
Cristofero & Johī Alleñ & Elizabēth ducentas librz sterlingor:.

From the original document in the Ipswich and East Suffolk Record
Office, Ref. No. xi/5/4.2; mentioned in the *Bulletin of the Institute
of Historical Research*, xx (1947), 226-227. I am very grateful to
the authorities of the Office for providing me a photographic copy of
the document. I have eliminated as much of the wordiness as possible.
The purport of this concord of fine is that Milton and John and Elizabeth Allen jointly transfer property in and near Rushmere to Dr. John
Wallace for two hundred pounds. It would seem as if the occurrence
of Milton's name among the judges before whom his own transfer of
property was being consummated must be a mistake; perhaps the scribe
who wrote the manuscript looked at the wrong line in this place and
exchanged names unintentionally.

[This is a final concord made in the court of our lord the
King at Westminster on the morrow of St. Martin (November
12) in the third year of the reign of James the Second . . . before Edward Herbert, Thomas Street, Edward Lutwich, and
Christopher Milton, Justices, and other faithful subjects . . .
between John Wallace, Doctor of Medicine, plaintiff, and Christopher Milton, Knight, one of the justices of the Bench of our
lord the King, and John Allen and Elizabeth his wife, defendants, concerning three messuages . . . and appurtenances in
Rushmere, Clopton, and Debach, from which a plea of convenience was entered between them in the same court. That is
to say that the aforesaid Christopher and John Allen and Elizabeth recognize the aforesaid tenements with their appurtenances

to be the property of the same John Wallace as that which the same John holds from the gift of the aforesaid Christopher and John Allen and Elizabeth . . . And in return for this recognizance, remission, quitclaim, guarantee, fine, and concord the same John Wallace has given to the aforesaid Christopher and John Allen and Elizabeth two hundred pounds sterling.]

1687. NOVEMBER 19. BROTHER CHRISTOPHER'S ROOM IN INNER TEMPLE IN QUESTION.

Inner Temple Bench Table Nouember 19ᵗʰ: 1687. . . .

That Mʳ: Purley attend Mʳ: Iustice Milton to know his pleasure when he intends to remove out of the Bench Chamber wherein he now is and that Clerke the Butler doe attend the said Mʳ: Purley.

From the records of the Inner Temple; Inderwick, III, 249. This is the last entry about Christopher Milton in these records.

1687. DECEMBER 29. BROTHER CHRISTOPHER BUYS OTHER PROPERTY IN RUSHMERE.

This Jndenture quadriptite made yᵉ Nyne & twentieth day of December . . . 1687 Between Sʳ Cristofer Milton of Rushmer Knight one of his Maᵗⁱᵉˢ Justices of his Court of Comon pleas at Westm' of the first pt John Allen of yᵉ same Towne Bricklayer & Elizabeth his Wife of yᵉ second pt John Wallace of Jpswich in yᵉ sd' County Doctor of Physick & Cave Beck of yᵉ same Towne Clerke of yᵉ third pt And Elizabeth Cutteris of Rushmer aforesaid Wȳdd of the fourth pt Whereas Jn the terme of Sᵗ Michael last past One ffyne sur conusans de droit cane ceo &c wᵗʰ Proclamacōns was had & levied by & between yᵉ aforesd' John Wallace p̄lt and yᵉ aforesd' Sʳ Christofer Milton & John Allen and Elizabeth his Wife Deforciants . . . of All that Capitall Mesuage or tenemᵗ . . . now in the tenure or occupacōn of yᵉ sd' Sʳ Christofer Milton and are scituate lyeing & being in Rushmer aforesaid and were lately purchased by yᵉ said Sʳ Christofer Milton of Jathniel Clark & others his trustees

And alsoe of All that Mesuage or tenem^t with ye houses . . .
now in the tenure or occupaċon of George Groome Thatcher
. . . in Rushmer aforesd' and were lately purchased by the sd'
Sr Christofer Milton of Rōbt Rednall of Jpswich aforesaid gent
. . . To & for the only vse & behoofe of ye sd' Sr Christofer Milton & of his heires & Assignes forever . . . In Witnesse whereof
ye parties first abovesd' to these p^rsent Jndentures have int-
changably set their hands & seals ye day & year first abovewrit-
ten/

[Signed:] John Wallace   John Allen   Elizabeth Allen
Cave Beck   X ye mark of Elisabeth Cuttris

From the original document now in the Ipswich and East Suffolk
Joint Record Office in Ipswich, England, Ref. No. xi/5/4.1; mentioned in the *Bulletin of the Institute of Historical Research*, xx (1947),
226-227. I am grateful to the kindness of Derek Charman, Esq., M.A.,
County and Borough Archivist, for making photostats of this and two
other documents about Christopher Milton in his office available to me.
Mr. Charman also helped me to read some sections which because of
creases were illegible in the photostat. This transaction seems to be another part of a complicated transfer of property to which that of November 12, 1687, also belongs. In the above transcript I have omitted
a great deal of the original document, much of which deals with the
other parties and not specifically with Milton.

1688. PUBLICATION OF FOURTH EDITION OF *PARADISE LOST*, ILLUSTRATED.

Paradise Lost. A Poem In Twelve Books. The Authour
John Milton. The Fourth Edition, Adorn'd with Sculptures.
London, Printed by Miles Flesher, for Jacob Tonson, at the
Judge's-Head in Chancery-lane near Fleet-street.
M DC LXXXVIII.

From the title page of my own copy; Masson, vi, 784-786. This
is a sumptuous illustrated edition, published by subscription and with the
names of hundreds of subscribers printed at the back. Though there
were of course many later editions, I shall omit further mention of them.
There were two other editions or issues in 1688.

(23) *Paradise lost* . . . pr. in fol. with cuts, *an.* 1688.
Wood, i, 883; Darbishire, p. 46.

1688. FEBRUARY 6-9. BROTHER CHRISTOPHER AS-
SIGNED TO NORFOLK CIRCUIT.

> *Norfolk* Circuit.
> Lord Chief Baron *Atkins.*
> Mr. Justice *Milton.*

London Gazette, February 6-9, 1687/8. The specific assignments
are: Aylesbury, Bucks, March 5; Bedford, March 7; Huntingdon,
March 9; Cambridge, March 10; Thetford, Norfolkshire, March 14;
Suffolk, March 17 (place unstated, but given in issue of February 9-13
as Ipswich).

1688. FEBRUARY 12. BROTHER CHRISTOPHER AR-
RANGES PROPERTY TRANSFER IN RUSHMERE WITH SIR
HENRY FELTON.

This Jndenture made the the twelfth day of ffebruary . . .
1687 Between Sr Christopher Milton of Rushmere in the County of Suff' Knight one of his Maties: Justices of the Court of
Comoñ Pleas at Westminister of the one parte And Sr Henry
ffelton of Playford in the said County Baronet of the other
parte Witnesseth That Whereas the said Sr Christopher Milton
by his deed indented beareing date the day before the date of
these p'ñtes for the consideracoñ therein mencõned Hath demised granted bargained and sold vnto the said Sr Henry ffelton
the seūall parcells of land in Rushmere aforesaid hereafter
mencõned . . . Normans Hills . . . Whites . . . Claypitts . . .
All wch demised p'mises lately were in the occupacõn of George
Groom of Rushmere aforesaid Thatcher . . . wch he lately held
of Robert Rednall of Ipwich who sold the said farm to the said
Sr Christopher Milton . . . To Have And to Hold all and
Singular the said fore demised peices or pcells of land wth their
appurtnants vnto the said Sr Henry ffelton . . . Now this Indenture further witnesseth that the said Sr Christopher Milton . . . Hath granted . . . vnto the said Sr Henry ffelton all
and Singular the said fore demised lands . . . To Have and to
Hold . . . In Witnesse whereof the said pties to these pñtes

have herevnto enterchangably sett their hands and seales the day and year first above written./

[Subscribed by] Henry Felton

From the original document in the Ipswich and East Suffolk Record Office, Ref. No. xi/5/4.3; mentioned in the *Bulletin of the Institute of Historical Research*, xx (1947), 226-227. This document is part of the same transfer of property to which the documents of November 12 and December 29, 1687, given above, also belong. A companion document with the present is Add. MS. 10,262 in the British Museum. It is of the same date and concerns the same people and properties, and it bears the endorsement: "1687 Feb^{ry} 12th 4: Jac. 2^d Release from Sr Henry ffelton [signed:] Chr̄ Milton."

1688. MARCH 8 AND 15. BROTHER CHRISTOPHER'S SON RICHARD CHOSEN TO STUDY FINES LEVIED ON RECUSANTS IN MIDLANDS.

The Lords Com^{rs}. of his Ma^{ts}. Treāry are humbly desired to direct the issueing out of severall Com^{ons}: to the severall persons hereinafter named with the Jnstruccōns agreed on to be thereunto annexed to enquire touching the Moneys levyed or received of or from any Recusant or other Dissenter whatsoever (and not accompted for unto his Ma^{ty}. or his late Royall brother) according to the forme and effect of the said Jnstructions. Viz. . . .

The like Com̄ission is desired for the Counties of Norfolke, Suffolke, Cambridge, Isle of Ely, and Citty of Norwich unto . . . Richard Milton of Jpswich Esqr.

Public Record Office, Treasury 54, Volume 12, pp. 262-264; *Calendar of Treasury Books, 1685-1689*, part 3, pp. 1803-1805. Richard Milton is one of 26 people named for this district.

1688. JUNE 25-28. BROTHER CHRISTOPHER ASSIGNED TO NORFOLK CIRCUIT.

Norfolk Circuit.

The Lord Chief Justice *Herbert*.

Mr. Justice *Milton*.

London Gazette, June 25-28, 1688. The specific assignments are: Aylesbury, Bucks, July 16; Bedford, July 18; Huntingdon, July 20;

Cambridge, July 21; Bury St. Edmunds, July 24; Norfolk, July 28; Norwich, the same day.

1688. JULY 6. BROTHER CHRISTOPHER RETIRES AS JUDGE, OR IS DISMISSED.

Whitehall, July 6. [The King has removed two justices of the King's Bench.] His Majesty has been also pleased, in considera- tion of the great Age and Infirmities of Sir *Christopher Mil- ton*, one of the Justices of the *Common Pleas*, to permit him to have his Writ of Ease, and has put in his place Sir *Thomas Jenner*, one of the Barons of the *Exchequer*.

London Gazette, July 5-9, 1688. This is the last occurrence of Christopher Milton's name in the *Gazette*. He was at this time nearly 73 years old, having been born on November 24 (?), 1615. As will be seen in the other versions of this action given below, the interpreta- tions of this retirement vary all the way from graceful compliment to certainty of his dismissal for inability or worse. Possibly Christopher's retirement had occurred a few days before the date of this announce- ment (see the following entries).

Judge Holloway and Judge Powell turned out for their opinion in the Bishops case, so was Street and Milton.

From "A Diary of Events in Ireland," under date of July 5, 1688, as quoted in the Historical Manuscripts Commission Calendar of the Manuscripts of the Marquess of Ormonde, N.S., Vol. VIII (1920), p. 353. The editor indexes "Milton" as Sir Christopher.

. . . his Years and Indisposition not well brooking the Fatigue of publick Imployment, he continued not long in either of these Stations [Baron of Exchequer and Judge], but having his *Quie- tus est*, retired to a Country Life, his Study and Devotion.

Phillips, p. vii; Darbishire, p. 53. Masson (VI, 762) explains this statement as "a euphemism for the fact that, on the 3rd of July, 1688, he was dismissed."

1688. NOVEMBER. ELIZABETH, DAUGHTER OF POET'S DAUGHTER DEBORAH, BORN IN IRELAND.

. . . Mrs. Elizabeth Foster, Grand-daughter of John Milton, . . . was born in Jreland in November 1688. . . .

From Thomas Birch's notes on May 14, 1754, *q.v.* This was the day of Mrs. Foster's burial, for which Birch conducted the funeral service.

1688. AFTER NOVEMBER. DEBORAH RETURNS FROM IRELAND TO ENGLAND.

[Deborah] went to live with a Lady, whom she call'd Lady *Merian*. This Lady going over to *Ireland*. . . . She liv'd with that Lady, till her Marriage, and came over again to *England* during the Troubles in *Ireland*, under King *James* II.

From Thomas Birch's notes on his conversations with Deborah's daughter Elizabeth Foster on February 11, 1738, *q.v.* Though Birch is indefinite in his dating, the fact that Elizabeth was born in Ireland in November, 1688 (as Birch wrote in his comment on her funeral on May 14, 1754, *q.v.*), means that Deborah and her husband must have been there still at that time. E. F. Rimbault discusses this matter in *Notes and Queries*, II, iii (1857), 265-266.

The text here is from Birch's 1738 edition.

1689. PUBLICATION OF ATTRIBUTED *PRO POPULO ADVERSUS TYRANNOS*.

Pro Populo Adversus Tyrannos: or the Sovereign Right and Power of the People over Tyrants, Clearly Stated, and plainly Proved. With some Reflections on the late posture of Affairs. By a true Protestant English-man, and Well-wisher to Posterity. London, Printed in the Year, 1689.

From the title page of the original edition. Attributed often to Milton; *e.g.*, in Wing's STC, M2165. See above, II, 95-96. This work is actually, except for a few changes, including the title, a reprint of Milton's *Tenure of Kings*. For a comparison of the two see Sensabaugh, pp. 127, 134-142, and W. R. Parker in *Modern Language Quarterly*, III (1942) 41-44.

(34) *The right of the People over Tyrants*. printed lately in qu.

Wood, I, 883; Darbishire, p. 47.

1691 . . . Much about which time was published under *Joh. Milton's* name *The right of the people over Tyrants*.

Wood, *Fasti Oxonienses*, I (1691), 885, *s.v.* Edmund Ludlow.

The Soveraign Right and power of the People over Tyrants clearly stated. The Author, **John Milton.** Quarto. Price 6d.

Term Catalogues, II, 361, under date of Easter Term, 1691. Either the date on the title page of the book is early, or this entry is late, or there were two issues of the book. The last of these three explanations seems the most unlikely. I suppose that there is no doubt that this title refers to the same book as the preceding ones.

1689. JANUARY 30. TRANSFER OF PRINTING RIGHTS IN MILTON'S PROSE WORKS.

30 Jany 1688 [*i.e.* 1688-9]

Awn Churchill. Entred . . . booke or coppy under the hand of Master Wardn CLAVELL entituled *Tracts of* **John Million** *of Divorce, Colasterion, Tetrachordon, Areopagitica, Notes on Griffith Sermon, True Religion, Heresey &c, Observacōns on Jicsk peace, pro populo Anglicano, et Salmatij Lat & Eng: defensio secundo lat Engl.; pro se contra Moram lat; Engl; epistola familiares lat & Eng on Rawleigh' Cabinet counsell Johannis Phillipis Angł responsio. Lat & Engl, Lrē Cromwelianee, Lat & Engl, of Rimerius herelius, of civill power.* Lycensed by RO: MIDGLY .... vj^d

Stationers' Registers, III, 345; Fletcher Facsimile, III, 20. The editor of the Registers makes the following comment on this masterpiece of confusion: "The person who made this entry had apparently never heard of John Milton or his works." "Jicsk" is a weird misspelling of "Irish"; "Rimerius herelius" may be the clerk's helpless rendering of "removing hirelings." The inclusion of both Latin and English rights in so many works cannot mean that English translations were already available, but only that the right to publish them was granted.

1690. FEBRUARY 11. BROTHER CHRISTOPHER'S PAPERS MENTIONED.

Whitehall 11th Feb^ry [1690]

S^r

J have received your letter of the 8th instant with some inclosed papers which seem to have belonged to the late Judge Milton and they containeing nothing of Moment if there be nothing else in the Trunke but what you mention J see noe reason for detaining it   J am

Sr Your humble Servant

Shrewsbury

[In the margin:] Mayor of Dover

Public Record Office, SP 44/97, f. 259; *CSP Dom, 1689-1690*, p. 456. The year, which does not appear in the manuscript (at least on my photostatic copy), is from *CSP*. The Earl of Shrewsbury was one of the chief Secretaries of State to William and Mary. This letter may have some connection with another of January 24, 1690, in which Shrewsbury asked the Mayor to search Francis Williamson for suspected papers (*CSP*, p. 428). Further communications on that subject appear under dates of January 26 and 28 and February 6. What papers of Milton's are concerned is left unexplained. By the word "late" the writer could have meant either that he thought (though mistakenly) that Christopher Milton was dead, or that Christopher had quitted active service (which was true).

1691. PUBLICATION OF ANTHONY WOOD'S LIFE OF MILTON.

Athenæ Oxonienses. An Exact History Of All The Writers and Bishops Who have had their Education in The most ancient and famous University Of Oxford . . . London: Printed for Tho. Bennet at the Half-Moon in S. Pauls Churchyard. MDCXCI. [Volume II is dated MDCXCII.]

Title page of the first edition, in which the life of Milton comes at I, 880-884. Miss Darbishire reprints the life at pp. 35-48.

1691. MARCH 24. AYLMER SELLS OTHER HALF RIGHT IN *PARADISE LOST* TO TONSON.

. . . and Aylmer afterwards sold . . . the other half on the 24th of March 1690, with a considerable advance of the price. . . .

Repeated from the main entry above under the transfer of the first half, August 17, 1683.

1692. TRANSLATION OF *DEFENSIO* IN ENGLISH PUB-
LISHED.

A Defence Of The People of England, By John Milton: In
Answer to Salmasius's Defence of the King. Printed in the Year
1692.

Title page of the copy in the Rutgers University Library; mentioned
in CM, VII, 563-564; Masson, IV, 258. This translation has been as-
scribed to a Mr. Washington of the Temple on the basis of a statement
by Toland (Darbishire, p. 155). But the translator is not named in the
book itself, and Toland gives no authority for his attribution. The prefatory "To the English Reader" in the edition of 1692 merely states
that this translation was *"long since made"* by an author *"since deceased"* (sig. A3). The Bohn edition of Milton's prose used this translation, but CM has a new one, keeping only phrases here and there from
1692. The identity of the translator is, however, virtually settled by
the existence of a copy carrying on the title page the inscription: "The
Gift of the Translator Joseph Washington of the Middle Temple";
see Emma Unger and William A. Jackson, *The Carl H. Pforzheimer
Library*, item 726. Mr. F. F. Madan, Esq., kindly informs me that this
inscribed copy is now in the Bodleian. In his "Revised Bibliography of
Salmasius's *Defensio Regia*," *Library*, 5th Series, IX (1954), 119, Mr.
Madan surmises that the printer omitted the name of the translator because the proclamation of August 13, 1660, forbidding reprints of the
book was still in force. He also suggests that the 1690 reprint of *Eikonoklastes* may have borne an Amsterdam imprint for the same reason.
Though he does not say so, he might have added the speculation that
perhaps the Toland edition of 1698 may have come within the same
reasoning.

Defensio pro populo Anglicano. *The same lately Translated
into English.*

Phillips, p. [liii]; not in Darbishire.

1692. NOVEMBER 26. LATIN DICTIONARY BASED PART-
LY ON MILTON REGISTERED.

November 26th 1692

Wm. Rawlins,	Entred ... booke or coppy under the hand of
Tho. Dring, and	Master Warden SIMS entitled *Linguae Ro-*
J. Place.	*manae Dictionarium Luculentum Novum.*
	A new Dictionary in five Alphabets ...

completed & improved from ye sevall workes of **Stephen Cooper Gouldman Holyoke** D[r] **Littleton** a large manuscript in three volumes of M[r] **John Milton** &c. In ye use of all wch for greater exactnesse recourse has alwaies been had to ye authors themselves. Lysenced, November 26th C. ALSTON .... vj[d]

Stationers' Registers, III, 411. This publication has already been mentioned above under date of 1655. Several further entries concerning this work occur in the Registers. On November 28 George Bright and Thomas Hookes, executors of John Wright, assigned one third right in this book to William Rawlins and Thomas Dring; on the same day Rawlins, Dring, John Place, John Lilly, and Thomas Rock (the two last being executors of Susanna Leigh, executrix of John Leigh) made a similar assignment to Christopher Wilkinson; and on the same day also Thomas Bassett, Richard Chiswell, William Rawlins, Thomas Dring, John Lilly, and Thomas Rock (the two last again as executors as before) made assignment to Christopher Wilkinson. Though not so stated, each assignment is presumably for a third or some other fraction. Later, on August 21, 1693, Wilkinson in turn made assignments of fractions in the same book to Rawlins, Dring, Chiswell, Place, Ben Tooke, Charles Harper, and William Crooke (Registers, III, 427-428). Wing (*STC*, L 2354) enters this title under "Linguae."

1693. FEBRUARY. PUBLICATION OF LATIN DICTIONARY BASED ON MILTON.

LINGUÆ *Romanæ Dictionarium Luculentum Novum.* A New Dictionary in Five Alphabets . . . compleated and improved from the several works of *Stephens, Cooper, Gouldman, Holyoke,* D. *Littleton.* A large MS., in three Volumes, of Mr. *John Milton,* etc. In the use of all which, for greater exactness, recourse has always been had to the Authors themselves. Quarto. Printed for **W. Rawlins** in St. *Bartholomew's Close*; **T. Dring** at the Harrow in *Fleet street*; **R. Chiswell** at the Rose and Crown in St. *Paul's* Churchyard; **C. Harper** at the Flower de luce in *Fleet street*; **W. Crook** at the Green Dragon, without Temple Bar; **J. Place** at Furnival's Inn Gate, in *Holborn*; and the executors of **S. Leigh.**

Term Catalogues, II, 440-441; Masson, VI, 813; Darbishire, pp. 339-340. Much of this material was used again in Robert Ainsworth's Latin dictionary of 1736. The manuscript seems to have disappeared.

1693. MARCH 22. BROTHER CHRISTOPHER BURIED IN IPSWICH.

1692 . . . Mar. 22th. Sr Christophere Melton of Rushmore was buried in the Church of this parish St Nicholas Ipswich.

Parish Registers of St. Nicholas, Ipswich, as printed by E. Cookson for the Parish Register Society, 1897, p. 167; Todd, I (1826), 259; Masson, VI, 762.

This may be an appropriate place to note two memorials to Christopher Milton. G. R. Clarke (*The History and Description of the Town and Borough of Ipswich*, Ipswich and London [1830], p. 226) says that the Theatre of his day was built on the spot where had stood "a Catholic chapel, for Judge Milton—the brother of the illustrious poet of that name—in the time of James II." Hugh H. L. Bellot (*The Inner Temple and Middle Temple*, London and New York, 1902, p. 195) remarks that "In one of the stained glass windows in the Hall [of the Inner Temple] there is a portrait of Sir Christopher, to remind us not so much of the successful lawyer as of the blind poet."

1693. DECEMBER 29. BROTHER-IN-LAW RICHARD POWELL MAKES WILL.

In the name of God Amen this twenty ninth day of December . . . Anno Dn̄i one thousand Six hundred ninety three I Richard Powell of the Jnner Temple London Esqr. One of the Readers of the same Temple . . . doe make and ordaine this my last Will and Testament . . . my body . . . to be buryed according to the fforme of the Church of England by Law established . . . Jtem J give and bequeath unto my deare and loveing wife Anne Powell all my moneys goods chattells rights credits and estates . . . belonging . . . to me . . . by force . . . of any Article or Articles . . . made upon the marriage of my late eldest Sonn Richard Powell since deceased . . . Jtem J give and bequeath all and every my Manno^rs Lands . . . unto my said deare wife . . . Signed sealed published by the abovenamed Richard Powell . . . in the presence of Esme Howard Geo ffawnt Thomas Newsham

Probatum fuit humoī Testament' apud London coram veñli viro Georgio Bramston Legum Doctore Surr̄o venlis et egregij viri Dnī Richardi Raines Militis Legū etiam Doctoris Curiæ Prærogat'. Cant'. Magr̄i Custodis Sive commissarij ltīme constituti tertio die mensis ffebruarij Anno Dnī (Style Angl) millīmo Sexcenm̄o nonagem̄o quinto Juramento Annæ Powell Relictæ dicti dēfti et Extrīcis in dicto Testo nominat' cui commissa fuit adm̄traco omniū et singulor̄ bonor̄ juriū et creditorum dicti dēfti de bene et fideliter administrando eadem ad Sancta Dei Evangelia Jurat'./

Prerogative Court of Canterbury, 18 Bond; *Genealogist*, II (1878), 314; Masson, VI, 751. The testator mentions in his will his sisters Anne Kingston, Sarah Pearson, Elizabeth Holloway, Elizabeth Howell, sister Shuter, and sister Scull (now Hereford); his wife's sister Jane Brokesby; his grandchild Elizabeth Powell; his cousin William Pudsey; and his godsons Richard Pearson and Hewett Holloway. The record shows, in addition to the probate given above, two further actions, evidently required by Mrs. Powell's failure, as a result of her death, to complete execution of the will. One is a commission to Jane Brokesby, sister of Mrs. Powell, dated June 27, 1704, to administer the will. The second is a similar commission, dated January 24, 1705 (probably 1705/6), to Samuel Grascome and Richard Holt, to take over administration as the result of the death of Jane Brokesby.

[A will of this sort was proved in London before the worshipful man George Bramston, Doctor of Laws, surrogate of the worshipful and excellent man Master Richard Raines, Knight, also Doctor of Laws, legally appointed Master Keeper or Commissary of the Prerogative Court of Canterbury, on the third day of the month of February in the year of our Lord (in English style) 1695, on the oath of Anne Powell, relict of the said deceased and executrix named in the said will, to whom was committed administration of all and singular the goods, rights, and credits of the said deceased, sworn on the holy gospels of God concerning well and faithfully administering the same.]

BEFORE 1694. DAUGHTER MARY DIES.

He had three Daughters who surviv'd him many years . . . *Anne* . . . *Mary* . . . and *Debora* the youngest, who is yet living. . . .

Phillips, pp. xl-xli; Darbishire, p. 76; Masson, VI, 751. Phillips's language clearly implies that Mary was dead at the time of his writing his memoir (published in 1694). She was living in 1678, as shown by Anne Powell's bequest in her will, dated on October 24 of that year. There is no more definite information as to the time of her death.

1694. NEPHEW EDWARD PHILLIPS PUBLISHES FOUR SONNETS, TRANSLATION OF *LETTERS OF STATE*, AND BIOGRAPHICAL MEMOIR.

Letters of State, Written by Mr. John Milton, To most of the Sovereign Princes and Republicks of Europe. From the Year 1649. Till the Year 1659. To which is added, An Account of his Life. Together with several of his Poems; And a Catalogue of his Works, never before Printed. London: Printed in the Year, 1694.

Title page of my own copy; Masson, I (1881), viii, and *passim*; CM, XIII (text of State Letters); Darbishire, pp. 49-82 (life and sonnets). The four sonnets first here published are those to Cromwell, Fairfax, Vane, and Cyriack Skinner ("*CYRIAC* this Three years day . . ."). All biographies of Milton depend considerably on this memoir.

1694. BROTHER CHRISTOPHER'S SON THOMAS IN CROWN OFFICE RECEIVES INCOME.

Crown Office. To Mr. Milton of the Crown office for fees there and for the King's servants, the Hanaper office, and the great seal—£873.1.9.; to the said Mr. Milton more as His Grace's free gift to him presenting His Grace with a gilt case to put the patent in — £5.0.0. ——————————— £878 1 9.

From the Duke of Bedford's account books for 1694 as quoted in Gladys S. Thomson's *Life in a Noble Household, 1641-1700*, New York, 1937, p. 334.

1694. JANUARY 12. SISTER'S SON-IN-LAW DAVID MOORE DIES.

Masson, VI, 774, based on Manning's *History and Antiquities of Surrey*, III, 229, and the Milton pedigree by Sir Charles Young, Garter King at Arms. This David Moore was the husband of Ann Agar, daughter of Milton's sister Ann Milton-Phillips-Agar, and her second husband, Thomas Agar, who had died in late 1673 and whose will had been proved on November 5 of that year. Moore's seat was Sayes House, Chertsey, and he was buried in Chertsey church. His wife Ann renounced administration of his effects in favor of their son Thomas Moore.

1694. OCTOBER 17. BROTHER CHRISTOPHER'S SON THOMAS BURIED.

Octob . . . 17 Thomas Milton out of fleet strete in the Chancell.

Parish Register of St. Dunstan in the West, London; summarized by Perceval Lucas in *Notes and Queries*, XI, vii (1913), 21-22. The last phrase indicates the place of burial in the church. On March 27, 1696 (*q.v.*), Thomas's widow appears as of St. Margaret's, Westminster.

1694. DECEMBER 3. ADMINISTRATION OF NEPHEW THOMAS MILTON'S ESTATE GRANTED TO RELICT MARTHA.

Tertio die em^t. com^o. Marthæ Milton rēlcæ Thomæ Milton nup poæ S^{ti}. Dunstani in Occidēn London dēfti hēntis &c ad adstrañd bona juῤ et crēd dcī def. De bene &c jurat'.

[In left hand margin:] Thomas Milton. [Mor]t' 6 Novemb: 1694

[In right hand margin:] London Inv^m. extum Tillotson 2do. 31 Dec: 1695.

Prerogative Court of Canterbury, Administration Act Book for 1694, f. 229; Perceval Lucas in *Notes and Queries*, XI, vii (1913), 21. If the reading "Mort'" is correct (my photostat shows only "t'"), which supports Lucas's statement that Thomas died on November 6, then something is wrong with the entry above about his burial in St. Dunstan's on October 17. Lucas speaks of Martha Milton as the daughter of Charles Fleetwood of Northampton; but R. W. B., in the same volume (p. 113), proves that she was the daughter of Sir William Fleetwood of Aldwinkle. John Tillotson had been Archbishop of Canterbury since 1691. It is just possible that Thomas Milton's acquaintance with and marriage to Martha Fleetwood may have come about through the distant relationship of Milton's first wife to the family. Anne Powell, Milton's mother-in-law, was the granddaughter of Richard Archdale,

merchant of London; the granddaughter of his brother Bernard Archdale of Oxford, Elizabeth Archdale, married John Fleetwood, son
and heir of Sir William Fleetwood of Great Missenden, co. Bucks.
See Henry F. Waters's collections of genealogical material on the Archdale family in his *Genealogical Gleanings in England*, I (1883), 316-
319. John Milton had been a friend of Charles Fleetwood; see above,
II, 53-54.

[On the third day there issued a commission to Martha Milton, relict of Thomas Milton, late of the parish of St. Dunstan
in the West, London, deceased, having, etc., for administering
the goods, chattels, and credits of the said deceased, sworn concerning well, etc.

Thomas Milton. Died (?) November 6, 1694.

London, inventory exhibited, Tillotson, for the second time,
December 31, 1695.]

1696. JANUARY (?). BROTHER-IN-LAW RICHARD POW-ELL DIES.

On February 3, 1695/6, Richard Powell's relict Ann proved his
will (see above under December 29, 1693); Masson, VI, 751. Masson
guesses that the death occurred in 1695, but it is more likely to be nearer
to the date of probate. But I have found no evidence of any exact date.

1696. MAY 27. DR. WILLIAM COWARD FILES MARRIAGE ALLEGATION TO MARRY POET'S BROTHER CHRISTO-PHER'S SON THOMAS'S WIDOW MARTHA.

27 Maij 1696

Which day Appeared psonally W^m. Coward of the pish of S^t
Andrew Holborne aged about 36 yeares & a Bacchelor & al-
leadged that he intended to marry with Martha Milton of the
pish of S^t. Marg^t. Westm^r. Widdow not knowing of any Jm-
pediment by reason of any p^rcontract Consanguinity Affinity or
otherwise to hinder the s^d. marriage of the truth of the p^rmises
he made Oath & prayed Licence to be marryed in the pish
Church of S^t. Marg^t. Westm̄ afores^d. or

Jurat' Coram me   Willm̄ Coward^e.

Tho: Lane

From the original in the Faculty Office of the Archbishop of Canterbury, London; Publications of the Harleian Society, XXIV (1886), 220; Perceval Lucas in *Notes and Queries*, XI, vii (1913), 21-22; Masson, VI, 763. I am not sure of the final "or" of the text though previous transcripts have so rendered it. Dr. Coward lived until 1724, when his will was proved in Ipswich on April 20. Elizabeth Milton, daughter of Thomas and Martha, lived until July 26, 1769.

1697. WIDOW WRITES TO FRIEND FOR INFORMATION FOR TOLAND'S LIFE.

I learnt som Particulars from a Person that had bin once his Amanuensis, which were confirm'd to me . . . by a Letter written to one at my desire from his last Wife, who is still alive.

Toland, I (1698), 5-6; Darbishire, p. 85. Toland does not name the correspondent, nor does the letter seem to be extant. See CM, XVIII, 524. The date, though not given, was probably not long before Toland wrote his life. The item is therefore filed here under 1697 as an approximate date.

1697. TOLAND VISITS POET'S DAUGHTER DEBORAH.

[Among sources for his life of Milton:] I learnt som Particulars from a Person that had bin once his Amanuensis, which were confirm'd to me by his Daughter now dwelling in *London*. . . .

Toland, pp. 5-6; Darbishire, p. 85. Though Toland does not identify the amanuensis, who may be any one of numerous persons, there is no doubt that he is saying that he talked with (or possibly had a letter from, though I think not) Deborah Milton. The date is not specified, and may quite possibly be earlier than 1697, or even as late as 1698 itself, the year when the life was published.

1697. FIRST COLLECTED EDITION OF ENGLISH PROSE WRITINGS.

The Works Of M^r. John Milton. [ornament] Printed in the Year MDCXCVII.

Title page of my own copy; J. F. Payne in the *Athenaeum*, 1898, I, 791-792; Wing, M2086. This large folio volume contains Milton's *Doctrine and Discipline of Divorce* (beginning on p. 1), *Tetrachordon* (p. 62), *Colasterion* (p. 127), *Judgment of Martin Bucer* (p. 153),

Of Reformation (p. 170), *Reason of Church Government* (p. 205), *Treatise of Civil Power* (p. 243), *Likeliest Means to Remove Hirelings* (p. 260), *Of Prelatical Episcopacy* (p. 284), *Animadversions* (p. 294), *Apology* (p. 325), *Ready and Easy Way* (p. 361), *Areopagitica* (p. 371), *Tenure of Kings* (p. 397), *Notes on Griffiths' Sermon* (p. 422), *Of True Religion* (p. 428), *Eikonoklastes* (p. 440), and *Articles of Peace* (p. 530). Most of the pieces here reprinted have their own individual title pages, usually dated 1697. There is no preface of any kind, nor does the title page give any further information about place of printing or name of printer. Mr. Payne thought it was published by Tonson and printed by Thomas Hodgkin, and that they left off their names for political reasons. There seems to be no connection between this volume and that of 1698 containing Toland's life of Milton (see below). The type, spelling, punctuation, use of title pages, etc., are all different. This volume contains no Latin writings.

1697. MARCH 6. A CHRISTOPHER MILTON SIGNS PARLIAMENTARY ORDER.

According to the Historical Manuscripts Commission's catalogue of the Manuscripts of the House of Lords for 1695-1697 (1903, p. 402), a Christopher Milton, along with others, signed on March 6, 1696/7, an order relating to the enlarging of the Fleet prison. This cannot of course be the poet's brother; and Christopher's son Christopher had died and been buried on March 12, 1668 (IV, 444). It may have been a relative.

1698. PUBLICATION OF TOLAND'S LIFE AND COLLECTED PROSE.

A Complete Collection Of The Historical, Political, and Miscellaneous Works Of John Milton, Both English and Latin. With som Papers never before Publish'd. In Three Volumes. To which is Prefix'd The Life of the Author, Containing, Besides the History of his Works, Several Extraordinary Characters of Men and Books, Sects, Parties, and Opinions. Amsterdam, Finish'd in the Year M.DC.XC.VIII.

Title page of the first edition. This life (I, 5-47), which has been used by almost every student of Milton's life, is reprinted in full in Darbishire, pp. 83-197. He says near the beginning that he got most of his materials from Milton's own writings, "som Particulars from a Person that had bin once his Amanuensis, which were confirm'd to me by his Daughter now dwelling in *London*, and by a Letter written to one at my desire from his last Wife, who is still alive. I perus'd the Papers of one of his Nephews, learnt what I could in Discourse with the other; and lastly consulted such of his acquaintance, as, after the best inquiry, I was able to discover." He adds very little factual material, however, to what preceding writers had gathered. He apparently merely contributed the life without having any part in editing Milton's works, for in the prefatory Life of James Harrington prefixed to Harrington's *Oceana and Other Works*, dated November 30, 1699 (published 1771; p. xxiv), he explains very carefully that "tho the history I wrote of MILTON's life be prefix'd to his works, yet I had no hand in the edition of those volumes; or otherwise his logic, his grammar, and the like, had not increas'd the bulk or price of his other useful pieces." The "Amsterdam" in the title page is, according to Miss Darbishire (p. 342), misleading, since the book was actually published in London. The only indication of Toland's authorship is the initials I. T. affixed to the end of the life. The life is dated at the end: "*Sept.* 3. 1698." The paging of this edition is continuous, but erratic. Some pages are skipped entirely in numbering; some are numbered on one side only like ancient folios. The life is paged separately. Some sets are bound in two volumes only. The "Life" was entered in the Stationers' Registers to John Darby, Jr., under date of December 15, 1698. Many of the single works in this edition bear individual title pages, some with dates as early as 1694 (*e.g., The History of Britain*). When the volumes are broken into parts and bound individually, as sometimes happens, the result is confusing.

1700. FEBRUARY 6. BROTHER CHRISTOPHER'S DAUGHTER-IN-LAW BENEFICIARY OF HER BROTHER'S WILL.

[William Fleetwood, son of Sir William Fleetwood of Aldwinkle, Northants, in his will of the above date makes his sister Martha, widow of Christopher's son Thomas, his chief beneficiary:] All the rest of my goods and chattells whatsoever I give and bequeath vnto my dearly beloved sister Mrs Martha Milton ... whom I doe declare and appoint full and sole Executrix of this my last Will and Testament.

Prerogative Court of Canterbury, 46 Noel; R. W. B. in *Notes and Queries*, XI, vii (1913), 113. The wording of the quoted section might make it seem that Fleetwood was unaware that Martha Milton had been widowed and had remarried. But in a memorandum of the same date at the end of the will he adds a bequest of £100 to his "brother" (*i.e.*, brother-in-law) Doctor William Coward. The will was proved on March 2, 1699 (*i.e.*, 1699/1700) by Martha Coward alias Milton, wife of William Coward, M.D.

1703. DAUGHTER DEBORAH'S SON CALEB NOW IN MADRAS, INDIA.

By June 2, 1703, the poet's grandson had moved to Madras, for on that day his son was baptized (*q.v.*). He had married a Mary Clark and was to settle down there, where he was to die in 1719. For a quick summary of the known events in his life see below under date of June 2, 1703.

1703. DAUGHTER DEBORAH'S DAUGHTER ELIZABETH COMES TO ENGLAND.

... M^{rs}. Elizabeth Foster ... was born in Jreland in November 1688, & was about 15 Years of Age when she came to England. ...

From Thomas Birch's notes on Elizabeth Foster's burial on May 14, 1754, below, *q.v.*

1703. JUNE 2. DAUGHTER DEBORAH'S SON CALEB'S SON ABRAHAM BAPTIZED IN INDIA.

Abraham Son of Caleb & Mary Clark, Baptiz'd by G Lewis, Ioseph Seotterall & Thos. Gray Godfathers, Susanna Defestro Godmother.

[Marginal entry:] June 2^d: Clark

From the original entry in the parish registers of St. George's Cathedral, Madras, India. I am deeply grateful to the Rev. R. L. Watson of the Cathedral, who kindly arranged to have this and a number of related entries photographed for me so that I could reproduce them exactly. These entries include the following: the baptisms of Mary Clark (March 17, 1707), of Isaac Clark (February 13, 1711), and of Mary Clark (April 5, 1727); the marriage of Abraham Clark and Anna Clark (September 22, 1725); and the burials of Mary Clark (December 15, 1716), of Caleb Clark (October 26, 1719), of Mary Clark (October 4, 1729), and of Abraham Clark (September 5, 1743). Most of these items have previously been published by Sir James Mackintosh (?) in the *Edinburgh Review* for October, 1815; by Hyde Clarke in the *Athenaeum* for March 13, 1880, p. 344; in British Museum Add. MS. 19,142, f. 79 (quoting from Chateaubriand's *Sketches of English Lit-*

erature, II, III); by John Bradshaw in the *Athenaeum*, 1892, II, 740-741; by Mrs. Frank Penny, *Fort St. George Madras*, London, 1900, pp. 136-138; in the *Genealogist*, New Series, xx, 1904, 61; and in Masson, VI, 755-761. Additional data from these sources include the fact that Caleb Clarke was for some time parish clerk of Madras (or Fort George); that his son Abraham visited England for a time, during which some person likewise named Abraham Clark was admitted to the Company of Weavers (May 9, 1709); and that though there is no record of the death of Isaac Clarke, it may well have occurred between 1746 and 1749, when the registers were not carefully kept. Apparently with the death of Abraham Clarke in 1743 all traces of this branch of Milton's family disappeared. I should add that Birch (1753 edition, p. lxxvi) had heard of Caleb's move to India, his marriage, and his two sons Abraham and Isaac, though he gives no dates.

In giving the rest of the entries listed above, I shall simply refer back to this note, rather than documenting each one separately, in order to save space.

Though my reproductions seldom give the year of the date, Mr. Watson has carefully checked each for me.

1704-1708. DAUGHTER DEBORAH APPEALS FOR AID, AND RECEIVES IT.

Only daughter of John Melton, author of *the Paradice Lost* [petitions Robert Harley, Secretary of State, saying that she is] in a very low and destitute condition, but is far more desirous to maintain herself by her care and industry than to be burdensome to any honourable person who generosity might induce to relieve her for the respect had to her late dear father.

From the Historical Manuscripts Commission report on the manuscripts of the Duke of Portland, Vol. VIII (1907), p. 388; these manuscripts are preserved (or were in 1907) at Welbeck Abbey. The date is set by the fact that Harley, later (1711) to become Earl of Oxford and Lord Treasurer, was Secretary of State between 1704 and 1708 (*DNB*). I have not seen the original manuscript.

Deborah Milton. Her I knew and often releivd. She is very like her Fathers picture; from her I had many particulars of her fathers life. Though she could read Greek and Latin she understood not one word.

A penciled note in Harley's copy of Wood's *Athenae Oxonienses*, and thought to be in his handwriting; described by the owner, Douglas

Macleane, in the *Saturday Review*, CXIX (1915), 114-115. Though undated, this note must be of a time corresponding to the abovementioned petition of Deborah's, except that of course Harley's generosity may have continued past the period of his service as Secretary of State.

1707. MARCH 17. DAUGHTER DEBORAH'S SON CALEB'S DAUGHTER MARY BAPTIZED.

Mary Daughter of Caleb & Mary Clark, Baptizd by G Lewis, Florence Gerald, Godfather Eleanor Boyd & Eliz^th. Cragg Godmothers.

[Marginal entry:] March 17 Clark.

From the parish registers of St. George's Cathedral, Madras; see note to entry of June 2, 1703.

1711. FEBRUARY 13. DAUGHTER DEBORAH'S SON CALEB'S SON ISAAC BAPTIZED.

Isaac Son of Caleb & Mary Clark, Baptiz'd by G Lewis

[Marginal entry:] 1710/11 Feb^ry. 13 Clark

From the parish registers of St. George's Cathedral, Madras; see note to entry of June 2, 1703.

1713. APRIL 11. WIDOW GIVES BOND TO RANDLE TIMMIS.

Noverint vniversi per p^rsentes nos Elizabēth Milton de Nantwich in Com̄ Cestr̄ vīd et Samuel Acton de Nantwich in Com̄ p̄^rd geñ teneri & firmiter Obligari Rano Timmis de Greasty in Com̄ p̄^rd yeom̄ in vigint' libris bonæ et legalis monetæ Magnæ Britanniæ Solvend eidem Rano Timmis aut suo certo Attornat Executor' vel Administrator' suis Ad quam quidem Soluconem bene et fideliter faciend' Obligamus nos et utrūqz nostrum per se pro toto et in solid Heredes Executores et Administratores nros et utrumqz nostrum firmiter per p^rsentes Sigillis ñris sigillat Dat undecimo die Aprilis Anno Regni Dñæ Annæ Dei gratia Magnæ Britanniæ ffranciæ & Hibniæ duodecimo fidei Defensor' &c' duodecimo Annoqz Dni' 1713

The Condicōn of this Obligacōn is such That if the above

bounden Elizabeth Milton and Samuel Acton or either of them
their or either of their Heires Executo^{rs} or Administrato^{rs} doe
well and truely pay or cause to be paid unto the above named
Randle Timmis his Executo^{rs} Administrato^{rs} or Assignes the
full sume of ten pounds with lawfull interest for the same of
good and lawfull money of Great Britain on ye eleventh day
of October next ensueing the date hereof Then this Obligacͦn
to be void or else to remaine in full force

Sealed and delivered

   in presence of   [Signed:] Elizabeth Milton [seal]

William Harrison,   S[amuel Acton   seal]

Ri: Wickstead

From the original document in the Manuscript Room of the New
York Public Library; Marsh, *Papers*, p. 25 (in full); Masson, VI, 746
(summary). Marsh noted that Acton's signature had been torn off even
in his day. He pointed out that Acton was minister of the General
Baptist Chapel at Nantwich, of which Mrs. Milton was a member. In
the upper left-hand corner of the sheet is a one-penny tax stamp.

This text occupies the front page of a sheet folded so as to make
four pages. The inside pages (2 and 3) are blank. On the fourth, of
which somewhat more than half has been torn away, is a record of
payments on the bond. There is no point in giving them in full, but
enough remains to show receipts for yearly payments of interest in 1713,
1714, 1715, 1718 (for three years), 1719, 1720 (?), 1721, 1722,
1723, 1724, 1725, and 1726(?).

[Know all men by these presents that we, Elizabeth Milton
of Nantwich in co. Chester, widow, and Samuel Acton of Nantwich in the county aforesaid, gentleman, are held and firmly
obligated to Randle Timmis of Gresty in the county aforesaid,
yeoman, in twenty pounds of good and legal money of Great
Britain, to be paid to the said Randle Timmis or his designated
attorney, executor, or administrator; to the making of which
payment well and faithfully we bind ourselves and each of us
for himself for the whole, and our heirs, executors, and administrators and both of us firmly by these presents for the
whole sum. Sealed with our seals. Given on the eleventh day of
April in the twelfth year of the reign of Anne, by the grace of

God Queen of Great Britain, France, and Ireland, Defender of
the Faith, etc., and in the year of our Lord 1713.]

1713. AUGUST 12. ADMINISTRATION OF CHRISTOPHER
MILTON'S SON RICHARD'S WILL GRANTED IN PART TO
JOHN TAYLOR.

[Marginal entry:] Richūs Milton deftus
Mense Augusti Anno Dnī 1713

Thomas providentiâ Divinâ Cantuariensis Archiepiscopus ...
Dilecto Nobis in Christo Johanni Taylor de Highgate in Comi-
tatu Middxīæ Hortulano Salutem Cum coram veñli viro Johanne Exton Legum Doctore Surrogato Præhonorandi viri
Dnī Caroli Hedges Militis Legum etiam Doctoris Curiæ Prærogativæ nostræ Cant'. Magistri Custodis sive Comissarij ltīme
constituti per Dnūm Edvardum Gould militem monstratum et
allegatum fuerit quendam Benjaminum Harison de Gippovico
in Com'. Suffolciæ Nantam per Jndenturam quandam Vicesimo
Sexto die mensis Julij Anno Dnī Millesimo Sexcentesimo Quin-
quagesimo primo datum concessisse et demisisse cuidam Gulielm-
mo Cross Londini Generoso ... All that the Mannor or Capitall Messuage called Norwoods ... in Sproughton within the
said county of Suffolk ... Cumqz præterea allegatum fuerit
quandam Jndenturam Secundo die mensis Octobris Anno ...
Dnī Millesimo Sexcentesimo Octogesimo Sexto factum fuisse
inter dictum Gulielmum Burrough de Gippovico prædicto Grocer' et dictum Carolum Burrough ex unâ parte et Richardum
Milton de Gippovico antedicto armigerum ex altera parte ...
Cumqz præterea allegatum fuerit dictum Richardum Milton
Hiberniâ abintestato nullo per eum condito Testamento fatis
cessisse cælibem habentem dum vixit et mortis suæ tempore
bona jura sive credita in diversis diæcesibus sive peculiaribus
Jurisdictionibus sufficientia ad fundandam Jurisdictionem Curiæ
nostræ prærogativæ Cant'. præd. nullasqz Lrās Adm^{nis} ....
Cumqz Surrogatus antedictus habitâ Maturâ consideratione
præallegatorum ad petitionem dicti Dnī Edvardi Gould Lrās

Adm^{nis}. bonorum jurium et creditorum dicti Richardi Milton dēfti quoad et quatenus concernant dictū Maneriū sive Messuagiam . . . ut præfertur concessi . . . Tibi Johanni Taylor de cujus fidelitate in hac parte confidimus primitus de bene et fideliter administrando bona jura et credita dicti Richī Milton dēfti quoad et quatenus concernant dictu Maneriū . . . Ac de pleno et fideli Jnventario eorundem . . . exhibendo . . . comittimus potestatem Teqz Johannem Taylor Administratorem bonorum jurium et creditorum dicti Richī Milton dēfti quoad et quatenus concernant dictū Manerium . . . sed non ultra nec aliter . . . nominamus ordinamus deputamus et constituimus per præsentes Dat Londini Duodecimo die mensis Augusti Anno Dnī Millesimo Septingentesimo Decimo Tertio Et Nr̄æ Translationis Anno Decimo Nono./.

Prerogative Court of Canterbury, Administration Act Books, 1713, ff. 184v-186; Perceval Lucas in *Notes and Queries*, XI, vii (1913), 21-22. The document recounts several indentures or other actions taken on property in Ipswich and elsewhere between 1651 and 1686, only one of which involves Richard Milton. It also provides information about the place of his death (Ireland) and at least, if not the date of his death, a date before which he must have been dead. I assume that "concessi" about three quarters through the quotation is a scribal error for "concessit."

[Richard Milton, deceased. August, 1715.

Thomas, by Divine Providence Archbishop of Canterbury, to our beloved in Christ John Taylor of Highgate in co. Middlesex, gardener, greetings. Whereas before the worshipful man John Exton, LL.D., Surrogate of the excellent man Master Charles Hedges, Knight, also Doctor of Laws, Master Keeper or Commissary of our Prerogative Court of Canterbury, legally constituted, it was shown and alleged by Master Edward Gould, Knight, that a certain Benjamin Harrison of Ipswich in co. Suffolk, sailor, by a certain indenture dated on July 26, 1651, had given and demised to a certain William Cross of London, gentleman, all that the manor or capital messuage called Norwoods in Sproughton, co. Suffolk; and whereas also it was alleged that a certain indenture had been made on October 2, 1686, between the said William Burrough of Ipswich aforesaid, grocer, and Charles Burrough on the one part and Richard Milton of Ipswich aforesaid, gentleman, on the other part; and whereas also it was alleged that the said Richard Milton had died intestate in Ireland, no will have been made by him, and unmarried, having while he lived and at the time of his death goods, chattels, or debts in various dioceses or particular jurisdictions enough to establish the jurisdiction of our Prerogative Court of Canterbury aforesaid, and that no letters of administration had been given hitherto; and whereas the aforesaid surrogate, mature consideration having been taken of the preallegations to the petition of the said Master Edward Gould, has, as it is asserted, granted letters of administration of the goods, chattels, and credits of the said Richard Milton, deceased, as far and as long as they concern the said manor or messuage— To you, John Taylor, of whose fidelity in this respect we are confident from the first, we commit the power of well and faithfully administering the goods, chattels, and credits of the said Richard Milton, deceased, as long and as far as they concern the said manor, and of exhibiting a full and faithful inventory of the same; and we name, ordain, depute, and constitute you by these presents administrator of the goods, chattels, and credits of the said Richard Milton deceased as long and as far as they concern the said manor, but no farther or otherwise. Given at London on August 12, 1713, and in the ninth year of our translation.]

1715. SISTER'S GRANDSON THOMAS MOORE KNIGHTED.

Masson, VI, 774-775, based on Manning's *History and Antiquities of Surrey*, III, 229, and the Milton pedigree by Sir Charles Young, Garter King at Arms. Sir Thomas married Elizabeth Blunden of Basingstoke, who bore him two children; and he died in 1735. From them have descended, says Masson, a number of Moores, Fitzmoores, and Dashwoods. At least two of these are connected with portraits of Milton now extant and of considerable claim to genuine contemporaneity; see the section on portraits above.

**1716. DECEMBER 15. DAUGHTER DEBORAH'S SON CA-
LEB'S DAUGHTER MARY BURIED.**

Mary the Daughter of Caleb Clarke, Bur^d. Decr. 15th: by M^r. Stevenson.

[Marginal entry:] Clarke Deborah, third Daughter of Milton, the Poet, by his first Wife, was married to Abraham Clarke, weaver, in Spitalfields, by whom she had issue the above Caleb Clarke, Clerk of this Parish, Anno 1717, born unto him sons and daughters as certified in this Register.

From the parish registers of St. George's Cathedral, Madras; see note to entry of June 2, 1703. Though this date has usually been given previously as 1706, and though the year itself does not appear on my photographic reproduction, the Rev. R. L. Watson has verified carefully that the year is 1716 and not 1706. He has also supplied some of the words of the marginal entry which are missing in my reproduction.

**1719. ADDISON VISITS AND BEFRIENDS DAUGHTER
DEBORAH.**

... Mr. *Addison* ... upon hearing she [Milton's daughter Deborah] was living, sent for her, and desired, if she had any Papers of her Father's, she would bring them with her, as an Evidence of her being Mr. *Milton*'s Daughter. But immediately upon her being introduc'd to him, he said, *Madam, you need no other Voucher; your Face is a sufficient Testimonial whose Daughter you are.* And he then made her a handsome Present of a purse of Guineas, with a promise of procuring for her an annual Provision for her Life; but he dying soon after, she lost the Benefit of his generous Design.

From an account of Mr. [John] Ward's visit to Deborah "at the House of one of her Relations, not long before her Death," communicated to Thomas Birch, who published it in his introduction to Milton's *Complete Collection of the ... Works*, 1738, I, lxi-lxii; Masson, VI, 752. Since Addison died on June 17, 1719, and since he died "soon after" the visit, it must have taken place some time in the early months of that year. There may possibly be some connection between Addison's interest in Deborah and the fact that his elder brother, Galston Addison, was governor of Madras while her son Caleb and his family were there, and that Caleb's son Abraham "came to *England* with the late Governor *Harrison*" (which could be a misprint for "Addison"); Birch, p. lxi; Masson, VI, 758. George Vertue repeats some of the details of this visit in his letter of August 12, 1721, quoted below. Some references in Richardson may possibly apply to Addison's visit, though they might also, since they name no names, apply to others. Richardson speaks (p. xxxii; Darbishire, p. 225) of two of Milton's daughters, especially "One, She that dy'd a few Years Since, and was so much Spoke of, and Visited and So Nobly Reliev'd for His Sake." In another section he mentions (p. xcix; Darbishire, p. 279) "That Daughter, who a few years since was So much Visited and Reliev'd for her Father's Sake, and for the Share She had in Producing the *Paradise Lost*, Reading and Writing for him. . . ." Or Richardson may equally well have been thinking of Queen Caroline's bounty in 1727, *q.v.*

1719. GRANDDAUGHTER ELIZABETH CLARKE MARRIES THOMAS FOSTER.

. . . M^rs. Elizabeth Foster, Grand-daughter of John Milton . . . married to M^r. Foster in 1719.

From Thomas Birch's account of the burial service for Elizabeth Foster on May 14, 1754, *q.v.*

Elizabeth, the youngest Child of *Deborah*, married Mr. *Thomas Foster*, a Weaver, and lives now in *Pelham-street* in *Spittle-fields*. She has had seven Children, viz. three Sons and four Daughters, who are now all dead.

From John Ward's account of his visit to Elizabeth Foster on February 10, 1738, *q.v.*

1719. JANUARY 27. BROTHER CHRISTOPHER'S DAUGHTER ANNE'S HUSBAND JOHN PENDLEBURY MAKES WILL.

Jn the Name of God Amen the Seven and twentieth day of January . . . Annoqz Domini 1718 J John Pendlebury of the Parish of ffarningham in the County of Kent Clerk . . . do make and ordain this my last Will and Testament . . . Jtem J do give and bequeath unto my Sister in Law M^rs. Mary Milton the Suɱe of one hundred pounds . . . Jtem J do give and bequeath unto my Sister in law M^rs. Katherine Milton the like Suɱe of one hundred pounds . . . And J do make and ordain my said dear Wife Ann Pendlebury Executrix of this my last Will and Testament and J do hereby give and bequeath all my Estate real and personal whatsoever and wheresoever unto my said dear Wife . . . but in case my said Executrix shall depart this life before me then J do hereby make and ordain my two Nephews John Lees living near the Conduit in Manchester and Samuel Rhodes of Safford in the Parish of Manchester joint Executors . . . Jn witness whereof J the said John Pendlebury have hereunto set my hand and seal the day and Year first above written: Jo: Pendlebury Signed Sealed . . . in the presence of us and in his presence . . . John Sharp Nicho: Sharp Watt: Loveden.

Probatum fuit hujusmodi Testamentum apud London decimo quarto die Mensis Januarij Anno Domini Millesimo Septingentesimo decimo nono coram Venerabilo et egregio Viro Johanne Bettesworth . . . Juramento Annæ Pendlebury Viduæ et Relictæ dicti defuncti et Executricis in dicto Testamento nominat' Cui commissa fuit administratio omnium et singulorum bonorum jurium. . . .

Prerogative Court of Canterbury, 16 Shaller; Perceval Lucas in *Notes and Queries*, XI, vii (1913), 21-22. The testator mentions also his nephews Collins Pendlebury and Johnson Lees, his niece Elizabeth Lees, and his sister Tabitha Rhodes, as well as his maid Elizabeth Collins.

[A will of this sort was proved in London on the 14th day of January in the year of our Lord 1719 before the worshipful and excellent man John Bettesworth . . . on the oath of Anne Pendlebury, widow and relict of the said deceased and executrix named in the said will, to whom was committed administration of all and singular the goods, chattels. . . .]

1719. October 26. Daughter Deborah's son Caleb Clarke buried in Madras.

Caleb Clarke Parish Clark, Bur^d October 26th by Charles Long.

[Marginal entry:] Clarke

From the parish registers of St. George's Cathedral, Madras; see note to entry of June 2, 1703.

1719. DECEMBER 9-14. BROTHER CHRISTOPHER'S DAUGHTER ANN'S HUSBAND JOHN PENDLEBURY DIES AND IS BURIED.

Here lies ye Body of ye Rev^d. M^r. IOHN PENDLEBERRY; 35 years Vicar of Farmingham who departed this life ye 9th day of Dec: 1719. in ye 66th. year of his Age. And ANN his Wife who departed this life ye 20th day of Feb: 1720/21.

Inscription on the gravestone at Farmingham, Kent. Though in my comments I retain the spelling Pendlebury as used by Masson, Lucas, and others, the regular spelling in the records is Pendleberry. I am grateful to the Vicar of Farmingham for cooperating with University Microfilms in the making of this and other Milton family records in Farmingham.

Mr John Pendleberry late Vicar of this parish was buried Decr. ye 14th. 1719.

And an affidavit was brought—Decr. ye 19th. 1719.

Entry in the parish register of Farmingham, Kent; summarized by Perceval Lucas in *Notes and Queries*, XI, vii (1913), 21-22. Affidavits of burial, submitted shortly after the burials themselves, were a regular procedure at this time in this place.

1720. JANUARY 19. BROTHER CHRISTOPHER'S DAUGHTER ANNE MAKES WILL.

Jn the Name of God Amen. the Nineteenth Day of January Anno Dnī 1719. J Anne Pendleberry of ffarningham in the County of Kent Widow . . . Do make and ordain this my last Will and Testament . . . ffirst J do give and bequeath unto my true and faithfull Servant Elizabeth Collins (now living with me) the Sume of ffive pounds . . . Jtem J do give and bequeath unto the poor people of the parish of ffarningham aforesaid the Sume of ffive pounds . . . All the rest of my Goods . . . J do give and bequeath unto my two Sisters M^rs. Mary Milton and M^rs. Katherine Milton whom J do make joint Executrixes of this my last Will and Testament . . . Jn Witness whereof J have hereunto Sett my hand and Seal the Day and year ffirst above written (the mark of M^{rs}. Pendleberry the Testatrix) . . . in the presence of us who have Subscribed our Names as Witnesses in her presence and at her request—Edward Tilson Katherine Moyce her mark, Walt: Loveden./.

Probatum fuit hujusmodi Testamentum apud London Decimo quarto die Mensis Aprilis Anno Domini Millesimo Septingentesimo Vicesimo primo coram Venerabili et egregio viro Johanne Bettesworth Legum Doctore Curiæ Prærogativæ Cantuariensis Magistro Custode sive Commissario legitime constituto Juramentis Mariæ Milton et Catharinæ Milton Executricium in dicto Testamento nominatarum quibus commissa fuit Administratio omnium et singulorum bonorum jurium et creditorum dictæ defunctæ de bene et fideliter Administrando eadem ad Sancta Dei Evangelia (vigore Commissionis) Jurat'./ Ex^{d}.

Prerogative Court of Canterbury, 74 Buckingham; Perceval Lucas in *Notes and Queries*, XI, vii (1913), 21-22.

[A will of this sort was proved in London on the fourteenth day of the month of April in the year of our Lord 1721 before the worshipful and excellent man John Bettesworth, LL.D., legally constituted Master Keeper or Commissary of the Prerogative Court of Canterbury, on the oaths of Mary Milton and Catherine Milton, executrixes named in the said will, to whom was committed administration of all and singular the goods, chattels, and credits of the said deceased after they had been sworn (by force of a commission) on the Holy Gospels of God concerning well and faithfully administering the same. Exhibited.]

1720. OCTOBER 22. WIDOW MAKES AGREEMENT WITH JOHN DARLINGTON ABOUT RENTING FARM AT BRINDLEY.

Articles of agreement indented had made Covenanted and agreed vpon this two & twentieth day of October in the seventh

Year of the Reigne of our Soveraigne Lord George by the Grace of God of Great Brittain ffrance and Jreland King Defend^r. of the ffaith &c' Annoqz Dñi 1720 Between Elizabeth Milton of Namptwich in the County of Chester Widdow of the one part and John Darlington of Brindley in the said County of Chester Yeoman of the other part as follows.

Impr̄is The said Elizabeth Milton for and in Consideracōn of the yearly Rent and other the Covenants and agreem^{ts}. hereinafter mencōned and reserved hath Demised Granted sett & to ffarme Let vnto the said John Darlington All That Messuage or Tenement scituate lyeing and being in Brindley āfd now in the holding or occupacōn of John Tomkins his assigns or vndertennants . . . To have and to hold . . . paying vnto the said Elizabeth Milton her Exec̄^{rs} or ass̄^s the yearly rent or sum̄e of thirty pounds of Lawfull Brittish Money . . . Jn witness whereof the partyes above said to these presents their hands and Seals have herevnto interchangeably put the day and year first within written.

Sealed and Delivered but it's agreed before the sealing and delivery that the said Elizabeth Milton shall keep and maintaine the premisses in Tennantable reparacōn during this Demise and then sealed and delivered in p^rsence of

[Signed:] Eiza Milton [seal]

[Signed:] John Darlington [seal]

　　Abraham Done
　　Jn°. Hollins.

[Endorsed:] Articles inter Mrs Milton & John Darlington [brace] Dated 22th. octob. 1720.

From the original document in the Manuscript Room of the New York Public Library; Marsh, *Papers*, pp. 26-29 (in full); Masson, VI, 747 (summary). The document bears a one-penny tax stamp. I have omitted much of the wordiness and detail of the original, but nothing of importance to the ordinary reader. There is no visible l in Mrs. Milton's first name in her signature.

1721. FEBRUARY 20-24. BROTHER CHRISTOPHER'S DAUGHTER ANN PENDLEBURY DIES AND IS BURIED.

. . . ANN his Wife who departed this life yᵉ 20ᵗʰ day of Feb: 1720/21.

Part of the inscription on the gravestone of John and Ann Pendlebury at Farmingham, Kent; see above under date of December 9-14, 1719, for the complete text.

Burials. 1720. . . . Feb. . . . 24. Ann Pendleberry Widow of Mr. John Pendleberry late Vicar of Farmingham. Aff. March. 1.

From the parish register of Farmingham, Kent; summarized by Perceval Lucas in *Notes and Queries*, XI, vii (1913), 21-22. The year must be 1721 because this page, headed 1720, begins with entries for May and works through to December before coming to January and the present entry for February. Immediately after this entry comes the new year-heading, 1721, in which the first entry is for September 12. "Aff." refers to affidavit of burial, which was regularly submitted shortly after the date of the burial itself.

1721. AUGUST 12. GEORGE VERTUE DESCRIBES VISIT TO POET'S DAUGHTER DEBORAH.

Mʳ Christian

Pray inform my Lord Harley that I have on Thursday last seen the Daughter of Milton the Poet. I carry'd with me two or three different Prints of Miltons picture which she immediately knew to be like her father. & told me her mother in Law (if living in Cheshire) had two pictures of him, one when he was a School boy. & the other when about twenty. she knows of no other picture of him. because she was several years in Ireland. both before & after his Death. she was the youngest of Milton's daughters by his first Wife. and was taught to read to her father several languages.

Mʳ Addison was desirous to see her once. & desir'd she woud bring with her Testimonials of her being Miltons daughter. But as soon as she came into the Room. he told her she needed none. her face haveing much of the likeness of the pictures he had seen of him.

For my part I find the features of her Face very much like the Prints. I showd her the Painting I have to Engrave which she believes not to be her Fathers picture. it being of a Brown Complexion & black hair & Curled-locks. on the contrary he was of a fair complexion a little red in his cheeks & light brown lanck hair.

I desire you woud acquaint Mr Prior I was so unfortunate to wait on him on Thursday Morning last just after he was gone out of Town. it was with this intent. to Enquire of him. if he remembers a picture of Milton in the late Lord Dorsetts Collection. as I am told this was. or if he can inform me how I shall enquire or know the truth of this affair. I shou'd be much obliged to him. being very willing to have all the certainty on that account before I begin to Engrave the Plate. that it may be the more satisfactory to the Publick as well as to my self.

The sooner you can communicate this the better. because I have to resolve, which I can't well do, till I have an Answer
which will much Oblige
your Friend to Command

Saturday Aug. 12. 1721/   Geo: Vertue/

British Museum Harl. MS. 7003, f. 176; Marsh, pp. 137-138; Masson, 1 (1881), 309. British Museum Add. MS. 5,016*, f. 71, is Thomas Birch's copy of the original. If Vertue visited Deborah on the Thursday preceding the date of this letter, he must have gone on August 10. On the identity of the picture which Vertue showed to her the extract from Blackburne below sheds some light.

One Instance of her [Deborah's] Tender Remembrance of him I cannot forbear relating. the Picture in Crayons I have of him was shown her After several Others, or which were Pretended to be His; when Those were shown, and She was Ask'd if She could recollect if She had ever seen Such a Face. No, No. but when This was Produc'd, in a Transport,—'tis My Father, 'tis my Dear Father! I see him! 'tis Him! and then She put her Hands to several Parts of Her Face, 'tis the very Man! Here, Here—

[315]

Richardson, p. xxxvi; Darbishire, p. 229. Though neither the date nor the name of the visitor is given, it is a reasonable guess that this anecdote refers to the same visit. It has strong similarities to the next following passage.

. . . about the year 1725 Mr. George Vertue, a worthy and eminent British antiquary, went on purpose to see Mrs. Deborah Clarke, Milton's youngest and favorite daughter, and some time his amanuensis, who then lodged in a mean little street near Moorfields, where she kept a school for children for her support. He took this drawing [Cipriani's etching of the Faithorne crayon drawing] with him, and divers paintings said to be of Milton, all which were brought into the room by his contrivance, as if by accident, whilst he conversed with her. She took no notice of the paintings; but when she perceived the drawing she cried out, 'O Lord! that is the picture of my father—how came you by it?' And, stroaking the hair of her forehead, added 'Just so my father wore his hair.' This daughter resembled Milton greatly.

Francis Blackburne, *Memoirs of Thomas Hollis*, 1780, pp. 619-620, as quoted in Marsh, pp. 138-139; Masson, VI, 755-756. In spite of the date 1725, this description may very likely refer to the same visit of 1721, since the 1725 is only a guess. The copy of Vertue's letter which Hollis got from the British Museum in 1761 and which Blackburne printed on pp. 113-114, was dated August 12, 172 , with the last digit of the year blank. He and Blackburne speculated whether it should be 1721, 1725, or 1729. The date 1725 in the text here is therefore probably only a wrong guess.

1724. MARCH 16. BROTHER CHRISTOPHER'S DAUGHTER-IN-LAW MARTHA'S SECOND HUSBAND DR. WILLIAM COWARD MAKES WILL.

Jn the Name of God Amen I William Coward of Ipswich in the County of Suffolk Doctor of Physick Do make & ordain this my last will & testament . . . [leaves main part of estate to executor William Ingham] (my Linnen & wearing apparrell excepted which I give to my Loveing wife Martha) my Personall Estate Subject nevertheless to the payment of twenty

pounds to my Said wife for mourning & also for the payment of
fourscore pounds a year to my Said wife without any Deduc-
cōns whatsoever during the term of her natural Life . . . In
Wittness whereof I the said William Coward have here unto
Sett my hand & Seal the Sixteenth day of March Anno Domini
One thousand Seven hundred & twenty Three./

William Coward./ . . .

Probat' apud Yoxford 20ᵐᵒ. die Aprilis 1724. . . .

From the original in the Ipswich and East Suffolk Record Office,
Ipswich, Archdeaconry of Suffolk, Beccles Register 1723-27, folio 3;
mentioned but not located by Perceval Lucas in *Notes and Queries*,
XI, vii (1913), 113. I am deeply indebted to Mr. G. M. T. Kirk-
wood of the Literary Department of the Principal Probate Registry
and to Mr. D. Charman, Archivist of the East Suffolk County Council, for their aid in helping me to find this document. Dr. Coward evidently died some time between March 16, the date of the will, and
April 20, the date of the probate.

[Proved at Yoxford (in Suffolk) April 20, 1724.]

1725. JUNE 16. WIDOW MAKES NEW AGREEMENT WITH JOHN DARLINGTON.

This Indenture made the Sixteenth Day of June in the Eleventh Year of the Reign of our Soveraigne Lord George by
the Grace of God of Great Brittain ffrance and Ireland, King
Defendᵉʳ of the ffaith &ct'. Annoqz Doṁ: 1725. Between John
Darlington of Brindley in the County Chester Yeoman of the
one parte and Elizabeth Milton of Namptwich Widdow of the
other parte Witnesseth that whereas the Rᵗ Honourable Lyo-
nell Earl Dysart of Helmingham in the County Suffolk and
the Rᵗ Honōble Grace Countess of Dysart by their Indenture
of Lease bearing date on or about the Tenth Day of May last
past Anno Doṁ: 1725 for the Consideration therein expressed
Did demise grant set and to ffarme lett unto the said John
Darlington All that Messuage or Tenement with the Appur-
tānces in Brindley in the said County of Chester now in the
possession of the said John Darlington . . . untill the full end
and term of the natural Lives of the aforesᵈ. Elizabeth Milton

and John and Abraham Darlington Sons of the s^d John Darlington . . . paying therefore Yearly . . . Twenty and Six Shillings of Lawfull Brittish Money . . . Now This Indenture Witnesseth, That the said John Darlington for and in Consideration
of the Surrend^{er} of a former Lease of the p^{r}misses before men-
c̄oned made to the s^d Elizabeth Milton . . . Hath granted bar-
gined sold . . . unto the said Elizabeth Milton all the Estate
right title Intrest property claime and demand whatsoever
which he the s^d John Darlington now hath or may might or
ought to have claime or demand off in or to the before men-
c̄oned p^{r}misses . . . To have and to hold . . . dureing her Natural Life . . . In Witness whereof I have hereunto put my hand
& Seal the day and year first above written.

    Sealed and delivered (the
       Stamps first observed)   John Darlington [seal]
      In the presence of: J
    Abraham Done   his   mark
    Sam̄^{l} Acton

From the original document in the Manuscript Room of the New
York Public Library; Marsh, *Papers*, pp. 29-32 (in full); Masson,
VI, 747 (summary). I have omitted as much as possible of the text without losing anything important to the meaning. A considerable section
is given to agreements about taking care of the land and the like. It
may be noted that though Darlington merely made his mark without
signing, he did sign in full the previous agreement of October 22, 1720.
Marsh points out that Grace, Countess of Dysart, was the daughter of
Sir Thomas Wilbraham, who appears in the bond of June 4, 1680,
above, as the recipient of Brindley property from Richard Minshull;
and that on her marriage to the Earl of Dysart the Brindley estate
passed into his family.

1725. SEPTEMBER 22. DAUGHTER DEBORAH'S SON CA-LEB'S SON ABRAHAM MARRIED.

    Abraham Clark and Anna Clark Married by Thomas Wen-
dey.

    [Marginal entry:] Sepr. 22^d Clark

From the parish registers of St. George's Cathedral, Madras; see
note to entry of June 2, 1703.

1727. QUEEN CAROLINE SENDS POET'S DAUGHTER DEB-
ORAH FIFTY POUNDS.

. . . her late Majesty Queen *Caroline* sent his Daughter, Mrs.
Clarke, fifty Pounds: and that she receiv'd several presents of
Money from other Gentlemen.

From Thomas Birch's account of his visit to Elizabeth Foster on
February 11, 1738, *q.v.* The date is uncertain. But if we could assume
that the queen's generosity was the result of the appeal in *Mist's Weekly Journal* for April 29, 1727, it would have to be between that date
and August 24 of the same year, when Deborah died. It may perhaps
have been this occasion rather than that of Addison's visit (see above
under date of before 1719) that Richardson had in mind in speaking
of Deborah's being "so Nobly Reliev'd."

She received presents likewise from several other gentlemen
[in addition to Addison], and Queen Caroline sent her fifty
pounds by the hands of Dr. Freind the physician.

Milton, *Paradise Lost*, ed. Newton, 1 (1749), lviii. Dr. Freind is
presumably John Freind (1675-1728), physician to Queen Caroline
in 1727 (*DNB*).

1727. APRIL 5. DAUGHTER DEBORAH'S SON CALEB'S
SON ABRAHAM'S DAUGHTER MARY BAPTIZED.

Mary Daughter of Abraham & Ann Clark, Baptiz'd by W
Leeke, Isaac George Godf^r. Rozaling George and Rozaling Lucy
Sequara Godm^rs.

[Marginal entry:] 1727 April 5 Clark

From the parish registers of St. George's Cathedral, Madras; see
note to entry of June 2, 1703.

1727. APRIL 29. PUBLIC APPEAL MADE FOR AID TO
MILTON'S DAUGHTER.

I wish heartily this fine Encomium of *Charity*, left by *Milton* [the writer has quoted *Paradise Lost*, XII, 581-587], may
prove the *Specifick*, to give Bread to his *only Daughter*, who
bows beneath the double Oppression of *Age* and *Penury*. It is
very hard that the Daughter of such a Man, who has left us a
Poem that is the Boast and Glory of our *English* Poetry, should

now be running the Course of her *seventy fifth* Year, supported only by the precarious Gifts of Providence, and the *Piety* of her Daughter, whose Husband is in no higher a Rank than that of a *Journeyman-Weaver*. . . .

I am excited to this Concern for her, by the Impressions of a late Visit made her, and a Detail of the several Disappointments she has undergone in Life, deliver'd from her own Mouth. I could not hear that a Daughter of *Milton* was still living, without a Curiosity of seeing her, and making some Enquiries about her Father. I was not, indeed, without some Doubts before I went, that she might have usurp'd the Title of such a Descent; but the Traces of her Father's Features appear so strong thro' her venerable Age, that they immediately silence all Doubts. The Resemblance strikes you with that Force, that I dare engage, any one who looks on the Print of *Milton* in *Mezzo tinto*, and then would go to see his Daughter, should be able to pick her out from amidst an hundred other Women of equal Age, and equally Strangers.

I could not help being touch'd at hearing, that as her Father was at one Time obliged to instruct young Gentlemen in the Learned Tongues; so she has been reduced to the Necessity, towards Part of a slender Support, to teach poor Infants the first Elements of Reading: A Fatigue, and an Assistance, that the Failure of Eyes and Strength has now robb'd her of!

. . . I would be loth to prescribe Limits to Generosity; but the Expence of a single *Masquerade* or *Opera Ticket*, retrench'd; nay, even the Price of a *Pantomime* and *Ropedancing* spared, by the gay Part of this Town, and applied to her Relief, would both set her at Ease and provide for her Funeral. I shall hope, that industrious and thriving *Bookseller*, who has got so many Thousand Pounds by the Copy of *Paradise lost*, will not be behind hand in his Contribution: 'Twill be but a bad Excuse for him to say, That it was her Father, not she, who wrote that admirable Poem. . . .

The Patrons of her distress'd Age, who will not think much of such a Labour, will find her by enquiring for Mrs. *Clark*, that being her Name of Widowhood, at Mr. *Foster*'s next Door to the *Blue-Ball* in *Pelham*-Street, *Spittlefields*.

I am, Sir, Your humble Servant,
PHILALETHES.

From *Mist's Weekly Journal*, No. 106, April 29, 1727, first page; Masson, VI, 754. "Philalethes" may be any one of a number of people, including Birch, Ward, and various others. If we may assume that Queen Caroline's gift was at least in part the result of this appeal, and that Voltaire was describing the general reaction to it, the response must have been excellent. Voltaire (as quoted in Masson, VI, 752) says: "I was in London when it became known that a daughter of blind Milton was still alive, old and in poverty, and in a quarter of an hour she was rich." In just about four months from the present date, Deborah was to die; see below under date of August 24, 1727.

1727. JUNE. DAUGHTER DEBORAH PRESENTS COPY OF *PARADISE LOST* TO FRIEND ELIZABETH LORD.

[(1) On flyleaf facing title page, in eighteenth-century (?) hand:] This Book was a presentation Copy from M^rs. Clarke, Miltons Daughter, who was his amanuensis to whom he dictated the Poem—Mrs. Clark presented it to her dear friend Miss Elizabeth Lord afterwards M^rs. Welwood—The presentation note was in M^rs. Clarke's hand writing (the same as the manuscript on the back of The Title page.) & it stated the Poem to be the Work of her dear father John Milton, the only one then in her possession, apologizing for her scribling on it, & she said she was the faithful scribe to whom he dictated the Poem after he had lost his sight—The Bookbinder has destroyed the Manuscript Note in binding the Book. it was dated Iune 1727.

C C.

[Along the margin of this page:] M^rs. Clarke died in August 1727—See Newtons Life of Milton. 4 Vols 8vo. London 1754.

[(2) Scattered notes on the title page:] Dear Mrs Lord Sighing on the plain I am plain oer' hills and

if you Will beleive me Tis not Sighing on the plain Songs nor' Son Sonnets cant relieue ye

Could j express [deleted]

This is the first Edition the Poem was not finished until 1668
—the 5 first Books were first published in 1667—

Eliza. Welwoold Her Book 1706

[(3) At the bottom of the last page of the poem:] the Mind
is its own place. [repeated along the margin]

Elizabeth Wellwood her Book Given her by Mrs Lord Milton Milton 1711

From annotations written on a copy of the 1669 title page edition
of *Paradise Lost* now in the Library of the Packer Collegiate Institute
in Brooklyn, New York. I wish to thank the Librarian, Miss Grace H.
Hilderbrand, for her kindness in arranging to supply me with photostatic copies of the title page, the flyleaf facing it, and the back page;
and Professor Thomas O. Mabbott for first calling my attention to
the location of this volume at the Institute. It is mentioned in Living-
ston's *Auction Prices of Books*, III, 225, and in *Book Prices Current*,
IV (1891), 448. The rambling notes quoted above, in addition to a
few others not worth mentioning, are scrawled in several handwritings
over the title page and elsewhere, except that the first paragraph quoted
is written in a businesslike hand. I cannot identify the "C. C." at the
end of this note.

1727. BEFORE AUGUST. WIDOW TELLS VISITORS ABOUT POET'S LIFE, FAMILY, AND CAREER.

[The poet's widow] died very old, about twenty years ago,
at Nantwich in Cheshire: and from the accounts of those who
had seen her, I have learned, that she confirmed several things
which have been related before; and particularly that her husband used to compose his poetry chiefly in winter, and on his
waking in a morning would make her write down sometimes
twenty or thirty verses: and being asked whether he did not
often read Homer and Virgil, she understood it as an imputation upon him for stealing from those authors, and answered
with eagerness that he stole from no body but the Muse who
inspired him; and being asked by a lady present who the Muse
was, replied it was God's grace, and the Holy Spirit that visited him nightly. She was likewise asked whom he approved
most of our English poets, and answered Spenser, Shakespear,

and Cowley: and being asked what he thought of Dryden, she said Dryden used sometimes to visit him, but he thought him no poet, but a good rimist: but this was before Dryden had composed his best poems, which made his name so famous afterwards. She was wont moreover to say, that her husband was applied to by message from the King, and invited to write for the Court, but his answer was, that such a behaviour would be very inconsistent with his former conduct, for he had never yet employed his pen against his conscience. By his first wife he had four children, a son who died an infant, and three daughters who survived him; by his second wife he had only one daughter, who died soon after her mother, who died in childbed; and by his last wife he had no children at all. His daughters were not sent to school, but were instructed by a mistress kept at home for that purpose: and he himself, excusing the eldest on account of an impediment in her speech, taught the two others to read and pronounce Greek and Latin and several other languages, without understanding any but English, for he used to say that one tongue was enough for a woman: but this employment was very irksome to them, and this together with the sharpness and severity of their mother in law made them very uneasy at home; and therefore they were all sent abroad to learn things more proper for them, and particularly imbroidery in gold and silver. As Milton at his death left his affairs very much in the power of his widow, tho' she acknowledged that he died worth one thousand five hundred pounds, yet she allowed but one hundred pounds to each of his three daughters. Anne the eldest was decrepit and deformed, but had a very handsome face; she married a master-builder, and died in childbed of her first child, who died with her. Mary the second lived and died single. Deborah the youngest in her father's life time went over to Ireland with a lady, and afterwards was married to Mr. Abraham Clarke, a weaver in Spittle Fields, and died in August 1727 in the 76th year of her age. She is said to have been a woman of good understanding and genteel behaviour, though in low circumstances. As she had been often called upon to read Homer and Ovid's Metamorphosis to her father, she could have repeated a considerable number of verses from the beginning of both those poets, as Mr. Ward, Professor of Rhetoric in Gresham College, relates upon his own knowledge: and another Gentleman has informed me, that he has heard her repeat several verses likewise out of Euripides. Mr. Addison, and the other gentlemen, who had opportunities of seeing her, knew her immediately to be Milton's daughter by the similitude of her countenance to her father's picture: and Mr. Addison made her a handsome present of a purse of guineas with a promise of procuring for her some annual provision for her life; but his death happening soon after, she lost the benefit of his generous design. She received presents likewise from several other gentlemen, and Queen Caroline sent her fifty pounds by the hands of Dr. Freind the physician. She had ten children, seven sons and three daughters; but none of them had any children, except one of her sons named Caleb, and one of her daughters named Elizabeth. Caleb went to Fort St. George in the East Indies, where he married, and had two sons, Abraham and Isaac; the elder of whom came to England with the late governor Harrison, but returned upon advice of his father's death, and whether he or his brother be now living is uncertain. Elizabeth, the youngest child of Mrs. Clarke, was married to Mr. Thomas Foster a weaver in Spittle Fields, and had seven children who are all dead; and she herself is aged about sixty, and weak and infirm.

Milton, *Paradise Lost*, ed. Thomas Newton, 1749, I, lvi-lviii; Masson, VI, 745-747 and *passim*. It is not quite clear whether Newton intends all this passage to belong together under his introductory phrase of "the accounts of those who had seen her" or not. It may be that that section ends with the sentence ending "his pen against his conscience." In either case, Newton for the most part repeats what we have already available from Birch and others. This account cannot be exactly dated because it is a combination of a number of different visits; the best we can do is therefore to date it before Mrs. Milton's death in 1727.

1727. AUGUST 22. WIDOW MAKES HER WILL.

Jn the Name of God Amen J Elizabeth Milton of Namptwich in the County of Chester Widdow being Weak in Body but of a good and sound Memory and Understanding Do make and Ordain this my last Will and Testament in Maner and fform ffollowing. That is to say. ffirst and Principally J Comend my [Body, *deleted*] Soul into the hands of Almighty God my maker, relying wholy on his grace for Salvation through the Merrits & Mediation of Jesus Christ my Saviour, And my Body to be decently Buryed att the Discretion of my herein after Named Executors And my Worldly goods J leave as ffolloweth.

And ffirst my Will is, That all my Just Debts Owing by me be punctualy paid and discharged by my Executors as also my ffuneral Expences which being done in the first place. Then as to the remainder and Overpluss of my Effects J give and Bequeath to my Nephews and Neices in Namptwich equaly to be devided amongst them. And hereby J revoke Añull and make voyd all former Wills by me made, And do make [and, *deleted*] Constitute and Appoint my loving ffreinds Samuel Acton, and John Allecock both of Namptwich Aforesaid my Executors of this my last Will and Testament Jn Wittness whereof J have hereunto put my hand and Seal this Twenty Second of August in the ffirst year of the Reign of our Soveraign Lord George the Second by the grace of God of Great Brittain ffrance and Jreland King And in the year of our Lord God 1727.

Signed Sealed and Delivered by   [signed] Elizabeth Millton.
the said Testator Elizabeth Milton   [seal]
who declared this to be and Contain
her last Will and Testament in presence
of us, who Subscrib'd our Names in the Sight
and Presence of the said Testator as Wittnesses
Richard Cooke
Uriah Rowley
Joseph Tomkins

10.° Oct' 1727.

Joēs Allecock unus Ēxtorm̄ in hum̄oj Testmō
noiātor' fidem fecit de bene &c.   pote
Samueli Acton alteri Ēxtori reservatâ.

coram Me   P. Gastrell

From the original document in the Cheshire Record Office in Chester; printed in Marsh's *Papers*, pp. 33-34; mentioned in Masson, VI, 747. There are certified copies in Joseph Hunter's collection in British Museum Add. MS. 24,501, f. 51, and in the Manuscript Room of the New York Public Library. I am grateful to Major F. G. C. Rowe, County Archivist of Cheshire, for his kindness in providing me with photostatic copies of Elizabeth Milton's will and the later inventory of it. Though Marsh's reading is essentially sound, he paid little attention to spelling according to the original manuscript, and for some reason he failed to read a few easily legible words. He also omitted the note at the end about the probate. He also abbreviated Mrs. Milton's signature, which actually appears in full as above, and in a most painful scrawl comprising a number of false starts for letters. The writing is so unlike that of her signatures of 1680 and 1681 that one suspects she was almost at the point of death when writing. The actual date of her death is unknown, though the heading of the inventory shows that it must have been before August 26, 1727.

There has been some question about a funeral sermon said to have been preached at the funeral of Mrs. Milton. In Isaac Kimber's *Sermons*, published in 1756, is one by Samuel Acton, one of the executors named here, on a Mrs. Milton, dated March 10, 1726. But even if we interpret 1726 as 1726/7, this date is far too early, since the will proves the widow of the poet to have been alive in August. And there is nothing in the sermon itself to identify the person about whom it was preached, so that it could be about almost anybody. On the other hand, in a book published some thirty years after the event the date might easily have been in error; and the fact that Acton was one of her executors gives additional reason for identifying the subject of the sermon with the poet's widow. On this matter see James Reed in the *Athenaeum*, 1849, p. 1046; J. F. Marsh, *ibid.*, p. 1065; Marsh's *Papers*, pp. 33-34; and Masson, VI, 747.

[October 10, 1727. John Allecock, one of the executors named in a will of this sort, gave his word about well etc., with power reserved to Samuel Acton, the other executor. Before me, P. Gastrell.]

[326]

1727. ABOUT AUGUST 23. WIDOW DIES.

A True and Perfect Inventory of of yᵉ Goods & Chattels of late Mʳˢ Eliz Miltton . . . this twenty sixth day of August 1727.

From the heading to the inventory of Elizabeth Milton's goods dated August 26, 1727, *q.v.* Since she was alive to sign her will on August 22 (*q.v.*), and is called the "late" Mrs. Milton on August 26, she must have died between those two dates. The 23rd is merely a chance selection of one.

Though the details of Mrs. Milton's death and burial are not known, Joseph Hunter said in 1857 (*Archaeological Journal*, XIV, 1857, 91) that the general tradition in Nantwich was that she was buried in the ground adjoining the chapel of the Anabaptists in Barker Street.

1727. BEFORE AUGUST 24. JOHN WARD VISITS DAUGH-TER DEBORAH.

Deborah [Clarke] . . . gave Dr. Ward, Professor of Rhetoric at Gresham-College, who saw her not long before her death, at the house of her relations, the following account, which he communicated to me, Feb. 10. 1737-8. "She informed me, that she and her sisters used to read to their father in eight languages; which by practice they were capable of doing with great readiness and accuracy, though they understood what they read in no other language but English; and their father used often to say in their hearing, 'one tongue was enough for a woman.' None of them were ever sent to school, but all taught at home by a mistress kept for that purpose. Isaiah, Homer, and Ovid's metamorphoses were books, which they were often called to read to their father; and at my desire she repeated a considerable number of verses from the beginning of both these poets with great readiness. I knew who she was, upon the first sight of her, by the similitude of her countenance with her father's picture. And upon my telling her so, she informed me, that Mr. Addison told her the same thing, upon her going to wait on him. For he, upon hearing she was living, sent for her, and desired, if she had any papers of her father's she would bring them with her, as an evidence of her being Mr. Milton's daughter. But immediately upon her being introduced to him, he said, 'Ma-

dam, you need no other voucher; your face is a sufficient testimonial whose daughter you are.' And he then made her a handsome present of a purse of guineas, with a promise of procuring
her an annual provision for her life; but he dying soon after,
she lost the benefit of his generous design. She appeared to be a
woman of good sense and a genteel behaviour, and to bear the
inconveniences of a low fortune with decency and prudence."

Thomas Birch, prefatory account to *The Works of John Milton*,
London, 1753, I, lxxvi; repeated with no substantial change from the
1738 edition of *A Complete Collection*, I, lxi-lxii; Masson, VI, 752-
754. The date must have been before August 24, 1727 (*q.v.*), when
Deborah died. For an account of Ward's visit to Deborah's daughter
Elizabeth Foster see below under date of February 10, 1738.

1727. AUGUST 24. DAUGHTER DEBORAH DIES.

Deborah . . . died *August* 24th, 1727, in the 76th year of
her age.

From John Ward's account of his visit to Elizabeth Foster on February 10, 1738, *q.v.*

. . . Deborah . . . was married to Mr. Abraham Clarke, a
Weaver in Spital-fields, and died August 24, 1727, in the 76th
year of her Age.

Milton, *Works*, ed. Birch, 1753, I, lxxvi.

1727. AUGUST 26. WIDOW'S ESTATE INVENTORIED.

A True and Perfect Inventory of of [sic] yᵉ Goods & Chattels
of late Mʳˢ Eliz. Miltton Appraisd by us whose Names are
Under Named this twenty sixth day of August 1727.

A pair Bedsteds & hangings ——————————	0. 18. 0
One feat^r bed & Boulster ————————— weigh'd 94ˡⁱ at 6ᵈ p ˡⁱ ———————————	2. 7. 0
2 Quilts & pair Blanketts ———————— old Patched Ones ———————————————	0. 10. 0
2 Teaspoons & 1 Silvʳ Spoon wᵗʰ a ————— Seal & stopper & bitts of Silver at ————— 5s p ˡⁱ. wᵈ 2 ˡⁱ ½ ——————————	0. 12. 6

1 Pencill Case	o.	3. 0
a Coffee; Copper Pott	o.	3. 0
1 Large Bible	o.	8. 0
2 Books of Parradice	o.	10. 0
Some Old Books & few Old Pictures	o.	12. 0
Mr Miltons Pictures & Coat of Arms	10.	10. 0
1 Tin Coffee Pott	o.	0. 8
A Totershell Knife & ffork		
wth other odd ones	o.	1. 0
tobbacoe Box	o.	0. 6
a old Blew shagg Coat	o.	01. 0
ye Best Shute head Cloathes	o.	3. 0
ye Worser Ditto	o.	1. 6
2 Pair Ruffles	o.	2. 0
2 Pair Spectables	o.	1. 6
In Money	o.	17. 0

31.   8. 4

John Wright
John Allecock

From the original document in the Cheshire Record Office at Chester; printed by John F. Marsh in *Transactions of the Historic Society of Lancashire and Cheshire*, VII (1855), 29*-31*. There are certified copies in Hunter's collection, British Museum Add. MS. 24,501, ff. 52-53, and in the New York Public Library Manuscript Room. Masson summarizes it at VI, 747-749. I have given here only a few out of the total of 108 items in the list, choosing those which may have had some direct relation to Milton himself or which give some indication of the way of life of Mrs. Milton. Though it is a temptation to include the whole list, it is too long. On the basis of this document, and with the aid of what he called "practised feminine judgment," Masson deduced that she lived in an apartment of one chamber and a scullery, uncarpeted but of ample size, and that her interests ran rather to cooking than to sewing. Some of the articles named above (such as the pictures, the coffee-pot, the knife and fork, and the tobacco box) survived for a long time and have been mentioned above in the section concerning "relics."

I am grateful to Major F. G. C. Rowe, County Archivist of Cheshire, for his kindness in providing me with photostatic copies of this document. Marsh's transcript needs a few corrections. Aside from trivial switches from "a" to "one," "the" to "y^e," and the like and vice versa, he made a number of omissions, copied some words and numbers incorrectly, and changed some words entirely. For example, in the selection above, Marsh omitted everything after "silver" in the fourth item about spoons and seal. He changed the value of a hair trunk from 5s. to 8s., that of two dale boxes from 2s. 6d. to 2s., and that of an old muff and case from 2s. to 4d. He reduced three dozen of glass bottles to two, created "petticoat" out of "coat" to accompany a Norwich gown, and altered Callamancoe to Calmianco for one of the widow's gowns. By leaving out the word "rod" he made the item of a window rod and ragged curtains rather meaningless. Worst of all, perhaps, he somehow altered the total value from the original £31. 8. 4 to £38. 8. 4. How he got "twad" out of "head" in "ye Best Shute head Cloathes" I cannot understand, nor can I understand the original term. Perhaps Marsh, at a loss in the same way, substituted "twad" (a queer form of "tweed"?) as something that might possibly make sense. At any rate, the readings given above are those of the original manuscript.

1727. OCTOBER 10. PROBATE OF WIDOW'S WILL.

TENORE *Præsentium Nos* Peregrinus Gastrell Arm^s̄ Legumq Baccalaureus *Reverendi in Christo Patris & Domini Domini* Samuelis *permissione divina* Cestriensis *Episcopi Vicarius in Spiritualibus Generalis & Officialis, principalis,* Necnon Decanus Ruralis Decanatus Ruralis de Namptwich Diœcñ Cestrien' *legitime fulcitus,* Notum *facimus quod hujusmodi Testamentum* Elizabethe Milton nuper de Namptwich in Cõm Cestriæ et Decanatu prædicto viduæ *defunctæ* Probatum *approbatum & insinuatum ac pro viribus & valore ejusdem pronunciatum fuit* Decimo *Die Mensis* Octobris *Anno Domini Millesimo Septingentesimo vicesimo* septimo, *ac Commissa fuit & est Executio dicti Testamenti juxta Tenorem & effectum ejusdem, ac Administratio Omnium & Singulorum Bonorum, Jurium Creditorum & Chattallorum ipsius defunctæ* (modo Inventario vero et pleno Eorundem confecto ad sum̄ quadraginta Librarum se non extendunt) Ioanni Allecock uni *Executorum in eodem Nominat'* (*primitus in debita Juris forma Jurat*) potestate Samueli Acton alteri Extōri Omnis Executionis hum̄oj Testm̄i in se acceptandi, cùm venerit idem petiturus reservatâ, Salvo jure cujuscunq, Dat' sub Sigillo (quo in hâc parte utimur) die Mensis Annoqz Dom p'dictis./

[stamp with crown and   [signed] Edvūs Roberts
letters I D]   Not' Pub^cus./

From the original in the Manuscript Room of the New York Public Library; Marsh, *Papers*, p. 34. Marsh has an additional signature at the end of which I can find no trace on my photostatic copy: "PER. [seal missing] GASTRELL." This document is partly printed and partly filled in by hand. With a few exceptions all the words given above in roman type are handwritten; this includes also the inflectional endings of words like "*defunctæ*" and "*Execut*orum," which of course had to be left open for masculine or feminine endings, singular or plural. The exceptions, which are printed in roman, are "TENORE," "Cestriensis," "Notum," and "Probatum." It seems odd that, with a careful inventory of the widow's effects already made about a month and a half previously (August 26), this document should speak as if it were yet to be completed. It is also odd that, with the inventory already totaling £31-8-4, the present document should specify that the total should not exceed £40. See also the entry about probate on the will itself above.

[By a copy of these presents we, Peregrine Gastrell, gentleman and bachelor of laws, principal general and official vicar in spiritual matters of the Reverend Father in Christ and lord the Lord Samuel, by divine permission Bishop of Chester, and legally appointed rural Dean of the rural deanery of Namptwich in the diocese of Chester, certify that a will of this sort, of Elizabeth Milton, widow, deceased, late of Namptwich in the County of Chester in the aforesaid deanery, was proved, approved, and entered, and that by virtue of the soundness and effectiveness of the same it was published on the tenth day of the month of October in the year of our Lord 1727; and execution of the said will according to the sense and meaning of the same, and administration of all and singular goods, rights, debts, and chattels of the said deceased (provided that by a true and full inventory of the same when completed they do not extend themselves to the sum of forty pounds) has been and is committed to John Allcock, one of the executors named in the same (he having first been sworn by due form of oath), with power reserved to Samuel Acton, another executor of the whole execution of a will of this sort, to be taken upon himself when the same shall come to seek it, and with the right of each person safe. Given under seal (which we use in this part) on the day of the month and the year of our Lord aforesaid.

Edward Roberts,
Notary Public.]

1729. OCTOBER 4. DAUGHTER DEBORAH'S SON CALEB'S SON ABRAHAM'S DAUGHTER MARY BURIED (?).

Mary Clark, Buried October the 4ᵗʰ. by Mʳ. Consett.

[Marginal entry:] Clark

From the parish registers of St. George's Cathedral, Madras; see note to entry of June 2, 1703. Since Mary Clark's parents are not named, it is not certain that she is of Milton's family. But she could very well be the Mary Clark whose baptism appears above under date of April 5, 1727.

1734. JONATHAN RICHARDSON PUBLISHES HIS LIFE OF MILTON.

Explanatory Notes and Remarks on Milton's Paradise Lost. By J. Richardson, Father and Son. With the Life of the Author, and a Discourse on the Poem. By J. R. Sen. London: Printed for James, John, and Paul Knapton, at the Crown in Ludgate-street, near the West-End of St. Paul's. M.DCC.XXXIV.

Title page of the first edition; reproduced in facsimile in Darbishire, p. 199; text in Darbishire, pp. 201-330.

I have finished my Lucubrations, my daily, early, pleasing task. . . . That book [by Milton] has from my youth made a considerable part of the happiness of my Life. . . . I accidentally took up the book when I was a youngster at Mr. *Riley*'s; 'twas his book. I have it still. I had never heard of *Milton*, but thenceforward neglected my favourite *Cowley* and all the rest. . . . I became a hearty Miltonian, and always shall be so, I believe. . . .

From a letter of Jonathan Richardson to Ralph Palmer dated May

3, 1732, as printed in the Sixth Report of the Historical Manuscripts Commission, Appendix, 1877 (papers of Sir Henry Ingilby, Bart., Ripley Castle, York), p. 395.

1737. MONUMENT BY RYSBRACK ERECTED IN WESTMINSTER ABBEY.

In the year of Our Lord Christ One thousand seven hundred thirty and seven This Bust of the Author of PARADISE LOST was placed here by William Benson Esquire One of the two Auditors of the Imprests to his Majesty King George the second formerly Surveyor General of the Works to his Majesty King George the first. *Rysbrack* was the Statuary who cut it.

Inscription on the monument to Milton in Westminster Abbey; Marsh, p. 172. John Michael Rysbrack (1693?-1770) was, according to the *DNB*, a foreign-born sculptor who came to England in 1720 and who placed many statues in Westminster Abbey. William Benson (1682-1754) was a critic and politician who generously patronized literature, and whose gift of the statue of Milton is memorialized in the *DNB*. In Milton's *Complete Collection of the . . . Works*, ed. Thomas Birch, 1738, I, lxiii, Birch mentions this statue as a monument which "is expected to be erected to our Author's Memory in *Westminster-Abbey.*" Newton speaks of it in his edition of *Paradise Lost*, I (1749), xlvi.

[Among moneys received and paid for monuments in the Abbey is the item:] John Milton ....21.0.0.

From the "Account of Dr Alured Clarke Treasurer of Collegiate Church of St Peter, Westminster, 1738," in Westminster Abbey Muniment 33,770.

E MARMORE IN ECCLESIA SANCTI PETRI APUD WESTMONAS-TERIUM ERECTORE GULIELMO BENSONO ARM. ANNO SALUTIS HU-MANÆ M DCC XXXVII. RYSBRACHIUS SCULPSIT.

Inscription on the reverse of a medal taken from the bust in Westminster Abbey, of which medal a copy is in my possession; see also Edward Hawkins, Augustus W. Franks, and Herbert A. Grueber, *Medallic Illustrations of the History of Great Britain and Ireland*, London, 1885, Vol. II, no. 524. The compilers of this volume state that Benson employed Rysbrach to erect this monument to the memory of Milton, that he engaged John Sigismund Tanner to engrave the medal, that he presented a copy on December 9, 1738, the anniversary of Milton's birthday, to the author of the best poem in praise of *Paradise Lost*, and that the likeness on the monument was based partly on the bust in the possession of Thomas Hollis and partly on a drawing by Faithorne. They also state (no. 525) that Hollis had one of these medals altered. The originals, in addition to the representation of Milton on the obverse, with the legend "IOHANNES. MILTONUS." surrounding it and "TANNER. F[ecit]." on the truncation, has the above-quoted legend on the reverse. Hollis had both legends erased on a turning-lathe and new engravings substituted. For the name on the front he substituted IOHN MILTON; for that on the back he substituted his favorite symbol, "an owl with expanded wings standing upon a palm branch, and his motto, BY. DEEDS. OF. PEACE." They consider this latter state of the medal unique, the former one rare.

A monument erected in 1737, to our author's memory in Westminster-Abbey, by William Benson Esq; one of the auditors of the imprest. . . .

Milton, *Works*, ed. Birch, 1753, I, lxxvii. In his edition of 1738 (I, lxiii) the corresponding passage reads: "A Monument is expected to be erected. . . ." The expectation had become rather old by this time, since Toland stated in 1698 that Milton was buried in the chancel of the church at St. Giles Cripplegate, "where the Piety of his Admirers will shortly erect a Monument becoming his worth, and the incouragement of Letters in King *William*'s Reign" (Toland, p. 46; Darbishire, p. 193). Mr. Edward L. Ruhe has reminded me of Toland's statement.

1738. ATTRIBUTED LETTER TO POLLIO (BY WILLIAM KING).

Miltonis Epistola ad Pollionem, 1738.

Title of a satire written by Dr. William King; attributed to Milton by Lowndes and others; *Notes and Queries*, v, iv (1875), 511, and v, v (1876), 75; CM, XVIII, 602. Thomas Birch has a note (British Museum Add. MS. 4,478c, f. 31) on this point under date of December 23, 1738: "Collocutus sum per plures horas cum—King L.L.D. Aulæ S. Mariæ Oxon. Principalis, cui ascribitur epistola Miltonis ad Pol[lionem]" (I talked for several hours with — King, LL.D., Principal of St. Mary Hall, Oxford, to whom is attributed Milton's Letter to Pollio). The last few letters of the last word are rubbed off in the manuscript.

1738. FEBRUARY 10. JOHN WARD VISITS POET'S GRANDDAUGHTER.

And here I shall take the Opportunity of giving a more exact

Account of *Milton's* Children and Descendants, communicated to me by my learned Friend, Mr. *John Ward*, F. R. S. and Professor of Rhetorick in *Gresham* College *London*; who just now [footnoted: "Feb. 10*th*, 1737/8"] received it from a Granddaughter of our Author.

Milton's first Wife was *Mary*, Daughter of *Richard Powell* Esq; Lord of the Manor of *Foresthill* in *Oxfordshire*. By her he had four Children, *viz.* 1. *Anne*, born *July* 29*th*, 1646. 2. *Mary*, born *October* 25*th*, 1648. 3. *John*, born *March* 16*th*, 1650, who died an Infant. 4. *Deborah*, born *May* 3*d*, 1652; of whom her Mother died in Childbed. The three Daughters all surviv'd him. *Anne* married a Master-Builder, and died in Childbed of her first Child, which died with her. *Mary* liv'd single. *Deborah* married Mr. *Abraham Clarke*, a Weaver in *Spittle-Fields*, and died *August* 24th, 1727, in the 76th year of her age. She had ten Children, *viz.* seven Sons and three Daughters. But none of them had any Children, except one of her Sons, nam'd *Caleb*, and the youngest Daughter, whose name is *Elizabeth*. *Caleb* went over to *Fort St. George* in the *East Indies*, where he married, and had two Sons, *Abraham* and *Isaac*. Of these *Abraham* the elder came to *England* with the late Governor *Harrison*, but return'd again upon advice of his Father's Death; and whether he or his Brother be now living, is now uncertain. *Elizabeth*, the youngest Child of *Deborah*, married Mr. *Thomas Foster*, a Weaver, and lives now in *Pelham-street* in *Spittle-fields*. She has had seven Children, *viz.* three Sons and four Daughters, who are now all dead.

Milton, *A Complete Collection of the . . . Works*, ed. Thomas Birch, 1 (1738), lxi; Masson, VI, 755-759.

1738. FEBRUARY 11. THOMAS BIRCH VISITS GRAND-DAUGHTER ELIZABETH FOSTER.

In my first visit to her [Elizabeth Foster] on the 11th of February, 1737-8. she gave the following particulars, which she had often heard from her mother, Mrs. Clarke, who meeting with very ill treatment from Milton's last wife, left her father, and went to live with a lady, whom she called Merian. This lady going over to Ireland, and resolving to take Milton's daughter with her, if he would give his consent, wrote a letter to him of her design, and assured him, that "as chance had thrown his daughter under her care, she would treat her no otherwise than as his daughter and her own companion." She lived with that lady, till her marriage, and came over again to England during the troubles in Ireland, under King James II. Milton's widow, though she owned, that he died worth 1500 l. yet allowed his three daughters but 100 l. each. Mrs. Foster informed me, that Milton's father was born in France. That Milton lost 2000 l. by a money-scrivener, whom he had intrusted with it; and that an estate of about 60 l. per Ann. at Westminster was taken away from him at the restoration, it belonging to the dean and chapter there. That his second wife did not die in childbed, as Mr. Philips and Toland relate, but above three months after of a consumption. That he kept his daughters at a great distance; and would not allow them to learn to write, which he thought unnecessary for a woman. That he seldom went abroad in the latter part of his life, but was constantly visited even then by persons of distinction, both foreigners and others. That there were three pictures of him; the first, painted while he was at school, which is that now in the possession of Charles Stanhope Esq; the second, when he was about twenty-five or twenty-six years of age; and the third, when he was pretty well advanced in age. That her late majesty queen Caroline sent his daughter, Mrs. Clarke, fifty pounds: and that she received other presents of money from several gentlemen.

Thomas Birch, prefatory life to *The Works of John Milton*, 1753, pp. lxxvi-vii; Masson, VI, 754. In Birch's notes (British Museum, Add. MS. 4,478c, f. 29v) he records: "Visited M[rs]. Foster, Grand-daughter of Milton." The visit must have taken place at Pelham Street, Spitalfields, where John Ward had called on her the day before. See also Birch's account below under date of January 6, 1750. This account repeats that in the edition of 1738 with no important change except for the addition of the clause about Stanhope.

1738. MARCH 1. THOMAS BIRCH'S LIFE OF MILTON (IN EDITION OF PROSE WORKS) PUBLISHED.

A Complete Collection of the Historical, Political, and Miscellaneous Works of John Milton: Correctly printed from the Original Editions. with an Historical and Critical Account of the Life and Writings of the Author; Containing several Original Papers of His, Never before Published. In Two Volumes. Vol. I. London: Printed for A. Millar, at Buchanan's Head, against St. Clement's Church in the Strand. M.DCC.XXXVIII.

Title page of the original. Birch's account, which bears his name at the heading, covers pp. i-lxiii, with appendixes on pp. lxiv-xcvii on the Pamela prayer and on the royal commission which Milton discusses in *Eikonoklastes*. A revised edition appeared in 1753.

Martii 1. The new Edition of Milton's Prose Works finish'd, & begun to be deliver'd to the Subscribers.

British Museum Add. MS. 4,478c (Birch's diary), f. 30, under the year 1738. I am indebted to Edward Ruhe for calling my attention to this entry and to the others given in the present note. Earlier in the same diary, under date of February 25, 1738, Birch wrote: "Jmpressio Vitæ Miltoni & Appendicis absoluta est" (f. 30) [The printing of the life of Milton and of the appendix is finished]. Later, under date of March 24 of the same year, he wrote: "Milton's Prose-Works advertis'd as publish'd" (f. 30v). Under date of September 1, 1739, he noted: "An Acc^t. of the new Edition of Milton's prose-Works publish'd in the *History of the Works of the Learned*" (f. 45v). According to an earlier note under date of August 25, 1737, "Incepi scribere Vitam Miltoni novæ Editioni Operum præ mittendam" (f. 26v) [I have begun to write the life of Milton to be prefixed to the new edition of his works]. Subsequent entries record the delivery of part of the life to the printer on January 13, 1738, and the correction of the first sheet on January 19.

1738. MARCH 4. FIRST THEATRICAL PRESENTATION OF *COMUS*.

1737/8 . . . Martii . . . 4 Milton's Mask first represented at the Theatre in Drury-Lane.

Thomas Birch's note, British Museum Add. MS. 4,478c, f. 30. In the same manuscript Birch tells how John Dalton, who adapted *Comus* for this presentation, visited him on January 27, 1738, to compare the printed text with "Autographo Miltoni nunc penes me" (Milton's autograph version, now in my possession); how Dalton read his "alteration" to Birch and the Richardsons, father and son, on February 1; how Birch attended the rehearsal of it on March 1; and how he dined afterwards on April 4 with Dalton. I am grateful to Mr. Edward Ruhe for showing me his copy of these notes.

This admirable piece [*Comus*] being adapted to the stage by Mr. John Dalton, now doctor of divinity, and prebendary of Worcester, by dividing it into scenes and acts, with proper additions and alterations, was exhibited at Drury-lane, on the 4th of March, 1738, where it was received for many nights with an applause, that did no less honour to the public taste, than to the name of Milton.

Milton, *Works*, ed. Birch, 1753, I, xvi.

1738. MARCH 24. BIRCH AGAIN VISITS ELIZABETH FOSTER AND HER BROTHER URBAN CLARKE.

Martii . . . 24 . . . Milton's Prose-Works advertis'd as publish'd. Went with Mr. Dalton to visit Milton's Grand daughter.

British Museum, Add. MS. 4,478c, f. 30v. For further notes on Dalton, see the entry above under date of March 4, 1738.

Mr. Urban Clarke, another of the sons of Deborah, was a weaver, and lived in Pelham-street Spital-fields, March 24, 1737-8; when I visited him and his sister, Mrs. Elizabeth Foster, the youngest daughter of Mrs. Clarke, and wife of Mr. Thomas Foster, by whom she had three sons and four daughters, who are all now dead.

Milton, *Works*, ed., Thomas Birch, 1753, I, lxxvi.

1742. GRANDDAUGHTER ELIZABETH FOSTER MOVES TO LOWER HOLLOWAY, LONDON.

J visited Mrs. Foster, Grand-daughter to Milton, who keeps a chandler's shop in Cock-Lane near Shoreditch-Church, wher she told me she had liv'd about a Year, having liv'd about seven Years at lower Holloway, after removing from Pelham Street Spittlefields, where I saw her in February 1737/8.

From Thomas Birch's notes of his visit to Mrs. Foster on January 6, 1749/50, *q.v.* Her brother Urban Clarke seems to have moved with her, since Birch says that he died at her house in Lower Holloway. So did her cousin Catherine, daughter of her great-uncle Christopher Milton; she made her will there on July 19, 1744, *q.v.*

1743. PUBLICATION OF STATE LETTERS AND DOCUMENTS FROM MILTON'S COLLECTION.

Original Letters And Papers of State, Addressed to Oliver Cromwell; Concerning the Affairs of Great Britain. From the Year MDCXLIX to MDCLVIII. Found among the Political Collections Of Mr. John Milton. Now first Published from the Originals. By John Nickolls, Jun. Member of the Society of Antiquaries, London. London: Printed by William Bowyer, And sold by John Whiston Bookseller, at Boyle's Head in Fleet-street. MDCCXLIII.

Title page of my own copy; Masson, vi, 814. These letters should not be confused with those that Milton wrote; they are incoming rather than outgoing. But they make a sizable collection, 164 folio pages. Though a few are from foreign countries, and some in Latin, the great majority are in English, many from places in England, and a number from agents of England abroad.

And though it cannot render them more authentic, to say that they had long been treasured up by the famous *Milton*, it may yet imply the use he conceived they might be of, and might one day intend to make of them, to illustrate either some particular or general history of his times. From him, they came into the possession of *Thomas Ellwood*, a person, who for several years was well acquainted with and esteemed by him: [here follows a brief account of Ellwood's friendship with Milton] ... All which may suffice to shew the probability of his putting these letters into his hands.

That history aforesaid of *Thomas Ellwood's Life*, written by himself to the year 1683, was published in octavo 1714, a year after his death, with a supplement concerning his writings and the remainder of his life by *J. W.* who was *Joseph Wyeth*, citizen and merchant of London, and for several years intimate

with him, into whose hands, among the other papers of the said
Ellwood, these letters fell; and through the hands of *J. Wyeth*'s widow they came into the possession of the present editor.

Original Letters, preface, p. iv; Masson, VI, 815.

1743. MAY 5 (?). ADMINISTRATION OF BROTHER CHRISTOPHER'S DAUGHTER MARY'S ESTATE GRANTED TO HER SISTER CATHERINE.

Mary Milton. On the fifth day Admcōn of th Goods Chattells and Credits of Mary Milton late of Highgate in the Parish
of Hornsey in the County of Mĩddᵽ Spinster decēd was granted
to Katharine Milton Spinster the natural and lawfull Sister
and only next of kin of the said decēd being first sworn duly to
adstēr

[After a bracket at the right are two dates, one on the top line
and the other on the bottom:] [1] Novʳ. [2] May 1743

Principal Probate Registry, London, Administration Act Book for
1742; Perceval Lucas in *Notes and Queries*, XI, vii (1913), 21-22.
Evidently Mary Milton had died shortly before, but the exact date is
not known. She seems to have been buried with her sister Anne Pendlebury at Farmingham, co. Kent; see her sister Catherine's will of July
19, 1744, below. The day of the month, which does not show on my
photostatic copy, is from Lucas, who however gives the year as 1742.

1743. SEPTEMBER 5. DAUGHTER DEBORAH'S SON CALEB'S SON ABRAHAM BURIED (?).

Abraham Clarke Soldier burᵈ. Septʳ. 5. by I. Feilde.

[Marginal entry:] Clarke.

From the parish registers of St. George's Cathedral, Madras; see
note to entry of June 2, 1703. Though this entry does not identify
Abraham Clarke, there is at least a reasonable likelihood that he is
Caleb's son.

1744. JULY 19. BROTHER CHRISTOPHER'S DAUGHTER CATHERINE MAKES WILL.

Jn the Name of God, Amen J Catherine Milton late of Highgate and now of Lower Holloway in the County of Middlesex

Spinster . . . do make this my last Will and Testament . . . my Body J commit to the Earth and desire it may be interred at Farmingham in the County of Kent as near as may be to my late Sister Mary Milton and J desire my Executors herein after named to lay a Broad Stone over my said Sister's Grave and mine . . . Jmprimis J give and bequeath unto my Cousin M^r. Thomas ffoster now of Lower Holloway aforesaid who married my Cousin Elizabeth Clarke who is Grand Daughter of my uncle the famous M^r. John Milton deceased the Sum of ffifty pounds   Jtem J give and bequeath unto my good ffriend Edward Yardley Archdeacon of Cardigan the Sum of two Hundred pounds Upon special Trust . . . that he . . . pay the said Sum . . . unto my said Cousin Elizabeth Foster to and for her own sole and seperate use and benefit notwithstanding her Coverture for my Will and Mind is that the said Sum of two Hundred Pounds or any part thereof nor any Jnterest or proceed thereof shall in any wise be controulable by him the said Thomas ffoster nor be liable or subject to the Debts Dues Claims or Demands whatsover that he owes . . . Jtem J give and bequeath unto my ffriend M^r. William Townsend of High-gate aforesaid the Sum of Thirty pounds Jtem J give and be-queath unto his Sister-in-Law M^{rs}. Alice Paradice the like Sum of Thirty pounds Jtem J give and bequeath unto my Cousin Ann Lambourne the Sum of fforty pounds But if she shall hap-pen to die in my Lifetime Then J give the s^d. Sum of fforty pounds unto her Brother M^r. Thomas Lambourne Jtem J give and bequeath unto M^{rs}. Musgrave the Sum of ten pounds . . . Jtem J give and bequeath unto M^{rs}. Ann Sandys of Highgate aforesaid the Sum of ten Pounds Jtem J give and bequeath unto the said M^r. Edward Yardley Archdeacon of Cardigan the Sum of Twenty five pounds And also my picture of our Saviour Christ on his Knees and my picture of Mary Magdalen Jtem J give and bequeath unto the poor of the parish of ffarm-ingham aforesaid the Sum of five pounds and to the poor of Darent parish near ffarmingham the like Sum of five pounds and to the poor of the parish of S^t. Nicholas in Jpswich the like Sum of five pounds and to the poor of the Hamlet of Highgate aforesaid five pounds to be distributed by and at the Discretion of the said M^r. Archdeacon Yardley Jtem J give and bequeath unto M^r. John Townsend Son of the said William Townsend the ffeatherbed and Bolster which J usually lye on Jtem J give and bequeath to my Cousin Elizabeth ffoster aforesaid the Bedstead worked Vallans Bases Curtains and all other ffurniture belonging to my said Bed Jtem Whereas J am possessed of and as Administratrix to my late Sister Mary Milton am solely interested in two Bonds given by William Bridges Esqr. deceased to my said Sister the one to secure to her two Hundred pounds with Jnterest for the same and the other to secure to her the payment of twelve pounds Yearly during the Term of her natural Life Now J do hereby give and bequeath to my two Executors herein after named both the said Bonds . . . and all the Rest and Residue of my Estate of what nature . . . J give and bequeath unto my said Cousin Thomas ffoster and . . . J make and appoint my said ffriend the Reverend M^r. Edward Yardley Archdeacon of Cardigan And my said Cousin Thomas ffoster Executors . . . Jn Witness whereof J have hereunto set my Hand and Seal this nineteenth day of July Anno Domini 1744—The Mark of Catherine Milton—Signed sealed . . . in the presence of us —Rich. Wall—John Collard—

Whereas I Catherine Milton . . . have . . . given and bequeathed to M^r. William Townsend . . . M^{rs}. Alice Paradise . . . M^{rs}. Musgrave . . . the poor of the parish of Darent . . . the poor of the parish of S^t. Nicholas . . . and to M^r. John Townsend . . . J do hereby revoke disanull and make void all the aforesaid Bequests . . . As to the other Legacys . . . J do hereby ratify and confirm . . . and desire that this may be taken as a Codicil to my said last Will . . . Jn Witness whereof J have hereunto set my Hand and Seal this eighth day of April Anno Dñi 1745—The Mark of Catherine Milton—Signed sealed . . . in the presence of . . . John Collard . . . Charles Dennett.

This Will was proved at London with a Codicil annexed before the worshipfull Robert Chapman Doctor of Laws Surrogate to the Right Worshipfull John Bettesworth also Doctor of Laws Master Keeper or Commissary of the prerogative Court of Canterbury lawfully constituted The Twenty third day of April in the year of our Lord One Thousand seven Hundred and fforty six By the Oaths of the Reverend Edward Yardley and Thomas ffoster the Executors named in the said Will To whom Administration of all and singular the Goods Chattells and Credits of the Deceased was granted being first sworn duly to administer./ Ex^d./.

Prerogative Court of Canterbury, 126 Edmunds; Perceval Lucas in *Notes and Queries*, XI, vii (1913), 21-22. Though the date of Catherine Milton's death is unknown, it must have been between April 8, 1745, the date of the codicil, and April 23, 1746, when her will was proved.

ABOUT 1745. GRANDSON URBAN CLARKE DIES.

Mr. Urban Clarke . . . lived in Pelham-street, Spital-fields, March 24, 1737-8; when I visited him and his sister, Mrs. Elizabeth Foster. . . . She removed from Pelham street, where she kept a Chandler's Shop, to lower Holloway, between Highgate and London, where she continued about seven years, and where her brother Urban died. . . .

Milton, *Works*, ed. Birch, 1753, I, lxxvi. The date is uncertain, but it must be somewhere between 1742, when Elizabeth Foster moved (see above under date of 1742), and January 6, 1749/50 (see below under that date, when Birch visited her and found out that Urban was dead). The present dating is otherwise a guess.

BEFORE 1749(?). THOMAS NEWTON VISITS GRAND-DAUGHTER ELIZABETH FOSTER.

Elizabeth, the youngest child of Mrs. Clarke, was married to Mr. Thomas Foster a weaver in Spittle Fields, and had seven children who are all dead; and she herself is aged about sixty, and weak and infirm. She seemeth to be a good plain sensible woman, and has confirmed several particulars related above,

and informed me of some others, which she had often heard
from her mother: that her grandfather lost two thousand pounds
by a money-scrivener, whom he had intrusted with that sum,
and likewise an estate at Westminster of sixty pounds a year,
which belonged to the Dean and Chapter, and was restored to
them at the Restoration: that he was very temperate in his eating and drinking, but what he had he always loved to have of
the best: that he seldom went abroad in the latter part of his
life, but was visited even by persons of distinction, both foreigners and others: that he kept his daughters at a great distance, and would not allow them to learn to write, which he
thought unnecessary for a woman: that her mother was his
greatest favorite, and could read in seven or eight languages,
tho' she understood none but English: that her mother inherited his head-akes and disorders, and had such a weakness
in her eyes, that she was forced to make use of spectacles from
the age of eighteen; and she herself, she says, has not been
able to read a chapter in the Bible these twenty years: that she
was mistaken in informing Mr. Birch, what he had printed
upon her authority, that Milton's father was born in France;
and a brother of hers who was then living was very angry with
her for it, and like a true-born Englishman resented it highly,
that the family should be thought to bear any relation to France:
that Milton's second wife did not die in childbed, as Mr. Philips
and Toland relate, but above three months after of a consumption; and this too Mr. Birch relates upon her authority; but
in this particular she must be mistaken as well as in the other,
for our author's sonnet on his deceased wife plainly implies,
that she did die in childbed. She knows nothing of her aunt
Philips or Agar's descendents, but believes that they are all extinct: as is likewise Sir Christopher Milton's family, the last of
which were two maiden sisters, Mrs. Mary and Mrs. Catharine
Milton, who lived and died at Highgate: and she herself is
the only survivor of Milton's own family, unless there be some
in the East Indies, which she very much questions, for she used

to hear from them sometimes, but has heard nothing now for several years; so that in all probability Milton's whole family will be extinct with her, and he can live only in his writings. And such is the caprice of fortune, this grandaughter of a man, who will be an everlasting glory to the nation, has now for some years with her husband kept a little chandler's or grocer's shop for their subsistence, lately at the lower Holloway in the road between Highgate and London, and at present in Cock Lane not far from Shoreditch Church.

Milton, *Paradise Lost*, ed. Thomas Newton, 1749, I, lviii-lix; Masson, VI, 760. Though Newton does not date his visit to Mrs. Foster, it was probably no great length of time previous to his writing. It is therefore tentatively dated 1749 here. He may quite likely, of course, have visited her more than once, and perhaps over a considerable period of time. In summarizing this visit, Birch (Milton's *Works*, 1753, I, lxxvii) speaks of it as having occurred "about two years ago." Either his memory was hazy, or he prepared this passage some time before the publication of his edition. Masson, on the other hand, assigns the visit to 1749 without question.

1749. THOMAS NEWTON PUBLISHES HIS EDITION AND LIFE OF MILTON.

Paradise Lost. A Poem, in Twelve Books. The Author John Milton. A New Edition, With Notes of various Authors, By Thomas Newton, D. D. Volume the First. London: Printed for J. and R. Tonson and S. Draper in the Strand. MDCCXLIX.

Title page of the original. Volumes I and II contain *Paradise Lost*, and Volume III (1752) the other poems. Newton's life of Milton covers pp. i-lxi of Volume I. Though largely dependent on previous accounts, it introduces some new facts derived from visits of Newton himself and of others to the poet's widow, to his daughter Deborah Clarke, and to her daughter Elizabeth Foster. Mr. Edward L. Ruhe tells me that among Thomas Warton's unpublished literary anecdotes in Trinity College, Oxford, is a remark that Isaac Hawkins Browne, author of *De Animi Immortalitate*, claimed to have "furnished Dr *Newton* with most of the Anecdotes in Milton's Life, particularly those that relate to his Wife and Daughters." Whatever truth there may be in Browne's assertion, it is clearly exaggerated, since Newton himself recounts visits to Milton's descendants which account for many of these anecdotes.

1749. JANUARY (?). GRANDDAUGHTER ELIZABETH FOSTER AND HUSBAND MOVE.

. . . M^rs. Foster, Grand-daughter to Milton, who keeps a chandler's shop in Cock-Lane near Shoreditch-Church, wher she told me she had liv'd about a Year, having liv'd about seven Years at lower Holloway, after removing from Pelham Street Spittlefields, where I saw her in February 1737/8.

From Thomas Birch's notes of January 6, 1750, *q.v.*; Masson, VI, 759.

1750. JANUARY 6. THOMAS BIRCH VISITS ELIZABETH FOSTER.

1749/50 January 6.

J Visited M^rs. Foster, Grand-daughter to Milton, who keeps a chandler's shop in Cock-Lane near Shoreditch-Church, wher she told me she had liv'd about a Year, having liv'd about seven Years at lower Holloway, after removing from Pelham Street Spittlefields, where I saw her in February 1737/8. Her Brother, M^r. Clarke died at her House at Lower Holloway, as did likewise at about 90 Years of age her Cousin M^rs. Milton, Neice of Milton, & Daughter of his Brother S^r. Xtopher Milton. J presented her 5 Guineas from M^r. Yorke. She shew'd me her Grand-Mother's Bible in 8vo. printed by Young in 1636, in a Blank Leafe of which Milton had enter'd in his own Hands the Births of his Children, as follows:

Anne my Daughter was born July the 29th. the day of the Monthly fast between six & seavn, or about half an hour after six the Ev'ning 1646.

Mary my Daughter was born on Wednesday Octob. 25 on the Fast Day in the Morning about 6 a Clock 1648.

My Son John was born on Sunday March the 16th. about halfe an howre past nine at night 1650.

My Daughter Deborah was born the 2^d. of May, being Sunday somwhat before 3 of the Clock in the morning 1652.

Jn another blank Leaf Milton wrote thus:

[346]

S. S. vocatur. Liber sacerdotalis ab Ambrosio.

Dionysius vocat Scripturam substantiam Sacerdotii nostri.

Sacræ Scripturæ s̄t Dei ad hoĩes litteræ.

Hausit è S. Script. atqz in primis è S. Paulo Ambrosius Doc-trinā suā, Vitæ Jnnocentiam, Comitate mixtam, Morum Gravi-tatem, Spiritum Episcopalem, imo Apostolicum.

Jn his Wife's Hand-writing,

J am the Book of Mary Milton.

D^r. Newton had been with her, & given her a Guinea some time ago; Mr Lauder lately, & D^r. Foster within these few Days.

She told me, that her great Uncle S^r. Xtopher Milton had, besides his two Daughters, who died unmarried, & had liv'd at Highgate, for many Years, had another, who was married to M^r. Pendleberry a Clergyman.

British Museum, Add. MS. 4,244 (Thomas Birch's notes), f. 52v-53; Hunter, p. 34; Masson, IV, 335; CM, XVIII, 275. I am grateful to Mr. Edward Ruhe for lending me his photostatic copy of this manu-script. Some of the items in this passage, especially those concerning the births of Milton's children, have already been given above in their ap-propriate places. The Dr. Foster mentioned may perhaps be James Fos-ter, nonconformist divine.

[The Holy Scripture is called a priestly book by Ambrose. Dionysius calls the Scripture the substance of our priesthood. The Holy Scriptures are the letters of God to men. Ambrose drew from the Holy Scriptures and primarily from St. Paul his doctrine, the innocence of his life, mixed with kindness, the gravity of his manners, and an episcopal, indeed apostolical, spirit.]

1750. APRIL 5. BENEFIT PERFORMANCE OF *COMUS* FOR GRANDDAUGHTER ELIZABETH FOSTER.

LIST *of* PLAYS *acted at the* Theatres. [1] DRURY LANE. . . . Plays. . . . *Apr.* . . . 5 Comus* . . .

[Note] *This play was performed for the benefit of Mrs *Foster*, grand-daughter of the author of Paradise Lost, of which we think it of use to posterity to give some further account, as, perhaps, an instance of greater or more rational regard to PoETRY was never shewn in any age. Upon an accidental intimation to the publick that such a person was living, (*Vol.* XIX. *p.* 563.) and not very happy in her circumstances a proposal to relieve her by a benefit was readily complied with by Mr *Garrick* and Mr *Lacy*, the managers of the theatre, who, on this occasion, receded from their right of security for the charges of the house. All those who had any share in the author's poetical works, and many other persons distinguished for their rank, or their abilities, contributed to promote ye design with their united endeavours. The 4th being the night first appointed, many inconvenient circumstances happened to disappoint the hopes of success; the managers therefore generously quitted the profits of another night, in which the theatre was expected to be fuller. —Mr *Samuel Johnson*, by whom the proposal to Mr *Garrick* was made, wrote an Occasional Prologue, (*See p.* 183.) which was afterwards printed for Mrs *Foster's* benefit.

Gentleman's Magazine, XX (for April, 1750), 152.

The account, which Dr. Newton gave of her [Elizabeth Foster], in his life of her grandfather, occasioned Comus to be acted on Thursday April 5, 1750. for her benefit, with a prologue by the learned and ingenious Mr. Samuel Johnson; which brought her clear about 130 l.

Milton, *Works*, 1753, ed. Birch, I, lxxvii.

In 1750, April 5, *Comus* was played for her [Milton's granddaughter Elizabeth Foster] benefit. She had so little acquaintance with diversion or gaiety, that she did not know what was intended when a benefit was offered her. The profits of the night were only one hundred and thirty pounds, though Dr. Newton brought a large contribution; and twenty pounds were given by Tonson, a man who is to be praised as often as he is named. Of this sum one hundred pounds was placed in the stocks, after some debate between her and her husband in whose name it should be entered; and the rest augmented their little stock, with which they removed to Islington. This was the greatest benefaction that *Paradise Lost* ever procured the author's descendants; and to this he who has now attempted to relate his Life, had the honour of contributing a Prologue.

Samuel Johnson, *Lives of the Poets*, London, n.d. (World's Classics), I, 114. Johnson's prologue, published in 1750, is reprinted in his *Poems*, ed. Smith and McAdam, Oxford, 1941, pp. 57-58.

[In 1750 Johnson] not only wrote a Prologue, which was spoken by Mr. Garrick before the acting of Comus at Drury-lane theatre, for the benefit of Milton's grand-daughter, but took a very zealous interest in the success of the charity. On the day preceding the performance, he published the following letter in the "General Advertiser," addressed to the printer of that paper:

"SIR,

"THAT a certain degree of reputation is acquired merely by approving the works of genius. . . .

"[But whoever wishes really to do a good deed] should appear at Drury-lane theatre to-morrow, April 5, when Comus will be performed for the benefit of Mrs. Elizabeth Foster, grand-daughter to the authour, and the only surviving branch of his family.

"N. B. There will be a new prologue on the occasion, written by the authour of Irene, and spoken by Mr. Garrick; and, by particular desire, there will be added to the Masque a dramatick satire, called Lethe, in which Mr. Garrick will perform."

James Boswell, *The Life of Samuel Johnson*, London, 1914 (Everyman's Library), I, 135; Masson, VI, 760. Masson comments that though Johnson estimated the return from the performance at £130, it was actually £147-14-6, out of which came expenses of £80, leaving a profit of only £67-14-6; but that contributions from various persons brought it up to £130. But see the next following entry.

1750. NOVEMBER 13. BIRCH AGAIN VISITS MILTON'S GRANDDAUGHTER.

On Tuesday I call'd upon Milton's Grand-daughter with a

present from a Friend. She shew'd me the Account of her Benefit play, which, including the 20 Guineas subscrib'd by Tonson,
brought her in clear £130: 4ˢ; the Charges of the House, &
other incidental Expences, amounting to about £73. She gave
me a particular Account of the Severities of her Grandfather's
last Wife towards his three Daughters by his first, the two
eldest of whom she bound prentices to Workers in Gold-Lace,
without his Knowledge; & forc'd the younger to leave his Family. Mrs. Foster confess'd to me, that he was no fond Father,
but assur'd me that his Wife's ill Treatment of his Children
gave him great Uneasiness; tho' in his State of Health & Blindness he could not prevent it.

Letter of Thomas Birch to Yorke, November 17, 1750, in British
Museum Add. MS. 35,397, f. 321v. I am grateful to Mr. Edward
Ruhe for a transcript of this entry. November 17, 1750, was a Saturday; so the preceding Tuesday was November 13. Yorke is probably
Philip Yorke (1720-1790), later to become second Earl of Hard-
wicke. In the manuscript the symbols for pounds and shillings appear
directly above the figures to which they pertain.

1750. DECEMBER. SUBSCRIPTIONS FOR GRANDDAUGH-
TER ELIZABETH FOSTER INVITED.

SUBSCRIPTIONS, for the relief of Mrs ELIZABETH FOS-
TER, grand-daughter to JOHN MILTON, are taken in by Mr
Dodsley, in *Pall-Mall*; Mess. *Cox* and *Collings*, under the
Royal Exchange; Mr *Cave*, at St *John's Gate, Clerkenwell*; and
Mess. *Payne* and *Bouquet*, in *Pater-noster row*.

Gentleman's Magazine, xix (for December, 1750), 563. This appeal appears in connection with an account of Lauder's essay on Milton's "Use and Imitation of the Moderns," which created such a stir.
Though Lauder's attacks on Milton as a plagiarist began in 1747 (*ibid.*,
xvii, 24), the above note is the earliest occurrence which I have found
of the invitation to assist Milton's granddaughter.

1753. DAUGHTER OF BROTHER CHRISTOPHER'S SON
THOMAS LIVING IN LONDON.

[Elizabeth Foster told Thomas Newton about 1749 that she
believed there were no living descendants of] Sir Christopher

Milton's family, the last of which, she says, were two maiden sisters, Mrs. Mary and Mrs. Catharine Milton, who lived at Highgate, and are both dead, one dying at Mrs. Foster's house at Holloway: but unknown to her, there is a Mrs. Milton living in Grosvenor's-street, the grand-daughter of Sir Christopher, and the daughter of Mr. Thomas Milton before-mentioned.

Milton, *Works*, ed. Birch, 1753, I, lxxvii; Masson, VI, 763. This lady died on July 26, 1769, *q.v.*

1753. BIRCH'S EDITION REPRINTED WITH ADDITIONS.

The Works of John Milton, Historical, Political, and Miscellaneous. Now more correctly printed from the Originals, than in any former Edition, and many Passages restored, which have been hitherto omitted. To which is prefixed, An Account of his Life and Writings. In Two Volumes. Vol. I. London: Printed for A. Millar, in the Strand. MDCCLIII.

Title page of the original. Birch's account of Milton appears in I, i-lxxviii. Though his name is absent from the title page, it appears at the heading of the account and on the table of contents. There are a good many changes from the edition of 1738, a number of which have been drawn on in the present work. Francis Blackburne (*Memoir of Thomas Hollis*, 1780, I, 364) says that Richard Baron was primarily responsible for this edition: "By the time Baron had thought of a new edition of Milton's prose works, he had taken a dislike to Birch as a trimmer; and did not, on that account, profit so much by the edition of 1738 as he might have done, particularly with respect to Birch's Life of Milton, which he altered in some few instances, not for the better."

1754. MAY 9. GRANDDAUGHTER ELIZABETH FOSTER DIES.

On Thursday last, May 9, 1754, died at Islington, in the 66th year of her age, after a long and painful illness, which she sustained with Christian fortitude and patience, Mrs. Elizabeth Foster, granddaughter of John Milton.

Masson, VI, 760-761. Masson says this notice comes from a "contemporary newspaper," which he does not identify, and which I have been unable to find. He also refers to *Hollis Memoirs*, p. 114.

A List *of* DEATHS *for the* Year 1754. . . .

MAY . . . 9. . . . Mrs Eliz. Foster, grand-daughter of the author of Paradise Lost.

Gentleman's Magazine, XXIV (May, 1754), 243.

1754. MAY 14. GRANDDAUGHTER ELIZABETH FOSTER, LAST LIVING DIRECT DESCENDANT, BURIED.

May 14. Tuesday. J attended the Funeral, & perform'd the Office of interring, of M[rs]. Elizabeth Foster, Granddaughter of John Milton, & the last of his Descendants. She died at her House, the sign of the Sugar Loaf, opposite to the Thatch'd House in Islington, of an Asthma & Dropsy on thursday afternoon May 9th. She was born in Jreland in November 1688, & was about 15 Years of Age when she came to England; & married to M[r]. Foster in 1719. She was buried in a Vault in Tindal's Ground in Bunhill fields.

British Museum Add. MS. 4,472 (Birch's notes), f. 3; mentioned by E. F. Rimbault in *Notes and Queries,* II, iii (1857), 265-266. In another notebook (Add. MS. 4,478c, f. 248v) Birch repeated this incident very briefly, writing under date of May 14, 1754: "Attended the funeral of M[rs]. Foster, Milton's Granddaughter." Mr. Edward Ruhe kindly called this note to my attention. With Mrs. Foster's death the direct line of descendants of Milton came to an end, though the families of his sister Anne and his brother Christopher have continued into the twentieth century.

1769. JULY 26. DEATH OF BROTHER CHRISTOPHER'S GRANDDAUGHTER.

List of Deaths for the Year 1769. . . . July . . . 26 . . . Mrs Milton, a descendant from the brother of Milton the great poet. She was house-keeper to Dr. Secker.

Gentleman's Magazine, XXXIX (1769), 367; Perceval Lucas in *Notes and Queries,* XI, vii (1913), 21. Lucas adds that this lady's name was Elizabeth, that she died in Covent Garden, aged 79, and that she was the daughter of Thomas and Martha Milton. He puts the date at July 24 instead of July 26. Dr. Secker is presumably Thomas Secker (1693-1768), appointed Archbishop of Canterbury in 1758. This lady is presumably the same as the daughter of Thomas Milton mentioned by Birch and entered above under the year 1753. But a manuscript pedigree of Milton in the Manuscript Room of the New York Public Library contains a curious note which seems to refer to a different granddaugther of Christopher Milton. After the genealogical notes on Christopher's family the writer adds below: "a grand daughter of Ch. Milton. marr^d. Iohn Lookup advocate Edinb." I can find no further information about her.

1825. PUBLICATION OF *CHRISTIAN DOCTRINE*.

Joannis Miltoni Angli De Doctrina Christiana Libri Duo Posthumi, Quos Ex Schedis Manuscriptis Deprompsit, Et Typis Mandari Primus Curavit Carolus Ricardus Sumner, A.M. Bibliothecæ Regiæ Præfectus. Cantabrigiæ, Typis Academicis . . . M.DCCC.XXV.

Title page of first edition; Masson, VI, 816 ff.; CM, XIV-XVII, with brief account of the manuscript (Public Record Office, MS. SP 9/61) at XVII, 425-431. The composition of this treatise is noticed above under the year 1655, and something about Daniel Skinner's abortive attempt to publish it in 1676. In 1823 it was discovered in the Public Record Office by Robert Lemon, Deputy Keeper of the State Papers. Except for a few minor and perhaps somewhat dubious items in CM, this is the last of Milton's known writings to reach publication.

[Two Posthumous Books of John Milton Englishman's Book on Christian Doctrine, which Charles Richard Sumner, A.M., Director of the Royal Library, took from the manuscripts and first arranged to have committed to type. Cambridge, at the University Press . . . 1825.]

A Treatise On Christian Doctrine, Compiled From The Holy Scriptures Alone; By John Milton. Translated From The Original By Charles R. Sumner, M.A. Librarian And Historiographer To His Majesty, And Prebendary Of Canterbury. Printed At The Cambridge University Press . . . 1825.

Title page of Sumner's translation of the preceding. This is the translation used in the Columbia Milton.

ADDITIONS AND CORRECTIONS TO
VOLUMES I-IV

PREFACE TO ADDITIONS AND CORRECTIONS

Since Volume I first appeared in 1949, I have been gathering additions and corrections from three sources: (1) the contributions of friends, (2) reviews, and (3) my own continuing research. In the following section I include appropriate material from these sources in order to make the volumes as accurate as possible. Though ignoring trivialities, I have attempted to correct every mistake of any importance. It is not easy to confess one's errors in print, especially when there are a good many of them, but it is my hope that the usefulness which this process may add to the work may outweigh the embarrassment. For that matter, the greater portion of this section consists of additions, frequently of material published since my volumes appeared in print. Since the index covers the whole volume, it includes all additions. A reader who notices an omission or error in a preceding volume should consult this one before assuming that the material he seeks is missing or is wrong.

I venture to suggest a method of using this section. I believe the owner of this set will find it worth while to go through Volumes I-IV and enter a check mark (or perhaps a page reference to the present volume) at each point for which a new item appears. Since the additions are designated by the volume, the page, and the location on the page where they belong, this task requires only a few hours. Simple additions and corrections involving only a few words can of course easily be written in directly.

I wish particularly to acknowledge here contributions from three friends who have searched my volumes with penetrating eyes and have generously given me the results of their examinations. To spare them the embarrassment of constant repetition of their names as well as to conserve space, I indicate my debts to them by their initials in parentheses. Thus (P) stands for Professor William R. Parker of Indiana University, the most indefatigable scrutinizer of my pages, (K) for Professor Maurice Kelley of Princeton University, and (R) for Mr. Edward L. Ruhe of Cornell University. This notation means either (1) that one of them has provided the material of the entry, (2) that he has pointed out an error, or (3) that he has made me consider it worth while to add material which I already had but had not printed.

VOLUME I

1. *after first caption, insert*:
Londini sum natus . . . . [I was born in London.]

Milton, *Defensio Secunda*, 1654, p. 60; CM, VIII, 118.   (P)

He was Born in *London*, in a House in *Breadstreet*, the Lease whereof, as I take it, but for certain it was a House in *Breadstreet*, became in time part of his Estate in the Year of our Lord, 1606.

Phillips, p. iii; Darbishire, p. 50. Phillips was off, as usual, on his date.
1. *first note, line 2, delete reference to Masson; insert*: Thomas Kerslake, in *Athenaeum*, January 5, 1884, p. 19.   (P)

1. *second text entry, for* Mr. *read* M^r.   *for* Iconoclastes *read* Jconoclastes   *for* Dec. *read* Dec:

2. *last note of first entry, add*:
Mr. Donovan Dawe, Principal Assistant Librarian of the Guildhall Library, writes to me that he thoroughly supports the idea that the White Bear was the property of Eton College, and points out that Kenneth Rogers expresses the same opinion in his article in the *London Topographical Record*, XVI (1932), 53.
3. line 1, *for London read Londinium*
3. *line 2, for* xlvii *read* xlviii   (P)   *Change period to semicolon and add*:
L. H. Chambers, *Marriages of Hertfordshire Persons: I All Hallows, Bread Street*, ed. W. Bruce Bannerman, London, 1913, as quoted in *Notes and Queries*, CXCIII (1949), 474; see also *ibid.*, VII, vi (1888), 324.
3. 1610, *father taxed, note, add*:

Dr. Leslie Hotson has called my attention to a passage in Kenneth Rogers's *The Mermaid and Mitre Taverns in Old London*, 1928, pp. 117-118, mentioning this record and noting the proximity of Milton's birthplace to these taverns, though Milton had nothing to do with them. Rogers interprets the record as meaning that Milton was assessed at six pounds and taxed for six shillings. The E 179 is the correct reference. Rogers adds that Black Spread Eagle Court, which has sometimes been identified with Milton's birthplace, "was on very old property of the Merchant Taylors' Company—'the Saracen's Head' in Bread Street, and there is no evidence that John Milton's father lived there, or that the Court was so-named before the Fire."

4. *first note, line* 5, *for* 24,491 *read* 24,490

4. *second note, line* 7, *after* Hesse *insert* or his son (P) *Add at end*: For the main entry about the music for the Polish prince see under the year 1601.

4. *insert*:

1612. PARENTS PRESENT FAMILY BIBLE (?).

Since the Authorized Version was so often reprinted, it is at least conjecturable that Milton's parents may have presented him, in the year of its publication, the family Bible often referred to in these volumes (British Museum Add. MS. 32,310). (P)

1612. MAY 15. FATHER DEPOSES IN CHANCERY ACTION BROUGHT AGAINST HIM BY WILLIAM SYMONDS.

John Milton of London Scr: the party dēft Aged 45. yeres or therabtᵽ sworne &c'/ 1 Jnter' That he knoweth the Complt 1 willm Symondᵽ and hath knowne him these fyve or six yeres past or therabtᵽ

That he this dēft had hertofore asmuch direccōn as possibly 2 Could be geven by word of mowth (as this dēft conceveth) from the p̄lt to put a bond in sute in the p̄ltᵽ name againste the Administratᵣs of Henry Corbet in the Jnter' named and the p̄lt dyd muche vrge and ymportune this deft to put the s̄d bond in sute saying that he would iustifye what Course soever this dēft should lawfully take for recovery of the dett vppon the s̄d bond wᵗʰowte lymiting this dēft to anye Courte or Course but leving the whole busynes to this dēftᵽ discrecōn/

That he this dēpt by such warrant as aforēs̄d Comenced sute 3 vppon the s̄d bond and as the p̄ltᵽ solicitᵣ disburssed the money

for Chargp of sute vppon the p̄ltp promise to repay the same to
this Dep̄t when the s̄d dett was recovered. and this dēft saith
that before he knewe of the Costp awarded againste the s̄d w^m
Symondp the p̄lt he this dēft dyd entend to p̄secute the s̄d sute
in the s̄d Willm Symondp his name. But at this Deftp owne
Costp vppon the aforēsd warrant and the s̄d Symondp his p̄mis
to repaye this Dēft such sumēs as he should disburse for Chargp
as aforēsd after Recovery had as aforēsd But some space of tyme
before the Costp awarded against the s̄d Symondp this Dēft
Certifyed the s̄d Symondp that by reson of his busynes in his
faculty he Could not follow the busynes anye longer in the
Chancery whervppon the s̄d w^m Symondp aunswered that he
would apoynte a frend of his that should followe yt effectualy
and shortly after one m^r Mayart of the Myddle Temple whoe
was a mere strang^r to this Dēft dyd vndertake to follow the s̄d
sute for the s̄d willm̄ Symondp vppon this dēftp promise to repaye vnto him such sumes of money as he the s̄d m^r Mayart
should disbursse in the s̄d sute wch this dēft was contented to
doe in respect of the aforēsd warrant & promis from the s̄d
Symondp

4 That he this dēft dyd never intreate the s̄d Cōmplt Symondp to
vndertake the s̄d sute or to reteyne an attorney in yt but told
him that he should doe well to followe his owne busynes him
self as other men dyd for whome this dēpt vsed to put owte
money as anye occasion of sute should be for the sume neith^r
was there reson why this dēpt should make such intrety to him
for this dēft dyd put forth the p̄ltp money at his speciall intrety
and as tuching the p̄tyes to whome yt was lent this deft at that
tyme toke them for verye sufficient men and had trusted one
of them wch was the principall being m^r Scryveñ for almost a
thowsand poundp at a tyme and had trusted the s̄d Scryven
vppon his owne security a little before wth forty poundp of this
dēftp owne money all wch was well repayd and when the s̄d
Scryveñ had the moneys for wch this sute ys cōmenced he dyd
not owe anye money to this deftp knowledg more then the

money now in question wch ys fyftye two poundℯ ten shillingℯ. Nevertheles because the plt alleged he had noe skyll to sue anye man and was lothe to pte wth anye more money till a Recovery were had vppon the s̄d bond and that after yt was recoūed then he would be willing to paye this deft anye mony wch he should disbursse in the s̄d sute and vppon his entrety as aforēsd for this deft to follow the sute. This deft for these resons tooke vppon him in the pltℯ name, & by such warrant as aforēsd to ease the p̄lt of that troble and Charge tyll a Recovery were had in the sute wch hathe synce fallen owte to this dēftℯ greate losse and Charge one waye wth another to the valewe of one hundred poundℯ as this dēft verely thinketh. But now of late the p̄lt (vppon some discontentmēt taken throughe the defaulte (as this dept thinketh) of the s̄d Mayart, whoe was put in trust to follow the s̄d sute in this ho: Courte) hath sayd that he loketh that this dept should loose the money he hath disburssed for him as a solicitor in the s̄d sute and allso paye him the fifty two poundℯ ten shillingℯ due vppon the s̄d bond althoughe the s̄d Symondℯ dyd accept of the s̄d bond and had the sume long in his owne Custody.

That to his knowledg he never sayd he would not leaue the sute 5 till he had recoūed the money for the s̄d Symondℯ or that this dēft sayd he would take the whole forfetur of the bond and satisfye him self for his Chargℯ and soe the s̄d w^m Symondℯ should haue his principall money as ys intended by this Jnter' But this dēft hath sayd that the partyes sued deserved no ffavo^r but rather to pay the penalty of the bond how beyt the p̄lt synce the sute com̄enced in this Courte dyd seale to a letter of lycence to one Thomas Dod one of the Dettors in the s̄d bond specifyed as expecting therby to further the paymēt of the s̄d lij^{li}x^s dett to him the s̄d Com̄plt

That he this dēft to his knowledg dyd never so affyrme as in 6 the Jnter' ys mencōed for the s̄d Symondℯ the Com̄plt hath allwayes iustifyed the s̄d sute and hath bene diligent in Cōming to this dēft to enquire how yt ℮ceded and well liked of the

Course this dēft toke therin saying that he hoped he should
meete wth them in thend or word℈ to that effect

7 That true yt ys this dēft dyd say he would haue bene at the
Charge to haue put in a Replicacōn to haue stopped the dēft℈
Davys and Stedmā from Recovering of Cost℈ against the p̄lt
yf this dēft had vnderstode so muche wth such proviso as afores̄d
that he this dēft might haue allowance therof from the p̄lt in
thend of the s̄d sute and vppon the s̄d Mayart℈ speches to this
dēft that the s̄d Davys & Stedmā would haue Cost℈ against the
p̄lt if a Replicacōn were not put into the Course this Dēft in-
treted m^r Mayart in any wise to p^rvent that danger wch he faithfully p^rmised to p^rvent but as yt semed made defalt therin
whervppon twenty nobles Cost℈ being geven (as this dept
thinketh) against the p̄lt yt hathe made the p̄lt thus to storme
in the matter and would lay the same Charge as all so all other
Charges of sute vppon this dēft. And furth^r sayth that this dēft℈
meaning was not to goe anye furth^r forward wth the sute in this
ho: Courte then only to stay Cost℈ as afores̄d vntill this dēft
had made more fyrme profe of the sufficency of the Admistra-
t^{rs} y^t are Chargable wth the dett in question/.

8 That yt was never this dēft℈ intent and meaning to vndertake
the s̄d sute as his owne proper sute or at his owne ꝑper Charge
or otherwise then to solycite the sute for the p̄lt as willing to
helpe him to his money agayne the best this dēft Could ꝓvyded
allwayes that vppon recovery in the s̄d sute this dēpt might haue
allowance of his disbursmēt℈ therin from the p̄lt wch this dēft
toke to be a Curtesye shewed to the p̄lt and more then ever this
dēft dyd yet to anye for whome he dealt in the like occasōn or
intendeth ever to do agayne and to the further Content℈ of this
Inter' he sayth as to the 5. Inter' p^rcedent he hath deposed

9 That he doth not rember whether he hath bene often told that
the s̄d w^m Symond℈ would not meddle wth the s̄d sute. Neither
dothe this deft rember that ever he sayd he would vndertake
to follow the s̄d sute as his owne sute and at his owne Charge
or w^{th}owte warrant and allowance from the p̄lt and ys sure that

he this dēft had never anye intent so to doe nor had anye reson
so to doe for the p̄lt ys of habilitye to be at the Charge of the
s̄d sute him self and the detters (as this deft) ys enformed are
suffycient for that dett and more if the p̄lt were but as diligent
to followe after them as of right apteyneth as he ys to troble
this dēft w^{th}owte Cause as this dēpt Conceveth whoe was all-
wayp willing to doe his best indevor to recover the s̄d dett for
the p̄lt and verely thinketh the p̄lt had saved the s̄d twenty
nobles Cost if m^r Mayart had bene as Carfull in the busynes as
he p̄mised this dēft to be and more &c

[signed] Jo: milton

Public Record Office, Chancery Town Depositions, C24/377/60;
not previously published. This document is peculiarly interesting because
Milton was evidently both a defendant and a witness. He refers to
himself first as defendant and then as deponent. As in many of these
items, I am indebted to Mr. Charles A. Bernau and Miss Nellie O'Far-
rell for help in finding and procuring a copy of this document. Though
my photostatic copy shows no date, Mr. John Philip Feil of Cornell University has kindly shown me a copy of the interrogatories on which it was
based, and which bear the heading "Johēs Milton iur' 15° Maij 1612.
Mat. Carew." (John Milton sworn May 15, 1612; Matthew Carew).
He has also found a decree dated April 29, 1612. He plans to publish
an account of these new documents soon.

5. *first note, add:*
Masson misdates this event August 16. (P)
7. *first note, add:*
These four songs are published with two others in *Six Anthems by John
Milton*, ed. G. E. P. Arkwright, London and Oxford (The Old Eng-
lish Edition, No. 22), 1900, with a biographical memoir from Masson.
They are here set for four (No. 1) or five voices, with an accompani-
ment for the lute or piano. The two additional songs are "When David
Heard," and "I am the Resurrection," which occur also in the Myriell
collection of 1616 (see below, pp. 11-12).

7. *January* 30, *transpose after next entry. Insert new entry:*
1614. FATHER PROBABLY TAKES AS APPRENTICES WILLIAM
BOWER AND RICHARD MILTON.

See the entry below, p. 36 (as revised), on their receiving their freedom in 1621. They would normally have begun their apprenticeship
seven years earlier. (P)

8. *first note, add*:

Fletcher (*The Intellectual Development of John Milton*, I, 1956) deals extensively with Milton's early education.

8. *August 3, note, delete reference to Masson.* (P)

9. *first note, add*:

One of Hamor's legacies was £300 to a Bathsheba Snelling, who probably married William Huet and appears in 1632 (p. 276) as Bersheba Huet. Henry F. Waters summarizes Hamor's will in *Genealogical Gleanings in England*, II (1902), 1012-1013. The will was proved on August 16, 1615. (P)

11. *December 3, note, line 3, for Londinum read Londinium*

11. *before first entry for 1616, insert*:

1616 (?). FATHER WRITES POEM IN PRAISE OF JOHN LANE'S CONTINUATION OF CHAUCER'S "SQUIRE'S TALE."

> *John Melton*, Cittisen of *London*:
>
> most loving of musick, to his frend J.L:
>
> Right well J knowe, that vnites, eightes, fyvths, thirdes,
>
> From discordꝑ; and cromatickꝑ, doe abhorr
>
> thoughe heavnlie reason, bares with those absurdꝑ
>
> To *musickes Class*, for love sake, to restor.
>
> but tell me Lane, how canst thow this approve?
>
> that wee presume on *musick*, with out Love?

Bodleian Library, MS. Douce 170, f. iv verso; printed in *John Lane's Continuation of Chaucer's "Squire's Tale*," ed. F. J. Furnivall, London, 1888 and 1890 (Publications of the Chaucer Society, Second Series, volumes XXIII and XXVI; this quotation is in XXIII, 8). The manuscript bears the title on f. iii: "*Spencers Squiers* tale; wch hath binn [?] lost allmost three hundred yeers. and sought by manie, is now brought to light by J L 1616." On f. 35 it contains the memorandum: "*This supplement to Chaucers Squiers tale, containinge .17. sheetes, hath Licence to be printed. March. 2. 1614. John Tauerner.*" (Italics used here indicate italic letters used in the manuscript in contrast to the English letters used for most of the writing.) Although apparently licensed for printing, Lane's poem was never published until 1888. Furnivall states in his note to this passage that Milton's poem does not appear in the second (1630) version of this poem, now Ashmole MS. 53 in the Bodleian. Other commendatory poems in the 1616 version are by Thomas Windham of Somersetshire, Edward Carpenter, Matthew Jefferies of Wells, and George Hancock of Somersetshire. Presumably the year of licensing is 1614/5.

14. first entry, father's poem to Lane, delete all of this entry on this page and insert the following revised reading:

Jf *virtewe* this bee not! what is? tell quick!

    for, *Childhode, Manhode, Old age,* thow doost write,

Loue, warr, and *Lustes* quelld, by arm *Heroick*;

    instancd in *Gwy* of *warwick* (knighthodes light.)

Heraltes record℈, and each sownd *Antiquarie,*

    for *Gwyes* trewe beinge, lief, death, eake hast sought,

to satisfye those w^{ch} *præuaricari*:

    Manuscript, Cronikel, (yf mote bee bought)

Coventries, Wintons, Warwickes monumentes,

    Trophies, Traditions delivered of *Guy,*

With care, cost, paine, as sweetlie thow present℈,

    toexemplifie the flowre of *Cheualrye.*

fro^{m} cradle, to the sadle, and the beere;

    for *Christian* immitation, all are heere.

J. M.

[At end of poem, fol. 132] This poem containinge a corrected historie of *Guy Earle* of *Warwick* in 87 leaves [the present contains 132] of large quarto, written by m^{r} *John Lane,* hath licence to bee printed. Jul: 13°. 1617.

John Tauerner.

as in ye original.

John Lane, *The corrected historie of Sir Gwy, Earle of Warwick,* 1621, British Museum Harl. MS. 5,243; Hunter, pp. 12-13; Todd, I (1826), 4; printed in John Lane's *Continuation of Chaucer's "Squire's Tale,"* ed. F. J. Furnivall, Publications of the Chaucer Society, Second Series, xxiii, London, 1888, ix; Masson, I, 43 (57); Brennecke, pp. 91-92. Todd suggests that the author may be Melton the astrologer. Brennecke transcribes "flowre" (line 12) as "powre," and "and" (line 13) as "to." In the original manuscript the words printed above in italics are in italic writing, the remainder in secretary hand. The writing may be Lane's. Hunter, in "Chorus Vatum," ii (British Museum, Add. MS. 24,489), 85 (143 by another numbering), calls this poem "really too bad to be quoted . . . very hobbling poetry indeed." Brennecke calls it Milton's only surviving verse. The Latin heading may be translated: "John Milton, citizen of London, to his friend on his travels, in praise of poetry, Greetings."

18. *first note, add*:

Kenneth Rogers gives information about the White Bear in (1) *Old Cheapside and Poultry: Ancient Houses and Signs*, London, 1931, pp. 42-44, and in (2) "Bread Street: Its Ancient Signs and Houses," *London Topographical Record*, XVI (1932), 52-76. In neither place does he connect Milton with the White Bear. But in *Old Cheapside* he gives a considerable history of the building, including the fact that Eton College sold it in 1874 but still receives a small quit-rent from the present owners, Messrs. P. B. Cow and Company. In the *Record*, in addition to the information about the subsidy list entered above under 1610 (p. 3), he repeats almost the same material.

19. *note, add*:

Fletcher (*The Intellectual Development of John Milton*, I, 1956, 33-38) reproduces the floor plans from Mr. Blakiston's article.

20. *first caption, for* GREAT-UNCLE *read* UNCLE   (P)

20. *first paragraph, line 3, for* grandmother Helen *read* mother Sara   (P)

20. *first note, last line, for* 1897 *read* 1879

20. 1618, *first caption, after* YOUNG *insert* (?)   (P)

21. *first note, add*:

Young was pastor of the English merchants at Hamburg from about 1620 or 1622 to 1628, when he returned to become vicar of Stowmarket. See A. G. H. Hollingsworth, *History of Stowmarket*, Ipswich, 1844, chapter 28.   (P)   Fletcher (*The Intellectual Development of John Milton*, I, 1956) devotes a chapter (10) to Young.

21. "*Early education*," *first note, add*:

Fletcher (*ibid.*) studies in detail in many chapters Milton's early introduction to languages, to mathematics, to music, and to other subjects in the curriculum.

23. *Janssen portrait, notes, add*:

Vertue's description of his visit comes in his letter of August 12, 1721 (printed below, V, 314), to Charles Christian; Masson, I (1881), 307. Stanhope bought the portrait for twenty guineas from the executors of the will of Milton's widow, according to Francis Blackburne's *Memoir of Thomas Hollis*, 1780, I, 95. Hollis himself bought it at the sale of Stanhope's effects on June 3, 1760. It apparently belonged later to a Mr. Lane, from whom Leigh Hunt bought it in 1812, according to a four-page printed description in the Pierpont Morgan Library. There should also be a reference here to the pioneer work on Milton portraits by John Fitchett Marsh ("On the Engraved Portraits and Pretended Portraits of Milton," *Transactions of the Historic Society of Lancashire* *and Cheshire*, XII, 1860, 135-188), which I have used constantly but often neglected to mention because so much of his work is incorporated in Williamson's *Milton Tercentenary*. Vertue's letter is British Museum Harleian MS. 7,003, f. 176; Add. MS. 5,016*, f. 11, is Birch's copy.

24. *line* 3, *for* witness *read* witnesses

25. *insert*:

FEBRUARY 19, 1619. MOTHER'S RELATIVE HESTER JEFFERY MARRIES.

On this date Hester Jeffery, cousin or niece of the poet's mother, married William Blackborow at St. Peter's, Cornhill, London; see *Notes and Queries*, x, xi (1909), 13. (P)

25. *note, lines* 3-4, *for* since they lived at this time in the same house *read* who held the lease of the entire White Bear building, and from whom Milton rented his rooms

28. *line* 1, *for Christiani homines read hominis Christiani*

32. *first note, line* 1, *for* 1641 *read* 1642

33. *first note, second paragraph, insert at beginning*: Priestly was buried on May 30 in the church of All Hallows, Bread Street; see the printed Registers, p. 178. (P)

33. *insert*:

MAY 6, 1620. FATHER PARTICIPATES IN ROWLEY-JEFFREY IN-DENTURE.

[John Crowley, in his answer dated February 10, 1622 (i.e., 1622/3) to the complaint of John Webster, tallowchandler of London, dated January 25, says that in the attempt to find money for real estate actions in Clavering, co. Essex] Willm Rowley having resorted to diûs Scriveñs in London to pcure him somuch money vpon vse after the rate of tenn poundes in the hundreth being one hundreth & twelue poundes or thereabout . . . wᵗʰ much importunacie pswaded this Defendᵗ to be bound by obligacoñ with & for him the said Willm Rowley to one John Jeffrie in the sofne of two hundreth poundes wᵗʰ con-dicoñ for paymᵗ of one hundreth and fiue poundes to him the said Jeoffrie his exec' or assignes oñ the eight daie of November then next followeing at the mancoñ howse of one John Mylton Scrivener in London And . . . the said Willm Rowley oñ or about the said sixt daie of Maie in the eightenth yeare of his Maties raigne of England ffrance & Jreland by this Jndenture of lease bearinge date the same sixt daie of Maie . . . did demise vnto this Def^t all that mesuage or teñt . . . in Claûing . . . To haue & hold . . . vnder & by ye yearlie rent of one peppcorne vppon a ₚuisoe . . . that if the said Willm̄ Rowley his heires exec' or admyñ should on the said eight daie of November then next ensueing paie or cause to be paid vnto the said John Jeoffrie one hundreth & fiue poundes at the said mancoñ howse of the said John Milton in London . . . That then the said demise should be void. . . .

[Dated at the top:] Jurat' io°. Febr: i622: *Char: Cæsar.*

Public Record Office, Chancery Proceedings, C2 James I/W21/45; first mentioned in print by R. G. Howarth in *Notes and Queries,* N.S. 1 (1954), 83, but without giving any quotations. The term "mansion house" means simply Milton's father's house or office (*O.E.D.*). The John Jeffrey who supplied the money may very well have been a relative of the poet's mother. The Latin means: "sworn February 10, 1622/3, before Sir Charles Caesar," a Master in Chancery.

36. *first note, add:*
F. J. Furnivall quotes about 20 lines of Lane's poem in his edition of John Lane's *Continuation of Chaucer's "Squire's Tale"* in the Publications of the Chaucer Society, Second Series, XXIII (London, 1888), ix-x. He reads the title as "Triton's Trumpet to the sweete moneths husbanded and moralized," 1621. The exact title on MS. Reg. 17b.xv is: "*Tritons Trumpet* to the twelve monethes husbanded and moralized by *John Lane.* poeticalie adducinge 1° The *seauen* deadlie sinnes practised into combustion. 2°. Theire remedie by theire contraries, the *virtues,* gratiously intendinge the *Golden meane*; so called of perfectinge to *felicitie.* 3°. The execrable *Vices* punished, alludinge eternalie. *Virtue perijt et inventa est.* 1621°." (Roman and italic type here signify secretary and italic writing respectively.) The Latin motto may be translated: "Virtue was lost and is found."

36. *Ravenscroft, note, add:*
Fletcher (*The Intellectual Development of John Milton,* 1, 1956, 350) quotes from Charles Butler's *Principles of Music,* 1636 (p. 4), an interesting reference to Ravenscroft's book, mentioning Milton as one of the contributors.

36. *last caption, delete and substitute:*

1621. FATHER'S APPRENTICES MADE FREE OF SCRIVENERS' COMPANY. (P)

36. *last line, add:*
Henry J. Sides (*Athenaeum*, May 1, 1880, p. 566) wonders whether Richard Milton mentioned here "may have been the scrivener's *first-born son* and the future head of the family, named after the old Oxfordshire yeoman, Richard Milton." He speculates also whether James Milton, apprentice of Francis Strange in 1596, may also have been a son, and therefore whether the family may still flourish. But Hyde Clarke (*ibid.*, June 12, 1880, p. 760) says that Richard was the son of Thomas and perhaps a nephew of the scrivener.

40. *September 2, caption, for* SEPTEMBER 2 *read* SEPTEMBER 3 (P)

40. *last note, last line, for* November 21 *read* November (P)

53. *February 7, caption, for* COLLEGE. *read* COLLEGE, OXFORD

Note, first word, for Cambridge *read* Oxford *next to last line, delete former* (P) The best study of Charles Diodati and his family is Donald C. Dorian's *The English Diodatis*, Rutgers University Press, 1950.

61. *last line, for* pounds *read* shillings
63. *second paragraph, line 3, for* witness *read* witnesses
66. *first caption, for* FATHER *read* FATHER'S SERVANT (P)

67. *first note. Though my photostat of this record is labeled merely* C24/501, *Professor Parker asks whether it should not be* C24/501/-105. *There should undoubtedly be a third number.*
67. *November 22, notes, first paragraph, add:*
Masson dated this event uncertainly but late in 1624; I, 81-82 (104-105). (P)
67. *November 22, notes, last paragraph, for* points out that *read* asks whether [Harris Fletcher, *The Intellectual Development of John Milton*, I, 1956, 394]

73. *signatures to document, first witness, for* Anne [?] *read* Sara (P)

73. *note, line 3, before* French *insert*: J. Holly Hanford in *Review of English Studies*, IX (1933), 58-60;

73. last line, add:

Bernard Quaritch bought this document in 1908 for £225 (London *Times*, June 5, 1908, p. 12d). A. M. Broadley reproduced the signatures in his *Chats on Autographs*, 1910, p. 302. The Manuscript Room of the New York Public Library, in a miscellaneous folder on Milton, has typed copies of published announcements of its sale by Sotheby, Wilkinson, and Hodge on January 30-February 1, 1918 (Catalogue of that date, item 282), and again on June 3-5, 1918 (item 569).

Professor Parker has now, I believe, been the first person to read correctly the name of the first witness above as Sara Milton, mother of the poet. He also tells me that Ralph E. Hone found a signature of Anne Milton Phillips on an indenture dated January 18, 1627 or 1628, in the Shrewsbury Public Library and Museum, and that Mr. Hone discussed it in his New York University doctoral dissertation on the Phillipses. Harris Fletcher (*The Intellectual Development of John Milton*, I, 1956) reproduces the signatures in photographic facsimile (plates 14, 15).

74. first note, add:

"Mr. *Bembo*" was John Benbow, who was buried at St. Martin's in the Fields on October 7, 1625, after having been in the Crown Office for forty years; see Masson, I (1881), 104. (P)

87. 1625, caption, for ESSAYS *read* ESSAY (P)

87. last note, delete; insert:

From a manuscript sheet found by A. J. Horwood with Milton's Commonplace Book and now in Netherby Hall, Longtown, Cumberland, according to "The Columbia Milton: Fourth Supplement," *Notes and Queries*, CXCV (1950), 245; reprinted in CM, I, 326-329 (the verse, with notes at 597-598), and XII, 288-291 (the prose, with notes at 390-391); see also XVIII, 643. See also Horwood's introduction to the revised edition of the reprint of the Commonplace Book in the Camden Society Publications, New Series, 1877, pp. 61-63; Masson, I (1881), 303-305; MacKellar, pp. 361-365; French, "The Autographs of John Milton," #1; Hugh C. H. Candy in the *Library*, Fourth Series, XV (1934), 330; *Complete Prose Works of John Milton*, ed. Don M. Wolfe, I (1953), 1034-1039 (ed. Maurice Kelley and Donald C. Mackenzie). An autotype reproduction made by Horwood and deposited in the Public Record Office bears the pressmark Autotypes/ Milton &c./ Fac. 6/ Library/ Shelf 156a. A photograph of this is in the British Museum, MS. Add. 41063 1, ff. 84-85. Horwood did not include this leaf in his facsimile edition of the Commonplace Book. The Latin may be translated: "(1) Elegiac Songs; By John Milton. (a) Rise; come, rise; it is now suitable; shake off light sleep. (b) Ignoble (sleep) ill befits a ruler. (2) Early in the morning flee quickly from your bed.

The proverb is trite with age." Though there is no definite clue to the dates of these writings, Harris Fletcher (*The Intellectual Development of John Milton*, I, 1956, 211) thinks that they come from Milton's grammar school period.

89. *January 16, note, last line, for* August, 1630 *read* October, 1631 (R)

94. *first note, first paragraph, add:*
Donald L. Clark treats extensively the question of Milton's being whipped by Chappell ("John Milton and William Chappell," *Huntington Library Quarterly*, XVIII, 1955, 329-350), and doubts whether he could have been, since only a praelector or a dean had this right. Professor Clark examines many phases of Milton's relationship with the college. For a sketch of Nathaniel Tovey (or Tovell) see Masson, I (1881), 130. Thomas Warton, in *The Life and Literary remains of Ralph Bathurst* (London and Oxford, 1761, p. 153), unaccountably identifies Dr. Thomas Bainbrigg, Master of Christ's, as the person who whipped Milton. The *DNB* article on Bainbrigg attributes Milton's rustication "perhaps" to him. (R)

94. *first note, second paragraph, line 3, for* living *read* being

95. *April 9 ff., first caption, after* GREEK, *insert* LATIN.

first note, add:
Perhaps we should add Spanish, which Francini in his ode prefixed to the 1645 *Poems* says Milton knew; see CM, I, 162-163 (P)

96. *line 1, for* brevior *read* breviora

97. *first note, add:*
See also below, III, 383. (P) Harris Fletcher (*The Intellectual Development of John Milton*, I, 1956, 385-391) points out that during the grammar school period Milton probably learned to fence, to dance, and to handle horses and hawks.

97. *second entry, line 1, after* Hall's *add* (?) (P)

99. *note, add:*
Professor Maurice Kelley has kindly pointed out to me several inexact transcriptions in this text, but since they involve only accents and punctuation, I omit giving them in detail. The same is true of the letter of May, 1626, below, pp. 104-105.

102. *last line, add:* I now believe Parker's argument stronger than when I wrote this note, and I would now move this poem down to p. 152, just after January 22, 1628.

103. *first caption, for* FOREST HILL *read* WHEATLEY (P)

103. *insert*:

1626. BROTHER CHRISTOPHER ADMITTED TO ST. PAUL'S SCHOOL (?).

Christopher Milton was admitted to Christ's College, Cambridge, February 15, 1631, after having been "grounded in letters under Mr. Gill in Paul's public school. . . ." See 1, 227. I have not searched for evidence of his admission, but if he took about five years at the school, he must have begun in about 1626.

106. *after first entry, add*:

. . . he left the University of his own accord, and was not expelled for misdemeanours, as his Adversaries have said.

Wood, 1, 880; Darbishire, p. 36.

112. *note, add*:

When Milton returned to Cambridge, he probably received Nathaniel Tovey (Tovell) as his tutor; see above, p. 94. (P)

117. *insert*:

JUNE 9, 1626. EDWARD ("LYCIDAS") KING ADMITTED TO CHRIST'S COLLEGE.

Masson, 1 (1881), 171. (P)

130. *second note, line 4, before* indicates *insert* probably

131. *second note, add*:

A. S. P. Woodhouse (*University of Toronto Quarterly*, XIII, 1943, 69) dates this prolusion shortly before May, 1628.

131. *May 25, caption, after* CONCERNING *insert* PROPERTY IN (P)

133. *last line, for* Convenco'rs *read* Convenco'is

135. *second line above caption, for* fourth day *read* fourth year (P)

135. *caption, for* £500 *read* £300

140. *second paragraph of text, line 5, for* goldbeater *read* goldsmith *so also in last paragraph, line* 3 (P)

143. *caption, for* LAND *read* PROPERTY (P)

147. *line 2, after* debt *insert* (or interest on it) (P)

147. *line 7, delete* probably (P)

148. *first note, add*:

What sounds like the original of this portrait is described as having been sold at Sotheby's on February 24, 1937, from the property of Lord Aldenham; it is described and reproduced in Sotheby's catalogue of that sale, lot 111, in which the Hobart-Faithorne oil was lot 355. The present one resembles the Onslow portrait of 1629, here attributed to Janssen also. It is said to be "inscribed below on the left '*J. Milton an: aet. suae* 20' " and to be "*signed with initials 'C. J.' fecit and dated 1627 on the right.*" The size of the picture, which is framed, is given as 29″ x 24″.

148. *mulberry tree, add*:

The *Gentleman's Magazine* (LXXXIV, 1814, II, 152) identified the tree as a walnut.

148. *second caption, delete; substitute*:

1628. FATHER'S APPRENTICE JOHN HATTON (OR HUTTON) MADE FREE OF SCRIVENERS' COMPANY.

149. *Latin prolusion, last line, after* serenissima *insert* fere (Milton's errata, 1674)

149. *note, add*:

A. S. P. Woodhouse (*University of Toronto Quarterly*, XIII, 1943, 69) dates this prolusion early in 1627.

152. *first note, line 7, before* sixth *insert* verses of the   (P)   *Add at end*:

Leicester Bradner suggests the possibility (*Musae Anglicanae*, 1940, p. 112) that Milton's devotion to Ovid may have led him to write a number of elegies more closely Ovidian than any which he published.

152. *De Idea Platonica, note, add*:

William R. Parker (*A Tribute to George Coffin Taylor*, 1952, pp. 113-131) dates this poem 1630-1632.

153. *insert*:

APRIL 2, 1628. FUTURE (SECOND) WIFE KATHERINE WOODCOCK CHRISTENED AT ST. DUNSTAN'S IN THE WEST.

See below, IV, 126.   (P)

153. *May 1, note, add*:

William R. Parker (*Review of English Studies*, XI, 1935, 281) dates this poem May, 1631. A. S. P. Woodhouse (*University of Toronto Quarterly*, XIII, 1943, 73) dates it in the spring of 1629.

156. *first note, add*:

William R. Parker (*A Tribute to George Coffin Taylor*, 1952, pp. 113-131) dates this elegy May, 1630.

159. *first note, add*:

Professor and Mrs. W. Arthur Turner, who edited Milton's letters for the Yale edition of Milton's *Complete Prose Works* (I, 1953, 313-317), accept Miss Chifos's date of 1630.

162. *Latin poem, note, add*:
In *A Tribute to George Coffin Taylor* (1952, pp. 113-131) Professor Parker dates this poem 1630-1632.

165. *italicized title, for Philosophi read Philosophiæ* (Milton's errata, 1674)

171. *note, add*:
Professor and Mrs. W. Arthur Turner, who edited Milton's letters for Volume I of the Yale *Complete Prose Works* of Milton (I, 1953, 313-315), believe that the reference to a "previous letter" is not to that dated May 20, 1628, in the original (above, pp. 158-159) but to another, now lost. Hence the change of date for that letter might have no effect on this.

175. *first note, add*:
Professor J. Max Patrick has kindly called my attention to a news item in the London *Times* for September 3, 1954, which states that this mulberry tree was recently "felled by a gale."

179. *first entry, note, add*:
William R. Parker (*Review of English Studies*, XI, 1935, 282-283) dates this prolusion before 1628. A. S. P. Woodhouse (*University of Toronto Quarterly*, XIII, 1943, 69) thinks that all Milton's prolusions are arranged chronologically in order of their composition.

179. *translation of Horace, note, add*:
In *The Intellectual Development of John Milton* (I, 1956, 238) Fletcher has revised his earlier opinion. He now thinks that Milton did the translation during his grammar school period, but revised it now and then until finally it reached "almost unbelievable perfection."

179. *fourth entry, caption, delete* APPRENTICED AS SCRIVENER *and substitute* MADE FREE OF SCRIVENERS' COMPANY (P)

182. *note 19, delete second sentence.* (P)

191. *first note, add*:
Though I use the term "Graduation Book," as Masson did, the proper designation of the book that Milton signed is now "University Subscription Books." (K)

204. *November 15, third paragraph, line 1, delete* probably *line 2: for* δεῳ *read* θεῳ (K)

205. *first note, line 5, for* July *read* June (P) *Add at end of note*:
Professor Fletcher has recently pointed out (*Journal of English and*

Germanic Philology, LV, 1956, 35-40) that Milton may have done the index as a guide to further work on literature such as the help which he may have given his nephew Edward Phillips in the preparation of the latter's *Theatrum Poetarum* (*q.v.*). The title reads: "Index omnium authorum qui in opere citantur, exceptes Homeri et Pindari Scholiaste. quos ubique citatos invenies" (an index of all the authors who are cited by the commentator in the work, except Homer and Pindar, whom you will find cited everywhere). The list is long because the marginal notes quote or refer to many classical authors.

207. *first note, last paragraph, add*:

Milton's daughter Deborah Clarke told Vertue that "her Mother-in-law living in Cheshire had two pictures of him . . . the other when about twenty"; this is from the same letter of Vertue to Christian mentioned above in the additional matter for p. 23. Thomas Hollis, who took Cipriani with him to visit Speaker Onslow on September 5, 1759, to make a copy of this portrait, had five hours of exciting conversation with Onslow about Milton and other men of his time; see Francis Blackburne at the reference cited above in this note.

Thanks to the kindness of the gentlemen to be named, I can now add some more recent information. The present Viscount Harcourt writes me that he still owns the copy by Van der Gucht, which is an oval 34" high by 30" broad, painted in oils in November, 1792, for George Simon, Earl Harcourt. In addition to the notes quoted above, it also carries one by the Viscount Harcourt's great uncle, Edward Harcourt, to say that as all trace of the original Onslow picture had been lost, he considered this copy far more valuable. Since this entry was made about 1870, whereas Marsh hinted in 1861 that the original Onslow picture was then extant, the probability is that it was destroyed between those two dates. Both the Viscount Harcourt and Lady Halifax, a daughter of the Earl of Onslow, believe that it was destroyed by fire. The Van der Gucht copy was exhibited in Paris in 1951 at the Exhibition held at the Bibliothèque Nationale entitled "Le Livre Anglais" which was organized by the British Council Fine Arts Committee. The Viscount Harcourt also gave permission to Dr. F. E. Hutchinson of All Souls College, Oxford, to reproduce the portrait in his *Milton and the English Mind* (English Universities Press, London, 1949), but Hutchinson's actual frontispiece is entirely different. The present Earl of Onslow regrets that he can add nothing about the original, except that he believes that the third Earl, grandson of Speaker Onslow, getting old and cranky, sold it near the beginning of the nineteenth century, allegedly for £4 to an unknown buyer, since which time all trace of it has been lost. E. K. Adams, Esq., of the National Portrait Gallery, informs me that the second Earl of Onslow exhibited the original at the British Institution in 1820, but that the third Earl, when asked about it in 1840, certified that he possessed no picture of Milton, but that

[375]

in 1827 or 1828 he sold a portrait of him supposed to be an original but considered by him as only a very bad copy. Mr. Adams nevertheless thinks that the picture which Onslow sold was probably the original. The buyer was a Mr. Moore, about whom nothing else seems to be known except that he bought several other pictures at the same sale. Since then several pictures claiming to be the lost one have turned up, but none with any credibility. Noel Blakiston, Esq., of the Public Record Office, believes it possible that even now the missing portrait may some day turn up.

214. *book on logic, note, add*:
For Milton's *Art of Logic* see under May, 1672.

214-215. FATHER RETIRES, *transfer this entry to p. 271, following one on the same subject there. The two were separated by error.*

225. *first note, first paragraph, add*:
See also Harris Fletcher's *Contributions*, p. 51; London *Times*, October 3, 1936; and *Notes and Queries*, CLXXI (1936), 445.

225. *Milton's Aratus, note, add*:
Maurice Kelley and Samuel D. Atkins have discussed this volume in *PMLA*, LXX (1955), 1090-1106. After a close study of the original volume in the British Museum (of which the press mark should be C.60.l.7), they have selected and printed 36 manuscript notes which they believe to be by Milton, giving their reasons and following up his references to the books from which he quotes. They conclude that Milton was a good student, and that his notes here were made at two periods: (1) 1631-1638, and chiefly 1631-1632; and (2) 1639-1652, and chiefly 1641-1642, when he went through the book a second time to teach his students.

225. *L'Allegro, note, first paragraph, add*:
William R. Parker (*Review of English Studies*, XI, 1935, 282) dates "L'Allegro" and "Il Penseroso" early in 1632. A. S. P. Woodhouse (*University of Toronto Quarterly*, XIII, 1943, 93) accepts Tillyard's date of 1631 (*The Miltonic Setting*, 1938, pp. 1-28) but censures me for having omitted to give Tillyard's reasons (*University of Toronto Quarterly*, XXI, 1952, 194). Ernest Sprott (*Milton's Art of Prosody*, Oxford, 1953), on the basis of metrics, dates the first 100 lines of "L'-Allegro" earlier than the "Epitaph on the Marchioness of Winchester" and the remainder after it, a conclusion which Ants Oras (*Notes and Queries*, CXCVIII, 1953, 332-333) rejects as based on unreliable evidence.

226. *Arcades, note, add*:
Lyla G. Hugill (*A Record of the Friends of John Milton*, University of Chicago dissertation, 1924, p. 106) thinks this work "another ex-

periment undertaken at Lawes's suggestion in the vacation of 1630."
William R. Parker (*Review of English Studies*, XI, 1935, 280) dates
it 1633. A. S. P. Woodhouse (*University of Toronto Quarterly*, XIII,
1943, 100) dates it in the summer of 1632. Donald C. Dorian (*The
English Diodatis*, 1950, pp. 145-150) gives a number of reasons for
believing that Milton was invited to do this poem as much through the
influence of the Diodatis, and especially Dr. Theodore, as through that
of Lawes.

227. *first note, add*:

Mr. Evans (*Modern Language Quarterly*, VIII, 1947, 10 and IX,
1948, 10 and 184) quotes four epitaphs on Hobson from James Jones's
Sepulchrorum Inscriptiones, 1727, I, 216-217, and comments further
on Milton's poems.

227. *insert*:

FEBRUARY 10, 1631. FATHER WITNESSES INDENTURE BETWEEN
FRANCIS AND JOHN FARLEY.

1630 This Jndenture made the Tenth day of ffebruarie in the
yeare of our Lord God One Thowsand Six hundred and Thirtie
And in the Sixte yeare of the reigne of our Soveraigne Lord
Charles by the grace of God King of England, Scotland, ffrance,
and Jreland Defender of the faith &c' *Betweene* ffrancis ffarley
of Bosbury in the County of Herefford Yeoman sonne and heire
of John ffarley late of Vpleadon in the Parrish of Bosbury
aforesaid Yeoman Deceased on thone part, And John ffarley
Citezen and Grocer of London Brother of the said ffrancis
ffarley on thother part/ [agree that Francis will convey to John
certain properties in the manor of Upleadon, alias Temple
Court, Herefordshire, in consideration of an annual rent of
twelve pounds, to be paid regularly every year] At the telling
howse scituate at the West end of the Royall Exchange within
the Cittie of London . . . At and vpon the ffeast day of the
Purificaċon of the blessed Virgin Mary Com̃only called Candle-
mas day. . . ./ Jn witnes whereof the said parties to these pñte
Jndentures Jnterchangeably have sett their hands and seales
Yeoven the day and yeares first above written:/

[Signed:] John ffarley

[Endorsed:] Sealed & deliũed in the pñce

of Jo: milton. scr./

Henry Rothwell svant to the s̄d Scr.'.

[Also endorsed:] John Farley Cou^t/

[Further endorsed:] The writeinge betweene John ffarley and ffraunc̦ ffarley all Cancelled./

From a photostatic copy of the original document now in the Hereford Public Library, provided for me through the kindness of the librarian, Penelope E. Morgan, F. L. A. According to the usual practice in such documents, the year is probably 1630/1 rather than 1629/30. The manuscript is labeled on the back, "L. C. Deeds 3232. No. 23." The text of the indenture is in the usual handwriting found in similar documents. John Farley's name at the foot of the indenture is presumably in his own hand, whereas on the back it is probably in the hand of Henry Rothwell, since it resembles the writing of his name. Milton's father's name is probably in his own hand, but very likely Rothwell wrote the text. The note about the cancellation of covenants is in a still different hand. "Cou^b" after the name of John Farley on the back probably means "covenant"; in other words, this is John Farley's copy of the covenant. This entry may be followed by a date, but it is no longer legible. This document is described briefly in the *Bulletin of the Institute of Historical Research*, XVIII (1941), 177.

228. *epitaph on Winchester, note, add*:
William R. Parker (*Modern Language Review*, XLIV, 1949, 547-550) thinks that the manuscript has considerable authority.

243. *August 25, note, line 4, for* LXVI, *read* LXVI, 262   (P)   *line 5: before* 1938 *insert* December 17,

257. *last caption, for* NOVEMBER, *read* AFTER NOVEMBER.

257. *last note, first line, for* as of this date *read* between this date and October, 1632. *The remainder of the note after the first sentence should be modified accordingly*.   (P)

259. *December 9, note, add*:
William R. Parker (*Review of English Studies*, XI, 1935, 278) feels sure that this sonnet was written in December, 1632. Merritt Y. Hughes assigns it to 1631 or 1632 (Milton's *Paradise Regained*, etc., 1937, p. 185). A. S. P. Woodhouse (*University of Toronto Quarterly*, XIII, 1943, 67) considers Parker "completely convincing," and repeats this stand in reviewing my volumes I and II (*ibid.*, XXI, 1952, 194). Their argument is that Milton is thinking of the time when Time has stolen away his age of 23 and made him 24. If they are right, this entry should be moved down to the bottom of p. 277. Donald C. Dorian suggests (*The English Diodatis*, 1950, pp. 122-123, 143) that Milton may be comparing himself with the swifter progress of Charles Diodati, who took his B.A. at the age of 16, his M.A. at 19, and his incorporation at

20, and who published his first poem at not more than the age of 15.

261. *epitaph on Shakespeare, note, add*:

Howard Parsons identifies the writer (*Notes and Queries*, CXCIV, 1949, 38) as James Mervyn. Arthur W. Secord (*Journal of English and Germanic Philology*, XLVII, 1948, 374) nominates James Mabbe. Donald C. Dorian speculates (*The English Diodatis*, 1950, pp. 155-156, 274) that the link between Milton and Shakespeare may have come through Charles Diodati's brother John, who was a beneficiary and an overseer of the will of the widow of Henry Condell, one of the printers of the First Folio.

265. *first note, line* 9, *after* Hanford in 1634. *insert*: Parker's note is in the *Review of English Studies*, XI (1935), 279. Professor and Mrs. Turner (Milton's *Complete Prose Works*, I, 1953, 318) agree with Parker. A. S. P. Woodhouse (*University of Toronto Quarterly*, XIII, 1943, 99-100) calls 1632 an "impossibly early date."

270. *insert*:

JUNE 30, 1632. BROTHER CHRISTOPHER ADMITTED TO INNER TEMPLE (?).

John and J. A. Venn (*Alumni Cantabrigienses*, III, 193) say that Christopher was admitted on this date. I know of no first-hand evidence. (P) The *DNB* gives the date as 1631.

271. *notes on father's move to Horton, add*:

British Museum Add. MSS. 36,358 (f. 217b) and 37,017 (ff. 3-6) contain water-color sketches said to be of Horton church, the poet's father's house, the dovecote, and the mother's tomb by John Buckler and his son and his grandson about 1817; they are described in *The Victoria History of the County of Buckingham*, III (ed. William Page, 1925), 281 and 246. There is a sentimentalized account of the house in Gordon W. J. Gyll's *History of the Parishes of Wraysbury . . . Horton . . . Colnbrook*, London, 1862, pp. 237-242, 250, 259, 261. Mr. Page says that the present Berkin Manor, the property and residence of Mrs. Tyrrell (at least in 1925), was built about the middle of the nineteenth century on the site of the Milton house, said to have been pulled down at the end of the eighteenth century except for the red brick dovecote. Since the buildings were said to be in Colnbrook rather than in Horton, I wrote to the then rector of Horton (Rev. T. D. Prentis, 1951), who informed me that neither he nor the minister at Colnbrook knew anything of such a location. Probably the explanation of the seeming inconsistency is that given by Mr. Page and later mentioned by Charles A. Toase in *Notes and Queries*, N.S. I (1954), 546: namely that until 1853 Colnbrook was a chapelry attached to the parish of Horton. But this explanation would still not account for the picture of Milton's mother's tomb, so called, whereas she is known to be buried in the Horton parish church (see below, p. 321).

Harris Fletcher has pointed out (*Journal of English and Germanic Philology*, LI, 1952, 154-159, and again in *The Intellectual Development of John Milton*, I, 1956, 405-414) that the long-standing conception of the Milton family as living tightly in London until 1632 and then retiring to Horton may be entirely wrong. Professor Fletcher believes that the "Musarum spatia" (haunts of the Muses) of Milton's letter of March 26, 1625, to Thomas Young, the "suburbani nobilis umbra loci" (noble shade of a suburban neighborhood) of Elegy I (line 50), and other similar references up at least through the "*E nostro Suburbano*" (from our suburban residence) of Milton's letter of December 4, 1634, to Alexander Gill prove that the family had at least a summer home outside the city as early as 1625 (the year of the plague), and perhaps as early as 1623. Further proof comes in Milton's father's describing himself a number of times between 1632 and 1635 as of Hammersmith (see pp. 276, 284, 285, 292). Whether this suburban retreat was Hammersmith for the whole period, or whether the family went to other spots is not clear. If Fletcher is right, perhaps the Miltons did not go to Horton until about 1635.

One further phase of this matter may be mentioned, though not very seriously. In 1913 Ezra Pound wrote (*Letters*, 1950, p. 28) that he was in Slough "for a week with the Hueffers in a dingy old cottage that belonged to Milton." But see the added note below for p. 321. A recent letter of inquiry to him brought no helpful information.

271. *after preceding addition, insert entry on father's move to Horton now erroneously printed on pp.* 214-215.

271. *July 3, caption and first line of note, for* GRADUATION BOOK *read* UNIVERSITY SUBSCRIPTION BOOKS   (K)

273. *second note, add*:
Phillips is confused in his geography: both Horton and Colnbrook are in Buckinghamshire.

273. *after selection from Wood, insert*:
[Milton would] make an excursion now and then to *London*, somtimes to buy Books, or to meet Friends from *Cambridg*.

Toland, p. 7; Darbishire, p. 88.   (R)
273. *last note* (*from Milton's Apology*), *line* 1, *for* 1641 *read* 1642.
274. *note, add*:
Marguerite Little ("Milton's *Ad Patrem* and the younger Gill's *In Natalem Mei Parentis*," *Journal of English and Germanic Philology*, XLIX, 1950, 345-351) finds a considerable debt in Milton's poem to Gill's.

William R. Parker (*A Tribute to George Coffin Taylor*, 1952, pp. 113-131) dates this poem between September 29 and November 29, 1634.

275. *Commonplace Book, notes, second paragraph, add*:
In his article in *PMLA* Hanford carefully analyzes the dates and the natures of the entries, which he divides into three large groups, naming the composition of each, and indexing all the entries at the end: (1) before 1639 and in Milton's hand; (2) between 1639 and 1652 and in Milton's hand; (3) after about 1650 and in the hands of amanuenses. He does not, however, date any entry earlier than 1636. This entry should probably more accurately appear under that year.

277. *first note, add*: According to the registers of All Hallows, Bread Street, Christopher Baron (or Barrowe) was buried on May 20, 1624 (Publications of the Harleian Society, Registers, XLIII, 1913, 180. If the elder Milton knew him, as he says, for 30 years, and if Baron lived in All Hallows parish for that period, perhaps Milton may have settled there as early as 1594. (P)

277. *last note, add*: A fire on the Bridge on February 12, 1632, destroyed about 60 houses. (P)

281. 1634, *first note, line 2, for* fall *read* summer *line 4, for* as late as *read* before *add at end*: A Thomas Agar and an Anna Phillips were married at St. Dunstan in the East on January 5, 1632 (Registers, Publications of the Harleian Society, LXIX, 115). (P) But if Masson is right that Agar and his preceding wife had a child as late as 1633, these cannot be the same people. Yet the similarity of names is very striking.

283. *end, add*:
Donald C. Dorian suggests (*The English Diodatis*, 1950, p. 268) that Milton's introduction into the Bridgewater circle may have come through the Diodatis, since Theodore was physician to most of them. He also queries (p. 276) whether the "certain shepherd lad" of Comus, line 618, may have been this same Theodore. On the other hand he also proposes his identification with Charles Diodati (p. 151), who was also a physician and who accompanied his father in visits to aristocratic patients to whom Henry Lawes also came. Harris Fletcher (ed. Milton's *Complete Poetical Works*, Houghton Mifflin Company, 1941, p. 103) believes that the reference in this line is "no doubt to Charles Diodati, who may have witnessed the performance" of *Comus*. Other identifications have been proposed, including Milton himself.

287. *last note, add*: The persons who acted in *Comus* are also named on the last page of the 1637 edition and on the title page of the Bridgewater Manuscript; Fletcher Facsimile, I, 299, 301. (P) There is a tradition that Lady Isabella Rich (daughter of the Earl of Holland and wife of Sir James Thynne) acted in *Comus* (K)

288. *translation of Psalm 114, first note, add*:

Harris Fletcher (*The Intellectual Development of John Milton*, I, 1956, 258-262) thinks that Milton made this translation as part of an exercise in grammar school, kept it by him for occasional revision as with his other early work, and finally discovered a version that satisfied him just before writing to Gill. In commenting on the slight changes between the versions of 1645 and 1673, which Fletcher attributes to Milton, he says of Milton, "He never tired of polishing them [his translations]."

291. *incorporated A. M., note, add*:
Mr. J. S. Phelip, Deputy Keeper of the University Archives at Oxford, kindly informs me that there is no record anywhere in the University of Milton's incorporation. Aubrey wrote to Wood on June 29, 1689 (Wood MS. F. 39, f. 386v, as quoted in Aubrey's *Brief Lives*, ed. Clark, II, 63): "Mr. Edward Philips tells me his uncle, John Milton, was Master of Arts of Cambridge, of Christ's College. He was never of Oxford." But either Wood did not get this letter in time to use it, or he did not believe it. (R)

294. *September 30, note, line 2, for Londinum read Londinium*
296. *Dion Chrysostom, note, add*:
There are manuscript textual corrections on pp. 177, 312, 321, 322. (K)

297. *first note, add*:
Henry F. Waters, who summarizes this will in *Genealogical Gleanings in England*, I (1901), 627, mistakenly calls this Richard Milton father of John.

302. *note, add*:
Raymond Delacourt mentioned this action and quoted a few sentences from it in *Notes aand Queries*, II, x (1860), 341, but without identifying it.

303. *Comus printed, change first five lines of text from italic to roman* (P)

Add to note: William R. Parker ("Contributions toward a Milton Bibliography," *Library*, 4th Series, XVI, 1935-1936, 431) believes that the printer of *Comus* was Augustine Mathewes.

304. *first note, add*:
The so-called Ludlow Castle copy of *Comus* at Harvard contains no markings.

304. *Milton's Heraclides, note, add*:
Harris Fletcher in *Philological Quarterly*, XXVIII (1949), 72, and in *Journal of English and Germanic Philology*, XLVII (1948), 182-187; Thomas O. Mabbott and others, "The Columbia Milton: Fourth Supplement," *Notes and Queries*, CXCV (1950), 246. Heraclides' name was by an oversight incorrectly spelled in the heading to this entry.

321. *April 6, first note, add*:

According to an article in the "Gardener's Chronicle" for August 21, 1886, as stated in *B T R News*, I, no. 6, June, 1950, pp. 2-4, "Milton's mother was buried on the cliff here [in Taplow, co. Bucks, near Slough]." The writer of the story in the *News* adds with amusement his discovery that the Sarah Jeffrey who was the heroine of this anecdote died in 1830. I mention it simply to warn readers not to pay any attention to it as a genuine biographical note about Milton's family. I am indebted to Dr. Ruth Mohl for this information.

322. *first note, add*:

In the New York Public Library Manuscript Room's miscellaneous folder on Milton is a clipping from the *Examiner* article, with photographs of Mr. Armstrong and of a page from the Bible showing manuscript notes (unreadable). The Bible is said to contain notes about Miltons named Sarah, Francis, Robert, and John, who lived about 1700.

342. *note, add*:

Professor and Mrs. Turner (Yale *Complete Prose Works* of Milton, I, 1953, 325) think that the month of this letter should be November, and that perhaps the printer misunderstood Milton's manuscript note, which might have read something like "2 IX 1637," in which IX means November.

344. *letter from Diodati, note, add*:

Donald C. Dorian (*The English Diodatis*, 1950, p. 163) thinks that Diodati's lost answer to Milton's letter of September 2 explained, for Milton's correction, that Diodati was not yet a practising physician but still studying with his father, as he had been since 1631, and acting as his father's assistant, though he was now just about ready to go into practice for himself.

346. *line 13, for* ἐνέταξε *read* ἐνεστάξε (Milton's errata, 1674)

347. *note, add*:

Professor and Mrs. Turner think that the date of this letter, like that of number 6 above (pp. 341-344) should be November instead of September.

354. *first entry for 1638, note, add*:

What connection, if any, this reputed Van Dyck has with an alleged portrait of Milton by Van Dyck now in the possession of Count Ivan N. Podgoursky in New York I cannot say. But such a portrait formed part of the Count's collection which was on exhibition through the Museum Association of Midwestern University at Wichita Falls, Texas, from September 25 to October 6, 1955. A reproduction is given on the fourth page of the catalogue of that exhibit. Probably this is an entirely different portrait, because the moustache, lace cuffs, and landscape which Williamson (pp. 84-85) describes do not show in this reproduction. I am indebted to Dr. French Fogle and to Rev. Claude A. Beeseley, President of the Museum Association, for information about this picture.

355. *first note, add*: In *The Inhabitants of London in 1638* (ed. T. C. Dale from Lambeth Palace MS. 272, London, 1931, p. 50), a John Milton, neighbor of John Lane, Edward Willoughby, and others, paid a rent of £25. I have no idea what relation, if any, this John Milton was to the poet.

355. *Lady Talbot, note, next to last line, delete* later (P)

355. *last note, first paragraph, add*:

R. B. McKerrow, on the other hand, in his *Introduction to Bibliography* (1928, pp. 218-219) believes that "The corrections appear to be those of a printer's reader." Some other references on this work are C. E. Sayle, *Early English Printed Books in the University Library,* Cambridge, II (1902), 1290, numbers 5829 and 5830; Williamson, *Milton Tercentenary,* p. 91; A. W. Pollard in the *Library,* 2nd Series, x (1909), 6; H. C. H. Candy, *ibid.,* 4th Series, XIII (1933), 192.

358. *Christopher marries, notes, second paragraph, line 3, for* July *read* June (P)

359. *letters of recommendation, first note, add*:

Donald C. Dorian (*The English Diodatis,* 1950, pp. 169-172) thinks that the Diodati family may have provided some of these letters, since various members of the family were friendly with Sir Henry Wotton, Hugo Grotius, John Hales, Galileo, and others.

359. *letter from Lawes, note, first paragraph, add*:

An autotype reproduction of this manuscript, together with those of Milton's early prose and verse pieces mentioned above on p. 87, was deposited by A. J. Horwood in the Public Record Office in 1876; its shelf-mark is Autotypes/ Milton &c./ Fac. 6/ Library/ Shelf 156a. Masson printed this letter first in the 1881 edition of Volume I, p. 736.

360. *April 1, first note, add*:

On Milton's acquaintance with Wotton and with John Hales (see p. 363, line 8), see the added note above for p. 359, letters of recommendation, first note.

361. *first note, lines 1-2, for* may well have been *read* was *Add at end*: The heading to Wotton's letter in Milton's *Poems* of 1645 is "The Copy of a Letter Writt'n By Sir HENRY WOOTTON, To the Author, upon the following Poem." (P)

363. *first note, add*:

Miss Lyla G. Hugill (*A Record of the Friends of John Milton,* University of Chicago doctoral dissertation, 1924, p. 185) interprets the Mr. R. of lines 22-23 as Robert Randolph, brother of the poet Thom-

as, and (p. 225) the learned friend of line 9 as Diodati. Professor
and Mrs. Turner (Milton's *Complete Prose Works*, ed. Don M.
Wolfe, I, 1953, 341) accept Robert Randolph as a possibility but prefer
Humphrey Robinson, who had published Milton's *Comus* the preceding year. They give no note on the learned friend.

368. *first note, add*: There is no mention of Milton, as one might
hope, in the Scudamore-Grotius correspondence in British Museum
Add. MS. 11,044, pp. 91 ff.

371. *insert*:

JUNE 28, 1638. MILTON VISITS SVOGLIATI ACADEMY (?).
A di. 8.

Il S^r. Bartolommei et il S^r. Buonmattei recitarono lero sonetti
e ci furono presenti li SS^ri. Alsso. e Giulio Pitti, il S^r. Mar^e. Vin-
cēzio Capponi, il S^r. Can^co. Vincenzio Bardi, il S^r. Lettor Siluestri,
L'Abate D. Eus°. il Gaddi, e un letterato Inglese che deside-
raua d'entrar nell' Accad^a. nella q̄le. oltre li altri ragionamj^ti.
litterarij, si esortò instantemj^te. dal Gaddi che si facessero d^e.
lezioni e oltre funzioni pubbliche che si frequētasse l'Accad^a.
e massime la prossima tornata nella q̄le si haueua a' dar l'ult°.
termine e conclusione.

Biblioteca Nazionale, Florence, Magliabecchiana MSS., Cl. IX, cod.
60, fol. 46v. I owe this reference to the kindness of Miss Edith P.
Hubbard, who found it in the original manuscript records of the Academy. She thinks it may perhaps refer to Milton, who might possibly
have arrived in Florence early enough for such a visit, though we
have tentatively placed his arrival in August or September of 1638.
In the absence of Milton's name this attribution can be only a guess.
Since the dating is probably New Style, this item is entered under Old
Style.

[(July) 8 (i.e., June 28, 1638).
Mr. Bartholommei and Mr. Buonmattei recited some of their
sonnets, and there were present Messrs. Alessandro and Giulio
Pitti, Marchese Vincenzio Capponi, Canon Vincenzio Bardi,
Reader Silvestri, Abate Eusebio, Gaddi, and an English man of
letters who wished to come to the meeting of the Academy, in
which, besides other literary discussions, there was a strong ex-
hortation by Gaddi that there should be some lectures and other

public functions, and that people should attend the meetings, especially the next one, in which would be given the final end and conclusion.]

I am grateful to my colleague Professor Remigio U. Pane for help in translating this difficult text.

JULY 5, 1638. ELECTED MEMBER OF THE SVOGLIATI ACADEMY (?).

A di 15

Nell' Accad^a., nella q̄le si trouarono li SS^{ri}. Aless°. Adimari, Aless°. e Giulio Pitti, Baccio Valori, Ben°. Buon Mattei, Fel°. Siluestri Fr. Rouai, Frescobaldi, Gaddi, Gir°. Bartolommei, Don V°. della Rena, furono proposti l'Ab°. D. Eusebio, et il S^r. . . . p̄ Accademici li q̄li vinsero non ostante una faua bianca; si strinse dal Gaddi la cosa d°. lezioni, siche si concluse, che il S^r. Rouai avanti passare il presente mese ne facesse una e non mj^{ti}. giorni doppo il S^r. BuonMattei. Si discusse di uarie imprese facendosi, e rifacendosi uarie obbiezioni e difficoltà, le q̄li risolute si ratificò a uoce quasi comune l'elezione già fatta della pianta de capperi.

furon' letti dal S^r. Adimari due nobili sonetti, e dal S^r. BuonMattei un piaceuole Prologo d'un suo Dramma.

Biblioteca Nazionale, Florence, Magliabecchiana MSS., Cl. IX, cod. 60, fol. 47. I owe this possible reference to Milton, like that of June 28 above, to Miss Edith P. Hubbard. It is no more certain than that, but equally possible. Like the preceding item, this is probably dated New Style.

[(July) 15 (i.e., July 5, 1638).

In the Academy, at which were present Messrs. Alessandro Adimari, Alessandro and Giulio Pitti, Baccio Valori, Benedetto Buonmattei, Feliciano Silvestri, Francois Rouai, Frescobaldi, Gaddi, Girolamo Bartolommei, Don Vincenzo dell Rena, there were proposed at this meeting the Abate Don Eusebio and Mr. . . . as members of the Academy, who won notwithstanding a white bean (i.e., blackball). The matter of lectures was pressed by Gaddi so that it was concluded that Mr. Rouai, before the end of the current month, should give one, and not many days later Mr. Buonmattei also. Various activities were discussed, and various objections and difficulties were presented, upon the resolution of which the choice already made of the caper plant was ratified almost unanimously.

Mr. Adimari read two noble sonnets, and Mr. Buonmattei read a pleasant prologue of a drama of his.]

I am grateful to my colleague Professor Remigio U. Pane for help in translating this Italian.

372. *first note, add:*
If the new entries for June 28 and July 5 actually refer to Milton, then the date of the present entry needs to be changed to June, with corresponding alterations in those for Nice, Genoa, Leghorn, and Pisa. On Clementillo see Edward Rosen, "A Friend of John Milton: Valerio Chimentelli . . . ," *Bulletin of the New York Public Library*, LVII (1953), 159-174. He points out that Chimentelli and Clementillo are two names for the same person.

373. *first paragraph, fourth line from end, for* Epistle, *read* Epistle;

373. *first note, add:*
Phillips made one mis-statement about the poems prefixed to Milton's volume: the "Elegant *Italian Canzonet*" is by Francini, not by Gaddi. (R)

374. *first note, line 2, for* translations *read* Psalm 114 (P)

375. *bottom, add:*
Edward Rosen (*Bulletin of the New York Public Library*, LVII, 1953, 173) questions the date of this entry since the poems are said in the title to have been composed in September, 1637. The reason for my dating, though not too strong, is that the time of Milton's visit in Malatesti's home town, Florence, would be the logical time for the author to give them to Milton. It is of course just possible that the figure 7 is an error for 8, but whether it is or not, this general period should be about right. Mr. Rosen also notes that the word "volume" in line 7 of paragraph 2 should be changed to "edition." I may also add that *La Tina* was reprinted in 1946. See also Blackburne's *Memoir of Thomas Hollis*, pp. 167, 491. (R)

376. *poem to Salsilli, note, add:*
Professor W. R. Parker (*A Tribute to George Coffin Taylor*, 1952, pp. 113-131) dates this poem November, 1638.

378. *after first note, add entry now printed at bottom of* II, 5 (P)
381. *first note, add:*

Selections from these letters are given below at II, 56, 60, 67, 70, 78. Donald C. Dorian (*The English Diodatis*, 1950, p. 282) believes that Elie Diodati may have provided Milton with a letter of introduction to Galileo. Though this particular letter has not been found, others of about this period from Elie Diodati are mentioned in letters from Galileo.

383. *fifth line from end, after* solidam *insert* a (Milton's errata, 1674)

384. *line* 15, *for* fuerat *read* fuerit (Milton's errata, 1674)

385. *note, add*:
Professor and Mrs. Turner (Milton's *Complete Prose Works*, I, 332) think that Milton's dating is New Style. If so, the English equivalent is August 31, and this entry needs to be moved to p. 371.

389. *September* 16, *note, add*:
If the date is New Style, the English equivalent is September 6.

390. *after first note, insert*:

Et ego, quid, inquam, nunc memorem tot agyrtas, tot empiricos, tot seplasiarios, tot circulatores, quos Romæ aut Venetiis iisdem penè verbis suas pyxides & pharmaca vendentes, præteriens audivi.

Milton, *Defensio Pro Se*, 1655, pp. 106-107; CM, IX, 156.   (P)

[And why, I ask, should I now recall the many mountebanks, quacks, perfume-sellers, and gypsies whom, as I passed through Rome and Venice, I heard selling their pill-boxes and potions in almost the same words?]

393. *after first caption, insert*:

die 30 pranzi st. in Coll°. nrō Ill^{ms}. D. N. Cary, frater Baronis de Faukeland. Doctor Holdingus Lancastrensis. D. N. Fortescuto. et Dñs. Miltonus cū famulo nobiles Angli. et excepti st. Laute.

From the original entry in the Travelers' Book, of which Professor Maurice Kelley kindly gave me a photostatic copy. Preceding the first word is what looks like a canceled "A." The date seems to have been first written 20 and later changed to 30. Possibly the 20 was Old (English) Style, in which case this entry needs to be redated October 20. The "cū famulo" which follows Milton's name is added over a caret. Since this is merely a revised reading of the present Latin, no additional translation is needed here.

394. *next to last line, after* lib. 20, *insert* [stanza 142] (my thanks to Professor Allan H. Gilbert)

401. *first note, add:*
Toland (p. 9) corrects the title of Tasso's poem to *Gierusalemme Conquistata* (Darbishire, p. 94) (P)

401. *Latin couplet, line 1, for mos read facies, mos* (R)

401. *insert:*
DECEMBER 30, 1638. FUTURE (THIRD) WIFE ELIZABETH MINSHULL BAPTIZED IN WISTASTON.

See below, IV, 381-383. (P)

403. *first caption, for* WARNING LETTERS *read* WARNINGS (P)

404. *third note, add:*
The quotation is from More's *Fides Publica*, 1655, p. 68.

408. *March 17, note, add:*
If the date is New Style, the English equivalent is March 7.

409. *first note, add:*
If the date is New Style, the English equivalent is March 14.

411. *note, add:*
Joseph McG. Bottkol discovered the holograph original of this letter in the Vatican library (*Barb. Lat.* 2181, ff. 57, 58) and published it with notes and photographic reproductions in *PMLA*, LXVIII (1953), 617-627. The original is dated March 29 instead of 30, and it is sealed with a wafer seal showing (Mr. Bottkol believes) a cipher for John Milton's name. There are many slight variations in punctuation, spelling, and the like, but only three verbal differences: "accipiuntur" to "arripiuntur" (410, 11), "publico" to "populo" (410, 28), and "Liberales" to "liberas" (411, 11).

414. *first caption, for* FLORENTINE *read* SVOGLIATI.

Add at end of note: Though I used the word "Florentine" in a general sense in the caption to this entry, Mr. Edward Rosen points out (*Bulletin of the New York Public Library*, LVII, 1953, 173) that another group in the city actually bore the title of Florentine Academy, so that my use of the name was unwittingly ambiguous.

414. *March 31, first note, add:*
If the date is New Style, the English equivalent is March 21.

[389]

414. *last entry, caption and translation, for* Bononia *read* Bologna.

418. *visit to Diodati, first note, add*:
Though Guillaume Fatio describes zestfully "Milton et Byron à la Villa Diodati" (*Nos Anciens et leurs Oeuvres*, ed. Jules Crosnier, Geneva, 1912, Series 12, Tome 2, *Recueuil Genevois d'Art*, 21-66), an idea which Masson also toys with (1 [1881], 832-833), Donald C. Dorian gives convincing evidence (*The English Diodatis*, 1950, p. 284) that Milton could hardly have stayed at the Villa Diodati since it did not come into the possession of the Diodati family until long afterwards. Milton frequently praised Geneva for its religious and civic virtues; see Patterson's *Index* and especially CM, IX, 202-205. Toland asserts (Darbishire, p. 95) that Milton, while at Geneva was "known to . . . *Ezechiel Spanhemius.*" But though it is likely that Milton met Frederick Spanheim (1600-1649), father of Ezekiel (1639-1710), there is no specific evidence. (P, in part)

419. *June 10, note, add*:
The date is not in Milton's handwriting. (K) If it is New Style, the English equivalent is May 31.

420. *return to England, first note, add*:
B. A. Wright (in *Modern Language Notes*, XXVIII, 1933, 308-314, and in *Review of English Studies*, N. S. II, 1951, 179-181) offers a different chronology of the whole Italian journey which, he believes, is more correct than Masson's and mine. The differences, however, are of course only a matter of months.

423. *index, insert prefatory note*: This index, unlike those in later volumes, does not cover the preface. (P)

424. *after* Bower, Thomas, *insert*: Bower, William, 36 (P)

427. Diodati, John, *first entry, for* father *read* uncle (P)

427. Diodati, Theodore, *after* M.D., *insert* father of Charles, (P)

429. Fortescue: *for* Mr. (or Lord) *read* Sir Nicholas the younger (P)

429. Gill, Alexander, *delete both entries; insert*:
Gill, Alexander, master of St. Paul's, 27-29, 90, 91, 227
Gill, Alexander, his son, 8, 27, 28, 53, 152, 157-159, 161, 162, 170-173, 288-290

432. Lane, John, *for* 44-49 *read* 43-49 (P)

433. Malcolm, *for London read Londinium*

434. Milton, Christopher, *for* 29 *read* 28

434. Milton, Elizabeth, *delete this entry* (P)

434. Milton, John, I. LIFE, *insert*:
buys books, 415

434. Milton, John, I, LIFE, Greek studies, *before* 384 *insert* 95,

435. 2. WRITINGS, "Ad Patrem," *before* 274 *insert* 95

436. 3. LETTERS, *insert*:
from Henry Lawes, 359
to unknown friend, 262

436. 4. ASSOCIATION BOOKS, *insert*:
Apologia pro Confessione, 179
Cardoyn, 419
Ovid, 52
Raleigh, 295
437. Milton, John, father, *bottom of first column, insert*:
poems to and from Lane, 13, 35
437. *insert*: Milton, Katherine (Woodcock), second wife, 215 (P)
437. Milton, Richard, scrivener, *after* 36, *insert* 279,
440. MS. Wood D 4, *before* 1 *insert* vii,
444. Talbot, Lady, *for* 354 *read* 355
445. Trinity College, *delete* 53,
445. *insert*: Trinity College (Oxford), 53

VOLUME II

1. *delete second entry, which inadvertently repeats that at* 1, 322.

2. *insert*:

DECEMBER 14, 1639. FATHER (?) WITNESSES WIDMER-WALLER INDENTURE.

This Jndenture made the ffowerteeneth Daye of December in the ffowerteeneth yeare of the Raigne of our Soveraigne Lord Charles by the grace of god of England Scotland ffrance and Jreland Kinge Defender of the faith &c Betweene William Widmer of the Parish of Chepinge Wycombe in the County of Buck gent Anne Waller of Beconsfeild in the said County of Buck Widdowe Edmund Waller the younger of Beconsfeild aforesaid Esqz Adrian Scroope of Wormesley in the County of Oxoñ Esquier & Thomas Widmer of Hugenden in the said County of Buck gent of the one part And Richard Widmer of Hugenden aforesaid Esqz of the other part [for 400 pounds make over specified property and other rights in Hugenden to Richard Widmer, excepting certain rights for Sir Edmund Verney, Sir Thomas Wenman, and Sir Robert Dormer, for 14 and 15 years from the previous Michaelmas; and William Widmer will pay 5 pounds yearly to Verney and Wenman and Dormer according to an indenture of 10 Charles I. Signed at the bottom by] Will: Widmer. [Anne] Waller: Edm: waller Adr[ian] Scrope

[Witnessed on the back for Adrian Scroope by] Jeffrey Goodchild [and] John Atherton

[Witnessed for William Widmer by] Thomas Style George Gosnold Henry: Bradley: Job Humfrey.

Sealed & delivered by the w^{th}in named Anne Waller & Edmund Waller in the p^{r}sence of Thomas Style John Milton Walter Waller

This note is entered through the kindness of Miss Emily Driscoll of 115 East 40th Street, New York, who generously allowed me to see it while in her possession. There is of course no proof that the John Milton of this document is either the poet or his father, but the location in Buckinghamshire would be suitable for him at this period. Edmund Waller is probably the poet, and Anne his mother. I believe this item has not previously been printed.

3. *poetic notebook, note, first paragraph, add*:
Thomas Birch (Milton's Prose *Works*, 1753, p. viii) describes how *Comus* and "other manuscripts of our poet, being found by the reverend Dr. Charles Mason, the present Woodwardian professor, among other papers, which once belonged to Sir Henry Newton Puckering, a considerable benefactor to the library of that college, were collected in 1736 into a volume, by the care and at the expence of Thomas Clarke, Esq; formerly fellow of that college, and now one of his majesty's council." Allan H. Gilbert develops this theme in "The Cambridge Manuscript and Milton's Plans for an Epic," *Studies in Philology*, XVI (1919), 172-176, showing numerous irregularities in the manuscript and concluding that it is "nothing more than a fortunate survival of a part of Milton's papers." William R. Parker made a careful study of "The Trinity Manuscript and Milton's Plans for a Tragedy" in the *Journal of English and Germanic Philology*, XXXIV (1935), 225-232.

4. *Commonplace Book. This entry, which by an oversight repeats some of the entry at I, 275, should be moved to that page and combined with that entry. Add the following sentence at the end of this entry*: Maurice Kelley (*Modern Language Notes*, LXIV, 1949, 522-525) prints two letters of 1682 from Daniel Skinner to Lord Preston, which help to explain how this book later came into the latter's possession.

5. *Dati and Francini. Transfer this entry to I, 378. In caption, for* POEMS *read* LINES, *since Dati's writing is in prose.* (P)

8. *first note, for* H. H. Fletcher *read* H. F. Fletcher *for p. 10 read p. 19*

9. *last note, add*:

Perhaps this selection from the "earliest" biography belongs with the Barbican house on p. 123. If so, that from Wood (pp. 10-11) should go with it. (P)

12. *poem on Lavinia, note, line 4, for* 1800 *read* 1801 *line* 5, *for* xci *read* xci) (P)

19. *note, line* 2, *for* octavo *read* quarto (P) *Add at end of note*: Donald C. Dorian (*The English Diodatis*, 1950, pp. 177, 286-287) thinks that Milton composed the poem "perhaps as soon as the closing months of 1639 or early in 1640," and questions whether lines 9-12 "Et jam bis . . .") refer to the time of Milton's return to England rather than of his writing. John T. Shawcross (*Modern Language Notes*, LXXI, 1956, 322-324) proposed the autumn of 1639 as the time of writing, on the ground that the two harvests mentioned in lines 9-13 refer to two *Italian* harvests, which occur in the Arno valley in March and August. Edmund Blunden published a new blank verse translation of the poem in the *University of Toronto Quarterly*, XXV (1955), 16-22.

28. *first note, line* 1, *for* 1641 *read* 1642 *line* 4: *for* 1629 *read* 1628 (P)

30. *last caption, for* 25 *read* 26-29 (P)

31. *April* 12, *caption, for* LICENSED *read* ENTERED (P)

32. *Of Reformation, text, line* 3, *for* written *read* Written (P)

33. *first note, add*:

William R. Parker ("Contributions toward a Milton Bibliography," *Library*, 4th Series, XVI, 1935-1936, 435) shows that the printers of this book were Richard Oulton and Gregory Dexter, who also printed *Of Prelatical Episcopacy* and *Animadversions*.

35. *after section on Of Reformation, add new items at end*: 20. Reformacōn touching church discipl.

British Museum, Add. MS. 28,954, fol. 9.

. . . he us'd frequently to tell those about him the intire Satisfaction of his Mind, that he had constantly imploy'd his Strength and Faculties in the defence of Liberty, and in a direct opposition to Slavery.

Toland, p. 46; Darbishire, p. 194. (R)

35. "The Head and the Wen," *note, add*:
But Peck makes it clear (p. 432) that he is quoting from *Of Reformation.* (P)

36. *first note, add*:
The Thomason copy makes other corrections as called for in the errata. A copy in the Bodleian (shelf mark D.12.6.Linc.) is inscribed on the title page: "Ex dono authoris accepi/ J [?]. H." [I received this as a gift of the author. J.H.] The initials are uncertain because the lower part is trimmed off. See also below, pp. 139-142. (P)

37. *Usher's Judgment, note, add*:
J. Max Patrick (*Huntington Library Quarterly,* XII, 1950, 303-311) believes that the earliest possible date must be May 24.

38. *first note, add*:
J. Max Patrick (*ibid.*) reasserts June or July as the date on the ground that Milton's work is an answer to Almoni rather than the reverse. William R. Parker ("Contributions toward a Milton Bibliography," *Library,* 4th Series, XVI, 1935-1936, 435) identifies the printers of this book as Richard Oulton and Gregory Dexter.

39. *end of section on Of Prelatical Episcopacy, insert*:

13. P^r^lat^ll^. Episcopacy.

British Museum, Add. MS. 28,954, fol. 9.

39. *May 31, note, add*: The date of this entry is from Almoni's preface.

41. *first note, add*:
William R. Parker ("Contributions toward a Milton Bibliography," *Library,* 4th Series, XVI, 1935-1936, 435) identifies the printers of this book as Richard Oulton and Gregory Dexter.

41. *end of section on Animadversions, insert*:

22. animadv. upon the Remonstrants def^ce^. ag^t^ Smectimnuus.

British Museum, Add. MS. 28,954, fol. 9.

52. *Malvezzi, note, add*:
The New York Public Library clipping has a note at the bottom: "Not Milton VHP" (probably Victor H. Palsits, Librarian). Joseph A. Bryant, Jr. (*Modern Philology,* XLVII, 1950, 217) doubts that Milton had anything to do with this volume.

52. *Fuller's criticism, text, line 1, for* One *read* And one (P)

54. *first caption, for* RICHARD *read* ROBERT (P)

56. *first note, add*:
Ralph H. Haug (Milton's *Complete Prose Works*, ed. Don M. Wolfe, I, 738) thinks that Milton began this pamphlet after August 4, 1641, and finished it by January 1, 1642. J. George (*Notes and Queries*, N.S. III, 1956, 157) disagrees and thinks Milton could not have begun earlier than November, 1641, because a letter of November 25, 1641, to Sir John Oglander from his son of the same name mentions "my Lord of Armagh's book, which to all rational men doth cleave the question concerning Episcopacy." Mr. George assumes that the book mentioned is *Certain Brief Treatises,* to which *The Reason of Church Government* is in part an answer, and that this letter both confirms the authorship of Archbishop Ussher and dates the first appearance of the book. The proof does not seem convincing. William R. Parker ("Milton, Rothwell, and Simmons," *Library*, 4th Series, XVIII, 1937-1938, 92) identifies the printer of the *Reason* as Edward Griffin the Younger.

56. *end of section on Reason of Church Government, insert*:
The Reason of Church-Government urged against Prelacy. In Two Books, 4*to*.

Phillips, p. [li]; not in Darbishire.

21. Reasons of Ch. Goverm^t. ag^t. P^{r}lacy.

British Museum, Add. MS. 28,954, fol. 9.

57. *note, third line of list of letters, for* Voltaire *read* Molière
59. *first note, all but the first two sentences of this note belongs more properly at* III, 351, *with merely a cross reference here. But add after the first two sentences*: William R. Parker ("Milton, Rothwell, and Simmons," *Library*, 4th Series, XVIII, 1937-1938, 92) identifies the printer of the *Apology* as Edward Griffin the younger.

59. *end of section on Apology, insert*:
23   apolog. for ye animadv.

British Museum, Add. MS. 28,954, fol. 9.

60. *first note, add*:
A copy with the signature of a seventeenth-century clergyman was advertised for £75 in Maggs Brothers' *Mercurius Britannicus*, No. 105 for February, 1951, item 660. Bound with other Milton books, it belonged to Walter Cradock. A man of this name (1606?-1659) was a Congregational minister and chaplain to Sir Robert Harley of Herefordshire (*D.N.B.*). There is no proof that it was a presentation copy from Milton.

62. *notes, second paragraph, add*:

Roland M. Frye (*Notes and Queries*, N.S. III, 1956, 200-202) collects much material from writings of the seventeenth century about whirlwind marriages, which the sober thinkers strongly deprecated as based on lustful infatuation and highly likely to result in trouble. For lack of any information to the contrary, he considers Milton's marriage in this class.

63. *notes, first paragraph, add*:

A. L. Rowse ("The Milton Country," in *The English Past*, New York, 1952) says (p. 95) that the manor house still stands and that he does not "think the manor house so much changed" (p. 111). In answer to my inquiry, since this statement contradicts mine in the text, he answered by referring me to the Estates Bursar of St. John's College, to which he said the property belonged. The Bursar, in return, stated that it was actually Lincoln College which owned the property, but as to the condition of the original house, referred me to the *Village Book* mentioned above. Since this book confirms (p. 12) the final demolition of the house in 1854, I fear we must face the fact that it no longer exists.

65. *Milton-Powell Bibles, first note, add*:

The page containing the Milton family records has been reproduced in *Facsimiles of Royal, Historical, and Literary Autographs in the . . . British Museum*, Series 1-5, London, 1899, #95; in Williamson, *Milton Tercentenary*, facing p. 1; and in a number of other books. Maurice Kelley made some additions and corrections to the Columbia Milton entries in *Modern Language Notes*, LXIII (1948), 539-540.

65. *Milton-Powell Bibles, second text, for* I *read* J *for* book *read* Book

66. *after first notes, insert*:

She [Elizabeth Foster] shew'd me [Thomas Birch, January 6, 1750] her Grand-Mother's Bible in 8ᵛᵒ. printed by Young in 1636, in a Blank Leafe of which Milton had enter'd in his own Hands the Births of his Children. . . .

From Birch's record of his visit to Elizabeth Foster, January 6, 1750, given more fully below under that date. The entries about the births of Anne, Mary, John, and Deborah have been quoted already in their appropriate places. (R)

70. *note, add*:

Donald C. Dorian (*The English Diodatis*, 1950, pp. 270-271) shows that there was a connection between the Leigh family and the Diodatis and also the Egertons. He infers that this relationship may have had something to do with Milton.

[396]

82. *insert*:

1643. ALLEGED LETTER TO GEORGE WITHER.

Lyle H. Kendall, Jr. ("A letter from John Milton to George Wither," *Notes and Queries*, CXCVIII, 1953, 473) suggests that the letter in Wither's *Se Defendendo*, 1643 (p. 3), signed "J.M." and rebuking Wither for having deserted Farnham Castle, was written by John Milton. But since the only basis of attribution other than the initials is the similar political and religious views of the two poets, the attribution carries little weight. Besides, Milton would be unlikely to be familiar with the gossip of county Surrey which is the basis of the letter.

84. *first note, add*:
The date at the end may be May 24. (P)

87. *first note, add*:
This volume is now in the University of Illinois Library, as listed in the program of its exhibition for 1953, p. 23, no. 61.

87. *August 1, first note, add*:
William R. Parker ("Milton, Rothwell, and Simmons," *Library*, 4th Series, XVIII, 1937-1938, 96) identifies the printers of this book as Matthew Simmons and Thomas Paine. Simmons later printed several other works by Milton.

91. *after last footnote, insert*:

15. Doct^{ne}. & Discip^{ne}. of Divorce.

British Museum, Add. MS. 28,954, fol. 9.

93. *first note, add*:
I am grateful to Mrs. George Vaughan Curtis and to Dr. Franklin M. Biebel, Director of the Frick Collection, for calling my attention to the fact that this portrait, at one time in the collection of Mrs. Edith Kingdon Gould, was sold at the American Art Association Galleries on January 12, 1929. I have not discovered the name of the purchaser. The sales catalogue reproduced the picture and described it as a miniature on enamel, 7/8 of an inch in height, set in a jeweled frame.

98. *last line, after* list. *insert*:
There are similar entries in the Rous copy in the Bodleian (Arch.G.e.-44; a change from my shelf-mark at II, 140), in a second Thomason copy (C.59.9.21 [17]), and in the Grenville copy in the British Museum (G 19,954). (K)

99. *insert*:

FEBRUARY 28, 1644. THOMAS YOUNG ALLUDES IN SERMON TO MILTON'S *DOCTRINE AND DISCIPLINE OF DIVORCE* (?).

Eminent governours have stained the glory of their government by enacting Lawes which stand in opposition to Gods Law:
Valentinian the great beginning to alienate his affection from his
royall consort (the cause I spare to relate) casting his affection
upon *Justina*, thereupon makes it free by Law for any, that
would, to have two wives, and after the promulgation of that
Law presently he married her: how inconsistent his Law was
with the Law of God, I need not speake.

Thomas Young, *Hopes Incovragement pointed at In A Sermon
Preached In St. Margarets Westminster, before the Honorable House
of Commons . . . February 28, 1643*, London, 1644, p. 32; quoted in
William Haller, *Liberty and Reformation in the Puritan Revolution*,
1955, p. 123. The Parliamentary order for printing this sermon which
appears on the back of the title page bears the same date (meaning, of
course, 1643/4), and the Thomason Catalogue dates the book also on
the same day. Professor Haller expresses the opinion that the occasion of
this passage was the second edition of Milton's divorce book, printed less
than a month previously (February 2), and also addressed to Parliament.
He says (p. 124) that Young "clearly drew the story of Valentinian's
decree from *Historia Ecclesiastica* of Socrates Scholasticus," from whom
Milton had inserted a quotation on the same subject in his Commonplace
Book (CM, XVIII, 150). Incidentally, Dr. Haller calls the translation
in this last reference wrong. For Milton's Latin "Digamian lege sanxit
Valentinianus. Socrat: 1.4.c. 30 græc.," the Columbia editors translate,
"Valentinian sanctioned by law a second marriage after the death of the
first wife." Dr. Ruth Mohl gives the entry (Milton's *Complete Prose
Works*, Yale University Press, I [1953], 400): "Valentinian sanctioned
bigamy by law. Socrat: Book 4. c[hapter] 30. [in the] Greek [text]."
She gives the full reference as Socrates Scholasticus, *Church History*
(*EHA*, Paris, 1544, f. 240v). She mentions by the way that Valentinian
was a murderer, self-indulgent, and vindictive. The connection with
Milton here is of course slight and debatable.

103. *first caption, for* 11 *read* 12

103. *first note, add*:
Though the date of the bond is, as I said, June 11, and though the
date set for payment of interest is the 24th (see I, 136, 137, 140), Milton's own account later gives the 12th as the date when payment was
due and by which date it was ordinarily paid (III, 358). Several other
accounts (I, 138-139) agree with his. (P)

103. *June 21, caption* (*and note, line 5*), *for* June 21 *read* June 24 (P)

103. *last note, line 6, for* 21 *read* 12

104. *July 1, add*:
This Mrs. Elijah (or Elizabeth, p. 115) Webster may possibly be Mrs. Christopher Milton's mother, Mrs. Isabel Webber, under another spelling. (P)

106. *after second note, insert*:

16. Iudgem^t. of M. Beucer.

British Museum, Add. MS. 28,954, fol. 9.

6. The Judgement of Martin Bucer.

Aubrey, f. 64; Darbishire, p. 11.

106. *August 13, note, line 4, for* 484. *read* 484; Parker, pp. 73-74. (P)

108. *first note, add*:
My text, which varies in a number of details from Parker's, is from the Thomason copy (E. 257), printed by F. L., whereas his is from that printed by I. D. (P)

112. *first note, add*:
In an edition of James Howell's *Familiar Letters* (1890-1892) J. Jacobs interprets the letter to Daniel Featley dated August 2, 1644, as commendation of Featley as author of this book. I take this note from the Temple Classics edition by Oliphant Smeaton (1903), II, 182-183 and 272. But there is no clear reference to Milton in the letter, and its date, if trustworthy, would not fit. (P)

113. *first note, line 5, for* nou. *read* nou: (K) *Add at end*: See also W. M. Clyde, "Parliament and the Press," *Library*, 4th Series, XIII (1932-1933), 399 ff., and XIV (1933-1934), 39-56; William Haller, "Before *Areopagitica*," *PMLA*, XLII (1927), 875 ff.; William Haller, *Tracts on Liberty in the Puritan Revolution, 1638-1647*, New York, 1934, 3 vols; F. S. Siebert, *Freedom of the Press in England 1476-1776*, University of Illinois Press, 1952, especially pp. 195-197; and W. W. Greg, *Some Aspects and Problems of London Publishing between 1550 and 1650*, Oxford, 1956.

113. *Latin paragraph, line 2, for* eóq; *read* eósq;

114. *at end of entry for Areopagitica, insert*:

14. Areopagitica for unlicenc'd Printing.—

British Museum, Add. MS. 28,954, f. 9.

114. *presentation Areopagitica, note, add*:
This copy may possibly be the one Birch described (1738, p. xxv; 1753, p. xxix; my quotation from the latter) as published "in November, as appears from a manuscript note on one of the copies presented by him to a friend." (P)

115. *first note, line 2, add to the two Bodleian copies a third, Milton's presentation copy to Rous, shelf-mark* Arch. G.e.44 (*formerly* 40 F.56.Th). (K) *Add also two copies in the Cambridge University Library*: Syn.7.64.121³³ *and* Bb.*9.47⁴ (E). (P)

115. *December 16, note, add*:
On Mrs. Webster see the note added to p. 104, July 1.

115. *December 21, transfer this entry to p. 164.* (P)
In line 2 of text, for second yᵉ *read* yᵗ *lines 3-4, for* yʷ *read* yᵘ *for* pleased *read* pleasd

In note, next to last line, for 1644 or 1645 read 1646 or 1647 Add at end of note: In the *Review of English Studies*, N.S. IV (1953), 221-233, Professor Turnbull dates this letter 1646.

118. *father and Anne Powell, note, last line, for* on *read* about (P)
120. *first note, add*:
A more likely identification is William Blackborow. (P)

120. *after second note, insert*:
What makes people say his first was a bad wife was because she did not like his studious life, and so went back to her father. Upon which Mʳ Milton travelled out after her 3 years and after his return, she came home to him.

British Museum, Add. MS. 4,320, fol. 232v. (R)

121. *Greek verse, note, add*:
William R. Parker, on the other hand, dates them 1634-1638 (*A Tribute to George Coffin Taylor*, 1952, pp. 113-131). But Harris Fletcher (*The Intellectual Development of John Milton*, I [Urbana, 1956], 262-263) agrees with Donald L. Clark that they are a survival of Milton's grammar school exercises.

123. *March 4, first note, add*:
William R. Parker ("Milton, Rothwell, and Simmons," *Library*, 4th Series, XVIII, 1937-1938, 99-100) believes that *Tetrachordon* was printed by two printers, probably Thomas Paine and Matthew Simmons. The unusually numerous watermarks and the unusual lapse in pagination suggest the work of two printers.

124. *at end of entry for Tetrachordon, insert*:
18. Tetrachordon.

British Museum, Add. MS. 28,954, fol. 9.

125. *at end of entry for Colasterion, insert*:
17. χολαστεριον.

British Museum, Add. MS. 28,954, fol. 9.

126. *first note, add*:
This volume was given to the library of Trinity College by Rev. Matthew Pilkington (1705-1765); see *Gentleman's Magazine*, LXII (1792), 900.

127. *May 8, last line of text, for* lust. *read* lust. . . .   (P)

128. *June 20, note, add*:
Sir Edmund Craster (*Bodleian Library Record*, v [1955], 130-146) sketches Rous's career as librarian and confirms Milton's designation of him (below, p. 140) as "the most learned man, and excellent judge of books," emphasizing his acquisition of several great collections of manuscripts and his excellent guidance of the Library through what Sir Edmund calls "without question the most difficult period the Library has ever endured, not excepting that of World War II."

128. *September, note, after first paragraph, insert*:
The Cornell University Library owns a copy of the first edition (1667) of *Paradise Lost* bound in wooden covers said to come from Milton's Barbican house. Both covers are elaborately carved, each with a central inscription surrounded by branches, presumably representing the Tree in the Garden of Eden, bearing both leaves and apples. The inscription on the front cover reads: "MILTON'S PARADISE LOST. 1667." That on the back cover reads: "1864 THIS COVER CARVED BY G. A. ROGERS IS FORMED OF A PART OF A BEAM OF THE HOUSE IN WHICH MILTON WAS BORN." Inside, on a leaf facing the title page, are two letters. The first reads: "London July 7 1868 George Alfred Rogers Esq. Dear Sir Will you have the kindness to inform me whether the inscription carved on the back of this First Edition of Milton's Works is correct & oblige Yours very truly Andrew D. White." Immediately under it is the second, which reads: "London 33 Maddox St. July 7. 68 Sir I carved the cover of this book out of oak which I myself procured from a beam in the house in the Barbican, in which Milton was born. Your Ob^t. Sv^t. George Alfred Rogers A D White Esqr." Though Milton was of course not born in the Barbican, I see no reason to doubt that Mr. Rogers may have got possession of a piece of wood from that house when it was torn down, and may have carved the covers from it. Mr. White, President of Cor-

nell University 1868-1875, who owned this volume and then gave it to Cornell, evidently wished to be sure about the identification of Milton's house, but received Mr. Rogers' ambiguous reply. It is quite possible that there may be other souvenirs of this house of Milton's which have never become publicly known.

130. *October* 17, *note, add*:

On Mrs. Webster see the note added to p. 104, July 1.

130. *last paragraph, line* 5, *delete* from life   (P)

131. *first note, add*:

W. W. Greg points out (*Modern Language Review*, XXXIX, 1944, 415) that though Professor Fletcher seems undecided as to whether Marshall made the drawing or the engraving or both [and my notes above have the same fault], it seems clear that he made the engraving from a picture already done in 1629. If so, despite the lack of similarity, it seems reasonably sure that it must have been made from the Onslow portrait.

135. *poem to Rosse, last line of verse, for* From *read* ffrō *for* Wholsome *read* wholsome   (K)

At end of note add:

Pickering and Chatto advertised a copy of this book (Catalogue 350, 1951, item 658) in which they stated that the date "has not been altered to 1643 [*sic*] as is usually the case."

136... *first paragraph, add*:

William R. Parker (*Review of English Studies*, XI, 1935, 281) objects to dating this poem later than 1645.

137. *first paragraph, add*:

The Bodleian copy Arch.F.f.9 has manuscript corrections almost certainly in Milton's hand on pp. 22, 28, 39, and (second numbering) 36.   (P)

137. *first note, fourth paragraph, add*:

Though Professor Fletcher (I, 149) thinks that the date of publication may be anywhere between August, 1645 (since Ruth Raworth proved the will of her husband on August 5) and January 2, 1645/6, W. W. Greg (*Modern Language Review*, XXXIX, 1944, 415) thinks it unlikely, though not impossible, that publication actually occurred before October 6, 1645, when the book was entered in the Stationers' Registers. I date the entry here from Thomason's note on his copy.

137. *at end of section on Poems, add*:

Poems upon several Occasions, both *English* and *Latin*, &c. Composed at several times.

Phillips, p. [lii]; not in Darbishire.

140. *first note, add:*
This volume contains several manuscript corrections. The *Doctrine and Discipline of Divorce* contained here is the second edition. (K, P)

142. *sonnet to Lawes, note, add:*
Willa McClung Evans, in a paper read at the Modern Language Association meeting in December, 1955 (summarized in the *Seventeenth Century News*, XIV, 1956, 7), argued that Milton's commendation of Lawes for fitting the music to the words was an implied criticism of the madrigalists, including even Milton's own father. She found further support of this interpretation in the preface to *Paradise Lost*.

143. *last note, add:*
The phraseology of the first paragraph is taken almost word for word from sections of Milton's *Doctrine and Discipline of Divorce*; see CM, III, 388, 479-480, 501-502. But "name" in the fifth line of the quotation seems to be a misprint for "nature."

144. *first line, for* Vid. *read* Vid.

153. *first note, line 2, for* boldface *read* gothic
153. *last note, add:*
Masson mistakenly dates this order July 16. (P)

159. *first note, add:*
Joseph Hunter makes a statement in his "Chorus Vatum" (IV, 189 [or 343]) which seems like a garbled version of this entry: "In the printed Catalogue of Compounders—12mo 1655—appears 'Milton, Christopher, Reading, Berkshire—80.6.0.'"

160. *first note, add:*
My colleague Professor Leslie A. Marchand, who recently examined a copy of the first edition of this work in the British Museum, tells me that he cannot find this entry in it. Presumably this whole entry should therefore be canceled.

163. *first caption, for* DECEMBER 16 *read* AFTER DECEMBER 12 (P)

163. *sonnet on Mrs. Thomason, note, add:*
The "16" preceding "Decem." in the title in the Trinity Manuscript is separately canceled. Since Smart has discovered that Mrs. Thomason was buried on December 12 and hence must have died several days earlier, Milton probably started to write "1646" but canceled it after writing the first two figures and made the heading more specific by adding the month (but not the day): "Decem. 1646." (P)

163. *insert:*
DECEMBER 17, 1646. JOHN HALL MENTIONS MILTON IN LETTER TO HARTLIB.

J had a loving & Modest express from Worthy Mr Milton, J desire to be enformed from y^u whether y^u suppose him willing to Entertain a Constant Correspondence or noe. . . .

S^r

Y^r obedient servant

Dec: 17   Jn Ch: Jes.

Munday   J Hall

From a letter of John Hall to Samuel Hartlib in the possession of Lord Delamere, by whose kind permission it is quoted here. This and several later quotations of December 21, 1646, and of January 4 and 8, February 7, and March, 1647, all from the Delamere papers, were first published by G. H. Turnbull in the *Review of English Studies*, N.S. IV (1953), 221-233. The present letter is on p. 227. I wish to thank Professor Turnbull for his kind cooperation in helping me to get photostatic copies of these letters. Since December 17, 1646, was Thursday rather than Monday, it is possible that what looks like a 7 may be a 4, or that Hall made a mistake. But the contents of the letter fit so well with others (below) of about this period that the year must be right.

169. *after first note, insert*:

1647. ATTRIBUTED *TREATISE OF MAGISTRACY.*

Seymour de Ricci (*The Book Collector's Guide*, 1921, p. 410) states, without comment, that Milton was the author of *A Treatise of Magistracy*, 1647. But since it favors Charles I and is attributed by both the Thomason Catalogue and Donald Wing (*STC*, P 2903) to Mary Pope, we need not take this attribution seriously.

170. *notes in Best, note, add*:
H. John MacLachlan (*Socinianism in Seventeenth-Century England*, Oxford, 1951, pp. 161-162) believes these notes genuinely Milton's autograph, and mentions additional notes on the verso of the title page not mentioned previously. But Maurice Kelley (*Library*, Fifth Series, V [1950], 49-51) rejects them as un-Miltonic.

172. *first note. Delete the second and third sentences* ("Mr. Martin notes . . . so dated") *and insert*: The copy of Cleveland's "The King's Disguise" in the Thomason collection is dated "Jan: 21 1646" (i.e., 1646/7) (Martin, II, 704). So Vaughan's poem can reasonably be dated January, 1647. (P)

174. *insert*:

JANUARY 4, 1647. JOHN HALL AGAIN WRITES TO HARTLIB ABOUT MILTON.

Worthy S^r . . .

    J gaue y^u an account of Mr Milton & Mr Worsley by Mr Blunden, J shall p^rsume to address my self to both next week.
. . .

S. Johns.   Y^r faithf: & Ready serv^t:
4. Jan 1646.   J Hall

    From a letter of John Hall to Samuel Hartlib in the possession of Lord Delamere; published by G. H. Turnbull in the *Review of English Studies*, N.S. IV (1953), 227. See the added note above under date of December 17, 1646.

JANUARY 8, 1647. JOHN HALL ASKS HARTLIB'S HELP IN MEET-
ING MILTON.

    Honor^d s^r . . .

    J beseech y^u be a means of my acquaintance wth Mr Milton & Worsley. . . .

S. Johns.   Y^r affect: serv^t to my vtmost
Jan: 8. 1646   J Hall

    From the same sources as the preceding note. The sentence given is actually a postscript following the signature.

    175. *note, add*:
In transcribing the name Rous in its various forms in this poem I unfortunately rendered the diaeresis inexactly, since Milton splits it in
curious fashion, putting one dot over the o and one over the u. W. W.
Greg criticizes Fletcher (*Modern Language Review*, XXXIX, 1944,
416-417) for ignoring it entirely, and points out that one argument for
Milton's having written this manuscript in his own hand might be this
peculiarity. He balances this point by calling the marginal correction of
"Graiæ" in line 71 (which is a rewriting of the same word because of
a blot in the text) "apparently in a different hand from the rest and is
probably Milton's own, since this is practically conclusive evidence
against the body of the text being autograph." But I cannot understand
why, aside from the fact that the same diaeresis occurs also in the inscription in the presentation copy of Milton's prose works to Rous
(above, p. 139), this peculiarity should be considered Miltonic rather
than the work of some other writer. If Milton used this marking, he
probably did so because some people also did; there is no assurance that
he invented it. On the other hand, the marginal "Graiæ" looks so
much like the same word in the text that this point also lacks conviction.
We still have no clear assurance whether or not the writing is Milton's.

177. *insert*:

FEBRUARY 7, 1647. JOHN HALL MENTIONS A SUPPOSED TRACT FROM MILTON.

Worthy s^r . . .

For ye tract of Jntelligence 'Tis polite, (& J suppose hath Come from Mr Milton) . . .

S. Johns.   Y^r most Ready freind to serv y^u.

Fej: 7. 1646   J Hall:

From a letter of John Hall to Samuel Hartlib in the possession of Lord Delamere; published by G. H. Turnbull in the *Review of English Studies*, N.S. IV (1953), 227. See the added note above under date of December 17, 1646. Before "polite" in the manuscript is "little," canceled. What the "tract of Jntelligence" is and what Milton's connection with it can have been is a mystery.

181. *insert*:

MARCH, 1647. JOHN HALL COMPLAINS OF MILTON'S STUBBORNNESS (?).

Dear & honord s^r . . .

J am sorry Mr Milto dos abundare suo sensu J wish J cold not Complain ye like of my dear Stanley. (To whom expect a lr as y^u desire next W.) But J hope J shall win on him when J come to Remain at London as J shall shortly. . . .

S^r Y^r sincere servt

Munday   J Hall

From a letter of John Hall to Samuel Hartlib in the possession of Lord Delamere; published by G. H. Turnbull in the *Review of English Studies*, N.S. IV (1953), 227-228, 231. See the added note above under date of December 17, 1646. Professor Turnbull points out that the Latin phrase in the first sentence is from Romans 14:5 (Vulgate), translated in the Authorized Version "fully persuaded in his own mind." Hall's meaning is not clear. The dating of this letter is from Professor Turnbull.

183. *last note, add*:

Lyla G. Hugill (*A Record of the Friends of John Milton*, University of Chicago doctoral dissertation, 1924) thinks (p. 57) that either Hartlib or Dury recommended Milton as a tutor for Richard Jones, since Dury married Lady Ranelagh's aunt. She also (p. 165) identifies Mr.

Packer as Philip Packer (1620-1683), who helped Aubrey collect information.

184. *letter from Dati. Delete this entry, which is an erroneous repetition of that on pp.* 170-171.

185. *April 7, note, line 4, after Clarendon insert State*
188. *note, add:*
In working out the date for publication in 1674, Milton may have made a mistake. In 1647 Easter fell on April 18, in 1674 on April 19. The Tuesday after Easter (the "Pascatis feriâ tertiâ" of the manuscript) was therefore April 20 in 1647 and April 21 in 1674. He may have confused the two and dated the letter April 21 when it should have been April 20. (P)

195. *insert:*

JULY 23, 1647. A MAJOR JOHN MILTON AUTHORIZED TO RECEIVE MONEY.

To the Worłł James Bunce Alderman m^r Richard Clyde and Coł Lawrence Bromfeild Threārs appointed by ordnance of Parliam^t of the 3° of June 1647 for the receiueing of fforty two thousand pound att Weauers hall London.

You are hereby desired by the Comittee for the Militia of the Citty of London &c to pay vnto Serieant Maior John Milton the sume of seauen pound tenn shiłłs for three Dutyes for Parliam^t and Citty within the Lines of Comunication from the 11th June last to this present day inclusiue as by accompts Appeareth for which this with his receipt shalbee yor Warr^t and Discharge Dated att Guild-hall London the 23th of July 1647/
[Signed:] Thomas Adams [and 9 others]

Public Record Office, SP 28/237. I owe this reference to the kindness of H. C. Cardew-Rendle, Esq., of Richmond, co. Surrey. This John Milton, who is surely not the poet, may be the same person as the one mentioned at I, 294, and II, 218.

200. *first note, add:*
Either this entry is placed too early or Phillips was mistaken when he wrote: "*Anne* his Eldest as abovesaid, and *Mary* his Second . . . were both born at his House in *Barbican*" (Phillips, p. xl; Darbishire, p. 76). It is just barely possible that Milton's move from Barbican to High Holborn came just after the birth of Mary, thus accounting for the

rather long period intervening between her birth and her baptism (II, 220). But by the time of her baptism the family must almost surely have been in High Holborn, since St. Giles in the Fields was much nearer that location than to Barbican. (R)

216. *January 17, note, add*:
The authorship of this book is generally attributed to Samuel Gott, and was so even as early as Milton's own day; see William London's Catalogue of September 25, 1658; Stevens, *Reference Guide*, #2657-2671; *Library*, Third Series, I (1910), 225-238; and Donald Wing, *STC*, G1355-1356.

217. *insert*:
MARCH, 1648. DIVORCE VIEWS ATTACKED.

A Catalogue of Strange Tenents, that are openly Asserted by divers Sectaries. . . .
MARRIAGE. . . .

191. That 'tis lawfull for a man to put away his wife for indisposition, unfitnesse, contrarietie of mind arising from a cause in nature unchangeable, disproportion and deadnesse of Spirit, something distastefull and averse in the immutable bent of nature; and man is a law to himselfe in this, being head of the other Sex, neither need he hear any Judge herein, but himselfe.

192. That it is lawfull for one man to have two wives at once.

A True and Perfect Picture of our Present Reformation, 1648, pp. 1, 16. I am indebted to Professor George Sensabaugh for this allusion, and to Mr. Richard H. Dillon of the Sutro Library in San Francisco for generously and promptly providing me with a photographic reproduction of this passage. The Sutro copy lacks the title page. It is noteworthy that these two paragraphs are almost verbatim copies of those in Edwards's *Gangræna* given above, II, 143. The date (March) is from the Thomason Catalogue (I, 605). (P)

220. *October 25, first note, add*:
See also Phillips's record in the note added to II, 200. (P)

222. *Greek quotation, line 2, for* πòρ *read* πàρ *12th line after quotations, for* dlla *read* (?) ella (K) *Professor Kelley has noted a few minor corrections in spelling and punctuation, but since they do not affect the meaning, I omit them.*

224. *first note, add:*

Masson (III, 691) identifies the Galilei of this letter as the astronomer's "natural son Vincenzo Galilei, also a man of talent."

225. *first note, add:*

A. K. Croston (editor, John Hall's *Advancement of Learning* [1649], Liverpool Reprints, No. 7, Liverpool, 1953, pp. 5-6, 26, 48, 51-52) finds what he considers to be several echoes from Milton's *Areopagitica* and *Of Education* in this book of Hall's. Though not convincing, they are worth considering.

225. *February 9, first note, add:*

On the numerous editions of this work see F. F. Madan in the *Bodleian Quarterly Record*, II (1920-1921), 27, 273; and his *New Bibliography of the Eikon Basilike*, Oxford Bibliographical Society, 1950.

226. *note, first paragraph, add:*

Francis F. Madan (London *Times Literary Supplement*, August 31, 1956, p. 511) has just acquired the copy of *Eikonoklastes* containing the original manuscript note in Anglesey's handwriting. In addition to the initials of the owner, Sir William Ashurst, on the title page, it bears two manuscript notes in his hand on a flyleaf: (1) "Being at the sale of the Earle of Anglesey library Eikon Basilike was there sold with the underwritt [the memorandum] by the Earle's own hand at the front of the booke which I tooke from the originall" and (2) "a true Coppy taken 16 No. 1686 and here incerted for the reason above Wm. Ashurst." Mr. Madan considers that this note "confirms the authenticity" of the memorandum "from a new and unimpeachable source."

226. *after notes, add:*

After much and long Enquiry and Consideration, the Truth seems to lye between the two Extreams, as in many other Cases. It is highly probable, that King *Charles* amidst his Solitudes and Sufferings did write most of those Essays or Meditations upon the particular Occasions, and soon after the special Times to which they are adapted: And that such Papers written by the King's own Hand were committed to a loyal Chaplain, Mr. *Edward Symonds*, Minister of *Rayne* in *Essex*, to convey them to the Press with all Privacy in *London* or elsewhere. But he being interrupted by Sequestration, and under a Necessity of flying and absconding, delivered the Royal Papers to his Friend and Neighbour Dr. *Gauden*, who being a Man of an enterprising Genius and a very luxuriant Fancy, and finding himself the more at Liberty by the Absence of Mr. *Symonds*, would not let them pass without somewhat of his own Additions, and (as he thought) Improvements of them. . . .

Upon the first Publication of the Ἐικὼν Βασιλικὴ the Book was taken for granted by all People to be the King's; and it is suppos'd that even Dr. *Gauden* himself was very industrious to have it so acknowledg'd. For in the first thirtieth of *January* Sermon, commonly imputed to Dr. *Gauden*, the Preacher ascribes this Book to the King in two several Passages, as if the Truth were intimately known to him. . . .

Some do from hence infer, that Dr. *John Gauden*, a daily Writer was likewise the Author of this Character [*The Faithful Yet Imperfect Character of . . . Charles I*, 1660], and did not then assume the Honour of being the sole Inventor of Ἐικὼν Βασιλικὴ, but dwells on it as if he had been much concern'd in it; and so he was in having dressed up the Original Papers, affix'd the Title, and convey'd the finish'd Copy to the Press. All this may be consistent with the different Relations of the King and the Doctor, being each the Author of that admirable Book.

White Kennett, *A Register and Chronicle*, 1728, I, 774-776.

227. *first note, add*:
Merritt Y. Hughes has contributed a cogent study of Milton's relation to these prayers in his "New Evidence on the Charge that Milton forged the Prayer in the *Eikon Basilike*," *Review of English Studies*, N.S. III (1952), 130-140. He points out that Dugard's edition was not the first to contain these prayers, that Parliament arrested Dugard, that the prayers were part of the intended contents of the book, and that they were included in later authorized editions. He concludes that Milton is far more likely to be innocent of the charges than some people have believed.

229. *first note, add*:
Merritt Y. Hughes has made an excellent study of this book in "Milton's Treatment of Reformation History in *The Tenure of Kings and Magistrates*" in R. F. Jones and others, *The Seventeenth Century*, 1951, pp. 247-263.

230. *second note, line 1, for* 10 *read* 11

232. *after first note, add*:
12. Tenure of Kings & Magistrates.

British Museum, Add. MS. 28,954, fol. 9.

232. *insert*:

AFTER FEBRUARY 13, 1649. PRESENTS COPY OF *TENURE* TO JOHN BRADSHAW (?).

Ex Dono Authoris ffeb. 1648

Inscription at the top of the title page of a copy of Milton's *Tenure of Kings*, 1649, now in the Exeter (England) Cathedral Library. The writing is very different from Milton's. Preceding and following the inscription are brackets which probably originally connected it with a signature above, which has unfortunately since been shaved off, probably in the process of rebinding, or perhaps by an autograph hunter. This volume forms part (volume II, number 18) of a five-volume collection of tracts in the Library said to have belonged formerly to Henry Bradshaw, Jr., who was an elder brother of John the regicide, and whose name appears on seven of the books. The history of the collection is somewhat hazy, and it is therefore only a guess that Milton presented the volume to John Bradshaw. But if he gave it to any Bradshaw, as seems likely in view of the history of the collection, John would be the likeliest member. Milton was later to write him at least two known letters, present him a copy of *Defensio Secunda*, mention one of his manuscripts in a wording which suggests that he had seen it, and receive a legacy in his will; see below, III, 322, 380, 381, 385-387, and IV, 47, 135-137, 287. Lower on the title page the printed "J. M." has been extended by a different hand, "(ilton)," and underneath it is pasted a small slip of paper in what looks like a seventeenth-century hand: "Miltons Tenure of Kings." I owe this note to the kindness of Professor Robert C. Bald, who first called the volume to my attention; Miss Marjorie P. Crighton of the Cathedral Library, who sent me some information about it and made a photostat of the title page for me; and Mrs. Audrey M. Erskine, also of the Library, who gave me further details.

236. *appointed secretary, note, add*:
Sotheby (*Ramblings*, facing p. 36) reproduces the record, but apparently from a different manuscript source, since the spellings do not agree with mine. On p. 35 he dates the appointment March 22, which must be an error.

237. *first note, last line, delete. Insert*: CLXXXI (1941), 289, and CLXXXII (1942), 96.

239. *March 26, Hamburg, caption, for* LETTER *read* LETTERS (*thanks to Professor J. Max Patrick*)

241. *line* 1, *for* westmonasteriensi *read* Westmonasteriensi
line 2, *for* Anglia *read* Angliæ   (K)

241. *first note, first paragraph, line* 1, *for* 153-154 *read* 133-134
241. *first note, after last paragraph, add*:
Mr. C. M. Williams has kindly written me from Oxford that he has found another manuscript of this letter in the Bodleian (Martin-Loder MSS., 3rd series, vol. XI, ff. 1-1v). Though varying somewhat in the greeting and the ending, it offers no significant variants in text. Mr. Williams identifies the handwriting as the same as that of the original manuscript in the Public Record Office. He also reports that the letter following this in the Bodleian manuscript is another to Hamburg, un-dated, complaining to the Senate at Hamburg about the activities of John Cochrane, a Royalist agent. Both are from the papers of Henry Marten. Mr. Williams thinks they were both translated and later cor-rected by Milton.

243. *line* 6, *for* their *read* thir   (K, P)

245, *first note, add*:
If, as F. F. Madan plausibly suggests in the *Library* (IX, 1954, 101), the date of Sarravius's letter is in New Style, then this entry should be redated April 6. Some interesting references to Salmasius's reaction to the English situation in 1649 and 1652 appear in the Clarendon state papers in the Bodleian, numbers 2, 4, 9, 11, and 783, as listed in W. D. Macray's *Calendar of the Clarendon State Papers*, II (1869), 1, 2, 143.
246. *first note, add*:
Kenneth Rogers gives some interesting items about the Rose in the article mentioned above, though he does not connect Milton very specifically with it beyond the note above. But he mentions a legal action taken by Elizabeth Bond, widow of Dennis, presumably the President of the Council of State, who died in 1658, concerning his lease of the White Rose in 1653. If Bond and Milton both had holdings in the same prop-erty, we may perhaps guess that their association in this piece of business may have had some connection with Milton's appointment in 1649 as Latin Secretary. But with our present limited knowledge of the details, this can be only a highly tentative guess.
246. *May* 11, *note, add*:
Madan reproduces the title page of the first edition in facsimile. In a later article (*Library*, Fifth Series, IX, 1954, 101-103) he dates the first publication about November, 1649, and considers Thomason's date of May 11 to mean 1650. My date may therefore be too early, though the Thomason Catalogue (I, 729) enters its copy under May 11, 1649.
251. *first note, line* 5, *for* French *read* German
256. *June* 11, *note, add*:
William Small of Botolph, Aldersgate, had been ordered arrested on June 8 on suspicion of holding correspondence with the enemy. On June

25, after the present order, he was ordered imprisoned in the Gatehouse. On June 27 his petition (not given) was laid aside for the present. On July 3 he was ordered discharged on entering recognizance to appear before Mr. Frost once a week, and on July 4 two sureties for him gave bond of £500 apiece for his appearance on July 11 and for his good behavior. On July 23 Pickering and Martin and Wallop were appointed to examine his business. No further entries about him appear. See *CSPD*, *1649-1650*, pp. 179, 208, 220, 243, 522, 535, 538. (P)

258. *August 10, first note, line 5, for 61 read* 194

259. *Eikon Alethine, notes, first paragraph, line 4, after* volume *insert* (which had formerly belonged to Thomas Hollis)

264. *line 6, add*:

There are similar corrections in at least five other copies. (P)

266. *after second note, insert*:

11. Εικονοκλάστης.

British Museum, Add. MS. 28,954, fol. 9.

267. *line 2, add*:

This entry needs to be changed. Since Hales's name appears only on the first tract, and since the binding together of the tracts may have occurred later, this should be regarded simply as an association copy of the 1645 edition of *The Doctrine and Discipline of Divorce*, and should be moved accordingly to p. 122, to follow the first entry on that page. (P)

268. *first note, add*:

Joseph A. Bryant (*Philological Quarterly*, XXIX, 1950, 15-30) disagrees with Professor Parks as to the date, which he thinks should rather be 1639-1641.

270. *November 5, note, add*:

Though the manuscript distinctly reads "vi" (six per cent) in the next to the last line, it is probably a mistake for "vii"; see below, pp. 302-303, where the amount is given both times as 7%. (P)

270. *insert*:

NOVEMBER 6, 1649. CLAUDE SARRAVIUS WRITES TO SALMASIUS ABOUT HIS *DEFENSIO*.

Vidimus hic Πρόσωπον τηλαυγὲς Defensionis Regiæ. Omnino magnus est iste tuus labor. . . . Typi sunt elegantes. . . .

Letter of November 6/16 from Sarravius to Salmasius printed in *Marquardi Gudii . . . Epistolæ*, ed. Pieter Burman, 1697, p. 216; quoted by F. F. Madan in "A Revised Bibliography of Salmasius's *Defensio Regia* and Milton's *Pro Populo Anglicano Defensio*," *Library*,

Fifth Series, IX (1954), 101. This statement about the arrival of part, if not all, of Salmasius's *Defensio* might seem to eliminate the earlier date which I have given above (p. 246), but I am not sure that it does. Sarravius continues for months (in later letters in this collection) to talk in terms of the fresh arrival of sheets of Salmasius's book. I suspect that at least some of the time he is talking about new editions. I must confess, however, that I have not found an earlier reference than the present, in his letters, to the appearance of the book. Incidentally, as Birch points out (Milton's *Works*, 1753, p. xxxiv), a number of these letters are full of opposition to Salmasius's defense of bishops, whom he had attacked acrimoniously in a book on presbyters and bishops in 1641.

[We see here the "glowing face" of your *Royal Defense*. That work of yours is very great. The type is elegant.]

NOVEMBER 12, 1649. LODGINGS IN WHITEHALL BEING ARRANGED.

To confer with Sir Jno. Hippesley as to accommodating Mr. Milton with the lodgings he has at Whitehall.

CSPD 1649-1650, p. 388. Though Masson and Raymond both missed this item, there was no excuse for my doing so, since it was in my notes; but I somehow overlooked it. I have not seen the original entry in the Order Books. (P)

273. *insert*:

NOVEMBER 16, 1649. WALTER STRICKLAND TRIES TO SUPPRESS SALMASIUS'S *DEFENSIO*.

Mr. F. F. Madan, Jr., in *A Revised Bibliography of Salmasius's Defensio* (*Library*, Fifth Series, IX, 1954, 102), says that on the above date Strickland applied to the Estates of Holland and West Friesland for suppression of Salmasius's *Defensio*, then in the press and daily expected to appear. (But see above, II, 246, under date of May 11, when this book seems already to have been available in England.) Madan's authority is *Register van Holland en Westvriesland, Van de Jaaren 1649 en 1650*. I have not seen the *Register*.

274. *insert*:

NOVEMBER 20, 1649. *EIKONOKLASTES* PRAISED IN JOURNAL.

The Reader may please to take notice of a book published the last weeke [*sic*] intituled IKONOCLASTES, in answer to a late book intituled EIKON BASILIKE, the portrature of his sacred Majesty in his solitudes and sufferings, wherein they who are not willing to be imposed upon, and would be content to be delivered from the danger of that Idolatry which many have committed, may see the gold taken off from that Idol, and that grosse hypocrisie, and incongruity, betweene those specious professions, and the late King's constant practise, sufficiently and clearly laid open by Mr. JOHN MELTON.

A Briefe Relation of Some Affairs, November 20, 1649, p. 96, as quoted by R. P. McCutcheon in "The Beginnings of Book-Reviewing in English Periodicals," *PMLA*, XXXVII (1922), 691-706. (P) I have not seen the original journal.

275. *second note, line 2, for Papers read State Papers line 3, for 500 read 32 Add at end*:
F. F. Madan quotes almost the same section (*Library*, 5th Series, IX, 1954, 103) from *Clarendon State Papers*, Oxford, 1773, II, 500.

275. December 16, caption, for 16 read 14

281. *first note, first paragraph, add*:
This portrait is now in the Victoria and Albert Museum in London. In response to my question, Leigh Ashton, Esq., Director, kindly informs me that though it bears the legend "JOHANNES MILTON AET . . . ANO 42 1650," it bears little resemblance to other accepted portraits of Milton and is no longer considered by the staff of the Museum to be an authentic picture of Milton.

282. *second edition of Eikonoklastes, note, add*:
Sonia Miller (*Journal of English and Germanic Philology*, LII, 1953, 214-220) contests Robertson's assertion (London *Times Literary Supplement*, June 15 and 22, 1951) that William Haller's edition of *Eikonoklastes* in the Columbia Milton is inferior to that in the Bohn edition. She also lists a number of pen-and-ink corrections from twelve copies which she has seen, though cautioning that we must not assume that these changes were made under Milton's direction. She calls Haller's text better because up to the Bohn edition each editor had merely copied the previous one, adding his own errors as he went along. William R. Parker ("Milton, Rothwell, and Simmons," *Library*, 4th Series, XVIII, 1937-1938, 101-103) identifies the printer of the second edition of *Eikonoklastes* as Thomas Newcombe, and thinks that Milton changed over from Matthew Simmons, printer of the first edition, because of Simmons's many errors in printing.

283. *first note, delete last paragraph; insert*:
This volume, offered for sale in 1950 by Thomas Thorp (Catalogue

557, item 1267, price £25) now belongs to Professor Donald S. Robertson of Trinity College, Cambridge, who described it in the London *Times Literary Supplement* for June 15 and 22, 1951. His article is summarized in the *Seventeenth Century News*, x (1951), 47. Mr. Robertson believes that the second inscription quoted above is in the hand of Robert Baron. He points out that there are numerous manuscript corrections in the text of the book. Thanks to his kindness in sending me photostatic copies of the inscriptions, I can substitute more accurate transcriptions than those at the bottom of p. 282:

[1] "for my very good ffrend m^r. William Thomas at Laherne. To be presented to the right ho:^{ble} the Earle of Carbery"

[2] "The above is supposed to be the hand-writing of Mr Milton," 284. *first note, add*:

This may be as appropriate a place as any to insert a note about one reader of *Eikonoklastes*, though English, in France. According to the *Memoirs of the Verney Family*, ed. Frances P. Verney, II (1892), 221, Sir Ralph Verney, who was in exile in France from 1643 to 1653, frequently sent back to England for books to read. One such book was Milton's *Eikonoklastes*. Though no date is given, it must have occurred between 1650 and 1653. (P)

286. *insert*:

JANUARY 7, 1650. HOLLAND AND WEST FRIESLAND BAN SALMASIUS'S *DEFENSIO*.

The *Chevalay* Gentlemen and Townes of *Holland* and west-*Frizeland*, representing the States of the same Land. To all that shall see or heare read these presents, hereby make knowne, That . . . in this Land were Printed, spread, or otherwise given out and made publique, all manner of naughty Libells, Pasquills, Dialogues, newes, invectives, raylings, and other such like Treatises . . . [scandalous to] Kings, Common-wealths, Princes, and Potentates of the Neighbouring Countreyes. . . . We have forbidden . . . to bring into this Land, such Pasquills . . . to publish, sell, or spread abroad, or utter, upon paine of forfeiture . . . and . . . upon forfeiture of five hundred Guilders. . . . And over and above to be punished according to discretion. . . .

And it is further made knowne to all, That we have forbidden, and by these doe forbid, the Printing, or Publishing in Print, or writing, the Buying, disposing, or uttering or publishing in any wise, of a certaine Booke or tractate Intituled, *DEFENSIO REGIA, PRO CARALO PRIMO*, &c. In what volume or Language soever it may be, upon forfeiture of all the said Books, and over and above, five hundred Guilders, and Correction according to discretion. . . .

Resolved and Concluded on, in the Hague, *under the great Seale, to be set up the* 17 *of January, in the yeare of our Lord.* 1650.

By Order of the States
Herst. Van Beaumont.

From a translation of the original proclamation in *A Briefe Relation*, no. 23, February 5-7 [*sic*], 1650, pp. 300-302; mentioned in F. F. Madan, "A Revised Bibliography of Salmasius's *Defensio*," etc., *Library*, 5th Series, IX (1954), 102, 112. Mr. Madan prints a facsimile of the Dutch original on p. 111. The ellipses here are mine. The translation seems accurate. Since the date of the proclamation is probably in New Style, the English equivalent is January 7.

286. *last note, add*:
Sotheby (*Ramblings*, facing p. 36) reproduces a facsimile of this order, but from a different manuscript.

291. *insert*:
JANUARY 10, 1650. SEVERAL EDITIONS OF SALMASIUS'S *DEFENSIO* NOW OUT; REPLY NEEDED.

Hague 10/20. *January*, 1650. . . .

I suppose Monsieur *Salmatius* his *defensio Regia*, is come to you, for there have been three or foure impressions of it already, notwithstanding the former seeming restraint of it.

I have read as I thinke scearce a more bitter and more art [*sic*] piece is extant, he may well be termed a Satyrist as he is by some, rather than a Royallist, though no greater fawner upon Royallitie; one cause being the Relation of two Sonnes, one with the Queene of *Bohemy* at the *Hague*, the other with the Queene of *Sweden*.

I question if he be godly for that he girds so much at Puritans, and Saincts, it had beene well for his honour to have kept still to those Subjects, *Deprimatu papæ, de Episcopis*, &c. But his Books, *De usuris, de coma*, and his *Defensio Regia*, discover him.

I say but this, because he hath the repute of beeing Learned, and his stile plausible, it were to be wish't that one of that Nation, which he calls fanatick would take up the Buckler against him in a Latine Style: its thought needfull with the soonest, for he plyes the Bellowes to incense all Princes against them whom he odiously styles, *Latrones, sicarios, homicidas, laniones, cacodæmones*, and what not.

From a foreign correspondent's report in *A Briefe Relation*, no. 20, January 22-29, 1650, pp. 262-263; summarized in F. F. Madan, "A Revised Bibliography of Salmasius's *Defensio*," *Library*, 5th Series, IX (1954), 102. Though the writer had probably not yet had time to hear about Milton's commission of January 8 to answer Salmasius, his last paragraph is remarkably apt. See also below under January 22. The Latin epithets mean approximately bandits, assassins, murderers, butchers, devils.

292. *insert*:
JANUARY 22, 1650. SALMASIUS'S *DEFENSIO* REPORTED POPULAR BUT EMBARRASSING IN PARIS.

Paris, 1. Feb. Stylo Novo. [January 22, English style]

Salmatius writes to his Friends here, that of his Booke concerning the late King of *England*; intituled *Defensio Regia*, foure impressions have beene sold already, and that a fifth was upon the Presse; the *Elzivers* having sold 2400 Copies in one fortnight, and had sent a great number of them to *Roüen* and Paris, but there are none of them yet arrived, nor any come to the *Louver* by Land, onely a Stationer of this Towne received one from *Bruxells*, which he sent for with an intent to Print it, and hath already begun it, and saith he will have done it in a fortnight: He would fayne have gotten a priviledge of the Chancellor, that none might Print it after him. But the Chancellour though he hath all those things in his owne hands, excused himselfe that he could not doe it without expresse Command of the King of *France* for it. It is beleived the State here is not willing to owne and countenance publiquely the Printing of that Booke so excessively full of injurious and virulent rayling against the Parliament of *England*, though tis like enough they may connive at the private printing and publishing of it.

From a foreign dispatch in *A Briefe Relation*, no. 22, February 5-7 [*sic*], 1650, pp. 299-300; summarized in F. F. Madan, "A Revised Bibliography of Salmasius's *Defensio*," etc., *Library*, 5th Series, IX (1954), 102. After the above section follows the English translation of the Dutch order banning Salmasius's book; see above under January 7.

292. *January 22-29, text, line 5, for* bustle *read* bussle *line* 12: *for* Memory *read* memory *for* Judge *read* Judge, (P)

293. *insert*:

JANUARY 29, 1650. *TENURE OF KINGS* MENTIONED.

As to those pretensions which other men make to power and rule over us, we found them but shadows or at best but dilute and washie supports of a sinking Common-wealth; we can expect no *operation* of that which is not in *being*, let the title or right to power be never so highly pretended; neither were we ever throughly perswaded that Government was any mans* freehold, or that many men might not serve providence in the administration of right to a Nation, and the promoving its welfare as well as any one, were his blood of never so high a colour, or his Grandeur never so pompous and Majestick.

[Marginal note:] *See the Tenure of Kings &c. I.M. *Princeps è Senatu oritur, Senatus è vobis. Otho in Tac. ad praetorianos.*

N. W., *A Discourse concerning The Engagement: or, The Northern Subscribers Plea*, London, 1650, p. 5. Thomason dates his copy of this tract "Jan. 29. 1649 [i.e., 1649/50]." I owe both the finding of this allusion and the text of it to Dr. Perez Zagorin through our mutual friend Professor Merritt Y. Hughes. (P)

[(Marginal note:) The prince originates from the senate, the senate from you. Otho, in Tacitus, to the pretorians.]

294. *note, add*:

John R. Moore (*Studies in Philology*, XLVIII, 1951, 17) says that

Samuel Wesley, "the only supposedly reliable evidence for the reality of such a club, charged that at Morton's academy for Dissenters his fellow-pupils had read Milton and defended King-killing." Mr. Moore refers to *A Defence of a Letter Concerning the Education of Dissenters*, London, 1704, pp. 4-5. See above, p. 67.

297. *first note, add*:

Through the kindness of Noel Blakiston, Esq., of the Public Record Office, and of Peter Walne, Esq., County Archivist of Berkshire at the Record Office, Shire Hall, Reading, I have learned that another copy of this letter of February 4 belongs to the Marquis of Downshire, who has deposited it in the Berks Record Office. It is identified as Trumbull Manuscripts, Miscellaneous Correspondence, Vol. XXII, no. 15. The text is said to be verbally identical with that given here.

298. *February* 15, *note, add*:

According to *The Carl H. Pforzheimer Library*, item 727, some copies with the additions are dated 1649. One is Bodleian Wood B. 29. (P)

299. *insert*:

FEBRUARY 20, 1650. WILLIAM DUGARD IMPRISONED FOR PLAN-NING TO PRINT SALMASIUS'S BOOK.

. . . ffebruarii 20ᵐᵘ 1649. Quo tempore, à Concilio novi-Statûs ab Archididascalatûs officio summotus, et in Carcerem Novæ-Portæ conjectus sum, ob hanc præcipuè causam, quòd Claudii Salmasii Librum (qui inscribitur Defensio Regia . . .) typis mandandum curaveram: Typographéo insuper integro spoliatus, ad valorem mille librarum. . . .

Guilielmus Dugard.

E Carcere Novæ-Portæ
Martii 7ᵐᵒ Anno Domini 1649.

From William Dugard's manuscript Scholars' Register, now in the possession of the Company of Merchant Taylors in London, pp. 179-180; printed in part in F. F. Madan's "A Revised Bibliography of Salmasius's *Defensio Regia*," etc., *Library*, 5th Series, IX (1954), 102. I am deeply grateful to Mr. Madan for finding the original manuscript for me when my attempts had failed, and for arranging to have photostats of these pages sent to me. Mr. Madan assumes, and I presume correctly, that 1649 means 1649/50.

[. . . February 20, 1649/50. At which time I was removed from the office of headmaster by the Council of the new state and thrown into Newgate Prison, chiefly for this reason, that I had arranged for the printing of Claudius Salmasius's book, which is entitled the *Royal Defense* . . . and I was stripped of my whole printing press, to the value of a thousand pounds. . . .

William Dugard.

From Newgate Prison, March 7, 1649/50.]

304. *April* 1, *note, add*: For the actual letter of April 2 see the second entry following this one.

307. *first note, two lines from end, for* 506 *read* 507

316. *notes, first paragraph, add*:
This warrant, now in the collection of the University of Illinois Library, is included in that library's catalogue of its Milton exhibition, 1953, p. 23, no. 62. It had previously been offered for sale in Emily Driscoll's catalogue of autographs and manuscripts, November, 1952, no. 14, item 200, for $800.

317. *last note, last sentence, for* Mr. Henry *read* Stern (II, iii, 256) (P)

318. *last note, line 2, after* 228, *insert* Stern, II, iii, 256; *last line, delete* Mr. Henry . . . this entry. (P)

320. *translation, last line, add closing bracket*

321. *first note, add*:
H. John McLachlan (*Socinianism in Seventeenth-Century England*, Oxford, 1951, pp. 189-190) discusses this situation briefly and adds some background. Leslie M. Oliver (*Harvard Library Bulletin*, VII, 1953, 119-121) notes a previous publication of the *Catechism* at Rakow in 1609, dedicated to James I of England, and probably at least in part printed in England. Mr. Oliver raises the question whether, if the place of printing is thus wrong, the date may not also be. In view of Leo de Aitzema's report (below, III, 206) that the printer told him that Milton had licensed the book, the "Note under the Hand" of Milton may be an official license of it for printing. Aitzema adds that Milton not only admitted having licensed it but also defended it on the basis of his previous defense of freedom of publication (presumably in *Areopagitica*).

321. *August* 14, *note, add*:
Vivian de Sola Pinto (*Peter Sterry*, Cambridge, 1934, p. 21) says that Peter Sterry was one of those included in this order to inventory records (though I have not found his name in the order). On this basis Mr. Pinto asserts of the friendship of Milton with Sterry that "We can be sure that Milton found Sterry a thoroughly congenial companion."

330. *insert*:
OCTOBER 28, 1650. *TENURE* MENTIONED IN *RESPUBLICA AN-GLICANA*.

... for a Parliament and State to call a Tyrant to account ...
This Doctor *Willet*, and *Paraeus* upon that place in the Epistle
to the *Romans, be subject to the higher powers, &c.* hold lawfull; and it is confirmed by a multitude of Protestant Divines,
and reasons, as you may see at large in a late treatise, entituled,
The tenor of Kings and Magistrates.

G. W., *Respublica Anglicana Or The Historie Of The Parliament
In their late Proceedings*, London, 1650, p. 41; mentioned by Merritt
Y. Hughes in "Milton's Treatment of Reformation History in *The
Tenure of Kings and Magistrates,*" in *The Seventeenth Century: Studies in the History of English Thought and Literature from Bacon to
Pope*, ed. R. F. Jones, Stanford, California, 1951, p. 262. Though
often attributed to George Wither, this book is written in a style so different from his that it can hardly be by him. The Thomason catalogue
dates the book October 28, 1650 (I, 815).

337. *bust by Simon, notes, after first paragraph, insert*:
It may be worth while to add here Hollis's note of July 30, 1757,
about his purchase of this bust, quoted in Blackburne's *Memoir*, II, 513-
514. "For an original model in clay of the head of Milton, £.9. 12s.
which I intended to have purchased myself, had it not been knocked
down to Mr. Reynolds by a mistake of Mr. Ford the auctioneer. Note,
about two years before Mr. Vertue died, he told me, that he had been
possessed of this head many years; and that he believed it was done by
one Pierce, a sculptor of good reputation in those times, the same who
made the bust in marble of Sir Christopher Wren, which is in the Bodleian library. My own opinion is, that it was modeled by Abraham Simon; and that afterwards a seal was engraved after it, in profile, by
his brother Thomas Simon, a proof impression of which is now in the
hands of Mr. Yeo, engraver in Covent-garden. This head was badly designed by Mr. Richardson, and then engraved by Mr. Vertue, and
prefixed to Milton's prose-works, in quarto, printed for A. Millar,
1753, [Baron's edition]. The bust probably was executed soon after
Milton had written his Defensio pro populo Anglicano." Blackburne
then adds: "Mr. Reynolds obligingly parted with this bust to Mr. Hollis for twelve guineas."
The officials of the National Portrait Gallery incline rather to Pierce
than to Simon as the sculptor, and to a date about 1660. D. T. Piper,
Esq., Assistant Keeper, has kindly shown me some notes being prepared
for a new catalogue, containing this information and also the comment
that perhaps the making of the bust was connected with an increasing
popularity of life-masks about the time of the Restoration. The Gallery,
by order of its trustees in 1925, had a cast made from a mould taken

from the original clay at Christ's College. From its cast, in turn, six further copies were taken, three of which are now respectively in the Victoria and Albert Museum, the Victoria Art Gallery in Melbourne, and the Scottish National Portrait Gallery. The Gallery's cast is 11 inches high. Professor Frank A. Patterson, I remember, used to have a bust of Milton, but whether it was one of the six taken from the Gallery's copy I do not know.

337. *last line, after* 79. *insert*:
Hollis considered the puncheon the work of Thomas Simon (Blackburne, II, 619-620). I have traced its history down to 1908, when it belonged to the Right Honorable Sir Joseph Cockfield Dimsdale, Bart., Chamberlain of London, who exhibited it in Stoke Newington; see *Stoke Newington Public Library. Milton Tercentenary. Catalogue of Exhibits*, 1908, p. 52. In answer to my inquiry several years ago, the Librarian of Stoke Newington kindly wrote to the present Baronet, Sir John Dimsdale, for further information, but was able to get none.

338. *first note, line* 4, *for* daughter, *read* daughter Deborah, to her daughter Elizabeth, *last line, add*: For further discussion of Milton's seals see V, 133-135.

340. *first caption, insert* FEBRUARY, *and move the entry to p.* 347.

345. *January* 20, *caption, for* 20 *read* 21

Add to note: Possibly the historical background given in the note for the next following letter (p. 346) is more relevant to the present one. (P)

346. *state letter to Cardenas, first note, add*:
Maurice Kelley found a contemporary manuscript copy of this letter in the Archivo General di Simancos, bearing the pressmark "Legajo 2528," and endorsed in Spanish as to be sent to His Majesty with the letter of February 15, 1652. See "The Columbia Milton: Fifth Supplement," *Notes and Queries*, CXCVII (1952), 378.

347. *January* 30, *note, line* 8, *after* numbers *delete* of

349. *February* 10, *note, line* 2, *after* Masson, IV, 231; *insert*: CSPD, *1651*, p. 40;

350. *first note, line* 2, *for* Salmasius *read* Needham

351. *first note, add*:
One of Salmasius's later jibes at Milton's authorship of this book is perhaps worth adding here. In his *Opus Posthumum*, 1660, p. 4 (repeated in Bayle, *Dictionnaire Historique et Critique*, 1697-1702, article on Milton, pp. 587-590), he doubts whether Milton had brains enough to write the book, and suggests that it may have been done by some little French schoolmaster ("Conscriptam enim esse à Ludimagistro quodam

Gallo de trivio, qui Londini pueros nihil sapere docet; nam Miltonum ipsum qui penitius noverunt, Latine scire, aut scribere posse, serio negant").

352. *first note, last paragraph, add*:

Mr. Madan has reissued his bibliography of 1923-24 with changes and additions as "A Revised Bibliography of Salmasius's *Defensio Regia* and Milton's *Pro Populo Anglicano Defensio*," in the *Library*, Fifth Series, IX (1954), 101-121.

354. *at end of entry on Defensio, add*:

4. Pro popl angl.   ɔtra Salmas.

British Museum, Add. MS. 28,954, fol. 9.

355. *presentation copy to Vane, note, add*:

The New York Public Library Manuscript Room miscellaneous folder on Milton contains a page from a catalogue of Charles Sawyer of London (No. 78, 1924, item 61), offering the Vane copy for sale for £250.

355. *last item (last eight lines on this page and first eight on p. 356), delete. This item appears more properly at* III, 66.

359. *last note, add*:

This paper of Anne Powell's was evidently thought of as being closely connected with Milton's petition of the same date (pp. 357-358 above), since in her deposition of June 4, 1656 (below, IV, 99), she says that she "did Joyne in p̄tic̄on with the said dēft [Milton] for the makeinge of her said Composic̄on and knoweth yᵗ her said late husbandę landę were thereupon freed from yᵉ sequestrac̄on. . . ."

363. *end of February, caption and first line of translation, for* Durer *read* Dury

364. *first note, line 1, for* 1659 *read* 1660

365. *after last line, insert*:

[When Milton's *Defensio* first reached Leipzig,] *dici non potest, quàm avidè à plerisque expetitus & perlectus fuerit, ut proinde mihi ejus tùm usus ad unam vix integram dieculam concederetur.*

Caspar Ziegler, *Circa Regicidivm Anglorum Exercitationes*, Leipzig, 1653, address to the kindly reader.

[It is impossible to express how eagerly it was sought for and devoured by many people, so that I could hardly get the use of a copy even for one whole little day (or space of time).]

Partly translated in Masson, IV, 534-535.

370. Cardenas, *for* 345 *read* 345, 346
370. *insert*: *Certain Brief Treatises*, 28-29
371. Chimentelli, Valerio, *before* 222 *insert* 187, 188, 191, *Delete entry for* Chimentelli the younger; *see Edward Rosen in Bulletin of the New York Public Library*, LVII (1953), 173.
373. Durer, *delete entry*.
373. Dury, John, *for* 321 *read* 321, 363
373. *before* Eyre, *insert*: "Exit Tyrannus," 319
375. Godwin, *for* 194 *read* 294
377. Hunter, *for* MS. *read* Add. MS. (*in both occurrences*)
379. Macray, *second title, after* Clarendon *insert* State   *before* 275 *insert* 185,
381. Milton, I. LIFE, *second line, for* 117, 118 *read* 117-119
381. I. LIFE, licensing, *for* 311 *read* 310, 311
381. I. LIFE, petition, *for* 322 *read* 322, 357
381. I. LIFE, *before* residences *insert*: puncheon and seal, *see under* VIII. POR-TRAITS
381. II. WRITINGS, *Complete Collection . . .* Birch, *delete* 154
382. *Literæ, before* 348 *insert* 346,
382. *Paradise Lost, before* 158 *insert* 50,
383. *Tetrachordon, for* 126 *read* 123-126
384. VIII. PORTRAITS, *before* Faithorne *insert* bust, 337
385. VIII. PORTRAITS, *add*: Vertue, 280
385. *before* Morley, Henry, *insert* Morley, George, 249
386. MS. SP 9/61, *for* 9/61 [*or* 194] *read* 9/194, the "Skinner MS."   (K)
392. *before* Slatford, *insert* Skinner MS., see MS. SP 9/194

VOLUME III

Preface, *line* 3, *for* to January, 1655 *read* through December, 1654

6. *March* 5, *note, line* 3, *after* Masson, IV, 313, *insert*: CSPD, *1651*, p. 70;

7. *March* 12, *note, add*:
On February 14 Gualter Frost was ordered by the Council of State to summarize English dealings with Hamburg for a report to Parliament, and to prepare a letter to the senate of Hamburg (*CSPD, 1651*, p. 47). Though a similar order was issued on May 27, presumably this letter had already been sent by then (*ibid.*, p. 219). If not, Milton's date is far from the time of actual sending.

9. *March* 19, *caption, for* LYONS *read* LEYDEN   (P)
10. *insert*:
MARCH 22, 1651. SALMASIUS REPORTED SICK IN SWEDEN.

Dicunt Salmasium nostrum in Suedia periculosissimo morbo laborare, quod valde me cruciat. . . .

Lut. Paris. Cal. April. CIƆ IƆC LI.

From a letter of Claude Sarravius to David Blondell, printed in *Marquardi Gudii . . . Epistolæ*, 1697, pp. 261-262. April 1, New Style, is March 22, English Style.

[They say that our Salmasius is suffering from a very dangerous illness in Sweden, which distresses me intensely.]

10. *last entry. This entry belongs with that for March 12 on p. 8. Delete the caption and all the note after the first sentence, and transfer the main entry and the identifying note to p. 8.* (P)

14. *March 30, note, delete last sentence. Insert*: On Salmasius's illness see entries below under dates of April 9, May 5, and June 1. See also addition to p. 10 above. (K, P)

16. *insert*:

APRIL 4, 1651. COUNCIL ORDER FOR TRANSLATION OF FOREIGN DISPATCHES.

That such dispatches as come to this Council from foreign parts in any foreign tongue are to be translated for the use of the Council.

Public Record Office, Order Books of the Council of State as quoted in Masson, IV, 314. I have not checked the original. But Masson is undoubtedly right in commenting that "This implies work for Milton." The version given in *CSPD, 1651*, p. 130, offers a few unimportant variant readings, chiefly the omission of "this" before "Council" (first occurrence) and "the" before the same word (second occurrence). (P)

16. *April 6, note, add*:

Since Thomason's copy was the Utrecht copy dated 1650 on the title page (Madan no. 4), he may have retained that date as the year of issue. (P)

F. F. Madan ("A Revised Bibliography of Salmasius's *Defensio Regia,*" *Library*, Fifth Series, IX, 1954, 116) interprets Thomason's substitution of "o" for "1" as meaning that "the edition was published before 25 March 1650/1." He also points out that the Commonwealth Arms printed on the title of this volume appears also on the title page of *Panegyrici Cromwello Scripti*, 1654, printed by Louis Elzevir in Leyden.

23. *May 2, caption, for 2 read 6. Transfer the whole entry to p. 24.*

27. *last two lines, and first five lines of figures on p.* 28. *Delete second and fourth set of equals-signs in each line.* (K)

28. *last line of solid paragraph, for* witness *read* wittness (K)

30. *first note, add:*

As J. W. Lever (*Review of English Studies*, XXIII, 1947, 101) and L. C. Martin (*Modern Language Review*, LI, 1956, 102-103) have suggested, the reading "nimium" on the last line of p. 29 may be a mistake for "minime," which would make better sense. The translation would then become, instead of "too often confused," "not the least confused throughout."

33. *second note, add:*

Patrick Young may possibly be the person intended because of Milton's presentation of copies of his works to Young; see II, 125-126. But it is not easy to see why Vossius should have thought of Patrick Young as Milton's teacher. (K)

34. *insert:*

ABOUT MAY-JUNE, 1651. MILTON'S *DEFENSIO* AND THAT OF SALMASIUS ISSUED TOGETHER WITH COMMON TITLE PAGE.

Claudii Salmasii Defensio Regia, Pro Carolo I. Rege Angliæ &c. Et Joannis Miltoni Defensio, Pro Populo Anglicano, Contrà Clavdii Anonymi, aliàs Salmasii Defensionem Regiam. Accesserunt huic editioni Indices locupletissimi. [Engraving of English royal arms: lion and unicorn, etc.] Parisiis, Apud viduam Mathvrini dv Pvis, Viâ Iacobæâ, sub signo Coronæ, M.DC.LI. Cvm Permissione.

Title page of British Museum copy 1477.b.59; mentioned in Parker, p. 33, and in *Christ's College Magazine*, XXXIII (1921), 3; listed with full title in F. F. Madan, "A Revised Bibliography of Salmasius's *Defensio*," etc., *Library*, 5th Series, IX (1954), 106-107. The individual title pages contained in this joint issue are Madan's Salmasius no. 7, *variant* ("Apvd Franciscvm Noel ... M.DC.L."), and Milton no. 3 ("Typis Du Gardianis. Anno Domini 1651."). Madan says that in some copies the joint title page reads 1650. Since he dates the Milton edition here included as "known to have been in existence by the end of April 1651," and adds that "its reissue with unsold copies of the *Defensio* may be dated a month or so later," the volume probably came out in about May or June, 1651.

[Claudius Salmasius's Royal Defense of Charles I, King of England, etc. And John Milton's Defense of the English People against the Royal Defense of Claudius Anonymous, alias Salmasius. Most copious indexes have been added to this edition. Paris, at the shop of the widow of Mathurin du Puis, Via Jacobaea, under the sign of the Crown, 1651. With permission.]

41. *line* 3, *for* style *read* pronouncement (From L. C. Martin in *Modern Language Review*, LI, 1956, 102-103.)

44. *note, add*:
This quotation from Salmasius also appears above at II, 362. (P)

50. *last note, for* 1651 *read* July, 1651

51. *insert*:

JUNE 26, 1651. JACOBUS MATTHIAS SCORNS MILTON'S *DEFENSIO*.

EPISTOLA X

De Miltoni scripto judicium.

THOMÆ BARTHOLINO   Hafniam.

INstar beneficii, fuit, quod Miltonum Salmasio adjunxeris. Si quid judico, nihil olim tam dispar fuit in armis Glauci et Diomedis. Pugnat Salmasius fortioribus telis, omniumq; seculorum consensum ad partes vocat. Alter verò obstitit, quà potest, circumit, discurrit, mutat in cornu pugnam, ut copias instruat provehendis turbidis consiliis pares. Ubi necessaria desunt argumenta, cavillis rem agit, & ut affectus suos ulciscatur, Salmasium modo grammaticum modo ardelionem vocat. Temporum nostrorum summa est infelicitas quod eius modi scribendi materiam suggerat. Calamis hactenus res acta est, aliter brevi argumentum illud tractabunt hinc Scoti illinc Angli, cum res ad manus atq; mucrones devenerit. Optarem Anglos eosdem successu pugnare, quo scripsit Miltonus, ut tandem temeritatis suæ pœnas luerent. Vertat se Miltonus in omnes, quot potest formas, nullis undis tantam gentis suæ labem eluet. Habet quidem speciosa subinde nomina, semper tamen velut funebre velum cadaver tegunt. Arhusij 6. Julii 1651.

Semper Tuus
Jacobus Matthias D.

Thomas Bartholinus, *Epistolarum Medecinalium . . . Centuria I. & II.*, Copenhagen, 1663, pp. 436-437; given in translation in Ethel Seaton's *Literary Relations of England and Scandinavia in the Seventeenth Century*, Oxford, 1935, pp. 107-108. Bartholinus (1616-1680) was a Danish biologist of some note and the son of one (Kaspar). The present letter is number 10 of the second hundred. Two hundred more were published in 1667. Bartholinus had evidently just sent his friend Matthias copies of both Salmasius and Milton. The date is probably New Style, which is June 26 in English style. (P)

[It was a great favor that you should have added the Milton to the Salmasius. If I can judge, there was never anything so unequal in the arms of Glaucus and Diomedes. Salmasius fights with the stronger weapons, and calls to his side the consensus of all the centuries. The other, to be sure, withstands him as best he can, walks around, runs up and down, changes his attack during the battle, that he may prepare troops fit for carrying out his violent schemes. Where necessary arguments fail, he resorts to scoffing; and to avenge his sufferings, he calls Salmasius first grammarian and then busybody. It is the chief unhappiness of our age that it furnishes material for writing of this sort. Hitherto the business has been done by pens, but in a short time the Scots on the one hand and the English on the other will carry on that debate in a different way, when the matter comes to hands and swords. I should hope that those English would fight with the same success with which Milton has written, so that they might finally pay the penalty for their great foolhardiness. Let Milton turn himself into all the forms he can, he will never with any waves wash away the great stain of his people. Now and then, to be sure, he has some plausible arguments, but they always, as it were, lay a funeral covering over the corpse. . . . Aarhus, July 6, 1651. Ever yours, Jacobus Matthias.]

[429]

58. *eighth line from bottom, for* monster (Milton) *read* monster (Salmasius)

59. *insert*:

JULY 8, 1651. EPHRAIM ELCOCK MENTIONS *TENURE OF KINGS AND EIKONOKLASTES.*

[1] So there is a sort of men, who in the beginning of civil Wars against Tyrants, are hot and active; but through sloath and unconstancy, and weakness of spirit, either fainting ere their own pretences, though never so just, be half attained, or through inbred falseness and wickedness, betray oft-times to destruction men of Noblest temper, joyned with them for causes, which they in their rash undertakings were not capable of: and that these men are such, they themselves may see, if they would view their faces in the Glasse held up to them by this worthy Authour, to answer whose Reasons I must refer them.

[Marginal note:] *Tenure of Kings and Magistrates*, p. 3.

[2] So that notwithstanding their professions and this shadow of reason, they must seek better Arguments before they can excuse themselves from being the Prophets of *Ahab's* Son, (for he that was the *Ahab* of our *Israel*, hath now shed his blood, where he began to shed the blood of *Naboth*.

[Marginal note:] Εἰκονοκλαστης, p. 37.

[3] *Non-Scribers* charge the takers of the *Engagement*, with sleight grounds. I will not say but some might engage upon such sandy foundations, as *Non-Scribers* speak of; but I dare withal confidently aver, that the most of such are to be found in *Non-Scribers* Folds, whose Pulpit-stuffe, both first and last, hath been the Doctrine and perpetual infusion of slavery and wretchedness to all their Hearers, that I may use the judicious censure of our *Iconoclastes. Et turpe est Doctori, cum culpa redarguit ipsum*, it is such guides sin and shame, that their people in the midst of such contentions for liberty, are no more acquainted with the nature of it.

Ephraim Elcock, *Animadversions on a Book, called, A Plea for Non-Scribers*, London, 1651, pp. 6, 5, 60 respectively. Thomason dated his copy "July 8th, 1651." I owe this allusion to Dr. Perez Zagorin through our mutual friend Professor Merritt Y. Hughes. (P)

65. *insert*:

AUGUST, 1651. *TENURE OF KINGS* MENTIONED.

. . . it followes not that if we speake of the DEMERIT OF BLOOD, . . . the Law of God accepteth any Judge, great or small, and if the Estate be above the King, as I conceive they are, though it be an humane Politick constitution, that the King be free of all co-action of Law, because it conduceth for the peace of that Commonwealth, yet if we make a matter of Conscience, for my part, I see no exception that God maketh, if men make, I crave leave to say, *A facto ad jus non sequitur*, thus far that honest publique Advocate. We see all *Scotchmen* are not of the bloud Royall, and when we heare this mans reasons, and those which other men have brought against exempting the King from the Co-action of the Law, answered, we shall then thinke men have some cause and ground for their heinous resentment of the proceedings against the late King, and for that great stirre they make in the world about them.

[Marginal note:] Junius Brutus, Ὑβρυστοδύκαι. I. M. Tenure of Kings, &c.

J. Drew, *The Northern Sub-Scribers Plea, Vindicated*, London, 1651, pp. 40-41. Thomason dated his copy August. I owe this allusion to Dr. Perez Zagorin through our mutual friend Professor Merritt Y. Hughes. (P)

77. *sixth line from bottom, after* morning *insert* early (P)

78. *October* 17, *translation, delete second sentence; insert*: He likewise sends apologies by a servant of Parliament, and the preceding is accordingly verified. (P)

82. *line* 4, *delete* to obtain this same end *and insert* with the idea of paying them a visit (P)

87. *translation, fifth line, delete* great return *and insert* fine (*from L. C. Martin* in *Modern Language Review*, LI, 1956, 102-103)

96. *line* 3, *for* which I wish could be hurried *read* as I would like to have it settled   (P)

104. *November* 19, *first line, for* αδενεία *read* ἀσθενείᾳ *third line, for* sua *read* suæ   (K)

104. *fifth line from bottom, for* Jeremy Picard or some other *read* an   (P)

106. *translation, line* 6, *for* points *read* reason   (P)

106. *last note, add*:
A copy of this order, signed by Gualter Frost, is in the archives at Oldenburg (Best 20, Tit. 38, No. 73, fasc. 6, No. 41).   (K)

108. *line* 3, *for* did *read* testified

115. *first note, line* 1, *for* 1652 *read* 1652, pp. 1316-1317   (P)
117. *notes, add*:
The correction of date looks like Milton's handwriting.   (K)

119. *before first entry, insert*:
1652. BIRTH OF BROTHER CHRISTOPHER'S SON JOHN (?).

The new entry given below under date of January 29, 1668, shows that John Milton, son of Christopher of Ipswich, was admitted to Pembroke College, Cambridge, on that date, at the age of 15. He must therefore have been born in or about 1652, or possibly in January, 1653.

121. *after note on Wood, insert*:
The late Reverend Mr. THOMAS BRADBURY, an eminent dissenting minister, used to say, that JER. WHITE, who had been Chaplain to OLIVER CROMWEL, and whom he personally knew, had often told him, "That MILTON was allowed by the Parliament a weekly table for the entertainment of foreign ministers, and persons of learning, *such especially as came from Protestant states*, which allowance was also continued by CROMWEL.["]

John Toland, *The Life of John Milton . . . with Amyntor*, ed. Thomas Hollis, London, 1761, p. 110 (Hollis's note).   (R)

134. *third line from bottom, for* must have happened the third time *read* probably happened through a third party   (P)

135. *first line, for* favorable *read* settled   *third line, for* when it reached him *read* as it was decided upon

136. *translation, line* 8, *for* Etruria *read* Tuscany   (P)

142. *confers with Mylius, translation, line* 3, *for* three hours earlier *read* before three o'clock   (P)

142. *January* 12, *caption, for* IMPRESSIONS OF *read* MEN-TIONS   (P)

149. *January* 20, *note, line* 3, *before* Since, *insert*:
The Columbia MS. also uses the date May 22, 1651. *Add at end*: This is the letter ordered by the Council on January 2; see above, p. 133. (P)

152. *translation, line*s 13-14, *for* should obtain . . . whole realm *read* was decided by a treaty of the whole Empire   (P)

158. *second note, add*:
The Council gave order on January 29 that the papers for the Dutch ambassadors should be ready tomorrow between 7 and 8 A.M. On February 20 the Council ordered the papers signed, translated into Latin, and sent (*CSPD, 1651-1652*, pp. 122, 149).   (P)

162. *insert*:
FEBRUARY 8, 1652. FAVORABLY MENTIONED BY THOMAS MAN-LEY.

But if your enemies are yet so stubborn that they will not be convinced thereby, let them peruse that excellent peece with a little seriousness, that cleerly declares the Prerogative of Kings, and evidently defends the Priviledges and liberty of the people.

Payne Fisher, *Veni; Vidi; Vici. The Triumphs of the Most Excellent and Illustrious Oliver Cromwell . . . done into English Heroicall Verse, by* T[homas]: *M*[anley]: *Jr.*, London, 1652, reprinted in Thomas Corser's *Collectanea Anglo-Poetica*, 1860-1861, Part IX, pp. 5-6. The original edition is dated February 8, 1652, by the Thomason Catalogue (1, 860). This reference comes from Paul B. Anderson.   (P)

172. *February* 12. *Thanks to the kindness of Professor Maurice Kelley, who allowed me to see a photostatic copy of the original letter from Milton to Whitelocke which he obtained from the Marquis of Bath, I can now offer a more correct reading through the following revisions:*

[433]

4 w^{ch}.] w^{ch}   received] receivd 5 Safeguard] Safeguard, 7
L^dship] L^dship,   Mr.] Mr   Neville] Nevill   8 desir'd]
desird   copy] Copy   11 enough] anough   13 with] wth 16
L^d.] L^d 21 successo^{rs}.] success^{rs}   22 W^{ch}.] W^{ch}   23 Y^r.] y^r
26 believe] beleive   leave.] leave   27 Feb.] Feb: 28 1651]
1651.   34 Volume xii;] Volume xii, f. 41;

173. *first note, add*: The signature is by proxy and not in Milton's
own hand. (K)

180. *first note, line 4, after* in *insert* the London *Times Literary
Supplement* (June 17, 1949, p. 397, together with that of the next
following English version) and in   (K)

191. *first note, line 3, after* the 19th. *insert*:
But the fact that Milton reports the action of Parliament as "heute"
(today) proves that the entry should properly be dated the 17th and
moved back with others of that date.   (P)

196. *translation, lines 3-4, for* must therefore . . . met by
them *read* they must apply for themselves, and would then be
received   (P)

198. *translation, line 6, for* my other eye *read* one eye   (P)

200. *sonnet on blindness, note, first paragraph, add*: Maurice Kelley
(*Modern Philology*, liv, 1956, 20-25) thinks that because this sonnet
follows that on Piedmont in the edition of 1673, it must be at least as
late, if not later, in composition, on the theory that Milton kept his
poems in order of composition in his notebooks. But since Dr. Kelley
agrees that Milton interchanged two other sonnets, it seems possible
that he may have done the same here. If he did reverse the order of
these two sonnets, there would be no barrier to supposing that the date
of composition of the sonnet on his blindness was 1652. I find it difficult to believe that it was not an early expression of his emotion over
the onset of total blindness.

202. *top note, add*:
Aitzema's dates are probably New Style, so that by English reckoning
they would be ten days earlier. But this difference does not affect the
main entry, which is only vaguely datable.   (P)

210. *first note, add*:
The original letter in the Riksarchivet at Stockholm ends: ". . . atqz
authoritate hisce literis Vndecimo Die Martij 1651/2. Westmonasterio
Datis Subscripsit et Parlamenti Sigillum imprimendum curavit [followed
by the signature:] Gulielm̄ Lenthall prolocut' parliam^{ti} Reipubl^e An-
glię." It bears another note, probably for filing purposes, repeating the
date of March 11, 1651[/2], and another, probably indicating the date

of receipt: ". . . 11. Maij, Aō 1652." On the outside is a good speci-
men of the Great Seal. Translation: ". . . and by authority William
Lenthall, Speaker of the Parliament of the Commonwealth of England,
signed and caused the seal of Parliament to be impressed on these letters, given at Westminster March 11, 1651/2."   (K)

210. *March* 21, *first note, add*:
The date of this letter is evidently a misprint for March 31, as is proved
by reference to it in the letter of August 10 (?), entered below on pp.
246-247; CM, XIII, 80-81. With this change of date the entry should
be moved to p. 211.   (P)

211. *March* 31, *note, add*:
On March 23 the Council ordered the Committee for Foreign Affairs to prepare an answer to the Spanish Ambassador (*CSPD, 1651-
1652*, p. 191). On March 29 the report was ordered to be considered
on the following day (*ibid.*, p. 198).

214. *first note, add*:
The original letter in the Rigsarkivet, Copenhagen, ends: "Datis Westmonasterio 13:°. Die Aprilis anno Dñi 1652. sub sigillo Parlamenti
subscripsit ejus nomine atqz Authoritate. [Signed:] Gulielm̄ Lenthall
plocut' Parliam̄ti Reipublicȩ Angliȩ." Translation: "Given at Westminster April 13, 1652, under the seal of Parliament and signed in its
name and by its authority by William Lenthall, Speaker of the Parliament of the Commonwealth of England."   (K)

220. *daughter Deborah born, line* 1, *for* Deborah *read* Dæ-
borah   (K)

221. *May* 5, *first note, add*:
Before the first word of the text there is a canceled His   (K)

226. *first note, last paragraph, add*:
Possibly in view of these dates it would be better to date the present
entry in July rather than in June.

229. *line* 10, *for* about *read* on   (P)

231. *first caption, for* July 19 *read* July 9   *Transfer the
entry to p. 230.*

At end of first note add: The equivalent date in English Style is
probably July 9.   (P)

232. *July* 29, *first note, add*:
On July 26 Thurloe was ordered by the Council to prepare a letter
to Tuscany (*CSPD, 1651-1652*, p. 346). By August 2 it had already
been sent (*ibid.*, pp. 353-354).

233. *notes, add*:
Possibly the date should be in July, toward the end, since the letter of
state of July 29 to Ferdinand II seems to have enclosed a copy.   (P)

247. *first note, add:*

The Committee for Foreign Affairs was ordered by the Council on July 23 to answer a letter from the ambassador, just received (*CSPD, 1651-1652*, p. 344). The Council passed a similar order on July 28 (*ibid.*, p. 349), after Parliament had given orders concerning the business. The Committee was ordered to answer another paper on August 6 (*ibid.*, p. 359), and others later.

250. *note, line 3, for* June 2 *read* June 5   (P)

256. *first note, add:*

Nethercot (p. 281), who reminds us that three people independently vouch for the mutual-assistance episode of Milton and Davenant (i.e., Richardson, through Pope and Betterton from Davenant himself; John Phillips, if he is the writer of the "earliest" biography; and Davenant's son William to Tonson), calls the story "the best authenticated of all these instances of ethical reversal—and the one treated most superciliously by the cynics . . . ."

257. *first note, add:*

This story of a life for a life becomes more complicated in Aubrey (ed. Clark, 1, 206-208). In addition to the story of the aldermen of York whom Davenant is said to have befriended and who later saved him, Aubrey adds two amusing anecdotes about the sparing of supposedly dangerous enemies of the state on the jesting grounds that they were not fit to be offered on the altar as sacrifices of state. He tells how Henry Marten saved Davenant on this plea, and how Lord Falkland in turn saved Marten by the identical ruse. Aubrey does not, however, unite Milton and Davenant in any one of these versions.

258. *first caption, for* AMBASSADOR *read* AMBASSADORS   (P)

258. *first note, add:*

The original letter, in the Rigsarkivet, Copenhagen, bears at the bottom a notation in what looks like an English hand of the nineteenth century (perhaps by the compiler of the reports of the Deputy Keeper of the Public Records) to the effect that this letter is in Milton's 1676 volume. Similar notations are found on the letters on pp. 267-268 and 273-274 below.   (K)

258. *last note, add:*

Other Portuguese papers were ordered translated (though not specifically by Milton) on October 12, October 21, and November 1 (*CSPD, 1651-1652*, pp. 437, 450, 464).   (P)

268. *second note, add:*

The original English text in Copenhagen is signed by James Harington, President of the Council of State, and countersigned by John Thurloe, Clerk of the Council.   (K)

271. *first note, line 2, for* 1652 *read* 1653   *line 3, for* 93 *read* 91 (P)

273. *November 9, note, add:*

The original letter in the Rigsarkivet, Copenhagen, ends: "Datis Westmonasterio Nono die Novembris Anno Dom: 1652. Sub sigillo Parlamenti subscripsit ejus nomine atqz Authoritate./. [Signed:] Gulielm Lenthall Prolocutor Parlamenti Reipub: Angliæ." Translation: Given at Westminster November 9, 1652, under the seal of Parliament, signed in its name and by its authority, by William Lenthall, Speaker of the Parliament of the Commonwealth of England. The Council on November 3 ordered this letter read, translated, signed, and delivered (*CSPD, 1651-1652*, p. 469). (P)

275. *first note, add:*

The Council approved the draft on November 23 and sent it to the Speaker for signature (*CSPD, 1651-1652*, p. 504). (P) There had also been earlier action. A letter of October 22 refers to an order of Parliament to release Cardi's ship (*ibid.*, p. 453). On November 10 Thurloe was ordered to prepare an answer to the Grand Duke in pursuance of this order (*ibid.*, p. 485).

275. *November 11, first note, add:*

Thurloe was ordered on November 5 to prepare this letter, and on November 10 some papers were ordered delivered on Friday next, which was November 12 (*CSPD, 1651-1652*, pp. 476, 486). These papers of November 11 presumably were or included those of November 5. The same record is true of the letter of the same date on p. 276. (P)

286. *December 14, first note, add:*

The Skinner version is dated December 19. For some odd reason the Council's Committee on Foreign Affairs did not order this letter until January 10, 1653 (*CSPD, 1652-1653*, p. 91).

300. *next to last line, after* a genuine Cooper. *insert:*

Leigh Ashton, Esq., Director and Secretary of the Victoria and Albert Museum, kindly informs me that he considers the Jones portrait an eighteenth-century imitation of a seventeenth-century piece (perhaps not even a copy but something worked up from the imagination), with a spurious S. C. "signature." The copy which he furnished me looks more unlike the Cooper original than like it.

303. *Peter English. This item should be dated February 2, 1654 (Thomason's copy), and moved to p. 355.* (P)

304. *first caption, for* ROWLANDS *read* ROWLAND (P)

307. *plans new edition, note, add:*

James Holly Hanford mentioned this possible projected edition in *Modern Philology*, XVIII (1920-1921), 477, as being intended for the fall and winter of 1653-1654. (K)

310. *January 8, first note, add:*

The Council approved this letter, ordered it sent to Parliament on December 15 and again on December 21, but only on January 11, 1653, ordered it delivered to the Venetian secretary (*CSPD, 1652-1653*, pp. 28, 45, 95). (P)

311. *last note, add*:
On January 6 the Committee for Foreign Affairs was ordered to prepare letters to ambassadors and foreign ministers, as the result of an act of Parliament of January 5, protesting the resort of English people to the houses of those officials for mass. On January 7 and again on January 12 Thurloe was ordered to draw up such papers, and on January 14 Fleming was ordered to deliver letters (probably these) to several ambassadors (*CSPD, 1652-1653*, pp. 84, 87, 99, 102). (P)

318. *first note, add*:
The Council ordered a translation of what is probably this letter made and sent on February 2 (*CSPD, 1652-1653*, p. 140). (P)

323. *line* 7, *for* and *read* &   *line* 8, *for* and *read* &   *line* 10, *for* Greek *read* Greeke   *next to last line of letter, for* emulation *read* æmulation   (K)

323, *note, line* 2, *before* French, *insert*:
CSPD, 1652-1653, p. 176;

328. *first note, first paragraph, add*:
A. K. Croston (ed. John Hall's *Advancement of Learning*, Liverpool, 1953, p. 2) points out that Hall signed his initials as author of *A True Account and Character of the Times* in 1647 in the form "N. LL." More conclusive evidence is the fact that John Davies of Kidwelly, Hall's intimate friend, in his account of Hall's life prefixed to Hall's *Hierocles upon the Golden Verses of Pythagoras Englished*, 1657 (sig. b5), states clearly that Hall wrote *A Letter Written to a Gentleman in the Country*. (P)

334. *July* 2, *caption, for* OLDENBURGH *read* DENMARK

334. *July* 2, *note, add*:
This or another letter to Frederick was ordered signed and sent on July 26 (*CSPD, 1653-1654*, p. 52). (P)

336. *line* 3, *for* 315 *read* 345   (K)
341. *insert*:
AUGUST 25-28, 1653. ALEXANDER MORE CLEARED BY SYNOD AT UTRECHT.

Synode Utrecht 1653.

Art. 26.

Les deputès de L'Eglise de Leyden ayant instammant requis

cette compagnie que n'obstant la litispendance du proces que M^r. Morus a intentè c̃re Elisabeth guerret membre de l'Eglise de Leyden et ce devant la Cour provinciale, La Compagnie voulut ouir lire certains escrits que leur Eglise leur avoit mis en mains et desquels la lecture avoit estè remise par la Synode passè jusques à ce present, La Compagnie apres avoir oui le contenu des dits papiers a jugè qu'il ne lui estoit apparue suffisante cause pour laquelle la libertè soit ostee aux Eglises de presenter la chaire au dit M^r. Morus.

From the articles of the Synod of Utrecht, September 3-6, 1653, among the "Actes des Synodes Wallons" in the Bibliothèque Wallonne in Leyden. I am grateful to Professor Kester Svendsen for his kindness in letting me have a photostatic copy of this article which he, in turn, obtained through M. Charles Cabanis, Conservateur of the Bibliothèque Wallonne. Professor Kelley calls my attention to Stern's reference to this Elizabeth Guerret or Guerrette (III, appendix 2, 299-300), who is probably the English maid known as Pontia or Bontia. Stern has a long appendix on the accusations brought against More in various synods and churches (III, 297-303). These materials need more investigation of the kind that Professor Svendsen is doing. The accents, in the text, which are all grave, are probably usually intended to be read as acute. The "en" of the final syllable of Leyden in both occurrences, like the preposition in the phrase "en mains" about half way through the selection, occurs as an abbreviated symbol which I cannot duplicate, but which resembles vaguely the form like a Greek letter rho which English writers of this period sometimes use for final "s" or "es." The date of the action, if New Style, is August 25-28 in English style. For references to this action see John Dury's letters at III, 368 and 370, and that of Heinsius at III, 344. The chair in the last clause is undoubtedly More's professorship.

[The deputies of the church of Leyden having urgently requested this company that, notwithstanding the pending action which M. More has brought against Elizabeth Guerret, a member of the church of Leyden, and that before the provincial court, the company would hear read certain writings which their church had entrusted to them and the reading of which had been deferred by the past synod to this present, the company, after having heard the contents of the said papers, has decided that it had not found sufficient cause for taking away from the churches the freedom of presenting the chair to the said M. More.]

343. *September 3, first note, add*:
If the date is New Style, the English equivalent is August 24, and this entry should be moved to p. 341. (P)

345. *insert*:
SEPTEMBER 14, 1653. OLAUS WORMIUS INQUIRES ABOUT SALMASIUS.

. . . we have learnt that Salmasius died in bitterness; tell me, did he finish his treatise against Milton?

From Olaus Wormius's letter of September 24, 1653, to his son Wilhelmus at Leyden, published in *Olai Wormii . . . Epistolae*, Copenhagen, 1751, p. 1119, as quoted (in translation) in Ethel Seaton, *Literary Relations of England and Scandinavia in the Seventeenth Century*, Oxford, 1935, p. 108. The date, if New Style, is September 14 in English style. (P)

346. *first note, add*:
William Jessopp was also engaged on the same day to help Thurloe (*CSPD, 1653-1654*, p. 205). (P)

348. *first caption, for* COUNT OF OLDENBURGH *read* FREDERICK III OF DENMARK (P)

348. *November 24, note, delete the second sentence and insert*: The Duke of Holstein was Frederick III, King of Denmark. *Delete the whole note after the third sentence.* (P)

349. *first note, add*:
The original letter in the Staatsarchiv, Zurich, ends: "Datis Westmonasterio xxviii°. die Novembris, Anno Domini. 1653. Subscripsit et Parlamenti sigillum imprimendum curavit. [Signed:] Franciscus Rous. Prolocutor Parlamenti Reipub. Angliæ." On the outside are various notes in Dutch and in Latin, probably for filing purposes. (K) Translation: Given at Westminster, November 28, 1653. Signed and caused to be sealed with the seal of Parliament by Francis Rous, Speaker of the Parliament of the Commonwealth of England.

On September 19 Scobell was ordered to send to the Council a draft letter prepared to be sent to Sweden and once read in Parliament; on September 26 the Committee for Foreign Affairs was ordered to consider it and report; on September 28 Lawrence was ordered to offer the draft to Parliament; on October 19 Fleming was ordered to summon the Swiss agent for an audience on Friday (October 21); on October

21 a paper was received from the Swiss minister and referred to the Committee for Foreign Affairs; on November 7 a letter of recredential to the cantons was approved and ordered translated, signed, and delivered to the agent J. J. Stockarus by Fleming; and on November 25 the letter now ready for the cantons was ordered delivered by Fleming to the agent (*CSPD, 1653-1654*, pp. 157, 166, 170, 207, 209, 235, 270). (P)

351. *Reason and Apology reissued, note, add*:
William R. Parker ("Milton, Rothwell, and Simmons," *Library*, 4th Series, XVIII, 1937-1938, 94), thinks that perhaps the printer of this joint issue was the T. C. who printed *Smectymnuus Redivivus*; see the next following entry.

352. *Nieremberg, note, lines 3-4, for* presumably . . . Nierembergius *read* probably in his *Flores Solitudinis* (P)

355. *Thurloe nominates, note, add*:
Cromwell approved these recommendations on February 3 (*CSPD, 1653-1654*, p. 458); see the next following entry. (P)

357. *insert*:
FEBRUARY 22, 1654. WHITELOCKE FINDS ADMIRATION OF MILTON IN SWEDEN.

February 22, 1653[/4]. . . . [At a dinner with Whitelocke Swedish people discussed] English authors, as Selden, Milton, the Viscount of St. Albans [Bacon], and others, whom they much admired and commended.

Bulstrode Whitelocke, *Journal of the Swedish Embassy*, 1855, I, 439-440; Ethel Seaton, *Literary Relations of England and Scandinavia in the Seventeenth Century*, Oxford, 1935, pp. 106-107. If Whitelocke uses Continental Style, this entry is February 12 by English reckoning. (P)

366. *March 27, note, add*:
Dr. Bernard Gagnebin gathers many interesting facts about this letter and about English relations with Geneva in his "Cromwell and the Republic of Geneva" in the *Proceedings of the Huguenot Society of London*, XVIII (1947-1952 [his own article appeared in 1948]), 158-180. He believes (p. 160) that the present letter was written "probably by Milton." He contributes a good deal of material from the Genevan archives. I first noticed this reference in the *Seventeenth-Century News*, IX (1951), 51.

376. *May 30, note, lines 9-11, delete* By what seems . . . copy of it. (P)

387. *insert*:

JUNE 5, 1654. *TENURE OF KINGS* QUOTED BY J. P.

All men naturally are born free, made at first to command, and not to obey; and so lived, until from the Spring of *Adams* transgression they fell among themselves to do violence and wrong; and foreseeing that such courses must needs tend to common destruction, they agreed by common consent to bind each other from mutual injury; and because a mutual faith was not sufficient unto mutual peace, therefore they ordained Authority by mutual consent, and betrusted some therewith to restrain by force and punishment the violation of common right, which Trustees were not so made to be their Lords and Masters, but Deputies and Commissioners to execute that Justice which else every man by the hand of Nature and Covenant must have executed for himself and for another; and why any man should have lordship or authority over others but for this common end, is not imaginable: Rulers were made by the people, not the people by them; they were made for the people, not the people for them; they are each particular mans Lord by their own consent for each mans peace, but they are servants to the whole for the good of all; no man is bound to the Ruler in any matter of common prejudice, but he is bound to them all in common preservation; the whole owe not their lives to any though never so great on Earth, the greatest oweth his life to the whole, and is made great by God and man for service, and not for Lordship sake: when such Trustees turn Tyrants, what are they but the greatest Traytors? Is not Treason the betraying of just Trusts? the greater the Trust, the greater the Treason, the worse the Traytor: What greater Trust then that of Government? which being once voluntarily and plenarily betrayed, the people are *ipso facto* discharged from their allegeance: The affirmation, that the whole people in one body is inferior to one single man who ever he be, is high Treason against the dignity of Mankind.

J.P., *Tyrants And Protectors Set forth In their Colours*, London, 1654, p. 8; quoted in slightly shorter form by Benjamin Boyce in *The*

Polemic Character, University of Nebraska Press, 1955, p. 41, who calls it a "cleverly pruned quotation" from Milton's *Tenure of Kings*. Boyce mentions the possibility that the author may be John Phillips. Wing gives the author as John Price. Though the writer gives no indication that he is drawing on Milton's writing, or that he is doing anything but composing his own ideas, his language here is almost identical with Milton's in *The Tenure of Kings*; see CM, V, 8-11. Professor Max Patrick first called this allusion to my attention. The date (June 5) is from the Thomason Catalogue (II, 69).

388. *first note, add*:
Another possibility is a pretended envoy from France named Jentilliot, who after some trouble was ordered on July 9, 1652, to leave the country within three days. On July 10 the time was extended by five additional days. See *CSPD, 1651-1652*, pp. 319-320, 324, 326. (P)

402. *June 28, delete period at end of text.*

402. *June 28, note, add*: The advertiser was Humphrey Moseley. (P)

404. *first note, lines 3-4, delete* (or perhaps a contemporary copy) *Add*: The original in the Niedersächsische Staatsarchiv, Oldenburg (Aa Grafschaft Oldenburg, Tit. 38, Nr. 83, fasc. 5, Bl. 97) ends: "Alba Aula Westmonasterij Vicesimo nono Junij. 1654. Illustrissimæ dignitatis vestræ Studiosissimus. [Signed:] Oliuer P." (K) Translation: Whitehall, Westminster, June 29, 1654, most zealous for your most illustrious dignity, Oliver, Protector. The handwriting of the signature makes this assuredly the original letter.

404. *last note, add*:
What seems to be a contemporary or continental copy of this letter has been found in the Niedersächsische Staatsarchiv at Oldenburg. It looks like an original except that the signature is not in Cromwell's hand. It ends: "Alba Aula Westmonasterij 29. Junij A° 1654 Jllustrissimæ Dignitatis vestr: Studiosissimus Oliver. P." (K) Translation: Whitehall, Westminster, June 29, 1654, most zealous for your most illustrious dignity, Oliver, Protector.

412. *July 25, first note, add*:
Yet he seems to have suffered the customary prolonged delay, for a letter of August 12 from Gravesend (*CSPD, 1654*, p. 297) shows that he was then still in England, though determined to sail on the following Monday, which was August 14.

414. *August 29, note, line 7, after* date *insert* of receipt (P) *Add at end*: The original letter in the Riksarchivet, Stockholm, ends: "Alba Aula Westmonasterij 29°. Augusti An. 1654./ Vester bonus Amicus. [Signed:] Oliuer P." Translation: Whitehall, Westminster, August 29, 1654. Your good friend. Oliver, Protector. The date of receipt on the outside reads: "21: Sept. 1654." (K)

[443]

415. *translation of Vlac's preface, lines 1-2, for* of considering More author of the *Clamor read* of careless, erroneous attribution of authorship (P)

417. *September 28, line 7, after* locis *insert* ipse (*Milton's errata*, 1674)

419. *note, add:*
The correct spelling of Thevenot's name, as Dr. Hanford shows, is Thévenin; his first name was François. But since there were several distinguished Frenchmen of the day named Thevenot, it would have been easy for Milton or Philaras to be confused about the spelling. Except Hanford, almost every writer on Milton since the seventeenth century has accepted the spelling in the text without question. (P)

421. *October, note, line 4, for* Masson. *read* Masson, but as I have shown on p. 412, the actual date is more likely as early as July. (P) My article mentioned in line 4 of this note was published in *Papers of the Bibliographical Society of America*, XLIX (1955), 262-268.

430. *insert:*

1654, October 16. Elizabeth, queen of bohemia, scorns milton and dury.

Sonne, I vnderstand that Dury meanes to pass by Heidleberg in his way from Suiss; I hope you uill neither see him nor suffer him to haue anie kinde of fauour or stay in your countrie, for though he be a minister, he is the basest rascall that euer was of that coat. He uritt and printed a booke, where he aproues the king my dear Brothers murther, which I haue read, and he has translated into french Milletons booke against the kings booke, so as I intreat you, not to see that rascall nor suffer his stay and if it be possible his passage thourough your countrie; I assure you, that if I were now at Heidleberg, and that he passed there, I would haue him soundlie basted, his coat shoulde not saue him, hauing dishonnoured it by his villanie, which is all I haue to say to you at this time onelie I pray, remember the ill condition I ame in who ame

your most affectionat Mother
E.

Hagh this 26./16. of Oct. [1654]

A letter of Elizabeth, Queen of Bohemia, to her son Charles Louis, Count Palatine, as printed in *Briefe der Elisabeth Stuart, Königen von Böhmen, an ihren Sohn, den Kurfürsten Carl Ludwig von der Pfalz*, Tübingen, ed. Anna Wendland, in *Bibliothek des Litterarischen Vereins in Stuttgart*, [band] CCXXVIII, 1902, pp. 51-52; quoted in part in J. G. Robertson, "Milton's Fame on the Continent," pp. 319-320. (R)

441. *first note, add*:
The original letter in the Riksarchivet, Stockholm, ends: "Dab: ex Aula Nostra Westmonasterij Octobris 27m°. An. 1654./ Vester bonus Amicus. [Signed:] Oliuer⁸. P." Translation: Given from our Hall of Westminster October 27, 1654. Your good friend, Oliver, Protector. The contemporary copy in the Staatsarchiv at Bremen has a similar ending except that instead of Cromwell's actual signature are simply the initials "O. P." in a scribal hand. The original also bears what is presumably the date of receipt on the outside: "die 23. Novemb 1654." (K)

441. *letter to Bremen, first note, add*:
The original letter in the Archivum Bremense in Bremen ends: "Dab: ex Aula Nostra Westmonasterij Octobris 27ᵐᵒ. An. 1654./ Vester bonus Amicus. [Signed:] Oliuer⁸ P." Translation: Given from our Hall of Westminster October 27, 1654. Your good friend, Oliver, Protector. (K)

443. *last caption, for 23 read 3. The last sentence of the note needs the same correction. The entry should be moved back to p. 442.* (P)

449-468. *index. Delete entirely the following entries, which were inserted when several additional pages of text were in proof; but when those pages were removed, the removal of these entries was overlooked. They appear early in Volume 4.*

For the same reason delete all page numbers above 446 under the following entries:

VOLUME IV

6. *work on theology, line* 2, *for* framing of *read* framing (K)

9. *sonnets to Skinner, notes, last paragraph, add*:
Maurice Kelley (*Modern Philology*, LIV, 1956, 24) makes a good case for dating the second of these sonnets as late as the middle or latter part of 1655.

16. *translation, lines* 7-9, *for* that the common people . . . accustomed to *read* how common people are accustomed to receive opinions not yet common

19. *March* 24, *first line of letter, for* accidit *read* acciderit (*Milton's errata*, 1674)

26. *letter to United Provinces, note, lines* 7-9, *for* Dab . . . Oliver P. *read* Dab: ex Aula Nostra Westmonasterij 25ᵗᵒ. Maij An. 1655./ Vester bonus Amicus. Oliuerˢ P. *Add at end*: The original letter in the Algemeen Rijksarchief in The Hague also bears the date of receipt: "9°. Junij 1655./"   (K)

34. *June* 7, *first note, add*:
The original letter in the Archives d'Etat de Geneve also bears an inscription at the top, probably by the receiving office for filing purposes: "7 Juin 1655 Oliv. Cromwell en envoyant 2000 liv. angl. p les vallées." Translation: June 7, 1655, from Oliver Cromwell, sending £2,000 English for the Valleys (of Piedmont).   (K)

Professor Kester Svendsen has kindly called my attention to a reference to this letter of state in Isaac Spon's *History of the City and State of Geneva*, London, 1687, p. 180. Under date of August 9, 1655, Spon writes: "The *Genevoises* received a Letter from *Cromwel*, written in the *Latin* Tongue. . . ." He then summarizes and partially translates this letter. Conceivably August 9 may be the date of receipt of the letter in Geneva, but it seems far too late even for that.

43. *letter to Louis XIV, note, add*:
The original letter (or more likely a contemporary copy) in Paris ends: "Dab: ex Aula Nostra Westmonasterij 31ᵐᵒ. Julij An. 1655./" Translation: Given from our Palace of Westminster, July 31, 1655. Since there is no signature, this is not likely to be the original. It bears endorsement at the top, probably for filing purposes in the Paris archives: "Lettre de Cromwell au Roy du 31 Juillet 1655" (Letter of Cromwell to the King of July 31, 1655). (K)

44. *letter to Mazarin, first note, add*:
The original letter in Paris ends: "Sum Ad Eminentiæ vestræ in serviendum paratissimus. [Signed:] Oliuer P. [at left side:] Ex Alba Aula Westmonasterij 31ᵐᵒ. Julij 1655./" Translation: I am most ready to serve your Eminence, Oliver, Protector. From Whitehall, Westminster, July 31, 1655. A note at the top, added in the receiving office presumably, reads: "Mʳ Leprotecteur a Son Eminence Du 31 Juillet 1655." (K)

47. *first note, add*:
A manuscript copy of this poem, which may be earlier than the printed versions, is in Bodleian MS. Rawl. Poet. 30. (K)

49. *first note, add*:
The Harvard College Library, in addition to a copy of the English translation of this declaration, has also a German translation, of which the title (chiefly in German type) reads as follows: "MANIFEST Oder Erklärung vorgebrachthen seiner Hochheit dem Protector OLIVIER CROMVEL, von seinen Räthen In dem Nahmen der Republic die Gerechtigkeit derselben gegen Spanien betreffend. Aus der Engelländischen in die Hochdeutsche Spraach überseltzt. Im Jahr M. DC. LV." Except for the omission of a few paragraphs, this sixteen-page pamphlet follows the original rather closely. The Harvard copy of the English translation also differs enough from that given here to be worth quoting: "A DECLARATION OF HIS HIGHNES, By the Advice of HIS COUNCIL; Setting forth, On the behalf of this Commonwealth, the Justice of their Cause Against SPAIN. Friday the 26. of October, 1655. Ordered by His Highness the Lord Protector, and the Council, That this Declaration be forthwith Printed and Published. Hen: Scobel, Clerk of the Council. EDINBURGH, Re-printed by Christopher Higgins, in Harts-Close, over against the Trone-Church. MDCLV."

56. *insert*:
1656. COLLECTED DIVORCE WORKS ADVERTISED.
Donald L. Clark ("John Milton and William Chappell," *Huntington*

Library Quarterly, XVIII, 1944-1945, 340, n. 41) points out that Edward Farnham advertised a collection of Milton's works on divorce in 1656 under the title: *The Works of Mr. John Milton, concearning Divorce, digested into one Volume.* This notice occurs in a catalogue of titles printed by Farnham as found in an anonymous English translation of William Chappell's *The Preacher, or the Art and Method of Preaching*, London, 1656 (Wing C 1957). The catalogue is inserted between the title page and the beginning of the text in copies in the Cambridge University Library and in the Union Theological Seminary. (P)

59. *end of page, insert*:

1656. *DEFENSIO* PRAISED BY FRENCH WRITER.

See entry under second edition of Parival's work below, addition to p. 249.

75. *first note, lines 6-7, for* Dab. . . . 1655/6 *read* Dab: e Palatio Nostro Westmonasterij 7mo. Februarij. An 1655/6. Ma^{tis}. Vestræ bonus Amicus. [Signed:] Oliuar^s P (Given from our Palace of Westminster February 7, 1655/6. Your Majesty's good friend, Oliver, Protector).

88. *lines 7-9, for* Watch out . . . with you *read* Watch out constantly that I never find it necessary to stir you up in these respects

91. *May 30, first note, add*:
The original letter in the Algemeen Rijksarchief in The Hague bears a heading, presumably added in filing in The Hague, repeating the date of sending and adding the date of receipt, "22. Junij 1656." (K)

92. *May 31, first note, add*:
The original letter in the Algemeen Rijksarchief in The Hague is headed, presumably by a clerk in the receiving office, in addition to the date of sending, with that of receipt, "13. 7^{br}. 1656." (K)

93. *line* 16, *for* disputionis *read* disputationis (*probably, though my microfilm shows only* disputi/nis)

94. *translation, lines* 3-4, *for* If I have . . . they are two *read* If you desire to know what my plans are in this retreat, they are two

101. *first note, add*:
A copy of Milton's *Tenure of Kings*, bound with this volume, contains an identical inscription. (P)

102. *letter to Sweden, first note, add*:
The original letter in The Hague bears in another hand the date of
receipt: "6. Julij. 1656." (K)

109. *Heimbach visit, second note, line 3, insert*:
It was sold at the Parke-Bernet Galleries on November 26, 1946, from
the collection of Mrs. J. B. Hirschhorn for $1,400.

111. *first note, add*:
The original letter in the Algemeen Rijksarchief in The Hague is endorsed, presumably in the receiving office, with the date of receipt: "22.
7^{br}. 1656." (K)

118. *September 26, Greek text, add smooth breathing above
first letter of second word.* (K)

122. *letter to Sweden, first note, lines 2-4, for* The original letter
. . . Oliver P." *read* The original letter, now in the Riksarchivet in
Stockholm, ends: "Ex Palatio Nostro Westmonasterij 22do. die Octo-
bris An. 1656. Ma^{tis}. Vestræ Bonus Amicus. [Signed:] Oliuer P."
Translation: from our Palace of Westminster October 22, 1656. Your
Majesty's good friend, Oliver, Protector. (K)

123. *first caption, for* ELIZABETH *read* KATHERINE (P)

128. *letter to Denmark, note, first paragraph, lines 2-3, for* The
official letter . . . Decembris." *read*: The official letter, now in the
archives in Copenhagen, ends: "Dab: ex Palatio Nostro Westmonasterij 4to. die Decembris An. 1656. Ma^{tl}: Vestræ amicitia ac Voluntate
conjunctissimus. [Signed:] Oliuer^{s} P" (translation: Given from our
Palace of Westminster December 4, 1656. Most closely joined to Your
Majesty in friendship and good wishes, Oliver, Protector). (K)

129. *December 28, line 2, for* qdam *read perhaps* qdem
(*though the manuscript could be either*).

139. *first note, add*:
Sir Charles Firth (*Oliver Cromwell and the Rule of the Puritans in
England*, World's Classics edition, 1953, p. 26) says that Cromwell
"saved Peregrine [*sic*] Spenser, the grandson of the poet, from trans-
plantation, not for the sake of the *Faery Queene*, but for the sake of
Edmund Spenser's *Dialogue on the State of Ireland*." He ignores Milton, and gives no proof.

154. *insert*:
JUNE 17 (?) 1657. MENTIONED IN HENRY STUBBE'S *CLAMOR*.
A heavy Work (this is the Doctors clinch) about *adducis*

malleum! And the Doctor in the management of it so deporteth himself, as *Smectymmuus* [sic] once did in a quarrel about the learned men the *Areopagi*, the defence whereof found work not only for the Gentlemen of the Assembly, but that excellent pen of Mr. *Milton*! . . .

Had not those *Grammarians*, who are, as I may *phrase* it with the *eloquent* Mr. *Milton, bonis authoribus transcribendis et divexandis nati*, varied the text, *Plautus* would have furnished us with a multitude of examples, wherein the *Substantive* and *Adjective* had not agreed in *gender*, as *eamus intro, non utibile* [now *utibilis*] *hic locus factis tuis*: and the like, which those *puny* criticks have altered. . . .

If the Doctor had considered his quotations, he must either fall into a gross *paralogisme ex particularibus*, or tell us that whatsoever the drag-net of "Authors (*antient* and *antick*, *Poets* and *prosaick* writers) hath drawn down, and tendered to us in gross, *prawn*, *Crabfish* and *Lobster*, Sea-weed, shells, shrubs, unpicked, ungarbled, this is the *RVLE* of Elegance. . . ."

Diverse men have diverse opinions concerning a *stile*; *Bembus* and *Barclay*, *Milton* (that glory of our English nation!) and *Salmasius* make use of a different sort of writing: yet who doubts but each did acquiesce in his own way as *best*?

Henry Stubbe (?), *Clamor, Rixa, Joci, Mendacia, Furta, Cachini, Or, A Severe Enquiry into the late Oneirocritica Published By John Wallis*, London, 1657, pp. 13, 16, 19, 45. I am indebted to Mr. Samuel I. Mintz for calling my attention to these passages, and to Mr. J. Max Patrick for his assistance. It was Mr. Patrick who noticed the third of the quotations as being an echo of Milton's "Whatsoever time . . . hath drawne down from of old to this present, in her huge dragnet, whether Fish, or Sea-weed, Shells, or Shrubbs, unpickt, unchosen, those are the Fathers" (*Of Prelatical Episcopacy*, CM, III, 82). The library of Goucher College, which has the only copy in this country so far as I know (Wing W563 lists it under Wallis and gives the British Museum as the only location), kindly allowed me to use it on inter-library loan. The date of the present entry comes from the introductory note to the reader, which is signed and dated on sig. A3: "*Oxon*. June 17. 1657. . . . *Henry Stubbe*." The book is one member of the contest among John Wallis, Thomas Hobbes, and others. The quotation from Milton in the second selection is from his first *Defensio* (CM, VII, 40), slightly altered: "bonis authoribus divexandis tantùm aut transcribendis natus" ("born only to pick good writers to pieces or transcribe them"). The brackets in the same selection stand thus in the original. I believe these passages in Stubbe have not previously been noticed as allusions to Milton.

155. *line* 15 *of letter, for* profitent *read perhaps* profitent[r] (*though nothing after the t shows on my photostat*).

157. *note, line* 4, *for* 17 *read* 16 (P)

159. *first note, line* 7, *for* I *read* II   *last line: for* brother *read* nephew

167. *first note, add:* H. M. Margoliouth (editor, Marvell's *Poems and Letters*, Oxford, 1952, I, xiv) accepts the evidence of Legouis and Miss Duncan-Jones and thinks that Marvell remained Dutton's tutor until 1657.

168. *first note, line* I, *after* Oliverius P." *insert:* It is countersigned at the bottom: "Jo: Thurloe." It bears outside what is presumably the date of receipt, entered in the receiving office: "9 Oct. 1657." (K)

170. *letter to Lubeck, first note, line* 4, *after* Oliverius P." *insert:* It is countersigned at the bottom: "Jo: Thurloe." (K)

170. *last caption, for* OLDENBURGH *read* DENMARK (P)

172. *last note, last line, add:*
V. de Sola Pinto (*Peter Sterry*, Cambridge, 1934, pp. 33-34) thinks it "just possible" that in 1657 Sterry was acting as assistant to Milton, perhaps replacing Philip Meadows, who had been sent as envoy to Denmark in February. He notes that on September 8 a Mr. Sterry, who could have been either Peter or his brother Nathaniel, was appointed to take Meadows' place. A few lines later Mr. Pinto refers to this speculation as "the fact that Nathaniel was assistant to Milton and Marvell," which "would probably mean that both the brothers were well acquainted with the two poets." Though Mr. Pinto refers to Masson (v, 71), he does not notice that Masson, in describing this business (v, 374), points out that the appointment of Sterry, whichever brother he was, did not take effect, but that it was Marvell who got the position. However, Mr. Pinto also reveals that among Sterry's extant manuscripts, now in the possession of Mrs. E. Poolman of Melbourne, Australia, one includes a transcript of the first seven lines of Milton's "At a Solemn Music."

173. *at end of entry on Marvell, add:*
Andrew Marvel . . . us'd to frequent him the oftenest of any body.

Toland, p. 38; Darbishire, p. 175.   (R)

176. *note, add*:
The date, September 23, is from Abbott, IV, 632.   (P)

177. *first caption, for* 25 *read* 29   (P)
177. *last entry. This entry belongs under* 1658 *and was put here by error. It should be transferred to p.* 237.

In line 6 of the note, for 1657 *read* 1658.   (P)

179. *line* 5, *for* temporumve locorū *read perhaps* locorūve temporum (*the words occur in the manuscript in the order given here, but there are faintly visible figures 1 and 2 over them, perhaps indicating an intention to reverse them*)

181. *October* 19, *second text, line* 2, *for* ye morning *read* y^e. morning   (K)

182. *first note, line* 5, *after* Oliverius P." *insert*:
It is countersigned at the bottom: "Jo: Thurloe." It also bears outside, probably written in the receiving office, both the date of writing and what I believe is the date of receiving, which seems (though difficult to read) to be "14 Nmbr̄e."   (K)
183. *first note, line* 5, *after* Oliver P." *insert*:
It is countersigned at the bottom: "Jo: Thurloe." At the head of the letter, presumably written by a clerk in the receiving office, are the dates of writing and of receipt, the latter being "6. 10^br. 1657."   (K)
188. *first note, line* 6, *after* Oliver^s P." *insert*:
It is countersigned at the bottom: "Jo: Thurloe." At the head, endorsed presumably in the receiving office, are the dates of sending and receiving. The latter reads: "28. Januarij 1658."   (K)

191. *quotation from "earliest" biography, line* 3, *for* happened *read* happend   (K)

195. *first note, last line, after* 1 *insert* (1749)   (P)
216. *last line, add*:
John T. Shawcross (*Notes and Queries*, N.S. III, 1956, 202-204) supports Professor Parker's thesis by the argument that Milton's heavy emphasis on the purity of his wife's mind is intended to offset the impurity of her body. "Only Mary would be considered impure of body," he thinks, "not Katherine," because Mary died too soon to have accomplished the Old Testament formula of purification (Leviticus 12:5), whereas Katherine lived 3½ months. Maurice Kelley, on the other hand

(*Modern Philology*, LIV, 1956, 24), from a careful study of the Trinity Manuscript, feels sure that the handwriting of this sonnet is that of Jeremie Picard, who wrote for Milton about 1658-1659, that therefore the sonnet dates from that period, and that the subject must therefore be Milton's second wife.

219. *March 30, first note, add*:

The letter of April 2 is signed "Oliuer⁵ P." and countersigned "Per mandatū Celsitudinis suæ. Jo: Thurloe" (by order of his Highness, John Thurloe). It bears the great seal, though an indistinct impression.

221. *first note, add*:

Professor Strathmann has recently presented evidence (London *Times Literary Supplement*, April 13, 1956, p. 228) on the basis of several manuscripts of *The Cabinet Council* (though they are always given other titles, usually "Observations Civil and Political") that this work was written, not by Raleigh at all, but by a T. B., who may be Thomas Blount, Sir Thomas Browne, Thomas Bedingfield, or some other.

223. *May 20, notes, add*:

The *DNB* uses the spelling Fauconberg rather than Falconbridge. (P)

236. *first note, first paragraph, add*:

Godfrey Davies (*The Restoration of Charles II*, Huntington Library, 1955, pp. 41-42) repeats the conventional interpretation of the figures, that Milton and Marvell "were first voted the nine yards, but then were reduced to six." He adds the comment that many people were scandalized by the cost and magnificence of the funeral, quoting passages to this effect from Cowley and Ludlow.

242. *insert*:

OCTOBER 14, 1658. ANOTHER JOHN (?) MILTON INVOLVED IN RUMOR OF SCANDAL.

[On this date the Navy Commissioners write to the Admiralty Comissioners about an abandoned child at Chatham, born some seven or eight weeks earlier, about whom] Mrs. Hudson, the midwife, affirmed that Mr. Milton's wife is the mother, and at her travail, the strumpet did say that Capt. Pett [Phineas] was the father, which is not denied.

CSPD, *1658-1659*, p. 155. Though it would be absurd to suppose that this rumor of scandal had any connection with the poet, whose wife had died some six months before this event, it is inserted here because the index to *CSPD* lists it with another entry under "Milton, John." No further information about the event seems to be available in the volume.

249. *insert*:

1659. *DEFENSIO* PRAISED BY FRENCH WRITER PARIVAL.

As war was made with the Pike; so was it also with the Pen. For *Salmasius*, wrote a Book in defence of the King of *England*; and a certain *Englishman* called *Milton*, who was not known before, and grew famous by entring the Lists with this triumphant Champion, most acutely, and elegantly answered it.

[Marginal note:] Milton *writes against* Salmasius.

Jean Nicholas de Parival, *The Historie Of This Iron Age* . . . *now rendred into English, by B. Harris, Gent.*, 2nd edition, 1659, p. 262. Professor Parker, who gave me this reference, says that substantially the same text occurs in the first edition of 1656, which I have not seen.

251. *Morus's move. Delete this entire entry, which duplicates that on pp. 75-76. Professor Kester Svendsen kindly called my attention to this oversight.*

253. *February* 16, *first note, line* 5, *after* (see below), *insert* as well as on February 14, (P)

269. *June* 9, *line* 1, *delete comma after Milton* (P)

270. *note, fourth line from bottom, for* thirty-five *read* thirty-one *third line, for* 1624 *read* 1628 (P)

273. *before entry for July 6, insert*:

JUNE 30, 1659. LETTER OF STATE TO DENMARK (?).

Parlamentum Reipublicæ Angliæ. Serenissimo Potentissimóque Principi ac Domino, D^{no}. Friderico Tertio Dei gratiâ Daniæ. . . . Cum Voluntate ac nutu summi rerum omnium. . . . Westmonasterio 30° Junij Anno 1659°. Gulièlmus Lenthall parliaṁti Reipublicæ Angliæ Prolocutor.

Not in any of the collections of Milton's letters; discovered by Maurice Kelley in the Rigsarkivet, Copenhagen, and published in *Modern Language Notes*, LXVII (1952), 18-19. The subject is the same as that in the preceding letter of the same date to Sweden, and in places the wording is identical. The writer comments on the return of Parliament to the ruling position in England, and names envoys from England to those countries: Edward Mountagu (later to be Earl of Sandwich), Algernon Sidney, Sir Robert Honywood, and Thomas Boone.

274. *White's Middle State, note, add*:
This volume has since been bought by the University of Illinois.   (K)

279. *item* 12, *line* 3, *for* a&untuatione *read* a ‿untuatione

285. *last two lines, for* Nature made . . . deserved *read* Nature caused Louis to be king and Mazarin to deserve to be

287. *December* 16, *note, line* 2, *for* died on November 22 *read* died on October 31 and was buried on November 22   (P)

290. *insert*:

1660(?). COSTAR MENTIONS MILTON'S PROSE.

J. J. Jusserand (*Shakespeare en France*, Paris, 1898, p. 107) and J. G. Robertson ("Milton's Fame on the Continent," *Proceedings of the British Academy*, III, 1907-1908, 320) say that Pierre Costar, in his *Mémoire des gens célèbres des pays étrangers*, mentions Milton but not as a poet. I have not seen the book and do not know its date, but Costar died in 1660.   (R)

293. *attack by Dunkin, note, add*:
Thomas Birch (ed. Milton's *Works*, 1753, p. lxxvii) transcribes this word as "scribbling," but offers no identification.

295. *first note, add*:
Kennett mirrors the confusion about this book by entering it under date of October, 1660, as "*Salmasius*, his Dissection and Confutation of *Milton*. Translated into *English*. [Marginal note:] London, 1660. 4to."

303. *first note, last line, for* Phillips *read* Phillipps

311. *after last note, add*:

The Fear of God and the King pressed; in a Sermon at *Mercer's* Chapel, on *Sunday March* 25, 1660. By *Matthew Griffith*, D. D.

In which Sermon shewing himself too zealous for the Royal Cause, before General *Monk* durst own it, he was to please and blind the fanatical Party, imprison'd in *Newgate*, but soon after released.

There was an Answer made to this by *John Milton*, entitled, *Brief Notes upon a late Sermon*, entitled THE FEAR OF GOD, &c. Whereupon came out a little Thing called *No blind Guides*, &c. addressed to the Author in two Sheets in *Roger L'Estrange his Apology. London* 1660 4to.

There was soon a second Edition of this Sermon, called *The Fear of God and the King,* to which he added *A brief historical Account of the Causes of our unhappy Distractions, and the only Way to heal them. London* 1660 8ᵛᵒ.

[Marginal note:] SUNDAY *Mar.* 25. *A Loyal Sermon; for which* Monk *committed the bold Preacher to* Newgate.

[Another marginal note to *The Fear of God*:] *Printed at* London, 1660. 4ᵗᵒ. Wood Athen. Oxon. II. 249.

White Kennett, *A Register and Chronicle,* 1728, I, 96.

313. *April* 3, *line* 4, *for* Answer *read* Answer   *line* 6, *for* him *read* him,   *line* 7, *for* Rabshakeh *read* Rabshakeh;   *line* 8, *for* united faculties *read* united faculties   *line* 9, *for* wickednesse *read* wickednesse   (P)

316. *April* 28, *note, delete last sentence.*
317. *mock funeral, note, add:*
I should perhaps have used Cunningham's version of this story rather than Warton's, since it must have been written much earlier. Though there is considerable confusion among two Alexander Cunninghams, the author of the *History* was probably dead by 1737 at the latest, and the manuscript of his book may be a good deal earlier. This fact increases to some extent the percentage of credibility in the story. His version follows: "Milton, Latin secretary to Cromwell, distinguished by his writings in favour of the rights and liberties of the people, pretended to be dead, and had a public funeral procession. The king applauded his policy in escaping the punishment of death, by a seasonable shew of dying." Since Warton's account is preceded immediately by an anecdote of the Calves Head Club, it is possible that some members of that group were Milton's accomplices in this hoax if it actually occurred.   (R)   But Professor J. Max Patrick ("The Arrest of Hugh Peters," *Huntington Library Quarterly,* XIX, 1956, 348) considers the whole story as unlikely as that of Hugh Peters, who is reputed to have crawled into bed with a Quaker woman, a Mrs. Peach, in childbed, in order to escape arrest. He relegates both episodes to the region of folklore with Mak's sheep in the Second Shepherds' Play.

322, *note, add:*
In connection with burning Milton's works, it may be appropriate here to quote Richard Baron's story, which he said he got from John Swale, a bookseller of Leeds: *"Many High-Church Priests and Doctors have*

laid out considerable Sums to destroy the prose works of Milton, *and have purchased Copies of his particular writings for the infernal pleasure of consuming them.* . . . Some Priests in that neighbourhood used to meet once a year, and after they were well warmed with strong Beer, they sacrificed to the flames the Author's *Defensio pro populo Anglicano*, as also This treatise against the EIKΩN." From Baron's Preface to *Eikonoklastes*, London, 1756, p. iv; Blackburne's *Memoir of Thomas Hollis*, 1780, pp. 62-63. (R)

323. *insert*:

JUNE 20, 1660. HOUSE OF COMMONS DEBATES MILTON'S FATE.

Mr. Powell (Berks) against Milton.

Sergeant Littleton for Thorpe.

Sir Henry [i.e., Heneage] Finch to lay aside Thorpe and take Corbet.

Mr. Palmer against Steele.

The question whether the question to be put upon Corbet voted aye being 20th man.

Quoted from the *Old Parliamentary History* by Godfrey Davies in "Milton in 1660," *Huntington Library Quarterly*, XVIII (1954-1955), 356. The significance of the vote is that whereas Milton might have become the 20th name among those to be excepted from the general pardon, Miles Corbet was chosen instead. Dr. Davies' article is full of interesting material about the events leading up to Milton's imprisonment and later release.

325. *first note, add*:
Though Masson does not quote this order, he refers to it at VI, 182. (P)

326. *first note, line 1, delete question mark. Line 5, after* author *add* of both books   *Add at end of note*:
The title page of *Royal and other Innocent Bloud* bears Starkey's name in full, which also appears at the end of the book, with the date (of writing), June 18, 1660. (P)

326. *July 14, text, line 3, for* and *read* and   (P)

327. *first note, add*:
Birch (1738, p. xxxvii; 1753, p. xlv) quotes this letter (in English translation) from the 1691 Cologne edition of Patin's *Lettres choisies* as dated July 13, 1660. (P)

333. *last entry. Move this entry to p. 371, under 1662. Add at end of note*:

Since the references in the verse are probably to the St. Bartholomew Sunday of 1662, when so many nonconforming ministers were ejected from their livings, this poem was probably written in that year. (R)

340. *note, add*:

Godfrey Davies ("Milton in 1660," *Huntington Library Quarterly*, XVIII, 1954-1955, 359) thinks that Milton's imprisonment began between August 13 (the date of the proclamation against him) and August 29 (when the Act of Pardon became law).

349. *December 15, second note, add*:

Godfrey Davies ("Milton in 1660," *Huntington Library Quarterly*, XVIII, 1954-1955, 359) adds another document here. He quotes Public Record Office Dockets Signet Office, Index 6812: "December 1660. A pardon granted to John Milton of the parish of St. Giles in the Field in the county of Middlesex, Gentleman. Signed by Mr. Secr. Nicholas."

Dr. Davies also offers some new solutions to the problems connected with Milton's imprisonment. He believes that Milton's friends (who were many and powerful) agreed, in order to keep Milton from being included among the twenty to be excepted from pardon, that he should be arrested, but thinks that this was intended to be only a token affair to allay criticism. Somewhere along the line, however, the signals went wrong, and the sergeant at arms made a real arrest, which changed the situation. Once in prison, Milton could escape only by bowing to the royal authority. We have no knowledge whether he was willing to do so or ever did. Perhaps he may have regretted that he had allowed his friends to supplicate for him. Perhaps the lack of information and the inaccuracies in the early biographies concerning this event may have arisen from the unwillingness of Milton and his friends to talk about what he may have considered an unworthy submission. The whole account is most interesting (*ibid.*, pp. 361-363). See also the article by Caroline Robbins in *Notes and Queries* for February 3, 1951.

351. *first note, add*:

See above, III, 257, and the added note for that page.

351. *extract from "J. T." letter, line 5: for & read* y^t *line 7: for* S^r *read* S^r.

353. *first note, add*:

Perhaps the last two lines of verse refer to Milton's latest publications like the *Accedence*, the *Art of Logic*, etc., as a kind of hack work done to keep body and soul together. If so, the date is after 1669, perhaps about 1672, and the entry should then be moved to that period. (P)

356. *bottom of page, insert*:

1661. FRANCIS KIRKMAN MENTIONS *COMUS*.

John Milton   Miltons Mask. M[asque].

Advertisement in a list of Kirkman's publications in drama appended to *Tom Tyler and His Wife*, London, 1661, p. 10. This advertisement, without Milton's name, was repeated in Kirkman's catalogue of 1671, p. 10. (P)

359, *first note, add*:
This Mr. Walker of the Temple may be William Walker, who entered Jesus College, Cambridge, on October 3, 1668, and was admitted to the Inner Temple on March 1, 1668/9 (Venn). It may also be the same William Walker who, then of St. Mary Aldermanbury, married there on September 5, 1700, a Sarah Milton of St. Mary White Chapel (Registers of St. Mary Aldermanbury). (P)

362. *June 6, note, last line, for 26 read* 27 (P)

363. *June 26, note, next to last line, for* June 1 *read* June 6 (P)

366. *last line, insert closing bracket after* Pennington (P)

367. *first note, add*:
The suggestion of Paget's authorship of this biography came first from Edward S. Parsons. See the entry about it under 1687. (I thank Professor James Holly Hanford for pointing out to me a possible wrong implication of my original note.)

369. *March 13, between caption and first entry, insert*:

4. A Letter under Chancellor *Hyde's* own hand, dated the 13*th* of *March*, 1661. wherein he expresses his uneasiness under the Bishop's [Gauden's] importunity, and excuses his inability yet to serve him: but towards the Conclusion it contains these remarkable words; *The Particular you mention has indeed bin imparted to me as a Secret; I am sorry I ever knew it: and when it ceases to be a Secret, it will please none but Mr.* Milton.

374. *insert*:
Toland, p. 29; Darbishire, pp. 148-149. (R)

1663. CHRISTIANUS FUNCCIUS MENTIONS MILTON AS POLITICAL AGITATOR.

J. G. Robertson, in "Milton's Fame on the Continent" (*Proceedings of the British Academy*, III, 1907-1908, 320) says that Funccius mentions Milton in his *Commentatio de Bibliothecis*, 1663, but I have not seen this book. Robertson says that Funccius knows Milton "only as a political agitator." (R)

377. *note, add*:
The friend of Salmasius whose opinion about his having defended a

good cause badly whereas Milton supported a bad one well was probably Heinsius; see the first note on p. 365 above.

381. *February* 11, *after caption, insert*:

Die p'āt [the day aforesaid, February 11]

Wch day psonally appeared John Milton of yᵉ parish of Sᵗ. Giles Cripplegate Londoñ geñt aged about 50 yeares and a widdower and alledged that he intendeth to marry with Elizabeth Minshull of yᵉ parish of Sᵗ. Andrew Holborne in yᵉ county of Mīdd mayden aged about 25 yeares and att her owne disposing and that he knoweth of noe Lawfull lett or impedimᵗ by reason of any p'contract consanguinity affinity or otherwise to hinder the s̄d intended marriage and of yᵉ truth hereof he offered to make oath & prayed Licence to be marryed in yᵉ parish church of Sᵗ. George in yᵉ Burrough of Southwark or Sᵗ. Mary. Aldermary. in London.

[Signed sprawlingly:] John Milton

[Marginal notes:] [1] John Milton & Eliz: Minshull

[2] Juratus Hen: Smyth. Sur:

[3] pñte Ja: Tayler norió pubió.

From the original manuscript in the Faculty Office. The second marginal note means that the marriage license allegation was sworn before Henry Smith, Surrogate; the third means in the presence of James Tayler, notary public. (K)

387. *lines 2 and 4, for* Gill *read* Gell (P)

389. *at end of entry about move to Bunhill, add*:

J had a mind to have seen miltons Books & mr Davenant [William, the poet's son] went with me in order to it; J was then in my prentiship & coud not goe except on a Holyday or Sunday, soe yᵉ next Sunday we went. mr milton was some time before then removed from Jewin street to moorefields near yᵉ Artillery ground & it being in yᵉ afternoon about sermon time, there was noe body at home, & soe we returned home. J have often since cast a look towards that street, & the houses were then thought such as any substantial trader or merchant might dwel in. This is not what the Dʳ [Bentley] represents him, as living in *a narrow dark Room or chamber* & as *poor & freind-less.*

From Jacob Tonson's letter to his nephew, date about 1731-1732, now in the Pierpont Morgan Library; Helen Darbishire, *The Manuscript of Milton's Paradise Lost Book I*, 1931, p. xiv. The Tonson visit must have occurred in about 1676. The sentence preceding the present quotation says: "Jt was a litle after miltons death he [William Davenant] told me this. . . ." Tonson was an apprentice between 1670 and 1677, and Davenant, who received the A.B. in 1677, was at Gray's Inn in 1676.

394. *insert*:

Before august 1, 1663. Milton talks to danish resident simon de petkum about salmasius and about divorce writings.

[Milton argued against Dury as to divorce, asserted he always wrote what he truly believed, and considered the posthumous book of Salmasius poorer than the preceding ones.]

Oluf Borck, *Itinerarium*, Royal Library, Copenhagen, Ny kgl. Saml., 4to, 373c, pp. 27-28, as summarized in Ethel Seaton, *Literary Relations of England and Scandinavia in the Seventeenth Century*, Oxford, 1935, p. 142. Whatever the date of the argument with Dury, the comment on Salmasius's book must be later than September, 1660, when it appeared. Probably the passage is the report to Petkum of a recent conversation of Milton's with Dury. See also the record, filed under 1674, of a conversation between Milton and a Danish agent. (P)

395. *insert*:

About october 20, 1663. Further news about alexander more's status.

Mr. Morus est suspendu pour un an: au bout de quel temps il pourra prescher partout hormis dan L'isle de France. C'est la l'arreste du sinode de Ronssi, il en a appellé a celuy de Berri. . . .

From a letter of Elie Bouhereau to Paul Baudry as quoted in *Proceedings of the Huguenot Society of London*, ix (1909-1911), 220. Though undated, the letter is marked "Receuë le 2 de Novembre 1663" (received November 2, 1663). October 30 is therefore an approximation of the time it was sent. Since the dating is probably New Style, the English equivalent is October 20.

[Mr. More is suspended for one year, at the end of which time he will be able to preach everywhere except in the Île-de-France. This is the decree of the synod of Ronssi; he has appealed to that of Berry. . . .]

395. *October 24, note, add*:
E. S. De Beer's new edition of the *Diary* gives what is presumably a more accurate rendering than that above (Oxford, 1955, III, 364-365). The only substantial change, however, is the addition of the following phrase at the end: "yet no way taint⟨e⟩d."

396. *before first entry for 1664, insert*:
1664. Alleged association copy of lawrence's *mercurius centralis*.

Ex dono Mrs. Royston.

Inscription said to be written on the license leaf of Thomas Lawrence's *Mercurius Centralis, or a Discourse of Subterranean Cockle, Muscle and Oyster-shels, Found in the digging of a Well at Sir William Doylie's in Norfolk, many foot underground and at considerable distance from the sea. Sent in a Letter to Thomas Brown, M.D.*, 1664. This volume, advertised for sale for £12 10s. in Catalogue 538 of Pickering and Chatto, Ltd., in 1936, item 611, is said also to bear on the opposite flyleaf a note by Thomas Thorpe, the bookseller, written from Britwell in 1867 and saying, "The inscription is I have no doubt in the handwriting of the Author of 'Paradise Lost.'" The compiler of the catalogue, however, doubts that Milton wrote this inscription, since he was blind in 1664. I owe this note to the kindness of Professor J. Max Patrick.

397. *Poor Robin, note, line 1, for 5 read 3*   (P)

398. *May 1, caption, for* preacher *read* reader (I thank Professor James Holly Hanford for this correction.)

399. *November 3, caption, for* foster *read* hopkins   (P)

400. *last note, third line from bottom, for* brother *read* brother-in-law

416. *insert*:
July 8, 1665. Brother-in-law richard powell gives bond for £120 to his mother.

Jtem J give vnto my sonne Richard Powell of the Inner

temple . . . Esqr one bond or obligacoñ of the penalty of one hundred and twenty pounds . . . wherein hee standeth bound vnto mee . . . which bond beareth date on or about the eighth day of July which was in the yeare of our Lord one thousand Six hundred Sixty and five. . . .

From Anne Powell's will of October 24, 1678, q.v.

418. *first note, add*:

The Pope-Richardson letter which initiated the hoax is dated July 18, 1737; it was probably aimed at fooling Richardson, a "connoisseur" of Milton, rather than Miltonists in general. But Thomas Birch, who was beginning his edition of Milton's prose at about that time, soon heard about it. His Diary (British Museum, Add. MS. 4,478c, f. 29r) has an entry for January 21, 1738: "Jnvisi Carolum Lyttleton Arm. qui me-cum communicavit Versus quosdam Miltoni scriptos tempore Pestis anno 1665, & observationes de Auctore Libri dicti *The whole duty of Man*" (I visited Charles Lyttelton, Esq., who communicated to me several verses of Milton written at the time of the Plague in the year 1665, and observations about the author of the book called *The Whole Duty of Man*). Six days later (*ibid.*) "J. Richardson Junr: ostendit mihi Literas A. Pope, in quibus sunt Versus Miltoni scripti tempore Pestis 1665" (Jonathan Richardson, Jr., showed me letters of Alexander Pope, in which are verses of Milton, written at the time of the plague, 1665). But less than a month later Lyttelton had discovered the fake and wrote to Birch as follows (Add. MS. 4,312, f. 270): ". . . J find J was imposed on in ye Little Piece of Milton's which J gave you. it was write by Ld Chesterfield & Pope in imitation of Milton's style, and J must say so much like ye original that it would have decieved a much better critick than myself. My Authority for it was a Letter shew'd me in Oxfordshire last Xtmas from a Gentleman on ye Road dated att Chalfont where he gravely tells his Friend He found it on a Glass there. Jf you have given copies of it to your Friends you will do well to undecieve y^m." The result was that in his edition of 1753 Birch omitted all mention of the poem. (R)

418. *September 25, caption, for 25 read* 29 (P)

419. *line 2, for* pishes *read* pishes

419. *first note, line 5, before* Alexander *insert* an (*Alexander Gill the elder had died in* 1635, *the younger in* 1642.) (P)

419. *insert*:

NOVEMBER 30, 1665. ALEXANDER MORE'S PREACHING DE-SCRIBED.

. . . Monsieur Morus qui nous avoit desja presché plusieurs fois sur ce texte, *Aujourdhuy si vous oyes sa voix n'endurcisses point vos coeurs*, le prit encore dimanche, mais ne s'attacha qu'au seul mot d'*Aujourdhuy*, sur quoy il prescha une heure et demie. Quelquefois je lui ay oui prendre des textes de quinze ou vingt verses. . . .

From a letter of Elie Bouhereau to Elie Richard, dated from Paris, December 10, 1665, as quoted in *Proceedings of the Huguenot Society of London*, IX (1909-1911), 233. Since the date is probably in New Style, the English equivalent is November 30.

[Mr. More, who had already preached to us several times on this text, "Today if you will hear his voice, harden not your hearts," took it again Sunday, but spent his time on just one word, "Today," on which he preached for an hour and a half. Sometimes I have heard him take texts of fifteen or twenty verses.]

419. *insert*:

1666. SCORED BY EVELYN (OR NICOL?) AS ADVOCATE OF TYRAN-NICIDE.

I appeal to the horrid Murther *committed on those Sacred Heads by* Clement, Chastel, Ravillac, *&c. if after those crimson* Tragedies *they had not each of them more then one* Compurgator; *The* Mariana's, Veruna's, Guignard's, *in our* Milton's, *our* Goodwin's *and our* Ascham's, *another spawn of these holy* Cleremontanians.

From the Dedicatory Preface of *The Pernicious Consequences Of The New Heresie of the Jesuites Against The King and the State. By an Advocate of Parliament*, 1666; mentioned but not quoted by E. S. de Beer in his edition of John Evelyn's *Diary*, III (1955), 364-365. Mr. de Beer attributes this book to Evelyn, but Donald Wing (*STC*, N 1138) gives the author as Pierre Nicol. I am grateful to Professor Wing for helping me to locate a copy of this work at Yale, and to the reference librarian at Yale for kindly sending me a photostatic copy of this allusion to Milton. The context is one of horror at the crimes of many people of various countries who have opposed kings by word or deed.

421. *June 6, caption, for* May 26 *read* May 27   (P)

423. *note, last line, for* 26 *read* 27   (P)

432. *May 22, note, lines* 4-5, *for* conveyed *read* detain   *line* 9, *for* 1662 *read* 1668   *line* 11, *delete* simply June, 1666, *and insert*: June 20, 1668, explaining that they cannot turn back the property without an order of court to protect them. There is also (5) a decree dated November 28, 1667, authorizing the defendants to deliver the property in question to the plaintiffs, and stating that the defendants are to be protected and saved harmless from any dispute arising from the transaction. There seems to be some mistake in the dates of items 4 and 5.

432. *June, Christopher's answer. Delete this entry.*

438. *at end of entry about publication of Paradise Lost, add*:
Now J here return you the manuscript coppy of ye first Book [of *Paradise Lost*] & there you wil find the several places he [Bentley] affirms were altered by ye printer; are exactly true to the coppy & J think it is plain that ye j^st edition was printed by this very coppy, wch was preserved onely uppon account of the License written before it, & was assignd over with the bond when Symonds sold ye Coppy to to [*sic*] Aylmere of whome J bought it, & though their is noe date to the License yet tis easy to know about ye time it was granted by having recourse to ye Companys book where it is entred & it must be before & near 1667, pray search & let me know it. Jf mr Aylmer is yet Living he may give you some account of this matter & particularly of Symons ye printer &c

As for Symons the person to whom milton sold ye coppy, he was not a poor Bookseller as ye D^r says (page 2) J remember him And he was lookt upon an able & substantial printer & J think his father a printer before him, & a strict dissenter, he lived near Aldersgate & milton in Jewin street pretty near him & they might be of acquaintance, & perhaps if ye former editions of miltons Books wer seen he might have been employed by him before, but this is onely conjecture.

From Jacob Tonson's letter to his nephew, date 1731-1732, now in the Pierpont Morgan Library; Helen Darbishire, *The Manuscript of Milton's Paradise Lost Book I*, 1931, p. xii. The manuscript of Book

I is also at the Morgan Library. This and a few other selections from the letter are printed in the present volume by the kind permission of the authorities of the Morgan Library. Tonson's guess about Simmons was good: he had printed *Bucer, The Tenure of Kings* (two editions), and *Eikonoklastes*; see above, II, 105, 228, 263, 298.

443. *last note, fifth line from bottom, for* daughter *read* son   *Add at end*: The identification of N. Skinnerz with Edward Skinner, brother of Cyriack, is evidently impossible, since, according to Venn, Edward died in 1657.   (P)

443. *insert*:

JANUARY 3, 1668. PETER DU MOULIN RECEIVES ROYAL AP-POINTMENT PARTLY BECAUSE OF UNCLE PIERRE'S BOOK AGAINST MILTON.

[1. Peter du Moulin petitions to the king that because of his ancestors' long service to the royal family, and because his uncle (Pierre, but not named)] att present Canon att Canterbury, is (as y^r pet^r: humbly conceiveth) well known to y^r Ma^{ty}: by his loyall endeavours in vindication of y^r Ma$^{ty's}$: late Royall father . . . [and because of his own training he begs the king] to conferr upon him y^e place of Assistant to y^e Master of y^e Ceremonyes w^{ch}: is now vacant. . . .

[2] CHARLES &c. . . . Wee haue thought fitt to appoint Our Trusty & Well beloved Peter Du Molin Esqr [as Assistant to the Master of the Ceremonies, Sir Charles Cotterell] . . . & for his Fee haue assigned unto him the sume of six shillings & eight pence . . . by the day. . . .   January 3^d 1667/8./
By his [Majesty's order] &c.
Arlington.

Public Record Office. The first selection is from SP 29/232, no. 19, and the second from SP 44/30, ff. 1-1v; *CSP Dom, 1667-1668*, pp. 154-155; K.H.D. Haley, *William of Orange and the English Opposition 1672-4*, Oxford, 1953, pp. 18-19. Though the first selection is undated, it must come before the second, which is the grant based on it. No. 20 in the same package as the first is a further petition by du Moulin; no. 21 seems to be a first draft of the warrant. Though none of these documents mention Milton by name, Haley assumes, and I believe rightly, that the petitioner refers to his uncle Pierre's writing against

Milton, which is presumably *Regii Sanguinis Clamor*; see above, III, 234 ff.

443. *insert*:
JANUARY 29, 1668. NEPHEW JOHN ADMITTED TO CAMBRIDGE.

John and J. A. Venn, *Alumni Cantabrigienses*, III, 193. On January 29, 1667/8, according to this record, John Milton, son of Christopher of Ipswich, was admitted pensioner of Pembroke College at the age of fifteen; he matriculated in 1668. This is probably the "John Melton gent." who was buried at Ipswich on December 29; see IV, 450. (P)

444. *March 12, note, add*:
John and J. A. Venn (*Alumni Cantabrigienses*, III, 193) mention a Christopher Milton who matriculated pensioner at King's College, Cambridge, in Lent, 1663; they give no further details. This could conceivably be the poet's nephew, but it seems most unlikely.

447. *note, add*: Probably this entry should be separated into two parts: (1) the first two thirds, through the quotation from Dryden, and (2) the last eight lines. If we can interpret "produc'd" (p. 447, line 2) as meaning "brought to attention," the first part would fit well with the year 1669. See also the addition below to this entry. The second part belongs to about 1693 or later. (P)

447. *end of page, insert*:
Dr. T. Robinson told me that it was my *L. Dorset* that made *P. Lost* first taken notice of: that he light upon it by Chance in Little Brittain, & reading a few lines was so pleas'd with it that he bought it for a Trifle, for it was then but waste Paper & when He came home read it many times over, & sent it to *Dryden* to know his opinion of it. *Dryden* had never seen it before, but brought it back to Him, & told Him *that Poet had cutt us all out*. This was yᵉ 4ᵗᵒ Ed. & abᵗ 2 years after yᵉ first Publication of yᵉ work. & My *Lᵈ Dorset* told it himself to Dr. Robinson at that Time at yᵉ Grecian Coffee House.

Manuscript note by Jonathan Richardson on p. cxix of the copy of his *Explanatory Notes . . . on . . . Paradise Lost*, 1734, in the London Library, as reprinted in V. de S. Pinto, *Sir Charles Sedley*, New York and London, 1927, p. 94. Richardson prefixed the following note: "This is a former account that I wrote down as soon as I came home." Pinto thus thinks that it is likelier to be accurate than the printed one given above. I am grateful to Professor Pinto for writing to me personally to call this note to my attention.

449. *June 28, line 1, for* Accidence *read* ACCIDENCE
line 6, for Street *read* street   (P)

453. Bonde, Christiern, *for* 80, 81, *read* 79-81
461. Heinsius, Nicholas, *for* 364 *read* 365
469. Milton, John, VIII. PORTRAITS, *add*: Woodcock, 57
472. MS. SP 9/61, *for* 9/61 *read* 9/194   *delete reference to page* 7   (K)
472. *insert*:
MS. SP 9/61 (PRO, "De Doctrina Christiana"), 7   (K)
478. Skinner MS., *for* 9/61 *read* 9/194   (K)
479. Stowe, *for* MS. *read* MSS.

APPENDIX: CHANCERY ACTIONS IN-VOLVING CHRISTOPHER MILTON AND HIS FAMILY.

The following actions are too incomplete and too far removed from connection with the life of the poet to belong in the body of this work. But it may be worth while to give the most compact summary possible of them in an appendix. The record is far from complete because I have had no opportunity to search for the missing parts. I gathered these items incidentally while concentrating on matters chiefly affecting John Milton. But some readers may find some of the details interesting and may wish to follow up these beginnings. I give at the end of each entry the call-numbers of the documents on which I base my summary. The order is chronological, based on the earliest action in each suit.

1. TROTT-MILTON, 1652. The original bill of John Trott is missing, and the record begins with a few miscellaneous decrees in 1652 and 1653. Christopher Milton's "further answer" of May 16, 1653, denies framing an assignment from John Raven to Thomas Willis in 1649 except to date it. Answers by Willis and by Thomas Agar in 1652 and 1653 reveal little. References: C7/399/63; C33/198/949, 1009, 1055; C33/199/38, 103, 730, 807, 877; C33/201/35, 275.

2. (canceled)

3. MILTON-HORNEBY, 1674. Christopher and Richard Milton sign an indenture to Joseph Horneby dated February 13, 26 Charles II (1673/4). Reference: C54.

4. MILTON-PILKINGTON, 1675. Christopher Milton and Richard Truelove allege on February 10, 1674/5, that James Caston of Swilland, co. Suffolk, left his estate by will of 1660 to the plaintiffs with the understanding that they should sell it and pay his legacies, and that they should sign a large bond to one Pilkington, rector of Swilland, as guarantee that they would do so. Now Mrs. Pilkington has assigned their bond to Samuel Humphries and William Willoughby, who refuse to surrender it though the plaintiffs have performed their task and can show receipts for their actions. Reference: C8/330/99.

5. MILTON-HASLEFOOT, 1685. Christopher Milton and nearly a dozen others complain on July 8, 1685, that though in July, 1675, William Walley (or Whalley) sold messuages in Essex to Milton and others, Walley's widow is now suing them for debt. Rebecca Haslefoot, daughter of Alice Walley, makes a long answer on May 10, 1686, but says little concerning Milton. Some interrogatories for witnesses, dated October 26, 1687, are signed by Richard Milton. References: C8/385/25; C22/126/12.

5. MILTON-ARDEN, 1693. On May 22, 1693, Thomas Milton of the Middle Temple, Deputy Clerk of the Crown, presents a bill against John Arden of London, who agreed to turn over his position as Clerk of the Peace in Stafford for about £90 to John Forster of the Middle Temple. Lacking money, Forster persuaded Milton to sign a bond for £80 in his support. Though he obtained the appointment and paid a large sum of money to Arden, they combine to sue him at the common law. After a demurrer and part answer from Arden dated November 10, 1693, and some delaying tactics, the court finally upholds Arden's objections and dissolves Milton's injunction against the common law suit. References: C8/547/80; C33/282/377v, 443v, 450.

6. HOSKINS-MILTON, 1695. William Hoskins complains on December 4, 1695, that Thomas Milton, late of the Middle Temple, and his wife Martha proposed to Martha Hoskins, spinster, to mortgage Rushmere to her for £600, but that Thomas Milton died before the money was paid. Martha Milton answers on May 20, 1696, that she is unaware of the Hoskins mortgage, but that Thomas during his lifetime borrowed £600 from Miles Fleetwood in 1691 and £200 from Henry Cooke in 1693, and that these sums were repaid after his death. Having married Martha Spencer [*sic*], he gave bond to Fleetwood to pay him £100 a year if they should not live together. But they did. When he died intestate in October, 1694, she took out an extent on the statute; she now claims the rest of the money due her. She includes an inventory of Thomas Milton's estate dated October 27, 1694. Mary and Catherine Milton also answer on the same day, saying that they know nothing about the Hoskins debt, but that on October 1, 1688, to raise £820 as provision for his younger daughters, Thomas Milton mortgaged Rushmere to Sir Henry Felton, by whose consent they still hold the premises. They refuse to pay Hoskins, but think Martha should pay. Evidently the plaintiff obtained a decree of foreclosure on Rushmere, but I have not found the document; see the Milton-Aston material below. References: C6/427/42; C33/285 [or 286]/747; C33/287 [or 288]/12.

7. HARRIS-MILTON, 1696. In response to a complaint from Rowland Harris, vintner (missing), and after at least two warnings from the court, Martha Milton answers that she doesn't know that her late brother John Younger owed Harris £300, though she heard that Harris secured an injunction against him. But in 1689 she lent him £100 at interest, for which he gave her a bond for £200. In gratitude for her care of him during his illness he gave her further bonds for £200 in 1695, on the basis of which, after his death, she seized his possessions and sold them. As his executrix she is trying to settle his estate despite obstructive tactics by Harris, but she denies that her brother's estate

amounted to any such ridiculous amount as £10,000. References: C7/148/7; C33/285 [or 286]/998v; C33/287 [or 288]/15v.

8. YOUNGER-MILTON, 1698. In what may be a continuation of the preceding action, Mary Milton submits her answer on July 15, 1698. Though she knows nothing about Thomas Milton's loan of £100 from John Younger, she thinks that the former died intestate, and that in settling his estate Martha Milton and her later husband William Coward acquired £1,300, more than enough to pay his debts, of which she submitted an inventory to the ecclesiastical court. Thomas possessed lands in Rushmere, in Cotton, co. Suffolk, but no more that she knows of. He mortgaged Rushmere to Hoskins for £100 and Cotton to Stap (or Slapp). Some leasehold lands descended to herself and her other sisters. Reference: C6/98/131.

9. MILTON-ASTON, 1701. Mary and Katherine Milton, spinsters, daughters of Sir Christopher deceased and sisters of Thomas, bring suit on July 18, 1701. (This may still be a continuation of number 7.) The estate of Christopher or Thomas Milton, including holdings in Rushmere, Cotton, and Bucklesham, co. Suffolk, was worth over £1,800, though Martha and Coward value it at far less. They have stirred up suits against the plaintiff by Hoskins and others (see no. 6 above?). Though Coward offered them £130 for their rights in Rushmere and gave bond for peaceful fulfillment, he now molests them. Various defendants, including Martha and Coward, answer, giving their ideas about Rushmere, about bonds and debts, and about various other acts. Martha and Coward deny instigating suits, deny that Martha recovered enough from Thomas Milton's estate to cover his debts, and give numerous details or assertions about debts and bonds. Their picture makes Rushmere look honeycombed with conveyances. References: C8/456/65; C8/595/60; C24/1244-5.

10. MILTON-THURSTON, 1714. Catherine Milton of London, spinster, sister of Thomas of the Middle Temple, enters her bill of complaint on April 14, 1714. Before his death in 1694 her brother Thomas, to make provision for her, conveyed property in London and elsewhere to Sir Adam Felton, Sir Compton Felton, and Thomas Thurston. But Thomas died intestate, Sir Adam is dead, and the others refuse her requests for information. She therefore begs a writ against them. Thomas Thurston, replying on June 22, 1714, thinks that Thomas had holdings in Rushmere, Cotton, Bucklesham, and Fleet Street, but never heard of any such bond or conveyance as the plaintiff mentions. Reference: C6/450/43.

As I said before, these records are distressingly incomplete and need considerable further research before they can begin to tell anything like the whole story of the events so sketchily mentioned. But they do add some interesting points to our knowledge of the Milton family. (1) They repeat some interesting names from earlier years, like Caston, Truelove, Fleetwood, and Agar. (2) They suggest the considerable financial complexities attending ownership or lease of property like Rushmere. (3) They hint at an odd relationship between Thomas and Martha Milton, and they give us an inventory of his estate at the time of his death. (4) They give us a glimpse of a more complicated life led by Martha Milton. (5) They reveal more data on the later lives of Mary and Catherine (or Katherine) Milton, spinster daughters of Christopher. They therefore invite additional research.

INDEX

Aarhus, Denmark, 429

Abbot, George, Archbishop of Canterbury, 54

Abbott, Wilbur C., 452

Abingdon, co. Berks, 149, 199

Academy, 39, 132, 144

Acton, Samuel, 303, 304, 318, 325, 326, 330, 332

Adam, 442

Adams, E. K., 134, 135, 375, 376

Adams, Frank O'B., 144

Adams, George, 255

Adams, John, gunner, 255

Adams, Joseph Quincy, Memorial Studies, 122

Adams, Thomas, 219, 220, 223, 407

Addison, Galston ("Governor Harrison"), 308, 324, 335

Addison, Joseph, 110, 135, 308, 314, 319, 324, 327, 328

Adimari, Alessandro, 386, 387

Admiralty, 207, 453

Aesop, *Fables*, 114

Agar, Anne Milton, poet's sister, see Phillips

Agar, Ann, poet's niece, see Moore

Agar, Mary Rugeley, 381

Agar, Thomas, poet's brother-in-law, 33, 34, 59-61, 153, 296, 381; his son Thomas, 33, 34, 61; other, 469

Agar family, 344, 472

Agnew, T., and Sons, London, 10

Ahab, 430; his son (Ahaziah?), 430

Ainsworth, Robert, 445; *Thesaurus Linguae Latinae*, 292

Aitken, G. A., see Marvell

Aitzema, Lieuwe van, 421, 434, 446

Akenside, Mark, 132

Akrigg, G. P. V., "The Curious Marginalia of . . . Stanhope," 122

Alasco, Albertus, see (1) Lasco and (2) Siradia

Albemarle, George Monck, Duke of, 69, 88, 455, 456

Alcock (Allecock), John, 325, 326, 329-331

Aldenham, Lord, 373

Aldersgate Street, London, 89, 90, 241, 412, 465

Aldrich, George, 3

Aldwinkle, co. Northants, 296, 300

Alford, Daniel, 93

All Hallows, Bread Street, 173, 175, 179, 182, 185, 212, 216, 367, 381; *Registers*, 367

All Saints Church, Oxford, 162, 163

All Souls College, Oxford, 375

Allam, Andrew, 146, 234, 235, 276-278

Allecock, see Alcock

Allegations for Marriage Licenses . . . Faculty Office, 262

Allen, Elizabeth, 282-284

Allen, John, bricklayer, 282-284

Allestree, Richard, *Whole Duty of Man*, 463

Allestry (Allestree), James, bookseller, 23, 24, 26, 45

Allnut, W. H., 162

Almoni, Peloni, 394

Alston, C., licenser, 292

Ambler, Humphrey, 180, 181

Ambrose, Saint, 347

American Art Association, 127, 397

Ames, William, 445

Ampthill, co. Bedford, 281

Amsterdam, Netherlands, 68, 238, 291, 299, 300

Anabaptists, 120, 327

Anchor (sign), 239

Anderdon, Mr., 93

Anderson, Paul B., 56, 433

Andrew, Saint, 212, 216

Angel (sign), 225, 235

Angles, East, 15

Anglesey, Arthur Annesley, first Earl of, 14, 18, 24, 116, 117, 409

Annesley, Arthur, see Anglesey

Anonymous life of Milton, see MS. Wood D 4

Antwerp, Belgium, 128, 131

Apollinarius, 445

Apologia pro Confessione, 391

Aratus, *Phenomena*, 376

Archaeological Institute, 134

Archaeological Journal, 131, 134, 327

Archdale, Bernard, 297

Archdale, Elizabeth, see Fleetwood

Archdale, Mary, 241

Archdale, Richard, 296, 297

Archdale, Thomas, 164

Archdale family, 297

Arden, John, 470

Areopagi, 450

[473]